EXTRAORDINARY PRAISE FOR
BERLIN 1961

"As time passes and the political geography of world power mutates, it is easy to forget the most fraught and dangerous crisis of the Cold War, which brought U.S. and Soviet tanks facing each other at close range. *Berlin 1961* is a gripping, well-researched, and thought-provoking book with many lessons for today."

—Dr. Henry Kissinger

"Frederick Kempe's compelling narrative, astute analysis, and meticulous research bring fresh insight into a crucial and perilous episode of the Cold War, bringing Kennedy and Khrushchev to life as they square off at the brink of nuclear war. His masterly telling of a scary and cautionary tale from half a century ago has the immediacy of today's headlines."   —Strobe Talbott, president, Brookings Institution

"History at its best. Kempe's book masterfully dissects the Cold War's strategically most significant East–West confrontation, and in the process significantly enlightens our understanding of the complexity of the Cold War itself."

—Dr. Zbigniew Brzezinski, national security advisor to President Jimmy Carter

"What an amazing drama this is! The showdown over Berlin in 1961 was the pivotal episode of the Cold War, far more important and illuminating than the Cuban Missile Crisis. It was a clash between two fascinating leaders, Kennedy and Khrushchev, whose misreading of each other holds lessons for today. Kempe's compelling narrative is a triumph of great writing and research."

—Walter Isaacson, president and CEO, The Aspen Institute, and author of
Einstein: His Life and Universe and *Benjamin Franklin: An American Life*

"An engaging, richly researched, thought-provoking book that captures the drama of, and challenges the conventional wisdom regarding, one of the Cold War's most decisive years. Frederick Kempe combines the 'You are there' storytelling skills of a journalist, the analytical skills of the political scientist, and the historian's use of declassified U.S., Soviet, and German documents to provide unique insight into the forces and individuals behind these events."

—General Brent Scowcroft, national security advisor to Presidents Gerald Ford
and George H. W. Bush

continued . . .

"Fred Kempe has masterfully captured the dramatic dimensions of a great story that shaped the world order for twenty-eight years. *Berlin 1961* is an important achievement."

—Chuck Hagel, distinguished professor, Georgetown University, and U.S. senator, 1997–2009

"*Berlin 1961* takes us to Ground Zero of the Cold War. Reading these pages, you feel as if you are standing at Checkpoint Charlie, amid the brutal tension of a divided Berlin."   —David Ignatius, columnist, *The Washington Post*

"Informed . . . His chronology of memos and meetings dramatizes events behind closed doors. . . . Kempe's history reflects balanced discernment about the creation of the Berlin Wall."   —*Booklist*

"Kempe . . . skillfully weaves oral histories and newly declassified documents into a sweeping, exhaustive narrative. . . . Likely the best, most richly detailed account of the subject, this will engross serious readers of Cold War history who enjoyed W. R. Smyser's *Kennedy and the Berlin Wall* but appreciate the further detail."

—*Library Journal*

"Good journalistic history in the tradition of William L. Shirer and Barbara Tuchman."   —*Kirkus Reviews*

"A significant contribution to our understanding of the Cold War. It also will enhance public appreciation of the role of diplomats and diplomacy, because *Berlin 1961* is as eminently readable as any good 'who done it.'"   —*American Diplomacy*

"An engaging study of the 1961 Khrushchev/Kennedy standoff over Berlin, presenting the drama in the journalistic, anecdotal, episode-by-episode mode . . . a readable narrative."   —*The Weekly Standard*

BERLIN 1961

KENNEDY, KHRUSHCHEV, AND THE
MOST DANGEROUS PLACE ON EARTH

Frederick Kempe

BERKLEY BOOKS
New York

THE BERKLEY PUBLISHING GROUP
Published by the Penguin Group
Penguin Group (USA) Inc.
375 Hudson Street, New York, New York 10014, USA
Penguin Group (Canada), 90 Eglinton Avenue East, Suite 700, Toronto, Ontario M4P 2Y3, Canada
(a division of Pearson Penguin Canada Inc.)
Penguin Books Ltd., 80 Strand, London WC2R 0RL, England
Penguin Group Ireland, 25 St. Stephen's Green, Dublin 2, Ireland (a division of Penguin Books Ltd.)
Penguin Group (Australia), 250 Camberwell Road, Camberwell, Victoria 3124, Australia
(a division of Pearson Australia Group Pty. Ltd.)
Penguin Books India Pvt. Ltd., 11 Community Centre, Panchsheel Park, New Delhi—110 017, India
Penguin Group (NZ), 67 Apollo Drive, Rosedale, Auckland 0632, New Zealand
(a division of Pearson New Zealand Ltd.)
Penguin Books (South Africa) (Pty.) Ltd., 24 Sturdee Avenue, Rosebank, Johannesburg 2196,
South Africa

Penguin Books Ltd., Registered Offices: 80 Strand, London WC2R 0RL, England

PRINTING HISTORY
G. P. Putnam's Sons hardcover edition / May 2011
Berkley trade paperback edition / January 2012

Berkley trade paperback ISBN: 978-0-425-24594-1

The Library of Congress has cataloged the G. P. Putnam's Sons hardcover as follows:

Kempe, Frederick.
    Berlin 1961 : Kennedy, Khrushchev, and the most dangerous place on earth / Frederick Kempe.
        p.   cm.
    Includes bibliographical references and index.
    ISBN 978-0-399-15729-5
    1. Kennedy, John F. (John Fitzgerald), 1917–1963.   2. Berlin (Germany)—Politics and government—
1945–1990.   3. Berlin Wall, Berlin, Germany, 1961–1989.   4. United States—Foreign relations—
Soviet Union.   5. Soviet Union—Foreign relations—United States.   I. Title.
    E841.K34   2011   2010033163
    943'.1550875—dc22

PRINTED IN THE UNITED STATES OF AMERICA

10 9 8 7 6 5 4 3 2 1

CONTENTS

PART II. **THE GATHERING STORM**

PART III. **THE SHOWDOWN**

FOREWORD

by General Brent Scowcroft

Historians have scrutinized the Cuban Missile Crisis of 1962 far more deeply than they have the Berlin Crisis that preceded it by a year. For all the attention given Cuba, however, what happened in Berlin was even more decisive in shaping the era between the end of World War II in 1945 and German unification and Soviet dissolution in 1990 and 1991. It was the Berlin Wall's rise in August 1961 that anchored the Cold War in the mutual hostility that would last for another three decades, locking us into habits, procedures, and suspicions that would fall only with that same wall on November 9, 1989.

Furthermore, there was a special intensity about that first crisis. In the words of William Kaufman, a Kennedy administration strategist who worked both Berlin and Cuba from the Pentagon, "Berlin was the worst moment of the Cold War. Although I was deeply involved in the Cuban Missile Crisis, I personally thought that the Berlin confrontation, especially after the wall went up, where you had Soviet and U.S. tanks literally facing one another with guns pointed, was a more dangerous situation. We had very clear indications mid-week of the Cuban Missile Crisis that the Russians were not really going to push us to the edge. . . .

"You didn't get that sense in Berlin."

Fred Kempe's contribution to our crucial understanding of that time is that he combines the "You are there" storytelling skills of a journalist, the analytical skills of the political scientist, and the historian's use of declassified U.S., Soviet, and German documents to provide unique insight into the forces and individuals behind the construction of the Berlin Wall—the iconic barrier that came to symbolize the Cold War's divisions.

History, sadly, does not reveal its alternatives. However, Kempe's important book prompts the reader to reflect on crucial questions regarding the Berlin Crisis that raise larger issues about American presidential leadership.

Could we have ended the Cold War earlier if President John F. Kennedy had managed his relationship with Nikita Khrushchev differently? In the early hours of Kennedy's administration, Khrushchev released captured U.S. airmen, published Kennedy's unedited inaugural address in Soviet newspapers, and reduced state jamming of Radio Free Europe and Radio Liberty broadcasts. Could Kennedy have more fully tested the possibilities behind Khrushchev's conciliatory gestures? If Kennedy had handled Khrushchev differently at the Vienna Summit in June 1961, would the Soviet leader have balked at the notion of closing Berlin's border two months later?

Or, on the other hand, as some have suggested: Is it possible that we should regard Kennedy's acquiescence to the communist construction of the Wall in August 1961 as the best of bad alternatives in a dangerous world? Kennedy famously said he preferred a wall to a war—and there was reason for him to believe that was the choice that confronted him.

These are not small matters.

Another question raised by Kempe's compelling narrative is whether we, in the richness of time, will look at the Cold War in a more nuanced manner than we do now. The Cold War was not simply a standoff against a Soviet Union bent on world domination; it was also driven by a series of self-reinforcing misinterpretations of what the other side was up to. *Berlin 1961*'s account of the miscommunication and misunderstandings between the United States and the Soviet Union at that crucial time makes one wonder whether we might have produced better outcomes if we had more clearly understood the domestic, economic, political, and other forces compelling our rival's behavior.

These are speculative questions no one can answer with any certainty. Yet raising them in the context of *Berlin 1961* is as relevant to navigating the future as it is to understanding the past. In the pages that follow are clues and cautions that are particularly timely during the first term of another young and relatively inexperienced commander in chief, President Barack Obama, who, like Kennedy, came to the White House with a foreign policy agenda aimed at engaging our adversaries more skillfully and understanding more reliably what lurks beneath seemingly intractable conflicts in order that we can better solve them.

I know something of such issues and challenges myself from our days dealing with Soviet leader Mikhail Gorbachev when I served as national security advisor in President George H. W. Bush's White House.

The two U.S. presidents who dealt with Gorbachev, Bush and Ronald Reagan, were very different men. However, both understood that nothing was more important in trying to end the Cold War than the ways in which they engaged their Soviet counterpart.

Despite labeling the Soviets "the evil empire," President Reagan engaged in five summit meetings with Gorbachev and worked on countless concrete agreements that helped build confidence between the two countries. As the Berlin Wall fell in 1989 and we worked to bring about German unification, President Bush resisted all temptations to gloat or breast-beat. He consistently sent the message that both sides were winning if the Cold War was ending. Through exercising such moderation in his public statements, he also avoided giving Gorbachev's enemies in the Soviet Politburo any excuse to reverse his policies or remove him from office.

One can do no more than speculate on how either a tougher or a more conciliatory Kennedy might have altered history in the Berlin of 1961. What is indisputable is that the events of that year put the Cold War back into a deep freeze at a time when Khrushchev's break with Stalinism might have presented us with the first possibilities of a thaw.

Berlin 1961 walks us through those events in striking new ways, exploring the fundamental natures of the two primary countries, the U.S. and the Soviet Union; the domestic political environments of each; and the crucial roles played by the personal characters of their leaders; and then weaving it all into the equally important stories of how those factors played out in the countries of East Germany and West Germany themselves.

It is an engaging, richly researched, thought-provoking book that captures the drama of the time in its colorful Berlin setting, and challenges the conventional wisdom regarding one of the Cold War's most decisive years.

INTRODUCTION:
THE WORLD'S MOST DANGEROUS PLACE

Who possesses Berlin possesses Germany, and whoever controls Germany
controls Europe.

Vladimir Lenin, quoting Karl Marx

Berlin is the most dangerous place in the world. The USSR wants to
perform an operation on this soft spot to eliminate this thorn, this ulcer.

Premier Nikita Khrushchev to President John F. Kennedy
at their Vienna Summit, June 1961

CHECKPOINT CHARLIE, BERLIN
9:00 P.M., FRIDAY, OCTOBER 27, 1961

There had not been a more perilous moment in the Cold War.

Undaunted by the damp, dangerous night, Berliners gathered on
the narrow side streets opening up onto Checkpoint Charlie. The next
morning's newspapers would estimate their numbers at about five hundred,
a considerable crowd considering that they might have been witnesses to
the first shots of a thermonuclear war. After six days of escalating tensions,
American M48 Patton and Soviet T-54 tanks were facing off just a stone's
throw from one another—ten on each side, with roughly two dozen more
in nearby reserve.

Armed with only umbrellas and hooded jackets against the drizzle, the crowd pushed forward to find the best vantage points toward the front of Friedrichstrasse, Mauerstrasse, and Zimmerstrasse, the three streets whose junction was Berlin's primary East–West crossing point for Allied military and civilian vehicles and pedestrians. Some of them stood on rooftops. Others, including a gaggle of news photographers and reporters, leaned out of windows from low-rise buildings still shell-pocked from wartime bombings.

Reporting from the scene, CBS News reporter Daniel Schorr, with all the drama of his authoritative baritone, declared to his radio listeners, "The Cold War took on a new dimension tonight when American and Russian fighting men stood arrayed against each other for the first time in history. Until now, the East–West conflict had been waged through proxies—German and other. But tonight, the superpowers confronted each other in the form of ten low-slung Russian tanks facing American Patton tanks, less than a hundred yards apart. . . ."

The situation was sufficiently tense that when an American army helicopter flew low overhead to survey the battleground, an East German policeman barked in panic, "Get down!" and an obedient crowd dived facedown on the ground. At other moments an odd calm reigned. "The scene is weird, almost incredible," said Schorr. "The American GIs stand by their tanks, eating from mess kits, while West Berliners gape from behind a rope barrier and buy pretzel sticks, the scene lit by floodlights from the eastern side while the Soviet tanks are almost invisible in the dark of the East."

Rumors swirled through the crowd that war was upon Berlin. *Es geht los um drei Uhr* ("It will begin at three in the morning"). A West Berlin radio station reported that retired General Lucius Clay, President Kennedy's new special representative in Berlin, was swaggering toward the border Hollywood-style to direct the first shots personally. Another story spread that the U.S. military police commander at Checkpoint Charlie had slugged an East German counterpart, and that both sides were aching for a gunfight. Still another account had it that entire Soviet companies were marching toward Berlin to end the city's freedom once and for all. Berliners as a breed were drawn to gossip even in the worst of times. Given that most of those in the crowd had experienced one if not two world wars, they reckoned just about anything could happen.

Clay, who had commanded the 1948 airlift that had rescued West Berlin from a three-hundred-day Soviet blockade, had set the current confrontation in motion himself a week earlier over an issue most of his superiors in Washington did not consider a war-fighting matter. Breaking with established four-power procedures, East German border police had begun to demand that Allied civilians present their identity cards before driving into the Soviet zone of Berlin. Previously, their vehicles' distinctive license plates had been sufficient.

Convinced from personal experience that the Soviets would whittle away at the West's rights like soft salami unless they were confronted on the smallest of matters, Clay had refused, and ordered armed escorts to muscle the civilian vehicles through. Soldiers carrying bayoneted rifles and backed by American tanks had flanked the vehicles as they wound their way through the checkpoint's low, zigzag, red-and-white-striped concrete barriers.

At first, Clay's tough approach was vindicated: the East German border guards backed down. Swiftly, however, Khrushchev ordered his troops to match U.S. firepower tank for tank and to be prepared to escalate further if necessary. In a curious and ultimately unsuccessful effort to preserve deniability, Khrushchev ordered that the Soviet tanks' national markings be obscured and that their drivers wear unmarked black uniforms.

When the Soviet tanks rolled up to Checkpoint Charlie that afternoon to halt Clay's operation, they transformed a low-level border contest with the East Germans into a war of nerves between the world's two most powerful countries. U.S. and Soviet commanders operating out of emergency operation centers on opposite sides of Berlin weighed their next moves as they anxiously awaited orders from President John F. Kennedy and Premier Nikita Khrushchev.

While leaders deliberated in Washington and Moscow, the American tank crews, commanded by Major Thomas Tyree, nervously sized up their opponents across the world's most famous East–West divide. In a dramatic nighttime operation on August 13, 1961, just two and a half months earlier, East German troops and police with Soviet backing had thrown up the first, temporary barriers of barbed wire and guard posts around West Berlin's 110-mile circumference in order to contain an exodus of refugees whose flight had threatened the continued existence of the communist state.

Since then, the communists had fortified the borderline with concrete blocks, mortar, tank traps, guard towers, and attack dogs. What the world was coming to know as "the Berlin Wall" was described by Mutual Broadcasting Network's Berlin correspondent Norman Gelb as "the most remarkable, the most presumptuous urban redevelopment scheme of all time . . . that snaked through the city like the backdrop to a nightmare." Journalists, news photographers, political leaders, spy chiefs, generals, and tourists alike swarmed to Berlin to watch Winston Churchill's figurative Iron Curtain assume a physical form.

What was clear to them all was that the tank showdown at Checkpoint Charlie was no exercise. Tyree had seen to it that his men had loaded their tanks' cannon racks that morning with live ammunition. Their machine guns were at half-load. Beyond that, Tyree's men had mounted several of their tanks with bulldozer shovels. During exercises in preparation for just such a moment, he had trained his men to execute a plan to drive into East Berlin peacefully through Checkpoint Charlie, which was permitted under four-power rights, then crash through the rising Berlin Wall upon their return—daring the communists to respond.

To produce warmth and steady their nerves, the U.S. tank drivers gunned their engines to a terrifying roar. However, the small Allied contingent of 12,000 troops, only 6,500 of whom were Americans, would stand no chance in a conventional conflict against the 350,000 or so Soviet soldiers who were within striking distance of Berlin. Tyree's men knew they were little more than a trip wire for an all-out war that could go nuclear faster than you could say *Auf Wiedersehen*.

Reuters correspondent Adam Kellett-Long, who had rushed to Checkpoint Charlie to file the first report on the showdown, worried as he monitored an anxious African American soldier manning the machine gun atop one of the tanks. "If his hand shook any harder, I feared his gun would go off and he would have started World War III," Kellett-Long thought to himself.

At about midnight in Berlin, or 6:00 p.m. in Washington, Kennedy's top national security advisers were meeting in emergency session in the White House Cabinet Room. The president was growing increasingly nervous that matters were getting out of control. Just that week, Kennedy's nuclear strategists had finalized detailed contingency plans to execute a nuclear first-strike on the Soviet Union, if necessary, which would leave America's adversary devastated and its military unable to respond. The president still had not signed off on the plans and had been peppering his experts with skeptical questions. But the doomsday scenarios colored the president's mood as he sat with National Security Advisor McGeorge Bundy, Secretary of State Dean Rusk, Secretary of Defense Robert McNamara, Chairman of the Joint Chiefs of Staff General Lyman Lemnitzer, and other key U.S. officials.

From there they phoned General Clay over a secure line in his map room in West Berlin. Clay had been told Bundy was on the line and wished to speak with him, so he was taken aback when he heard the voice of Kennedy himself.

"Hello, Mr. President," Clay said loudly, abruptly ending the buzz behind him in the command center.

"How are things up there?" Kennedy asked in a voice designed to be cool and relaxed.

Everything was under control, Clay told him. "We have ten tanks at Checkpoint Charlie," he said. "The Russians have ten tanks there, too, so now we're equal."

An aide then handed General Clay a note.

"Mr. President, I've got to change my figures. I've just been told that the Russians have twenty more tanks coming up, which would give them exactly the total number of tanks that we have in Berlin. So we'll bring up our remaining twenty. Don't worry about it, Mr. President. They've matched us tank for tank. This is further evidence to me that they don't intend to do anything," he said.

The president could do the math as well. Should the Soviets escalate their numbers further, Clay lacked the conventional capability to respond. Kennedy scanned the anxious faces of his men in the room. He propped his feet up on the table, attempting to send a message of composure to men who feared matters were spinning out of control.

"Well, that's all right," said the president to Clay. "Don't lose your nerve."

"Mr. President," responded Clay with characteristic candor, "we're not worried about our nerves. We're worrying about those of you people in Washington."

A half-century has passed since the Berlin Wall rose, midway through the first year of the Kennedy administration, yet it is only now that we have sufficient distance and access to personal accounts, oral histories, and newly declassified documents in the U.S., Germany, and Russia to more confidently tell the story of the forces that shaped the historic events of 1961. Like most epic dramas, it is a story best told through time (the course of a calendar year), place (Berlin and the world capitals that shaped its fortune), and particularly people.

And few relationships between the two leading figures of their day have been as psychologically fraught or involved characters of such sharp contrasts and colliding ambitions as John F. Kennedy and Nikita Khrushchev.

Kennedy walked onto the world stage in January 1961 after winning the closest U.S. election since 1916 on a platform of "getting America moving again" following two terms of Republican President Dwight D. Eisenhower, whom he had accused of allowing Soviet communists to gain a dangerous edge both economically and militarily. He was the youngest president in American history, a forty-three-year-old American son of privilege, raised by a multimillionaire father of boundless ambition whose favored son, Joseph Jr., had died at war. Though handsome, charismatic, and a brilliant orator, the new president suffered afflictions that ranged from the adrenal insufficiency of Addison's disease to often crippling back pain exacerbated by a war injury. Though outwardly confident, he would be wracked by uncertainty about how best to engage the Soviets. He was determined to be a great president of the caliber of Abraham Lincoln and Franklin Delano Roosevelt, yet he worried they had only found their place in history through war. In the 1960s he knew that would mean nuclear devastation.

An American president's inaugural year often can be perilous, even when its occupant is a more experienced one than Kennedy, as the burdens of a dangerous world are passed from one administration to another. And during Kennedy's first five months in office, he would suffer several self-inflicted wounds, from his mishandling of the Bay of Pigs invasion to the Vienna Summit, where by his own account Khrushchev had outmaneuvered and brutalized him. Yet nowhere were the stakes higher for him than in Berlin, the central stage for U.S.–Soviet competition.

By temperament and upbringing, Khrushchev was Kennedy's opposite. The sixty-seven-year-old grandson of a serf and son of a coal miner was impulsive where Kennedy was indecisive, and bombastic where Kennedy was measured. His moods alternated between the deep-seated insecurity of a man who had been illiterate until his twenties and the bold confidence of someone who had risen to power against impossible odds while rivals faded, were purged, or were killed. Complicit in his mentor Joseph Stalin's crimes before renouncing Stalin after his death, in 1961 Khrushchev was vacillating between his instinct for reform and better relations with the West and his habit of authoritarianism and confrontation. It was his conviction that he could best advance Soviet interests through peaceful coexistence and competition with the West, yet at the same time pressures were growing on him to escalate tensions with Washington and by whatever means necessary stop the outflow of refugees that threatened to trigger East Germany's implosion.

Between the establishment of the East German state in 1949 and 1961, one of every six individuals—2.8 million people—had left as refugees. That total swelled to 4 million when one included those who had fled the Soviet-occupied zone between 1945 and 1949. The exodus was emptying the country of its most talented and motivated people.

In addition, Khrushchev was racing against the clock as 1961 began. He faced a crucial Communist Party Congress in October, at which he had reason to fear his enemies would unseat him if he failed to fix Berlin by then. When Khrushchev told Kennedy during their Vienna Summit that Berlin was "the most dangerous place in the world," what he meant was that it was the spot most likely to trigger a nuclear superpower conflict. Beyond that, Khrushchev knew that if he botched Berlin, his rivals in Moscow would destroy him.

The contest between the key supporting German actors to Khrushchev and Kennedy was just as charged, an asymmetrical conflict between East German leader Walter Ulbricht and his failing country of seventeen million people, and West German Chancellor Konrad Adenauer and his rapidly rising economic power of sixty million.

For Ulbricht, the year would be of even greater existential importance than it was for either Kennedy or Khrushchev. The so-called German Democratic Republic, as East Germany was officially known, was his life's work, and at age sixty-seven he knew that without radical remedy it was heading for economic and political collapse. The greater that danger, the more intensively he schemed to prevent it. Ulbricht's leverage in Moscow was growing in rough proportion to his country's instability because of the Kremlin's fear that East German failure would cause ripples across the Soviet empire.

Across the border in West Germany, the country's first and only chancellor, Konrad Adenauer, was, at age eighty-five and after three terms, waging war simultaneously against his own mortality and against political opponent Willy Brandt, who was West Berlin's mayor. Brandt's Social Democratic Party represented to Adenauer the unacceptable danger of leftist takeover in the coming September elections. However, Adenauer considered Kennedy himself to be the greatest threat to his legacy of a free and democratic West Germany.

By 1961, Adenauer's place in history would seem to have been assured through the phoenix-like rise of West Germany from the Third Reich's ashes. Yet Kennedy considered him a spent force upon whom his U.S. predecessors had relied too much at the expense of closer relations with Moscow. Adenauer, in turn, feared Kennedy lacked the character and backbone to stand up to the Soviets during what he was convinced would be a decisive year.

The story of *Berlin 1961* is told in three parts.

Part I, "The Players," introduces the four protagonists: Khrushchev, Kennedy, Ulbricht, and Adenauer, whose connecting tissue throughout the year is Berlin and the central role the city plays in their ambitions and fears. The early chapters capture their competing motivations and the events that set the stage for the drama that follows. On his first morning in the Lincoln Bedroom, Kennedy wakes up to Khrushchev's unilateral release of captured airmen from a U.S. spy plane, and from that point forward the plot is driven by the two leaders' jockeying and miscommunication. Meanwhile, Ulbricht works behind the scenes to force Khrushchev to crack down in Berlin, and Adenauer navigates life with a new U.S. president whom he mistrusts.

In Part II, "The Gathering Storm," Kennedy reels from the botched U.S. effort to overthrow Castro at the Bay of Pigs and sees an opportunity to recover his endangered foreign policy standing through an arms buildup and a summit meeting with Khrushchev. The greatly increased refugee exodus from East Germany sharpens the crisis for Ulbricht, who intensifies his scheming to close the Berlin border. Ever mercurial, Khrushchev transforms himself from courting to undermining Kennedy at the Vienna Summit, where he tables a new, threatening Berlin ultimatum and expresses mock sympathy about his adversary's demonstrated weakness. Kennedy is left disheartened by his own poor performance and grows preoccupied with finding ways to ensure that Khrushchev doesn't endanger the world by miscalculating American resolve.

"The Showdown," the book's third and final part, documents and describes the dithering in Washington and the decisions in Moscow that result in the stunning nighttime August 13 border-closure operation and its dramatic aftermath. Privately, Kennedy is relieved by the Soviet action and hopes that the Soviets will become easier partners with the East German refugee matter solved. He quickly learns, however, that he has overestimated the potential benefits of a Berlin Wall. Dozens of Berliners engage in desperate escape attempts, some with deadly outcomes. Internationally, the crisis intensifies as Washington debates how best to fight and win a nuclear war,

Moscow wheels its tanks into place, and the world holds its breath—just as it would again a year later when the ripples of Berlin 1961 would result in the Cuban Missile Crisis.

Sprinkled throughout the narrative are vignettes of Berliners themselves, who are buffeted by their involuntary role in a decisive moment of Cold War history: the survivor of multiple Soviet rapes who tries to tell her story to a people who just want to forget; the farmer whose resistance to land collectivization lands him in prison; the engineer whose flight to the West ends with her victory at the Miss Universe pageant; the East German soldier whose leap to freedom over coils of barbed wire, with his arm releasing his rifle in mid-flight, becomes the iconic image of liberation; and the tailor who is gunned down while trying to swim to freedom, the first victim of East German shoot-to-kill orders for would-be escapees.

Early in 1961, it was just as unthinkable that a political system would put up a wall to contain its people as it was inconceivable twenty-eight years later that the same barrier would crumble peacefully and seemingly overnight.

It is only by returning to the year that produced the Berlin Wall and revisiting the forces and the people surrounding it that one can properly understand what happened and try to settle a few of history's great unanswered questions.

Should history consider the Berlin Wall's construction the positive outcome of Kennedy's unflappable leadership—a successful means of avoiding war—or was the Wall instead the unhappy result of his missing backbone? Was Kennedy caught by surprise by the Berlin border closure, or did he anticipate it and perhaps even desire it because he believed it would defuse tensions that might lead to nuclear conflict? Were Kennedy's motivations enlightened and oriented toward peace, or cynical and shortsighted at a time when another course of action might have spared tens of millions of Eastern Europeans from another generation of Soviet occupation and oppression?

Was Khrushchev a true reformer whose efforts to reach out to Kennedy following his election were a genuine effort (that the U.S. failed to recognize) to reduce tensions? Or was he an erratic leader with whom the U.S. could never have done business? Would Khrushchev have backed off from the plan to build a Berlin Wall if he had believed Kennedy would resist? Or was the danger of East German implosion so great that he would have risked war, if necessary, to shut off the refugee flow?

The pages that follow are an attempt to shed new light, based on new evidence and fresh insights, on one of the most dramatic years of the second half of the twentieth century—even while we try to apply its lessons to the turbulent early years of the twenty-first.

BERLIN 1961

North Sea

DENMARK

Berlin

POLAND

EAST GERMANY

Bonn

NETHERLANDS

BELGIUM

LUX.

WEST GERMANY

CZECHOSLOVAKIA

FRANCE

AUSTRIA

SWITZERLAND

Falkenberg
rracks uprising

State Security
Directorate compound

S o v i e t   S e c t o r

ry headquarters
Stasi headquarters
e

To People's Army
headquarters

Soviet High Commission

0 Miles   5

0 Kilometers   5

Spree

Oberspree
Cable Works

RLIN WALL
w CANAL

E A S T   G E R M A N Y

adquarters
ying forces

© 2011 Jeffrey L. Ward

PART I

THE PLAYERS

1

KHRUSHCHEV:

COMMUNIST IN A HURRY

We have thirty nuclear weapons earmarked for France, more than enough
to destroy that country. We are reserving fifty each for West Germany and
Britain.

Premier Khrushchev to U.S. Ambassador Llewellyn E. Thompson Jr.,
January 1, 1960

No matter how good the old year has been, the New Year will be better
still. . . . I think no one will reproach me if I say that we attach great
importance to improving our relations with the USA. . . . We hope that
the new U.S. president will be like a fresh wind blowing away the stale air
between the USA and the USSR.

One year later, Khrushchev's New Year's toast, January 1, 1961

THE KREMLIN, MOSCOW
NEW YEAR'S EVE, DECEMBER 31, 1960

It was just minutes before midnight, and Nikita Khrushchev had reason
to be relieved that 1960 was nearly over. He had even greater cause for
concern about the year ahead as he surveyed his two thousand New Year's
guests under the towering, vaulted ceiling of St. George's Hall at the Kremlin.
As the storm outside deposited a thick layer of snow on Red Square and

the mausoleum containing his embalmed predecessors, Lenin and Stalin, Khrushchev recognized that Soviet standing in the world, his place in history, and—more to the point—his political survival could depend on how he managed his own blizzard of challenges.

At home, Khrushchev was suffering his second straight failed harvest. Just two years earlier and with considerable flourish, he had launched a crash program to overtake U.S. living standards by 1970, but he wasn't even meeting his people's basic needs. On an inspection tour of the country, he had seen shortages almost everywhere of housing, butter, meat, milk, and eggs. His advisers were telling him the chances of a workers' revolt were growing, not unlike the one in Hungary that he had been forced to crush with Soviet tanks in 1956.

Abroad, Khrushchev's foreign policy of peaceful coexistence with the West, a controversial break with Stalin's notion of inevitable confrontation, had crash-landed when a Soviet rocket brought down an American Lockheed U-2 spy plane the previous May. A few days later, Khrushchev triggered the collapse of the Paris Summit with President Dwight D. Eisenhower and his wartime Allies after failing to win a public U.S. apology for the intrusion into Soviet airspace. Pointing to the incident as evidence of Khrushchev's leadership failure, Stalinist remnants in the Soviet Communist Party and China's Mao Tse-tung were sharpening their knives against the Soviet leader in preparation for the 22nd Congress of the Communist Party of the Soviet Union. Having used just such gatherings himself to purge adversaries, all Khrushchev's plans for 1961 were designed to head off a catastrophe at that meeting.

With all that as the backdrop, nothing threatened Khrushchev more than the deteriorating situation in divided Berlin. His critics complained that he was allowing the communist world's most perilous wound to fester. East Berlin was hemorrhaging refugees to the West at an alarming rate. They were a self-selecting population of the country's most motivated and capable industrialists, intellectuals, farmers, doctors, and teachers. Khrushchev was fond of calling Berlin the testicles of the West, a tender place where he could squeeze when he wanted to make the U.S. wince. However, a more accurate metaphor was that it had become his and the Soviet bloc's Achilles' heel, the place where communism lay most vulnerable.

Yet Khrushchev betrayed none of those concerns as he worked a New Year's crowd that included cosmonauts, ballerinas, artists, apparatchiks, and ambassadors, all bathed in the light of the hall's six massive bronze chandeliers and three thousand electric lamps. For them, an invitation to the Soviet leader's party was itself confirmation of status. However, they buzzed with even greater than usual anticipation, for John F. Kennedy would take office in less than three weeks. They knew the Soviet leader's traditional New Year's toast would set the tone for U.S.–Soviet relations thereafter.

As the Kuranty clock of the sixteenth-century Spasskaya Tower ticked over Red Square toward its thunderous midnight chime, Khrushchev generated his own heat inside St. George's Hall. He hand-clasped some guests and bear-hugged others, nearly bursting from his baggy gray suit. It was the same energy that had carried him to power from his peasant birth in the Russian village of Kalinovka near the Ukrainian border, through revolution, civil war, Stalin's paranoid purges, world war, and the leadership battle following Stalin's death. The communist takeover had provided many Russians of humble beginnings with new opportunities, but none had survived as skillfully nor risen as far as Nikita Sergeyevich Khrushchev.

Given Khrushchev's increased capability to launch nuclear-tipped missiles at the West, it had become a consuming occupation of U.S. intelligence agencies to fathom Khrushchev's psychological makeup. In 1960, the CIA had assembled some twenty experts—internists, psychiatrists, and psychologists—to scrutinize the Soviet leader through films, intelligence files, and personal accounts. The group went so far as to inspect photo closeups of Khrushchev's arteries to assess rumors of their hardening and his high blood pressure. They concluded in a highly classified report—which later would reach President Kennedy—that despite Khrushchev's mood swings, depressions, and drinking bouts (which they reported he had recently brought under greater control), the Soviet leader exhibited the consistent behavior of what they called a "chronic optimistic opportunist." Their conclusion was that he was more of an ebullient activist than, as many had believed until then, a Machiavellian communist in Stalin's mold.

Another top-secret personality sketch prepared by the CIA for the incoming administration noted Khrushchev's "resourcefulness, audacity, a good sense of political timing and showmanship, and a touch of the gambler's instinct." It warned the newly elected Kennedy that behind the often buffoonish manner of this short, squat man lay a "shrewd native intelligence, an agile mind, drive, ambition and ruthlessness."

What the CIA didn't report was that Khrushchev took personal responsibility for Kennedy's election and was now seeking the payoff. He boasted to comrades that he had cast the deciding vote in one of America's closest presidential elections ever by refusing Republican entreaties that he release three captured American airmen—the downed U-2 pilot, Francis Gary Powers, and two crew members of an RB-47 reconnaissance plane shot down by the Soviets over the Barents Sea two months later—during the height of the election campaign. Now he was working impatiently through multiple channels to land an early summit meeting with Kennedy in hopes it would solve his Berlin problem.

During the campaign, the Soviet leader's instructions to his top officials had been clear, regarding both his desire for a Kennedy win and his distaste for Richard Nixon, who as Eisenhower's anticommunist vice president had humiliated him in Moscow during their so-called Kitchen Debate over the relative advantages of their two systems. "We can also influence the American presidential election!" he had told his comrades then. "We would never give Nixon such a present."

After the election, Khrushchev had crowed that by refusing to release the airmen he had personally cost Nixon the few hundred thousand votes he would have required for his victory. Just a ten-minute walk from his Kremlin New Year's party, the American captives languished as a reminder of Khrushchev's electoral manipulation inside the KGB's Lubyanka Prison, where the Soviet leader was keeping them as political pawns to be traded at some future moment for some other gain.

As the countdown to his New Year's toast continued, Khrushchev bathed in the crowd more like a populist politician than a communist dictator. Though still vigorously youthful, he had aged with the accelerated speed of so many other Russians, having already turned gray at age twenty-two after a serious illness. As he bantered with comrades, he often threw back his nearly bald head and exploded in mirth at one of his own stories, unself-consciously showing bad teeth with a center gap and two golden bicuspids. Closely cropped gray hair framed a round, animated face with three large warts, a slit scar under his pug nose, red cheeks with deep laughter lines, and dark, piercing eyes. He waved his hands and spoke short, staccato sentences in a loud, high-pitched, nasal voice.

He recognized many faces and asked after comrades' children by name: "How is little Tatyana? How is tiny Ivan?"

Given his purpose that evening, Khrushchev was disappointed not to find among the crowd Moscow's most important American, Ambassador Llewellyn "Tommy" Thompson, with whom he had remained close despite the decline of the U.S.–Soviet relationship. Thompson's wife, Jane, apologized to Khrushchev that her husband was home nursing ulcers. It was also true that the ambassador was still smarting from his encounter with the Soviet leader at the previous New Year's gathering, when an inebriated Khrushchev had nearly declared World War III over Berlin.

It had been two in the morning when Khrushchev, in an alcoholic haze, escorted Thompson, his wife, the French ambassador, and Italy's Communist Party leader into a newly built anteroom of St. George's Hall, curiously decorated with a running fountain filled with colored plastic rocks. Khrushchev spat at Thompson that he would make the West pay if it didn't satisfy his demands for a Berlin agreement that would include Allied troop withdrawal. "We have thirty nuclear weapons earmarked for France, more than enough to destroy that country," he said, tilting his head toward the French ambassador. He added for good measure that he was reserving fifty each for West Germany and Britain.

In an awkward attempt to restore a lighter mood, Jane Thompson had asked how many rockets Khrushchev had earmarked for Uncle Sam.

"That's a secret," Khrushchev had said with a wicked smile.

In an attempt to reverse the degenerating tone, Thompson had offered a toast to the upcoming Paris Summit with Eisenhower and its potential for improved relations. The Soviet leader, however, only escalated his threats, discarding his commitment to Eisenhower that he would refrain from any unilateral disruptions over Berlin until after the Paris meeting. Thompson was able to end the vodka-soaked session only at six in the morning, when he walked away knowing superpower relations would depend on Khrushchev's inability the next morning to recall anything he had said that night.

Thompson had dispatched a damage-control cable to President Eisenhower and Secretary of State Christian Herter that same morning, relating Khrushchev's remarks while at the same time declaring they should not be "taken literally," given the Soviet leader's intoxicated condition. He offered that the Soviet merely wished "to impress upon us the seriousness" of the Berlin situation.

A year later, and with Thompson safely at home, Khrushchev was in a more sober and generous spirit as the clock struck twelve. Following the bells welcoming the arrival of 1961, and the lighting of the forty-foot New Year's tree inside St. George's Hall, Khrushchev raised his glass and offered a toast that would be taken as doctrinal direction by party leaders and repeated in diplomatic cables around the world.

"Happy New Year, comrades, Happy New Year! No matter how good the old year has been, the New Year will be better still!"

The room exploded in cheers, embraces, and kisses.

Khrushchev ritually toasted the working people, the peasants, the intellectuals, Marxist-Leninist concepts, and peaceful coexistence among the world's peoples. In a conciliatory tone he said, "We consider the socialist system to be superior, but we never try to impose it on other states."

The hall grew silent as he turned his words to Kennedy.

"Dear Comrades! Friends! Gentlemen!" said Khrushchev. "The Soviet Union makes every effort to have friendly ties with all peoples. But I think no one will reproach me if I say that we attach great importance to improving our relations with the USA because this relationship greatly molds others. We would like to believe that the USA strives for the same outcome. We hope that the new U.S. president will be like a fresh wind blowing away the stale air between the USA and the USSR."

The man who a year earlier had counted the atomic bombs he would drop on the West was striking a peacemaker's pose. "During the election campaign," Khrushchev told the crowd, "Mr. Kennedy said if he had been president he would have expressed regret to the Soviet Union" about sending spy planes over its territory. Khrushchev said he as well wanted to put "this lamentable episode in the past and not go back to it. . . . We believe that by voting for Mr. Kennedy and against Mr. Nixon, the American people have disapproved of the policy of Cold War and worsening international relationships."

Khrushchev raised his refilled glass. "To peaceful coexistence among nations!"

Cheers.

"To friendship and peaceful coexistence among all peoples!"

Thunderous cheers. More embraces.

Khrushchev's choice of language was calculated. The repetitive use of the term "peaceful coexistence" was at the same time a declaration of intent toward Kennedy and a message of determination to his communist rivals. Recognizing Soviet economic limits and new nuclear threats, Khrushchev, in his famous secret speech at the 20th Congress of the Communist Party in 1956, had introduced the new thinking that communist states could peacefully coexist and compete with capitalist states. His opponents, however, favored a return to Stalin's more aggressive notions of world revolution and more active preparations for war.

As 1961 opened, the ghosts of Stalin endangered Khrushchev far more than any threat from the West. After his death in 1953, Stalin's bequest to Khrushchev had been a dysfunctional Soviet Union of 209 million people and dozens of nationalities stretching over one-sixth of the world's landmass. World War II's battles had depleted a third of the Soviet Union's wealth and had left some 27 million dead while destroying 17,000 Soviet towns and 70,000 villages. That didn't count the millions Stalin had killed previously through man-made famine and his paranoid purges.

Khrushchev blamed Stalin for then launching an unnecessary and costly Cold War before the Soviet Union had been able to recover from its previous devastation. In particular, he condemned Stalin for the botched Berlin blockade of 1948, when the dictator had underestimated American resolve and overestimated Soviet capabilities at a time when the U.S. still retained its nuclear monopoly. The result had been the West's breaking of the embargo, then the 1949 creation of NATO and the founding in the same year of a separate West Germany. What accompanied that was an American commitment to dig into Europe for a longer stay. The Soviet Union had paid a high price because Stalin, in Khrushchev's view, "didn't think it through properly."

Having extended the olive branch to Kennedy through his New Year's toast, a still-sober Khrushchev at two a.m. took aside West German Ambassador Hans Kroll for a private talk. For Khrushchev, the sixty-two-year-old German was the second most important Western ambassador after the absent Thompson. However, the two men were far closer personally than Khrushchev was to the American envoy, connected both by Kroll's Russian fluency and his conviction, not unusual for Germans of his generation, that his country was more closely connected culturally, historically, and potentially also politically to Moscow than to the U.S.

Accompanied by Deputy Premier Anastas Mikoyan and Presidium member Alexei Kosygin, Khrushchev and Kroll retreated to the same odd anteroom where the Soviet leader had threatened Thompson one year earlier. That year as well, Kroll had stormed out of the New Year's celebration in protest after the Soviet leader used his toast to condemn West Germany as "revanchist and militaristic."

This time, however, Khrushchev was in a seductive mood, and he summoned a waiter to pour Kroll Crimean champagne. While nursing a light Armenian red wine, the Soviet leader explained to Kroll that under doctor's orders he was not drinking vodka or other hard drinks. Kroll savored such personal exchanges with Khrushchev, and it was his practice at such moments to draw him near physically and speak in hushed tones to underscore their closeness.

Kroll had been born four years later than Khrushchev in the then Prussian town of Deutsch Piekar, which in 1922 would be ceded to Poland. He learned his first Russian while fishing as a boy on the river that divided the German and Czarist empires. His first two years as a diplomat in Moscow had come in the 1920s when post–World War I Germany and the new communist Soviet Union, then two of the most vilified countries in the world, struck the Rapallo agreement that broke their diplomatic isolation and formed an anti-Western, anti–Versailles Treaty axis.

Kroll's view was that European hostilities could only be calmed through an eventual accord enabling West Germany and the Soviet Union—"the two most powerful countries in Europe"—to get along better with each other. He had worked in that direction since leading the East–West trade department of the Economics Ministry in 1952, when West Germany was only three years old. His convictions had brought him into frequent conflict with the United States, which remained wary that too cozy a relationship could open the way to a neutral West Germany.

Khrushchev thanked Kroll for his help the previous autumn in getting West German Chancellor Konrad Adenauer to approve new economic agreements with the communist world, including the renewal of an East–West German trade accord, which had been interrupted a few months earlier. Though East Germany was the Soviet client, Khrushchev considered West Germany to be of far greater importance to the Soviet economy, due to the unique access it provided him to modern machinery, technology, and hard-currency loans.

So the Soviet leader raised his glass in a toast to what he called the Federal Republic of Germany's remarkable postwar reconstruction. Khrushchev told Kroll that he hoped Chancellor Adenauer would use his growing economic strength and thus greater independence from the U.S. to distance himself from Washington and further improve relations with the Soviets.

Kosygin then asked Kroll for permission to raise his own toast, which the ambassador granted. "You are for us the ambassador for all the Germans," he said, reflecting Khrushchev's own view that the Soviet Union would be far better off if it had been the West Germans, with all of their resources, who had become their allies, rather than the burdensome East Germans with their constant economic demands and substandard goods.

Khrushchev then laced this seduction with a threat. "The German problem must be solved in 1961," he told Kroll. The Soviet leader said he had lost his patience with the U.S. refusal to negotiate a change to Berlin's status in a manner that would allow him to stop the refugee flow and sign a war-ending peace treaty with East Germany. Mikoyan told Kroll that "certain circles" in Moscow were increasing their pressure on Khrushchev to the point that the Soviet leader could not resist their demands much longer to act on Berlin.

Kroll assumed Mikoyan was referring to what had become known within Soviet party circles as the "Ulbricht lobby," a group that had been greatly influenced by the East German leader's increasingly strident complaints that Khrushchev was not defending Germany's socialist state with sufficient vigor.

Made more agreeable by all the Soviet compliments and champagne, Kroll conceded that the Soviet leader had demonstrated remarkable patience over Berlin. He warned Khrushchev, however, that if the Soviets unilaterally upset the Berlin status quo, the result would be an international crisis, and perhaps even military conflict with the U.S. and the West.

Khrushchev disagreed. He shrugged that the West would respond with "a short period of excitement" that would quickly recede. "No one in the world will declare war over Berlin or the German question," he told Kroll. Khrushchev, knowing Kroll would report the conversation to the Americans and his superiors, said he would prefer a negotiated agreement to taking unilateral action, but he stressed, "That will depend on Kennedy."

At four in the morning, Khrushchev ended the meeting and then paraded Kroll, Kosygin, and Mikoyan through the still-dancing crowd, which paused and opened an aisle for them to walk through.

Even as experienced an ambassador as Kroll never knew which of Khrushchev's frequent threats to take seriously. Yet the manner in which Khrushchev had raised the Berlin issue that evening convinced him that the year ahead would bring a confrontation over the matter. He would relay that view to Adenauer—and through him to the Americans. It was clear to Kroll that Khrushchev had concluded that the risks of inaction were growing greater than the dangers of action.

However, the way the year would play out—cooperation or confrontation—would depend on the dilemma that lay at the heart of Khrushchev's thinking on Berlin.

On the one hand, Khrushchev remained certain that he could not afford a military competition or war with the Americans. He was committed to negotiating a peaceful coexistence with the U.S. and was reaching out to the new American president in hopes of brokering a Berlin deal.

On the other hand, Khrushchev's meeting with West German Ambassador Kroll demonstrated the growing pressure on him to solve his Berlin problem before it became a larger threat, both to the Soviet empire and, more immediately, to his own leadership.

For that reason, Khrushchev was a communist in a hurry.

And that was not his only Berlin problem. The Berliners themselves despised him, resented Soviet soldiers, and were weary of their occupation. Their memories of the postwar period were only bad ones. . . .

Marta Hillers's Story of Rape

Marta Hillers's only consolation was that she had refused to put her name on the extraordinary manuscript in which she had so meticulously recounted the Soviet conquest of Berlin during the cold spring of 1945. It had been a time when her life—like that of tens of thousands of other Berlin women and girls— had become a nightmare of fear, hunger, and rape.

Published for the first time in German in 1959, the book had brought to life one of the worst military atrocities ever. According to estimates extracted from hospital records, between 90,000 and 130,000 Berlin women had been raped during the last days of the war and the first days of Soviet occupation. Tens of thousands of others had fallen victim elsewhere in the Soviet zone.

Hillers had expected the book to be welcomed by a people who wanted the world to know that they, too, had been the victims of war. However, Berliners had responded with either hostility or silence. The world still felt little sympathy for any pain inflicted on a German people who had brought the world so much suffering. Berlin women who had lived through the humiliation had no desire to recall it. And Berlin men found it too painful to be reminded of their failure to protect their wives and daughters. Early 1961 was a time of complacency and amnesia in Soviet-dominated East Germany and East Berlin, and there seemed little reason to get worked up about a history that no one had the power to change or the stomach to digest.

Perhaps the German response should have been no surprise to Hillers, given the shame she herself expressed in signing her memoirs, Eine Frau in Berlin (A Woman in Berlin), *only as "Anonyma." She'd published them only after marrying and safely moving to Switzerland. The book had not circulated or been reviewed in East Germany, and only a few copies had been smuggled across to the communist zone in suitcases stuffed full of Western fashion magazines and other more escapist literature. In West Berlin, Anonyma's memoirs sold poorly, and reviews accused her either of anticommunist propaganda or of besmirching the honor of German women—something she would insist that Soviet soldiers had done just fine long before her.*

One such review, buried on page 35 of West Berlin's Tagesspiegel, *bore the headline:* A DISSERVICE TO BERLIN WOMEN / BEST-SELLER ABROAD— A FALSIFIED SPECIAL CASE. *What irritated the reviewer, who accused the author of "shameless immorality," was the book's uncompromising narrative that so richly captured the cynicism of the postwar months. Judgments like that of* Der Tagesspiegel *prompted Hillers to remain underground and to prohibit any new editions of the book from being published during her lifetime, which ended at age ninety in 2001.*

She would never know that, following her death, her book would be republished and become a best-seller in several languages, including the German edition in 2003. Nor would she ever have the satisfaction of knowing her story would be made into a major German movie in 2008 and become a favorite of feminists everywhere.

Back in 1961, Hillers was more concerned with dodging the reporters who were trying to hunt her down from the few clues in her published pages. The book revealed that she was a journalist in her thirties, had lived in the Tempelhof district, had spent sufficient time in the Soviet Union to speak some Russian, and was "a pale-faced blonde always dressed in the same winter coat." None of that had been enough to identify her.

Still, nothing better captured the German attitude of the time toward their occupiers than the substance of Hillers's book and Berliners' aversion to reading it. The East German relationship to their Soviet military occupiers, who still numbered 400,000 to 500,000 by 1961, was a mixture of pity and dread, complacency, and amnesia. Most East Germans had grown resigned to their seemingly permanent cohabitation. Among those who hadn't, many had fled as refugees.

The East German pity toward their Soviet occupiers, whom they considered inferior to them, came from what they could see with their own eyes: undernourished, unwashed teenagers in soiled uniforms who would drop to the ground to retrieve the unfinished stubs of their discarded cigarettes or trade their service medals and gasoline for any form of consumable alcohol that would help them briefly escape their miserable existence.

The pity was also stirred by the occasional alarms that accompanied desperate attempts at desertion. For the teenage soldiers, the brutality of officers, hazing by fellow soldiers, and the cold and overcrowded quarters occasionally became too much to bear.

Their barracks, built during the Third Reich or earlier, housed three times the number of soldiers that Hitler had ever bunked there. The latest escape had come after an insurrection on New Year's Eve, when a barracks uprising in Falkenberg had resulted in the escape to West Berlin of four soldiers and the dispatch of Soviet search parties along the Berlin border. Stories circulated of Soviet troops setting alight barns and other structures where deserters had gone in hiding—burning the escapees alive alongside farm animals.

That only increased a deeply ingrained German dread of the Soviets.

That dread had grown after the events of June 17, 1953, when Soviet troops and tanks had put down a workers' revolt after Stalin's death that had shaken the young East German state to its fragile foundations. As many as 300 East Germans had died then, and a further 4,270 were imprisoned.

Yet the deeper roots of East German terror were found in the events that Hillers had described. There was a reason why women in East Berlin froze up whenever a Soviet soldier passed by or when East German leader Walter Ulbricht spoke on the radio of the enduring friendship with the Soviet people.

Hillers described why outsiders had so little sympathy for what German women had suffered—and why many Germans wondered whether some vengeful God had delivered this punishment of rape in retribution for their own misbehavior. "Our German calamity," Hillers wrote during the first days of occupation, "has a bitter taste—of repulsion, sickness, insanity, unlike anything in history. The radio just broadcast another concentration camp report.

The most horrific thing is the order and the thrift: millions of human beings as fertilizer, mattress stuffing, soft soap, felt mats—Aeschylus never saw anything like that."

Hillers despaired at the stupidity of Nazi leaders who had issued orders that liquor should be left behind for advancing Soviet troops on the theory that inebriated soldiers would be less dangerous adversaries. If it had not been for Soviet drunkenness, Hillers wrote, Berlin women would have suffered only half as much rape at the hands of Russians who "aren't natural Casanovas" and thus "had to drown their inhibitions."

With characteristic power, she described one of the many times she'd been raped and how it had driven her to seek protection.

The one shoving me is an older man with gray stubble, reeking of brandy and horses . . . No sound. Only an involuntary grinding of teeth when my underclothes are ripped apart. The last untorn ones I had.

Suddenly his finger is on my mouth, stinking of horse and tobacco. I open my eyes. A stranger's hands expertly pulling apart my jaws. Eye to eye. Then with great deliberation he drops a gob of gathered spit into my mouth.

I'm numb. Not with disgust, only cold. My spine is frozen: icy, dizzy shivers around the back of my head. I feel myself gliding and falling, down, down through the pillows and the floorboards. So that's what it means to sink into the ground.

Once more eye to eye. The stranger's lips open, yellow teeth, one in front half broken off. The corners of the mouth lift, tiny wrinkles radiate from the corners of his eyes. The man is smiling.

Before leaving he fishes something out of his pants pocket, thumps it down on the nightstand, and without a word, pulls the chair aside, and slams the door shut behind him. A crumpled pack of Russian cigarettes, only a few left. My pay.

I stand up—dizzy, nauseated. My ragged clothes tumble to my feet. I stagger through the hall . . . into the bathroom. I throw up. My face green in the mirror, my vomit in the basin. I sit on the edge of the bathtub, without daring to flush, since I'm still gagging and there's so little water left in the bucket.

It was at that point that Marta Hillers made her decision. She cleaned herself up a bit and went to the street to hunt for a "wolf," a higher-ranking Soviet officer who would become her protector. She concluded it was better to be abused by just one Russian on a regular basis than by an unending string of them. Like millions of other Germans, Hillers was reaching an accommodation with an occupation she could not resist.

Only years later would researchers try to reconstruct the full horror of that time. Between the late summer and early autumn of 1945, a minimum of 110,000 women between the ages of twelve and eighty-eight had been raped. Some 40 percent of the victims were raped on multiple occasions. One in five of the rape victims became pregnant, roughly half of these gave birth, and the other half had abortions, often without anesthesia. Thousands of women killed themselves for the shame of having been raped or out of fear of being the next victims. Some 5 percent of all Berlin newborns in the following year would be "Russenbabys." Across Germany, the number would be 150,000 to 200,000 children.

It was as these children were first becoming teenagers, in 1958, that Khrushchev would provoke what would become known as the Berlin Crisis.

2

KHRUSHCHEV: THE BERLIN CRISIS UNFOLDS

West Berlin has turned into a sort of malignant tumor of fascism and revanchism. That's why we decided to do some surgery.

Nikita Khrushchev, at his first press conference as premier,
November 27, 1958

The next President in his first year is going to be confronted with a very serious question on our defense of Berlin, our commitment to Berlin. It's going to be a test of our nerve and will. . . . We're going to be face-to-face with the most serious Berlin crisis since 1949 or 1950.

Senator John F. Kennedy, in a presidential campaign debate with
Vice President Richard Nixon, October 7, 1960

PALACE OF SPORTS, MOSCOW
MONDAY, NOVEMBER 10, 1958

On an unlikely stage and before an unsuspecting audience, Nikita Khrushchev launched what the world would come to know as "the Berlin Crisis."

Standing at the center of Moscow's newest and grandest field house for indoor sports, the Soviet leader told a gathering of Polish communists that he planned to renounce the postwar agreements that had been the basis for Europe's fragile stability. He would abrogate the Potsdam accord that had been signed with wartime allies and unilaterally change Berlin's occupied status, with the aim of liquidating the city's western part altogether, and removing all military forces from the city.

The venue for his remarks, the Palace of Sports, which rested beside Lenin Central Stadium, had opened to great fanfare two years earlier as a state-of-the-art stage to show off Soviet athletic accomplishment. Since then, however, its most memorable moment had been the stunning defeat of the Soviets by the Swedes at the 1957 ice hockey world championships, which had been tainted by the boycott conducted by the U.S. and other Western hockey powers in protest against the Soviet crackdown in Hungary. The Swedish victory had come after a defenseman had head-blocked a puck before the goal, producing a gusher of blood and the championship.

Khrushchev's Polish audience had anticipated far less drama. Having stayed on in Moscow following a celebration of the forty-first anniversary of the Bolshevik revolution, they had expected the routine rhetoric of one of communism's countless friendship meetings. Instead, they sat in stunned silence as Khrushchev declared, "The time has obviously arrived for the signatories of the Potsdam Agreement to discard the remnants of the occupation regime in Berlin and thereby make it possible to create a normal situation in the capital of the German Democratic Republic."

The Poles weren't the only surprised party. Khrushchev had failed to give advance notice either to the Western signatories of the Potsdam agreement or to his socialist allies, including the East Germans. He had acted without even seeking the blessing of his own Communist Party leadership. Only shortly before the speech did Khrushchev share what he planned to say with the leader of the Polish delegation, the stunned Communist Party First Secretary Władysław Gomułka. If Khrushchev meant what he said, Gomułka feared he could trigger a war over Berlin.

Khrushchev explained to Gomułka that he was acting unilaterally because he had wearied of Berlin diplomacy that was leading nowhere. He was prepared to risk a confrontation with the West, and he argued that he was in a better position to succeed than Stalin in 1948 because Moscow had now overcome the American nuclear weapons monopoly. Under a project called "Operation Atom," Khrushchev would deploy a nuclear deterrent on East German territory within weeks. Twelve medium-range R-5 missiles would give Khrushchev the capability to respond to any U.S. nuclear attack on East Germany with counterstrikes on London and Paris—if not yet New York. Without reference to those still-secret weapons, Khrushchev told Gomułka, "Now the balance of forces is different. . . . Today America has moved closer to us; our missiles can hit them directly." Though not literally true, the Soviet leader was newly in a position to annihilate Washington's European allies.

Khrushchev did not share any details about the timing or implementation of his new Berlin plan, because he had not worked them out yet himself. What he told his Polish audience was that the Soviets and the Western Allies, according to his plan, would over time remove all their military personnel from East Germany and East Berlin. He would sign a war-ending peace treaty with East Germany and then hand over all Soviet functions in Berlin to that country, including control of all access to West Berlin. Thereafter, U.S., British, and French soldiers would need to seek East German leader Walter Ulbricht's permission to enter any part of Berlin by road or air. Khrushchev told the Palace of Sports crowd he would consider any resistance to East Germany's exercise of these new rights—which could include blocking air and road access to West Berlin—as an attack upon the Soviet Union itself and its Warsaw Pact alliance.

Khrushchev's shocking escalation of the Cold War had three sources.

Above all, it was an attempt to win the attention of President Eisenhower, who had been disregarding his demands for Berlin negotiations. It seemed that no matter what Khrushchev did, he could not win the respect of American officials that he so craved.

His party rivals rightly argued that the U.S. had given him scant credit and no reward for a series of unilateral measures he had taken to reduce Cold War tensions since Stalin's death. He had gone far beyond simply replacing the concept of inevitable war with peaceful coexistence. He had also cut Soviet troop numbers unilaterally by 2.3 million men between 1955 and 1958, and had withdrawn Soviet forces from Finland and Austria, opening the way for those countries' neutrality. He had also encouraged political and economic reform among Soviet satellites in Eastern Europe.

The second source of Khrushchev's impulsive Berlin move was his growing confidence in power after having put down the so-called anti-party coup against him in June 1957, led by former premiers Vyacheslav Molotov and Georgy Malenkov and his onetime mentor, Lazar Kaganovich. They had attacked him partly because of just the sort of reckless leadership style he was now demonstrating over Berlin. Unlike Stalin, he hadn't killed them but exiled them to lesser roles far from Moscow's power center: Molotov to Mongolia as ambassador, Malenkov to Kazakhstan to run a hydroelectric plant, and Kaganovich to the Urals to direct a small potassium factory. He thereafter removed from power his popular defense minister Marshal Georgy Zhukov, whom he also suspected of plotting against him.

To justify his bold action on Berlin, he had told his party leadership just four days before his speech that the U.S. had already abrogated the Potsdam accord first, by bringing West Germany into NATO in 1955, and then by preparing to give it nuclear weapons. After outlining his plan of action, he closed the meeting without taking the usual vote of his Presidium on matters of such significance, having sensed the possibility of opposition.

The third source of Khrushchev's speech was Berlin itself, where the refugee bleed was accelerating. Despite his greater self-assurance in power, Khrushchev knew from personal experience that problems in the divided city could end careers in Moscow. Shortly after Stalin's death, Khrushchev had used the threat of East German implosion to help destroy his most dangerous rival, former secret police chief Lavrentiy Beria, after Soviet troops put down the East German workers' uprising of June 17, 1953.

At the time, Khrushchev had been only a dark horse candidate for Stalin's succession among the collective leadership that had replaced the dictator. He was a foreign policy neophyte who saw German policy primarily through a domestic political lens. As part of his power play, Beria had led a proxy campaign against Stalinist East German leader Walter Ulbricht and his harsh policy of *Aufbau des Sozialismus*, or "construction of socialism."

Ulbricht had been countering internal opposition and the growing refugee numbers through escalated arrests and repression, forced collectivization of farms, accelerated industrial nationalization, greater military recruitment, and expanded censorship. The result had been an even greater outflow of refugees in the first four months of 1953—122,000 East Germans, twice the rate of the previous year. The March 1953 figure of 56,605 was six times larger than a year earlier.

At a decisive party leadership meeting, Beria had said, "All we need is a peaceful Germany. Whether it is socialist or not isn't important to us," even if it were "united, democratic, bourgeois and neutral." Beria wanted to negotiate substantial financial compensation from the West in exchange for Soviet agreement to a neutral, unified Germany. He had even assigned one of his most loyal lieutenants to explore such a deal with Western countries. "What does it amount to, this GDR?" Beria had asked, using the abbreviation for East Germany's misleading official name. "It's only kept in existence by Soviet troops, even if we do call it the German Democratic Republic."

The post-Stalin collective leadership did not heed Beria's call to abandon the socialist cause in East Germany, but it did demand that he reverse what it called his "excesses." Following Soviet orders, Ulbricht stopped new agricultural collectives and ended large-scale political arrests; introduced an amnesty for many political prisoners; reduced the repression of religious freedoms; and expanded the production of consumer goods.

Khrushchev took little active part in the debates that produced this abrupt policy change, but he also didn't oppose the reforms. He then watched the loosening of Stalinist controls inspire an uprising that might have prompted East Germany's collapse if Soviet tanks had not intervened.

A little more than a week after the uprising, Khrushchev masterminded the June 26 arrest of Beria. Among other charges, Khrushchev argued that Beria had been willing to abandon socialism altogether in a Germany that had been conquered at such great Soviet human cost during World War II. At the party plenary that sealed Beria's fate and set in motion events that resulted in his execution, fellow communist leaders branded him as an unreliable socialist and called him a "filthy people's enemy who should be expelled [from the party] and tried for treason." It called his willingness to give up East German socialism a "direct capitulation to the imperialist forces."

Khrushchev came away from the Beria experience with two lessons he would never forget. First, he had learned that political liberalization in East Germany could result in the country's collapse. Second, he had seen that Soviet mistakes made in Berlin could end careers in Moscow. Three years later, in 1956, Khrushchev would grease his own rise to power by renouncing Stalinism's criminal excesses at the 20th Party Congress. However, he would never forget the contradictory lesson that it was only Stalinist-style repression that had saved East Germany and allowed him to remove his most dangerous adversary.

In the first days following Khrushchev's Palace of Sports speech, President Eisenhower chose not to respond publicly, hoping, as had happened so often in the past, that the Soviet leader's bluster would not be accompanied by concrete action. Khrushchev, however, would not be ignored. Two weeks after the speech, on America's Thanksgiving Day, he transformed his Berlin speech into an ultimatum that would require a U.S. response. He had softened some of his demands to gain his Presidium's backing in a declaration delivered to the embassies of all interested governments.

Khrushchev backed off from his threat to immediately discard all Soviet obligations under the Potsdam agreement. Instead, he would give the West six months to negotiate with him before unilaterally altering the city's status. At the same time, he fleshed out his plan to demilitarize and neutralize West Berlin in a manner that would leave it both outside the Soviet bloc and the West.

Khrushchev summoned U.S. correspondents, who were in their Moscow apartments carving Thanksgiving turkeys, to tell them about some knife-work he planned of his own. During his first press conference as premier, evidence itself of Berlin's growing significance to him, Khrushchev told reporters, "West Berlin has turned into a sort of malignant tumor of fascism and revanchism. That's why we decided to do some surgery."

Referring to the text of the twenty-eight-page diplomatic note, Khrushchev told the correspondents that it had been thirteen years since the war had ended, and thus it was time to accept the reality of two German states. East Germany would never give up socialism, he said, nor would West Germany ever succeed in absorbing East Germany. Hence, he was giving Eisenhower a choice: within six months, he could negotiate a peace treaty that would demilitarize and neutralize West Berlin, or Moscow would act unilaterally to achieve the same outcome.

Khrushchev's son Sergei, then twenty-three years old, worried that his father was giving Eisenhower no escape route from a collision course that could lead to nuclear conflict. He told his father that the Americans would never accept his proposed terms. Although Russians were known as chess players, Sergei knew that in this case—as in so many others—his impetuous father had not thought out his next move.

Khrushchev laughed off Sergei's fears: "No one would start a war over Berlin," he said. He told Sergei all he wanted was to "wring consent" out of the U.S. to start formal Berlin negotiations and preempt the exasperating diplomatic process of an "incessant exchange of notes, letters, declarations and speeches."

Only by setting a tight deadline, Khrushchev told his son, could he move both sides toward an acceptable solution.

"What if we can't find it?" Sergei asked.

"We'll look for another way out," Khrushchev said. "Something will always turn up."

In answer to similar doubts posed by his longtime interpreter and foreign policy adviser, Oleg Troyanovsky, Khrushchev paraphrased Lenin when he explained that he planned to "engage in battle and then see what happens."

KHRUSHCHEV'S KREMLIN OFFICE, MOSCOW
MONDAY, DECEMBER 1, 1958

A few days after Thanksgiving, during one of the most extraordinary meet-ings ever between a Soviet leader and an American politician, Khrushchev made clear that his Berlin ultimatum for the moment was far more about getting President Eisenhower's attention than it was about altering Berlin's status.

Giving him only a half hour's notice, Khrushchev summoned visiting Minnesota Senator Hubert H. Humphrey to his Kremlin office for the lon-gest meeting any American official or elected politician had ever had with any Soviet leader. Though scheduled for only an hour from three p.m., their talks ended just before midnight, after an eight-hour, twenty-five-minute exchange.

To show off his knowledge of matters American, Khrushchev ex-pounded on the local politics of California, New York, and Humphrey's home state of Minnesota. He joked about "the new McCarthy"—not anti-communist Joe but the left-of-center congressman Eugene, who would later run for president. He shared with Humphrey a secret "no American has heard of," telling him of the successful test of a Soviet five-million-ton hy-drogen bomb using only a tenth of the fissionable material previously re-quired to produce an explosion of its magnitude. He also spoke about the development of a missile with a 9,000-mile range, for the first time sufficient to strike U.S. targets.

After asking Humphrey to name his native city, Khrushchev bounced to his feet and drew a bold blue circle around Minneapolis on a map of the United States hanging on his wall—"so that I don't forget to order them to spare the city when the rockets fly." Khrushchev struck Humphrey as a man infected with personal and national insecurity, "somebody who has risen from poverty and weakness to wealth and power but is never wholly confi-dent of himself and his new status."

In recounting his meeting the following day to Ambassador Thompson, so that the U.S. envoy could relay it to President Eisenhower, Humphrey said Khrushchev returned perhaps two dozen times to the matter of Berlin and his ultimatum, which the Soviet leader said had followed "many months of thought." Humphrey concluded the chief purpose of their marathon meeting was "to impress him with the Soviet position on Berlin and to convey his words and thoughts to the President."

Khrushchev wielded an arsenal of metaphors to describe the city. It was alternatively a cancer, a knot, a thorn, and a bone in his throat. He told Humphrey he intended to cough the bone loose by making West Berlin a "free city" that would be demilitarized and guaranteed by United Nations observers. To convince Humphrey he wasn't trying to trick the U.S. into giving up West Berlin to communist control, he recalled at length how he had personally ordered the withdrawal of Soviet troops from Austria in 1955, thus ensuring its neutrality. Khrushchev told Humphrey that at the time he had argued to Foreign Minister Molotov that Russian troops were only useful in Austria if he intended to expand westward, and he didn't want to do that. So, he said, "a neutral Austria was established and a source of conflict was removed."

His argument was that Soviet behavior in Austria should serve for Eisenhower both as a model for West Berlin and as reassurance about its future. Because of that, he said, the U.S., Britain, and France had no need to leave any troops in Berlin. "Twenty-five thousand troops in Berlin are of no importance unless you want to make war," he said in a calm voice. "Why do you maintain this thorn? A free city, a free Berlin, could lead to the breaking of the ice between the USSR and the USA."

Khrushchev insisted to Humphrey that by solving the Berlin problem, he and Eisenhower could improve their personal relationship and together achieve a historic thaw in the Cold War. And if the U.S. president didn't like the details of his Berlin plan, Khrushchev told Humphrey, he would be open to a counterproposal. Khrushchev said he could accept any alternative suggestions from Eisenhower as long as they didn't include either German unification or "the liquidation of the socialist system in East Germany." For the first time, he was painting his red lines for any Berlin talks.

Khrushchev shifted so rapidly between seduction and threats that Humphrey was reminded of his father's treatment for chilblains back in South Dakota, which involved the frequent shifting of his feet between hot and cold water. "Our troops are there not to play cards, our tanks are not there to show you the way to Berlin," Khrushchev blurted to Humphrey at one point. "We mean business." At the next moment, however, the Soviet leader's eyes would moisten as he spoke with dripping sentimentality about losing a son in World War II and his affection for President Eisenhower. "I like President Eisenhower," he told Humphrey. "We wish no evil to the United States or to Berlin. You must assure the President of this."

Eisenhower responded to Khrushchev's Berlin ultimatum just as the Soviet leader had hoped. He signed on to a four-power foreign ministers' meeting in Geneva, which East and West German representatives would attend as observers. Although progress there proved disappointing, Eisenhower thereafter invited Khrushchev to be the first Soviet Communist Party leader to visit the United States.

Khrushchev congratulated himself, considering Eisenhower's agreement to receive him in the capitalists' lair "as a concrete result of the Berlin pressure he had been exerting on the Western powers."

He felt he had finally extracted from America the respect he so profoundly craved for himself and his homeland.

KHRUSHCHEV'S U.S. VISIT
SEPTEMBER 15–27, 1959

As the departure date for his trip to America drew closer, Khrushchev grew increasingly concerned that his hosts were planning a "provocation," a damaging slight upon his arrival or at other points during his visit. That in turn could be used against him at home by his now silenced but far from vanquished rivals as evidence that his high-profile U.S. visit was both naive and harmful to Soviet interests.

For that reason, Khrushchev's considerations about how he would negotiate Berlin's future in the U.S. were secondary to his scrutiny of every aspect of the itinerary to ensure he didn't suffer what he referred to as "moral damage." Though Khrushchev was a communist leader ostensibly representing the proletariat vanguard, his advance team demanded that he be treated with the pomp and circumstance of a visiting Western head of state.

Khrushchev balked, for example, when he learned his most crucial talks with Eisenhower would occur at a place called "Camp David," a place none of his advisers knew and which sounded to him like a *gulag*, or internment camp. He recalled that in the first years after the Revolution, the Americans had brought a Soviet delegation to Sivriada, in the Turkish Princes' Islands, where the stray dogs of Istanbul had been sent to die in 1911. Thinking to himself that "the capitalists never missed a chance to embarrass or offend the Soviet Union," he feared "this Camp David was . . . a place where people who were mistrusted could be kept in quarantine."

Khrushchev only agreed to the meeting after his advance team, following investigation, reported that the Camp David invitation was a particular honor, as Eisenhower was taking him to a country *dacha* built by Roosevelt in the mountains of Maryland during World War II. Khrushchev would later express shame about how the episode revealed Soviet ignorance. More important, however, was what it said about the potent mixture of mistrust and insecurity with which Khrushchev approached every aspect of his relationship with the U.S.

Disregarding the advice of his pilot, Khrushchev flew across the Atlantic in a still-experimental Tupolev Tu-114, which had not yet passed its required tests and had microscopic cracks in its engine. Despite the risks, Khrushchev insisted upon this means of travel, as it was the only aircraft in the Soviet fleet that could reach Washington nonstop. He would thus arrive aboard a plane that had the world's largest passenger capacity, longest range, greatest thrust, and fastest cruising speed. That said, Soviet fishing boats, cargo ships, and tankers formed a line under the plane between Iceland and New York as a potential rescue party should the engine fissures expand and force a crash landing at sea.

Khrushchev would recall later that his "nerves were strained with ex-citement" as he looked from the window of his plane as it circled over its landing area and he considered the trip's deeper significance: "We had fi-nally forced the United States to recognize the necessity of establishing closer contacts with us. . . . We'd come a long way from the time when the United States wouldn't even grant us diplomatic recognition."

For the moment, Berlin was an afterthought to this larger national pur-pose. He relished the notion that it had been the might of the Soviet econ-omy, its armed forces, and the entire socialist camp that had prompted Eisenhower to seek better relations. "From a ravaged, backward, illiterate Russia, we had transformed ourselves into a Russia whose accomplishments had stunned the world."

To Khrushchev's relief and delight, Eisenhower greeted him at Andrews Air Force Base outside Washington, D.C., with a red carpet and a twenty-one-gun salute. Khrushchev would later recall that he was "immensely proud; it even shook me up a bit. . . . Here was the United States of America, the greatest capitalist power in the world, bestowing honor on the repre-sentative of our socialist homeland—a country which, in the eyes of capital-ist America, had always been unworthy or, worse, infected with some sort of plague."

It was more a result of this improved mood than any deeper Berlin strategy that moved Khrushchev to tell President Eisenhower during their first meeting on September 15 that he would like to "come to terms on Germany and thereby on Berlin too." Without providing further details, Khrushchev said, "We do not contemplate taking unilateral action." For his part, Eisenhower called the Berlin situation "abnormal," language the Soviet leader considered encouraging for Berlin talks that would come at the end of the trip.

The coast-to-coast journey that followed was marked by dramatic highs and lows that illustrated both sides of Khrushchev's complex emotional relationship with the U.S.: the eager suitor seeking approval from the world's greatest power, and the insecure adversary scanning for the slightest offense.

He and his wife, Nina Petrovna, sat between Bob Hope and Frank Sinatra during a lunch at Twentieth Century–Fox, at which Marilyn Monroe wore her tightest dress, but the Soviet leader railed like a spoiled child at being denied entry to Disneyland—wondering whether it was because the amusement park had cholera or a missile launching pad. Khrushchev saw conspiracy in the choice of Russian-born Jewish movie mogul Victor Carter as his Los Angeles escort, blaming much of what went wrong in the city on the evil intent of the émigré whose family had fled Rostov-on-Don.

His trip had nearly ended on his first day in California, when Khrushchev struck back at conservative Los Angeles Mayor Norris Poulson during a late-night speech at a star-studded banquet. Looking to score domestic political points, the mayor had refused the appeal of Henry Cabot Lodge Jr.—the U.S. ambassador to the United Nations and Khrushchev's companion throughout the trip—that he remove anticommunist lines that the Soviet leader would find offensive. "It took us only twelve hours to get here," Khrushchev said in response, asking that his plane be prepared for departure. "Perhaps it will take us even less time to get back."

The climactic Camp David meeting began badly, as Khrushchev and Eisenhower engaged in two days of acrimonious talks over everything from the threat of nuclear war (Khrushchev said he didn't fear it) to discriminatory rules on what technology Americans could sell Moscow (Khrushchev sneered that he didn't need low-tech U.S. help to make shoes or sausages). Eisenhower prevented a breakdown in talks when he flew his guest by helicopter to his Gettysburg ranch and presented him with one of his cattle as a gift. In return, Khrushchev invited Eisenhower and his grandchildren to visit the Soviet Union.

The following morning, Khrushchev agreed to abandon his Berlin ultimatum of the previous year in exchange for Eisenhower's commitment that he would enter talks on Berlin's status with the aim of achieving a solution that would satisfy all parties.

With unusual candor, Khrushchev shared with Eisenhower that he had only issued a Berlin ultimatum as "the result of the high-handed attitude of the U.S. toward the USSR, which had led the Soviets to think that there was no alternative." He said he needed a disarmament agreement with the U.S., as it was hard enough to feed his country without having to bear the costs of an arms race. The two men then compared notes about how their military establishments were pushing them each toward ever larger arms purchases, always blaming the aggressive posture of the other country.

Talks nearly collapsed again when Khrushchev insisted on a joint communiqué to capture their agreement on Berlin negotiations, but demanded the U.S. side take out language that "there would be no time limit on them." After a difficult exchange, Eisenhower accepted Khrushchev's terms as long as he could mention at their joint press conference the Soviet leader's agreement to abandon his Berlin ultimatum, which Khrushchev would confirm if the media asked.

For his part, Eisenhower agreed to what Khrushchev had most wanted: a four-power Paris Summit on Berlin and disarmament issues. For Khrushchev, the agreement immunized him against critics who argued his "peaceful coexistence" policy toward the West had been without result— and provided incontrovertible proof that his course was improving the Soviet Union's global standing.

Elated by the U.S. trip and the prospect of a summit, Khrushchev preemptively cut Soviet armed forces by a further 1.2 million men in December, the largest-percentage reduction since the 1920s. Reports that France's Charles de Gaulle and West Germany's Konrad Adenauer were rolling back Eisenhower's willingness to negotiate Berlin's status did not dampen Khrushchev's self-congratulatory optimism.

SVERDLOVSK, SOVIET UNION
SUNDAY, MAY 1, 1960

Just eight months after his American journey, what Khrushchev heralded as the "spirit of Camp David" exploded over Sverdlovsk in the Ural Mountains when a Soviet surface-to-air missile brought down a spy plane.

Initially, Khrushchev celebrated the incident as a triumph of Soviet antiaircraft technology and a change of luck. As recently as three weeks earlier, his air defense forces had failed to bring down the advanced, high-altitude CIA plane even though the Soviets knew exactly where it was flying. While in pursuit on that earlier occasion, a MiG-19 Soviet fighter had crashed in Semipalatinsk near a secret nuclear testing site that the U-2 plane was photographing. Two newly developed high-altitude interceptors also could not catch up to the U-2 as it collected images of the Tyumatom ballistic missile site.

Up until that point, a frustrated Khrushchev had kept the U.S. intrusions secret from the world so as to avoid having to admit Soviet military failure. Now that his forces had shot down the U-2, he gleefully toyed with the Americans by saying nothing about the incident while the CIA put out a false cover story—one it would later be forced to withdraw with embarrassment—that a weather plane had gone missing over Turkey.

Within days, however, Khrushchev recognized that the U-2 incident posed greater dangers to him than to the Americans. Political enemies whom he had neutralized after putting down the 1957 coup against him began to regroup. Mao Tse-tung publicly condemned Khrushchev's wooing of the Americans as "communist betrayal." Though still speaking privately, Soviet party officials and military brass more confidently questioned Khrushchev's troop reductions. They argued that Khrushchev was undermining their ability to defend the homeland.

Years later, Khrushchev would concede to the American physician A. McGhee Harvey, a specialist who was treating his daughter, that the U-2 incident proved to be the watershed event after which he "was no longer in full control." From that point forward, Khrushchev found it harder to defend himself against those who argued that he was too weak in the face of the militaristic and imperialist intentions of duplicitous Americans.

At first, Khrushchev tried to keep on track the Paris Summit that was scheduled to occur two weeks after the U-2 event—a meeting that he had worked so hard to organize as a crowning moment of his rule. Khrushchev told domestic critics that if they pulled out, they would only be rewarding U.S. hard-liners like CIA chief Allen Dulles, who, he argued, had ordered the flights to undermine Eisenhower's genuine peace efforts.

Eisenhower removed Khrushchev's last political cover at a press conference on May 11, just five days ahead of the summit. To reassure Americans that their government had acted responsibly and under his complete control, Eisenhower said he had personally approved Gary Powers's U-2 flight—as he had with each and every one of the sensitive missions. Such risks were necessary, he said, because Soviet secrecy made it impossible to assess Moscow's intentions and capabilities through any other means. "We are getting to the point where we must decide whether we are trying to prepare to fight a war or prevent one," he told his national security team.

By the time he landed in Paris, Khrushchev had concluded that if he couldn't get a public apology from Eisenhower, he would have to prompt the collapse of the Paris talks. It was politically safer for him to abandon the summit than to go ahead with a meeting that was destined to fail, and by then it also was clear the U.S. would offer none of the concessions he was seeking on Berlin.

Though Eisenhower refused to apologize in Paris for the U-2 mission, he tried to avoid a summit collapse by agreeing to stop the flights. He went an important step further and proposed an "open skies" approach that would allow United Nations planes to monitor both countries with overflights. Khrushchev, however, could never accept such a proposal because it was only secrecy that protected his exaggerations about Soviet capabilities.

In what would be the one and only session of the summit, Khrushchev uncharacteristically stuck to the language of a prepared forty-five-minute harangue that proposed a six- to eight-month postponement of the conference so that it would resume only after Eisenhower had left power. He also withdrew his invitation for Eisenhower to visit the Soviet Union. Without forewarning the other leaders at the summit, Khrushchev then petulantly refused to attend the second session the following day. He instead retreated with Defense Minister Rodion Malinovsky to the French village of Pleurs-sur-Marne—where Malinovsky had stayed during World War II —to drink wine, eat cheese, and talk about women. Well lubricated, the Soviet leader returned to Paris that afternoon to declare the summit's collapse.

His crowning public act came during a nearly three-hour farewell press conference at which he slammed his fist so hard on a table that it toppled a bottle of mineral water. Assuming the catcalls that followed came from West German reporters, he called them "fascist bastards we didn't finish off at Stalingrad." He said if they continued to heckle him, he would hit them so hard "there won't be a squeal out of you."

Khrushchev was so unhinged by the time he debriefed Warsaw Pact envoys in Paris that he employed a crude joke in relating to them the outcome of the summit. It concerned the sad story of a Tsarist soldier who could fart the melody to "God Save Russia" but experienced an unfortunate accident when forced to perform the tune under duress. Khrushchev's punch line was that the ambassadors could report to their governments that his own pressures applied in Paris had similarly made Eisenhower shit in his pants.

Poland's ambassador to France, Stanisław Gaevski, concluded from the session that the Soviet leader "was just a bit unbalanced emotionally." For the sake of East–West relations, Gaevski wished Khrushchev had never come to Paris.

For all his theatrics, however, Khrushchev had too much at stake to abandon his course of "peaceful coexistence" with the U.S. He had given up on Eisenhower but not yet on America. Though the U-2 had undermined his summit, he could not let it undercut his rule.

On his way back to Moscow, Khrushchev stopped in East Berlin, where he replaced his Paris scowl with a peacemaker's smile. Though originally scheduled to speak to a crowd of 100,000 in Marx-Engels Square, after the Paris debacle East German leaders had moved the event to the safer confines of the indoor Werner-Seelenbinder-Halle, where Khrushchev spoke to a select group of 6,000 communist faithful.

To the surprise of U.S. diplomats who had expected Khrushchev to escalate the crisis, Khrushchev sounded an unexpected note of patience until the Americans could elect a new president. "In this situation, time is required," he said, adding that the prospects for a Berlin solution would then "ripen better."

Khrushchev then began preparations for his return trip to the U.S. under dramatically changed circumstances.

ABOARD THE *BALTIKA*
MONDAY, SEPTEMBER 19, 1960

Khrushchev's damp welcome on a rickety New York dock demonstrated just how much had changed since his grand reception by President Eisenhower at Andrews Air Force Base just a year earlier. Instead of flying to America aboard the Soviets' most advanced passenger aircraft, which was in the shop for repairs, he had traveled aboard the *Baltika*, a vintage 1940 German vessel seized as reparations after the war.

To compensate and send a message of communist solidarity, Khrushchev had drafted as fellow passengers the leaders of Hungary, Romania, Bulgaria, Ukraine, and Byelorussia. His mood swings during the voyage were violent. At one point he fought off depression while preoccupied by fears that NATO might sink his unprotected vessel, yet on another occasion he joyously insisted the Ukrainian party boss Nikolai Podgorny entertain fellow passengers by dancing a *gopak*, a national dance performed with strenuous leg kicks from the squatting position.

When one of the Soviet sailors jumped ship while approaching the American shore, then sought asylum, Khrushchev shrugged in response, saying, "He'll find out soon enough how much it costs and what it tastes like in New York." Other indignities would follow. Khrushchev was received in the harbor by union demonstrators from the International Longshoremen's Association, who waved huge protest signs from a chartered boat. The most memorable: ROSES ARE RED, VIOLETS ARE BLUE, STALIN DROPPED DEAD, HOW ABOUT YOU?

Khrushchev was infuriated. He had dreamed of arriving like America's earliest discoverers, whom he had read about as a boy. Instead, the unionist boycott left the *Baltika* to be moored by its own crew and a handful of unskilled Soviet diplomats on the East River's dilapidated Pier 73. "So, another dirty trick the Americans are playing on us," Khrushchev complained.

The only saving grace was Khrushchev's control of his home press. *Pravda* correspondent Gennady Vasiliev filed a story speaking of a happy crowd (there was none) lining the shore on a bright and sunny morning (it was raining).

None of that dampened the energy Khrushchev would invest in the trip. Speaking before the UN General Assembly, he would unsuccessfully demand the resignation of Secretary General Dag Hammerskjöld (who would die the next year in a plane crash in Africa), and be replaced by a troika of a Westerner, a communist, and a nonaligned leader." On the last day of his stay, in an iconic act that would be history's primary recollection of the visit, he removed a shoe in protest of a Philippine delegate's reference to communist captive nations and banged it on his UN table.

By September 26, only a week into Khrushchev's trip, the *New York Times* reported that a nationwide survey showed the Soviet leader had made himself the focal point of the presidential election campaign and had helped make foreign policy the premier concern of U.S. voters. Americans were measuring which of the candidates, Richard Nixon or Senator John F. Kennedy, could best stand up to Khrushchev.

Khrushchev was determined to use his considerable leverage more wisely than in 1956, when Soviet Premier Nikolai Bulganin's praise of the Soviets' favored candidate, Adlai Stevenson, had helped the winning Eisenhower–Nixon ticket. In public, Khrushchev hedged his bets, saying that both candidates "represent American big business . . . as we Russians say, they are two boots of the same pair: which is better, the left or the right boot?" When asked whom he favored, he safely said, "Roosevelt."

But behind the scenes, he worked toward Nixon's defeat. As early as January 1960, over vodka, fruit, and caviar, Soviet Ambassador to the U.S. Mikhail Menshikov had asked Adlai Stevenson how Moscow might best help him defeat Nixon. Was it better for the Soviet press to praise him or criticize him—and on which topics? Stevenson responded that he did not

expect to be a candidate—and he then prayed that news of the Soviet proposition would never leak.

Yet both parties so deeply recognized Khrushchev's potential to swing
votes, either by design or by accident, that each reached out to him.

Republican Henry Cabot Lodge Jr., who had grown close to Khrushchev during his first U.S. trip, had flown to Moscow in February 1960 to
convince the Soviet leader that he could work with Nixon. Lodge, who
would become Nixon's running mate, said, "Once Mr. Nixon is in the White
House, I'm sure—I'm absolutely certain—he'll take a position of preserving
and perhaps even improving our relations." He asked Khrushchev to remain
neutral, realizing any endorsement would only cost Nixon votes.

By autumn, the Eisenhower administration had increased its appeals to
Khrushchev to release Gary Powers and the RB-47 airmen who had been
shot down over the Arctic. Khrushchev recalled later that he had refused
after calculating that the election was so close any such move might have
swung the outcome. "As it turned out, we'd done the right thing," he would
say later. Given the margin of victory, he said, "The slightest nudge either
way would have been decisive."

The Democrats were also at work to influence Khrushchev. W. Averell
Harriman, President Roosevelt's former ambassador to Moscow, recommended through Ambassador Menshikov that Khrushchev be tough on
both candidates. The surest way to elect Nixon was to praise Kennedy in
public, he said. The timing of the meeting, less than a month before the
election and while Khrushchev was still in the U.S., demonstrated the Democrats' recognition of Khrushchev's electoral influence.

As guarded as he was in public, Khrushchev was explicit with underlings. "We thought we would have more hope of improving Soviet–American
relations if John Kennedy were in the White House." He told colleagues
that Nixon's anticommunism and his connection with "that devil of darkness [Senator Joe] McCarthy, to whom he owed his career," all meant "we
had no reason to welcome the prospect of Nixon as President."

Though Kennedy's campaign rhetoric was hawkish against Moscow,
the KGB chalked that up less to conviction than to political expedience

and the influence of his anticommunist father, Joe. Khrushchev welcomed Kennedy's calls for nuclear test ban negotiations and his statement that he would have apologized for the U-2 incursions if he had been president when they occurred. More to the point, Khrushchev believed he could outmaneuver Kennedy, a man whom his foreign ministry had characterized as "unlikely to possess the qualities of an outstanding person." The consensus in the Kremlin was that the young man was a lightweight, a product of American privilege who lacked the experience required for leadership.

The candidates continued to shower attention on Khrushchev as he monitored their campaign from his suite at the Soviet Mission at Sixty-eighth Street and Park Avenue, where he would occasionally appear on the balcony of a turn-of-the-century mansion built originally for the banker Percy Pyne. In the initial Kennedy–Nixon debate in a Chicago TV studio on September 26—the first live-broadcast presidential debate ever—Kennedy's opening statement before sixty million American viewers spoke directly to Khrushchev's New York stay and "our struggle with Mr. Khrushchev for survival."

Though the debate was to have been about domestic issues, Kennedy worried that the Soviet Union was churning out "twice as many scientists and engineers as we are" while the U.S. continued to underpay its teachers and underfund its schools. He declared that he would do better than Nixon in keeping America ahead of the Soviets in education, health care, home construction, and economic strength.

During their second debate on foreign policy on October 7 in Washington, D.C., the candidates focused squarely on Khrushchev and Berlin. Kennedy predicted that the next president "in his first year is going to be confronted with a very serious question on our defense of Berlin, our commitment to Berlin. It's going to be a test of our nerve and will." He said that President Eisenhower had allowed American strength to erode and that he, if elected, would ask Congress to support a military buildup, because by spring or winter "we're going to be face-to-face with the most serious Berlin crisis since 1949 or 1950."

During the campaign, Adlai Stevenson had counseled Kennedy to avoid discussing Berlin altogether because it would be "difficult to say anything very constructive about the divided city without compromising future negotiations." So Kennedy had raised Berlin in only half a dozen speeches. Yet before a national television audience the subject was impossible to avoid, particularly after Khrushchev had told United Nations correspondents he wanted the U.S. to join a summit on Berlin's future shortly after elections—to be followed by a UN General Assembly meeting on the matter in April.

During their third debate on October 13, Frank McGee of NBC News asked both candidates whether they would be willing to take military action to defend Berlin. Kennedy responded with his clearest statement of the campaign on Berlin: "Mr. McGee, we have a contractual right to be in Berlin coming out of the conversations at Potsdam and of World War II that has been reinforced by direct commitments of the President of the United States. It's been reinforced by a number of other nations under NATO. . . . It is a commitment that we have to meet if we are going to protect the security of Western Europe, and therefore on this question I don't think there is any doubt in the mind of any American. I hope there is not any doubt in the mind of any member of the community of West Berlin. I'm sure there isn't any doubt in the mind of the Russians. We will meet our commitments to maintain the freedom and independence of West Berlin."

For all Kennedy's apparent conviction, Khrushchev sensed the makings of compromise. Kennedy talked of U.S. contractual rights in Berlin but not of moral responsibility. He wasn't sounding the usual Republican clarion call to free captive nations. He wasn't even suggesting that freedom should spread across the city's border to East Berlin. He had spoken of *West* Berlin and of *West* Berlin alone. Kennedy was talking about Berlin as a technical and legal matter, points that could be negotiated.

Before Khrushchev could test Kennedy, however, he had to put his communist house in order and neutralize rising challenges on two fronts—China and East Germany.

MOSCOW
FRIDAY, NOVEMBER 11, 1960

It was understandable that at first the West overlooked the importance of the world's largest-ever meeting of communist leaders, given that it was characterized primarily by two weeks of mind-numbing and redundant speeches from eighty-one party delegations from around the world. Behind the scenes, however, Khrushchev was working to neutralize the challenge China's Mao Tse-tung was mounting to his leadership of world communism—and to gain support within the party for a new diplomatic effort with President-elect Kennedy.

Soviet foreign policy strategists saw their two priorities as the Sino–Soviet alliance and peaceful coexistence with the West, very much in that order. Foreign Minister Andrei Gromyko had argued it would be a mistake to lose Beijing without gaining anything reliable from the U.S., yet that was precisely what had happened during 1960. The Soviet embassy in Beijing reported to Khrushchev that the Chinese were using the aftermath of the U-2 incident and the Paris Summit failure to oppose Khrushchev's foreign policy "for the first time directly and openly."

Mao opposed Khrushchev's foreign policy of peaceful coexistence with the West and sought a course of more intense confrontation both over Berlin and across the developing world. The Chinese delegation had come to Moscow determined to gain increased Kremlin support for national liberation movements and assorted leftists—from Asia and Africa to Latin America.

Now that relations had broken down with the U.S., a number of Soviet officials privately argued that Khrushchev should make a bolder strategic bet on the Chinese. What only a few of them knew, however, was that the personal animosity that had grown between Khrushchev and Mao would make that impossible.

By Khrushchev's own account, he had disliked Mao since his first visit in 1954 for the fifth anniversary of the People's Republic. Khrushchev had complained about everything from the endless rounds of green tea ("I can't take that much liquid") to what he regarded as his host's ingratiating, insincere courtesy. Mao was so uncooperative during their talks that Khrushchev had concluded upon returning to Moscow, "Conflict with China is inevitable."

When a year later West German Chancellor Konrad Adenauer raised concerns with Khrushchev about an emerging Sino-Soviet alliance, Khrushchev dismissed that prospect and pointed to his own concerns about China. "Think of it," he had said. "Already six hundred million of them and every year twelve million more. . . . We have to do something for our people's standard of living, we have to arm like the Americans, [and] we have to give all the time to the Chinese who suck our blood like leeches."

Mao had shocked Khrushchev with his readiness for war with the U.S., irrespective of the devastation it might bring. Because the Chinese and Soviets together had a vastly greater population, Mao had argued to Khrushchev that they would emerge victorious. "No matter what kind of war breaks out—conventional or thermonuclear—we'll win," he had told Khrushchev. "We may lose more than three hundred million people. So what? War is war." Using what the Soviet leader considered the crudest possible term for sexual intercourse, Mao told Khrushchev the Chinese would simply produce more babies than ever before to replace the dead. Khrushchev came to consider Mao "a lunatic on a throne."

Khrushchev's 1956 repudiation of Stalin and of his personality cult had strained the relationship further. "They understood the implications for themselves," Khrushchev said of the Chinese. "Stalin was exposed and condemned at the Congress for having had hundreds of thousands of people shot and for his abuse of power. Mao Tse-tung was following in Stalin's footsteps."

The downward spiral in relations accelerated in June 1959 when Khrushchev reneged on a pledge to give the Chinese a sample atomic bomb while at the same time moving to improve relations with the Americans. Mao told fellow party leaders that Khrushchev was abandoning communism to make pacts with the devil.

Khrushchev further strained ties when he returned to China shortly after his 1959 U.S. trip to celebrate the tenth anniversary of the People's Republic. Instead of simply praising Mao's revolution, Khrushchev used a state banquet as well to congratulate himself for reducing world tensions through the "Camp David spirit" that he had created with Eisenhower.

On the same trip, Mao blew a cloud of cigarette smoke in Khrushchev's face while he talked—though he knew the Soviet leader hated nothing more—and mocked him for what he called disorganized rambling. Mao's efforts to humiliate Khrushchev reached their low point at an outdoor pool where he took him for further discussions. The champion swimmer Mao dived in the deep end and performed laps gracefully while Khrushchev floundered in the shallows with the help of a life ring tossed in by Chinese aides. On the drive home from the pool, Mao told his physician that he had so tormented Khrushchev it was like "sticking a needle up his ass."

Khrushchev knew he had been set up: "The interpreter is translating, and I can't answer as I should. It was Mao's way of putting himself in an advantageous position. Well, I got sick of it. All the while I was swimming, I was thinking, 'The hell with you.'"

The first sign of how much uglier matters would get between Mao and Khrushchev had come five months earlier, on June 20, 1960, in Bucharest, where the Romanians had hosted fifty-one national communist delegations for their 3rd Party Congress. Just two days before the gathering, Khrushchev had announced that he would attend after failing to bridge differences with a Chinese delegation that had visited Moscow en route to the Romanian capital. His participation turned an insignificant, provincial party meeting into the most open warfare yet between leaders of the two most powerful communist states. To prepare the ground, Boris Ponomarev, chief of the International Department of the Soviet Central Committee, had circulated Moscow's case against Mao's "misjudgment of the current global situation" in the form of an eighty-one-page "Letter of Information" for Congress delegates. In it, Khrushchev explained his intention to continue his disputed course of peaceful coexistence with the new U.S. president.

With Mao absent from Bucharest, his counterthrust was delivered by

Peng Zhen, the head of the Chinese delegation and a legendary communist who had guided resistance to Japanese occupation and ultimately the communist capture of Beijing in 1948.* Peng stunned delegates with the fierceness of his unprecedented attack on Khrushchev, which he supported by circulating copies of a lengthy correspondence the Soviet leader had sent to Mao that year. The Soviet leader's letter shocked delegates in two respects: the crude language with which Khrushchev spewed venom at Mao, and the Chinese breach of confidentiality in sharing the private communication with others.

Khrushchev turned as vicious as veteran delegates had ever seen him in a final, closed session. He attacked the absent Mao as "a Buddha who gets his theory out of his nose" and for being "oblivious of any interests other than his own."

Peng shot back that it was now clear Khrushchev had organized the Bucharest meeting only to attack China. He said the Soviet leader had no foreign policy except to "blow hot then cold toward the imperialist powers."

Khrushchev was livid. In a furious, impulsive froth, he issued overnight orders that would undo Soviet economic, diplomatic, and intelligence-gathering interests in China that had taken years to establish. "Within the short span of a month," he decreed, he would withdraw 1,390 Soviet technical advisers, scrapping 257 scientific and technical cooperation projects, and discontinuing work on 343 expert contracts and subcontracts. Dozens of Chinese research and construction projects came to a stop, as did factory and mining projects that had begun trial production.

Despite all that, the Bucharest communiqué had been crafted to carefully hide from the West the truth about the head-on collision of communism's leaders. That would be harder to conceal at the November follow-on meeting in Moscow, which included many of the same delegates but was far larger and at a higher level.

Khrushchev's intense lobbying before the meeting and cajoling during

---

*In the 1990s, Peng would come to be considered one of "the Eight Immortals of the Chinese Communist Party."

the conference kept the Chinese in check. Only a dozen country delegations among the eighty-one sided with China's objections to Khrushchev's course of liberalizing communism at home and peaceful coexistence abroad. Still, even that level of opposition to Soviet rule was unprecedented.

With Mao in Beijing, Khrushchev and Chinese General Party Secretary Deng Xiaoping locked horns behind closed doors at the Kremlin's St. George's Hall. Khrushchev called Mao a "megalomaniac warmonger." He said Mao wanted "someone you can piss on. . . . If you want Stalin that badly, you can have him—cadaver, coffin, and all!"

Deng attacked the Soviet leader's speech, saying, "Khrushchev had evidently been talking without knowing what he was saying, as he did all too frequently." It was an unprecedented personal insult to the communist movement's acknowledged leader on his own turf. Mao's new ally, the Albanian leader Enver Hoxha, made the most vicious of all the speeches, saying Khrushchev had blackmailed Albania and was trying to starve his country into submission for remaining true to Stalin.

In the end, the Soviets and the Chinese negotiated a ceasefire. The Chinese had been surprised by the support the Soviet leader could still muster and retreated, having seen the futility of splitting the communist movement at such a crucial moment. The Chinese reluctantly accepted Khrushchev's notion of peaceful coexistence with the West in exchange for the Soviet leader's agreement to increase support for capitalism's opponents across the developing world.

The Soviets would resume assistance to China and thus keep construction work going on 66 of the 155 unfinished industrial projects they had begun. However, Mao didn't get what he most wanted: high-end collaboration on military technology. Mao's interpreter Yan Mingfu viewed the agreement as only "a temporary armistice. In the long run, events were already out of control."

With the Chinese temporarily in check, however, Khrushchev moved to protect his East German flank.

THE KREMLIN, MOSCOW
WEDNESDAY, NOVEMBER 30, 1960

Ulbricht sat forward and erect in his chair, listening skeptically as Khrushchev briefed him on his strategy for handling Kennedy and Berlin in
1961. The East German leader had peppered Khrushchev with three letters
since October, each increasingly critical of Khrushchev's failure to counter
his country's growing economic difficulties and refugee bleed with a more
determined response.

Having given up hope that Khrushchev would act on Berlin at any
point soon, Ulbricht had begun to act unilaterally to tighten his control
over Berlin. For the first time, East Germany was requiring that diplomats
accredited to West Germany seek permission from East German authorities
to enter East Berlin or East Germany—and in one high-profile incident had
turned back Walter "Red" Dowling, the U.S. ambassador to West Germany.
The East German moves directly contradicted Soviet efforts to expand diplomatic and economic contacts with West Berlin and West Germany. So on
October 24, Khrushchev had angrily ordered Ulbricht to reverse the new
border regime. Ulbricht had reluctantly complied, but tensions between the
two men continued to grow.

The Soviet ambassador in East Berlin, Mikhail Pervukhin, complained
to Khrushchev and Foreign Minister Gromyko that Ulbricht was disregarding Kremlin directives with ever greater frequency. A second secretary in the
Soviet embassy, A. P. Kazennov, cabled his bosses in Moscow a warning that
the East Germans might shut down travel across the border altogether to
stop the increased refugee flow. Pervukhin reported to Moscow that a host
of Ulbricht measures limiting movement and economic interaction between the two parts of the city had demonstrated the East German leader's
"inflexibility."

Ulbricht had created a new National Defense Council to better defend
his country's security, and he had named himself to chair it. On October
19, the new council discussed potential measures to seal the Berlin border

through which so many refugees were flowing. Though the West considered Ulbricht a Soviet puppet, it was increasingly the East German leader who was trying to pull Moscow's strings.

In his most recent letter on November 22, Ulbricht had complained to Khrushchev that the Soviets were sitting on their hands while his economy was crumbling, refugees were fleeing, West Berlin freedom was becoming an international cause célèbre, and West Berlin factories were supplying the West German defense industry. He told Khrushchev that Moscow must change course "after years of tolerating an unclear situation." Waiting to act on Berlin until after Khrushchev could organize a summit with Kennedy, Ulbricht argued, simply played into American hands.

Khrushchev assured a skeptical Ulbricht that he would force the Berlin issue early in the Kennedy administration. What he wanted was not another four-power summit, he said, but a one-on-one meeting with Kennedy where he could more effectively achieve his ends. He told Ulbricht he would resort to another ultimatum at an early stage if Kennedy showed no willingness to negotiate a reasonable agreement in the first months of his administration.

Though Ulbricht remained distrustful, he was heartened by Khrushchev's declaration of determination to force the Berlin issue so early. At the same time, the East German leader warned Khrushchev that his repeated promises of action on Berlin were losing credibility. "Among our population," he told Khrushchev, "there is already a mood taking shape where they say, 'You [Khrushchev] only *talk* about a peace treaty, but don't *do* anything about it.' We have to be careful." The East German client was lecturing his Soviet master.

Ulbricht wanted Khrushchev to know that time was running out. "The situation in Berlin has become complicated, not in our favor," he said. He told Khrushchev that West Berlin's economy was rapidly growing stronger, illustrated by the fact that some 50,000 East Berliners crossed the border each day to work for the West's higher wages. The tension in the city was growing in rough proportion to the widening gap in living standards between East and West.

"We still have not taken corresponding countermeasures," Ulbricht complained. He said he was also losing the battle for the minds of the intelligentsia, a great number of whom were leaving as refugees. Ulbricht told Khrushchev he couldn't compete because West Berlin teachers earned some 200 to 300 marks more a month than teachers in the East, and doctors earned twice the Eastern salaries. He didn't have the means to match such salaries, and lacked the ability to produce sufficient consumer goods—even if he could provide East Germans with the money to buy them.

Khrushchev promised Ulbricht further economic assistance.

The Soviet leader shrugged. Perhaps he would have to put Soviet rockets on military alert as he maneuvered to alter Berlin's status, but he was confident the West would not start a war over the city's freedom. "Luckily, our adversaries still haven't gone crazy; they still think and their nerves still aren't bad." If Kennedy would not negotiate, Khrushchev told Ulbricht, he would move forward unilaterally, "and let them see their defeat."

With an exasperated sigh, Khrushchev told Ulbricht, "We must be finished with this situation sometime."

3

KENNEDY:
A PRESIDENT'S EDUCATION

We can live with the status quo in Berlin but can take no real initiative
to change it for the better. To a greater or lesser degree, the Soviets and
East Germans can, whenever they are willing to assume the political
consequences, change it for the worse.

Martin Hillenbrand, State Department chief of German affairs,
transition memo to President Kennedy, January 1961

So let us begin anew, remembering on both sides that civility is not a sign
of weakness, and sincerity is always subject to proof.

President Kennedy, inaugural address, January 20, 1961

OVAL OFFICE, THE WHITE HOUSE, WASHINGTON, D.C.
THURSDAY MORNING, JANUARY 19, 1961

The oldest president in U.S. history reckoned it was time to introduce
the youngest man ever elected to the office to the most fearsome part
of the job. It was Inauguration Eve, and in less than twenty-four hours,
President Dwight D. Eisenhower, age seventy, would hand off America's
nuclear football to Senator John F. Kennedy, age forty-three, transferring to
him the most destructive capability any single country had ever possessed.

And he would have it at a time when Eisenhower feared that miscalculation over numerous U.S.–Soviet flashpoints around the world, the most sensitive of them all being Berlin, could trigger a nuclear exchange. So Eisenhower planned to take Kennedy aside for a private chat on how such a war would be conducted, a session he would close with a memorable bit of show-and-tell using the paraphernalia of the world's most powerful individual.

Eisenhower worried about Kennedy's readiness for such responsibility. Among friends, he dismissed Kennedy as "Little Boy Blue" or "that young whippersnapper" when he wasn't mocking him as "that young genius." As Supreme Commander of all Allied forces in Europe during the last two years of World War II, Eisenhower had overseen the invasion and occupation of France and Germany. As a Navy lieutenant, Kennedy had piloted nothing more significant than a PT boat, a torpedo-bearing vessel so small that its squadrons were called "mosquito fleets."

It was true; Kennedy had been decorated as a war hero after saving the lives of eleven crew members, but only after he had inexplicably allowed his PT-109 to be rammed by a lumbering Japanese destroyer. Eisenhower's military friends didn't buy the "dark-of-night, fog-of-war" explanation, and instead suspected Kennedy of negligence, though he was spared an investigation.

Eisenhower doubted young Kennedy ever would have achieved the presidency without his father Joe's deep pockets and insatiable parental ambition. During the war, Joe Sr. had tasked his cousin Joe Kane, a Boston political insider, to game the electoral viability of both his eldest son Joe and Jack. It also was his father who placed the story of Jack's bravery with author and family friend John Hersey. Its publication in *Reader's Digest* and then the *New Yorker* helped launch Jack's political career. A year after Jack's anointment as a hero, Joe Jr. died in action while piloting an experimental, high-risk bombing mission. He was supposed to have ejected from an explosive-laden B-24 Liberator before the plane, now a guided missile, continued by remote control toward a German V-bomb base—but it detonated prematurely. Those who knew the family best wondered if his death hadn't ultimately been the result of the sibling rivalry their father had nurtured over the years. A reckless gamble to outdo his younger brother may have cost Joe Jr. his life.

On the cold, overcast morning, Kennedy pulled up to the White House at 8:57, after an eight-minute drive from his Georgetown home. It was a rare show of punctuality for the habitually tardy Kennedy. The morning newspapers were sprinkled with Kennedy family biographies and artists' renderings of Cabinet wives' elegant ball gowns. The dowdy Eisenhower era was over. On a more serious note, General Thomas S. Power, chief of the Strategic Air Command, announced that for the first time the U.S. would conduct round-the-clock nuclear-armed bomber flights to keep America in a constant state of readiness against surprise attack.

Ahead of the meeting, Kennedy's transition chief, legendary Washington lawyer Clark Clifford, had sent Eisenhower's people a list of issues that Kennedy wished to discuss, since they might bite him during his first days in office: Laos; Algeria; the Congo; Cuba; the Dominican Republic; Berlin; disarmament and nuclear test talks; basic economic, fiscal, and monetary policies; and "an appraisal of war requirements versus capabilities."

That last point was Kennedy's shorthand for an issue that had come to occupy him more the closer he got to occupying the Oval Office: "How would I fight a nuclear war, if it comes to that." He wasn't at all certain he or the American people—the voters required for his reelection—would be willing to deliver on solemn U.S. commitments to defend Berlin if those commitments required the risk of a nuclear war that could cost millions of American lives.

After their first transition meeting on December 6, Eisenhower had revised some of his negative views of Kennedy. Eisenhower told Democratic political operative George E. Allen, a Clifford friend, that he had been "misinformed and mistaken about this young man. He's one of the ablest, brightest minds I've ever come across." Though still uneasy about Kennedy's youth and lack of experience, Eisenhower had been comforted by Kennedy's grasp of the issues he would be facing.

Kennedy had been less taken with "Ike," whom he referred to among friends as "that old asshole." He told his younger brother Bobby, who was to become his new attorney general, that he had found the outgoing president to be intellectually ponderous and inadequately informed about issues he should have known intimately.

Kennedy believed the Eisenhower administration had accomplished little of consequence, having treaded water in a dangerous riptide of history that could pull the U.S. under. The most obvious example was the festering problem of Berlin. He was designing his presidency for greater accomplishment, taking as his role models Abraham Lincoln and Franklin Roosevelt. In contrasting Eisenhower with Kennedy, French Ambassador Hervé Alphand saw the president-elect as a man who had "an enormous memory of facts, of figures, of history, he had complete knowledge of the problems he had to discuss . . . a will to achieve for his country and for the world a great design, to be, in other words, a great President."

There were two great obstacles to his quest for greatness: his lack of any clear mandate after the narrowest electoral victory since 1886, and the fact that Lincoln and Roosevelt had found their place in history through war, a horrifying prospect to be avoided, since these days that could mean a nuclear holocaust.

Kennedy was perplexed that he had been elected with only a fraction less than 50 percent of the vote, over a man like Nixon, whom he considered so personally unappealing. "How did I manage to beat a guy like this by only a hundred thousand votes?" he complained to friend Kenneth O'Donnell, who would become a White House aide.

And his coattails had been short. Though the Democrats had kept their commanding majorities in Congress, they had lost one Senate seat and twenty House seats. The Southern Democrats, who had gained the most, would form a caucus with the Republicans in favor of a hard line toward the Soviets and Berlin. Kennedy likely would not have won at all had he not in the campaign been more hawkish toward Moscow than Nixon. To further burnish his conservative anti-Soviet credentials, and perhaps to prevent release of damaging intelligence about his past, Kennedy had also made the unconventional decision to keep in office Eisenhower's CIA and FBI directors, Allen Dulles and J. Edgar Hoover. A curious similarity between Kennedy and Khrushchev was emerging: both were being coaxed by their domestic constituencies more toward confrontation than conciliation.

His meager margin over Nixon made Kennedy all the more keen to observe Eisenhower that day, figuring he could learn a great deal from the calm and reassuring manner that had won the outgoing president two terms and such widespread public affection. Kennedy would have to build his personal popularity as quickly as possible to take on all the issues in front of him.

During his transition briefings on nuclear strategy, nothing concerned Kennedy more than the fact that Eisenhower had left him such limited and inflexible war-fighting options. Should the Soviets overrun Berlin, Kennedy had no alternative to either a conventional conflict that the Soviets invariably would win or an all-out atomic exchange that he and America's allies would be reluctant to fight. For that reason, it would have seemed natural for Berlin contingencies to have been at the top of Kennedy's agenda that morning.

Instead, the two teams focused far greater attention on the raging conflict in Laos and the growing danger that the Southeast Asian country could fall into communist hands as the first of multiple dominoes. Though the crisis in Berlin was of greater significance, Kennedy had been told time and again that that situation was a frozen conflict without a foreseeable solution, and thus his initial energies were best spent on other matters.

A transition document prepared by the Eisenhower team for Kennedy warned the new president—a man who prided himself on big thinking— that it was the small issues he had to watch out for regarding Berlin, everything from detailed agreements ensuring unfettered travel to and from West Berlin to a host of arcane practices under four-power agreements that protected West Berliners' rights and Allied presence.

"Current Soviet tactics," the memo said, "are to seek to win Berlin by whittling away at the Western position to make it hard for us to demonstrate that the real issue in each minor incident is the survival of free Berlin. Our immediate problem is to counter these 'salami tactics.' . . . We have tried in every way possible to convince the Soviets that as a last resort we would fight for Berlin." The paper warned the president-elect that he would face an early effort by Khrushchev to revive Berlin talks, with the aim of gaining the withdrawal of Western troops from the city.

However, Eisenhower's team had no good advice for Kennedy about how he could more effectively deal with all this, aside from simply standing his ground. "No one has yet been able to devise an acceptable and nego-tiable formula to solve the Berlin problem separate from a solution for Germany as a whole," the transition document said. For the moment, the U.S. position was that Germany should someday be unified through free elections across West and East Germany—and no one anticipated that hap-pening at any point soon, if at all. Hence, the memo said, "the principal Western tactic has been to gain time and demonstrate determination to protect West Berlin, while seeking a basis for solution. The problem is in-creasingly one of convincing the USSR that the Western Powers have the will and the means to maintain their position."

Martin Hillenbrand, the director of the State Department's Office of German Affairs, put it more sharply in his own transition memo. He led a Berlin task force established by Eisenhower after Khrushchev's 1958 Berlin ultimatum, and it met almost daily on issues large and small. It included representatives of most agencies of the U.S. government, as well as the French, British, and German ambassadors.

"We can live with the status quo in Berlin but can take no real initiative to change it for the better," he wrote. "To a greater or lesser degree, the So-viets and East Germans can, whenever they are willing to assume the po-litical consequences, change it for the worse.... However impelling the urge to find some new approach to the problem, the ineluctable facts of the situation strictly limit the practical courses of actions open to the West."

What Kennedy was hearing from multiple sources was that the stirring message of change that had gotten him elected didn't apply to Berlin, where his advisers were asking him to defend an unsatisfying status quo. It went against all his instincts, and his promises to the electorate to bring creativ-ity to the problems the Eisenhower administration had failed to address. After weighing his options, Kennedy elected to put Berlin on a back burner while he addressed issues where it seemed he could find quicker agreement.

So Kennedy's priority with Moscow would be the pursuit of nuclear test ban talks, which he saw as a confidence-building measure to warm up the chilly U.S.–Soviet relationship. Kennedy's logic was that once he had improved the overall tone of relations through arms negotiations, he could then return to the more intractable matter of Berlin. That would give rise, however, to what would become the first and greatest point of disagreement between Kennedy and Khrushchev—the pace and priority of negotiating a Berlin solution.

Even before he entered the White House, Kennedy was learning that the reality of dealing with Berlin as a sitting president was a world away from the hard-line rhetoric he had employed as a senator and presidential candidate. In February 1959, Kennedy had appealed to the Eisenhower administration to do more to prepare America for the "extremely serious" prospect of an armed showdown over West Berlin's freedom.

The following August, while putting pieces in place for his presidential run, Kennedy had declared himself prepared to use the atomic bomb to defend Berlin, and he accused the Soviets of trying to push the Americans out of Germany. "Our position in Europe is worth a nuclear war because if you are driven from Berlin, you are driven from Germany," he said in a television interview in Milwaukee. "And if you are driven from Europe, you are driven from Asia and Africa, and then our time will come next. . . . You have to indicate your willingness to go to the ultimate weapon."

In an article published by the Hearst newspapers within hours of his victory at the Democratic National Convention in June 1960, Kennedy had written, "The next President must make it clear to Khrushchev that there will be no appeasement—no sacrifice of the freedom of the people of Berlin, no surrender of vital principle."

Yet "indicating willingness" in Milwaukee as a barnstorming senator and pledging "no appeasement" as a nominated candidate was a long way from nuclear weapons use as president. And Soviet nuclear capabilities were improving—while Moscow's conventional superiority around Berlin remained overpowering.

The president had only 5,000 troops in West Berlin, with 4,000 British and 2,000 French—so 11,000 Allied troops in all—arrayed against CIA estimates of some 350,000 Soviet troops either inside East Germany or within striking distance of Berlin.

The last National Intelligence Estimate—the authoritative assessment from the U.S. intelligence community—that had been done on Soviet capabilities spoke with worry about shifting strategic trends that could undermine the U.S. position in Berlin by the end of Kennedy's first term. It predicted a Soviet emergence from strategic inequality by 1965 primarily through the buildup of their intercontinental ballistic missile force and nuclear defense systems. It said the Soviets would then be emboldened to challenge the West in Berlin and elsewhere around the world.

The CIA document warned Kennedy about the mercurial nature of Khrushchev, who would use "alteration of pressure and accommodation as the regular pattern of Soviet behavior." It predicted that Khrushchev would play the role of suitor in the early days of the Kennedy administration, but that if that failed, he would "resort to intensified pressure and threats in an attempt to force the West into high-level negotiations under more favorable conditions."

So, with Berlin on hold, Eisenhower briefed Kennedy more deeply on Laos. A three-way civil war between Pathet Lao communists, pro-Western royalists, and neutralists had raised the possibility of communist takeover. The danger was clear: Kennedy's first weeks in office could be spent on a military engagement in a landlocked, tiny, impoverished country about which he cared little. The last thing Kennedy wanted was to send troops to Laos as his first foreign policy initiative. He would have preferred it if the Eisenhower administration had dealt with the issue before it left office. But as it had not done so, Kennedy wanted to know Eisenhower's thinking and preparations for military response.

Eisenhower portrayed Laos as "the cork in the bottle," a place where he felt the U.S. should intervene, even unilaterally, rather than accept a communist victory that could spread a contagion across Thailand, Cambodia, and South Vietnam. "This is one of the problems I'm leaving you that I'm not happy about," Eisenhower apologized. "We may have to fight."

Kennedy was struck by Eisenhower's relaxed manner as he discussed war scenarios. Nothing brought that home more than Eisenhower's fifty-minute private tutorial for the incoming president on nuclear weapons use. Eisenhower's personal effects had mostly been removed from the Oval Office into which he brought Kennedy. Some boxes lay stacked in corners, and the carpet had golf cleat damage from Eisenhower's putting sessions.

Eisenhower briefed Kennedy on issues ranging from running covert operations to the kind of emergency procedures that were the commander in chief's personal domain: how to respond to immediate attack and authorize atomic weapons use. Eisenhower showed Kennedy how to work the codebook and manipulate the computer device in its satchel that would launch a nuclear attack—the so-called football that was always near the president.

It was the most intimate exchange possible between an outgoing and incoming president in the nuclear age.

Eisenhower made no reference to Kennedy's mistaken statements during the campaign that the outgoing president had allowed a dangerous "missile gap" to emerge in favor of the Soviets. Eisenhower hadn't corrected Kennedy at the time, much to candidate Nixon's consternation, instead preferring to protect national security secrets and avoid giving the Kremlin an excuse to arm up even faster.

Now, however, Eisenhower calmly assured Kennedy that the U.S. still enjoyed an overwhelming military advantage, particularly due to submarines armed with nuclear-tipped missiles. "You have an invaluable asset in Polaris," he said. "It is invulnerable."

The Polaris could reach the Soviet Union from undetectable positions in various oceans, he said. Because of this, Eisenhower thought the Soviets would have to be mad to risk nuclear war. The downside, Eisenhower said, was they just might be mad. If you judged Soviet leaders by the brutality they had used against their own people and enemies during and after World War II, Eisenhower reckoned that nuclear inferiority might not stop fanatical communists from attacking under the right circumstances. Eisenhower spoke of the Russians more as animals to be tamed than as partners with whom one could negotiate.

Like a child showing off a favorite toy to a new friend, Eisenhower then ended his Kennedy tutorial with a demonstration of how quickly the president could be whisked from Washington by helicopter in case of emergency.

"Watch this," he said.

Eisenhower picked up a special phone, dialed a number, and said simply, "Opal Drill Three." He put down the phone and smiled, asking his visitor to consult his watch.

In less than five minutes, a Marine Corps chopper landed on the White House lawn. It whirred on the ground just a short stroll from where they sat. As Eisenhower took Kennedy back into the Cabinet Room, where their top people remained assembled, he joked, "I've shown my friend here how to get out in a hurry."

In the presence of their staffs, Eisenhower warned Kennedy that presidential authority would not always be such a magic wand.

Kennedy smiled. Eisenhower's press secretary later said that Kennedy showed considerable interest in the "dry run." Although his responsibilities were sobering, the powers Kennedy would soon have were intoxicating. As he drove off, he looked back with satisfaction at the building that would soon be his home.

WASHINGTON, D.C.
INAUGURATION DAY, FRIDAY, JANUARY 20, 1961

The snow began to fall at noon, shortly after Kennedy left his meeting with Eisenhower. Washington dealt badly with inclement weather, even when it was on a preinaugural footing. Traffic snarled. Two-thirds of the sold-out crowd didn't show for the inaugural concert that evening at Constitution Hall. The National Symphony started its performance a half hour late because so many of its musicians were caught in traffic or blocked by drifts. Frank Sinatra's star-studded gala began only after a two-hour delay.

Yet by the clear, cold, sunny morning of January 20, a battalion of soldiers and plows had cleared the eight inches of snow. The skies opened and provided perfect lighting for the most intricately planned and most widely televised inaugural show in history. Some 140,000 feet of cable ran to fifty-four television circuits, covering the inaugural from thirty-two locations, from the oath to the last parade float. Some six hundred extra telephones had been scattered around strategic locations for reporters. However else the Kennedy administration would differ from its predecessors, it would present the most televised commander in chief in history, all in living color.

When Kennedy traveled with his wife, Jackie, in their limousine the day before the inauguration, when he sat in the bathtub that evening, and again over breakfast the next morning after four hours of sleep, the president-elect reviewed time and again the latest version of his inaugural address. Whenever he could find a moment, he familiarized himself more deeply with each of its tightly crafted 1,355 words, honed through more drafts and rewrites than any speech he had ever delivered.

Back in November, he had told his chief wordsmith, Ted Sorensen, to keep the speech short, nonpartisan, optimistic, uncritical of his predecessor, and focused on foreign policy. However, when they worked through the final draft—a process which got under way only a week before the speech would be delivered—he still found it too long and domestic for his liking. He told Sorensen, "Let's drop the domestic stuff altogether. It's too long anyway." His view: "Who gives a shit about the minimum wage anyway?"

The more difficult decision was, what message to send Khrushchev? Though nuclear war with the Soviets was unthinkable, negotiating a just peace seemed unfathomable. Kennedy had campaigned from the hawkish side of a Democratic party that still hadn't resolved its internal dispute about whether engagement or confrontation was the best way to deal with the Soviets.

Dean Acheson, who had been President Truman's secretary of state, represented the Democratic party's hard-liners, who were convinced Khrushchev was still pursuing Stalin's goal of world domination. Other Democrats—Adlai Stevenson, Averell Harriman, Chester Bowles—saw Khrushchev as a genuine reformer whose primary aim was to reduce his military budget and improve Soviet living standards.

Kennedy's inaugural speech would place him squarely in the indecisive middle of the debate, reflecting his uncertainty about whether he would be more likely to make history by confronting the Soviets or by making peace with them. It was that same ambiguity that had fed Kennedy's reluctance since his election to respond to Khrushchev's many efforts through multiple channels to establish a private conduit and schedule an early summit meeting.

On December 1, 1960, Kennedy had sent an early but indirect plea for patience to the Soviet leader through his brother Robert, who had met with a KGB officer posing as a correspondent for the newspaper *Izvestia* in a presidential transition office in New York. At age thirty-five, Bobby had been his brother's campaign manager and was soon to become his attorney general, so the KGB officer had no reason to doubt it when Bobby said he was speaking for his brother.

The Soviet reporter never filed a story to his newspaper but he did send an account to his KGB superiors, which likely also reached Khrushchev, as an indication of the Kennedy administration's foreign policy direction. It contained several messages. Bobby said the president-elect would pay great attention to the relationship, and he thought a test ban treaty agreement could be concluded in 1961. He said that Kennedy shared Khrushchev's desire for a face-to-face meeting, and that he wanted to repair the harm done to the relationship under Eisenhower.

Less encouraging to Khrushchev was Kennedy's intention to handle Berlin far more slowly than the Soviet leader wanted. The new president would need two to three months before he could engage in a summit, Bobby said. "Kennedy is seriously concerned about the situation in Berlin and will strive to find the means to reach a settlement of the Berlin problem," said the KGB report on the meeting. "However, if in the next few months the Soviet Union applies pressure on this question, then Kennedy will certainly defend the position of the West."

Still, that did not dissuade Khrushchev from continuing to press for an early meeting. A few days later, on December 12, Soviet Ambassador Mikhail Menshikov invited Bobby for lunch at Moscow's Washington embassy.

The ambassador, whom U.S. officials derisively called "Smiling Mike," cut a comic figure with his modest intelligence and supreme confidence. His fractured English once produced a much-maligned toast to the women attending a Georgetown cocktail party: "Up your bottoms!" However, the direct messages he carried from Khrushchev made even his detractors take his invitations seriously.

Menshikov argued to Bobby that U.S.–Soviet misunderstandings were often a result of the two countries' leaders leaving crucial matters to mid-level officials. He said Kennedy and Khrushchev were unique individuals who together could find a way around their bureaucracies to achieve historic outcomes. He thus urged Bobby to get his brother to embrace the idea of an early meeting between the two nations' leaders, to achieve a "clear and friendly understanding."

Two days after meeting with the president's brother, Menshikov reached out with much the same message to Khrushchev's favorite American, Averell Harriman, the U.S. ambassador to Moscow under President Franklin Roosevelt. A day later, Menshikov again pressed his campaign for an early Khrushchev–Kennedy meeting through the well-connected *New York Times* correspondent Harrison Salisbury. "There is more to be gained by one solid day spent in private and informal talks between Khrushchev and Kennedy," he told the reporter, "than all the meetings of underlings taken together."

Kennedy was the target of some similar lobbying from two-time presidential candidate Adlai Stevenson, an erstwhile rival, who was trying to position himself for a major administration job. Stevenson phoned Kennedy at his father's house in Palm Beach to volunteer himself as a middleman who could fly to Moscow immediately after the inauguration and put matters on track with Khrushchev. "I think it's important to find out whether he wants to expand the Cold War," Stevenson told Kennedy.

Kennedy did not take the bait. Stevenson had failed to endorse Kennedy's nomination before the time of the Democratic convention, and that had likely cost him the post of secretary of state that Kennedy had dangled as incentive. If that weren't enough, anticommunists on Capitol Hill considered the former Illinois governor an appeaser. And Kennedy was unwilling to run his foreign policy in anyone's shadow. Beyond that, West German Chancellor Konrad Adenauer had made clear through press leaks that what worried him most about the Kennedy administration was the prospect they would bring in someone as soft on Moscow as Stevenson to lead his foreign policy. So Kennedy made Stevenson ambassador to the United Nations instead, and he would not take up his offer of mediation with Khrushchev.

Weary of Khrushchev's lobbying barrage, Kennedy asked his friend David Bruce, whom he had tapped as ambassador to London, to help him frame a response to Khrushchev's extended hand. Bruce was a veteran diplomat who had run America's spy service in London during the war, and he had been Harry Truman's ambassador to Paris.

After much eating and drinking at Menshikov's residence on January 5, the Soviet ambassador gave Bruce a letter without letterhead or signature, which Menshikov said held his personal thoughts. Its unmistakable message: Khrushchev urgently wanted a summit and would go to great lengths to arrange it.

Menshikov told Bruce that Khrushchev believed under the Kennedy administration, the two countries could "resolve existing and dangerous differences." However, the Soviet leader believed they could only relax tensions once the two great powers at the top levels had agreed on a program for peaceful coexistence. He said this would revolve around "two outstanding problems"—achieving disarmament and solving "the German question, including West Berlin." Khrushchev wanted to meet Kennedy before the incoming president sat down with West German Chancellor Konrad Adenauer and British Prime Minister Harold Macmillan, meetings Menshikov said he had heard were scheduled for February and March.

Bruce told the Soviet ambassador that the meetings with those key U.S. allies would occur later than that, but this did not alter Khrushchev's underlying message: He hoped Kennedy would depart from the usual protocol of consulting with allies before meeting with his adversary. Menshikov said that Khrushchev was willing to accelerate preparations for such a meeting through either private or official conduits. As further incentive, Menshikov sent Bruce a hamper full of his country's best vodka and caviar after the meeting. A few days later, he invited Bruce to lunch again to underscore his message.

Just nine days before his inauguration, Kennedy had sought from George Kennan—whom he would make his ambassador to Yugoslavia—further advice about how to handle this flurry of Soviet communication. Kennedy had been communicating on Soviet matters with Kennan, the legendary former U.S. ambassador to Moscow, since January 1959. In one letter, Kennedy had praised Kennan for standing against the "extreme rigidity" toward Moscow of Dean Acheson, President Truman's secretary of state.

Kennan had inspired the U.S. foreign policy of Soviet communist "containment" with his long telegram from Moscow as a diplomat, which was followed by his famous and anonymously written *Foreign Affairs* article in July 1947, "The Sources of Soviet Conduct." Yet Kennan now opposed the hard-line doctrines toward Moscow that he had done so much to inspire. He thought the U.S. and its allies were now strong enough to enter into talks with Khrushchev, and he complained about U.S. militarists who had misinterpreted his thinking.

During the campaign, Kennan told Kennedy that as president he should "heighten the divisive tendencies within the Soviet bloc by improving relations with Moscow," not through formal summits and agreements but rather by using private channels of communication with the Soviet government, aimed at reciprocal concessions. "These things are difficult," Kennan had said, "but they are not, I reiterate, not impossible." He said such contacts helped end the Berlin blockade in 1948 and the Korean War. He had urged Kennedy in an August 1960 letter that, should he be elected, his administration should "move quickly and boldly in the initial stages of its incumbency, before it becomes enmeshed in the procedural tangles of Washington and before it is itself placed on the defensive by the movement of events."

Kennedy wrote back that he agreed with most of Kennan's recommendations. Now that he was about to be president, however, he wanted guidance of a more concrete and immediate nature. While speaking to Kennan on a flight from New York to Washington on his private jet, the *Caroline*,

Kennedy briefed Kennan on the barrage of Soviet messages and then showed him the Menshikov letter.

Kennan frowned as he read. He concluded by the letter's stiff and tough language that it had been drafted in Khrushchev's office but cleared by a wider circle that included both those who were for and those who were against closer relations with the U.S. Contrary to his earlier advice that Kennedy move fast to open up a dialogue with Moscow, he now told Kennedy the Soviets had no right to rush him in this manner, and that the president-elect should not respond before taking office. That said, Kennan suggested he should at that time communicate privately with Khrushchev, breaking Eisenhower's habit of making almost every exchange with Khrushchev public.

Asked by Kennedy why Khrushchev was so eager to meet with him, Kennan said with characteristic insight that the U-2 incident and the growing intensity of the Chinese–Soviet conflict had weakened the Soviet leader, and he needed a breakthrough with the U.S. to reverse that trend. Khrushchev, Kennan explained, "hoped by the insertion of his own personality and the use of his powers of persuasion he could achieve such an agreement with the United States and recoup in this way his failing political fortunes."

For Kennedy, it was the clearest and most convincing explanation of Khrushchev's behavior he had heard. It coincided with his own understanding that domestic politics drove foreign policy issues more than most Americans understood—even in the authoritarian Soviet Union. It made sense to Kennedy that Khrushchev was seeking help to improve his imperiled political standing at home, but that was insufficient reason for Kennedy to act before he was ready. The president-elect again determined that Khrushchev could wait—and so could Berlin.

Thus, Kennedy's inaugural address would be his first communication with the Soviet leader on Berlin, however indirect and shared with tens of millions of others. The most compelling line was also the one most quoted in Berlin newspapers the following day: "We shall pay any price, bear any burden, meet any hardship, support any friend, oppose any foe to assure the survival and the success of liberty."

Yet Kennedy's soaring rhetoric concealed a dearth of policy direction with regard to the Soviets. Kennedy was leaving all options open. Multiple rewrites altered only nuance, putting his indecision in more memorable form and excising language his speechwriter Ted Sorensen had drafted that might appear too soft toward the Soviets.

A first version read, for example: ". . . nor can two great and powerful nations forever continue on this reckless course, both overburdened by the staggering cost of modern weapons."

Kennedy, however, did not want to call the U.S. course either "reckless" or unsustainable. So the final text took those two ideas out and instead read: ". . . neither can two great and powerful groups of nations take comfort from our present course—both sides overburdened by the cost of modern weapons."

An initial draft read: "And if the fruits of cooperation prove sweeter than the drugs of suspicion, let both sides join ultimately in creating a true world order—neither a Pax Americana, nor a Pax Russiana, nor even a balance of power—but a community of power."

A final text nixed the notion of a "community of power" with the communists, which congressional hawks would have called naive. The final version read: "And if a beachhead of cooperation can push back the jungle of suspicion, let both sides join in creating a new endeavor, not a new balance of power, but a new world of law. . . ."

He mentioned no countries or places by name—neither the Soviet Union, nor Berlin, nor any other. The German newspaper *Die Welt* praised the "new wind" from America, which was "hard but refreshing. What we Germans notice, though: No word on Berlin!"

Instead of mentioning Khrushchev by name, Kennedy spoke only of those "who would make themselves our adversary," having changed the word "enemy" to "adversary" at the suggestion of columnist friend Walter Lippmann. Kennedy prescribed projects of potential cooperation: exploration of the heavens and oceans, negotiation of arms control and inspection regimes, and cooperation in science to cure disease.

There was enough in the speech to please America's hard-liners. Arizona

Senator Barry Goldwater of Arizona applauded enthusiastically after the line about paying any price for liberty. Having achieved no progress in getting his boss an early meeting with Kennedy, Soviet Ambassador Menshikov sat impassively throughout with a gray hat pulled down over his eyes, a white scarf pulled up over his neck, and his frame wrapped in a large, gray overcoat.

Just as important as his words that day was Kennedy's appearance, which in the competition for global favor was more than a superficial factor. The world was inspired by the charismatic smile that lit up a face bronzed during his preinaugural vacation in Florida. What no one sensed was Kennedy's underlying ill health: he had swallowed a cocktail of pills that day for his bad stomach and his aching back, and he had taken an extra dose of cortisone to control the telltale swelling that came with his treatments for Addison's disease. As he had looked in the mirror just four days before his swearing-in, Kennedy had spoken with shock to his secretary, Evelyn Lincoln, about the impact of his treatments. "My God, look at that fat face," he said. "If I don't lose five pounds this week, we might have to call off the Inauguration."

Evelyn Lincoln would help monitor the multiple medications for a young president who in many respects was far less healthy than Khrushchev, twenty-three years his senior. Kennedy could only hope that the KGB operatives digging up whatever they could find on the true state of his health did not discover the truth. To knock down rumors about his illnesses, the Kennedy team had put two doctors before the press. And just two days before the inauguration, the magazine Today's Health, working from a report issued by the Kennedy team, had covered the president-elect's medical history more extensively than it had any other previous president's. It quoted his physicians on his "superb physical condition" that made him "quite capable of shouldering the burdens of the Presidency." The article said that the fact he had overcome his many ailments demonstrated "his barbwire toughness." It said he drank and smoked little, that he enjoyed an occasional cold beer at dinner, and that his only cocktail was a daiquiri. He didn't smoke cigarettes—only a cigar now and again. It reported authoritatively that he kept his weight at 165 pounds and that he had no special diet, which concealed the fact that he preferred bland foods because of a bad stomach.

A closer read left plenty of reason for concern. The article listed adult health issues that included "attacks of jaundice, malaria, sciatica, and two back injuries." All it said about his Addison's disease, without mentioning it by name, was that Kennedy takes "medication by mouth for the aftermath of adrenal insufficiency and has an endocrinologic examination twice a year." It noted he wore a quarter-inch lift in his shoes "and even beach sandals" to ease back pain caused by a slightly shorter left leg.

Perhaps never in American presidential history had youthful image and ailing reality stood in such contrast. While others at the inauguration wore top hats and heavy coats against the chill, Kennedy took the oath of office without overcoat or hat. With only an electric space heater to warm him in an open reviewing box, he watched the inaugural parade for more than three hours with his new vice president, Lyndon Johnson.

The next morning's papers around the world painted the portrait of Kennedy that he wanted. Columnist Mary McGrory of the *Washington Evening Star* compared him to a Hemingway hero. "He has conquered serious illness. He is as graceful as a greyhound and can be as beguiling as a sunny day."

Yet for all Kennedy's success at shaping media coverage ahead of his inauguration, he would quickly discover he had less influence over the actions of Soviet leader Nikita Khrushchev. When Kennedy woke up at about eight in the Lincoln Bedroom on his first morning in office, he found that atop the congratulatory cables from around the world was the offer of an inaugural gift from Moscow that would be the first gambit in U.S.–Soviet relations during his presidency. Given the right conditions, Khrushchev would release the two airmen of the RB-47 reconnaissance plane who had been sitting in a Soviet prison since their capture the previous summer.

It would be an early introduction for Kennedy to the world of U.S.–Soviet intrigue that swirled around Berlin, a place where, he would quickly learn, even seeming victories often contained hidden dangers.

The "Sniper" Comes In from the Cold

David Murphy, the chief of the Central Intelligence Agency's Berlin base, was hungry for success stories. So his heartbeat accelerated when he heard that his most valuable asset—a Polish agent with the code name of Heckenschütze, *or* Sniper—*had phoned the secret number he had been given for emergencies over the Christmas holidays. Certain that his cover had been blown, Sniper wanted to defect. "Are you ready to give me and my wife protection?" he asked.*

Murphy had warned the CIA station's special Berlin switchboard operators that if they missed Sniper's call on the number that was designated only for him "they would be on the next boat home." The caller had only said he was passing on the message on behalf of a Herr Kowalski, a code that began a set of prearranged responses. Sniper had planned his defection well. First, he had deposited perhaps three hundred photographed documents—including the names of several hundred Polish agents and organizational tables—in Warsaw at a dead drop inside a hollowed-out tree trunk near his home. The CIA had already recovered the treasure trove.

Now it was the early afternoon of January 4, and a senior CIA official who had flown in from Washington was waiting with other operatives at the American consulate in Berlin, where they had arranged that Sniper would come in from the cold. The consulate, which was open to civilians, rested conveniently beside the military section of a U.S. compound on West Berlin's Clayallee. Murphy had already arranged for an impressive office, wired with microphones and recorders, where Sniper would have his first debriefing.

Murphy would recall later that he and deputy John Dimmer felt even greater tension than was usual for such high-profile cases, partly because after two years of receiving letters from Sniper—sometimes valuable though often indecipherable—no one had yet met the mysterious agent nor knew who he really was. Beyond that, Murphy's Berlin Operations Base—known in clandestine cables by its acronym BOB—had been fighting a losing battle in the world's most important and extensive spy war in a city that hosted more foreign and domestic intelligence agents than any other place on Earth.

The CIA also needed a victory after having just lost its only penetration agent inside Soviet military intelligence, Colonel Pyotr Popov, through either sloppiness or infiltration. And by any measure, the United States was being outspied by Soviet and East German services in Berlin. The problem, in Murphy's view, was that the CIA was a relative newcomer to the espionage business and too often combined the fierce determination of the youthful with the dangerous naiveté of the uninitiated. In that respect, Murphy reckoned BOB reflected the optimistic if not always fully professional American character as the United States embraced a more global role. Berlin was a place where both Murphy's spies and America in general had been doing a lot of growing up in the decade and a half since World War II.

Murphy's most insuperable competitive problem was recruiting local talent, and in that respect he had fallen far behind both Moscow's KGB and the East German Ministry for Security. The sad truth was that it was far easier for the communists to infiltrate the West's open society, to manipulate key individuals, and to plant agents than it was for the CIA to operate within Ulbricht's strictly controlled and monitored East Germany.

The CIA had evolved rapidly from the wartime Office of Strategic Services into America's first peacetime civilian intelligence service. It had drawn together in a single agency both clandestine operations and intelligence analysis. By comparison, the KGB was both more experienced and more extensive. It was a proficient external and internal intelligence service that had been forged during the Russian Revolution, then battle-hardened through Stalin's purges and war with Nazi Germany. Despite the Soviet Union's distracting political power struggles, it had operated with stunning continuity and ongoing successes.

Murphy's most immediate concern was the increasing effectiveness of the East German secret police, which in just a decade and a half was already outperforming its predecessor, the Gestapo, as well as the KGB. A widening army of internal informants, a data-gathering system of German efficiency, and a broad network of agents in key Western positions of influence were allowing Ulbricht and Moscow to foil many CIA case efforts before they could even get started.

With BOB already operating in full-alert status, a caller phoned at 5:30 p.m. saying that Kowalski would arrive in a half hour. The caller asked that Mrs. Kowalski be given special attention—the first indication that Sniper was not coming alone. At 6:06 p.m., a West Berlin taxi dropped off a man and woman, each of them carrying small bags. The chief of the station's Eastern European branch watched briefly as they apprehensively walked toward the consulate entrance, and then quickly ushered them inside.

As is so often the case in the spy business, matters were not what they had initially seemed. Sniper explained that the woman was not his wife but his mistress and that he would want asylum for her as well. He then asked that she be removed from the debriefing room because she knew him only as the Polish journalist Roman Kowalski. In fact, he said, he was Lieutenant Colonel Michael Goleniewski, who until 1958 had been the deputy chief of Polish military counterintelligence. He had acted as a double agent, reporting not only to the CIA but also to the KGB on anything the Poles might be hiding from their Soviet masters.

The CIA would whisk him by military aircraft on the following day to Wiesbaden, West Germany, and then on to the United States. Goleniewski would provide the names of countless Polish and Soviet intelligence officers and agents. He would help unearth a spy ring at the British Admiralty, uncover George Blake as a KGB spy in British intelligence, and expose Heinz Felfe, a KGB agent who had served as chief of West German counterintelligence. Of potentially greater importance, Goleniewski pointed to the presence of an undiscovered mole burrowed deep in U.S. intelligence.

There was only one problem: even before his briefings had ended, mental illness began to cloud Goleniewski's credibility. He drank to excess and played Victrola records of old European songs at high volume. He would later insist *that he was Tsar Nicholas II's son, Alexei, the only surviving heir of the Romanov imperial family, and that Henry Kissinger was a KGB spy. The most senior CIA operatives would never agree upon whether he was a genuine defector or a Soviet provocateur.*

Kennedy was entering a world of intrigue and deception for which he had only inadequate preparation.

4

KENNEDY:

A FIRST MISTAKE

The United States Government was gratified by this decision of the Soviet Union and considers that this action of the Soviet Government removes a serious obstacle to improvement of Soviet–American relations.

John F. Kennedy, at his first press conference as president, on the Soviet release of captured U.S. airmen, January 25, 1961

Each day, the crises multiply. Each day, their solution grows more difficult. Each day, we draw nearer the hour of maximum danger. I feel I must inform the Congress that our analyses over the last ten days make it clear that, in each of the principal areas of the crisis, the tide of events has been running out—and time has not been our friend.

President Kennedy, five days later, in his State of the Union Address, January 30, 1961

THE KREMLIN, MOSCOW
10:00 A.M., SATURDAY, JANUARY 21, 1961

Nikita Khrushchev summoned the U.S. ambassador to Moscow, Tommy Thompson, to the Kremlin at ten a.m., or two in the morning in Washington, where President Kennedy had not yet returned to the White House from his inaugural revelry.

"Have you read the Inaugural Address?" Thompson asked. Khrushchev appeared weary to Thompson, as if he had spent the entire night awake. His voice was hoarse.

Not only had he read the speech, Khrushchev said, but he would ask Soviet newspapers to print the entire text the following day, something no Soviet leader had done for any previous U.S. president. "*If* they will agree to do so," Khrushchev said with the satisfied chuckle of someone who knew Soviet editors did as he dictated.

Khrushchev then nodded to Deputy Foreign Minister Vasily Kuznetsov, signaling that he should read Thompson the English version of an aide-mémoire that contained his inaugural gift for Kennedy: "The Soviet Government, guided by a sincere desire to begin a new phase in relations between the Soviet Union and the U.S., has decided to meet the wishes of the American side in connection with the release of two American airmen, members of the crew of the RB-47 reconnaissance airplane of the U.S. Air Force, F. Olmstead and J. McKone."

Kuznetsov said the Soviets would also transfer to the U.S. the body of a third airman that had been recovered after the plane was shot down.

Khrushchev had carefully calculated precisely how and when to execute the offer, timing it on Kennedy's first day in office for maximum impact to demonstrate to the world his goodwill for the new administration. However, he would at the same time continue the incarceration of U-2 pilot Gary Powers, who, unlike the RB-47 fliers, had already been convicted of espionage and sentenced to ten years after a show trial in August. The cases couldn't have been more different in Khrushchev's mind. For him, the U-2

incident was an unforgivable violation of Soviet territory that had undermined him politically and humiliated him personally ahead of the Paris
Summit. He would exact a higher price for Powers at another time.*

Back in November and just after Kennedy's election, when asked by an
intermediary how the Soviet leadership could best pursue a "fresh start" in
relations, former U.S. Ambassador to Moscow Averell Harriman had urged
Khrushchev to release the airmen. In any case, Khrushchev's thoughts had
been running in that direction. The pilots had served their electoral purpose. They could now play a diplomatic role in jump-starting a more positive U.S.–Soviet relationship.

The aide-mémoire said Khrushchev wanted to "open a new page in
relations," and that past differences should not interfere with "our joint
work in the name of a good future." Khrushchev said he would release the
airmen as soon as Kennedy approved the draft Soviet statement on the matter and promised to prevent future aerial violations of Soviet territory and
ensure the freed airmen would not be used for anti-Soviet propaganda. If
Kennedy did not accept his terms, Khrushchev made clear he would try the
two men on espionage charges—as he had done with Powers.

Thompson improvised a response without seeking instructions from
Kennedy, whom he would not disturb during his first night in the Lincoln
Bedroom. Thompson said he appreciated the offer, but the U.S. maintained
that the RB-47 had been shot down outside Soviet airspace. The U.S. thus
could not accept wording in the Soviet draft that amounted to a confession
of a deliberate incursion.

Khrushchev was in a flexible mood.

"Each side is welcome to maintain its own view," he said. The U.S. could
make whatever statement it wished.

With that settled, Thompson and Khrushchev then engaged in one of
their frequent exchanges on the merits of their respective systems. Thomp-

---

*Powers was not released until more than a year later, on February 10, 1962, when he was
exchanged on Glienicke Bridge in West Berlin for Colonel Rudolf Abel—the alias for the captured
legendary Russian spy William Fischer, whose exploits were such that his face would later appear
on a Soviet postage stamp.

son complained about a January 6 speech in which Khrushchev had portrayed the U.S.–Soviet struggle as a zero-sum game of class struggle around the world. Yet the two men tangled in an amicable manner that reflected an improved atmosphere of cooperation.

Khrushchev joked that he would cast his vote for Thompson to stay on as ambassador under Kennedy, an extension Thompson wanted but had not yet received. The Soviet leader winked that he was unsure whether his intervention with Kennedy would be helpful.

Thompson laughed that he also had his doubts.

When Khrushchev's offer to release the airmen reached Kennedy, the new president was suspicious. He asked National Security Advisor Mc-George Bundy whether he was "missing a trick." After weighing the dangers, however, Kennedy concluded he could not pass up the opportunity to bring the American airmen home and show such dramatic results with the Soviets in the first hours of his presidency. He would take Khrushchev's offer.

Secretary of State Dean Rusk sent Thompson the president's positive response two days after Khrushchev made his offer.

In the meantime, Khrushchev had served up a menu of other unilateral conciliatory gestures. As promised, *Pravda* and *Izvestia* ran the full, uncensored text of Kennedy's inaugural address, including even the parts Khrushchev did not like. Khrushchev reduced the jamming of Voice of America radio. He would allow five hundred elderly Soviets to join their families in the U.S., he approved the reopening of the Jewish theater in Moscow, and he gave the green light for the creation of an Institute for American Studies. He would allow new student exchanges and would pay honoraria to American writers for their pirated and published manuscripts. The state and party media reported in a celebratory chorus on the Soviet people's "great hopes" for improved relations.

Thompson saw how delighted Khrushchev was at having taken the initiative in U.S.–Soviet relations. What he didn't anticipate was how quickly Kennedy would come to dismiss Khrushchev's gestures, partly on the basis of a misreading of one of Thompson's own cables.

It would be the first mistake of the Kennedy presidency.

NEW STATE DEPARTMENT AUDITORIUM, WASHINGTON, D.C.
WEDNESDAY, JANUARY 25, 1961

Even as the thirty-fifth president of the United States prepared to trumpet
the release of the U.S. airmen at the triumphant first press conference of his
five-day-old presidency, he had also received new information from Moscow
that made him question Khrushchev's true motivations. Eager to be useful
to Kennedy, Ambassador Thompson, in a cable designed to prepare the
president for his first media encounter, had drawn attention to the inflam-
matory language of a secret Khrushchev speech on January 6: "I believe the
speech should be read in its entirety by everyone having to do with Soviet
affairs, as it brings together in one place Khrushchev's point of view as
Communist and propagandist. If taken literally, [Khrushchev's] statement
is a declaration of Cold War and is expressed in far stronger and more explicit terms than before."

What Thompson failed to tell Kennedy and his superiors was that there
was nothing at all new in what Khrushchev had said. The Soviet leader's
so-called secret speech was little more than a belated briefing to Soviet
ideologists and propagandists on the conference of eighty-one Communist Parties the previous November. The Kremlin had even published a
shortened version two days before Kennedy's inauguration in the party
publication *Kommunist*, though that had gone unnoticed in Washington.
Khrushchev's call to arms against the U.S. in the developing world was less
an escalation of the Cold War, as Thompson suggested, than it was the result
of a tactical agreement with the Chinese to prevent a diplomatic breakdown. Lacking that context, Kennedy concluded Khrushchev's words were
"game changing." He thought he had found the clue to unlock, to paraphrase Churchill, the enigma inside the riddle of Khrushchev.

Kennedy's interpretation of the speech was prompting him to devalue
and distrust all of Khrushchev's conciliatory gestures.

The president had initially responded to Khrushchev's moves with positive signals of his own. The U.S. had lifted a ban on Soviet crabmeat imports, it had resumed civilian aviation talks, and it had ended U.S. Post Office censoring of Soviet publications. Kennedy had also ordered his most senior military officers to tone down their anti-Soviet rhetoric.

Beyond that, President Kennedy was learning from his initial intelligence briefings that Moscow wasn't as threatening an adversary as the candidate Kennedy had said it was. He had learned in ever greater detail how wrong his charges had been that the Soviets had created a "missile gap" in Moscow's favor.

Yet none of that altered Kennedy's conviction that Khrushchev's speech was profoundly revealing and aimed quite personally at him. Though that shift in thinking would significantly color his State of the Union message in five days' time, Kennedy was not yet ready to volunteer his shifting thoughts on Khrushchev at his press conference—and no one asked. Reporters had not anticipated much news that day, since it was a sufficient sensation that Kennedy was hosting the first presidential press conference ever to be broadcast live on television and radio across the nation. It was a dramatic departure from Eisenhower's practice of recording his press conferences and then releasing them only after careful editing.

Given the unprecedented media demand to attend, Kennedy staged the gathering in the newly built State Department auditorium, a cavernous amphitheater that the New York Times called "as warm as an execution chamber," with its deep well between the president's raised podium and the reporters. He saved the news from Moscow for the last of three prepared announcements. The Times would report the next day that a low whistle of astonishment rose from the room when Kennedy said two RB-47 fliers, who had been imprisoned and interrogated for six months, already were en route home from Moscow by air.

Kennedy lied that he had promised nothing in return to Khrushchev for the airmen's release. The truth was that he had agreed to Khrushchev's demand to extend the ban on spy flights over Soviet territory and, once the airmen landed, to keep them away from the media. Kennedy radiated calm self-satisfaction. His first public encounter with the Soviets had ended well. His statement contained much the same language he had cabled to Khrushchev: "The United States Government was gratified by this decision of the Soviet Union and considers that this action of the Soviet Government removes a serious obstacle to improvement of Soviet-American relations."

But among friends and advisers, Kennedy was growing so fixated on the January 6 Khrushchev speech that he would read loudly and frequently from a translated version he carried around with him—at Cabinet meetings, at dinners, and in casual conversations—always requesting comments afterward. Thompson had advised Kennedy to distribute the speech to his top people, and Kennedy did so, instructing them to "read, mark, learn and inwardly digest" Khrushchev's message.

"You've got to understand it," he would say time and again, "and so does everybody else around here. This is our clue to the Soviet Union."

The text spoke of Kremlin support for "wars of liberation or popular uprisings . . . of colonial peoples against their oppressors across the developing world." It declared that the Third World was rising in revolution and that imperialism was weakening in a "general crisis of capitalism." In one of the lines Kennedy most liked to quote, Khrushchev said, "We will beat the United States with small wars of liberation. We will nibble them to exhaustion all over the globe, in South America, Africa, and Southeast Asia." Referring to Berlin, Khrushchev promised he would "eradicate this splinter from the heart of Europe."

With its timing just ahead of his inauguration, Kennedy falsely concluded that Khrushchev's policy shift was designed specifically to test him and thus required a response. Thompson had fed that thinking in his advice to the president on how to handle potential media questions. "Solely from a tactical point toward the Soviet Union," Thompson had said, "it might be advantageous for the President to take the line that he cannot understand why a man who professes to wish to negotiate with us publishes a few days before his inauguration what amounts to a declaration of Cold War and determination to bring about the downfall of the American system."

It was true enough that the Soviets and Chinese had agreed on a more active and militant policy toward the developing world. Then Secretary of State Christian A. Herter had told President Eisenhower that the communist gathering sounded "a number of danger signals which the West would do well to heed, such as a call for the strengthening of the might and defense capability of the entire socialist camp by every means." Herter, however, dismissed the ritual call for a continuation and intensification of the Cold War as "nothing new."

Eisenhower had heard so much similar bluster from Khrushchev during his presidency that he had shrugged off this latest version. Lacking this experience and overly confident in his own instincts, Kennedy magnified what Eisenhower had dismissed. He thus overlooked the most important point of the communist gathering, and one that would have been far more helpful to understanding Khrushchev's predicament than his rhetoric. Herter had told Eisenhower that what was most significant was the unprecedented measure of success the Chinese had achieved in challenging Soviet leadership of world communism—despite four months of Moscow's lobbying to contain Mao's views.

Kennedy's first miscue in office regarding the Soviets had several sources. Thompson's cable had played a role. Kennedy was also drawn instinctively to a more hawkish approach to the Soviets due to the popularity of such a course among American voters, his father's anticommunist influence, and his search for a rallying cause around a presidency he had promised would be "a time for greatness." His personal take on history had also played a role. His senior honors thesis at Harvard, published in July 1940, had been about British appeasement of the Nazis at Munich. Playing on his hero Churchill's book *While England Slept*, he had called it *Why England Slept*.

Kennedy would not be caught napping.

The president was seeking a great challenge, and Khrushchev seemed to be providing it. His administration had not formally reviewed its policy toward the Kremlin nor held a major policy meeting on how to deal with Khrushchev. Despite that, Kennedy was sharply altering course from his inaugural speech's studied ambiguity toward the Soviets ten days earlier to the drafting of one of the most apocalyptic State of the Union messages ever delivered by an American president.

Kennedy began by listing all the U.S. domestic challenges, from seven months of recession to nine years of falling farm income. "But all these problems pale when placed beside those which confront us around the world." Reading language he had scribbled himself onto a final draft, he said: "Each day, the crises multiply. Each day, their solution grows more difficult. Each day, we draw nearer the hour of maximum danger. I feel I must inform the Congress that our analyses over the last ten days make it clear that, in each of the principal areas of the crisis, the tide of events has been running out—and time has not been our friend."

Though new intelligence provided him during those intervening ten days had shown him that China and the Soviet Union were increasingly at loggerheads, he insisted, based on the January 6 speech, that both "had forcefully restated only a short time ago" their ambitions for "world domination."

He asked Defense Secretary Robert McNamara "to reappraise our entire defense strategy."

Kennedy could not have more obviously linked himself rhetorically to his heroes Churchill and Lincoln in this perceived hour of danger. Churchill had said, "Sure I am of this, that you only have to endure to conquer." Lincoln's Gettysburg Address had framed the Civil War as one that was testing whether "a nation conceived in liberty and dedicated to the proposition that all men are created equal . . . can long endure."

Placing himself directly in the same crosshairs of history, Kennedy told the Congress and the nation: "Before my term has ended, we shall have to test anew whether a nation organized and governed such as ours can endure."

It was memorable rhetoric based on a false understanding.

THE KREMLIN, MOSCOW
MONDAY, JANUARY 30, 1961

Khrushchev was still waiting for an answer to his multiple pleas for an early summit with Kennedy when the president's State of the Union address delivered him the first of several perceived indignities. Two days later, Khrushchev suffered what he considered the further humiliation of watching Kennedy's America test-launch its first Minuteman intercontinental ballistic missile.

Four days after that, McNamara shamed Khrushchev again—while at the same time embarrassing the White House—by dismissing as "folly," during a Pentagon press briefing, Khrushchev's declaration that he was expanding his missile superiority against the U.S. In both missile technology and overall striking potential, the U.S. still enjoyed a considerable edge. McNamara said the two countries had about the same number of missiles in the field, and though he didn't mention the U.S. superiority of 6,000 warheads to about 300 for the Soviets, he nevertheless had publicly called Khrushchev's bluff.

After his failed negotiation track with Eisenhower in 1960, Khrushchev had taken significant political risk in openly praising Kennedy's election, freeing the airmen, offering other gestures, and reaching out to the new president for an early summit. Kennedy's dismissive response, his ICBM test launch, and McNamara's statement reinforced the charges of Khrushchev's enemies that he was naive about American intentions.

On February 11, Khrushchev returned earlier than scheduled from a trip to Soviet farming regions for an emergency Presidium meeting, where his rivals called for a policy shift to address what they regarded as new American militancy.

The Soviet leader had to rethink his approach. He had failed in his desire to meet with Kennedy before the new president could establish his course toward Moscow. The Soviet leader could not afford to appear weak after Kennedy's startling State of the Union. Khrushchev immediately altered his tone toward Kennedy and his administration, replacing it with aggressive talk about Soviet nuclear capabilities. The Soviet media shifted course as well.

The Kennedy-Khrushchev honeymoon had ended before it had begun. Misunderstandings were souring the relationship between the world's two most powerful men before Kennedy had even chaired his first meeting on Soviet policy.

CABINET ROOM, THE WHITE HOUSE, WASHINGTON, D.C.
SATURDAY, FEBRUARY 11, 1961

Twelve days after his State of the Union, Kennedy called together his top Soviet experts for the first time to lay the groundwork for administration policy. He had placed the horse firmly behind the cart.

He would not be the first or last newly elected U.S. president to be forced through a speaking schedule to set a policy direction before a formal policy review. Though the administration was only twenty days old, those who attended the meeting—representing both a tougher and more accommodating policy toward Moscow—realized Khrushchev's early gestures and Kennedy's tough response had already set a lurching train in motion that they now hoped to steer.

The long-awaited meeting would provide insight into both Kennedy's hunger for knowledge and his continued indecision about how to deal with Khrushchev, irrespective of his speech's apparent clarity. The president had summoned to the Cabinet Room Vice President Lyndon Johnson, Secretary of State Dean Rusk, National Security Advisor McGeorge Bundy, U.S. Ambassador to Moscow Thompson, and three former ambassadors to Moscow: Charles "Chip" Bohlen, who continued as the State Department's resident Russia expert; George Kennan, Kennedy's new ambassador to Yugoslavia; and Averell Harriman, whom Kennedy had made "ambassador at large."

The days leading up to the session had produced a flurry of preparatory cables and meetings. Thompson had been busiest of all, sending in a series of long telegrams designed to educate the new president and his administration on all aspects of his greatest foreign policy challenge. Kennedy had decided to keep Thompson on as ambassador, in large part due to his unique access to Khrushchev. This was his first trip to Washington, D.C., since that decision had been made. Thompson was delighted to serve a president who not only was a fellow Democrat but had already demonstrated he would read his cables far more closely than Eisenhower had ever done.

At age fifty-six, Thompson lacked the charm of his predecessor Bohlen and the brilliance of Kennan. But no one doubted his knowledge or pedigree. He had won the U.S. Medal of Freedom and had endeared himself to the Soviets for remaining in Moscow as a U.S. diplomat during the most gruesome days of the Nazi siege after the American ambassador had fled.

Thompson had been at the table in the postwar years for almost every important negotiation concerning the Soviets, from Potsdam in July 1945 through talks over Austria's independence in 1954 and 1955. He was known for his steady hand, whether at poker with embassy personnel or at geopolitical chess with the Soviets. Thompson argued it was time for Kennedy to decide "our basic policy toward the Soviet Union."

Privately, Thompson had been critical of Eisenhower's failure to pick up on the post-Stalin efforts to ease Cold War tensions. He agreed with Khrushchev's view that his efforts to reduce tensions had gone unrewarded. Thompson had cabled home in March 1959, "We have refused these overtures or made their acceptance subject to conditions he as a Communist considers impossible." Explaining Khrushchev's decision to launch the Berlin Crisis in late 1958, Thompson said, "We are in the process of rearming Germany and strengthening our bases surrounding Soviet territory. Our proposals for settling the German problem would in his opinion end in dissolution of the Communist bloc and threaten the regime in the Soviet Union itself."

In the days ahead of the February 11 meeting, Thompson was careful to provide a more nuanced and complex understanding of Khrushchev than he had done ahead of Kennedy's State of the Union. He considered Khrushchev the least doctrinaire and best of all possible Soviet leadership alternatives. "He is the most pragmatic of the lot and is tending to make his country more normal," wrote Thompson in the sparse language of the diplomatic cable. Pointing to Khrushchev's Kremlin opposition, Thompson warned that the Soviet leader could disappear within Kennedy's term "from natural or other causes."

Regarding Berlin, Thompson cabled that the Soviets cared more about the German problem as a whole than they did about the fate of the divided city. Thompson said Khrushchev wanted above all to stabilize communist regimes throughout Eastern Europe, "particularly East Germany, which is probably the most vulnerable." He said the Soviets were "deeply concerned with German military potential and fear West Germany will eventually take action, which will face them with the choice between world war and retreat from East Germany."

Thompson conceded that no one could predict with any accuracy Khrushchev's intentions regarding Berlin, but it was Thompson's best judgment that the Soviet leader would try to settle the problem during 1961 due to increased pressure from the Ulbricht regime, which felt endangered by Berlin's increased use as an escape route for refugees and as a base for Western spy and propaganda activities. Thompson said Khrushchev would be influenced on Berlin by other issues, ranging from what sorts of trade incentives Kennedy offered to the extent of domestic pressures on him. Thompson said Khrushchev "would be disposed not to bring matters to a head" on Berlin before German elections in September if Kennedy could give him some hope that real progress could be made thereafter.

In one cable after another, Thompson tried to provide a crash tutorial for the new administration on how to handle the Soviets regarding Berlin. He was also in competition with other voices, who were prescribing tougher measures against Moscow. Walter Dowling, the U.S. ambassador to West Germany, cabled from Bonn that Kennedy had to be sufficiently tough with the Soviets so that Khrushchev would see there was "no painless way for him to undermine the Western position in Berlin," and that any attempt to do so held as many dangers for Moscow as it did for Washington.

In Moscow, however, Thompson was arguing that the Kennedy administration had to devise better nonmilitary methods to fight communism. He said the president had to ensure that the U.S. system worked well, had to be certain the Western alliance's member states remained united, and through deeds needed to demonstrate to the developing world and newly independent former colonies that the future belonged to the U.S. and not the USSR. He worried about U.S. mistakes in Latin America at a time when the Chinese challenge was forcing the Soviets to rejuvenate their "revolutionary posture."

"I am sure we would err if we should treat the Communist threat at this time as being primarily of a military nature," he wrote in a cable that got particular traction in Washington. "I believe the Soviet leadership has long ago correctly appraised the meaning of atomic military power. They recognized major war is no longer an acceptable means of achieving their objectives. We shall, of course, have to keep our powder dry and have plenty of it, for obvious reasons."

As if to counterbalance Thompson, Kennedy announced on February 9 that he was bringing out of retirement Harry Truman's secretary of state, Dean Acheson, a hard-liner who was convinced from years of experience that one could counter the Kremlin only with a policy of strength. At Kennedy's behest, one of America's best-known hawks would lead the administration studies on Berlin, NATO, and the related issues of balancing conventional versus nuclear weapons in any future military contingencies with the Soviets. Though Acheson would not join the meeting convened two days after his appointment, he would soon provide the antidote to Thompson's more accommodating stance.

The February 11 meeting would become typical of how the new president would reach decisions. He would bring together the top minds on an issue and then let them fire off sparks while he provoked them with probing questions. In making sense of it later in a top-secret account titled "The

Thinking of the Soviet Leadership," Bundy organized the subjects under four headings: (1) the general condition of the Soviet Union and its leadership; (2) Soviet attitudes toward the U.S.; (3) useful American policies and attitudes; and finally and most important, (4) how best Kennedy could enter negotiations with Khrushchev.

Bohlen was surprised to discover that Kennedy, after having spoken so stridently in his State of the Union, possessed so few prejudices about the Soviet Union. "I've never heard of a president who wanted to know so much," said Bohlen. Kennedy had little interest in the arcane subtleties of Soviet doctrine but instead wanted practical advice. "He saw Russia as a great and powerful country and we were a great and powerful country, and it seemed to him there must be some basis upon which the two countries could live without blowing each other up."

The men arrayed before him differed fundamentally in their views about Moscow. Bohlen worried that Kennedy underestimated Khrushchev's determination to expand world communism. Kennan had doubts about whether Khrushchev was really in charge. He said the Soviet leader confronted "considerable opposition" from Stalinist remnants who opposed negotiation with the West, and thus Kennedy needed to deal with the "collective." Thompson argued that although the government was a collective enterprise, it was increasingly one of Khrushchev's making. He thought only grave failures in foreign affairs or agricultural production could threaten Khrushchev's political control. There he saw problems, as Khrushchev could be facing a third successive year of bad harvests.

Thompson argued that the U.S. "hope for the future" was the evolution of Soviet society into one that was more sophisticated and consumer-driven. "These people are becoming bourgeois very rapidly," he said. Based on long conversations with Khrushchev, Thompson argued that the Soviet leader was trying to buy time to allow the Soviet economy to progress in that direction. "For this he really wants a generally unexplosive period in foreign affairs."

For that reason, Thompson said, Khrushchev badly wanted an early meeting with the president. Though he had responded to the U-2 incident as a blow to his pride, prompting him to cut off communication with the White House, Khrushchev now was eager to move forward again. Thompson thought Kennedy should be open to such a meeting, since Khrushchev's foreign policy relied so much on his personal interaction with counterparts.

Others in the room were more cautious, wondering what value could come from meeting with a Soviet leader who was calling the U.S. "the principal enemy of mankind." Bohlen opposed Khrushchev's suggestion that the meeting should take place during a UN session, "because the Soviet leader cannot resist a rostrum." Harriman reminded Kennedy that protocol required he meet first with his allies.

Whatever the timing, Kennedy made increasingly clear to the men in the room that he wanted the meeting with Khrushchev. He felt he could unlock the potential of his presidency only once he had met with the Soviet leader. As he had told his aide and longtime friend Kenneth O'Donnell, "I have to show him that we can be just as tough as he is. I can't do that sending messages to him through other people. I'll have to sit down with him, and let him see who he's dealing with." Beyond that, other countries— including close U.S. allies—were acting cautiously on crucial issues until they saw how Kennedy and Khrushchev came to terms.

Kennedy told the group he wanted to avoid a full-fledged "summit," which he interpreted as something that was necessary only when the world was threatened by war or when leaders were ready to sign off on major agreements that lower-level officials had precooked. What he wanted was a personal, informal meeting to get a firsthand impression of Khrushchev and thus better make judgments about how to deal with him. Kennedy wanted to open up wide channels of communication with the Soviets to prevent the sort of miscalculation that had led to three wars in his lifetime. Nothing worried him more in the nuclear age than this threat of miscalculation.

"It is my duty to make decisions that no adviser and no ally can make for me," he said. To ensure that those decisions were well-informed, said Kennedy, he needed the sort of in-depth, personal knowledge he could get only from Khrushchev. At the same time, he also wanted to present U.S.

views to the Soviet leader "precisely, realistically, and with an opportunity for discussion and clarification."

Ten days later, on February 21, the same group of experts and senior officials assembled again, and by that time all had agreed that Kennedy should put pen to paper and invite Khrushchev to meet. Khrushchev had floated the possibility of a March get-together in New York around a special UN disarmament session. To head off that option, Kennedy would suggest a spring meeting in a neutral European city, either Stockholm or Vienna. When he hand-delivered Kennedy's letter in Moscow, Thompson would explain to Khrushchev that the president needed the time before then to consult with allies.

On February 27, Bundy instructed the State Department in the president's name to prepare a report studying the Berlin problem. The report should deal with the "political and military aspects of the Berlin crisis, including a negotiating position on Germany for possible four-power talks."

That same evening, Thompson arrived in Moscow with President Kennedy's letter. It had taken the ten weeks of transition after Kennedy's election and first month of his presidency before Kennedy had been ready to respond to Khrushchev's multiple attempts to gain an audience and his several gestures aimed at improving relations.

But by the time Thompson phoned Foreign Minister Gromyko to arrange a time to deliver the long-sought Kennedy response, Khrushchev was no longer interested. The Soviet leader had to resume his agricultural tour of the Soviet Union, Gromyko said, and thus could not receive Thompson either that evening or the next morning before his departure. Gromyko's frosty tone could not have transmitted Khrushchev's snub more clearly.

Thompson protested to Gromyko about the importance of the letter he carried. He said he would "go anywhere at any time" to see Khrushchev. Gromyko replied that he could guarantee neither the place nor the time. Thompson's extension as ambassador had been based in no small part on his vaunted access to Khrushchev, so he was sheepish as he reported the situation back to Washington.

Khrushchev delivered a speech the following day in Sverdlovsk that reflected his surly mood: "The Soviet Union has the most powerful rocket weapons in the world and as many atomic and hydrogen bombs as are needed to wipe aggressors from the face of the Earth," he said.

It was a long way from his New Year's toast about Kennedy's presidency as "a fresh wind" in relations. Kennedy's misreading of Khrushchev's intentions and the Soviet leader's angry response to perceived slights had undermined a brief opportunity to improve relations.

Thompson would have to fly to Siberia to try to prevent matters from turning even worse.

And in Germany itself, things were not going any better.

5

ULBRICHT AND ADENAUER:
UNRULY ALLIANCES

Whatever elections show, the age of Adenauer is over. . . . The United
States is ill-advised to chase the shadows of the past and ignore the
political leadership and thinking of the generation which is now coming
of age.

John F. Kennedy on West German Chancellor Konrad Adenauer,
in Foreign Affairs, *October 1957*

West Berlin is experiencing a growth boom. They have increased wages
for workers and employees more than we have. They have created more
favorable living conditions. . . . I am only saying this because we need to
deal with the real situation and draw its consequences.

Walter Ulbricht, General Secretary of the East German Socialist
Unity Party, in a meeting with the Politburo, January 4, 1961

History would record that Walter Ulbricht and Konrad Adenauer were
the founding fathers of two opposing Germanys, men whose striking
differences, both personal and political, would come to define their era.

In the first weeks of 1961, however, one important similarity drove
their actions: Both leaders fundamentally distrusted the men upon whom
their fates depended—Nikita Khrushchev in the case of Ulbricht and John F.
Kennedy for Adenauer. In the year ahead, nothing mattered more to the

German leaders than managing these powerful individuals and ensuring that their actions did not undermine what each German considered his legacy.

At age sixty-seven, Ulbricht was a cold, introverted workaholic who avoided friendships, distanced himself from family members, and pursued his strict, Stalinist version of socialism with a relentless focus and an unwavering distrust of others. "He was not much liked in his youth and that didn't improve as he grew older," said Kurt Hager, a lifelong fellow communist campaigner who would become the party's chief ideologist. "He had not the slightest understanding of jokes."

Small in stature and cramped in demeanor, Ulbricht regarded Khrushchev as ideologically inconsistent, intellectually inferior, and personally weak. Though the West posed many threats, nothing endangered his East Germany more immediately than what he considered Khrushchev's wavering commitment to protecting its existence.

For Ulbricht, the lesson of World War II—which he had spent primarily in Moscow exile—was that, when given a choice, Germans had become fascists. Determined never to allow his countrymen that sort of free will again, he placed them within the unyielding guardrails of his repressive system, enforced by a secret police system that was both more sophisticated and more extensive than Hitler's Gestapo. His life's purpose was the creation and now the salvation of his communist state of 17 million souls.

At age eighty-five, Adenauer was an eccentric, shrewd, dryly humorous, and orderly man who had survived all the chaotic stages of Germany's previous century: the Imperial Reich, Germany's first unification, the Weimar Republic's chaos, the Third Reich, and now Germany's postwar division. He had seen most of his political allies die or fade from the scene, and he worried that Kennedy lacked the historical context, policy experience, and personal character to stand up to the Soviets in the style of his predecessors, Presidents Truman and Eisenhower.

Adenauer shared with Ulbricht a distrust of German nature, but his remedy was to lash his country irretrievably to the U.S. and the West through NATO and the European Common Market. As he would explain later, "Our task was to dispel the mistrust harbored against us everywhere in the West. We had to try, step-by-step, to reawaken confidence in Germans. The precondition for this . . . was a clear, steady, unwavering affirmation of identity with the West" and its economic and political practices.

As the first and still the only freely elected West German chancellor, Adenauer had helped construct from Nazi ruins a vibrant, democratic, free-market state of sixty million people. His objective was to sustain that construct until the West was strong enough to gain unification on its own terms. More immediately, he was seeking a fourth term in September with the rejuvenated purpose of a politician who felt vindicated by history.

Both Ulbricht and Adenauer were simultaneously central actors and needy dependents—both driving and being driven by events—as the ways they spent the first days of 1961 illustrate.

"GROSSES HAUS," COMMUNIST CENTRAL PARTY HEADQUARTERS,
EAST BERLIN
WEDNESDAY, JANUARY 4, 1961

Standing before a secret emergency session of his ruling Politburo, Walter Ulbricht scratched his goatee unhappily and contradicted his optimistic, public New Year's message of just three days earlier.

Speaking to his subjects, he had spouted socialist triumph, extolled the success of his farm collectivization, and boasted that he had enriched East Germany economically in the previous year while improving its standing around the world. However, the situation was far too serious to risk employing the same lies on his leadership, who knew better, and whom he needed for his struggle against an opponent whose resources seemed to be expanding with every hour.

"West Berlin is experiencing a growth boom," Ulbricht complained. "They have increased wages for workers and employees more than we have. They have created more favorable living conditions, and they have to a great degree rebuilt the main parts of the city, while construction in our part continues to lag." The result, he said, was that West Berlin was "sucking out" the East Berlin workforce, and that more of East Germany's most talented youth were studying in West Berlin schools and watching Hollywood movies in its theaters.

Ulbricht had never been so clear with his comrades about the enemy's rising fortunes or their own declining position. "I am only saying this, because we need to deal with the real situation and draw its consequences," he said, laying out his plans for a year during which he wished to shut off the refugee flow, bolster the East Berlin economy, and protect his East Germany from the spies and propagandists operating from West Berlin.

One speaker after the other rose to support Ulbricht and provide additional reasons for concern. A Magdeburg district party secretary said he had only solved a Christmas tree shortage over the holidays through an emergency harvest. His citizens blamed a shoe and textile shortage on the party's redirection of insufficient supplies to the more politically sensitive major cities of Karl-Marx-Stadt and Dresden. Politburo member Erich Honecker complained that the West's attractions were draining East Germany's sports movement, for which he was responsible, of its best athletes, a serious threat to its Olympic ambitions. Bruno Leuschner, the head of state planning and a concentration camp survivor, said East Germany would only avoid collapse if it got an immediate billion-ruble credit from the Soviets. He reported that he had recently returned from Moscow, where just the technical documents to work out the required scale of Soviet help had filled a twin-engine, Ilyushin Il-14 military cargo plane. East Berlin party boss Paul Verner, a former metalworker, said he could do nothing to stop the continued flight of his city's most skilled workers.

Ulbricht's party lieutenants drew a picture of a country heading toward inevitable collapse. As long as so much of the country's productive capacity was walking out the door as refugees, they complained, they could do little to reverse the trend. Their increasing dependence on the West Berlin economy for suppliers had only made them more vulnerable. Karl Heinrich Rau, the minister in charge of East Germany's trade with the West, argued that Ulbricht could not accept Khrushchev's position that they wait until the Soviet leader had his summit with Kennedy before he dealt with the growing problems. They had to act now.

With unusual candor before his party comrades, an exasperated Ulbricht condemned Khrushchev for his "unnecessary tolerance" of the Berlin situation. Ulbricht knew the KGB would get a report on what he told his Politburo, but he nevertheless pulled no punches. The dangers of Khrushchev's displeasure mattered far less to him than those of his continued inaction. Ulbricht reminded his colleagues that he had been the first to declare openly that all of Berlin should be considered part of East German territory, and that Khrushchev had only later come to agree with him.

Again, Ulbricht said, he would have to take the lead.

The West would not know until years thereafter—through the release of secret East German and Soviet documents—how crucial Ulbricht's actions during the first days of 1961 would be in shaping everything that followed. That said, his decision to escalate his pressure on Khrushchev, despite the potential political perils for himself, was consistent with a career during which he had repeatedly overcome Soviet and internal opposition to create a state that was more Stalinist than even Stalin had envisioned.

Like his mentor Stalin, Ulbricht was unusually short, standing at just five feet, four inches, and like Stalin he had a physical peculiarity that helped define his misshapen personality. For Stalin, the scars were pockmarks, a limp, and a crippled left arm from childhood disease. Ulbricht's enduring defect was his distinctive squeaky falsetto voice, born of a diphtheria infection when he was just eighteen. He hammered home his harshest points in a high-pitched, often indecipherable Saxon dialect, leaving listeners waiting for him to calm down and drop an octave or two. His anti-imperialist rants—most often delivered while he wore crumpled suits and shirts with clashing ties—had made him such an object of derision during the 1950s that he had become the butt of jokes among East German citizens (in their bolder or more inebriated moments) and West Berlin cabaret comedians alike. Perhaps in response, Ulbricht had shortened his speeches and begun to wear more neatly pressed double-breasted suits with silver ties. However, those changes had done little to alter his public image.

Like Stalin, Ulbricht was an organizational zealot who remembered people's names and closely cataloged their loyalties and personal foibles. It was useful data for manipulating friends and destroying enemies. He lacked rhetorical skill and personal warmth, deficits that made it impossible for him to ever gain public popularity, but he compensated with methodical organization skills that would be crucial to running a centrally planned, authoritarian system. Though his East Germany provided a far smaller canvas than that of Stalin's Soviet empire, he shared the Soviet dictator's knack for taking and holding power against all odds to achieve improbable outcomes.

Ulbricht was also a man of precision and habit. He started every day with ten minutes of calisthenics and preached to his countrymen in rhyming slogans about the value of regular exercise. Before skating on winter evenings across his private lake with his wife, Lotte, he demanded that the staff smooth the surface so that it did not show a scratch. The fact that Ulbricht, *unlike* Stalin, did not execute his real or perceived enemies did not alter the single-minded purpose with which he had imposed a Bolshevik system on the Soviet-occupied third of a broken postwar Germany. And he had done so against the instructions of Stalin and other Kremlin officials, who had doubted their own particular style of communism would take among Germans, and thus dared not impose it.

Ulbricht had no such qualms. Almost from the hour of Nazi Germany's collapse, Ulbricht's vision had shaped the Soviet-occupied zone. At six in the morning on April 30, 1945, just hours before Hitler's death, a bus picked up the future East German leader and ten other German leftists—known as the *Ulbricht Gruppe*—from the Hotel Lux, the wartime hostelry for exiled communist leaders. Ulbricht's assignment from Stalin was to help create a provisional government and rebuild the German Communist Party.

Wolfgang Leonhard, the youngest member of the group at age twenty-three, observed that from the moment they landed, "Ulbricht behaved like a dictator" over local communists, whom he considered unfit to rule postwar Germany. Ulbricht had fled Nazi Germany to fight in the Spanish Civil

War before retreating to exile in Moscow, and he didn't hide his disdain for German communists who had remained inside the Third Reich but who had done so little to bring down Hitler—leaving the job to foreigners.

Ulbricht provided a preview of his leadership style when he received a group of a hundred communist district leaders in May 1945 to provide them with their orders. Several of them stood to argue that their most urgent task was to heal the social wounds from widespread incidents of Soviet soldiers raping German women. Some called upon Ulbricht to provide doctors with permission to abort the resulting pregnancies. Others sought a public condemnation of the Red Army's excesses.

Ulbricht snapped. "People who get so worked up about such things today would have done much better to get worked up when Hitler began the war," he said. "Any concession to these emotions is for us quite simply out of the question. . . . I will not allow the debate to be continued. The conference is adjourned."

As would happen so often in the future, Ulbricht's would-be opponents remained silent, assuming he had Stalin's blessing. The truth was that Ulbricht exceeded Stalin's orders from the beginning. One example came in 1946 when the Soviet dictator asked Ulbricht to fully merge his Communist Party of Germany, or KPD, with the less doctrinaire Social Democratic Party, SPD, to create a single Socialist Unity Party, or SED. Instead, Ulbricht purged enough of the SPD's key figures to ensure his own leadership and a more dogmatic party than even Stalin had sought.

As late as April 1952, Stalin had told Ulbricht, "Although two states are being currently created in Germany, you should not shout about socialism at this point." Stalin preferred a unified Germany with all its national resources, one that would exist outside America's military embrace, rather than Ulbricht's rump state inside the Soviet bloc. Ulbricht, however, had his own plans, and he campaigned to create a distinct and Stalinist East Germany through the nationalization of 80 percent of the industry and the exclusion from higher education of the children of so-called bourgeois parents.

By July 1952, Stalin had embraced Ulbricht's plan for a draconian period of forced collectivization and greater social repression. Ulbricht's convictions only grew deeper after Stalin's death, when he survived at least two efforts by liberalizing party comrades to unseat him. Both failed after Soviet military interventions put down first the East German and then the Hungarian uprisings of 1953 and 1956—rebellions that had been inspired by reforms that Ulbricht had opposed.

Just as Ulbricht had been more determined than Stalin to create a Stalinist East Germany, he was also more determined than Khrushchev to protect his creation. Speaking to his Politburo on January 4, 1961, he bluntly blamed East Germany's own shortcomings for 60 percent of all refugee departures. He declared that the party had to address housing shortages, low pay, and inadequate pensions, and that it must reduce the workweek from six to five days by 1962. He complained that 75 percent of those fleeing their country were under twenty-five years old, evidence that East German schools were not properly preparing young people.

The most important action of the Politburo's emergency session was its approval of Ulbricht's plan to create a highest-level working group whose purpose would be to design plans to "fundamentally stop" the refugee bleed. Ulbricht put his three most loyal, reliable, and resourceful lieutenants on the job: Minister for State Security Erich Honecker, Interior Minister Karl Maron, and Erich Mielke, the head of his vast secret police operation.

Having circled the communist wagons at home, he was ready to turn his attention to Khrushchev.

FEDERAL CHANCELLERY, BONN
THURSDAY, JANUARY 5, 1961

By tradition, Catholic and Protestant orphans arrived first to congratulate Konrad Adenauer on his eighty-fifth birthday. Shortly after ten in the morning, two boys dressed as dwarfs and a girl clad as Snow White entered the cabinet hall, where West Germany's first and only chancellor was receiving well-wishers. One dwarf wore a red cap, blue cape, and red pants, and the

other was dressed in a blue cap, red cape, and blue pants. Both shrank behind their identical white beards as the nuns pushed them forward to greet
one of German history's great men, who sniffled badly with a lingering cold.

The chancellor's friends were convinced that Adenauer's inconsolable
concerns about Kennedy's victory had worsened his illness, contracted before the election, from a cold to bronchitis and then to pneumonia. He was
only now recovering. Though the chancellor had publicly praised Kennedy
with false effusiveness, he feared privately that Americans had elected a man
of dangerously flawed character and insufficient backbone. His intelligence
service, the Bundesnachrichtendienst, had provided Adenauer with reports
of Kennedy's sexual infidelities, a weakness the communists would know
how to exploit. Yet Kennedy's undisciplined personal behavior was just one
of many reasons Adenauer concluded that Kennedy, forty-two years his
junior, was "a cross between a junior naval person and a Roman Catholic
Boy Scout," both undisciplined and naive at the same time.

Adenauer knew Kennedy had little higher regard for him. The incoming president considered the chancellor a reactionary relic whose considerable influence in Washington had constrained U.S. flexibility in negotiations
with the Soviets. Kennedy preferred that Adenauer be replaced in the upcoming elections by his Social Democrat opponent, Willy Brandt, the
charming and handsome Berlin mayor, who at age forty-seven was presenting himself as the German Kennedy.

Adenauer faced four challenges in 1961: managing Kennedy, defeating
Brandt, resisting Khrushchev, and wrestling with the inescapable biological
fact of his own mortality. Nevertheless, the chancellor smiled with delight
as Snow White and the dwarfs recited memorized rhymes about animals of
the forest and their love for him. The children presented him with home-
made gifts, and Adenauer, after wiping his dripping nose with a handker-
chief, handed each of them some of his favorite Sarotti chocolates.

One of the great men in German history would be photographed for
the next day's newspapers standing ramrod stiff and looking oddly serious
between two frightened-looking children in the attire of a Brothers Grimm
fairy tale.

Call it the banality of success.

Adenauer's young country was growing more robust by the month. The average annual growth of per capita income in the decade leading up to 1961 had been 6.5 percent. The country had reached full employment, driven by a manufacturing boom of everything from cars to machine tools, and it was now the world's third-largest exporter. No other developed country was performing as well.

For all that accomplishment, Adenauer was an unlikely hero of sometimes comical contradictions. He was a buttoned-down man who sang German drinking songs with relish, a proper Catholic who like Churchill napped naked at midday, and a fierce anticommunist who ran his democracy with authoritarian zeal. He craved power but vacationed frequently on Italy's Lake Como when the stress grew too great. He championed Western integration just as intensely as he feared U.S. abandonment. He loved Germany but feared German nationalism.

Dean Acheson, President Truman's secretary of state, spoke of his longtime friend Adenauer as a man of "stiffness and inscrutability" who at the same time valued nothing more than good gossip or a close male friendship, which he opened up to cautiously but then nurtured over years irrespective of the individual's continued position. Said Acheson, "He moves slowly, gestures sparingly, speaks quietly, smiles briefly, and chuckles rather than laughs when amused." He particularly valued Adenauer's sharp wit deployed against politicians who refused to learn history's lessons. "God made a great mistake to limit the intelligence of man but not his stupidity," Adenauer often told Acheson.

On the morning of his birthday celebration, Adenauer walked briskly to the cabinet hall, where he would receive his guests. An automobile accident in 1917 had left the chancellor with a medically rebuilt, parchment-like face that appeared more Tibetan than German. He had high cheekbones and blue, oriental eyes set apart by the flat bridge of his uneven nose. Some likened his profile to that of the Indian on the American nickel.

Adenauer's twelve years in power had already equaled the length of Hitler's reign, and he had used that time to undo much of the harm his

predecessor had inflicted on Germany. While Hitler had excited nationalism, genocidal racism, and war, Adenauer projected a sense of serene and
peaceful belonging to Europe, with himself as Germany's custodian within
the community of civilized nations.

Just eight years after the Third Reich's collapse, *Time* magazine had
made Adenauer its Man of the Year in 1953, calling his Germany "a world
power once more . . . the strongest country on the continent save Soviet
Russia." He had built on that reputation since then, joining NATO and negotiating diplomatic relations with Khrushchev in Moscow in 1955, then
easily leading his Christian Democrats to reelection with an absolute majority in 1957.

It was his conviction that the division of Germany and Berlin was
more a consequence of East–West tension than its cause. Thus, the only safe
way to reunite Germany was through European reunification as part of
the Western community, and only after a larger U.S.–Soviet détente could
be achieved. Adenauer thus had dismissed Stalin's offer in early March 1952
that Germany be reunified, neutralized, demilitarized, de-Nazified, and
evacuated by occupying powers.

Adenauer's critics complained that this wasn't the act of a visionary
leader but rather the choice of an opportunistic politician. And it was true
that the Catholic Rhinelander likely would have lost Germany's first elections if the Protestant Prussians who dominated eastern Germany had
joined in the vote. That said, Adenauer's suspicion of Russian motivations
was real and consistent. As he explained later, "The aim of the Russians was
unambiguous. Soviet Russia had, like Tsarist Russia, an urge to acquire or
subdue new territories in Europe."

In Adenauer's view, it was failing Allied determination after the war that
had allowed the Soviets to swallow up a big piece of prewar Germany and
install subservient governments across Eastern Europe. That had left his
western Germany "between two power blocs standing for totally opposed
ideals. We had to join the one or the other side if we did not want to be
ground up between them." For Adenauer, neutrality had never been an op-

tion, and he wished to join the side that shared his views of political liberty and personal freedoms.

Over the two days of his birthday celebration, choreographed more for a monarch than a democratic leader, Adenauer received European leaders, ambassadors, German Jewish leaders, political party chiefs, union bosses, editors, industrialists, folkloric groups in colorful costumes, and his political opponent Willy Brandt. Cologne's archbishop bestowed blessings. Defense Minister Franz Josef Strauss led a delegation of generals.

Time was allotted like scarce rations: family members got twenty minutes, cabinet members ten, and lesser mortals five. Adenauer had fumed in protest when the West German press reported, on the basis of leaks from inside his own government, that it was because of his fragile health that Adenauer's eighty-fifth birthday celebration had been extended over two days, thus providing him sufficient recovery time between visitors. The real cause for the prolonged observance, Adenauer insisted, was that his protocol people couldn't cram into a single day the hordes who wanted to congratulate *Der Alte*, or "the Old Man," as his countrymen endearingly knew him.

Hovering darkly over the entire celebration were Adenauer's concerns about Kennedy. Few issues differentiated the Kennedy administration from the Truman and Eisenhower presidencies more than their attitudes toward Adenauer and his West Germany.

During his election campaign, Kennedy had said of Adenauer, "The real trouble is that he is too old and I am too young for us to understand each other." But the problem went beyond the fact that Adenauer was one year short of being twice Kennedy's age. More telling were differences of character and background that gave them little common ground upon which to build other than their shared Catholicism.

Kennedy had been born into a life of wealth and privilege and as an adult had surrounded himself with glamour and beautiful women. He impatiently sought new ideas and solutions to old problems. Adenauer had been raised in the austere, late-nineteenth-century home of a stern civil servant father who had survived the Battle of Königgrätz, the largest military confrontation until that time in Europe, which had opened the way to German unification. Adenauer prized order, experience, and reflection, while he distrusted Kennedy's reliance on flair, instinct, and razzmatazz.

President Eisenhower had considered Adenauer one of the great men of twentieth-century history, a man who had countered nationalist and neutralist instincts among Germans. In Eisenhower's view, Adenauer helped provide both the philosophy and the means for the Western containment of Soviet communism, arguing that greater Western military strength had to be a prerequisite for successful negotiations with the Soviets.

Eisenhower's National Security Council summed up its admiration for Adenauer in a top-secret report handed to the Kennedy transition team. "The main German development of 1960 was a marked increase in self-reliance and independence," said the NSC's Operations Coordinating Board, which implemented foreign policy across all U.S. agencies. It said West Germany had emerged as a national state and was no longer viewed by its population as a temporary construct pending unification. Instead, it said, West Germany was "successor to the Reich and the essential framework of the reunited Germany of the future."

It gave the "firmly established rule of Adenauer" full credit for creating a country that was so successful that even the wayward Social Democrats had abandoned doctrinaire socialism and accommodation with the Soviets in order to give themselves an electoral chance. The group praised West Germany's sound and strong economy, its hard currency, its export success, and its home market, which all together had produced a labor shortage even while the population was increasing.

U.S. Ambassador to Bonn Walter Dowling joined the enthusiasm for Adenauer in his own transition memo. "His self-confidence, fed by the conviction that his grasp of the political verities has been fully vindicated by the events of recent years, is unimpaired. At eighty-five, he still identifies his exercise of political power with the well-being and destiny of the German people. He sees his victory in the coming elections as necessary to the continued security and prosperity of the country." Dowling's bottom line:

"Adenauer remains the controlling influence at the center of political life, his political instincts still acutely alive."

None of that swayed Kennedy from his contrasting view, first laid out in an article in *Foreign Affairs* in the autumn of 1957 and still circulated and read with concern by those closest to Adenauer. The then junior senator from Massachusetts complained that the Eisenhower administration, like Truman's before it, "let itself be lashed too tightly to a single German government and party. Whatever elections show, the age of Adenauer is over." He thought the socialist opposition had proved its loyalty to the West and that the U.S. had to prepare for democratic transitions across Europe. "The United States is ill-advised to chase the shadows of the past and ignore the political leadership and thinking of the generation which is now coming of age," Kennedy had written.

The Eisenhower National Security Council portrayed Adenauer not as history's shadow but as a man whose influence had only grown with his increased parliamentary majority from the 1957 elections. With France's de Gaulle turning more nationalist and anti-American, the NSC regarded Adenauer as the crucial link both for continued European integration and closer transatlantic relations. Beyond that, Adenauer's Defense Minister Franz Josef Strauss had vigorously pursued a military buildup that was making West Germany the largest European contingent in NATO, with 291,000 men, eleven divisions, and modern weapons systems.

But at the same time the NSC sounded warning bells about trends that could endanger the relationship, strains that could grow more pronounced should the personal links erode between the men who ran both countries. West Germans were tiring of their prolonged division, the report said, and were beginning to doubt whether they could rely on Washington's commitment. They despaired that the most likely U.S.–Soviet conflict would be fought on their territory and over German corpses.

Kennedy's election had fed Adenauer's fears of being abandoned by the U.S., which had only increased since the death in May 1959 of his friend and staunchest U.S. supporter, John Foster Dulles, Eisenhower's secretary of state. Adenauer calmed his restless nights only with larger doses of sleeping tablets. Adenauer dismissed Kennedy's brilliant young advisers, known by others as "New Frontiersmen," as "Harvard prima donnas," theoreticians who "had never served at the political front."

Adenauer was painfully aware of Kennedy's doubts about him. As far back as 1951, after then Congressman Kennedy made his first political visit to Germany, the young man had concluded it was Social Democratic leader Kurt Schumacher, and not Chancellor Adenauer, who was "the strongest of Germany's political figures." Schumacher, who had lost narrowly in West Germany's first elections two years earlier, would have been ready to take Stalin's deal of unification for neutrality and thus forgo both deeper West European integration and NATO membership. Acheson had considered Schumacher a "bitter and violent man" determined to weaken Germany's links with the West. Even after his death in 1952, Schumacher's Social Democrats continued to oppose West Germany's NATO membership in 1955.

It wasn't the first time Kennedy had gotten Germany wrong. While traveling through Europe as a student in 1937, four years into Hitler's rule, he had written in his diary: "Went to bed early . . . The general impression seems to be there will *not* be a war in the near future and that France is much too well prepared for Germany. The permanence of the alliance of Germany and Italy is also questionable."

Adenauer's successful 1957 campaign slogan and his advice to Eisenhower on Berlin and the Soviets were the same: *No experiments.* Yet Kennedy's campaign had been all about experimentation; he believed underlying changes in Soviet society offered the chance of more fruitful negotiations. "We should be ready to take risks to bring about a thaw in the Cold War," he said at the time, suggesting a new approach to the Russians that might end "the frozen, belligerent, brink-of-war phase . . . of the long Cold War."

Adenauer considered such talk naive, an attitude that had hardened following his historic trip to Moscow in 1955 to open diplomatic relations and free German prisoners of war. Adenauer had held out hope that he could bring home as many as 190,000 POWs and 130,000 German civilian captives out of the 750,000 who were believed to have been captured or kidnapped and then imprisoned.

Nothing in Adenauer's life had prepared him for the verbal abuse and battering talks that followed. When the Soviets informed their German visitor that only 9,628 German "war criminals" remained in Soviet gulags, Adenauer asked what had become of the rest. "Where are they?" Khrushchev had exploded. "In the ground! In the cold, Soviet ground!"

Adenauer had been shaken by "a man who was, without a doubt, crafty, shrewd, clever, and very savvy, yet at the same time crude and without compunctions. . . . He pounded his fist on the table, half wildly. So I showed my fist as well, and that is what he understood."

Khrushchev got the better of Adenauer, gaining de facto recognition of East Germany in exchange for so few living POWs. For the first time, Adenauer accepted that there would be two ambassadors from the two Germanys in Moscow. The physical strain from the trip left Adenauer with double pneumonia. *Die Zeit* correspondent Countess Marion Dönhoff wrote, "The freedom of 10,000 was bought at the price of the servitude of 17 million." The U.S. ambassador to Moscow, Charles Bohlen, wrote, "They traded prisoners for the legalization of the division of Germany."

Having never forgotten this unsettling encounter, Adenauer worried Kennedy would fare even worse with Khrushchev, though the stakes would be far higher. For that reason, Adenauer had only badly hidden his preference for Nixon over Kennedy. Adenauer even sent Nixon a condolence letter after he lost the election, saying, "I can only imagine the way you feel now." The suggestion was clear: he shared Nixon's pain.

However, on his eighty-fifth birthday, Adenauer briefly put aside such concerns and basked in the adulation of admirers.

The morning began as Adenauer had choreographed it at a Mass read by his son Paul at St. Elisabeth Hospital in Bonn, followed by a breakfast with doctors and nurses. He then joined a Catholic service in Rhöndorf, a neat village of tidy homes with well-tended flower boxes just across the Rhine from Bonn, where he had settled in retreat from the Nazis in 1935. The official explanation for choosing Bonn as West Germany's provisional capital was to avoid the greater permanence that would have been associated with a major city. However, Germans knew the choice also suited Adenauer's lifestyle.

In Bonn, things were as Adenauer liked them—unruffled and in their place. The crisis of Berlin some four hundred miles away was real, but Adenauer seldom visited the city, the Prussian charms of which were lost on the Rhinelander. He considered Germany, like ancient Gaul, to be a country of three parts defined by its chosen alcoholic beverage. He called Prussia the Germany of schnapps drinkers, Bavaria the land of beer drinkers, and his Rhineland a place of wine drinkers. Of the three, Adenauer believed only wine drinkers were sober enough to rule the others.

The chancellor's office window looked out upon barren winter trees to the morning shimmer of the Rhine. His room was simply decorated: an old grandfather clock, a Winston Churchill painting of a Greek temple (a personal gift from the artist), and a fourteenth-century sculpted Madonna, presented to him by his Cabinet on his seventy-fifth birthday. Roses that Adenauer raised and cut himself rested in a delicate crystal vase on the shiny surface of the polished credenza behind his desk. If he had not been a politician, he told friends, he would have been a gardener.

His birthday celebration ran according to the same sense of order, aside from Adenauer's indulgence of twenty-one grandchildren. They romped through his Cabinet Hall as West Germany's President Heinrich Lübke praised the irreversible nature of the chancellor's achievements. Economics minister Ludwig Erhard declared that, thanks to Adenauer, the German people had rejoined the community of free peoples.

In all, Adenauer received 300 guests and 150 gifts during his two-day celebration. But no visit was more revealing than that of Berlin Mayor Willy Brandt, who at age forty-seven was both Adenauer's opponent and his opposite. Born Herbert Frahm, the illegitimate son of a Lübeck shop assistant, he was a lifelong leftist who had fled the Gestapo to Norway, where he changed his name for safety. When the Germans invaded Norway, he relocated to Sweden and remained there until the war's end.

That Brandt was paying his respects was a reflection of how far West

German politics had come. The Social Democrats had concluded that their policy platform of neutrality and closeness to the Soviets would never get them elected. So in 1959 at their Bad Godesberg party conference, and again in November 1960, when they elected Brandt as their leader, they revised their domestic program and embraced West Germany's NATO membership.

The SPD's shift to the right could not have been more apparent at Adenauer's birthday procession. A year earlier on Adenauer's birthday, the Social Democrat press service had accused him of abusing power and acting autocratically and cynically in executing his country's highest office. A mid-ranking official had dropped off some carnations. This year Brandt himself visited, and SPD parliamentary leader Carlo Schmid personally delivered eighty-five red tea roses.

Still, Adenauer did not trust the conversion of Brandt or his socialists. He considered Brandt a particularly treacherous opponent due to his charm and significant political skills, and because he represented the more electable center of the Social Democratic Party. So Adenauer applied one of his political maxims: he portrayed his most dangerous foe as the most despicable of characters and questioned the origins of his birth and the genuineness of his patriotism. Adenauer told his party's ruling council, "Consideration must now be given to what can be said about Brandt's background. . . ." He told another party gathering later, "Whoever wants to be chancellor must have character and a clean past, because the people must trust him."

When Brandt asked Adenauer to his face whether such unfriendly competition was really necessary, the chancellor protested with false innocence, "I would tell you, if I had anything against you," and then he continued conspiring against Brandt. Some questioned whether Adenauer at his age should seek another term, but nothing injected him with more youthful energy than the necessity of defeating the socialists.

In a New Year's radio interview, Adenauer set the standard low for what would constitute success in 1961. When pressed about his ambitions, he said, "I would say that 1961 will have twelve months. No one can dispute that. What will happen in those twelve months no one in the world knows. . . . Thank God that the year 1960 did not bring any catastrophe down upon our heads. And we want to work hard and diligently in 1961 as before. I hope 1961 will also be free of catastrophes for us."

So that was *Der Alte*'s fondest dream: a year free from disaster—providing more time to erode the Soviet bloc through his policy of strength and Western integration. He was convinced Khrushchev would test Kennedy in 1961 and that Germany's future would lie in the balance. At a Cabinet meeting he held on the fringes of his birthday celebration, he said, "We will all need to keep our nerves. No one will be able to do that by himself. We have to do that in a common effort."

At the end of the long celebration, Adenauer's secretary Anneliese Poppinga remarked that the chancellor must feel wonderful seeing such adulation.

Waving his hand, Adenauer said, "Do you really think so? A good feeling? When you are as old as I am, you stand alone. All the people I knew, all those I cared for, my two wives, my friends, are dead. No one is left. It is a sad day."

As he scanned stacks of written congratulations with her, he spoke of the stress of the year ahead: the trips in the coming days to Paris, London, and Washington, and the need to keep Brandt down and Berlin free. "Old people are a burden," he said. "I can understand those who talk so much about my age and who want to be rid of me. Don't let all the attention today fool you. Most don't know how I am and that I remain so healthy. They think that with my eighty-five years I must be tottering and not right in my head."

He then laid his papers to the side, stood, and said with a sigh to his secretary in his flawless Italian, *"La fortuna sta sempre all'altra riva"*—Good fortune always lies on the far side of the river.

Yet even in Adenauer's darkest moments, he knew the buoyant Federal Republic of Germany, through the irrepressible dynamism of its economy and the free agency of its people, was winning the struggle against communism. No matter what dangers Adenauer foresaw from President Kennedy's inexperience or Mayor Brandt's socialism, none of them amounted to the existential threat facing Ulbricht's East Germany: the refugee exodus.

The Failed Flight of Friedrich Brandt

Friedrich Brandt was hiding in his family barn's hayloft when the East German Volkspolizei burst through the front door of his nearby home. Brandt knew his crime: he was resisting the state-mandated collectivization of his family farm, which had been the Brandt property and livelihood through four generations.

Brandt's wife wept and his thirteen-year-old son Friedel stood in stony silence while police ransacked every room, dumping out drawers, overturning mattresses, cutting open picture frames, and tipping over bookshelves in the pursuit of incriminating evidence. However, they already had all the proof they required in a letter that Farmer Brandt had written several weeks earlier to East German President Wilhelm Pieck.

Brandt was confident that Pieck, a trained carpenter whom he considered a hardworking man of integrity, would protect his country's farmers and their property if only someone would tell him about collectivization's excesses and its costs to agricultural production:

Dear President Wilhelm Pieck:

Municipal council representatives have revoked my right to farm despite the fact that my grains and harvest are maintained at the highest standards while potatoes are rotting in the fields that have been harvested by the collectivized state farmers under the supervision of Master Farmer Gläser.

I beg to know why the police have confiscated all my farm equipment and inventory. They have taken my beautiful young horses to be slaughtered. I consider this a criminal act of robbery and beg for your assistance and an investigation into these events as soon as possible. And if that is no longer possible, then I ask for an exit permit

so that I may leave the GDR in order to live out my twilight years
quietly and recover from this land of injustice. For freedom and unity!

Friedrich Brandt

Brandt was just one among thousands of East Germans who had fallen victim to Ulbricht's accelerated efforts at agricultural collectivization and the completion of his industrial nationalization under his second five-year plan for 1956–1960. The East German leader had executed the Stalinist plan with a vengeance after two efforts by reformers to oust him had been defeated, and the uprisings of 1953 and 1956 showed Soviet leaders that the cost of a too-liberal East German leadership was dissolution.

The first two years of the plan had introduced an impressive 6,000 agricultural cooperatives—which quickly became known by the abbreviation LPG, short for the lengthy German name Landwirtschaftliche Produktionsgenossenschaft. For Ulbricht, that was insufficient, as 70 percent of all arable land still belonged to the country's 750,000 privately owned farms. So in 1958 and 1959, the Communist Party sent agitation teams to villages throughout the country to cajole and threaten the locals into "voluntary" collectivization. By the end of 1959, the state set unachievable quota measures for those farmers who remained private. The State Security Directorate then began to imprison farmers who resisted collectivization.

Brandt had been one of the few holdouts. The state sector's 19,000 LPGs and dozens of other state farms controlled 90 percent of the arable land by then and produced 90 percent of its agricultural products. It was a remarkable achievement for Ulbricht, coming while he reduced private enterprise's share of total industrial production to only 9 percent. The cost, however, was that tens of thousands of the country's most skilled business leaders and farmers had fled the country, and state enterprises were being run by individuals more skilled at party fealty than at effective management.

Having terrorized the Brandt family, the People's Police left his farm before even trying to find their missing suspect. They had restricted his and his wife's ability to travel or flee to the West by taking their identity papers, which left them naked in a country of frequent, random document checks. Authorities would return later to arrest Herr Brandt for resisting collectivization and conspiracy to commit the further crime of Republikflucht, *or flight from the Republic, which carried a prison sentence of three years.*

So Brandt decided to leave the country that night, joining the four million who had left the Soviet zone and then East Germany from war's end until 1961. To avoid possible police inspections on public transport, he rode his bicycle for four hours through the night to the home of his wife's sister in East Berlin near a border crossing on a bridge over the Teltow Canal. She offered to conceal him, but after a short conversation Brandt decided to make his way west before the border posts had his description or police began checking the homes of his relatives the next morning. The odds were good that Brandt would be spared any identity check, along with the tens of thousands of others who safely crossed the open border each day for work, shopping, and social visits.

After she heard the next day from her sister about her husband's decision, Brandt's wife decided to flee as well, along with her son. With their farm lost and her husband likely to be already safely in the West, it was an easy decision. Her sister, with whom she shared a resemblance, provided her with identity papers with which she could travel. If she was caught, to protect her sister she would say she had stolen the documents. Life meant nothing to her without her Friedrich.

When stopped by East German police on the same bridge her husband likely had crossed, she collapsed on the ground and cried from the tension. She was certain she had been found out. But luck was on her side that evening. In the random ways that determined East German life, the border police gave Frau Brandt's papers only a cursory look and allowed her to pass.

When she arrived with her son at the Marienfelde refugee camp in West Berlin, the administrator running the registration office said no one of her husband's name or description had arrived. After she waited and worried for three days, a friend arrived from their village and reported that Friedrich Brandt had been captured and jailed before he could cross the border. The charge was one that Ulbricht was employing frequently: "endangerment of the public order and antisocial activities." In a touch of irony, authorities had further justified his imprisonment by pointing to his letter's slanderous contention that East Germany was a land of injustice.

Brandt's village friend urged her to remain in the West, but she protested: "What should I do alone with the boy in the West? I cannot allow Friedrich to sit in a jail there with no one to help him."

She returned home the next morning with her boy, hoping she could still land a job on the collective farm to sustain their diminished family while Friedrich was in prison. Their brief freedom became years of quiet desperation as they disappeared into East Germany's drab society, quietly awaiting his release.

Friedrich Brandt's arrest was a small victory for Ulbricht. But he knew he would lose the larger war on refugees without far more decisive help from Khrushchev.

6

ULBRICHT AND ADENAUER:

THE TAIL WAGS THE BEAR

We are a state, which was created without having and still does not have a
raw material base, and which stands with open borders at the center of
the competition between two world systems. . . . The booming economy
in West Germany, which is visible to every citizen of the GDR, is the
primary reason that in the last ten years around two million people have
left our republic.

Walter Ulbricht in a letter to Premier Khrushchev,
January 18, 1961

The probe which we carried out shows that we need a little time until
Kennedy stakes out his position on the German question more clearly and
until it is clear whether the USA government wants to achieve a mutually
acceptable resolution.

Khrushchev's response to Ulbricht, January 30, 1961

EAST BERLIN
WEDNESDAY, JANUARY 18, 1961

Walter Ulbricht had never written a letter of greater consequence. Though it was marked SECRET, Ulbricht knew that what he was about to send to Khrushchev would also circulate among all the top Soviet leadership. Separately, he would forward copies to other communist allies who might support the new pressure he was placing on the Soviet leader.

Every word of the East German leader's fifteen-page correspondence was written for maximum impact. Just two short months after their last meeting in Moscow, Ulbricht had again lost faith that Khrushchev would get the job done in Berlin. He rejected Khrushchev's plea for patience, feeling his problems were growing too rapidly to be laid aside until Khrushchev could test relations with Kennedy.

"Since Comrade Khrushchev's statement on the West Berlin question in November 1958, two years have flown by," Ulbricht complained. In a brief concession to Khrushchev, the East German leader acknowledged the Soviet leader had used the time to convince more countries that "the abnormal situation in West Berlin must be eliminated." But he spent most of the letter arguing why it was finally time to act on Berlin and how to do so. Even Moscow's NATO adversaries, Ulbricht argued, knew negotiations to change West Berlin's status "are unavoidable."

Conditions in the coming year favored communist action, Ulbricht argued, because Adenauer would want to avoid a disruptive conflict before his September elections, and Kennedy would go to great lengths to prevent a confrontation during his first year in office.

Ulbricht then brazenly issued what he called "GDR demands." Writing more as the ruler than the ruled, Ulbricht listed in detail what he expected of Khrushchev in the coming year. He wanted him to end postwar Allied occupation rights in West Berlin, bring about the reduction and then withdrawal of Western troops, and ensure the removal of Western radio stations and spy services with all their subversive influences.

His catalog of expectations was lengthy, touching on issues small and large. From Khrushchev, he sought the transfer to East Germany of all the state functions in Berlin that were still controlled by the four powers, ranging from postal services to air control. In particular, he wanted control of all air access to West Berlin from West Germany, which would provide him with the capability to shut down the daily scheduled and chartered flights that were ferrying tens of thousands of refugees to new homes and better-paying jobs in West Germany.

If Ulbricht could control all access to West Berlin, he could also squeeze it and over time erode its viability as a free, Western city. Ulbricht knew he was suggesting something similar to Stalin's failed Berlin Blockade of 1948, but he used Khrushchev's own arguments that the Soviets would be more likely to succeed this time because Moscow had closed the gap on Western military superiority and faced a less determined adversary in Kennedy than had been the case with Truman.

On three matters, Ulbricht demanded that Khrushchev make immediate decisions and announce them publicly.

The tail was furiously trying to wag the bear.

First, he wanted Khrushchev to issue a statement that Moscow would ratchet up Soviet economic assistance to the GDR to show the West that "economic blackmail" against his country could not succeed. Second, he appealed to Khrushchev to announce that there would be an East German–Soviet summit in April to raise the standing of Ulbricht and his country in negotiations with the West. Finally, he demanded that the Soviet leader convene a Warsaw Pact summit to rally Moscow's allies to support East Germany militarily and economically. Thus far, Ulbricht complained, these countries had been unhelpful bystanders. "Although they report in the press about these problems," wrote Ulbricht, "they basically feel uninvolved in this matter."

Ulbricht reminded Khrushchev that it was the Soviets who had stuck East Germany with such an impossible starting point from which Ulbricht now had to defend the Kremlin's global standing. "We are a state," he lectured Khrushchev, "which was created without having and still does not have a raw material base, and which stands with open borders at the center of the competition between two world systems."

Ulbricht groused to Khrushchev that the Kremlin had deeply damaged East Germany during the first ten postwar years by extracting economic resources through reparations, including the complete withdrawal of factories, while the U.S. had built up West Germany through the enormous financial support and credits of the Marshall Plan.

Perhaps reparations had been justified at the time, Ulbricht conceded, given all of the Soviets' wartime suffering and the need to strengthen the Soviet Union as the world communist leader. But now, Ulbricht argued, Khrushchev should recognize how much such measures had damaged East Germany in its competition with West Germany. From the war's end through 1954, Ulbricht said, the per capita investment in West Germany had been double that in East Germany. "This is the main reason that we have remained so far behind West Germany in labor productivity and standard of living," he wrote.

In short, Ulbricht was telling Khrushchev: *You got us into this mess, and you have the most to lose if we don't survive, so now help get us out.* Ulbricht escalated the economic demands he had made in November, which Khrushchev had mostly accepted. "The booming economy in West Germany, which is visible to every citizen of the GDR, is the primary reason that in the last ten years around two million people have left our republic," he said, adding that it was also what allowed the West Germans to apply "constant political pressure."

An East German worker had to labor three times as long as a West German to buy a pair of shoes, *if* he could find them at all. East Germany had 8 cars per 1,000 people, compared with 67 per 1,000 in West Germany. The East German official growth rate of 8 percent came nowhere near measuring the real situation for most citizens, since the figures were inflated by heavy industrial exports to the Soviets that did nothing to satisfy consumers at home. The result in 1960, when West German per capita income was double that of East Germans, was a 32 percent increase in refugees, from 140,000 to 185,000, or 500 daily.

Because of all that, Ulbricht appealed to Khrushchev to dramatically reduce the remaining East German reparations to the Soviet Union, and to increase supplies of raw materials, semifinished goods, and basic foodstuffs like meat and butter. He also sought new emergency loans, having already asked Khrushchev to sell gold to help East Germany. "If it is not possible to give us this credit, then we cannot maintain the standard of living of the population at the level of 1960," he wrote. "We would enter into such a serious situation in supplies and production that we would be faced with serious crisis manifestations."

Ulbricht's message to Khrushchev was clear: *If you don't help now and urgently, you will face the prospect of another uprising.* Khrushchev had barely survived the 1957 coup attempt that had followed Budapest, so Ulbricht knew the Soviet leader could not ignore his warning.

Ulbricht was combining maximalist demands with threats of dire consequences if Khrushchev failed to act. His letter might offend the Soviet leader, but that was the least of Ulbricht's worries. Khrushchev's failure to act could bring the end of East Germany—and of Ulbricht.

On the same day, Ulbricht sent an indirect but just as unmistakable message through Khrushchev's nemesis: Beijing.

Ulbricht did not seek Khrushchev's permission, nor did he provide prior notice before dispatching a high-level mission to China's capital, led by Politburo member and party loyalist Hermann Matern. Given Ulbricht's insider knowledge of Khrushchev's ugly dispute with Mao, it was an unfriendly act in both timing and execution.

It was only the inescapable flight route through Moscow that alerted the Soviet leadership to the mission. Yuri Andropov, then the Politburo member responsible for Socialist Party relations, asked to be briefed on the trip during the delegation's airport layover. Matern insisted the mission's purpose was purely economic, and Ulbricht knew Khrushchev could not object at a time when East Germany's needs were growing and the Kremlin was complaining about the cost of satisfying them.

But everything about the trip's timing and choreography was political. In China, the group was received by Vice Premier Chen Yi, Mao's confidant and a legendary communist commander during the Sino-Japanese War and marshal of the People's Liberation Army. He told Matern that China regarded its Taiwan problem and Ulbricht's East German problem as having "very much in common." They both involved areas of "imperialist occupation" of integral pieces of communist countries.

In a direct challenge to Khrushchev, the East Germans and the Chinese agreed to assist each other in their efforts to recover these territories. The Chinese view was that Taiwan was the eastern front and Berlin the western front of a global ideological struggle—and Khrushchev was faltering in both places as world communist leader. Beyond that, Chen promised that China would help get the Americans out of Berlin because the situation there affected all other fronts in the global communist struggle.

Chen reminded the East Germans that communist China had shelled the Taiwanese islands of Quemoy and Matsu in 1955, causing a crisis during which Eisenhower's Joint Chiefs had considered a nuclear response. This happened, he said, not because China had wanted to increase international tensions, but rather because Beijing had needed "to show the USA and the whole world that we have not come to terms with the current [Taiwan] status. We as well had to remove the impression that the USA is so powerful that no one dares to do something and one must come to terms with all of its humiliations."

His suggestion was that the same determination was now necessary regarding Berlin.

The warmth of the East German–Chinese exchange was in sharp contrast to the Sino–Soviet chill that had set in. Ulbricht knew from his November meeting with Khrushchev in Moscow how competitive the Soviet leader felt toward Mao, and he had already played that card to successfully increase Moscow's economic support. Khrushchev had declared at the time that he would provide East Germany with the sort of economic assistance Mao could not, creating joint enterprises with the East Germans on Soviet territory—something the Soviets had done with no other ally. "We aren't

China," he declared to Ulbricht. "We are not afraid of giving the Germans a boost. . . . The needs of the GDR are our needs."

Three months later, the Chinese were becoming an ever greater problem for Khrushchev, despite the apparent truce he had negotiated with them at the November gathering of Communist Parties in Moscow. While the East Germans were in Beijing seeking economic assistance, China was in Tirana encouraging xenophobic Albanian leader Enver Hoxha to break with the Soviet Union. During the Fourth Congress of the Albanian Communist Party, from February 13 to 21, Albanian communists had torn down public portraits of Khrushchev and replaced them with those of Mao, Stalin, and Hoxha. Never had a Soviet leader suffered such humiliation in his own realm.

Ulbricht's course of greater diplomatic pressures on Khrushchev had its risks.

The far more powerful Khrushchev might have decided it was finally time to replace Ulbricht with a more submissive and obedient East German leader. He might have decided the China mission had crossed some impermissible line. However, Ulbricht had gambled correctly that Khrushchev had no good alternatives.

THE KREMLIN, MOSCOW
MONDAY, JANUARY 30, 1961

Khrushchev's response landed on Ulbricht's desk twelve days after the East German leader had written to him and, by coincidence, on the day of John F. Kennedy's State of the Union speech. Given the impertinence of Ulbricht's demands, Khrushchev's letter was surprisingly submissive.

The Soviet leader reported to Ulbricht that the Central Committee "has discussed your letter carefully" and that Moscow's leaders agreed with much of it. The fact that Khrushchev had shared it with party bosses showed that he recognized the gravity of Ulbricht's criticisms and the urgency of his requests. That said, Khrushchev again asked Ulbricht to contain his mounting impatience.

"Currently, we are beginning to initiate a detailed discussion of these questions with Kennedy," he wrote. "The probe which we carried out shows that we need a little time until Kennedy stakes out his position on the German question more clearly and until it is clear whether the USA government wants to achieve a mutually acceptable resolution."

The Soviet leader conceded that the extreme measures Ulbricht had suggested in his letter "under the circumstances" would prove necessary. "If we do not succeed in coming to an understanding with Kennedy, we will, as agreed, choose together with you the time for their implementation."

Ulbricht had achieved less than he had sought, but more than he might have considered probable. Khrushchev again would ratchet up economic assistance. The Soviet leader would also convene a Warsaw Pact meeting on Berlin. Of all Ulbricht's demands, Khrushchev refused to agree only to the East German–Soviet summit.

Khrushchev had accepted Ulbricht's diagnosis of the problem, and he had not rejected the steps Ulbricht had suggested toward a cure. Ulbricht could be satisfied that he had penetrated and influenced Soviet Communist Party thinking on Berlin at the highest levels.

Khrushchev was still buying time to work the new American president. However, Ulbricht had put all the pieces in place to move forward decisively at the moment Khrushchev's efforts to negotiate a Berlin deal with Kennedy failed. And the East German leader was certain they would.

In the meantime, Ulbricht would put his team to work on contingencies.

THE WHITE HOUSE, WASHINGTON, D.C.
FRIDAY, FEBRUARY 17, 1961

The clouds were already gathering around the U.S.–West German relationship when Foreign Minister Heinrich von Brentano di Tremezzo walked into the Oval Office with his satchel full of Adenauer's concerns.

For several years, Americans had been warming to the West Germans, impressed by their embrace of U.S.-style freedoms. Now, however, public opinion was turning more negative again, fed by media reports about the impending trial in Israel of Nazi war criminal Adolf Eichmann, and publicity around William L. Shirer's best-selling book, *The Rise and Fall of the Third Reich*, with all its sordid new details about the not-so-distant German past.

The West German foreign office had warned Adenauer at the beginning of the year: "There are still some resentments and suspicions which lie dormant under the surface, but which are ready to break out under certain stimuli." In exasperation at the shifting mood, West German ambassador Wilhelm Grewe told a group of U.S. journalists at a conference of the Atlantik-Brücke, an institution created to bring the two countries closer, that they had "to choose whether they consider us as allies or a hopeless nation of troublemakers."

Kennedy's briefing papers for the Brentano meeting warned the president that his visitor was coming to express Adenauer's concern that his administration might sell out West German interests in Berlin in exchange for a deal with the Soviets. "The Germans are acutely aware that vital aspects of their destiny are in hands other than their own," said the position paper, signed by Secretary of State Dean Rusk. It advised Kennedy to both reassure Brentano of continued U.S. commitment to West Berlin's defense and share with him as much of the president's thinking as possible about the possibility of Berlin negotiations with Moscow.

Given past experience, however, U.S. officials distrusted their West German partners' ability to keep a secret. American intelligence services assumed that their West German counterparts were infiltrated and thus unreliable. "While frankness is desirable particularly in view of the chronic German sense of insecurity," the Rusk memo said, "the German government does not have a good record for retaining confidences."

Detractors said that Brentano—a fifty-seven-year-old bachelor whose life was his job and its trappings—was little more than the genteel, cultured instrument of the strong-willed Adenauer, and the foreign minister did little to alter this impression. Adenauer was determined to run his own foreign policy, and no independent actor could remain long in Brentano's job. Where Brentano and Adenauer did differ was their attitude regarding

Germany's European calling. While Brentano was of a younger generation that considered Europe as Germany's natural destiny, Adenauer regarded European integration more as a means of suppressing German nationalism.

Kennedy opened what would be a stiff meeting with Brentano by speaking from a script about "the appreciation of the U.S. government for the cooperation and friendship of the German government during the past years." He very much wanted to arrange a meeting soon with Adenauer, he said, and hoped "that all mutual problems would be worked out satisfactorily."

Adenauer's political opponent Willy Brandt had already manipulated matters so that he would arrive in Washington ahead of Adenauer in March for a personal meeting with Kennedy, a breach of the usual protocol that put the head of an Allied government before any city mayor. Rusk had supported the Brandt visit to keep "freshly before the world our determination to support West Berlin at all costs." He wanted the Adenauer meeting to follow as closely thereafter as possible to avoid giving the impression that Kennedy favored Brandt in upcoming German elections, which of course he did.

Kennedy reassured Brentano that his failure to mention Berlin by name in the inaugural address or in his State of the Union, a matter that had become such an issue in the German press, "did not by any means signify a lessening of United States interest in the Berlin question." He said he had merely wanted to avoid provoking the Soviets at a time of relative calm in the city. Kennedy told the foreign minister that he expected Moscow to renew pressure on Berlin in the coming months, and he wanted Brentano's suggestions about how one could best counter "the subtle pressures" Moscow was likely to exert.

Brentano said Berlin's absence from Kennedy's speeches was of such little concern that it had not even been in talking points Adenauer had given him. He agreed there was no reason yet to raise the Berlin question, but added, "We would have to deal with it sooner or later." Brentano frowned, declaring, "The leaders of the Soviet Zone cannot tolerate the symbol of a free Berlin in the midst of their Red Zone." He told Kennedy that East German leaders "will do all in their power to stimulate the Soviet Union to action with regard to Berlin."

On the positive side, Brentano estimated that 90 percent of the East Berlin population opposed the East German regime, which he called the region's second-harshest communist system after that of Czechoslovakia. His message was that the people in both Germanys heavily favored its Western version and therefore would over time support unification.

Kennedy probed deeper. He worried the Soviets would unilaterally sign a separate peace treaty with East Germany and then cut short West Berlin's freedom, maintaining the status quo for only a brief period in order to mollify the West.

Brentano agreed such a course was probable, so Kennedy asked what the NATO allies should do about it.

Brentano described to Kennedy his chancellor's "policy of strength" approach, and said the Soviets would "hesitate to take drastic steps with regard to Berlin as long as they know that the Western Allies will not tolerate any such steps." As long as Kennedy remained firm, he said, the Soviets "may continue to threaten but will not take any actual steps for some time to come." However, Brentano agreed that recent U.S. setbacks in the Congo, Laos, and Latin America all increased the chance that the Soviets would test Kennedy over Berlin.

As if to prove Brentano's point, Khrushchev simultaneously escalated pressures on Adenauer in Bonn.

FEDERAL CHANCELLERY, BONN
FRIDAY, FEBRUARY 17, 1961

Ambassador Andrei Smirnov's urgent requests for meetings with Adenauer were seldom good news.

It was invariably Smirnov, Khrushchev's envoy in Bonn, who was the vehicle for the Soviet leader's bullying. So the West German chancellor was already apprehensive upon receiving Smirnov's demand for an immediate meeting, considering that its timing coincided with his foreign minister's visit to the White House.

More often than not, Smirnov was a charming and courteous diplomat who delivered the fiercest communication with a calm demeanor and outside the public spotlight. A rare exception had come the previous October, when he had exploded in rage at the comments of Adenauer's number two, Ludwig Erhard, to a visiting delegation of two hundred African leaders from twenty-four countries, many of them newly independent. "Colonialism has been overcome," Erhard had said, "but worse than colonialism is imperialism of the Communist totalitarian pattern."

Before storming out of the hall, Smirnov rose from the audience and shouted, "You talk about freedom, but Germany killed twenty million people in our country!" It was a rare public display of the enduring Russian resentment toward Germans.

This time Smirnov's task was a more familiar one. He was presenting Adenauer with a nine-point, 2,862-word aide-mémoire from Khrushchev that would provide the most compelling evidence yet during the Kennedy administration that Khrushchev had again turned confrontational on Berlin. Soviet intelligence reports tracked Adenauer's doubts regarding Kennedy's reliability, and Khrushchev was wagering that Adenauer might be more susceptible to Soviet entreaties than he had been under the more dependable Truman or Eisenhower.

"An entirely abnormal situation has emerged in West Berlin, which is being abused for subversive activities against the German Democratic Republic, the USSR and other socialist states," the Khrushchev document said in clear, undiplomatic language. "This cannot be allowed to go on. Either one continues down the path of an increasingly dangerous worsening of relations between countries and military conflict, or one concludes a peace treaty."

The aide-mémoire, written in the tone of a personal letter from Khrushchev to Adenauer, called Berlin the most important issue in Soviet–German relations. It criticized what it called ever louder and more emphatic popular support in West Germany for revising postwar agreements that had ceded a third of the Third Reich's territory to the Soviet Union, Poland, and Czechoslovakia. "If Germany now has different borders than it had before the war, it has only itself to blame," the letter said, reminding Adenauer that his country had invaded its neighbors and killed "millions upon millions."

Though the aide-mémoire had been delivered by the Soviet ambassador to Adenauer, its tough message was intended just as much for Kennedy. In unmistakable fashion, the Soviet leader was declaring that he had lost all patience with Western dithering. First, he complained, the U.S. had asked the Soviets to wait for Berlin talks until after its elections, then Moscow was told to wait until Kennedy could settle into his job, and now Moscow was being asked to wait again until after West German elections.

"If one gives in to these tendencies," Khrushchev wrote, "it could go on forever."

The letter closed with Khrushchev's characteristic cocktail of seduction and threats. He appealed to Adenauer to use "all his personal influence and his great experience as a statesman" to secure European peace and security. If matters turned more confrontational, however, the letter reminded Adenauer that the current correlation of military forces provided the Soviet Union and its friends with all the force they required to defend themselves.

The letter scoffed at West Germany's appeal for disarmament at a time when Adenauer was quickly building up his military forces and seeking nuclear weapons while trying to transform NATO into the fourth nuclear power. It scolded Adenauer over talk that his party's coming election campaign would focus on anticommunism. "If that is really the case," the letter said, "you . . . must be aware of the consequences."

The Kennedy administration was not yet a month old, but Khrushchev had already shifted course on Berlin. If Kennedy was unwilling to negotiate an acceptable deal with him, Khrushchev was determined to find other ways to get what he wanted.

PART II

THE GATHERING

STORM

7

SPRINGTIME FOR KHRUSHCHEV

West Berlin is a bone in the throat of Soviet–American relations. . . .
If Adenauer wants to fight, West Berlin would be a good place to begin
conflict.

Premier Khrushchev to U.S. Ambassador Llewellyn E. Thompson Jr.,
March 9, 1961

It seems more likely than not that the USSR will move toward a crisis on
Berlin this year. All sources of action are dangerous and unpromising.
Inaction is even worse. We are faced with a Hobson's choice. If a crisis is
provoked, a bold and dangerous course may be the safest.

Former Secretary of State Dean Acheson, memo on Berlin for
President Kennedy, April 3, 1961

NOVOSIBIRSK, SIBERIA
SUNDAY, MARCH 9, 1961

Nikita Khrushchev was in poor condition and foul temper.

The Soviet leader's face was ashen, his body slumped, and his eyes
lifeless—an appearance in such contrast to his usual brash buoyancy
that it shocked U.S. Ambassador Llewellyn "Tommy" Thompson and his
two travel companions, the young U.S. political counselor Boris Klosson
and Anatoly Dobrynin, the Soviet foreign ministry's top America hand.

It had taken Thompson ten days of pleading before he'd succeeded in winning an audience with Khrushchev to deliver the president's first private letter to the Soviet leader, which included a long-awaited invitation to meet. Even then, Thompson had to fly 1,800 miles to catch up with Khrushchev in Akademgorodok, the vast science city Khrushchev had ordered to be built outside Novosibirsk on the West Siberian plain.

Khrushchev's aspiration in Siberia had been to create the world's leading center of scientific endeavor, but like so many of his dreams, this one, too, had fallen short. Just that week he had fired a geneticist whose theories he disliked, and he had ordered four of nine stories chopped off the plans for a new academy so that it conformed to a more standard Soviet size. Akademgorodok's frustrations only added to a growing list of Soviet failures that were taking a toll on the Soviet leader's confidence.

Khrushchev's ongoing agricultural tour of the country had taken a physical and emotional toll, making him all the more aware of his country's economic shortfalls. Albania had shifted its allegiance from Moscow to China in a heretically public manner, a worrisome crack in Khrushchev's leadership of world communism. Moscow's ally in the Congo, Patrice Lumumba, had been murdered, for which Khrushchev blamed UN Secretary-General Dag Hammarskjöld.

More fundamentally, the capitalist world was proving far more resilient than his propagandists had predicted. Decolonization in Africa had failed to damage the West's standing in the developing world as much as his experts had envisioned. For all the Soviet efforts to divide the alliance, NATO's integration was deepening, and the West German Bundeswehr was expanding its capabilities so quickly that it was altering the European military balance. Both in his rhetoric and his defense spending, President Kennedy was acting more anticommunist than Eisenhower. And each month, the East German refugee numbers hit new records. If Khrushchev's luck didn't turn soon, the Soviet leader had to worry that his October Party Congress would become a struggle for survival.

Facing such an array of new challenges, Khrushchev agreed to meet Thompson only after the U.S. ambassador had leaked to *New York Times* correspondent Seymour Topping—and to any number of diplomats in Moscow—that the Soviet leader was giving him the cold shoulder at a time when Kennedy was trying to reach out. On March 3, Topping had reported dutifully that Thompson had been frustrated in his efforts to pass Khrushchev a crucial message from Kennedy in hopes of "seeking to head off a serious mishap in relations." Topping wrote that Thompson had a new mandate "to initiate a series of exploratory conversations looking to substantive negotiations on a range of East-West differences."

Even after that, Khrushchev agreed only reluctantly to see Thompson. Khrushchev's adviser Oleg Troyanovsky had seen his boss's high hopes for a new start in U.S.–Soviet relations come "quickly to evaporate" in the four months since Kennedy's election. There were few better barometers of the U.S.–Soviet temperature than Troyanovsky, the ever-present Khrushchev adviser who had attended Sidwell Friends School in Washington, D.C., while his father served as the first Soviet ambassador to Washington in the mid-1930s. He could quote Marx and speak American slang with equal fluency.

Troyanovsky had seen Khrushchev weary of the Kennedy waiting game, having lost the opportunity he had sought to reach the new American leader before he could be infected by what Khrushchev considered Washington's anti-Soviet bias. A little less than a year after the U-2 incident and the failed Paris Summit, Khrushchev could not politically afford another failed meeting with an American president. Yet that now seemed the most likely outcome of any such summit, given Kennedy's determination to drag his feet on Berlin and to press for a nuclear test ban agreement that the Soviet military didn't want. Khrushchev was already in hot water with his military brass over troop cuts, and they would resist any measures that would constrain their nuclear development or leave them open to intrusive inspections.

Khrushchev's farm visits en route to Novosibirsk had fed his discontent. A new Soviet statistical yearbook showed the Soviet Union had achieved some 60 percent of America's gross national product, but that was certainly an exaggeration. The CIA pegged it at closer to 40 percent, and other experts estimated that the Soviet economy's size was no more than 25 percent of the U.S. level. Agricultural productivity was but a third of the U.S. level, and shrinking.

During his travels, Khrushchev had seen the ugly truth behind overly optimistic reports from provincial sycophants. Soviet farming was failing because of erratic planting, bad harvests, and dreadful distribution systems that often left crops to rot. Every week Khrushchev fumed at a new list of incompetent subordinates, some of whom fudged numbers to conceal their failures while others conceded their shortcomings but failed to fix them. In confessing his inadequacy, one party secretary named Zolotukhin, from the western Russian provincial capital of Tambov on the Tsna River, pulled down his trousers and asked Khrushchev three times to lash him.

"Why is it that you want your pants whipped off to show us your ass?" Khrushchev had barked. "Do you think you will give us some sort of thrill? Why would we keep such secretaries?"

At one local Communist Party gathering after another, Khrushchev demanded his underlings match American economic and agricultural benchmarks and exceed U.S. milk and meat productivity, goals that had been his fixation since his 1959 visit to the American heartland. When comrades questioned the wisdom of benchmarking against imperialists, Khrushchev said America was "the highest stage of capitalism," while Soviets were only just getting started building the foundation for the house of communism— "and our bricks are production and consumer goods."

The Soviet public's awareness of the country's failings had produced a bumper crop of humor, told in the food lines as Khrushchev hopscotched the country:

Q. What nationality were Adam and Eve?

A. Soviet.

Q. How do you know?

A. Because they were both naked, had only an apple to eat, and thought they were in paradise.

Some of the jokes involved the new U.S. president:

President John Kennedy comes to God and says: "Tell me, God, how
    many years before my people will be happy?"
"Fifty years," replies God.
Kennedy weeps and leaves.
Charles de Gaulle comes to God and says: "Tell me, God, how many years
    before my people will be happy?"
"A hundred years," replies God.
De Gaulle weeps and leaves.
Khrushchev comes to God and says: "Tell me, God, how many years
    before my people will be happy?"
God weeps and leaves.

As sour as Khrushchev's mood had been when Thompson arrived, it
worsened as the Soviet leader read the Russian translation of Kennedy's
letter. Khrushchev could not find a single word on Berlin. Speaking calmly
and wearily, Khrushchev told Thompson that Kennedy must understand
that he would never back off his demand to negotiate "the German question." Over time, Khrushchev said, he had converted Eisenhower to the
realization that Berlin talks could not be avoided, but then U.S. militarists
"deliberately exploded relations" with their U-2 flight.

Under instructions not to be drawn on Berlin, Thompson responded
only that Kennedy was "reviewing our German policy and would wish to
discuss it with Adenauer and other allies before reaching conclusions."

Fed up with what he considered U.S. delay tactics, Khrushchev scoffed at
the notion that the world's most powerful country must consult with anyone before acting, given his own dismissive treatment of Warsaw Pact allies. "West Berlin is a bone in the throat of Soviet–American relations,"
Khrushchev told Thompson, and it would be a good time to remove it. "If
Adenauer wants to fight," he said, "West Berlin would be a good place to
begin conflict."

Though Kennedy was not ready to negotiate Berlin with Khrushchev, the Soviet leader eagerly laid out his own negotiating position for Thompson so that he could relay it to the president. He told Thompson that he was ready to stipulate in any agreement that West Berliners could maintain the political system of their choice, even if it was capitalism. However, he said, the Americans would have to take the notion of German unification off the table, even if both the U.S. and Soviets might desire it over time. Abandoning the language of unification was necessary, he said, if the Soviet Union and the U.S. wanted to sign a war-ending treaty that recognized both Germanys as sovereign states.

For his part, Khrushchev assured Thompson he would not expand the Soviet empire any farther westward, but he also wanted Washington to refrain from any rollback of what was already his. Employing a voice calculated to project intimacy between old friends, Khrushchev told Thompson it was his "frank desire" to improve relations with Kennedy and make nuclear war impossible. However, he said, he could not do so alone.

Khrushchev was pushing Thompson far beyond his approved talking points. The American ambassador warned Khrushchev not to expect rapid change in the U.S. position on Berlin, further cautioning the Soviet leader that if he acted unilaterally he would only increase tensions. "If there is anything which will bring about a massive increase in U.S. arms expenditures of the type which took place at the time of the Korean War," Thompson said, "it would be the conviction that the Soviets are indeed attempting to force us out of Berlin."

Khrushchev dismissed Thompson's warning. "What attracted the West so much to Berlin anyway?" he countered.

It was because America had given its solemn commitment to Berliners, Thompson responded, and thus it had its national prestige invested in their fate.

Khrushchev shrugged that it was only Germany's World War II capitulation that had brought Western powers to Berlin. "Let us work out together a status for West Berlin," he said. "We can register it with the UN. Let us have a joint police force on the basis of a peace treaty which can be guaranteed by the four powers, or a symbolic force of four powers could be stationed in West Berlin." Khrushchev said his only precondition was that East Berlin would have to be left out of any such planning, as the Soviet zone of the city would remain the capital of East Germany under any new plan.

Because Berlin lacked political significance for Moscow, Khrushchev repeated that he would provide the U.S. whatever guarantees it wanted to protect its prestige and ensure West Berlin's current political system. He was prepared to accept West Berlin as a capitalist island in East Germany, he said, because in any case the Soviet Union would surpass West Germany in per capita production by 1965, and then surpass the United States five years later. To further illustrate West Berlin's insignificance, Khrushchev said that since the Soviet population grew each year by 3.5 million, the total population of West Berlin at two million was just "one night's work" for his sexually active country.

Playing devil's advocate, Thompson responded that even if West Berlin were unimportant to the Soviets, "Ulbricht was very much interested," and would be unlikely to endorse Khrushchev's guarantee for its democratic, capitalist system.

With a dismissive wave of the hand, as if swatting away a troublesome gnat, Khrushchev said he could compel Ulbricht to approve whatever he and Kennedy would decide.

In an effort to find safer ground than Berlin, Thompson changed the subject to U.S.–Soviet trade liberalization. On that matter, he did have an offer he hoped would mollify Khrushchev. He said the U.S. was hoping to lift all restrictions on Soviet crabmeat imports to the United States.

Instead of embracing the gesture, Khrushchev shot back his outrage at a recent U.S. decision to cancel, on national security grounds, the sale to Moscow of advanced grinding machine tools. "The USSR can fly its rockets without U.S. machines!" he snarled. He railed further against the delayed approval of a urea fertilizer factory sale, also due to its potential military application, ostensibly for chemical weapons. Khrushchev said such urea technology was so widely available that he already had purchased three such plants from Holland.

However, no amount of fertilizer could approach the importance of Berlin to Khrushchev, and the Soviet leader returned to the issue time and again until Thompson reluctantly engaged him. He assured Khrushchev that the president knew the situation was unsatisfactory to both sides, was "re-examining the whole problem of Germany and Berlin," and would be "disposed to do something to help relaxation." But Thompson repeated that he could not reflect Kennedy's views until the president had consulted personally with allies—and he would do that during meetings in March and April before their own proposed summit.

Khrushchev complained that Kennedy did not understand fully what was at stake in Berlin. If he and Kennedy could sign a treaty ending the city's postwar status, he told Thompson it would calm tensions all around the world. If they were unable to solve their Berlin disagreements, however, their troops would continue to confront each other in a situation "not of peace but of armistice." Khrushchev dismissed Kennedy's notion that arms reduction talks could build the confidence necessary to take on the more difficult matter of Berlin. Quite the contrary, he said; only U.S. and Soviet troop withdrawal from Germany would create the right atmosphere for weapons cuts.

After so many weeks of angling to meet Kennedy, Khrushchev now balked at the president's invitation. He said only that he was "inclined to accept" Kennedy's offer to get together the first week of May, some two months away, following visits to Washington by Britain's Macmillan and West Germany's Adenauer, and after a stop Kennedy would make in Paris to see de Gaulle. Kennedy had offered as a venue either Vienna or Stockholm. Although he preferred Vienna, Khrushchev said, he would not rule out Sweden. The Soviet leader shrugged that it would be useful to get to know Kennedy, noting they had met only briefly in 1959 when the then senator had arrived late for the Soviet leader's visit to the Senate Foreign Relations Committee. Without accepting or declining the invitation, however, Khrushchev told Thompson it "would be necessary to work out a reason for the meeting."

At the end of the lunch that followed, Khrushchev raised a glass of his favorite pepper-flavored vodka in a lukewarm toast to Kennedy that was in striking contrast to his enthusiastic New Year's message. Khrushchev dispensed with the usual wishes for Kennedy's health: "Being so young, he does not need such wishes." Having withdrawn his invitation to Eisenhower to visit the Soviet Union a year earlier, he regretted the time still was not ripe for him to extend his country's traditional hospitality to Kennedy and his family.

Thompson returned by plane that evening to a snow-blanketed Vnukovo Airport in Moscow, and his driver whisked him over icy streets to the embassy, where Thompson cabled Washington his report. Although Thompson had been on the move for eighteen hours, adrenaline surged through him as he typed.

In Thompson's experience, Khrushchev's fixation on Berlin had never been so single-minded. The Soviet leader had convinced Thompson he would no longer delay action. "All my diplomatic colleagues who have discussed the matter consider that in the absence of negotiations, Khrushchev will . . . precipitate a Berlin crisis this year," he wrote.

A week later, Thompson urged his superiors in another cable to accelerate their contingency planning for a Soviet move on Berlin. Relations between Khrushchev and the Kennedy administration were so bad, the ambassador argued, that the Soviet leader might feel he had much to gain and very little to lose over Berlin. Thompson added, however, that Khrushchev still wanted to avoid provoking a military confrontation with the West, and would instruct the East Germans not to interfere in any way with Allied military access to the city.

Thompson listed the sources of growing U.S.–Soviet tensions that had accumulated during the Kennedy administration's first weeks: The Kremlin lacked interest in the U.S. proposal of a nuclear test ban agreement; it considered Kennedy more militant than Eisenhower with his increased arms budget; it worried about new U.S. preparations for guerrilla warfare in the developing world; and it was displeased with the Kennedy administration's increased restrictions on selling the Soviets sensitive technologies. The Kremlin was particularly irked by Kennedy's personal and public commitment to provide more support for Radio Free Europe, which was proving an effective tool in preventing communist regimes' monopoly on information. In Africa and South America, wrote Thompson, proxy confrontations would continue and perhaps increase.

Laying out his thoughts for President Kennedy on what might be the focus of his likely meeting with Khrushchev, Thompson wrote: "Discussion of the German problem will be the main point of the exercise so far as [Khrushchev] is concerned. It would be at that meeting or shortly thereafter that the Soviet leader would set his course on Berlin." Thompson thought the president's challenge would be to convince a doubtful Khrushchev that the U.S. would fight rather than abandon West Berliners. On the other hand, a tough stance alone could not avoid confrontation. Khrushchev would force the issue ahead of his October Party Congress, Thompson predicted, and if he did so, "it could involve the real possibility of world war, and we would almost certainly be led back to an intensified Cold War relationship."

Thompson repeated his conviction that the risks of dealing with Khrushchev must be weighed against the reality that the U.S. had no good alternative. For all his downsides, said Thompson, Khrushchev "is probably better from our point of view than anyone likely to succeed him." It was thus in America's interest to keep Khrushchev in power, though Thompson conceded that his embassy knew far too little about the Kremlin's inner workings to provide any reliable advice on how Kennedy could influence Communist Party struggles.

With uncanny clairvoyance, Thompson then added: "If we expect the Soviets to leave the Berlin problem as is, then we must at least expect the East Germans to seal off sector boundary in order to stop what they must consider the intolerable continuation of the refugee flow through Berlin."

With that thought, Thompson may have been the first U.S. diplomat to predict the Berlin Wall.

Thompson then proposed a negotiating position that he thought the Soviets might be willing to accept—and which would allow Washington to regain the initiative. He suggested that Kennedy propose to Khrushchev an interim deal on Berlin under which the two Germanys would have seven years to negotiate a longer-term solution. During that time, and in exchange for a Soviet guarantee of continued Allied access to West Berlin, the U.S. would give the Soviets assurances that West Germany would not try to recover eastern territories it had lost after World War II.

With that deal, Thompson said the East Germans could stop the refugee flow, which he argued would be in American as well as Soviet interests because the rising numbers threatened to destabilize the region. Fleshing out his plan, Thompson proposed as confidence-building measures the reduction of Western covert activities conducted from Berlin and the shutting down of RIAS, the U.S. radio station that beamed reports into the Soviet zone from West Berlin. Even if Khrushchev rejected such a U.S. offer, Thompson argued that the simple act of making it would allow Kennedy to win over public opinion and thus make it more unpalatable for Khrushchev to act unilaterally.

Kennedy, however, disagreed with his ambassador's sense of urgency. He and his brother Bobby were beginning to suspect that Thompson was falling victim to the State Department's malady of "clientitis" and was associating himself too readily with Soviet positions. The president conceded to friends that he still didn't "get" Khrushchev. After all, Eisenhower had ignored the Soviet leader's Berlin ultimatum of 1958 without paying any real price. Kennedy didn't see why the urgency should be any greater now.

The best minds in the U.S. intelligence community reinforced that view. The United States Intelligence Board's Special Subcommittee on the Berlin Situation, the spy world's authoritative group on the issue, said Khrushchev was "unlikely to increase tensions over Berlin at this time." They said Moscow would increase its pressures only if Khrushchev thought by doing so he could force Kennedy into high-level talks. Their bottom line: if Kennedy demonstrated that increased Soviet threats wouldn't impress him, Khrushchev would not escalate in Berlin.

So once again the president decided Berlin was an issue that could wait. Two other matters had also begun to shape his thinking. First, Dean Acheson was about to deliver to the president his first report on Berlin policy, and it would provide the hawkish antidote to Thompson's softer line.

Kennedy was also growing increasingly distracted by a matter closer to home. His top spies were putting the final pieces in place for an invasion of Cuba by exiles trained and equipped by the CIA.

WASHINGTON, D.C.
MONDAY, APRIL 3, 1961

Acheson's paper, the first major Kennedy administration reflection on Berlin policy, landed on Secretary of State Dean Rusk's desk the day before British Prime Minister Harold Macmillan arrived in Washington. Characteristically, President Truman's secretary of state had timed its delivery for maximum impact, laying down a hard line at the front end of a parade of Allied visitors.

Acheson's central argument was that Kennedy had to show a willingness to fight for Berlin if he wished to avoid Soviet domination of Europe and, after that, Asia and Africa. Wielding words like weapons, Acheson wrote that if the U.S. "accepted a Communist takeover of Berlin—under whatever face-saving and delaying device—the power status in Europe would be starkly revealed and Germany, and probably France, Italy and Benelux would make the indicated adjustments. The United Kingdom would hope that something would turn up. It wouldn't."

Acheson knew Kennedy well enough to be confident that the president both trusted his judgment and shared his suspicions of the Soviets. While searching for a secretary of state during the transition, Kennedy had sought the advice of his Georgetown neighbor Acheson. With a gaggle of photographers outside his home, the president-elect told Acheson he "had spent so much time in the past few years knowing people who could help him *become* president that he found he knew very few people who could help him *be* president."

Acheson then helped dissuade Kennedy from considering Senator William Fulbright, who he said "was not as solid and serious a man as you need for this position. I've always thought that he had some of the qualities of a dilettante." He instead steered Kennedy to the man eventually chosen, Dean Rusk, who during the Truman years had capably helped Acheson fight appeasement and resist communism in Asia as his assistant secretary of state for Far Eastern Affairs. Concerning other Cabinet and ambassadorial roles, Acheson blessed some names and torpedoed others, playing the Washington blood sport he so savored. He also turned down Kennedy's offer to become ambassador to NATO, saying he preferred maintaining his free agency and lawyerly income without "all these statutes operating on me."

That said, Acheson was pleased to be reestablishing his influence in government through a leading role in thinking through two of America's highest priorities: NATO's future and the related matters of nuclear weapons use and Berlin's defense. Acheson's place in history was already sealed because of his leading role in creating the International Monetary Fund, the World Bank, and the Marshall Plan. He had been the primary designer of NATO—altering America's aversion to entangling alliances—and with George Marshall had conceived the Truman Doctrine of 1947 that set America's course as "leader of the free world," whose mission globally would be to fight communism and support democracy. Still, being invited back into the mix by Kennedy was a pleasing confirmation for Acheson that his capabilities remained both relevant and required.

Even at almost age sixty-eight, Acheson still cut a captivating figure. As impeccably dressed as he was informed, he liked to tell friends that he lacked the self-doubt that so afflicted his opponents. With his bowler hat, wicked grin, steel-blue eyes, and upturned mustache, he would have been noticeable enough. However, he stood out all the more due to his long-legged, slender, six-foot frame. Quick-witted and intolerant of fools, Acheson had brought to his new Berlin study the determination to outmaneuver and outmatch the Soviets that had so distinguished his career. It was that hard line that had formed such a curious bond between Acheson and President Truman—the Yale-educated, martini-drinking son of an Episcopal rector and the plain-speaking Midwestern politician without a college degree.

Shortly after Kennedy's election, Acheson had scolded Truman playfully in a letter that addressed the former president's concerns about Kennedy's Catholicism. "Do you really care about Jack's being Catholic?" he had asked Truman, who dismissively called Kennedy "the young man." Acheson told Truman he had never cared that de Gaulle and Adenauer were Catholic. "Furthermore," Acheson said with knowing understatement, "I don't think he's a very good Catholic."

Since Kennedy had hired him in February, Acheson had intensively reviewed all the options for Berlin contingencies. He agreed with Thompson that a showdown was likely during the calendar year, but that's where their agreement ended. He counseled the president to show greater strength and abandon any hope of a negotiated solution that could improve upon the status quo. "All sources of action are dangerous and unpromising," Acheson said. "Inaction is even worse. We are faced with a Hobson's choice. If a crisis is provoked, a bold and dangerous course may be the safest."

Eisenhower had rejected Acheson's advice, which at the time had been offered from outside government, that he respond more robustly to Moscow's repetitive tests of America's commitment to Europe and Berlin with a conspicuous military buildup. Acheson hoped to get more traction with Kennedy. He had already won over Rusk and Bundy, and he could count as allies the two other most influential administration officials on Berlin matters, the Pentagon's Paul Nitze and the State Department's Foy Kohler.

Most controversially, Acheson argued in his memo that the threat of general nuclear war might no longer be sufficient to deter Khrushchev in Berlin—if it ever had been. Acheson argued that Khrushchev's reluctance to act thus far had been based more on his desire to avoid a breakdown in relations with the West than on a conviction that the U.S. would risk atomic war to defend Berlin. Thus Acheson was prescribing for Kennedy a significant conventional buildup in Europe while at the same time counseling him to persuade the Allies, and in particular the West Germans, "to agree in advance to fight for Berlin."

Acheson listed for Kennedy what he had concluded were Khrushchev's five primary objectives regarding Berlin:

1. To stabilize the East German regime and prepare for its eventual international recognition.
2. To legalize Germany's eastern frontiers.
3. To neutralize West Berlin as a first step and prepare for its eventual takeover by the German Democratic Republic.
4. To weaken if not break up the NATO Alliance.
5. To discredit the United States or at least seriously damage its prestige.

Agreeing with Adenauer, Acheson was convinced the Berlin problem had no solution short of unification, and that unification could not be achieved until far into the future and through a consistent demonstration of Western strength. Therefore, no agreement with Moscow on Berlin was currently available to Kennedy that would not make the West more vulnerable, so talks had no purpose.

Berlin was "the key to power status in Europe," Acheson argued, and thus a willingness to defend it was central to keeping the Kremlin in check elsewhere. Whatever course Kennedy took, Acheson counseled the president to "choose quickly what constitutes grounds for fighting on Berlin" and get America's allies to agree to those criteria.

Acheson's bottom line for Kennedy: "We must content ourselves for the time being with maintaining the status quo in Berlin. We could not expect Khrushchev to accept less—we ourselves should not accept less."

His groundbreaking paper then concentrated on the most appropriate military means—within U.S. capability—to deter Khrushchev. The threat of nuclear attack had long been the U.S.'s ace in the hole, but Acheson's heresy was to argue that it was not a real capability because it was "perfectly obvious" to the Russians that Washington would not risk the lives of millions of Americans over Berlin. Acheson noted that some military leaders advocated as an alternative the "limited use of nuclear means—that is, to drop one bomb somewhere."

He dismissed that idea as quickly as he had raised it: "If you drop one bomb, that wasn't a threat to drop that bomb—that was a drop—and once it happened, it either indicated that you were going on to drop more, or you invited the other side to drop one back." That struck Acheson as "irresponsible and not a wise step adapted to the problem of Berlin."

So Acheson tabled a proposal for Kennedy designed to make Western determination unmistakable. He wanted the president to substantially increase conventional forces in Germany so that the Soviets would see more clearly the U.S. commitment to Berlin's defense—a course that could not have been more in contrast to Thompson's notion of a seven-year moratorium during which the two Germanys negotiated their differences. Through this buildup, he said, "we would have made too vast a commitment to back down in any way—and if there was any backing down, they would have to do it."

Acheson conceded that reducing America's reliance on nuclear deterrence had its risks, but added that "it was the only way of showing that we meant business without doing something very foolish." His proposal was not to increase forces in Berlin, where they would be trapped and be of little use, but to bring in three or more divisions elsewhere in Germany. He would ratchet up U.S. reserves by as many as six divisions and provide more transport for all those new soldiers to descend on Berlin in an emergency.

Defense Secretary McNamara embraced Acheson's paper. Kennedy took it seriously enough to use it as the basis to order a new Pentagon examination on how to break any new Berlin blockade. Acheson knew, however, that an important constituency would oppose his views: America's allies. The French and Germans would argue against any dilution of a nuclear deterrent that they believed was all that ensured long-term U.S. commitment to their defense. And the British wanted a greater emphasis on negotiations with the Soviets, a course Acheson opposed. As the Allies couldn't even agree among themselves about how best to defend Berlin, Acheson's advice to Kennedy was to decide his course unilaterally and present it to the Allies as a fait accompli.

In advance of the Macmillan meeting, Bundy rushed to Kennedy what he called his friend Acheson's "first-rate" paper. He advised Kennedy that he must make sure that his British visitors, known for being "soft" on Berlin, understood that he was determined to stand firm. Rusk echoed Acheson in saying Berlin talks had failed in the past and there was no reason to think they had any greater chance now to succeed.

Almost overnight, Acheson had taken the initiative on Berlin, filling a vacuum in the administration. Drawing upon that, National Security Advisor Bundy counseled Kennedy to politely consider any schemes London "may dream up, but in return we should press hard to get a commitment of British firmness at the moment of truth."

OVAL OFFICE, THE WHITE HOUSE, WASHINGTON, D.C.
WEDNESDAY, APRIL 5, 1961

British Prime Minister Macmillan was taken aback when Kennedy nodded toward Acheson and asked him to explain why, regarding the Soviets and Berlin, he believed a confrontation was likelier than reaching an acceptable compromise solution. The president was surrounded by his top national security team as well as U.S. Ambassador to London David Bruce. Among others, Macmillan had brought along Foreign Secretary Sir Alec Douglas-Home. Yet they all turned toward Acheson, and one of the world's most colorful diplomatic showmen launched a performance that unsettled the British.

Kennedy did not say whether he shared Acheson's hard-line views, although Macmillan had to presume that he did. Acheson prefaced the discussion with the disclaimer that he had not reached final conclusions in his Berlin study, but he then vigorously laid out precisely what he had decided. Kennedy listened without comment.

Macmillan and Acheson were almost the same age, and Acheson's attire, upper-class mannerisms, and Anglo-Canadian background would have suggested a cultural compatibility in any other setting. But the two men could not have differed more in their diagnosis of how to deal with the Soviets. Macmillan had lost none of his enthusiasm for just the sort of high-level Moscow talks that Acheson had consistently said would have little value, all the way back to an executive session of the Foreign Relations Committee in 1947 when Acheson said, "I think it is a mistake to believe that you can, at any time, sit down with the Russians and solve questions."

Acheson listed what he called his "semi-premises":

1. There was no satisfactory solution to the Berlin problem aside from a resolution more broadly of Germany's division. And it did not seem such a solution was anywhere near.
2. It was likely the Soviets would force the Berlin issue within the calendar year.
3. There was no negotiable solution Acheson could imagine that could put the West in a more favorable position regarding Berlin than it had at the moment.

Thus, he said, "we must face the issue and prepare now for eventualities. Berlin is of the greatest importance. That is why the Soviets press the issue. If the West flunks, Germany will become unhooked from the alliance."

The president did not interrupt Acheson's presentation, and because of that neither did anyone else. Acheson said negotiations and other non-military remedies, which everyone in the room knew were the British preference, were insufficient. There must be a military response, Acheson said, but what should it be, and under what circumstances?

Macmillan and Lord Home contained their dismay. They had just been in Paris, where they'd heard de Gaulle—who was already trying to lure Adenauer into a Gaullist view of Europe that permanently excluded the British—also vehemently oppose Berlin talks with the Soviets. The British didn't want Kennedy on the same page.

At age sixty-seven, Macmillan had grown increasingly convinced that most of London's aspirations in the world depended on its ability to influence Washington. That in turn relied on how he would interact with America's new president. A keen student of history, Macmillan had come to realize that Americans represented "the new Roman Empire and we Britons, like the Greeks of old, must teach them now to make it go. . . . We can at most aspire to civilize and occasionally to influence them." But how did he get Kennedy's consent to play Rome to Macmillan's Greece?

After Prime Minister Anthony Eden's political collapse following the Suez Crisis, his successor Macmillan had wagered much on rebuilding a "special relationship" with the U.S. through his friendship with President Eisenhower, first forged during World War II. Macmillan had played a crucial role as an "honest broker" in convincing President Eisenhower to engage with Khrushchev on Berlin's future through summitry, and he had considered the Paris Summit's collapse to be a personal defeat. He had begged Khrushchev unsuccessfully not to abandon the talks.

It was in this context that Macmillan had been gathering as many data points as he could find on Kennedy so that he could better design an approach to a man who was twenty-four years his junior. Macmillan had worried to columnist friend Henry Brandon that he would never be able to replicate the unique connection he had had with Eisenhower, a man of the same generation with whom he had shared war's cruel experiences. "And now there is this cocky young Irishman," he had said.

Eisenhower's ambassador to London, John Hay "Jock" Whitney, had warned Macmillan that Kennedy was "obstinate, sensitive, ruthless and highly sexed." However, their behavioral differences would surface only many months later, when Kennedy shocked the monogamous, puritanical Scot with the impertinent question, "I wonder how it is with you, Harold? If I don't have a woman for three days, I get a terrible headache. . . ."

What concerned Macmillan more than the age and character differences he had with Kennedy was the possibility that the president might be overly influenced by his anticommunist, isolationist father. Perhaps the most disliked U.S. ambassador ever to the Court of St. James's, Joseph Kennedy had warned President Roosevelt not to overdo U.S. backing for Britain against Hitler and be "left holding the bag in a war in which the Allies expect to be beaten." So Macmillan was relieved when his research turned up that Kennedy's hero was the interventionist Churchill—a point they had in common.

To further influence Kennedy's thinking, during the transition Macmillan had written the president-elect a letter that proposed a "Grand Design" for the future. While Macmillan had formed his bond with Eisenhower based on their common memories of war, he had determined on the day of Kennedy's election that he would base his approach to the new president on intellect. So he set out to sell himself "as a man who, although of advancing years, has young and fresh thoughts."

Written with a publisher's deft touch, Macmillan appealed to Kennedy's vanity by quoting from the president's earlier writings before sketching out a dangerous era ahead in which the "free world"—the United States, Britain, and Europe—could only vanquish the growing appeal of communism through the steady expansion of economic well-being and common purpose. Thus, he regarded closer transatlantic coordination to create joint monetary and economic policies as being more critical than political and military alliances.

Since he had written that letter, Macmillan had not gained much traction for his "Grand Design" in preparatory visits to allies. De Gaulle in Paris sympathized with Macmillan's views but stubbornly opposed his desire to bring Britain into the European Common Market. When they met in London, the British prime minister found even less support from Adenauer. Macmillan concluded that the flourishing West Germany had grown too "rich and selfish" to understand his proposal. Ahead of Macmillan's White House meeting, Kennedy discovered he had misplaced his copy of the "Grand Design." It took a White House search to unearth it in the nursery of Caroline, his three-year-old daughter.

Despite Macmillan's initial concerns, he and Kennedy had already begun to form a closer bond ahead of their Washington meeting than the British prime minister had anticipated, a product of shared wit, breeding, and brains—and Macmillan's intentional efforts. They were also related by marriage: Kennedy's sister Kathleen had married Macmillan's nephew. Like Kennedy, Harold Macmillan had known wealth from birth and enjoyed its license for independent thinking and eccentricity. The prime minister was elegant and tall, at six feet, and had a toothy British smile under a guardsman's mustache. He wore his hand-cut suits as casually as his intellect. Macmillan liked Kennedy's emphasis on bravery in his book *Profiles in Courage*, as he had himself been wounded three times during World War I. While waiting for rescue at the Battle of the Somme with a bullet in his pelvis, he had read Aeschylus in the original Greek.

To the prime minister's relief, he and Kennedy had hit it off ten days earlier when the president had issued him a last-minute invitation to Key West, Florida, to exchange ideas on how to address an unfolding crisis in Laos. Kennedy had listened sympathetically to Macmillan's advice that he should stay clear of military intervention in Laos, and the prime minister was encouraged to see the president manage the generals around him— instead of being managed *by* them. Macmillan had been taken by Kennedy's "great charm . . . and a light touch. Since so many Americans are so ponderous, this is a welcome change."

Yet that positive beginning in Key West only made Macmillan and Lord Home all the more concerned about Kennedy's apparent militancy toward the Soviets as expressed and encouraged by Acheson.

When thinking about how to defend Berlin, Acheson said the Brits should focus on the three military alternatives: air, ground, and nuclear. Given that the nuclear option was "reckless and would not be believed," Acheson talked mostly about the other two. He dismissed an air response, as Soviet "ground-to-air missiles have been brought to a point where aircraft cannot survive. Thus there could be no test of will in the air. The Russians would just shoot down the planes with their rockets."

Acheson was driving home his view that the U.S. and its allies really had only one possible credible response to a Berlin showdown, and that was a conventional ground offensive to "show the Russians that it was not worthwhile to stop a really stout Western effort." To pull that off, Acheson said, would require a significant military buildup. Acheson crisply listed the possible military countermeasures to a Berlin blockade of one sort or another, including the dispatching of a division down the Autobahn to reopen access to Berlin with force. If blocked, said Acheson, then the West would know where it stood and could rearm and rally allies as it did during the Korean War.

Kennedy told Macmillan, whose body language of lifted eyebrows and sideways glances revealed his skepticism, that he had not yet fully considered Acheson's views. That said, he agreed with his new adviser that Berlin contingency planning was not yet "serious enough," given the growing likelihood of some sort of confrontation.

Macmillan focused his opposition on Acheson's proposed response to a Berlin blockade, of sending a division up the Autobahn, as it "would be a very vulnerable body if moving on a narrow front." It inevitably would have to spread beyond the Autobahn if trouble started, he said, and that would raise a host of difficulties. When pressed by Kennedy, however, he agreed with Acheson's view that the Berlin Airlift could not be repeated because of improved Soviet antiaircraft capability.

U.S. and British officials then hashed out what new military planning and training would be required to allow more intensive preparation for Berlin contingencies. Secretary Rusk welcomed British–U.S. bilateral planning but suggested that the West Germans, with their expanded military capability and willingness to help defend Berlin, should be brought in "rapidly." Lord Home frowned his dissent. The British distrusted the Germans far more than did the Americans, convinced that Adenauer's intelligence service and other government structures were riddled with spies. Though Lord Home was happy enough to discuss Germany's future with the Americans, he was not ready to do the same with the Germans.

Home wanted to shift the Americans from their focus on military contingencies to consideration of potential openings for Berlin talks with the Kremlin. He argued that Khrushchev had made only one public commitment that limited his room for maneuver, and that was to end Berlin's occupation status. Lord Home believed Khrushchev "could get off this hook" if the Allies signed a treaty that would leave the status quo in place for a period of ten years or so, but that over time this would alter Berlin's status.

"Khrushchev is not on a *hook*," Acheson shot back, "and thus does not have to be taken off one."

Acheson had no patience for what he considered British spinelessness toward Moscow. He sharply reminded Home that Khrushchev "is not legalistic. Khrushchev is pushing to divide the Allies. He is not going to make any treaty that would help us. Our position is good as it is and we should stick by it." Acheson worried that even consideration of signing a treaty with East Germany, which would serve only Soviet interests, "will undermine the German spirit."

The tension between Home and Acheson infused the room.

After an awkward silence, Rusk agreed with Acheson that any talk about accepting such a treaty would be "starting down a slippery slope." He said the U.S. had to make clear it was in Berlin as a result of war, and not "by the grace of Khrushchev." The U.S., Rusk insisted to the British, was a great power that would not be driven out of Berlin.

Home warned his American friends of the public opinion consequences in the West if Khrushchev openly proposed what might seem a reasonable change in Berlin's legal status and the West failed to put forward any alternative approach. Western presence had to be put on a new legal basis, he argued, as the current "right of conquest" justification for Berlin occupation was "wearing thin."

Perhaps, Acheson fired back again at Home, "it is our power that is wearing thin."

Much the same group reconvened the next morning, although mercifully for the British, Acheson was absent on a mission. However, his spirit remained in the room. President Kennedy wanted to know from his U.S. and British experts why Khrushchev had not acted on Berlin thus far. What made him hold off?

"Was it the danger of the Western response?" he asked.

Lord Home said he thought Khrushchev "wouldn't lay off much longer."

Ambassador Charles E. "Chip" Bohlen agreed. The State Department's leading Soviet specialist, who had been ambassador to Moscow from 1953 to 1957, believed the rising Chinese challenge and "strong importunities from the East Germans" were forcing Khrushchev into a more militant position. It wasn't that the Soviets cared so much about Berlin, Bohlen insisted, but that they had concluded its loss could lead to the unraveling of their entire Eastern empire.

Kennedy brought the discussion back to Acheson's paper. If Khrushchev had been contained by the threat of a military confrontation with the West, Kennedy said, "we should consider how to build up this threat. On Berlin, we have no bargaining position. Thus we ought to consider, as Mr. Acheson suggested yesterday, how to put the issue to Khrushchev as bluntly as possible."

With the return of Acheson's ghost, the group gamed Khrushchev's next likely move and the West's potential response. The British didn't see how talks could be avoided, while most of the U.S. contingent doubted their utility. Kennedy's ambassador to the United Kingdom, David Bruce, a former intelligence officer who had been Eisenhower's ambassador to West Germany, said that the United States could not cede its few remaining rights in Berlin. "We cannot disregard the consequences that would flow in Central Europe and in West Germany from weakening on Berlin," he said.

As his meetings with Kennedy neared an end, Macmillan was dissatisfied. He still did not know, he said, at what point the West "would break" and take action against Russian moves on Berlin. Without such a clear line, he feared that Kennedy could be drawn into a war he didn't want, over far too little cause—and might then drag Britain into the hostilities.

Differing with Acheson, Kennedy responded that he believed it was the nuclear deterrent effect that "keeps the Communists from engaging us in a major struggle on Berlin." Thus, he said, it was necessary to keep the fact of that deterrent "well forward."

Macmillan, however, wondered what would happen in West Germany after Adenauer died—whether the Berlin game might be lost to the Soviets under a less resolute leader. "Sooner or later, say in five or ten years, the Russians might try to offer the West Germans unity in return for neutrality," he ventured, repeating Britain's stubborn doubts about German reliability.

Bohlen told Macmillan that he thought the time was past when West Germans would take "the bait of neutrality." The Soviets as well, he said, could no longer afford to let socialism go down the drain in East Germany. Bruce argued that the larger issue for the moment was that East German refugees were "weakening all that goes to make up the normal life of a state," with 200,000 leaving in 1960, and some 70 percent of those from vital age groups.

A final internal memorandum on the meeting papered over the two sides' dispute. It noted that both the U.S. and the UK expected an escalation of the Berlin Crisis in 1961, that they agreed the loss of West Berlin would be catastrophic, and that they believed the Allies needed to make clearer their seriousness over Berlin to the Soviets. The document also called for intensified planning of military contingencies.

In the brisk spring sunshine of the White House Rose Garden, Kennedy stood by Macmillan and read a one-page joint statement that spoke of a "very high level of agreement on our estimate of the nature of the problems which we face." It glossed over the considerable disagreements with mushy language, saying that the two men agreed on "the importance and the difficulty of working toward satisfactory relations with the Soviet Union."

Macmillan had achieved little with Kennedy. What he gained was that Kennedy had endorsed Britain's efforts to join the Common Market as part of his "Grand Design," a crucial voice of support given French opposition. The two men also had further built a personal bond through two long, private talks.

Despite that, Macmillan had failed in many of his most important aims. Kennedy had opposed Britain's efforts to get China into the United Nations, and had made it clear that, unlike Eisenhower, he did not intend to use Macmillan as an intermediary with Moscow. Most important, the Americans planned to convene a summit with a Soviet leader for the first time on European territory without inviting their British or French allies to participate. It seemed Kennedy had clearly bought Acheson's line that London was too soft on Berlin.

British officials surprised the Americans by leaking to their home press that the Kennedy–Macmillan talks were "rough, touchy," in many ways inconclusive, and certainly more difficult than the communiqué suggested.

And much worse was to follow.

8

AMATEUR HOUR

The European view was that they were watching a gifted young amateur practice with a boomerang, when they saw, to their horror, that he had knocked himself out. They were amazed that so inexperienced a person should play with so lethal a weapon.

Dean Acheson on President Kennedy's handling
of the Bay of Pigs debacle, June 1961

I don't understand Kennedy. Can he really be that indecisive?

Premier Khrushchev to his son Sergei after the Bay of Pigs

THE WHITE HOUSE, WASHINGTON, D.C.
FRIDAY, APRIL 7, 1961

I t was Washington's first warm spring day, the perfect temperature for President Kennedy's walk through the White House Rose Garden with Dean Acheson. Kennedy had suggested the stroll, explaining to Acheson that he sought urgent advice. Though Kennedy was in shirtsleeves, Acheson remained his usual formal self in jacket and bow tie. In his only compromise with the weather, Acheson removed his bowler hat and carried it under his arm.

Truman's former secretary of state expected Kennedy to quiz him on his ongoing NATO or Berlin projects, as he was leaving the next day for Europe to brief the Allies on his progress. Instead, Kennedy said he had another, more pressing matter in mind. "Come on out here in the garden and sit in the sun," the president said, directing Acheson to a wooden bench, then settling down beside him. "Do you know anything about this Cuba proposal?"

Acheson conceded he did not even know there was a Cuba proposal.

So Kennedy sketched out the plan that he said he was considering. A force of 1,200 to 1,500 Cuban exiles—soldiers who had been trained by the CIA in Guatemala—would invade the island. They would be supported by the air cover of B-26 bombers, also flown by exiles. The idea was that once the exiled Cubans established a beachhead, as many as 7,000 insurgents and other Castro opponents already on the island would rise up in revolt. Without requiring the use of American troops or aircraft, the U.S. would remove Fidel Castro from power and replace him with a friendly regime. The plan had been hatched by the Eisenhower administration, but it had been revised in Kennedy's early weeks. It was supported throughout by U.S. intelligence equipment, trainers, and planners.

Acheson did not hide his alarm. He said that he hoped the president wasn't serious about such a crazy scheme.

"I don't know if I'm serious or not," Kennedy said. "But this is the proposal and I've been thinking about it, and it is serious in that sense. I've not made up my mind but I'm giving it very serious thought."

In truth, the president had already given the plan his go-ahead almost a month earlier, on March 11, 1961. He had signed off on the last details on April 5, just two days before his conversation with Acheson. He had altered only two important aspects, having moved the landing place to allow for a less spectacular invasion, and ensuring that there was a suitable airfield nearby for tactical air support. Otherwise, "Operation Mongoose" was much the plan that the Eisenhower administration had passed down to Kennedy.

Acheson said he would not "need to phone Price Waterhouse" to determine that Kennedy's 1,500 Cubans were no match for Castro's 25,000 Cubans. He told Kennedy such an invasion could have disastrous consequences for America's prestige in Europe and for relations with the Soviets over Berlin, where they likely would respond with their own aggression.

Yet it was precisely because of Berlin that Kennedy wanted there to be no obviously American assets involved. He wanted to avoid giving the Soviets any pretext to do something similarly disruptive in Berlin.

The two men talked awkwardly for a little longer before Acheson left the Rose Garden without having exchanged a word with the president about anything other than Cuba. As he left for Europe, Acheson dismissed the Cuban matter from his mind, as "it seemed like such a wild idea."

He was confident wiser minds would prevail.

RHÖNDORF, WEST GERMANY
SUNDAY, APRIL 9, 1961

West German Chancellor Konrad Adenauer's concerns about how to manage his relationship with Kennedy had grown so great that he summoned his friend Dean Acheson to meet with him in Bonn to talk strategy before his visit to the U.S. a few days later.

Legions of Germans were out for Sunday walks on pathways under the flowering fruit trees beside the Rhine River as Adenauer, in a less leisurely manner, sped by them with Acheson in his Mercedes from the airport to his home. The chancellor savored high-speed drives in the well-engineered German cars that had become such an export hit, and Acheson held tightly to his seat as Adenauer's driver accelerated to keep pace with a lead jeep.

A soldier sat in the jeep's open back, providing directions with outstretched paddles. If the soldier extended a paddle out to his right, it was a sign to Adenauer's driver that he was going to pass traffic by driving up over the sidewalk. If he pointed one up to the left, it meant the driver would scatter oncoming traffic as he passed to that side. Acheson smiled grimly at Adenauer and noticed that "the old man was just having a wonderful time."

A small group of Adenauer's neighbors had gathered to applaud the legendary political couple's arrival at the chancellor's home in the Rhineside village of Rhöndorf. The eighty-five-year-old Adenauer looked to the zigzag stairway heading up the hill about a hundred feet from the street to his door and said to his sixty-seven-year-old guest, "My friend, you are not as youthful as you were the first time we met, and I must urge you not to take these steps too fast."

"Thank you very much, Mr. Chancellor," Acheson replied, smiling. "If I find myself wearying, may I take your arm?"

Adenauer chuckled. "Are you teasing me?"

"I wouldn't think of doing so." Acheson smiled. The good-natured banter was an elixir for Adenauer's troubled spirit.

Acheson spent much of the day calming an Adenauer whom he found "worried to death—just completely worried" about Kennedy. Adenauer's greatest concern was that Kennedy was scheming to make a peace deal behind his back with the Russians on any number of issues that would sell out German interests and abandon Berliners. He worried as well about the rise of a new hostility among Americans toward Germans after years of postwar healing, inflamed by the shocking revelations of William Shirer's newly published book, *The Rise and Fall of the Third Reich*, and the imminent trial of Nazi war criminal Adolf Eichmann in Israel.

Beyond that, Adenauer said, he was disturbed by reports that the Kennedy administration was shifting its deterrence strategy from its overwhelming reliance on nuclear weapons to the relatively new notion of "flexible response." That would involve a greater emphasis on conventional weaponry in all military contingencies regarding Berlin. Though such a policy change could have significant impact on West German security, the Kennedy administration had neither consulted nor briefed Adenauer or other West German counterparts.

As he argued against the new strategy, what Adenauer didn't realize was that Acheson was one of its leading proponents and architects. Adenauer was convinced the West could only contain Moscow if Khrushchev was certain a Soviet move on Berlin would prompt a devastating U.S. nuclear response. He feared that Moscow would regard any change in the U.S. approach as an invitation to test Washington's resolve. Though he did not say so to Adenauer that day, Acheson disagreed because he doubted any U.S. president would ever risk millions of American lives for Berlin—and he reckoned Khrushchev knew that as well.

So Acheson instead focused his efforts on reassuring Adenauer that Kennedy was as determined as his predecessors had been to defend West German and West Berlin freedoms. Acheson briefed Adenauer in some detail on the Kennedy administration's military contingency planning regarding Berlin and on Kennedy's own skepticism about Russian intentions.

Adenauer sighed with satisfaction. "You have lifted a stone from my heart."

But at the same time, Acheson had to disappoint the chancellor about one of his fondest dreams. For the moment, Kennedy had rejected the plan considered by Eisenhower to place a fleet of U.S. Polaris missile submarines under NATO control, thus making the alliance a fourth nuclear power. The U.S., Britain, and France would keep their monopoly. Instead, Kennedy would put five or more Polaris submarines at the disposal of NATO, but under U.S. fleet commanders, and with caveats on their use so restrictive and the process of using them so complicated that it would fail to satisfy Adenauer's desire for a more easily accessible nuclear deterrent.

In short, Kennedy's evolving view toward handling Berlin military contingencies—reflected in KGB reports at the time from Paris and elsewhere—was that he wanted to ensure that any Berlin conflict remained local in character and would not escalate into a world war. That required not only backing off American reliance on nuclear arms in any Berlin confrontation, but also opposing the notion of NATO possession of atomic weapons.

Adenauer closed the day in typical fashion, inviting his guest to the rose garden to play the Italian bowling game of bocce. Removing his jacket but leaving on his tie, with sleeves rolled down, Adenauer looked disarmingly formal as he began the precision throwing game by tossing the smaller "jack" ball forward, then following it with larger balls, the goal being to land closest to the initial throw.

When Acheson was near victory, the chancellor changed the rules and began to carom shots off the sideboards.

At Acheson's protests, Adenauer smiled: "You are now in Germany—in Germany I make the rules."

Acheson smiled, knowing his mission had achieved its aim. He had reduced Adenauer's alarm over Kennedy, he had predelivered whatever disappointing news Adenauer would get in Washington in a more palatable manner, and he had set a more promising tone for the first Adenauer–Kennedy meeting.

What Acheson couldn't control were two events that would overshadow Adenauer's visit: a historic Soviet space shot and the U.S. debacle in Cuba.

PITSUNDA PENINSULA, SOVIET UNION
TUESDAY, APRIL 11, 1961

On the day of Adenauer's flight to Washington, Khrushchev was in retreat at his villa in Sochi, on the Pitsunda Peninsula of the Black Sea's eastern coast, where he was resting and receiving regular updates on the Soviet plans to put the first man in space the following morning. He had also begun preparations for the 22nd Communist Party Congress in October.

Khrushchev would later explain his frequent retreats from public to Pitsunda by saying, "A chicken has to sit quietly for a certain time if she expects to lay an egg." Though the metaphor had a negative connotation in English, Khrushchev described its meaning in a positive manner: "If I have something to hatch, I have to take the time to do it right." Pitsunda was where he caught his breath in the rush of history or wrote a few pages of it himself. It had been there, between his walks through the pine grove and past cabanas on the beach, that he had crafted his 1956 speech breaking with Stalin. He liked to introduce guests to his ancient trees, many of which he had given human names, and to show off his small indoor gym and private, glass-enclosed swimming pool.

It was a measure of how important Khrushchev considered relations with Kennedy that amid all his other demands that morning he had still been willing to receive Walter Lippmann, the legendary seventy-one-year-old American columnist, and his wife, Helen. It was not just Lippmann's national influence and access to Kennedy that endeared him to Khrushchev, but also the fact that his columns had been consistently friendly to the Soviets.

With the schedule for the space launch firmed up, however, Khrushchev passed word to Lippmann on the tarmac in Washington, in the first-class cabin of his plane to Rome, that their meeting would be postponed. "Impossible," Lippmann boldly responded in a scrawled reply to Soviet Ambassador Menshikov.

By the time the Lippmanns landed, Khrushchev had decided he would see them, but he would not breathe a word concerning plans for his potentially historic space launch with the cosmonaut Yuri Gagarin the following morning.

Khrushchev had accelerated the original May Day launch date after a training accident on March 23 killed the flight's intended cosmonaut, Lieutenant Valentin Bondarenko. Shortcuts taken by the Soviets to rush their first man into space ahead of the Americans had likely contributed to Bondarenko's death, which came after flames engulfed his oxygen-rich training chamber. The Soviets did not disclose any of the details of the accident. They did not even announce the cosmonaut's death, and airbrushed Bondarenko from all photographs of the Soviet space team.

Undaunted, Khrushchev grew all the more determined, and further accelerated the Soviet target launch date to April 12. The timing was chosen to keep Moscow ahead of the U.S. Project Mercury mission that was scheduled to launch astronaut Alan Shepard into space on May 5. If the flight succeeded, Khrushchev would not only make history but also get a badly needed political boost. If Gagarin's mission failed, Khrushchev would bury all evidence of the launch.

Oblivious to that background drama, Lippmann and his wife arrived at Khrushchev's sanctuary at 11:30 in the morning, and would remain for eight hours of walking, swimming, eating, drinking, and talking before spending the night.

Lippmann savored his access to U.S. and world leaders, and it didn't get any better than meeting the communist world's leader in his Black Sea lair. Before he had begun writing a column, Lippmann had been an adviser to President Woodrow Wilson and was a delegate to the 1919 Paris Peace Conference, which resulted in the Treaty of Versailles. Lippmann had coined the phrase "Cold War" and was the leading U.S. voice suggesting that Washington accept the new Soviet sphere of influence in Europe. Moscow's interest in Lippmann was so great that a KGB spy ring in the U.S. was working through his secretary, Mary Price, to gather information on his sources and subjects of interest, an infiltration Lippmann had not yet discovered.

The tall, large-boned Lippmann towered over the short, squat Khrushchev as they walked the compound. In a lively afternoon game of badminton, however, the fiercely competitive Khrushchev teamed up with the Lippmanns' portly female minder from the foreign ministry and thrashed the more athletic Lippmanns, who were surprised by his agility. Khrushchev viciously and repeatedly struck the shuttlecock only a few inches above the net, often aiming at his opponents' heads.

During a lunch break, Khrushchev's second-in-command, Anastas Mikoyan, joined the group for a three-and-a-half-hour conversation the focus of which was so exclusively on Berlin that Lippmann, like Ambassador Thompson before him, concluded that for the Soviet leader, nothing matched the importance of Berlin's future.

White House, State Department, and CIA officials had briefed Lippmann before his departure, so he was able to float a trial balloon on their behalf. Lippmann questioned why Khrushchev considered the Berlin matter such an urgent affair. Why not negotiate a Berlin standstill of five to ten years, during which the U.S. and the Soviet Union could attend to their relationship's other problems and create an atmosphere more conducive to a Berlin agreement?

When Khrushchev sharply dismissed the notion of further delay, Lippmann pressed him for reasons.

A German solution, said Khrushchev, must come before "Hitler's generals with their twelve NATO divisions get atomic weapons from France and the United States." Before that could happen, Khrushchev said he wanted a peace treaty setting in stone the current frontiers of Poland and Czechoslovakia and guaranteeing the permanent existence of East Germany. Otherwise, Khrushchev insisted, West Germany would drag NATO into a war aimed at unifying Germany and restoring its prewar eastern frontier.

Lippmann took mental notes while his wife scribbled down the conversation verbatim. Both tried to remain sober by pouring out the considerable amounts of vodka and Armenian wine that Mikoyan served them into a bowl the Soviet leader had provided them in an act of mercy.

Time and again, with Kennedy as his intended audience, Khrushchev told the Lippmanns he was determined to "bring the German question to a head" that year. Lippmann would later report to his readers that the Soviet leader was "firmly resolved, perhaps irretrievably committed, to a showdown" over Berlin to stop the gusher of refugees and to save the communist East German state.

Khrushchev laid out his Berlin thinking to Lippmann in three parts, offering greater detail than he had previously provided for public consumption. Lippmann's three-part report on their talks would win him a second Pulitzer Prize—and appear in 450 newspapers.

First, Khrushchev told the columnist, he wanted the West to accept "there are in fact two Germanys" that would never be reunited. The U.S. and the Soviet Union therefore should codify through peace treaties the three elements of Germany: East Germany, West Germany, and West Berlin. This would fix by international statute West Berlin's role as a "free city." Thereafter its access and liberty could be guaranteed, he said, by symbolic contingents of French, British, American, and Russian troops and by neutral troops assigned by the United Nations. The four occupying powers would sign an agreement with both Germanys that would produce that outcome.

Because Khrushchev doubted Kennedy would accept this option, he sketched for Lippmann what he called his "fallback position." He would accept a temporary agreement that provided the two German states perhaps two or three years during which they could negotiate a loose confederation or some other form of unification. If the two sides reached a deal during that period of time, it would be written into a treaty. If they failed, however, all occupation rights would end and foreign troops would leave.

If the U.S. refused to negotiate either of his first two options, Khrushchev told Lippmann, his "third position" was to sign a separate peace treaty with East Germany that gave Ulbricht full control over all West Berlin access routes. If the Allies resisted this new East German role, Khrushchev said he would bring in the Soviet military to blockade the city entirely.

To cushion the blow of this threat, Khrushchev told Lippmann he would not precipitate a crisis before he had the chance to meet Kennedy face-to-face and discuss the matter. In other words, he was opening his negotiations with the president through the columnist.

Assuming his unassigned role of U.S. co-negotiator, Lippmann suggested to Khrushchev a five-year moratorium on Berlin talks during which the current situation would remain frozen, which he knew from his pre-trip briefings was Kennedy's preference.

Khrushchev waved his hand dismissively. Thirty months had passed since his Berlin ultimatum, he said, and he would not agree to that long a delay, nor was he willing to let the Berlin matter go unsettled before his October Party Congress. His deadline for a Berlin solution was the fall or winter of 1961, he said.

Khrushchev told Lippmann that he didn't believe Kennedy was making decisions anyway. He summed up the forces behind Kennedy in one word: Rockefeller. He thought it was big money that manipulated Kennedy. Despite "their imperialistic nature," he felt these capitalists could be won over with common sense. If they were forced to choose between a mutually advantageous agreement or Soviet unilateral action or war, Khrushchev said that he thought the Rockefeller crowd would cut a deal.

Khrushchev said he was ready to call the Americans' nuclear bluff. "In my opinion," he said, "there are no such stupid statesmen in the West to unleash a war in which hundreds of millions would perish just because we would sign a peace treaty with the GDR that would stipulate a special status of 'free city' for West Berlin with its 2.5 million population. Such idiots have not yet been born."

At the end of the day, it was the Lippmanns and not Khrushchev who flagged and retreated to bed. Khrushchev embraced each of them with overpowering hugs before they returned, tired and drunk, to their hotel room in nearby Garga. Lippmann noticed none of the weariness in Khrushchev that Ambassador Thompson had seen just a month earlier. Nothing, how-

ever, would energize the Soviet leader as much as the news he would hear
the following morning.

PITSUNDA PENINSULA, SOVIET UNION
WEDNESDAY, APRIL 12, 1961

Khrushchev had only one question when Sergei Korolyov, the legendary
rocket designer and head of the Soviet space program, phoned him with
the good news: "Just tell me, is he alive?"

Yes, Korolyov declared, and even better than that, Yuri Gagarin had
returned to Earth safely after becoming the first human in space and the
first human to orbit the Earth. The Soviets had called his mission *Vostok*,
or "East," to drive home the point of their rise. And the project had achieved
its purpose. To Khrushchev's delight, during the 108-minute flight, Gagarin
had whistled a patriotic tune composed by Dmitri Shostakovich in 1951:
"The Motherland hears, the Motherland knows, where her son flies in the
sky." Over the protests of military leaders, the euphoric Soviet leader spontaneously promoted Gagarin two ranks to major.

Khrushchev exploded with joy and pride. As had been the case with the
Sputnik mission in 1957, he had again beaten the Americans in the space
race. At the same time, he had demonstrated a missile technology with
unmistakable military significance, given Soviet advances in nuclear capability. Most important, *Vostok* provided him with the political booster
rocket he badly needed ahead of his October party conference—effectively
neutralizing his enemies.

A banner headline in the official newspaper *Izvestia*, whose entire issue
was devoted to the flight, read: GREAT VICTORY, OUR COUNTRY, OUR SCIENCE,
OUR TECHNIQUE, OUR MEN.

Khrushchev exulted to his son Sergei that he would stage a grand event
that would allow the Soviet people to celebrate a real hero. Sergei tried to
talk his father out of an immediate return to Moscow, given the toll the
stressful year already had taken on his health, but Khrushchev would not

be dissuaded. The KGB hated the idea of crowds they could not completely control, but Khrushchev would not heed their warnings either.

The Soviet leader ordered the biggest parade and national celebration since World War II's end on May 9, 1945. His sense of triumph was so great that he spontaneously jumped into the open limousine that drove Gagarin and his wife down Leninsky Prospekt to Red Square. On sunlit streets, they together waved to cheering crowds who climbed trees and hung out of windows for better views. Roadside balconies so groaned with people that Khrushchev feared they would collapse.

From atop the Lenin Mausoleum, Khrushchev used his cosmonaut's nickname as he declared, "Let everyone who's sharpening their claws against us know . . . that Yurka was in space, that he saw and knows everything." He scorned those who had belittled the Soviet Union and thought Russians went "barefoot and without clothes." Gagarin's flight seemed as much a personal confirmation for Khrushchev of his leadership as it was a message to the world about his country's technological capability. The peasant boy who had been illiterate and shoeless had outdone Kennedy and his far more advanced country.

More than three weeks later, Project Mercury would make Alan Shepard the second human and first American in space. History would always record that Khrushchev and Yurka got there first.

WASHINGTON, D.C.
WEDNESDAY, APRIL 12, 1961

Adenauer's timing could not have been worse.

The West German chancellor landed in Washington just a few hours after Yuri Gagarin had parachuted to safety in Kazakhstan. He sat in the Oval Office with a president who was eager to get him out of town and get on with the invasion of Cuba.

All the more awkward, Adenauer had arrived in Washington roughly a month after the visit of Willy Brandt, the Berlin mayor, with the speaker of the Berlin Senate Egon Bahr. It was almost unprecedented that a newly elected U.S. president would schedule a meeting with key opposition representatives of an Allied country before he had met with the national leader, but such was the nature of the strained Kennedy–Adenauer relationship.

Kennedy had told Brandt that "of all the legacies of World War II which the West had inherited, Berlin was the most difficult." Yet the president said he could think of no good solution to the problem, and neither could Brandt. "We will just have to live with the situation," Kennedy had said.

Brandt joined the list of those who were telling Kennedy that Khrushchev would be likely to act to change Berlin's status before his October Party Congress. To test Western resolve, Brandt said the East Germans and Soviets were increasing their harassment of civilian and military movement between the two sides of Berlin. If the Soviets again blockaded West Berlin, he said the city had built up stockpiles of fuel and food that would last for six months. This would give Kennedy time to negotiate his way out of any Berlin difficulty.

Brandt had used his forty minutes in the Oval Office to try to instill in Kennedy a greater passion for the cause of Berlin's freedom. He called West Berlin a window to the free world that had kept alive East German hopes for eventual liberation. "Without West Berlin this hope would die," he said, and American presence was the "essential guarantee" for the city's continued existence. Brandt was relieved to hear Kennedy for the first time reject the Soviet proposal of a UN–protected "free city" status for West Berlin, an outcome Kennedy had been rumored to support. For his part, Brandt assured Kennedy that his Social Democrats' earlier flirtations with the Soviets over neutrality were a thing of the past.

A month later, Kennedy's conversations with Adenauer would be less congenial. Kennedy asked Adenauer many of the same questions he had posed to Brandt, but with less satisfying a result. When asked what the Soviets might do during 1961 in Berlin, Adenauer told Kennedy, "Anything or nothing could happen," noting that he was not a prophet. Adenauer said that when Khrushchev issued his six-month ultimatum in November 1958,

Master and mentor: Joseph Stalin stands with Moscow Communist Party boss Nikita Khrushchev in 1936 at the Shchelkovo aerodrome. (*Sovfoto*)

Khrushchev waves to a Los Angeles crowd during a 1959 trip to the U.S., the first state visit ever of the Soviet Union's premier. (*Frank Bauman/Library of Congress*)

Khrushchev with President Dwight Eisenhower, Nina Khrushchev, and Soviet Foreign Minister Andrei Gromyko in 1959. (*ITAR-TASS/Sovfoto*)

Ambassador to Great Britain Joseph Kennedy in 1938, flanked by sons Joe Jr. and John, in Southampton, England. (*President's Collection/JFK Library*)

Changing of the guard: Eisenhower gives pointers to the man who will become America's youngest president the next day. (*Abbie Rowe/JFK Library*)

Walter Ulbricht in exile: The future East German leader got to know Khrushchev while in Soviet exile during World War II. Here Ulbricht and fellow German communist Erich Weinert (left and right, respectively) try to persuade soldiers to defect. (*Sovfoto*)

Khrushchev and Ulbricht at the 5th Congress of the Socialist Unity Party, East Berlin, 1958. (*Sovfoto*)

At the time of the Berlin crisis, Chancellor Konrad Adenauer, in his third term, was the first and still only elected leader of the Federal Republic of Germany. (*Library of Congress*)

"Der Alte" poses with orphans dressed as Snow White and two of her dwarfs as part of a two-day eighty-fifth birthday celebration in January 1961. (*Bundesarchiv*)

As an inaugural gift, Khrushchev released two captured U.S. airmen from Soviet prison. Here, JFK greets Captains Freeman B. Olmstead (second from left) and John McKone and their wives at a private reception. (*AP Photo*)

Kennedy with Dean Acheson, Truman's secretary of state, whom he recruited for Berlin and NATO advice. (*AP Photo/Tom Fitzsimmons*)

A tale of two cities: East Berlin. Elderly women look out from apartment buildings pockmarked from World War II street battles. (*USIS/National Archives*)

A war-damaged store on Alexanderplatz stands in contrast to the propaganda sign in the background: "The stronger the German Democratic Republic, the more certain is peace in Germany." (*USIS/National Archives*)

A tale of two cities: West Berlin. Nightlife on the Kurfürstendamm.
(*USIS/National Archives*)

Fashionable West German
women outside the
Ku'damm's most famous
watering hole, the
Café Kranzler.
(*USIS/National Archives*)

February 11, 1961. President Kennedy convenes the first meeting of his Kremlin experts for a brainstorming session. Clockwise from left: Ambassador to the Soviet Union Llewellyn "Tommy" Thompson, Vice President Johnson, Ambassador-at-Large W. Averell Harriman, State Department adviser Charles Bohlen, Secretary of State Dean Rusk, JFK, and Soviet expert George Kennan. (*AP Photo/Harvey Georges*)

Kennedy dispatched Ambassador Thompson to Moscow in late February with his first letter for Khrushchev—which the premier refused to receive for ten days. (*Abbie Rowe/ JFK Library*)

March 13. Breaking with protocol, Kennedy meets with Berlin Mayor Willy Brandt, the West German opposition leader, before seeing Chancellor Adenauer. (*Library of Congress*)

April 5. Kennedy takes a stroll with British Prime Minister Harold Macmillan during a break in their talks in Washington, where the president would surprise his ally with the administration's hard line on Berlin. (*Robert Knudsen/JFK Library*)

April 15. Adenauer and Kennedy praise each other at a press conference—though neither trusts the other. (*Abbie Rowe/JFK Library*)

April 16. Johnson throws a barbecue for Adenauer at his Texas ranch—and on the way to the airport, tells him about the Bay of Pigs operation then under way. (*AP Photo*)

April 22. Kennedy and Eisenhower meet at Camp David to discuss the aftermath of the Bay of Pigs disaster. (*Robert Knudsen/JFK Library*)

Khrushchev travels the Soviet Union on an "agricultural tour," drumming up local support for the coming October Party Congress. (*Novosti/Sovfoto*)

A Soviet spy at Hyannis Port. In a rare photo, military intelligence agent Georgi Bolshakov (second from right) sits with JFK, an interpreter, and Khrushchev's son-in-law Alexei Adzhubei (right). Before the Vienna Summit, Bolshakov began secret talks with Robert Kennedy as a conduit between the president and Khrushchev. (*Cecil Stoughton/JFK Library*)

June 1961, Washington. A reinjury of his back caused JFK much pain at the Vienna Summit. He was usually careful not to be photographed on crutches. (*Abbie Rowe/JFK Library*)

May 31. Children waving American flags welcome Kennedy to Paris.
(*USIA/JFK Library*)

The First Couple, dressed for a formal dinner in their honor at the Élysée Palace. (*USIA/JFK Library*)

June 3, Vienna. Kennedy and Khrushchev shake hands on the first day of their historic talks. (*USIA/JFK Library*)

It began all smiles. (*Sovfoto*)

Khrushchev quickly came to dominate the discussion. (*Cornell Capa/Library of Congress*)

They broke for dinner at the Schönbrunn Palace, where Khrushchev was charmed by Jackie. (*USIA/JFK Library*)

But the mood of the talks remained tense. At the end, Kennedy left feeling battered and defeated by the premier. (*USIA/JFK Library*)

no one had expected him to be so patient, and still he had not delivered on his threats.

Kennedy wanted to know what Adenauer believed the U.S. reaction ought to be if the Soviet Union did sign a separate peace treaty with East Germany, assuming Khrushchev did so without interfering with access to Berlin.

Adenauer delivered an elderly man's lecture to the young president about how complicated the legal situation was regarding Germany. Was the president aware, he asked, that there still had been no peace treaty signed by the four powers with Germany as a whole? Was the president aware, he inquired further, of "the little-known fact" that the Soviet Union still maintained military missions in parts of West Germany? The three Allies had asked Adenauer not to say much about this, the chancellor said, as they also kept such outposts in East Germany, which enabled them to gather intelligence.

Since his boss had failed to answer Kennedy's direct question, Foreign Minister Brentano assessed Soviet alternatives. The first possibility was that of another Berlin blockade, which he thought unlikely. The second was the Soviet transfer of control over Berlin to the East German leadership, followed by harassing tactics impeding access to the city, an outcome Brentano considered more probable. So Brentano suggested contingency planning for that possibility.

Given such a case, Adenauer said West Germany would stand by its military commitments under NATO and intervene to defend Western forces against Soviet attack. "If Berlin fell, it would mean the death sentence for Europe and the Western World," said Brentano.

What followed then was a complex discussion about which parties had what legal rights under what contingencies in a Berlin crisis. What rights did West Germany have in international law over Berlin? What rights did it want? What rights did the four powers have to supply and defend Berliners? What was the essence of the NATO guarantee for Berlin? When might it be exercised, and by whom? At what point did the West go nuclear in a Berlin conflict?

All those questions required work, Adenauer said.

Kennedy fidgeted as he listened impatiently to the translation.

For Adenauer, the solution to the Berlin Crisis was to reinforce the division of the city into East and West to match that of Germany as a whole. In his mind, West Germany's integration into the West was a prerequisite for eventual unification, as it would provide a better chance to negotiate from strength. He told Kennedy that West Germany had no interest in entering bilateral talks with the Soviets. "In the great game of the world," he said, West Germany was "after all only a very small figure." He needed a fully committed America, however, in order for his approach of refusing direct talks with Moscow on Berlin to work.

Kennedy said he was concerned about the $350 million "gold drain" each year caused by keeping U.S. troops in Germany, a situation not helped by the appreciation of the deutsche mark. He called it "one of the major factors in our balance of payments accounts." He wanted the chancellor to help him reduce U.S. costs in Germany and to increase German procurements of military and other goods in the United States. The president wasn't seeking direct budgetary relief from Adenauer, as had been rumored the previous December after the visit of Eisenhower Treasury Secretary Robert Anderson. But he did want a richer West Germany to provide more support for lesser-developed countries, in part to reduce this global burden for the U.S. Adenauer agreed to that and other economic measures that would lighten the U.S. load.

The discussion over the budget impact of the U.S. security guarantee for West Germany marked an important shift. Kennedy was less personally committed to Germany than his predecessors, and beyond that he believed a more prosperous Germany should also be more capable of offsetting U.S. costs.

The communiqué at the end of the Kennedy–Adenauer sessions was limp. It was vague concerning their points of agreement and left out entirely the issues where the sides differed. The correspondent of the German magazine *Der Spiegel* reported that Adenauer had been bitterly disappointed by a visit that did nothing to address Bonn's major concerns. He said the three long meetings between Adenauer and Kennedy over two days "had eaten up the bodily strength of the West German chancellor, and had annihilated his political plans." Adenauer, he said, walked down the White House steps following their talks "visibly exhausted, his suntanned face seemingly ashen-yellow against his sunken torso."

Der Spiegel reported that the Kennedy administration had not satisfied Adenauer's request to spend the weekend after his White House meetings with his friend President Eisenhower in Pennsylvania. Instead, the magazine said, Kennedy's people "banned" Adenauer to Texas and "Vice President Johnson's out-of-the-way cattle farm."

For all the rising economic success of his country, Adenauer was suffering from the declining currency of his own leadership in Washington. The U.S. allies with whom he had executed the Marshall Plan, had rebuilt his country, had joined NATO, and had stood down the Soviets were mostly out of power. His closest co-conspirator, John Foster Dulles, had died two years earlier. A couple of German reporters had swallowed the White House spin that Adenauer and Kennedy had formed a deeper personal bond, but there was no evidence to support it.

At the end of the visit, Kennedy stepped out onto the White House lawn in the raw cold of Washington's April dampness to praise the Adenauer to whom he had given so little. "History will deal most generously with him," Kennedy said. "His accomplishments have been extraordinary in binding the nations of Western Europe together, in strengthening the ties which link the United States and the Federal Republic."

Adenauer returned Kennedy's favor, calling the man he so deeply doubted a "great leader" who carried "huge responsibility for the fate of the free world."

Little noticed was Adenauer's later response to a reporter's question at the National Press Club about a rumored concrete wall that might be built along the Iron Curtain. "In the missile age," Adenauer said after a short pause, "concrete walls don't mean very much."

STONEWALL, TEXAS
SUNDAY, APRIL 16, 1961

At high noon on a sunny Sunday, Adenauer rode off by plane from Washington with his daughter Libet and Foreign Minister Brentano to Austin, Texas. From there he would helicopter some sixty miles to Stonewall, population about five hundred, Vice President Johnson's birthplace and home of his LBJ ranch. Adenauer was trading a world of real problems for one of almost mythical attraction to Germans—the open spaces of America and the Old West made popular by the best-selling novels written by German author Karl May (who, by the way, had never visited America).

Johnson's central Texas of ranches and wooded hills had been settled by German pioneers a century earlier, and their ancestors warmly welcomed the *Bundeskanzler* with signs bearing messages such as WILLKOMMEN ADENAUER and HOWDY PODNUR. Father Wunibald Schneider staged a special afternoon Mass in German for Adenauer at Stonewall's St. Francis Xavier Church.

When Adenauer visited nearby Fredericksburg, where German was still widely spoken, he said in his native tongue that he had "learned two things in his life. A man can become a Texan, but a Texan can never stop being one. And second, there is only one thing larger than Texas in the world, and that is the Pacific Ocean." The crowd loved it, as did Johnson. With star German reporters in tow, Adenauer was using Texas as an antidote for his Washington disappointments and a campaign stop for his forthcoming elections. Though never happy being Kennedy's errand boy for lower-profile missions, Johnson nevertheless followed Kennedy's instructions that he "butter up" Adenauer, even though the vice president would have preferred being in Washington to push for his harder line on Cuba.

Adenauer was savoring some sausage at a Texas barbecue in two giant tents down by the Pedernales River that ran through the LBJ ranch at about the same time the CIA-supported Brigade 2506, loaded with arms and supplies, converged on its rendezvous point forty miles south of Cuba. Johnson put a ten-gallon hat on the chancellor's head, which Adenauer cocked for a memorable photo that would appear in all the major German newspapers. Johnson gave him a saddle and spurs and praised how bravely Adenauer had been riding the horse of freedom through the Cold War. Adenauer enthused about how much he felt at home in Texas.

On their drive to the airport for Adenauer's Monday, April 17, departure, Johnson took a phone call from Kennedy. He passed the president's greetings to the chancellor and the fact that Kennedy regarded West Germany as a "great power." Johnson then whispered to Adenauer that an uprising had begun in Cuba, triggered by an invasion of exiles, information just provided by Kennedy.

One would have to wait for developments, Johnson told Adenauer.

THE WHITE HOUSE, WASHINGTON, D.C.
TUESDAY EVENING, APRIL 18, 1961

With Adenauer safely back in Bonn, President Kennedy took a break from his unfolding Cuba crisis to put on a white tie and tails and sip champagne with members of Congress and their spouses at the White House. They all basked in the elegance and charm that the Kennedys had brought to Washington.

Most of Kennedy's guests didn't know that the previous morning 1,400 Cuban exiles, armed and trained by the CIA in Guatemala, had begun their landing at the Bay of Pigs, nor that the operation was already heading for disaster.

Two days earlier, eight B-26 bombers with Cuban markings, launched from a secret CIA air base in Puerto Cabezas, Nicaragua, had failed in their preparatory strikes for the assault. They had destroyed only five of Castro's three dozen combat planes, leaving the landing party's boats vulnerable even before they had run aground on unanticipated coral reefs.

Castro's fighters sank two freighters loaded with ammunition, food, and communication gear. Many of the U.S.-backed Cuban brigade's men had landed in the wrong locations, and all had insufficient supplies. On the morning of the white-tie gala, National Security Advisor McGeorge Bundy had delivered to Kennedy the bad news: "The Cuban armed forces are stronger, the popular response is weaker, and our tactical position is feebler than we had anticipated."

Nevertheless, the Marine Band played on that evening, striking up "Mr. Wonderful." A singer belted out the lyrics from the Broadway hit as the perfect couple with their perfect smiles, the president and the First Lady, descended red-carpeted stairs to enormous applause.

Jackie danced with senators. The president schmoozed, elevated by popularity ratings that still exceeded 70 percent.

At 11:45 p.m., the president pulled away from his guests for a meeting that would be the last chance to save the failing Cuba mission. It was a scene out of Hollywood: the president and his Cabinet members in white tie talking battle plans with a military leadership in their most formal dress uniforms, medals dripping from their chests. Meanwhile, in Cuba, men they had sent into battle were being cut apart. Although Kennedy had tried to preserve deniability by refusing to use American soldiers or planes in the operation, his fingerprints were all over the unfolding calamity.

Most of the military brass in the room had been in their jobs under Eisenhower when in January 1960 he had approved the plan to overthrow Castro. Allen Dulles, the sixty-eight-year-old CIA director whom Kennedy had kept on from the Eisenhower administration, was overseeing the operation. He had produced the first plan for the assault, modeled on a successful 1954 coup in Guatemala that had toppled a leftist government using 150 exiles and U.S. pilots flying a handful of World War II fighter planes. The CIA men involved in Guatemala had also served as Dulles's point men for the new Cuba plan.

Most important at the meeting was Richard Bissell, who was the sort of high-intellect, high-class, high-secrecy figure that appealed to the Kennedy brothers' spy world fascination. The tall, stooped former Yale economics professor was CIA director of plans and had direct charge of the Cuban operation. Sophisticated and self-deprecating, he had amused Kennedy by describing himself as a "man-eating shark" when the two men had first met over a dinner put on for the new president by CIA officers at the all-male Alibi Club.

Now working for Kennedy, Dulles and Bissell had put the final touches on a plan for a high-profile amphibious landing of some 1,400 exile soldiers. The notion was that the assault force's success would somehow trigger an anti-Castro uprising among what U.S. intelligence estimated to be 25 percent of the population, spurred by 2,500 members of resistance organizations and 20,000 sympathizers.

Kennedy had never questioned their numbers, yet had ordered changes in the plan that had weakened its chances of success. He had altered the landing site from Trinidad, a Cuban town on the south-central coast, to the Bay of Pigs on the argument that the new site would allow a less spectacular nocturnal landing with less chance of opposition. Kennedy had insisted there be no air or other support traceable to the U.S. and had reduced the initial air strike from sixteen to eight planes—again, to "play down the magnitude of the invasion." Berlin had factored in the president's considerations: he wanted to avoid providing Khrushchev with any pretext for Soviet military action in the divided city through a too-direct U.S. involvement in the Cuban invasion.

Kennedy's last-minute changes to the operation had required such quick fixes that the result was a number of oversights. No one had anticipated the Bay of Pigs' treacherous coral reefs. Nor had anyone thought to replace the earlier site's escape route for insurgents into the mountains, should matters go amiss. Also, leaks had been widespread. Already, on January 10, the *New York Times* had splashed a three-column headline across its front page: U.S. HELPS TRAIN AN ANTI-CASTRO FORCE AT SECRET GUATEMALAN AIR-GROUND BASE. Then, just hours ahead of the invasion, Kennedy had to intervene through aide Arthur Schlesinger to get the *New Republic* magazine to withhold a story that richly and accurately detailed the Cuban invasion plans.

"Castro doesn't need agents over here," Kennedy had complained. "All he has to do is read our papers."

The April 17 invasion had produced a sharp exchange of letters between Kennedy and Khrushchev. The Soviet leader, not yet knowing how badly the operation was going, fired a warning shot on April 18 at 2:00 p.m. Moscow time in the most threatening language he had yet employed with Kennedy. Making the Cuba–Berlin link, he said, "Military armament and the world political situation are such at this time that any so-called 'little war' can touch off a chain reaction in all parts of the globe."

Khrushchev wasn't buying Kennedy's disclaimers, saying it was a secret to no one that the U.S. had trained the invasion force and supplied the planes and bombs. Warning Kennedy about the chances of a "military catastrophe," Khrushchev vowed, "There should be no mistake about our position: We will render the Cuban people and their government all necessary help to repel armed attack on Cuba."

Kennedy had responded to Khrushchev at about 6:00 p.m. Washington time on the same day. "You are under a serious misapprehension," he protested to the Soviet leader. He recited all the reasons Cubans found the loss of their democratic liberties "intolerable," and how that had bred growing resistance to Castro among more than 100,000 refugees. That said, he stood by the fiction of American noninvolvement and warned Khrushchev to also keep his hands off. "The United States intends no military intervention in Cuba," he said, and if the Soviets intervened in response, then the United States would honor its obligations "to protect this hemisphere against external aggression."

With that exchange fresh in his mind, Kennedy resisted all calls for greater American involvement. He rejected Bissell's argument that he should urgently provide the exiles with limited U.S. air cover, with which Bissell argued victory could still be had. Bissell said all he required were two jets from the aircraft carrier USS *Essex* to shoot down enemy aircraft and support the stranded force.

"No," said the president.

Just six days earlier, Kennedy had been irritated when aides expressed doubts about the mission. "I know everybody is grabbing their nuts on this," he had said. Now he was just as annoyed when told by the people who had gotten him into this mess that he couldn't succeed without escalating military action in a manner that would more clearly show the U.S. hand.

"The minute I land one Marine, we're in this up to our necks," he told Bissell. "I can't get the United States into a war and then lose it, no matter what it takes." Moreover, Kennedy didn't want another "American Hungary," a situation in which the U.S. was perceived to have encouraged an uprising that in the end it did nothing to defend. "And that's what it could be, a fucking slaughter. Is that understood, gentlemen?"

If the president didn't want to use warplanes, argued Chief of Naval Operations Admiral Arleigh Burke, a hero of World War II and the Korean War, he could use a U.S. destroyer's guns to help the Cuban brigade. Known as "31-knot Burke" for his tendency as admiral to drive his destroyers at boiler-breaking speed, Burke now wanted Kennedy to push up the throttle. He said Kennedy could change the whole course of battle if just one destroyer "knocked the hell out of Castro's tanks," which he insisted would be a relatively easy task.

"Burke," the president fumed, "I don't want the United States involved in this."

"Hell, Mr. President, we *are* involved," retorted Burke, speaking with the tone of a four-star to a young PT boat captain. He had seen often enough how political indecision could cost lives and shift battle outcomes.

Kennedy ended the three-hour meeting at 2:45 a.m. with a weak compromise. He approved a plan that would send six unmarked jets to protect the exile force's B-26s as they dropped supplies and ammunition. But the bombers arrived an hour ahead of the U.S. escorts, and the Cubans shot down two of the planes.

When it was all over, Castro had killed 114 of the CIA's trainees and had taken 1,189 prisoners. He had gained his enemies' surrender after three days of fighting.

Acheson immediately grasped the negative impact Kennedy's Cuba failure would have on Khrushchev's thinking and on Allied confidence. He considered it "such a completely un-thought-out, irresponsible thing to do."

Speaking before diplomats at the Foreign Service Institute, he said, "The European view was that we were watching a gifted young amateur practice with a boomerang, when they saw, to their horror, that he had knocked himself out." He told his audience the Europeans were "amazed that so inexperienced a person should play with so lethal a weapon."

With a tone of dismay, Acheson wrote to his former boss Truman after returning from his Europe trip, referring to his Rose Garden meeting with Kennedy but without mentioning the president's name. "Why we ever engaged in this asinine Cuban adventure," he said, "I cannot imagine. Before I left it was mentioned to me and I told my informants how you and I had turned down similar suggestions for Iran and Guatemala and why. I thought that this Cuban idea had been put aside, as it should have been."

He told Truman that the impact of Cuba on European thinking about Kennedy would be profound. "The direction of this government seems surprisingly weak," he said of Kennedy. "So far as I can make out the mere inertia of the Eisenhower plan carried it to execution. All that the present administration did was to take out of it those elements of strength essential to its success. Brains are no substitute for judgment. Kennedy has, abroad at least, lost a very large part of the almost fanatical admiration which his youth and good looks have inspired." Acheson told Truman that Washington was "a depressed town," where "the morale in the State Department has about struck bottom."

Reports of Acheson's comments to diplomats-in-training made their way back to Kennedy, who asked to see a full transcript of the meeting. From that point forward, Acheson noticed "an unfortunate effect" on Kennedy's trust in him and a sharp reduction in his level of personal access.

Acheson's colorful criticism had cut too close to the bone.

MOSCOW
THURSDAY, APRIL 20, 1961

Khrushchev could hardly believe his good fortune.

He had known in advance that Kennedy would act in Cuba, and he had told columnist Lippmann as much at Pitsunda. Yet never in his fondest dreams had he anticipated such incompetence. In his first major foreign test, the new U.S. president had lived down to Khrushchev's lowest expectations. Kennedy had demonstrated weakness under fire. He had lacked the backbone to cancel Eisenhower's plans or the character to make them work as his own. He had lacked the resolve to bring to a successful conclusion an action of so much importance to American prestige.

Though Kennedy had avoided giving Khrushchev a pretext for a tit-for-tat response in Berlin, at the same time, through his failure, he had provided the Soviet leader valuable intelligence on the sort of man who was leading the U.S. "I don't understand Kennedy," Khrushchev said to his son Sergei. "Can he really be that indecisive?" He compared the Bay of Pigs unfavorably to his own bloody but bold intervention of Soviet troops in Hungary to ensure the country remained firmly in the communist sphere of influence.

That said, Khrushchev was concerned by the possibility that CIA chief Dulles, whom he had blamed for the U-2 incident the year before, might have executed the invasion to undermine preparations for a U.S.–Soviet summit. Khrushchev was also sufficiently self-centered to believe Kennedy may have launched his Cuban landing to humiliate the Soviet leader on his April 17 birthday. Instead of ruining his celebration, however, Kennedy's failure would provide Khrushchev with an unanticipated gift.

The KGB reports on Kennedy that followed struck Khrushchev as simultaneously encouraging and troubling. On the positive side, the KGB was reporting from London—apparently from sources at the American embassy—that Kennedy had been telling colleagues in the wake of Cuba that he regretted having kept on Republicans like Dulles as CIA chief and

C. Douglas Dillon at Treasury. At the same time, however, Khrushchev wondered what the Cuban operation said about the nature of the Kennedy presidency. Was the president really in control, or was he being manipulated by anticommunist hawks like Dulles? Was Kennedy himself a hawk? Or, more likely, did the botched plan suggest that Kennedy was perhaps something even more dangerous—an incalculable and unpredictable adversary?

Whatever the truth, what was indisputable was that Khrushchev's fortunes had shifted dramatically for the better in the space of a single week. Very little could have provided a more dramatic shift in momentum than the combination of the Gagarin space triumph and the Bay of Pigs setback. It had been just six weeks since Khrushchev had met Ambassador Thompson in Siberia and relayed his reluctance to accept Kennedy's invitation for a summit meeting.

Now that Kennedy had been so weakened, Khrushchev was more inclined to risk drawing him into the ring.

Although the Soviet leader's luck had changed far faster than he could have imagined, he knew he had to move faster still. The situation on the ground in Berlin remained stubbornly unchanged. A whole new generation was congregating in Berlin, eager to soak up the sights and atmosphere of the only city in the world where they could watch the world's two feuding systems compete openly and without mediation.

Khrushchev wanted to take no chances about where it would all lead.

Jörn Donner Discovers the City

What drew young Finnish writer Jörn Donner to Berlin was his conviction that the place was more of an idea than it was a city. For that reason, it served his postgraduate lust for adventure and inspiration far better than any of the available alternatives.

Paris's Left Bank had Sartre and his disciples, Rome's Via Veneto offered its Dolce Vita, and nothing could rival London's Soho when it came to Donner's search for the combined attractions of learning and debauchery. Yet only Berlin could provide Donner such a unique window on the divided world in which he lived.

Donner considered the difference between East and West Berliners to be purely circumstantial, and thus they served as the perfect laboratory mice for the world's most important social experiment. They had been the same Berliners shaped by the same history until 1945, when an abrupt application of different systems left one side with the decadent vices of prosperity and the other with the virtues of a straitjacket. Berliners had always been pinched geographically between Europe and Russia, but the Cold War had transformed that map into a psychological and geopolitical drama.

Twenty years later, Donner would produce Ingmar Bergman's film Fanny and Alexander, and it would win four Academy Awards. But, for the moment, he fashioned himself as a modern-day Christopher Isherwood, and, having just completed his studies at the University of Stockholm, he wanted to launch his artistic career by chronicling Berlin as the living history of his times.

Isherwood's Goodbye to Berlin had tracked the improvised street battles between communists and Nazis during the 1930s that were the prelude to World War II and the Holocaust. Donner regarded the story he would tell of no less historic significance, though the role of Berliners themselves would be more as passive bystanders to the high politics that surrounded them.

Germans disparagingly employ the term Berliner Schnauze, or "Berlin snout," to describe Berliners' irreverent boisterousness, and none of that had been lost during their postwar occupation. Author Stephen Spender described Berliners' apparent Cold War courage this way: "If Berliners show a peculiar fearlessness which excites the almost unbelieving wonderment of the world, that is because they have reached that place on the far side of fear, where, being utterly at the mercy of the conflict of the great powers, they feel there is no use being afraid, and therefore they have nothing to be afraid of."

In the cold damp of the West Berlin subway, Donner studied the unpleasant, incurious Berlin faces that were at the center of his drama. Though the fate of humanity might be decided in their city, Donner found Berliners curiously apathetic, as if the reality were too much for them to absorb.

In a search for the right metaphor to describe the divided city, Donner would later apologize to his readers that he could not resist "the sleepwalker's almost automatic mania" to describe Berlin's division through the contrasting nature of its two most prominent avenues—West Berlin's Kurfürstendamm and East Berlin's Stalinallee.

Like West Berlin, the Ku'damm (as locals called it) had emerged from the chaos of the postwar years full of restless energy, neon lights, aspirational fashion, and new cafés and bars competing for expanding wallets. Like East Berlin, the Stalinallee concealed the underlying fragility of its society with its centrally planned neoclassical grandeur, which dictated everything from each apartment's size to the width of its hallways and height of its windows. State security directives determined precisely how many informants would be planted among what number of residents.

Though the heart of the Ku'damm was but four kilometers long, that stretch contained seventeen of the country's most expensive jewelers, ten car dealers, and the city's most exclusive restaurants. War widows begged on corners where they knew the city's finest citizens would pass. One such spot was directly before Eduard Winter's Volkswagen showroom, where Berlin's richest man was known to sell thirty cars a day when not running his Coca-Cola distributorship.

Isherwood, whose book gave rise to the movie Cabaret, spoke of prewar

Ku'damm as a "cluster of expensive hotels, bars, cinemas, shops . . . a sparkling nucleus of light, like a sham diamond, in the shabby twilight of the town." The Cold War atmosphere remained much the same, though postwar reconstruction had introduced the sharper concrete and glass architectural edges of the 1950s.

The Ku'damm's seedier side had also survived the war. In one tawdry bar, called The Old-Fashioned, Donner observed a Düsseldorf businessman licking the ear of a blond bar girl until she wearily drew back and his lips fell into her armpit. Berlin was a place where Germans came to pursue their pleasures in anonymity and without curfew, from its transvestite bars to more conventional amusements. What happened in Berlin stayed in Berlin.

Across town in communist East Berlin, Donner found the Ku'damm's alter ego. In 1949, in honor of Stalin's seventieth birthday, Ulbricht renamed the city's grand Frankfurter Strasse for the dictator, and it would keep his name through November 1961, even though he was dead and had been renounced by Khrushchev.* During World War II's final days, Soviet soldiers had hung Nazis from trees that lined the street, often fastening to their corpses identifying papers with the inscription: HERE HANGS SO-AND-SO, BECAUSE HE RE-FUSED TO DEFEND WIFE AND CHILD.

Ulbricht had rebuilt the street as Stalinallee to be a showcase for the power and capabilities of communism, "the first socialist road of Germany," whose purpose was to provide "palaces for the working class." So construction crews from 1952 to 1960 produced a long row of eight-story apartment houses of Stalinist monumental architecture. Wartime rubble was transformed into high-ceilinged flats with balconies, elevators, ceramic tiling, marble staircases, and—a luxury at the time—baths in every apartment. To provide a sufficiently wide and long promenade for military marches, builders made Stalinallee a tree-studded, six-lane, ninety-meter-wide, two-kilometer-long highway. Stalinallee would provide the backdrop for the annual May Day parade, but it also was where the 1953 workers' uprising gained its momentum.

Only a short distance from Stalinallee, Donner described the quiet des-

---

*It would be renamed Karl-Marx-Allee that November.

peration of East Berliners who had passed through the ravages of World War II, only to again land on the wrong side of history. The Raabe-Diele was one of the oldest pubs in Berlin and sat on Sperlingsgasse, a narrow lane still blocked in the middle by wartime ruins that had not yet been cleared. It had but three tables, a counter, benches along the walls, and simple, tattered chairs.

Its sole proprietor was Frau Friedrich Konarske, who at age eighty-two had worked the same counter for fifty-seven years. She would not discuss her own sad life but happily gossiped with Donner about her clientele, all men save for a loud, forty-something woman who drank straight shots while recounting her stomach operations.

"Ten drunk men are better than one half-sober female," complained Konarske.

Two middle-aged men strummed their guitars at a table by the window and sang sentimental songs. As they prepared to go home, a man with a hunchback shouted a last request in a squeaky voice. "Play 'Lili Marlene.' That's what I want to hear. And then I'll buy you a round."

The best-dressed man in the bar—and who, because of that, the others took to be a Communist Party member or state security officer—shouted his objection on the grounds that the song had been one of Hitler's favorites.

The hunchback protested angrily, "What's that? 'Lili Marlene' was played during the war in order to give voice—yes, to give voice—to the longing of the soldiers for peace. It has nothing to do with Nazism." And it was true: the song had been written during World War I by soldier Hans Leip while he marched to the Russian front from Berlin. The hunchback protested that even Americans and Englishmen loved the song.

"It's a universal melody!" shouted an inebriated young man who looked like he had been a boxer, with his large, flat nose, cauliflower ears, and fingertips yellowed by nicotine. One after another of Frau Konarske's clientele sounded agreement in an uprising against the supposed communist, but the singers still hesitated, as momentary acts of defiance could result in long jail sentences.

Made courageous by drink, the boxer type threatened the well-dressed man: *"If you don't want to listen, you can leave."* He then began to sing the first verse alone, after which the two musicians joined in, followed by one additional voice after the other, until the entire pub joined in song around the still-silent man in the dark suit who sipped his beer.

Frau Konarske offered drinks on the house. She then took Donner aside and showed him the small, framed text behind her on the wall, dating from World War II. It read: WE SHALL GO TO OUR DEATH JUST AS NAKED AS WE CAME INTO THE WORLD.

She asked the stranger, *"Do you think that anyone will take over my place after I am gone? All my relatives and friends are in West Germany. Do you think they want to come over to East Berlin and work in a little hole from ten in the morning until two at night?"*

She answered her own question: *"No."*

9

PERILOUS DIPLOMACY

The American government and the president are concerned that the Soviet leadership underestimates the capabilities of the U.S. government and those of the president himself.

Robert Kennedy to Soviet military intelligence agent
Georgi Bolshakov, May 9, 1961

Berlin is a festering sore which has to be eliminated.

Premier Khrushchev to U.S. Ambassador Llewellyn E. Thompson Jr.,
at the Ice Capades in Moscow, on the goal of the
Vienna Summit, May 26, 1961

WASHINGTON, D.C.
TUESDAY, MAY 9, 1961

Wearing a white shirt, a loosened tie, and a jacket held casually over one shoulder, U.S. Attorney General Robert Kennedy bounded down the steps of the side entrance to the Department of Justice on Pennsylvania Avenue and extended his hand to Soviet spy Georgi Bolshakov.

"Hi, Georgi, long time no see," the attorney general said, as if reacquainting himself with a long-lost friend, though he had met him only briefly once, some seven years earlier. Beside Kennedy stood Ed Guthman, the Pulitzer Prize–winning reporter who had become his press officer and sounding board. Guthman had arranged the unprecedented meeting through the man who had delivered Bolshakov by taxi and stood beside him, New York *Daily News* correspondent Frank Holeman.

"So shall we take a walk?" Kennedy asked Bolshakov. The attorney general's casual manner was disarming, considering the unconventional, unprecedented contact he was about to initiate. He nodded to Guthman and Holeman to stay behind as he and the Russian spy walked onto the Washington Mall in the spring evening mist, making small talk about the magazine that Bolshakov had been editing that day.

At Kennedy's suggestion, the two men sat on a secluded patch of lawn, the air scented with freshly mowed grass. The U.S. Capitol stood in the background to one side, and the Washington Monument to the other, with the Smithsonian Castle's front gate directly behind them. Lovers on early evening walks and small groups of tourists looked to the rain clouds above, which threatened a storm.

Bolshakov described his closeness to Khrushchev, and he offered himself up as a more useful and direct contact to the Soviet leader than Moscow's ambassador to the United States, Mikhail Menshikov, whom Bobby and his brother had come to consider a clown.

Bobby told Bolshakov that his brother was eager to meet with Khrushchev, and that he hoped to improve communication in the run-up to their first meeting so that the two sides could get the agenda right. The attorney general said he already knew about Bolshakov's links to some of Khrushchev's top people and was confident he could play that role, if he was willing. "It would be great if they receive information firsthand, from you," Bobby said. "And they, I believe, would have a chance to report it to Khrushchev."

After a roll of thunder, Kennedy joked, "If a bolt of lightning kills me, the papers will report a Russian spy killed the president's brother. It could trigger a war. Let's get away from here." They first walked briskly and then accelerated to a run to escape the downpour, regrouping in the attorney general's office after riding up in his private elevator. They removed their wet shirts and continued their conversation while wearing undershirts and sitting in a tiny room with two armchairs, a refrigerator, and a small library.

Thus began one of the most unique and—even years thereafter—only partially understood relationships of the Cold War. From that day forward, the attorney general and Bolshakov would communicate frequently—during some periods as often as two or three times monthly. It was an exchange that went almost entirely unreported and undocumented, an omission Robert Kennedy would later regret. He never took notes at the meetings, and reported on them directly and only orally to his brother. Thus the Bolshakov–Kennedy exchanges can be reconstructed only imperfectly through a dissatisfying Robert Kennedy oral history, Soviet records, Bolshakov's partial recollections, and the memories of several others who were involved at one point or another.

President Kennedy had approved of his brother's initial meeting with Bolshakov without consulting or advising any of his chief foreign policy advisers or Soviet experts. That reflected the Kennedys' increased distrust of his intelligence and military apparatus following the Bay of Pigs, their penchant for clandestine activities, and their desire to put the pieces in place as carefully as possible for a smooth summit meeting.

For Khrushchev, however, Bolshakov was more of a useful pawn than a significant player. On a complex chessboard, Khrushchev could deploy Bolshakov to draw out Kennedy without revealing his own game. From the beginning, the structure of the exchange provided the Soviet leader with an advantage. President Kennedy could learn from Bolshakov only what Khrushchev and other superiors had provided him to transmit, while Bolshakov could extract much more from Bobby Kennedy, who so intimately knew the president and his thinking.

Bolshakov was just one of two channels Khrushchev was working to reach Kennedy in early May, and while top Soviet officials engaged in both to their maximum benefit, their U.S. counterparts knew only about the formal contact made five days earlier. It was then that Foreign Minister Andrei Gromyko had telephoned Ambassador Thompson with Khrushchev's belated response to Kennedy's letter of two months earlier, inviting the Soviet leader to a summit meeting.

Gromyko had apologized to Thompson that Khrushchev himself could not personally transmit his interest. The Soviet leader was leaving Moscow for yet another trip to the provinces to put the pieces in place for his October Party Congress, and he would not return until May 20. But speaking on Khrushchev's behalf, Gromyko said the Soviet leader "deplored the fact that discord" had grown between the two countries over the Bay of Pigs and Laos.

Reading carefully scripted language, Gromyko said, "If the Soviet Union and the U.S. do not consider that there is an unbridgeable gulf between them, they should draw the appropriate conclusions from this, namely that we live on one planet and therefore ways should be found to settle appropriate questions and build up our relations." Motivated by that end, Gromyko said Khrushchev was now ready to accept Kennedy's invitation to meet, and believed "bridges have to be built which would link our countries."

What Gromyko wanted to know from Thompson was whether the Kennedy invitation "remains valid or is being revised" after the Bay of Pigs. Though Gromyko had posed the question politely, its underlying message was an impertinent one. He was asking whether Kennedy still dared meet with Khrushchev after having so badly shot himself in the foot in Cuba.

With that, Khrushchev's approach to President Kennedy had entered its third stage. The first had been Khrushchev's initial flurry of efforts to meet Kennedy directly after the U.S. election and during his first days in office. The second had been Khrushchev's withdrawal of interest following the new president's hawkish State of the Union message. Now Khrushchev was again eager to meet and press his perceived advantage over a now weakened opponent.

Thompson put down the phone and prepared a cable. He immediately concluded that if the president wished to reverse a perilous worsening of relations, the dangers of agreeing to such a meeting were far outweighed by its necessity. Thompson followed his 4:00 p.m. secret telegram reporting on his conversation with Gromyko with a similarly classified message to Secretary Rusk that urged the president to grasp Khrushchev's extended hand. Critics would argue that Kennedy was walking like wounded prey into a bear trap, but Thompson suggested Kennedy reveal publicly that he had issued the invitation to Khrushchev long before the Bay of Pigs, and that the Soviet leader was only now responding.

Thompson then laid out his arguments in favor of the meeting:

- The very prospect of such a summit would prompt the Soviets to take a "more reasonable approach" to issues such as Laos, nuclear testing, and disarmament.
- A face-to-face meeting would be the best place for Kennedy to influence crucial decisions of the October Party Congress that could set the stage for the superpower relationship for years to come.
- Because Mao Tse-tung opposed such U.S.–Soviet consultations, Thompson suggested the "mere fact of meeting will exacerbate Soviet–Chinese relations."
- Finally, showing the world a willingness to talk directly to Khrushchev would influence public opinion in a way that would make it easier for Kennedy to maintain a strong U.S. position in favor of defending West Berlin's freedoms.

Despite the negative turn in relations with Moscow, Thompson also argued that Khrushchev had not fundamentally altered his desire to do business with the West, nor had he abandoned his foreign policy doctrine of peaceful coexistence. Thompson often worried about being labeled by his Washington critics as a Khrushchev apologist, but he nevertheless argued that the Soviet leader had not initiated confrontation with the West in the Third World but had merely taken advantage of U.S. setbacks in Cuba, Laos, Iraq, and the Congo.

However, too much was at stake for Kennedy to agree to such a summit without preconditions that would more thoroughly test Soviet intentions—and avoid further foreign policy mistakes. Through diplomatic probes, Kennedy wanted to determine whether Khrushchev genuinely wished to improve relations.

After a day of reflection, Kennedy responded cautiously to Thompson through Rusk. Rusk wanted the ambassador to tell Khrushchev that the president "remains desirous" to meet the Soviet leader and hoped they could still do so by early June in Vienna—the Soviets' preferred location. Kennedy regretted, however, that he couldn't yet make a firm decision but would do so before Khrushchev returned to Moscow on May 20.

What followed were the conditions.

Most important, Rusk cabled that Thompson should relay to Khrushchev that the chances for such a summit weren't good if the Soviets didn't change their approach to the ongoing conflict in Laos. The Geneva talks were beginning the following week, and Kennedy wanted to end the war and achieve a neutral Laos. But the Soviets had been stalling in Geneva while fighting escalated.

Special envoy Averell Harriman, who was leading the U.S. delegation in Geneva, had reported to Kennedy that he doubted Khrushchev was ready to accept a neutral Laos because the "commies in Geneva are full of confidence and appear utterly relaxed about achieving their goals in Laos." The Soviets, Harriman said, were maneuvering to put the U.S. in the unacceptable position of having to attend the conference before they had an effective ceasefire, hardly the actions of a country that would engage usefully in a summit meeting.

Beyond that, Rusk told Thompson that "for domestic political reasons," the president wanted Khrushchev to provide some prospect that he would work toward Kennedy's goal of achieving a nuclear test ban agreement during their Vienna talks. Furthermore, the president wanted assurance that any public statement in Vienna would exclude reference to Berlin, a matter he was unprepared to negotiate.

Three days later, President Kennedy was test-driving the same message via his brother as RFK sat in his undershirt with Bolshakov at the Justice Department.

It suited Bolshakov fine that Bobby had picked May 9—a national holiday in Moscow—for their first, furtive meeting. Though it was just another workday in Washington, the Soviet embassy's staff had the day off to celebrate the sixteenth anniversary of the Nazi defeat. That served Bolsha-kov's purpose of concealing even from his closest comrades the ultrasecret conduit to President Kennedy that he had established.

In going forward with the contact, Bolshakov had disregarded the op-position of his nearest superior, the station chief, or *rezident*, at the embassy for Soviet military intelligence, the GRU. For Bolshakov's boss, it was un-thinkable that a mid-level Soviet agent would establish the most important U.S.–Soviet intelligence back channel imaginable. In meeting with Robert Kennedy, Bolshakov was connecting with a man who was at the same time the president's brother, his closest confidant, and his attorney general, thus overseeing all the counterintelligence activities of the FBI.

What gave Bolshakov the confidence to nevertheless pursue such a high-level mission was the sanction of the Soviet leader himself through Khrushchev's son-in-law, Alexei Adzhubei, editor of the newspaper *Izvestia* and Bolshakov's friend. Adzhubei had recommended Bolshakov to Khru-shchev as someone who could help counsel him when he was planning his first trip to the U.S. in 1959. (Until shortly before then, Bolshakov had loy-ally served Marshal Georgy Zhukov, the decorated war hero and defense minister whom Khrushchev had purged.)

What followed was Bolshakov's new posting to the U.S. under the cover of embassy information officer and editor of the English-language Soviet propaganda magazine *USSR*. It would be Bolshakov's second tour in Wash-ington, the first having come under cover as correspondent for the news agency TASS from 1951 to 1955.

For a cloak-and-dagger operative, Bolshakov had an unusually high profile as Washington society's favorite Soviet. He was a gregarious, hard-drinking bon vivant with wisps of black hair, piercing blue eyes, and a central-casting Russian accent. His friends and acquaintances included a number of Kennedy circle insiders: *Washington Post* editor Ben Bradlee; reporter Charles Bartlett, who had introduced the president to his wife, Jacqueline; the president's chief of staff, Kenny O'Donnell; his special coun-sel, Ted Sorensen; and his press secretary, Pierre Salinger.

However, Bolshakov's most important link to Kennedy had been Frank

Holeman, a Washington journalist who had been close to Nixon and was now trying to ingratiate himself with the Kennedy administration. With his six-foot-eight frame, Southern accent and manners, deep voice, and ever-present bow tie and cigar, he was known by colleagues as "the Colonel." Though only forty years old, Holeman was a Washington fixture, having covered presidents Roosevelt, Truman, Eisenhower, and now Kennedy. He knew Washington was all about contacts, and he had them everywhere.

Bolshakov had worked Holeman as an unpaid informant from the time they had met at a 1951 Soviet embassy lunch in the American correspondent's honor. Holeman had endeared himself to the Kremlin by blocking a National Press Club effort to ban Soviet journalists from membership in response to the Czech government's jailing of the entire Associated Press bureau in Prague. Explaining why he had done so, Holeman joked that the club should be a place where all parties could "swap lies." He then went even further on behalf of the Soviets, landing club membership for a new Soviet press officer, an individual likely to be a spy.

When Bolshakov returned to Moscow in 1955, he handed off the Holeman contact to his GRU successor, Yuri Gvozdev, whose cover was as a cultural attaché. Gvozdev had passed through Holeman, who described himself as the Soviets' "carrier pigeon," a crucial message that the Eisenhower administration should not overreact to Khrushchev's November 1958 Berlin ultimatum because Khrushchev would never go to war over Berlin. Working through Holeman, Gvozdev also helped lay the groundwork for Nixon's visit to the Soviet Union thereafter, handling negotiations over the conditions.

When Bolshakov replaced Gvozdev in 1959, he reacquainted himself with Holeman and the two struck up such a close friendship that their families often got together socially. As fortune would have it, Holeman had been close for some years to the new attorney general's press secretary, Ed Guthman, to whom he had been passing on the most interesting aspects of his conversations with Bolshakov. Guthman in turn had reported the gist of those talks to Robert Kennedy. With Guthman's blessing, Holeman on April 29 first floated the possibility of a meeting when he asked Bolshakov,

"Don't you think it would be better to meet directly with Robert Kennedy so that he receives your information at first hand?"

Ten days and countless conversations later, Bolshakov sensed something important was up when Holeman asked if he would join him for a "late lunch" at about four p.m.

"Why so late?" Bolshakov asked.

Holeman explained he had tried to reach Bolshakov several times over the course of the day but that the holiday duty officer had told him Bolshakov was at the printing office, finishing the new edition of his magazine.

A short time later, after they had settled into the chairs in the corner of a cozy, inconspicuous Georgetown restaurant, Holeman looked at his watch. When Bolshakov asked whether it was time for him to go home, Holeman said, "No, it's our time to go. You have an appointment with Robert Kennedy at six."

"Damn it," said Bolshakov, looking at his old suit and frayed shirt cuffs. "Why didn't you tell me before?"

"Are you afraid?" asked Holeman.

"Not afraid, but I'm not ready for such a meeting."

"You are always ready." Holeman smiled.

At the Justice Department, Bobby told the Soviet his brother worried that tension between the two countries was caused in large degree by misunderstanding and misinterpretation of each other's intentions and actions. Through the Bay of Pigs experience, Bobby said, his brother had learned about the dangers of taking action based on bad information. He told Bolshakov that his brother had made a mistake after the Bay of Pigs in failing to immediately fire the senior officials responsible for the operation.

"The American government and the President," said Bobby, "are concerned that the Soviet leadership underestimates the capabilities of the U.S. government and those of the President himself." The message he wanted Bolshakov to relay to the Kremlin could not have been clearer: If Khrushchev tried to test his brother's resolve, the president would have no choice but to "take corrective action" and introduce a tougher approach toward Moscow.

He told Bolshakov, "At present, our principal concern is the situation in Berlin. The importance of this issue may not be evident to everybody. The President thinks that further misunderstanding of our opinions on Berlin could lead to a war." Yet, he added, it was precisely because of the complications of the Berlin situation that the president didn't want the Vienna meeting to focus on a matter where it would be so difficult to achieve progress.

What the president wanted, Bobby told Bolshakov, was for Khrushchev and his brother to use the meeting as a chance to better understand each other, to create personal ties, and to outline a course to further develop their relationship. He wanted real agreements on matters like the nuclear test ban. On Berlin, however, he believed in delaying significant diplomatic steps until both sides had had more time to thoroughly study the matter.

For an individual who had only been called to join the meeting a couple of hours earlier, the Soviet seemed well prepared to respond. If the top U.S. and Soviet leaders met, Bolshakov said, Khrushchev would then consider "substantial" concessions on nuclear testing, and would also offer progress on Laos. Bolshakov did not comment on RFK's insistence that Berlin remain off-limits in any summit decisions, which Bobby may have misinterpreted as agreement.

Encouraged by Bolshakov's response, Bobby sketched out a potential nuclear test ban deal. The two countries had been negotiating at lower levels since 1958, but their sticking point was verification. The U.S. had sought without success the right to inspect sites in the Soviet Union. Bobby proposed a unilateral concession under which the U.S. would cut in half, from twenty to ten, the number of inspections it was demanding each year on each other's territory to investigate seismic events. The condition for this agreement, he said, would be that neither side would veto the creation of an international commission that could monitor complaints.

Behind Bobby's proposal lay a growing U.S. fear that the Soviets were digging holes so deep and large that they could conceal a weapons test. The most annual inspections Moscow had been willing to accept previously were three. And Moscow wanted any verification to be performed by a "troika"—three officials representing the Soviet bloc, the capitalist West, and the Third World. U.S. officials had opposed that approach as it would have granted a Soviet representative a de facto veto. Said Bobby, "The President does not want to repeat the sad experience of Khrushchev's meeting with Eisenhower at Camp David and hopes that this forthcoming meeting will produce concrete agreements."

Playing the role of suitor, Bolshakov said nothing that would make Bobby believe the president's preconditions for a summit were unacceptable to Khrushchev. There was only one problem: Bolshakov was a mere message carrier who could not know Khrushchev's mind as well as Bobby knew that of his brother.

The perils to the U.S. of the Bolshakov–Bobby Kennedy contact were deep and multiple. Bolshakov could deceive on Moscow's behalf without knowing he was doing so, while Bobby was far less likely to engage in disinformation and, even if he had tried, would have been less skilled in doing so. Beyond that, Bolshakov almost undoubtedly was tailed by FBI agents. Reports back from field agents on their meetings could have increased FBI boss J. Edgar Hoover's suspicions of the Kennedys.

Finally, Bolshakov lacked Bobby's license to horse-trade. And because JFK would keep the contacts secret even from his own top Cabinet members until after the Vienna Summit, he had no independent means to verify Bolshakov's reliability. Moscow not only controlled what Bolshakov could discuss, it also determined the precise manner in which he would raise issues. If Robert Kennedy raised a matter for which Bolshakov was unprepared, the Soviet spy would respond that he would consider the issue and get back to the attorney general later.

The most important messages Bolshakov brought back from his first meeting with Bobby relayed the president's readiness for a summit, his fear that the Soviet leader perceived him as weak, his aversion to negotiating Berlin's status, and his desire above all else to achieve a nuclear test ban deal. Bobby came away from the initial contact unable to provide his brother any greater insight into Khrushchev. He was at the same time gaining the false impression that Khrushchev was ready to accept his brother's conditions.

After five hours of conversation, Bobby gave Bolshakov a ride home. Kept awake by adrenaline, the Soviet operative stayed up all night before cabling a full report to Moscow early the next morning. Through Bolshakov, Khrushchev knew far better what Kennedy hoped to achieve through a summit and what he feared about it. At the same time, he had effectively misled the president about what the Soviet side was willing to accept.

MOSCOW
FRIDAY, MAY 12, 1961

Eager to close agreement for a Vienna Summit, Khrushchev rapidly satisfied Kennedy's desire for confidence-building gestures.

In Geneva, Soviet officials negotiating Laos reached agreement with British representatives on a formula to defuse an impending crisis. The result would be a fourteen-nation conference on Laos in Geneva, with the goal of an end to hostilities and a neutral Laos.

On the same day, Khrushchev delivered a speech in Tbilisi, in the Soviet republic of Georgia, that senior State Department officials considered the most moderate Soviet statement on U.S.–Soviet relations since the U-2 incident the previous May. Repeating language he had used in his acceptance of Kennedy's summit invitation, Khrushchev said, "Although President Kennedy and I are men of different poles, we live on the same Earth. We have to find a common language on certain questions."

On that day, too, Khrushchev sent a letter to Kennedy accepting his invitation of nearly two months earlier to a summit meeting. The letter made no mention of a nuclear test ban, though it touched upon areas where they might make progress, such as Laos. However, Khrushchev was not willing to lay Berlin to the side. He said he did not seek unilateral advantage in the divided city, but wanted through their meeting to remove a "dangerous source of tension in Europe."

Now it was Kennedy's move.

WASHINGTON, D.C.
SUNDAY, MAY 14, 1961

Not wanting to appear rushed, Kennedy took forty-eight hours to reply. He was unhappy about Khrushchev's failure to embrace the test ban issue and his insistence on discussing Berlin. The Soviet leader's letter had walked away from Kennedy's preconditions as relayed by Bobby to Bolshakov. Yet for all the perils, Kennedy saw no option but to agree to the meeting.

Khrushchev's Tbilisi speech and his gestures on Laos were encouraging. However, the awkward truth was that what could be one of the most decisive meetings since World War II was less than one month off and there would be little time for the two sides to reach agreement on what diplomats referred to as the summit's "deliverables." To veteran diplomats, the president's haste looked restless and naive.

Kennedy sent cables to his closest allies informing them of the upcoming meeting, knowing particularly the Germans and the French would be skeptical of his plan. To the distrustful Adenauer, he wrote, "I would assume you would share my view that since I have not previously met Khrushchev, such an encounter would be useful in the present international situation. If the meeting in fact takes place, I would expect to inform you of the content of these discussions with Khrushchev, which I anticipate will be quite general in character."

Preparations went into high gear for what everyone knew would be a historic meeting—the first such summit of the television age. Despite Kennedy's efforts to avoid the Berlin issue, his foreign policy team was coming to accept that it would define the president's first year in office far more than Cuba, Laos, a nuclear test ban, or any other issue.

On May 17, State Department Policy Planning staff member Henry Owen captured the growing consensus of the administration. "Of all the problems the administration faces, Berlin seems to me the most pregnant with disaster." He suggested putting more money into the fiscal year 1963 budget for conventional arms and the defense of Europe, "to enhance our capability to deal with—and thus perhaps deter—a Berlin Crisis."

Two days later, on May 19, the Kennedy administration officially announced what the press had been reporting from leaks for several days: The president would meet with Khrushchev in Vienna on June 3 and 4 after seeing de Gaulle in Paris.

Western European and U.S. commentators worried that a weakened president was heading to Vienna at a disadvantage. The intellectual weekly *Die Zeit* compared Kennedy to a traveling salesman whose business had fallen on bad times and who was hoping to improve his prospects by negotiating directly with the competition. In its review of European opinion, the *Wall Street Journal* said Kennedy was projecting the "strong impression . . . of a faltering America desperately trying to regain leadership of the West in the Cold War." The influential Swiss daily *Neue Zürcher Zeitung* despaired that the summit was being badly prepared by the Americans, and that Kennedy had abandoned his prerequisite that the Kremlin demonstrate a changed attitude before any such meeting take place.

Although Vienna was technically neutral ground, European diplomats still considered Austria to be far closer to the Russian sphere of influence than the alternative of Stockholm. "Thus there is an impression of Kennedy going to see Khrushchev at a place as well as a time of Khrushchev's choosing," said the *Neue Zürcher Zeitung*. It saw a damaged U.S. president "rushing about to patch up his alliances and coming meekly to Austria to meet the powerful Russian leader face-to-face."

EAST BERLIN
FRIDAY, MAY 19, 1961

Sensing the wind shift in his favor, East German leader Walter Ulbricht moved with greater confidence in Berlin. The Soviet ambassador in East Germany, Mikhail Pervukhin, complained to Foreign Minister Gromyko that Ulbricht, without Kremlin approval, was ratcheting up pressure on West Berlin through heightened identity controls of civilians.

"Our friends," said the ambassador, employing the term used by Moscow for its East German allies, "would now like to establish such control on the sectoral border between Democratic West Berlin which would allow them to, as they say, close 'the door to the West,' reduce the exodus of the population from the Republic, and weaken the influence of economic conspiracy against the GDR, which is carried out directly from West Berlin." He reported that Ulbricht wanted to slam shut the Berlin sectoral border, in contradiction to Soviet policy.

Khrushchev worried Ulbricht might go so far that he would prompt the Americans to cancel the Vienna Summit, so he asked Pervukhin to restrain his increasingly impatient and insolent East German client.

WASHINGTON, D.C.
SUNDAY, MAY 21, 1961

President Kennedy began to fear he was walking into a trap.

Two weeks ahead of the summit, Robert Kennedy again reached out to Bolshakov, this time on a Sunday when their meeting would be less noticed. The attorney general invited the Soviet spy to Hickory Hill, his brick country house in McLean, Virginia, for a two-hour conversation.

Bolshakov laid out the Soviet position, having memorized with great skill five pages of detailed briefing notes before his meeting. His recall was remarkable, and his informal manner masked the fact that his conduit role was still unfamiliar terrain.

Bobby made clear he was speaking for the president. He told Bolshakov to call him only from a pay phone when making contact, and to name himself only to his secretary and his press spokesman Ed Guthman. On occasions when Bolshakov didn't want to risk telephoning himself, Holeman did so for him, saying to Guthman, "My guy wants to see your guy." Bobby told Bolshakov that only his brother knew of their meetings—and that he approved of them.

By contrast, Bolshakov's role was now becoming known to a larger circle of Soviet officials. The GRU relayed all Bolshakov's reports to Anatoly Dobrynin, the foreign ministry official who headed the group of Soviet advisers for the Vienna talks. One of Bolshakov's Moscow bosses wrote with astonishment about the May 21 meeting with Bobby Kennedy, "The situation when a member of the U.S. government meets with our man, and secretly, is without precedent." Moscow was sending directions to its embassy and its intelligence operatives on how to ensure that the meetings were kept secret from the U.S. press and the FBI.

Bobby told Bolshakov he had been disappointed that Khrushchev had not had more to say in his letter to the president about the possibility of a nuclear test ban treaty. He offered a concession to Bolshakov: Washington would accept the troika of inspectors that the Kremlin wanted—representing the Soviet, Western, and nonaligned world—but Russia could have no veto over what could be inspected.

Bolshakov encouraged Bobby to think he had been given more leeway to negotiate than actually was the case. He said the Soviets would accept fifteen unmanned detection stations on Soviet soil, which came closer to what had become the American demand of nineteen.

Seeking a further bond with Khrushchev, Bobby said he and his brother agreed in principle with the Soviets on what they regarded as the historic German problem and sympathized with their fear of German revanchists. He said the president shared Soviet opposition to the notion of a nuclear Germany trying to recover its eastern territories. "My brother fought them as enemies," Bobby told Bolshakov. The two sides only disagreed on the remedies, he said.

Bolshakov and Bobby Kennedy continued their meetings as close to a week before the Vienna Summit. Perhaps for that reason it took only a day for Moscow to respond to President Kennedy's request that the two leaders include more tête-à-têtes at the summit, attended only by interpreters.

However, it would not be until two days after the final Bolshakov meeting before the Vienna Summit that Khrushchev would send the clearest message of all regarding how determined he was to negotiate Berlin's future.

For that, he would use the official channel of Ambassador Thompson in Moscow. He wanted no one to mistake his intention to force the issue.

PALACE OF SPORTS, MOSCOW
TUESDAY, MAY 23, 1961

By coincidence, Khrushchev would make clear that he intended to bring the Berlin matter to a head in the same sports field house where he had launched the Berlin Crisis two and a half years earlier before an audience of Polish communists.

Within minutes of Ambassador Thompson's arrival with his wife in Khrushchev's box at a guest performance of the American Ice Capades, the Soviet leader complained that he had seen enough ice shows to last a lifetime. So he escorted the Thompsons to a private room for dinner, explaining that his invitation to them had all along been an excuse to discuss Vienna.

Thompson did not take notes, but he would have no trouble afterward recalling the conversation in a cable to Washington. Against the background sound of American music, skates scraping on ice, and the crowd's applause, Khrushchev delivered an unmistakable message. Without a new agreement on Berlin, he told Thompson, he would take unilateral action by fall or winter to give control of the city to the East Germans and end all Allied occupation rights.

Khrushchev dismissed Kennedy's focus on nuclear disarmament, which he said would be impossible as long as the Berlin problem existed. If the U.S. used force to interfere with Soviet aims in Berlin, he said, then it would be met with force. If the U.S. wanted war, it would get war. Thompson had seen this saber-rattling side of Khrushchev before, but coming just days ahead of the Vienna meeting it was more unsettling.

Khrushchev shrugged, however, saying that he did not expect conflict. "Only a madman would want war and Western leaders were not mad, although Hitler had been," he said. Khrushchev pounded the table and talked of the horrors of war, which he knew so well. He could not believe Kennedy would bring on such a catastrophe because of Berlin.

Thompson countered that it was Khrushchev, not Kennedy, who was creating the danger by threatening to alter the Berlin situation.

Though that might be true, Khrushchev said, if hostilities were to break out, it would be the Americans and not the Soviets who would have to cross the frontier of Eastern Germany to defend Berlin and thus begin the war.

Time and again during their dinner, Khrushchev said that it had been sixteen years since the Great War had been won, and that it was time to put an end to Berlin's occupation. Khrushchev reminded Thompson that in his original 1958 Berlin ultimatum he had demanded satisfaction within six months. "Thirty months have now passed," he said, fuming at Thompson's suggestion that matters could be left as they currently stood in Berlin. The U.S. was trying to damage Soviet prestige, and this could not be allowed to continue, Khrushchev said.

Thompson conceded that the U.S. could not stop Khrushchev from signing a peace treaty with East Germany, but the important question was whether the Soviet leader would use that moment to interfere with the U.S. right-of-access to Berlin. While Khrushchev was floating a trial balloon for the Vienna Summit of a tougher approach on Berlin, Thompson as well was testing what was likely to be Kennedy's response.

Thompson also said U.S. prestige everywhere in the world was at stake in its commitments to Berliners. Moreover, Washington feared that if it gave in to Soviet pressure and sacrificed Berlin, West Germany and Western Europe would be the next to fall. "The psychological effect would be disastrous to our position," he told Khrushchev.

Khrushchev scoffed at Thompson's words, repeating what had become his frequent refrain: Berlin was really of little importance to either America or the Soviet Union, so why should they get so worked up about changing the city's status?

If Berlin were of such little significance, retorted Thompson, he doubted that Khrushchev would take such an enormous risk to gain the upper hand in the city.

Khrushchev then put forward the proposal that he planned to present in Vienna: Nothing would prevent the U.S. from continuing to have troops in the "free city" of West Berlin. All that would change was that Washington in the future would have to negotiate those rights with East Germany, he said.

Thompson probed, asking what elements of the problem troubled Khrushchev most, suggesting it might be the refugee problem. Khrushchev brushed aside that notion and said simply, "Berlin is a festering sore which has to be eliminated."

Khrushchev told Thompson that German reunification was impossible and that in fact no one really wanted it, including de Gaulle, Macmillan, and Adenauer. He said de Gaulle had told him not only that Germany should remain divided, but that it would be even better if it were divided into three parts.

The soft-spoken Thompson saw no option but to return Khrushchev's threat or be misinterpreted as giving him the green light on Berlin. "Well, if you use force," said Thompson, "if you want to cut off our access and connections by force, then we will use force against force."

Khrushchev responded calmly and with a smile. Thompson had misunderstood him, he said. The mercurial Soviet said he didn't plan to use force. He would simply sign the treaty and put an end to the rights the United States had won as "the conditions of capitulation."

Thompson's later cable to Washington on his ice rink face-off reflected little of the importance of what he had just heard. For Khrushchev, it had been a dress rehearsal for what would follow. Thompson, however, played down Khrushchev's bluster. He wrote that the Soviet leader was outlining in detail for the first time how a permanent division of the city might take place without violating American rights. Thompson repeated his conviction that Khrushchev would not force the Berlin issue until after his October Party Congress. In Vienna, Thompson reckoned, Khrushchev would "slide over the Berlin problem in a sweetness-and-light atmosphere."

Thompson nevertheless suggested that Kennedy in Vienna offer Khrushchev a Berlin formula that would enable both sides to save face, as the problem would likely come to a head later in the year. Otherwise, he wrote, "war would hang in the balance."

On the same day, Kennedy was getting a different reading from Berlin. The head of the U.S. Mission there, diplomat E. Allan Lightner Jr., said Moscow could "live with Berlin status quo for some time," and that Khrushchev had no timetable for action. Thus, argued Lightner, Kennedy could deter Khrushchev in Vienna by sending a sharp message that the U.S. was determined to defend the city's freedom, and that "the Soviets should keep their hands off Berlin."

Lightner wanted to ensure that Kennedy knew the consequences of showing weakness in Vienna. "Any indication the President is willing to discuss interim solutions, compromises, or a *modus vivendi*," he said, "would reduce the impact of warning Khrushchev of the dire consequences of his miscalculating our resolve."

WASHINGTON, D.C.
THURSDAY, MAY 25, 1961

Like an author seeing the first unsatisfying drafts of his presidency, Kennedy opted to deliver a second State of the Union speech on May 25—"a Special Address to the Nation on Urgent National Needs"—just twelve weeks after the first. It reflected his recognition that before Vienna and after the Bay of Pigs, he needed to set the stage by sending Khrushchev an unmistakable message of resolve.

Bobby Kennedy had used one of his Bolshakov meetings to forewarn Khrushchev that although the president's rhetoric in the speech would be harsh, this didn't lessen his brother's desire to cooperate. However, the Bolshakov channel was not a sufficient means to convey a message of strength that was intended as much for a domestic audience as for Khrushchev.

Standing before a joint session of Congress and a national television audience, Kennedy explained that American presidents had on occasion during "extraordinary times" provided a second State of the Union during a single year. These were such times, he said. As the United States was responsible for freedom's cause in the world, he declared that he was going to unveil "a freedom doctrine."

The president's forty-eight-minute midday speech was interrupted by applause seventeen times. He stressed the need to maintain a healthy American economy, and he celebrated the end of the recession and beginning of recovery. He spoke of the world's southern hemisphere as the "lands of the rising peoples"—Asia, Latin America, Africa, and the Mideast—where the adversaries of freedom had to be countered on "the world's great battleground."

Kennedy called for a defense spending increase of some $700 million to expand and modernize the military, to overtake the Soviets in the arms race, and to reorganize civil defense with a threefold increase in money for fallout shelters. He wanted to enlist 15,000 more Marines and put a greater focus on fighting guerrilla wars in the Third World by expanding the supply of howitzers, helicopters, armored personnel carriers, and battle-ready reserve units. Most important, he declared that the United States by the end of the decade would put a man on the moon and return him to Earth. It was a race he was determined to win against the Soviets, who had put the first satellite and man into space.

With the Vienna Summit just nine days off, his message to the American people was that the world was growing more dangerous by the hour, that America had a global responsibility as freedom's champion, and that it thus must accept the sacrifices required. He set the bar low for what could be achieved with so difficult an adversary, saving just one paragraph for discussion of the Vienna meeting.

"No formal agenda is planned and no negotiations will be undertaken," he said.

MOSCOW
FRIDAY, MAY 26, 1961

Directly responding to what he perceived as Kennedy's shot across his bow, Khrushchev called together his most critical constituency, the Communist Party's ruling Presidium. As usual, his decision to bring the stenographer to the meeting was a sign to its attendees that he intended to say something significant.

He told his Presidium colleagues that Kennedy was "a son of a bitch." Despite that, he attached great significance to the Vienna Summit because he would use it to bring to a head what he referred to as "the German question." He outlined the solution that he would propose, using much the same description that he had employed with Ambassador Thompson.

Could the steps he was proposing to change Berlin's status prompt nuclear war? he asked his fellow Soviet leaders. Yes, he answered, and then he outlined why he considered such a conflict to be 95 percent unlikely.

Only Anastas Mikoyan among his party chieftains dared differ with the Soviet leader. He argued that Khrushchev underestimated the American willingness and ability to engage in conventional war over Berlin. Shifting from previous attacks that focused more on West Germany and Adenauer as the threat, Khrushchev told those gathered that the United States was the most dangerous of all countries to the Soviets. In his love-hate relationship with America, he had turned the needle back to loathing in preparation for the Vienna Summit, a clear indication to his leadership of what outcome he expected.

Khrushchev repeated his increasingly obsessive view that although he was meeting with Kennedy, it was the Pentagon and the CIA that ran the United States, something he said that he had already experienced during his dealings with Eisenhower. He said it was for this reason one could not trust that American leaders could make decisions based on logical principles. "That's why certain forces could emerge and find a pretext to go to war against us," he said.

Khrushchev told his comrades that he was prepared to risk war and that he also knew how best to avoid it. He said America's European allies and world public opinion would restrain Kennedy from responding with nuclear weapons to any change in Berlin's status. He said de Gaulle and Macmillan would never support an American lurch toward war because they understood that the Soviets' primary nuclear targets, given the range of Moscow's missiles, would be in Europe.

"They are intelligent people, and they understand this," he said.

Khrushchev then laid out exactly how the Berlin situation would unfold after the six-month ultimatum he would issue in Vienna. He would sign a peace treaty unilaterally with the East German government, and then he would turn over to it all the access routes to West Berlin. "We do not encroach on West Berlin, we do not declare a blockade," he said, thus providing no pretext for military action. "We show that we are ready to permit air traffic but on the condition that Western planes land at airports in the GDR [not West Berlin]. We do not demand a withdrawal of troops. However, we consider them illegal, though we won't use any strong-arm methods for their removal. We will not cut off delivery of foodstuffs and will not sever any other lifelines. We will adhere to a policy of noninfringement and noninvolvement in the affairs of West Berlin. Therefore, I don't believe that because the state of war and the occupational regime are coming to an end it would unleash a war."

Mikoyan was alone in warning Khrushchev that the probability of war was higher than the Soviet leader estimated. Out of respect for Khrushchev, however, he put it at only a slightly greater 10 percent rather than Khrushchev's 5 percent. "In my opinion, they could initiate military action without atomic weapons," he said.

Khrushchev shot back that Kennedy so feared war that he would not react militarily. He told the Presidium they perhaps would have to compromise in Laos, Cuba, or the Congo, where the conventional balance was less clear, but around Berlin the Kremlin's superiority was unquestionable.

To ensure this became even more so, Khrushchev ordered Defense Secretary Rodion Malinovsky, Soviet Army Chief of Staff Matvei Zakharov, and Warsaw Pact Commander Andrei Grechko—who sat before him—"to thoroughly examine the correlation of forces in Germany and to see what is needed." He was willing to spend the rubles required, he told them. Their first move had to be increasing artillery and basic weapons, and then they had to be ready to reposition more weaponry if the Soviet Union was provoked further. He wanted a report from his commanders in two weeks' time about how they would plan to execute a Berlin operation, and he expected within six months to be able to match his tough words in Vienna with an improved military capability.

Mikoyan countered that Khrushchev was backing Kennedy into a dangerous position where he would have no option but to respond militarily. Mikoyan suggested that Khrushchev continue to allow air traffic to arrive in West Berlin, which might make his Berlin solution more palatable to Kennedy.

Khrushchev disagreed. He reminded his comrades that East Germany was imploding. Thousands of professionals were fleeing the country each week. A failure to take firm action to stop this would not only make Ulbricht anxious but raise doubts among its Warsaw Pact allies, who would "sense in this action our inconsistency and uncertainty."

Not only would Khrushchev be willing to shut down the air corridor, he said, looking toward Mikoyan, but he would also shoot down any Allied plane that tried to land in West Berlin. "Our position is very strong, but we will have, of course, to really intimidate them now. For example, if there is any flying around, we will have to bring aircraft down. Could they respond with provocative acts? They could. . . . If we want to carry out our policy, and if we want it to be acknowledged, respected and feared, it is necessary to be firm."

Khrushchev ended his war council with a discussion of whether he should exchange gifts with Kennedy in Vienna, according to the usual protocol.

Foreign Ministry officials suggested he give President Kennedy twelve cans of the finest black caviar and phonographic records of Soviet and Russian music. Among other gifts, his aides had a silver coffee service in mind for Mrs. Kennedy. They wanted Khrushchev's approval.

"One can exchange presents even before a war," Khrushchev responded.

HYANNIS PORT, MASSACHUSETTS
SATURDAY, MAY 27, 1961

Kennedy lifted off in a rainstorm aboard Air Force One from Andrews Air Force Base, bound for Hyannis Port. In just three days he would land in Paris and meet de Gaulle, and in just one week's time he would be in Vienna with Khrushchev. His father had decorated the president's sleeping quarters with pictures of voluptuous women—a practical joke from a fellow womanizer just before his son's forty-fourth birthday.

Kennedy was retreating to the family compound to briefly celebrate and bury himself in his briefing books on issues ranging from the nuclear balance to Khrushchev's psychological makeup. What U.S. intelligence services painted was a picture of a man who would try to charm him one moment and bully him the next; a gambler who would test him; a true-believing Marxist who wanted to coexist but compete; a crude and insecure leader of peasant upbringing and cunning who above all was unpredictable.

The president could only hope that Khrushchev's background briefings on U.S. leadership were less revealing. His back pain was as bad as at any time in his administration, made worse by an injury he had suffered during the ceremonial planting of a tree in Canada a few days earlier. Alongside his paperwork, he would pack anesthetic procaine for his back, cortisone for his Addison's disease, and a cocktail of vitamins, enzymes, and amphetamines for flagging energy and other maladies.

He was using crutches, though never in public, limping around like an already injured athlete preparing for a championship match.

10

VIENNA:

LITTLE BOY BLUE MEETS AL CAPONE

So we're stuck in a ridiculous situation. It seems silly for us to be facing an atomic war over a treaty preserving Berlin as the future capital of a reunified Germany when all of us know that Germany will probably never be reunified. But we're committed to that agreement, and so are the Russians, so we can't let them back out of it.

President Kennedy to his aides as he soaked in his bathtub,
June 1, 1961, Paris

The U.S. is unwilling to normalize the situation in the most dangerous spot in the world. The USSR wants to perform an operation on this sore spot—to eliminate this thorn, this ulcer—without prejudicing the interests of any side, but rather to the satisfaction of all peoples of the world.

Premier Khrushchev to President Kennedy, June 4, 1961, Vienna

PARIS
WEDNESDAY, MAY 31, 1961

For all the adoring French crowds, grand Gallic meals, and media hype generated by a thousand correspondents covering his trip, President Kennedy's favorite moments in Paris were spent submerged in a giant, gold-plated bathtub in the "King's Chamber" of a nineteenth-century palace on the Quai d'Orsay.

"God, we ought to have a tub like this in the White House," the president said to his troubleshooter Kenny O'Donnell, as he soaked himself in the deep, steaming waters to relieve his excruciating back pain. O'Donnell reckoned the vessel was about as long and wide as a Ping-Pong table. Aide David Powers suggested that if the president "played his cards right," de Gaulle might give it to him as a souvenir.

So began what the three men would come to refer to as their "tub talks" in the vast suite of rooms of the Palais des Affaires étrangères, where de Gaulle had put up Kennedy for his three-day stay in Paris en route to Vienna. During the breaks in the president's packed schedule, Kennedy would soak and share his latest experiences with his two closest friends in the White House, veterans both of World War II and his political campaigns. By title, O'Donnell was White House appointments secretary, but his long relationship with the Kennedys had begun when he was Bobby's roommate at Harvard. Powers was Kennedy's affable man Friday who kept him amused, on schedule, and well supplied with sexual partners.

Between 500,000 and 1 million people had lined the streets to welcome the world's most famous couple that morning, depending on who was counting the crowd (the French police being more conservative than the White House press office). Considering de Gaulle's frosty relationship with Kennedy's predecessors Eisenhower and Roosevelt, his warm reception for Kennedy was a departure. De Gaulle suspected that all U.S. leaders wanted to undermine French leadership of Europe and supplant it with their own. That said, he was happy to bask in the celebrity of the First Couple, whose images adorned the covers of all the major French magazines. The difference in age also helped, allowing de Gaulle to play his preferred role of the wise, legendary man of history taking this young, promising American under his wing.

At Orly Airport at ten that morning, de Gaulle had welcomed Kennedy on a giant scarlet carpet, flanked by fifty black Citroëns and a mounted honor guard of Republican Guards. All six feet, four inches of Le Général rose from his car in his double-breasted business suit as the band played "The Marseillaise."

"Side by side," reported the *New York Times*, "the two men moved all day through Paris—age beside youth, grandeur beside informality, mysticism beside pragmatism, serenity beside eagerness."

The cheers grew so loud as the two men drove along Boulevard Saint-Michel on the Left Bank of the Seine that de Gaulle persuaded the U.S. president to rise in the rear seat of their open-top limo, eliciting an even greater roar. Despite a chill wind, Kennedy rode bareheaded and with only a light topcoat. He dressed no more warmly that afternoon as rain drenched the two men in their sweep up the Champs-Élysées, an indignity de Gaulle bore without complaint.

Behind all that misleading theater was a U.S. president who was entering the most important week of his presidency as a weary, wounded commander in chief who was inadequately prepared and insufficiently fit for what would face him in Vienna. Khrushchev would be scanning for Kennedy's vulnerabilities after the Bay of Pigs, and there were plenty for the picking.

At home, Kennedy was facing violent racial confrontations that had broken out in the American South as African Americans grew more determined to end two centuries of oppression. The immediate problem revolved around the "Freedom Riders," whose efforts to desegregate interstate transportation had won only tepid support from the Kennedy administration and were opposed by nearly two-thirds of Americans.

Abroad, Kennedy's failure in Cuba, unresolved conflict in Laos, and tensions building around Berlin made his Paris–Vienna trip all the more fraught with risk. Kennedy was making the mental connection to Berlin even while wrestling with racial affairs at home. When Father Theodore Hesburgh, a member of his Civil Rights Commission, questioned the president's reluctance to take bolder steps to desegregate the United States, Kennedy said, "Look, Father, I may have to send the Alabama National Guard to Berlin tomorrow, and I don't want to do it in the middle of a revolution at home."

It seemed just another of his presidency's early misfortunes that Kennedy had seriously reinjured his back muscles while planting a ceremonial tree in Ottawa, and the pain had grown worse on the long flight to Europe. It had been the first time since his spinal fusion surgery in 1954 that he was hobbling around on crutches. To protect his image, he refused to use the props in public, but that only aroused more pain when he was in France, by putting even greater pressure on his back.

Kennedy's personal physician, Janet Travell, who accompanied him to Paris, was concerned about his heightened suffering and the impact his treatments might have on everything from mood to endurance during the trip. The president had already been taking five baths or hot showers a day to ease his pain. Though Americans didn't know it, the real purpose of his famous Oval Office rocking chair was that it helped relieve the throbbing of his lower back, into which doctors had been shooting procaine, a potent cousin of novocaine, for nearly a decade. Travell was also treating him for chronic adrenal ailments, high fevers, elevated cholesterol levels, sleeplessness, and stomach, colon, and prostate problems.

Years later, Travell would recall that Paris was the beginning of "a very hard period." Travell would give Kennedy two to three shots a day in Paris. White House doctor Admiral George Burkley was worried because the procaine soothed the president through only a temporary numbness that was followed by even greater soreness, requiring ever larger doses and ever stronger narcotics. Burkley had prescribed more exercise and physical therapy, but Kennedy preferred the quicker fix of the drugs.

Travell kept an ongoing "Medicine Administration Record" to track the cocktail of pills and shots she provided the president: penicillin for urinary infections and abscesses, Tuinal to help him sleep, Transentine to control diarrhea and weight loss, and assorted other remedies, including testosterone and phenobarbital. What she couldn't log were the more unconventional administrations of a more unconventional medic who had traveled more secretly to Paris and Vienna.

Known as "Dr. Feelgood" to his celebrity patients, who included Tennessee Williams and Truman Capote, Dr. Max Jacobson provided injections that contained hormones, animal organ cells, steroids, vitamins, enzymes, and—most important—amphetamines to combat fatigue and depression.

Kennedy was so pleased with Jacobson's remedies that he had recommended them as well for Jackie after the difficult November delivery of their son John-John—and again to boost her stamina before the Paris trip. On the night of their grand state dinner with de Gaulle at Versailles, Dr. Feelgood administered Kennedy his customary shot. The diminutive, red-cheeked, dark-haired doctor then wandered through the First Couple's suite of rooms to Jackie's bedroom, where she was choosing an elegant French gown designed by Givenchy over a dress designed by the American Oleg Cassini, to drive home her connection to the host country.

She cleared the room when Dr. Jacobson arrived, and he put a needle in her behind and injected a fluid that would help her glow incandescently through a six-course dinner in the Hall of Mirrors. Truman Capote would later praise Jacobson's treatments: "You feel like Superman. You're flying. Ideas come at the speed of light. You go 722 hours straight without so much as a coffee break."

However, the potential national security consequences of these concoctions for the commander in chief were considerable coming just before his crucial meeting with the Soviet leader. Besides the addictive nature of what Kennedy was consuming, the potential side effects included hyperactivity, hypertension, impaired judgment, and nervousness. Between doses, his mood could swing wildly from overconfidence to bouts of depression.*

---

*Dr. Jacobson would lose his medical license in 1975. Another patient of his, Kennedy friend Mark Shaw, died at the young age of forty-seven in 1969 as a result of "acute and chronic intravenous amphetamine poisoning."

At Bobby's urging, the president would later provide Jacobson's concoctions to the Food and Drug Administration for analysis. Kennedy was untroubled when the FDA said Dr. Feelgood was shooting him up with steroids and amphetamines. "I don't care if it's horse piss," Kennedy said. "It works."

In strategizing for Paris, Kennedy had three primary purposes, and they all had to do with Vienna and its impact on Berlin. First, he wanted de Gaulle's advice about how best to manage Khrushchev in Vienna. Second, he wanted to know how the French leader would recommend that the Allies wrestle with the next Berlin crisis, which he was beginning to believe was likely. Finally, Kennedy wanted to use the Paris trip to burnish his public image and thus strengthen his hand for Vienna.

When Kennedy briefed de Gaulle on Khrushchev's threats regarding Berlin as delivered to Thompson at the Ice Capades, de Gaulle dismissed them with a wave of the hand. "Mr. Khrushchev," he declared dismissively, "has been saying and repeating that his prestige is engaged in the Berlin question and that he must have a solution within six months, and then again in six months and then still again in another six months." The Frenchman shrugged. "If he had wanted a war over Berlin, he would have acted already."

De Gaulle told Kennedy that he considered Berlin primarily a psychological question: "It is annoying to both sides that Berlin should be located where it is; however, it is there," he said.

The Kennedy–de Gaulle meeting was already off to a better start than previous U.S. presidential sessions with the French leader. Eisenhower had warned Kennedy that de Gaulle endangered the entire Atlantic alliance with his nationalist disdain for the U.S. and NATO. Franklin Roosevelt had compared de Gaulle's vicious temper to that of Joan of Arc. "The older I get," Eisenhower told Kennedy, "the more disgusted I am with them—not the French people but their governments."

In contrast to his predecessors, Kennedy had two advantages in dealing with the French leader: his willingness to play the role of de Gaulle's junior and the impact of his wife's Sorbonne education and her French-language fluency on the vain general. After she chatted amicably with de Gaulle over lunch about the Bourbons and Louis XVI, de Gaulle turned to Kennedy and enthused, "Your wife knows more French history than most French women."

Safely back in his golden tub, Kennedy told his friends, "De Gaulle and I are hitting it off all right, probably because I have such a charming wife."

KIEVSKY STATION, MOSCOW
SATURDAY, MAY 27, 1961

While Kennedy endured the Paris whirlwind, Khrushchev was making the 1,200-mile trip from Moscow to Vienna in a more leisurely fashion aboard a specially equipped six-car train. He would make barnstorming stops in Kiev, Prague, and Bratislava—and would be cheered at rural stations all along the train's path.

Communist Party cells had gathered a crowd of thousands to see him off at Moscow's Kievsky Station, where Khrushchev took Ambassador Thompson aside for a last exchange before departure. In a cable that would report on their brief chat, Thompson hit a strained note of optimism. "I believe Khrushchev will wish the meeting with the president to be a pleasant one," he wrote, "and that he will desire if possible to make some proposal or take some position on some problems which have the effect of improving the atmosphere and relations. I find it extremely difficult, however, to imagine what this could be."

As Khrushchev boarded the train, a young girl rushed forward to present him a huge bouquet of red roses. Ever impulsive, Khrushchev summoned the U.S. ambassador's wife, Jane, and, with the crowd cheering, presented her the flowers.

Without confidence, Thompson told the press gathered there, "I hope everything will go well." Privately, Thompson had begun to worry that Kennedy was heading for an ambush on Berlin issues. The latest clue was a stridently worded editorial in the official government newspaper *Izvestia* that had declared on the day of Khrushchev's departure that the Soviet

Union could not wait any longer for Western agreement before acting on Berlin.

Khrushchev swelled with pride as he waved to enthusiastic crowds gathered alongside the tracks of the countless stations the train passed, many of them decorated with welcoming flags, posters, and streamers. Khrushchev was particularly taken by a crimson banner that covered the entire front of the provincial station at Mukachevo in the Ukrainian region near his birthplace. It had been inscribed in Ukrainian: MAY YOU LIVE WELL, DEAR NIKITA SERGEYEVICH!

In Kiev, thousands cheered him as he toured the city and laid a wreath on the grave of its beloved poet Taras Shevchenko. At Čierna, the first stop inside Czechoslovakia, the country's party leader Antonín Novotný had seen to it that his giant portrait hung beside that of Khrushchev at every turn. A band played both national anthems to the crash of cymbals and blare of trumpets. Uniformed Young Pioneers, the party's youth organization, filled Khrushchev's arms with flowers while pretty girls with embroidered blouses offered the traditional welcome gift of bread and salt.

His hosts in Bratislava carefully choreographed his final stop before Vienna. Public buildings were draped in banners: GLORY TO KHRUSHCHEV— UNSHAKABLE CHAMPION OF PEACE. He and Novotný spoke to the crowds about finding a "final solution" to the Berlin problem, oblivious to whatever parallels there might be to Hitler's "final solution" for the Jews. Locals celebrated the eve of the Vienna meetings with a fireworks display over the medieval castle in the ancient town of Trenčín, where Soviet troops in April 1945 had captured the Gestapo headquarters.

In a final, precautionary touch, Khrushchev delayed his train's departure to Vienna from Bratislava until two p.m., four hours later than had been planned. Having received reports of the throngs that celebrated Kennedy in Paris, Khrushchev's people concluded they could only ensure a respectable reception in Vienna if communist worker unions could assemble their workers near the end of the workday.

PARIS
WEDNESDAY, MAY 31, 1961

Acting as a self-appointed tutor, de Gaulle recounted for Kennedy how he managed Khrushchev during his most irascible moments. He warned Kennedy that it was inevitable Khrushchev would threaten war at some point in their Vienna talks.

De Gaulle recalled how he had told the Soviet leader: You pretend that you seek détente. If such is the case, proceed with détente. If you want peace, start with general disarmament negotiations. Under the circumstances, the entire world situation may change little by little and then we will solve the question of Berlin and the entire Germany question. However, if you insist on raising the question of Berlin within the context of the Cold War, then no solution is possible. What do you want? Do you want war?

Khrushchev had then replied to de Gaulle that he did not want war.

In that case, the Frenchman had told him, do nothing that can bring it about.

Kennedy doubted dealing with Khrushchev would be that easy. Kennedy told the French leader, for example, that he knew de Gaulle wanted his own nuclear weapons capability because he doubted that the U.S. ever would risk New York for Paris—let alone for Berlin—in a nuclear exchange with Moscow. If the general himself so deeply doubted American resolve, why would Khrushchev feel otherwise? Kennedy wondered.

De Gaulle would not be drawn. This was a moment for a clear American message of resolve to Khrushchev, irrespective of whether the French leader believed it himself. "It is important to show that we do not intend to let this situation change," de Gaulle said. "*Any* retreat from Berlin, *any* change of status, *any* withdrawal of troops, *any* new obstacles to transportation and communication, would mean defeat. It would result in an almost complete loss of Germany, and in very serious losses within France, Italy and elsewhere." Beyond that, de Gaulle told Kennedy, "If [Khrushchev] wants war, we must make clear to him he will have it." The French leader was confident that if Kennedy refused to retreat before Soviet dictates, Khrushchev would never risk a military confrontation.

What worried de Gaulle more was the Soviet and East German approach of slowly eroding the Western position in Berlin so that "we would have lost without seeming to have lost but in a way which would be understood by the entire world. In particular, the population of Berlin is not made up exclusively of heroes. In the face of something which they would interpret as our weakness, they might begin to leave Berlin and make it into an empty shell to be picked up by the East."

It struck Kennedy that de Gaulle was free to speak so bravely about Berlin because France did not have to shoulder America's security burden there. De Gaulle was being so vague about possible remedies that Kennedy tried to provoke a more detailed response. Kennedy said he was a practical man who wanted de Gaulle to be specific about the point at which the French leader would go to war over Berlin.

De Gaulle said he wouldn't go to war over either of the issues currently in question: if the Soviets unilaterally signed a peace treaty with East Germany or changed four-power procedures in the city to give East Germans greater sovereignty over East Berlin—for example, by handing them the right to stamp travel documents at border crossings. "This is in itself no reason for a military retaliation on our part," he said.

So Kennedy pressed the great Frenchman further: "In what way, therefore, at what moment, shall we bring pressure to bear?" The president complained that the Soviets and East Germans had a multitude of ways to complicate the Berlin situation, perhaps even causing West Berlin's ruin, but using methods that would not trigger a Western response. "How do we answer that?" he wondered.

De Gaulle said the West should only respond militarily if the Soviets or East Germans acted militarily. "If either [Khrushchev] or his lackeys use force to cut our communications with Berlin, then we must use force," he said.

Kennedy agreed, but he did not believe as de Gaulle did that any weakening of the Western position in Berlin would be a disaster. He said it would be a blow "which would not be mortal but would be serious" to Western Germany and all of Europe.

Kennedy sought de Gaulle's advice on how he in Vienna could best convince Khrushchev of Western firmness, given that the Soviet leader so doubted U.S. resolve following the Bay of Pigs. He wanted to know what the French leader thought of U.S. and Allied contingency plans to respond to any new Berlin blockade with a demonstration of approximate company strength, and, if that failed, then of brigade strength.

Given Soviet conventional superiority around Berlin, de Gaulle told Kennedy he could deter the Soviets only with a willingness to use nuclear weapons, which was precisely what the president wanted to avoid.

"What we must make clear is that if there is any fighting around Berlin, this means general war," de Gaulle said.

By the time of their grand Élysée Palace banquet that evening, Jack and Jackie, as the French press called them, had taken the country by storm. They sat down that evening with three hundred other guests in the mirrored, tapestried dining hall around an immense table covered by a single table-cloth of white organza and gold embroidery, giving rise to the Kennedys' wonder over how one could create such an object. The Republican Guard symphony orchestra played everything from Gershwin to Ravel, each number embodying some deeper U.S.–French meaning.

In his comments, Kennedy joked about how much French influence he had in his life. "I sleep in a French bed. In the morning my breakfast is served by a French chef, I go to my office, and the bad news of the day is brought to me by my press secretary Pierre Salinger, not in his native [French] language, and I am married to a daughter of France."

The view through long French windows was to a rainy evening outside where palace lawns and grand fountains turned emerald green in spotlights. The after-dinner reception expanded to a thousand guests, whom the *Washington Post* report portrayed as "indescribably elegant." The French men were peacocking with bright sashes across shirtfronts, giant stars and crosses pinned to their tailcoats, and rows of miniature medals pinned on lapels. The women wore long gloves and jewels, and a few dowagers were richly tiaraed.

Yet the star that evening was Jackie, wearing a Directoire-styled gown of pale pink and white straw lace. Alexandre, hairdresser to the Parisian elite, whispered to the *New York Times* that he had cut an inch from the First Lady's hair and trimmed her bangs for that evening, creating the look of "a Gothic Madonna." For the next evening's dinner at Versailles, Alexandre promised something more evocative of Louis XIV, with diamond flame clips sticking through her hair to "give her a fairy-like air."

Kennedy's mother, Rose, "slim as the proverbial wand," wore a floor-length Balenciaga gown of white silk appliquéd with pink flowers that had real diamonds in their centers. Paris publications gushed at how refreshingly European all the Kennedys were.

During their "tub talk" the following day, Kennedy reflected with his friends on de Gaulle's observation that the West could never keep West Berlin free without a willingness to use the nuclear bomb.

"So we're stuck in a ridiculous situation," Kennedy said through the steam. "It seems silly for us to be facing an atomic war over a treaty preserving Berlin as the future capital of a reunified Germany when all of us know that Germany will probably never be reunified. But we're committed to that agreement, and so are the Russians, so we can't let them back out of it."

VIENNA
SATURDAY, JUNE 3, 1961

Kennedy's advance team had choreographed the president's arrival in Vienna in a manner calculated to unsettle Khrushchev, who had expressed jealousy to his team about Kennedy's ever-rising global popularity. The more the Soviets opposed a grand Kennedy airport arrival and motorcade, the more O'Donnell had insisted upon it. After each Soviet objection, he had added more limousines and flags.

Vienna basked in the competition for its attention. Never had a high-level meeting between heads of state attracted so much international media attention. At least 1,500 reporters with all their equipment and supporting staff would be on hand to cover the two men and their meetings.

Photographers furiously snapped shots of the two men's historic first encounter at 12:45 p.m. on the red-carpeted steps of the U.S. ambassador's residence, where they posed under the canopy of the gray stucco building with its brown stone columns. A small, circular graveled courtyard stood behind them, blocked from public view by thick firs and weeping willows heavy with the day's rain.

Just minutes earlier, the Soviet premier had swung his squat legs out of his black Soviet limousine while Kennedy had bounded lightly down the steps to retrieve him. Kennedy showed no sign of his chronic pain, which was dulled by shots, pills, and a tightly strung corset. After so much anticipation, the initial Kennedy–Khrushchev encounter was unavoidably awkward.

In the practiced tone of the political campaign trail, Kennedy issued a reflexive greeting in his Boston bray, "How are you? I'm glad to see you."

"The pleasure is mutual," said Khrushchev through his interpreter.

The bald top of the communist world leader's head reached only to Kennedy's nose. O'Donnell would later recall how sorry he was that he had not brought a movie camera to record the moment. It struck him that Kennedy was studying "the stubby little Soviet leader" a little too obviously.

Kennedy stood back, one hand deep in his jacket pocket, and slowly looked Khrushchev up and down with unconcealed curiosity. Even as photographers shouted requests for more posed handshakes, Kennedy continued ogling Khrushchev as if he were a game hunter stumbling upon a rare beast after years of tracking.

Khrushchev muttered something to Foreign Minister Gromyko and then moved inside.

In chronicling the first Kennedy–Khrushchev encounter, *New York Times* reporter Russell Baker wondered how much the greetings had differed in Vienna 146 years earlier as Metternich, Talleyrand, and other European leaders gathered to build a century of European stability at their Congress of Vienna. "Here in the home of the waltz, schmaltz, hot dogs and Habsburgs, the two most powerful met today in a music room," he wrote.

The *Wall Street Journal* introduced the two men as boxers coming into a heavyweight ring: "The American President is a younger man by a generation, highly educated, while Khrushchev was brought up in the school of hard knocks, his main political ambitions ahead of him rather than behind him. The confrontation of these two men, as powerful in their time as Napoleon and Alexander I were when they met on a raft in the river Niemen to redraw the map of Europe in 1807, against the background of old Vienna, once a power center in its own right, now the capital of a small state that only desires to be left alone in peace, clearly possesses the element of drama."

The *Journal* opined that "the least worst" outcome would be if Kennedy simply stuck to his commitment that he had come only to acquaint himself with Khrushchev and would not negotiate with him over Berlin or anything else.

European newspapers rang with the historic consequence of it all. The influential Swiss newspaper *Neue Zürcher Zeitung* regretted that, against its advice, Kennedy had come unprepared to meet with an unrepentant Kremlin boss. The German intellectual paper *Die Zeit* reported from Vienna, "The question that the West faces is the same as the one Demosthenes described in his speech to the Athenians against Philip of Macedonia: When another man stands before you with a weapon in his hand and at the head of a great army claiming to come in peace but really intent on war, what can you do but assume a defensive position?"

Six years earlier, the Austrians had signed their state treaty with the four wartime Allies, which allowed them to escape the fate of neighboring Warsaw Pact states and establish a free, sovereign, democratic, and neutral country. So the Viennese were particularly taken with their newly found stage as neutral ground for a superpower powwow. Herbert von Karajan was conducting Wagner at the Staatsoper, and Viennese cafés and streets overflowed with locals out for a gossip and in hopes of a glimpse of their visitors.

Viennese teenager Monika Sommer scribbled in her diary that she and her friends regarded Kennedy as a "pop idol." She had tacked his photograph on her bedroom wall, sorry that her country didn't provide such role models. Teenager Veronika Seyr was more unsettled by all the hoopla surrounding the summit. Having witnessed Soviet brutality in Budapest during the crackdown just five years earlier, the increased police presence all around Vienna frightened her. Perched in a cherry tree, she watched Soviet fighter planes and helicopters circle the city as Khrushchev arrived. Terrified by the prospect of a new invasion, she fell to the ground and lay on her back for some time "like a beetle," still watching the helicopters overhead.

Anticipating two long days of exchanges, Kennedy opened his discussions with Khrushchev with some small talk about their first meeting at the Senate Foreign Relations Committee in 1959 during the Soviet leader's first visit to the United States.

In an initial thrust of one-upmanship that would come to characterize their talks, Khrushchev said he remembered the meeting as well, though he had "no opportunity to say much except hello and good-bye" to Kennedy because the then senator had arrived so late. The Soviet leader reminded Kennedy that he had remarked at the time, showing his foresight, that he had heard Kennedy was a young and promising politician.

Kennedy reminded Khrushchev that he also had said at the time that Kennedy looked too young to be a senator.

The Soviet leader questioned Kennedy's memory. Normally, Khrushchev said, he "did not say such things because young people want to look older and older people like to look younger." Khrushchev said he also had looked younger than his age before graying prematurely at age twenty-two.

Khrushchev laughed that he would "be happy to share his years with the President or change places with him."

From that opening exchange, Khrushchev was setting the tone and pace of their conversations by answering Kennedy's short statements and questions with his longer interventions. To gain an early upper hand, the U.S. side had wanted the first day's talks to be at the U.S. ambassador's residence, and the Soviets had accepted that the two men would move to Soviet territory on Day Two. However, it was Khrushchev who was making himself most at home.

In an attempt to reassert some control, Kennedy outlined his hopes for their talks. He said he wanted their two powerful countries—though "allied with other countries, having different political and social systems, and competing with each other in different parts of the world"—to find ways to avoid situations that could lead to conflict.

Khrushchev responded by detailing what he called his long-standing efforts "to develop friendly relations with the United States and its allies." At the same time, he said, "the Soviet Union did not wish to reach agreement with the U.S. at the expense of other peoples because such agreement would not mean peace."

The two men had agreed to leave any discussion of Berlin to their second day, so their initial talks focused on the general relationship and disarmament issues.

Khrushchev said his greatest concern was that the U.S. was trying to leverage its economic superiority over the Soviets in a way that could prompt conflict, a veiled reference to the Soviet world's growing dependence on Western trade and credits. He said he would make the Soviet Union richer than the U.S. over time, not by acting as a predator, but by better tapping its own resources.

Khrushchev took little note of Kennedy's brief comment on how impressed he had been by improving Soviet economic growth rates before the Soviet leader took charge of the conversation again. He complained that John Foster Dulles, Eisenhower's secretary of state from 1953 to 1959 and a Soviet opponent, had tried to liquidate communism. He said Dulles, whose name he spat out like a curse, resisted "both *de facto* and *de jure*" the recognition that both systems could continue to exist beside each other. Khrushchev told Kennedy that during their talks he "would not try to convince the President about the advantages of Communism, just as the President should not waste his time [trying] to convert him to capitalism."

In pre-summit conversations, Ambassador Thompson had warned Kennedy to avoid ideological debate with Khrushchev, a course that would consume valuable time and one that he believed Kennedy could not win against a lifelong communist with years of experience in dialectical debate. However, Kennedy came to Vienna much too convinced of his own powers of persuasion to resist the temptation.

Khrushchev's remarks raised "a very important problem," said Kennedy. The president called it a matter of "very serious concern to us" that Khrushchev believed it was acceptable to try to eliminate free systems in countries associated with the United States but objected to any efforts by the West to roll back communism in the Soviet sphere of influence.

Employing his calmest voice, Khrushchev told Kennedy this was "an incorrect interpretation of Soviet policy." The Soviet Union was not imposing its system on others but merely riding the wave of historic change. With that, Khrushchev launched into a history lecture on everything from feudalism to the French Revolution. He said the Soviet system would triumph on its merits, although he added that he was certain Kennedy thought just the opposite. "In any event, this is not a matter for argument, much less for war," he said.

Continuing to disregard his experts' advice, Kennedy decided again to lock swords with the Soviet leader on ideology. The president would later explain that he believed he had to successfully engage Khrushchev in ideological debate if he was to be taken seriously on other issues. "Our position is that people should have free choice," Kennedy told Khrushchev. What concerned the president was that minority governments that did not express the will of the people—governed by friends of Moscow—were seizing control in places of interest to the U.S. "The USSR believes that is a historical inevitability," Kennedy said, while the U.S. did not. Kennedy worried that such situations could bring the USSR and the U.S. into military conflict.

Khrushchev wondered whether Kennedy "wanted to build a dam preventing the development of the human mind and conscience." If so, Khrushchev said, it "is not in man's power. The Spanish Inquisition burned people who disagreed with it, but ideas did not burn, and eventually triumphed. Thus if we start struggling against ideas, conflicts and clashes between the two countries will be inevitable."

The Soviet leader was savoring the exchange. In an awkward effort to find a point of agreement, Kennedy argued that communism could remain lodged where it was now, namely places like Poland and Czechoslovakia, but could not be accepted anywhere the Soviets were not already installed. American officials who would read the transcripts later would be shocked that Kennedy was going further than any president before him in his expressed willingness to accept the existing division of Europe into spheres of influence. Kennedy seemed to be suggesting that he would mortgage the future of those seeking freedom in Warsaw Pact countries if the Kremlin would abandon hope of expanding communism elsewhere.

Khrushchev challenged Kennedy's apparent belief that the Soviet Union was responsible for all communist development in the world. If Kennedy was saying that he would oppose the advance of communist ideas anywhere they did not currently exist, Khrushchev argued, then indeed "conflicts will be inevitable."

Initiating yet another tutorial for his wayward student, Khrushchev reminded Kennedy that it was not, after all, Russians who had originated communist ideas but rather the German-born Karl Marx and Friedrich Engels. He joked that even if he should renounce communism—something he made clear to Kennedy that he had no intention of doing—its concepts would continue to develop. He asked Kennedy to agree that it was "essential for the peaceful development of the world" that the president recognize communism and capitalism as being the world's two primary ideologies. Naturally, Khrushchev said, either side would be happy if its ideology spread.

If the summit was going to be decided by which side controlled more of the conversation, Khrushchev had taken a commanding early lead. Nothing in Kennedy's past had prepared him for Khrushchev's immovable force. Yet Thompson, who watched with other senior U.S. officials from the sidelines, knew from previous experience that the Soviet leader was just warming up.

"Ideas should not be borne on bayonets or on missile warheads, bayonets now being obsolete," Khrushchev said. In a war of ideas, he said, Soviet policy would triumph without violent means.

But wasn't it true, Kennedy said, that "Mao Tse-tung had said that power was at the end of a rifle"? Kennedy had been briefed on growing Sino–Soviet disagreements, and he was probing.

"I don't believe Mao could have said that," Khrushchev lied, having experienced himself Mao's lust for war with the West. He said Mao "was a Marxist, and Marxists are always against war."

Trying to get back to his agenda of reducing tensions and securing peace, Kennedy said what he wanted to avoid was a miscalculation between the U.S. and the Soviet Union that would cause both countries to "lose for a long time to come," a reference to the long radiation afterlife following a nuclear exchange.

"Miscalculation?"

Khrushchev spat out the word like a terrible taste.

"'Miscalculation'! 'Miscalculation'! 'Miscalculation'! All I ever hear from your people and your news correspondents and your friends in Europe and every place else is that damned word 'miscalculation.'"

The word was vague, Khrushchev sputtered. What was the meaning of this word, "miscalculation"? He kept repeating the word for effect. Did the president want him "to sit like a schoolboy with hands on top of the desk"? he asked. Khrushchev protested that he could *not* guarantee communist ideas would stop at Soviet borders. Yet, he said, "we will not start a war by mistake.... You ought to take that word 'miscalculation' and bury it in cold storage and never use it again."

A stunned Kennedy sat back and absorbed the storm.

Kennedy tried to explain what he had meant by using the word. Referring to World War II, he said, "Western Europe had suffered because of its failure to foresee with precision what other countries would do." The U.S. had failed to foresee Chinese actions recently in Korea. What he wanted from their meeting was "to introduce precision in judgments of the two sides and to obtain a clearer understanding of where we are going."

Before their lunch break, Khrushchev would have the last word.

He believed the purpose of their conversation was to improve and not worsen relations. If he and Kennedy should succeed in that effort, "the expenses incurred in connection with the meeting would be well justified." If not, the money would have been wasted and the hope of the people frustrated.

As participants looked at their watches, they were surprised that it was already two p.m.

Khrushchev remained in full voice over a lunch of beef Wellington in the U.S. ambassador residence's dining room, lubricated by his mostly vodka dry martini. He regaled the long table, at which each man had nine aides and senior officials, about matters ranging from farm technology to space travel.

Khrushchev boasted about Gagarin's flight as the first man in space, but he conceded that Gagarin's masters at first did not want to trust him with the spacecraft's controls. It had seemed too much power for one individual.

Kennedy suggested that the U.S. and USSR should consider a joint moon expedition.

After an initial rejection, Khrushchev reconsidered, saying, "All right, why not?" It seemed to be the first progress of the day.

At the end of the lunch, Kennedy lit a cigar and threw the match behind Khrushchev's chair.

The Soviet leader feigned alarm. "Are you trying to set me on fire?" he asked.

Kennedy assured him he wasn't.

"Ah," said Khrushchev with a smile, "a capitalist, not an incendiary."

Khrushchev's raw energy was overpowering Kennedy's more subtle charms.

The two men's after-meal toasts reflected the unbalanced nature of their earlier conversations. Kennedy was brief and complimentary of Khrushchev's "vigor and energy," hoping for fruitful meetings.

The Soviet leader responded at greater length. He talked about how the two countries had the combined power to stop by joint effort any war any other country might start. He spoke of his initially good relationship with Eisenhower. Although Eisenhower had taken responsibility for the U-2 spy flight incident that undermined their relationship, Khrushchev said he was "almost sure that Eisenhower had not known about the flight" but had accepted blame "in the spirit of chivalry." Khrushchev declared the flight to have been orchestrated by those who wished to worsen U.S.–Soviet relations—and they had succeeded.

He spoke of his desire to receive Kennedy in the Soviet Union "when the time was ripe." But he then condemned the visit of his previous guest, former Vice President Nixon, who thought "by showing the Soviet people a dream kitchen, a kitchen that did not exist nor would ever exist in the U.S., he would convert the Soviet people to capitalism." Only Nixon, he said, "could have thought of such nonsense."

Khrushchev told Kennedy that he took full credit for Nixon's electoral defeat, which had been gained because he had refused to release the imprisoned American airmen whom his troops had shot down. If he had released them, Khrushchev said, Kennedy would have lost the presidency by at least 200,000 votes.

"Don't spread that story around," Kennedy said, laughing. "If you tell everybody that you like me better than Nixon, I'll be ruined at home."

Khrushchev raised his glass to the president's health and said how he envied his youth. Yet Kennedy bore the backache of a much older man under his corset. The benefit of his morning shot from "Dr. Feelgood" was wearing thin. The procaine, vitamins, amphetamines, and enzymes could not counteract the weight of Khrushchev's onslaught.

After lunch, Kennedy invited Khrushchev for a stroll in the garden with interpreters only. Thompson and others had advised Kennedy that Khrushchev would be more pliable when he wasn't around other Soviet officials before whom he felt he had to perform.

Kennedy's friends O'Donnell and Powers watched the superpower stroll from a second-floor window at the residence. Khrushchev circled around Kennedy, snapping at him like a terrier and shaking his finger, while Kennedy strolled casually on the lawn beside him, stopping now and then to say a few words, withholding any upset or anger.

O'Donnell downed an Austrian beer and condemned himself again for not having brought a camera. He was close enough to see how hard the stroll was on Kennedy's back. The president winced as he leaned over to better hear the far shorter Khrushchev.

When the two men returned inside, Kennedy suggested that he and Khrushchev continue talking privately for a time with interpreters before their aides rejoined them. Happy with how matters were unfolding, Khrushchev agreed.

Kennedy wanted to further explain his fear of "miscalculation." In another awkward effort to bond with the Soviet, Kennedy conceded he had made a misjudgment "with regard to the Cuba situation."

Kennedy said he had to make judgments that would drive U.S. policy based on what the USSR would do next around the world, just as Khrushchev had to "make judgments as to the moves of the U.S." So, Kennedy said, he wanted to use their meeting to gain "greater precision in these judgments so that our two countries could survive this period of competition without endangering their national security."

Khrushchev countered that dangers only arose when the U.S. misunderstood the sources of revolution, which he insisted were homegrown and not invented by the Soviets. He seized upon the example of Iran, a U.S. ally, where the Soviet Union "does not want a revolution there and does not do anything in that country to promote such a development."

Khrushchev said, however, that "the people of the country are so poor that the country has become a volcano and changes are bound to occur sooner or later. The Shah will certainly be overthrown. By supporting the Shah, the United States generates adverse feelings toward the United States among the people of Iran and, conversely, favorable feelings toward the USSR."

He then turned to Cuba. "A mere handful of people, headed by Fidel Castro, overthrew the Batista regime because of its oppressive nature," he said. "During Castro's fight against Batista, U.S. capitalist circles . . . supported Batista, and this is why the anger of the Cuban people turned against the United States. The President's decision to launch a landing in Cuba only strengthened the revolutionary forces and Castro's own position." Said Khrushchev, "Castro is not a communist, but U.S. policy can make him one."

Referring to his own life, Khrushchev said he had not been born a communist. "It was the capitalists who made me a communist." Khrushchev scoffed at President Kennedy's notion that Cuba could endanger American security. Could six million people really be a threat to the mighty U.S., the Soviet leader wondered.

Khrushchev challenged Kennedy to explain to him what sort of global precedent he might be setting by arguing that the U.S. should be free to act as it wished regarding Cuba. Did that mean the USSR would be free to meddle in the internal affairs of Turkey and Iran, who were allies of the U.S. and had American bases and rockets? Through the Bay of Pigs invasion, Khrushchev argued, "the U.S. has set a precedent for intervention in the internal affairs of other countries. The USSR is stronger than Turkey and Iran, just as the U.S. is stronger than Cuba. This situation may cause 'miscalculation,' to use the President's term."

Khrushchev's voice hung on that dreaded word for emphasis.

Turning Kennedy's words on himself, Khrushchev agreed both sides should agree "to rule out miscalculation." This is why he was "happy that the President had said that Cuba was a mistake."

Kennedy attempted again to appease the growling bear. He conceded Khrushchev's point that if Iran's current prime minister didn't improve his people's lot, "there would be important changes in that country as well." Having been challenged on Cuba, Turkey, and Iran, Kennedy felt compelled to respond. He protested that he had not been a fan of Batista, but his concern now was that Castro would transform Cuba into a base for regional trouble. Although it was true that the U.S. had military installations in Turkey and Iran, Kennedy said, "these two countries are so weak that they could be no threat to the USSR, no more than Cuba to the U.S."

When U.S. officials read the transcripts of the two leaders' exchanges a few days later, they were again shocked by what followed. In reference to Cuba, Kennedy wondered how Khrushchev would respond if a government friendly to the West established itself in Poland. "It was critical to have the changes occurring in the world and affecting the balance of power take place in a way that would not involve the prestige of the treaty commitments of our two countries," he said. What Kennedy was suggesting was that because of Poland's Warsaw Pact treaty obligations, it was off-limits for American interference.

It was once again the furthest any U.S. president ever had gone with a Soviet counterpart in recognizing the division of Europe as acceptable and permanent. To balance this apparent concession, Kennedy added that the days would be numbered for Soviet bloc leaders who failed to produce better living standards and education for their people. At the same time, Kennedy was saying that the U.S. would not meddle where the Kremlin's prestige was in question—and Moscow ought to play by the same rules.

Khrushchev shot back that American policy was inconsistent, then apologized to the president that he wasn't criticizing Kennedy personally, as he had only been in the White House a very short time. The Soviet leader again returned to the subject of Iran, and said that for all the U.S. emphasis on democracy, Washington supported the Shah, "who says his power was given to him by God. Everybody knows how this power was seized by the Shah's father, who had been a sergeant in the Iranian Army and who had usurped the throne by means of murder, plunder and violence. . . . The United States is spending vast sums of money in Iran but that money does not go to the people; it is plundered by the Shah's entourage."

Hammering away further at what he condemned as American hypocrisy, Khrushchev turned to Washington's support for Spanish dictator Franco. "The U.S. knows how he came to power and yet it supports him," said Khrushchev. "The United States supports the most reactionary regimes and this is how the people see U.S. policy." He conceded that Castro might indeed become a communist, though he didn't start that way. Khrushchev felt that U.S. sanctions had turned him toward Moscow.

Kennedy was in over his head. For all Kennedy's willingness to debate Khrushchev, he had failed to challenge the Soviet leader where he was most vulnerable. He had not condemned the Soviet use of force in East Germany and Hungary in 1953 and 1956. Worse, he had not posed the most important question of all: Why were hundreds of thousands of East German refugees fleeing to a better life in the West?

At the end of the first day's talks, Kennedy returned to the subject of Poland and argued that democratic elections there might well replace the current Soviet-friendly government with one that was closer to the West. Khrushchev feigned shock. It was not respectful, he said, for Kennedy "to speak that way about a government the U.S. recognizes and with which it has diplomatic relations." He argued that Poland's "election system is more democratic than that in the United States."

Kennedy's subsequent effort to differentiate between America's multiparty system and single-party Poland was lost on Khrushchev. The two men could not agree on the definition of democracy, let alone on whether Poland had one.

Kennedy and Khrushchev circumnavigated the globe geographically and philosophically with Khrushchev thrusts and Kennedy parries on issues ranging from Angola to Laos. Khrushchev's biggest concession of the day would be agreement to accept a neutral, independent Laos—a deal that their underlings would negotiate on the Viennese sidelines. Uncharacteristically, he demanded little from Kennedy in exchange.

Khrushchev was clearing out the underbrush for what he wanted to be the next day's all-consuming focus: Berlin.

Kennedy declared an evening break at 6:45, after six hours of nearly uninterrupted discussion. Weary and drawn, Kennedy noted the lateness of the hour and suggested that the next agenda item, the question of a nuclear test ban, could be discussed that night over dinner with the Austrian president, so that most of the following day could be given over to Berlin. Kennedy also gave Khrushchev the option of discussing both issues the following day.

Kennedy wanted to ensure that Khrushchev didn't stray from his pre-summit commitment to discuss a test ban, something he knew was of little interest to Moscow, before they took on Berlin.

With Kennedy glancing at his watch, Khrushchev pounced on the mention of Berlin. He said he would agree to discuss nuclear testing only in the context of general disarmament issues. That was an approach Kennedy opposed for the simple reason that a test ban could be agreed upon quickly, while concluding far-reaching arms reduction agreements could consume years of negotiation.

Regarding Berlin, Khrushchev said his demands would have to be satisfied the following day or he would move unilaterally. "The Soviet Union hopes that the U.S. will understand this question so that both countries can sign a peace treaty together," he said. "This would improve relations. But if the United States refuses to sign a peace treaty, the Soviet Union will do so and nothing will stop it."

After a Soviet limo drove Khrushchev away, a dazed Kennedy turned to Ambassador Thompson on the U.S. residence steps and asked, "Is it always like this?"

"Par for the course," said Thompson.

Thompson restrained himself from telling the president how much better matters might have gone had he taken the advice he had been given to avoid ideological debate. Thompson knew the next day's Berlin discussion was likely to be even more difficult.

It was only the halftime break at the Vienna Summit, but it was already clear that Team USA was losing.

Kennedy had reinforced Khrushchev's impression of his weakness. "This man is very inexperienced, even immature," Khrushchev told his interpreter Oleg Troyanovsky. "Compared to him, Eisenhower is a man of intelligence and vision."

In the years that followed, then Vienna-based U.S. diplomat William Lloyd Stearman would teach students about the summit's lessons in a lecture he called "Little Boy Blue Meets Al Capone." He thought that title captured the naive, almost apologetic approach Kennedy had followed in the face of Khrushchev's brutal assaults. He believed the Bay of Pigs had cut into the president's confidence at the summit and had made Khrushchev feel that "Kennedy was now his pigeon."

Stearman's insights were better informed than most observers' because he was regularly briefed in Vienna by his friend Martin Hillenbrand, who was the note-taker at the Kennedy–Khrushchev meeting. Stearman's view was that the talks had gone astray partly because Kennedy had been so ill served by his key advisers.

Stearman dismissed Secretary of State Rusk as an Asia expert who lacked sufficient judgment on Soviet issues. National Security Advisor Bundy was more cerebral than decisive, Stearman believed. Missing at the heart of the administration were advisers who could bring Kennedy the sense of historic moment and accompanying strategic direction that Dean Acheson and John Foster Dulles had supplied Truman and Eisenhower.

By Stearman's account, Kennedy had also hurt his chances of success during the pre-summit planning by going around his national security staff and doing much of the planning secretly between Bolshakov and his brother Bobby. When the talks began to head in the wrong direction, Kennedy lacked backup staff with adequate knowledge of the preparations to help him change direction.

Mercifully, the U.S. embassy residence where Kennedy was staying also had a bathtub, though it was more modest than the gilded basin of Paris. As Kennedy soaked, O'Donnell asked the president about the awkward moment at the beginning of the day when he was sizing up the Soviet leader on the residence steps.

"After all the studying and talking I've done on him in the last few weeks, you can't blame me for being interested in getting a look at him," he said.

Was he different than forecast? asked O'Donnell.

"Not really," said Kennedy, but then he corrected himself. "Maybe [he was] a little more unreasonable [than expected]. . . . From what I read and from what people told me, I expected him to be smart and tough. He would have to be smart and tough to work his way to the top in a government like that one."

Dave Powers told the president that he and O'Donnell had watched from the second-floor window as the Soviet leader went after him during their walk in the garden. "You seemed pretty calm while he was giving you a hard time out there."

Kennedy shrugged. "What did you expect me to do?" he asked. "Take off one of my shoes and hit him over the head with it?" He said Khrushchev had been battering him on Berlin in an effort to wear him down over the issue. Khrushchev had questioned how the U.S. could support the notion of German unification. The Soviet leader had said he lacked all sympathy for Germans, who had killed his son in the war.

Kennedy had reminded Khrushchev that he had lost his brother as well, but the U.S. would not turn its back on West Germany nor pull out of Berlin. "And that's that," Kennedy had told Khrushchev.

Kennedy told his friends about Khrushchev's tough response to his concerns about the possibility of *miscalculation* on either side leading to war. "Khrushchev went berserk," he said. He told O'Donnell that he would make a mental note to stay away from the word during the rest of their talks.

A ustrian President Adolf Schärf had a protocol problem to solve before his grand gala dinner that evening at Schönbrunn Palace. Which of the two leaders' wives should sit at his right? he wondered.

On the one hand, Khrushchev had freed Vienna from the possible fate of a divided Berlin by allowing it to embrace independence and neutrality through the Austrian state treaty of May 15, 1955. Because of that, Khrushchev's wife, Nina, had earned pride of place. Yet the Viennese loved the Kennedys, and Austrians, despite their neutrality, felt that where they belonged was the West.

In a diplomatic compromise, Schärf would seat Madame Khrushchev to his right at the dinner, and Mrs. Kennedy would have the honored position for the second half of the evening, during performances in the music room.

It was Austria's coming-out party. More than six thousand Viennese crowded around the floodlit gates of the 265-year-old palace to watch Kennedy and Khrushchev arrive. The palace staff had waxed the parquet floor to a perfect sheen and scrubbed the windows until they sparkled. The most valuable of the antiques were removed from the museum's display rooms and positioned for use. Staff collected flowers from the palace gardens and arranged them so generously on the tables that they perfumed the entire hall. The tables were set with the "Gold Eagle Service," a priceless porcelain collection with the Austrian double-headed eagle embossed on a white background that had been used by Emperor Franz Joseph.

Aside from the fact that the meals were served cold, the Austrians patted themselves on the back on an evening well done. The evening's guests noticed how Jackie and Nina had hit it off. Jackie wore a floor-length pink sheath dress. Designed by Oleg Cassini, the gown was sleeveless and low-waisted. Nina dressed in a dark silk dress laced with a faint golden thread—a more proletariat choice.

Their husbands struck the same contrast. Kennedy was in black tie and Khrushchev in a plain dark suit and checkered gray tie. Waiters in white gloves, knee breeches, and gold braid moved through the corridors and across the spacious rooms bearing silver trays laden with drinks.

"Mr. Khrushchev," a photographer asked, "won't you shake hands with Mr. Kennedy for us?"

"I'd like to shake *her* hand first." Khrushchev grinned and nodded to the president's wife.

Associated Press reporter Eddy Gilmore scribbled that beside Jackie "the tough and often belligerent Communist leader looked like a smitten schoolboy when the ice thaws along the Volga in springtime." Khrushchev went out of his way to sit beside Jackie while the chamber ensemble of the Vienna Philharmonic played Mozart and then the Vienna State Opera's dance company performed the "Blue Danube" waltz.

Kennedy's performance was not nearly as graceful. Just before the music began, he lowered himself onto a chair, only to find that it already held Khrushchev's wife. He stopped just short of landing in her lap.

He smiled an apology. The Vienna Summit wasn't going well at all.

11

VIENNA:

THE THREAT OF WAR

The U.S. is unwilling to normalize the situation in the most dangerous spot in the world. The USSR wants to perform an operation on this sore spot—to eliminate this thorn, this ulcer. . . .

Premier Khrushchev to President Kennedy, Vienna, June 4, 1961

I never met a man like this. I talked about how a nuclear exchange would kill seventy million people in ten minutes and he just looked at me as if to say, "So what?" My impression was he just didn't give a damn if it came to that.

President Kennedy to reporter Hugh Sidey, Time, *June 1961*

SOVIET EMBASSY, VIENNA
10:15 A.M., SUNDAY, JUNE 4, 1961

Standing before the Soviet embassy, Nikita Khrushchev shifted from side to side like a boxer eager to come back out of his corner after having won the opening rounds. A wide grin revealed the gap in his front teeth as he thrust out his small, plump hand to greet Kennedy.

For all the Soviet state's working-class pretensions, Moscow's embassy was unashamedly imperial. Acquired by Tsarist Russia in the late nineteenth century, its neo-Renaissance facade opened up to a grand entry hall of natural granite and marble. "I greet you on a small piece of Soviet territory," said Khrushchev to Kennedy. He then threw out a Russian proverb whose meaning escaped Kennedy: "Sometimes we drink out of a small glass but we speak with great feelings."

After some nine minutes of small talk, none of it memorable, Khrushchev took his American guests through a pillared corridor to a wide staircase that led to the second floor. There they sat on sofas in a twenty-foot-square conference room with red damask walls.

The manner in which the two men had spent the morning ahead of their second day's meeting spoke to their differences. The Catholic Kennedys had listened to the Vienna Boys' Choir and had taken Mass from Cardinal Franz König in the Gothic magnificence of St. Stephen's Cathedral. The First Lady's eyes had welled up as she fell to her knees to pray. When the Kennedys emerged from worship, a throng cheered on the cobblestoned square outside. At about the same time, a far smaller and less enthusiastic crowd watched with curiosity as the leader of the atheist Soviet Union laid a wreath at the Soviet war memorial at the Schwarzenbergplatz. Locals knew it bitterly as the "monument to the unknown rapist."

In the conference room where the two delegations gathered, the matching red curtains were pulled shut. They concealed the embassy's tall and broad windows and created an atmosphere of gloom, keeping out the day's bright sun. Kennedy began with the same sort of small talk he had employed the first day, asking the Soviet premier about his childhood. Khrushchev had no interest in discussing his peasant origins with this child of privilege. So he was curt, saying only that he was born in a Russian village near Kursk, less than ten kilometers from the Ukrainian border.

Shifting quickly to the present, he said the Soviet Union had recently found very large deposits of iron ore near Kursk, estimated at 30 billion tons. He said total reserves were likely to be ten times greater than that. By comparison, he reminded Kennedy, total iron ore deposits of the U.S. were only a fraction of that, at 5 billion tons. "Soviet deposits will be sufficient to cover the needs of the entire world for a long time to come," he said.

In the first minutes of Day Two in Vienna, Khrushchev had turned what might have been a personal exchange about family matters into a boast about his country's superior resource base. He did not ask about the president's upbringing, about which he knew quite enough. Impatiently, he suggested they move on to the day's purpose: discussing Berlin and its future.

In its edition of that morning, the London *Times* had quoted a British diplomat on his concerns about the Vienna Summit. "We hope the lad will be able to get out of the bear cage without being too badly mauled," he had said. And Khrushchev had come out at the beginning of the second day with his claws bared. Despite progress their delegations had made overnight on Laos, he was unwilling to seize upon the issue as an example of how the two sides could reduce tensions.

U.S. and Soviet foreign secretaries and their staffs had reached agreement that they would accept a neutral Laos. It was a concession that could be politically costly to Khrushchev, as it would be opposed by the Chinese, the North Vietnamese, and the Pathet Lao, the Laotian communist movement. Instead of embracing Kennedy over the accord, however, Khrushchev accused him of "megalomania and delusions of grandeur" for insisting that the U.S. would continue to safeguard its commitments in Asia.

Beyond that, Khrushchev resisted all of Kennedy's efforts to steer talks toward nuclear test ban issues. He rejected the president's logic that only an overall improvement of relations could open the way to an eventual Berlin settlement. For Khrushchev, Berlin had to come first.

Pushing for the test ban, Kennedy drew upon a Chinese proverb: "A journey of a thousand miles begins with one step."

"You seem to know the Chinese very well," Khrushchev said.

"We may both get to know them better," responded Kennedy.

Khrushchev smiled. "I know them well enough now," he said. It was an unusual slip for the Soviet, a brief glimpse into his frustration with Mao.

However, the Soviets would doctor the final transcript, which would be provided to Beijing, adding another sentence that Khrushchev actually had never said to Kennedy: "China is our neighbor, our friend, and our ally."

The most important exchange of the summit began with a Khrushchev warning. The Soviet leader prefaced his statement by saying Moscow had waited as long as it could for a Berlin solution. He said the position he was about to outline regarding Berlin would "affect the relations between our two countries to a great extent and even more so if the U.S. were to misunderstand the Soviet position."

At that point, both men's advisers sat forward, knowing that everything else had been foreplay for this moment. "Sixteen years have passed since World War II," said Khrushchev. "The USSR lost twenty million people in that war and much of its territory was devastated. Now Germany, the country which unleashed World War II, has again acquired military power and has assumed a predominant position in NATO. Its generals hold high offices in that organization. This constitutes a threat of World War III, which would be even more devastating than World War II."

For that reason, he told Kennedy, Moscow refused to tolerate any further delay regarding Berlin, because only West German militarists would gain from it. He said German unification was not a practical possibility and that even Germans didn't want it. So the Soviets would begin to act from the "actual state of affairs, namely, that two German States exist."

Khrushchev told Kennedy that it was his preference to reach agreement personally with *him* on a war-ending treaty that would alter Berlin's status. If that wasn't possible, however, he would act alone and end all postwar commitments made by the Soviets. He said thereafter West Berlin would be a "free city" where U.S. troops could remain, but only coexisting with Soviet troops. The Soviets would then join the U.S. in ensuring "what the West *calls* West Berlin's freedom." Moscow would also be "agreeable" to the presence of neutral troops or UN guarantees.

Kennedy began his response by thanking Khrushchev for "setting forth his views in such a frank manner." Shot up with painkillers and amphetamines and snug in his corset, Kennedy realized Khrushchev had just delivered what amounted to a new ultimatum on Berlin. That required a clear and sharp response. It was a moment Kennedy had prepared for, and he measured each word carefully.

He stressed that the two men were talking no longer about lesser issues such as Laos but rather about the far more crucial topic of Berlin. This place was "of greatest interest to the U.S. We are in Berlin not because of someone's sufferance. We fought our way there." And though the U.S. casualties in World War II had not been as high as those of the Soviet Union, Kennedy said, "we are in Berlin not by agreement of East Germans but by contractual rights. . . .

"This is an area," said Kennedy, "where every President of the U.S. since World War II has been committed by treaty and other contractual rights and where every President has reaffirmed his faithfulness to those obligations. If we were expelled from that area, and if we accepted the loss of our rights, no one would have any confidence in U.S. commitments and pledges. U.S. national security is involved in this matter, because if we were to accept the Soviet proposal, U.S. commitments would be regarded as a mere scrap of paper."

At the Vienna Summit until that point, words had tumbled over each other without consequence. Yet now note-takers sat forward, precisely scribbling their leaders' verbatim comments. The world's two most powerful men were facing off over their most intractable and explosive issue.

It was the stuff of history.

"West Europe is vital to our national security and we have supported it in two wars," Kennedy said. "If we were to leave West Berlin, Europe would be abandoned as well. So when we are talking about West Berlin, we are also talking about West Europe."

What was new for the Soviets was Kennedy's repeated emphasis on the qualifying word of "West" in front of Berlin. No U.S. president had previously differentiated so clearly between his commitment to all of Berlin and to *West* Berlin. In perhaps the most important manhood moment of his presidency, Kennedy had made a unilateral concession. He reminded Khrushchev that the Soviet leader in their first day's talks had agreed that "the ratios of [military] power today are equal." So he thought it "difficult to understand" why a country like the Soviet Union, with such considerable achievements in space and economy, should suggest that the U.S. leave a place of such vital interest where it was already established. He said the U.S. would never be willing to agree to give up rights it had "won by war."

Khrushchev's face reddened, as if it were a thermometer measuring a rise in his internal temperature. He interrupted to say that he understood Kennedy's words to mean the president did not want a peace treaty. He spat derisively that Kennedy's statement on U.S. national security sounded like "the U.S. might wish to go to Moscow [with its troops] because that too would, of course, improve its position."

"The U.S. is not asking to go anywhere," Kennedy responded. "We are not talking about the U.S. going to Moscow or of the USSR going to New York. What we are talking about is that we are in Berlin and have been there for fifteen years. We suggest that we stay there."

Returning to a course he had tried a day earlier without success, Kennedy explored a more conciliatory path. He said that he knew the situation in Berlin "is not a satisfactory one." That said, added Kennedy, "conditions in many parts of the world are not satisfactory," and it was not the right time to change the balance in Berlin or in the world more generally. "If this balance should change, the situation in West Europe as a whole would change, and this would be a most serious blow to the U.S.," he said. "Mr. Khrushchev would not accept similar loss and we cannot accept it either."

Until that point, Khrushchev had largely held his usual bombast in check. Yet now his arms were waving, his face turned crimson, and his voice rose to a truculent pitch as his words tumbled out in staccato spurts like angry machine-gun fire. "The U.S. is unwilling to normalize the situation in the most dangerous spot in the world," he said. "The USSR wants to perform an operation on this sore spot—to eliminate this thorn, this ulcer—without prejudicing the interests of any side, but rather to the satisfaction of all peoples of the world."

The Soviet Union was not going to change Berlin by "intrigue or threat" but by "solemnly signing a peace treaty. Now the President says that this action is directed against the interests of the U.S. Such a statement is difficult to understand indeed." The Soviets did not want to change existing boundaries, he argued, but were only trying to formalize them so as to "impede those people who want a new war."

Khrushchev spoke derisively of Adenauer's desire to revise Germany's borders and regain territory it had lost after World War II. "Hitler spoke of Germany's need for *Lebensraum* to the Urals," he said. "Hitler's generals, who had helped him in his designs to execute his plans, are [now] high commanders in NATO."

He said the logic of the U.S. needing to protect its interests in Berlin "cannot be understood and the USSR cannot accept it." He told the president he was sorry, but that "no force in the world" would stop Moscow from moving forward on its peace treaty.

He repeated again that sixteen years had passed since the war. How much longer did Kennedy want Moscow to wait? Another sixteen years? Perhaps thirty years?

Khrushchev looked around the room at his colleagues and then said with a wave of his arm that he had lost a son in the last war, that Gromyko had lost two brothers, and that Mikoyan had also lost a son. "There is not a single family in the USSR or the leadership of the USSR that did not lose at least one of its members in the war." He conceded that American mothers mourn their sons just as deeply as do Soviet mothers, but that while the U.S. had lost thousands, the USSR had lost millions.

He then declared: "The USSR will sign a peace treaty and the sovereignty of the GDR will be observed. Any violation of that sovereignty will be regarded by the USSR as an act of open aggression" with all its attendant consequences.

Khrushchev was threatening war, just as de Gaulle had predicted. The American delegation sat in stunned silence as they awaited Kennedy's response.

The president calmly asked whether access routes to Berlin would remain open after the Soviets had agreed to such a peace treaty. Kennedy had already decided he could accept an outcome under which the Soviets concluded a treaty with the East Germans but did nothing to impede Western rights in West Berlin or Allied access to the city.

Khrushchev, however, said the new treaty *would* alter freedom of access. That crossed Kennedy's red line.

"This presents us with a most serious challenge and no one can foresee how serious the consequences might be," said Kennedy. He said it was not his wish to come to Vienna only to "be denied our position in West Berlin and our access to that city." He said he had hoped relations between the U.S. and the Soviet Union could be improved through the Vienna Summit, but instead they were worsening. Kennedy said it was Moscow's business if it wanted to transfer its rights in Berlin to the East Germans, but the president could not allow Moscow to give away American rights.

Khrushchev began to probe the U.S. position. He wanted to know if an interim arrangement still might be possible along the lines that Eisenhower had discussed with him—something that protected the prestige of both countries. All sides could set a time limit of six months for the two Germanys to negotiate a unification arrangement. If they failed during that time—and Khrushchev was convinced they would—"anyone would be free to conclude a peace treaty."

Khrushchev said that even if the U.S. disagreed with the Soviet proposal, it should understand "the USSR can no longer delay" and would take action by year's end that would make all access to West Berlin subject to East German control. He based his right to act on a statistical analysis of the difference in the price the two sides had paid to defeat the Germans—the 20 million–plus people the Soviets had lost in World War II, compared to only 143,000 U.S. military dead.

Kennedy said it was those losses that motivated him to avoid a new war.

Repeating the word that he so hated, the Soviet leader reminded Kennedy of his worry that the Soviets might "miscalculate." It seemed to Khrushchev it was the Americans who were in danger of miscalculation. "If the U.S. should start a war over Berlin, let it be so," he said. "That is what the Pentagon has been wanting. However, Adenauer and Macmillan know very well what war means. If there is any madman who wants war, he should be put in a straitjacket!"

Kennedy's team was stunned again. Now Khrushchev had used the word "war," and he had done so three times. That was unheard-of in diplomatic discussions at every level.

As if to close the matter, Khrushchev flatly stated that the USSR would sign a peace treaty by the end of the year, altering Western rights in Berlin for all time, but that he was confident common sense and peace would prevail.

The Soviet leader had not yet responded to what amounted to a Kennedy proposal, so the president probed again. Kennedy stressed that he would not regard a peace treaty in itself as a belligerent act if Khrushchev left West Berlin untouched. "However, a peace treaty denying us our contractual rights *is* a belligerent act," he said. "What *is* belligerent is transfer of our rights to East Germany."

It was increasingly clear what Kennedy was saying: Do what you want to with what is yours, but do not touch what is ours. If the U.S. ceded anything on *West* Berlin, the world "would not regard [the U.S.] as a serious country." But as East Berlin was Soviet territory, he was suggesting that the USSR would be free to do as it pleased there.

Khrushchev did not acknowledge at the time what would later look like the makings of a deal that had been offered by Kennedy. Instead, the Soviet leader replied that the USSR "would never, under any conditions, accept U.S. rights in West Berlin after a peace treaty had been signed."

He then lashed out at what he considered U.S. mistreatment of the Soviet Union after the war. Khrushchev said the U.S. had deprived the USSR of reparations, rights, and interests in West Germany. Beyond that, he said the U.S. practiced a double standard by refusing to negotiate a war-ending peace treaty with East Germany although it had signed just such an agreement with the Japanese in 1951—without consulting with Moscow in preparing the document. Deputy Foreign Minister Andrei Gromyko had led the Soviet delegation at the conference, where it had tried to stall the treaty and then refused to sign while complaining that the U.S. had not invited the Chinese and was creating an anti-Soviet, militaristic Japan.

Kennedy countered that Khrushchev had publicly declared he would have signed the Japan treaty if he had been in power at the time.

For Khrushchev, however, the point wasn't what he *might* have done but rather that the U.S. had not even sought Soviet agreement. Khrushchev called Kennedy's approach regarding Berlin a similar one of "I do what I want."

Khrushchev said he had seen enough of that sort of U.S. behavior. Moscow would sign its treaty with East Germany, he said, and the price would be great if the U.S. thereafter violated East German sovereignty over access to Berlin.

What he wanted, Kennedy countered, was not a conflict over Berlin but an overall mending of East–West German relations and of U.S.–Soviet relations, so as to permit over time a solution to the whole German problem. He said he did not wish "to act in a way that would deprive the Soviet Union of its ties in Eastern Europe," again reassuring Khrushchev, as he had done the first day, that he would do nothing to upset the balance of power in Europe.

Kennedy noted that the Soviet leader had called him a young man, and the president suggested that Khrushchev was trying to take advantage of his relative inexperience. However, Kennedy said, he had "not assumed office to accept arrangements totally inimical to U.S. interests." Khrushchev repeated that the only alternative to unilateral action would be an interim agreement under which the two Germanys could negotiate and after which all Allied rights would disappear. That would "give the semblance of responsibility for the problem having been turned over to the Germans themselves." But as they would not agree to unification, Khrushchev was certain the outcome would be the same.

With an actor's sense of dramatic timing, Khrushchev then presented Kennedy a document, an aide-mémoire on the Berlin question, whose purpose was to give his ultimatum official force. No one on Kennedy's team had prepared the president for such a written Kremlin initiative. Bolshakov had not even hinted at such a move. Khrushchev said the Soviet side had prepared it so that the U.S. could study the Soviet position and "perhaps return to this question at a later date, if it wished to do so."

With that bold move, Khrushchev had put himself on a collision course with Kennedy over Berlin. He had acted in part because Kennedy, in clinging to the status quo, had not shown even Eisenhower's willingness to negotiate the issue. That was difficult enough for Khrushchev to accept under Eisenhower, and before the U-2 incident. But now it was impossible.

The morning had passed quickly.

While Khrushchev and Kennedy retreated to a tense lunch, their wives were out doing the town. In front of the Pallavicini Palace on the sun-bathed Josefsplatz, a crowd of a thousand had gathered to get a glimpse of the two women heading for lunch. A slight murmur greeted the Soviet, followed by an outburst of cheers for Jackie. Two American reporters felt sorry for the crowd's inattention to Nina, so as the Viennese shouted, "Ja-kee! Ja-kee!" they countered with their own chant of "Nina!" But it gained no following.

Reuters correspondent Adam Kellett-Long, who had been sent from Berlin to cover the summit, was horrified as he heard photographers shout at Jackie to stick out her breasts for more alluring shots. "And she did!" he recalled later. "She behaved like Marilyn Monroe or a film star. She was lapping it up."

From the upstairs window of the restaurant, the two women looked down on the crowd. Jackie appeared very much like a fashion magazine illustration in her navy blue suit, black pillbox hat, and four strands of pearls and white gloves. Soviet press spokesmen didn't release what Nina was wearing, but the *New York Times* described her as looking like the housewife for whom Jackie's fashion magazines were produced. None of that disturbed Nina Petrovna, who found Jackie's conversation intelligent and who thought she "looked like a work of art." She held Jackie's gloved hand aloft standing before the crowd in the window frame of their restaurant—a warmth that was absent from their husbands' last supper.

The two men conversed about weapons manufacturing and arms policies. Khrushchev said he had scrutinized the president's May message to Congress in which he had dramatically increased defense spending. He said that he understood the U.S. could not disarm, controlled as it was by monopolists. However, he said, the U.S. buildup would force him also to increase the size of Soviet armed forces.

In that context, Khrushchev returned to their chat over lunch a day earlier at which he said he would consider a joint moon project. He regretted that such cooperation would be impossible as long as there was no disarmament. Khrushchev would not leave even this thin strand of new cooperation on the table.

Kennedy said perhaps they could at least coordinate the timing of their space projects.

Lacking conviction, Khrushchev shrugged that such a course might be possible. He then lifted a glass of sweet Soviet champagne to Kennedy.

He joked that "natural love is better than love through intermediaries," and that it was good the two men had now talked directly to each other.

He wanted the president to understand that the new Soviet ultimatum on Berlin "would not be directed against the U.S. or its allies." He compared what Moscow was doing to a surgical operation, which was painful to the patient but necessary for survival. Mixing his metaphors, he said Moscow "wants to cross that bridge and it will cross it."

Khrushchev conceded that U.S.–Soviet relations would sustain "great tensions" but that he was certain "the sun will come out again and will shine brightly. The U.S. does not want Berlin, neither does the Soviet Union. . . . The only party really interested in Berlin as such is Adenauer. He is an intelligent man but old. The Soviet Union cannot agree to having the old and moribund hold back the young and vigorous."

As he toasted Kennedy, Khrushchev conceded that he had put the president in a difficult position, as allies would question his decisions on Berlin. He then dismissed the influence and interests of allies, noting that Luxembourg should cause Kennedy no problem, just as the Soviet Union's own unnamed allies "would not frighten anyone."

Khrushchev then raised his glass and noted that Kennedy as a religious man would say, "God should help us in this endeavor." Khrushchev said he would rather raise his own drink to common sense rather than to God.

Kennedy's return toast focused on the two men's obligations in a nuclear age when the effects of a conflict "would go from generation to generation." He stressed that each side "should recognize the interests and the responsibilities of the other side."

The gift Kennedy had brought the Soviet leader rested before them on the table, a model of the USS *Constitution*, whose guns, the president said, had a range of only a half-mile. In the nuclear age, where guns were intercontinental and the devastation would be far more horrible, Kennedy said leaders could not allow war to happen.

Kennedy referred to their setting in neutral Vienna, and he said that he hoped they would not leave a place that so symbolized the possibility of finding equitable solutions after having increased dangers to both sides' security and prestige. "This goal can be achieved only if each is wise and stays in his own area," he said.

There it was again: Kennedy's solution to the Berlin Crisis. He was once more suggesting the Soviet could do whatever he wished on his own ground. It was a negotiating point he had repeated several times during the day in different forms—and now he had employed it within his closing toast.

To take some of the sting out of that as a final word, Kennedy recalled that he had asked Khrushchev what job he had had when he was forty-four, the president's current age. The Kremlin boss had said he was head of the Moscow Planning Commission. Kennedy joked that he would like to head the Boston Planning Commission at age sixty-seven.

"Perhaps the President would like to become head of the planning commission of the whole world," Khrushchev sneered.

No, said the president. Just Boston.

With their two days of talks ending so badly, Kennedy took a last stab at a more positive outcome. He asked Khrushchev for one more post-lunch meeting alone with their interpreters.

"I can't leave here without giving it one more try," Kennedy told Kenny O'Donnell.

When the president's staff told him that that would throw them off their scheduled departure, Kennedy barked that nothing in the world could be more important at the moment than getting matters right with Khrushchev. "No, we're not going on time! I'm not going to leave until I know more." Throughout his life, Kennedy had depended on his charm and personality to overcome obstacles. Yet none of that had broken through Khrushchev's force field.

Kennedy opened their last, short exchange by acknowledging the importance of Berlin. However, he hoped that Khrushchev, in the interest of relations between their two countries, "would not present him with a situation so deeply involving our national interest." He underscored yet again "the difference between a peace treaty and the rights of access to Berlin." He hoped relations would unfold in a way that would avoid direct confrontation between the U.S. and the Soviet Union.

Yet with Kennedy already in his chokehold, Khrushchev squeezed harder. If the U.S. insisted on its rights, thus violating East German borders after the signing of a peace treaty, "force would be met by force," he declared. "The U.S. should prepare for that, and the Soviet Union will do the same."

Before leaving Vienna, Kennedy wanted to understand clearly the options the Soviet was leaving him. Under the interim arrangement that Khrushchev had suggested, would U.S. military forces in Berlin remain, along with free access to the city? Kennedy asked.

Yes, for six months' time, responded Khrushchev.

And then the forces would have to be withdrawn? Kennedy asked.

Khrushchev said that was so.

The president said that either Khrushchev did not believe the U.S. was serious or the situation was so "unsatisfactory" to him that he believed he needed this "drastic action." Kennedy said he would see British Prime Minister Macmillan in London on his way home and would have to tell him that he was faced with the unhappy alternative of accepting a Soviet fait accompli on Berlin or confrontation. Kennedy said he had the impression that Khrushchev was leaving him with the only alternatives of conflict or capitulation.

Khrushchev suggested that in order for Kennedy to save face, U.S. and Soviet troops could be maintained in Berlin not as occupation forces but subject to East German control and registered with the United Nations. "I want peace," Khrushchev said. "But if you want war, that is your problem. It is not the USSR that threatens with war, it is the U.S."

Kennedy's extension of their meeting wasn't going well. "It is you, and not I, who wants to force a change," the president protested, avoiding Khrushchev's provocative use of the word "war."

It was as if two teenage boys with nuclear sticks were arguing over who was trying to pick a fight with whom.

"In any event," said Khrushchev, "the USSR will have no choice but to accept the challenge. It must respond and it will respond. The calamities of a war will be shared equally.... It is up to the U.S. to decide whether there will be war or peace." Kennedy, he said, could tell this to Macmillan, de Gaulle, and Adenauer.

Khrushchev said his decision on Berlin was "irrevocable" and "firm": a peace treaty with East Germany by December with all its consequences on Allied control of West Berlin, or an interim agreement that would lead to the same outcome.

"If that is true, it's going to be a cold winter," said Kennedy.

For all the power of Kennedy's single-sentence summation, he got even that wrong. His troubles would come much earlier.

BERLIN

SUNDAY AFTERNOON, JUNE 4, 1961

While Khrushchev and Kennedy engaged in angry exchanges about the possibility of war in Berlin, Berliners themselves were out in droves on the first sunny, dry weekend after a month of rain. They were riding in cars and on motor scooters, in the elevated train and subway, heading for Berlin's many parks and lakesides to swim, sail, play, and enjoy the sun.

The Berlin newspapers were calling it "beautiful summit weather," and the consensus was that a meeting of the two leaders controlling their fate was more likely than not to reduce tensions. Berliners from both sides of the city filled West Berlin's cinemas in the evening to see the latest releases: *Spartacus*, with its four Oscars; *Ben-Hur*, with Charlton Heston; and *The Marriage-Go-Round*, with James Mason and Susan Hayward. The film ads reminded East Berliners that their soft East marks would be accepted in a one-to-one exchange for entrance—the best bargain in town.

In the East, Walter Ulbricht was weathering a bread shortage and was out with the people celebrating the communist youth organization's Children's Day. With little news from the Vienna Summit, the papers were filled with photographs and accounts of the two wives' joint Vienna outings.

Fewer refugees registered during the Vienna Summit weekend than at any time for the last many years, because East Germans were holding out hope that the Vienna talks would bring a change for the better.

When asked what he expected from the talks, Ulbricht said he was adopting a wait-and-see attitude. Mayor Willy Brandt told his citizens, "Our good cause is in good hands with President Kennedy. . . . The best we can hope for is that some of the misunderstandings that might give rise to new threats and dangers in the future are cleared up."

VIENNA
SUNDAY AFTERNOON, JUNE 4, 1961

Having just threatened him with war, Khrushchev smiled broadly as he bid farewell to a frowning, shell-shocked Kennedy on the Soviet embassy's steps. Photographers caught their contrasting moods for the next day's papers.

Khrushchev knew he had won the day, even if he could not yet know the consequences. He would recall later that Kennedy "looked not only anxious, but deeply upset . . . Looking at him, I couldn't help feeling sorry and a little bit upset myself. I hadn't meant to upset him. I would have liked very much for us to part in a different mood. But there was nothing I could do to help him. . . . As one human being toward another, I felt bad about his disappointment. . . .

"Politics is a merciless business," Khrushchev concluded.

The Soviet leader could guess what U.S. hard-liners would argue when they discovered how poorly Kennedy had performed. "We've always said the Bolsheviks don't understand the soft language of negotiations," Khrushchev reckoned they would say. "They understand only power politics. They tricked you; they gave your nose a good pull. You got a good going-over from them, and now you've come back empty-handed and disgraced."

After seeing off Kennedy at the airport, Austrian Foreign Minister Bruno Kreisky visited with Khrushchev. "The President was very gloomy at the airport," said Kreisky. "He seemed upset, and his face had changed. Obviously the meeting did not go well for him."

Khrushchev said he had also noticed Kennedy's sour mood and told Kreisky that Kennedy's problem was that he "still doesn't quite understand the realignment of forces, and he still lives by the policies of his predecessors—especially as far as the German question is concerned. He's not ready to lift the threat of world war which hangs over Berlin. Our talks were helpful in that they gave us a chance to sound each other out and get to know each other. But that's all, and it's not enough."

With the two days of meetings so fresh in his mind, Khrushchev recounted for Kreisky much of his dialogue with Kennedy—knowing Kreisky would pass word of his triumph to other European leftists, including Berlin Mayor Willy Brandt.

In contrast to Kennedy, Khrushchev left Vienna in as unhurried a manner as he had arrived. While the Soviet leader joined a dinner given in his honor by the Austrian government, Kennedy licked his wounds en route to London.

K ennedy was brutally honest about his poor performance. As he drove away from the Soviet embassy with Secretary Rusk in his black limo, with presidential and American flags fluttering on its wings, he banged the flat of his hand against the shelf beneath the rear window. Rusk in particular had been shocked Khrushchev had used the word "war" during their acrimonious exchange, a term diplomats avoided and invariably replaced with any number of less alarming synonyms.

Despite all the president's pre-summit briefings, Rusk felt Kennedy had been unprepared for Khrushchev's bullying brutality. The extent of Vienna's failure would not be as easy to measure as the Bay of Pigs fiasco. There would be no dead exile combatants in a misbegotten landing area who had risked their lives in the expectation that Kennedy and the United States would not abandon them. However, the consequences could be even bloodier. Confirmed in his suspicions of Kennedy's weakness, Khrushchev might engage in just the sort of "miscalculation" that could lead to nuclear war.

Kennedy carried with him to London and Prime Minister Macmillan the aide-mémoire that detailed the Soviet demands for a German settlement within six months, "or else." If the Soviets made it public, as Kennedy had to assume they would, his critics would accuse him of having walked into a Berlin trap in Vienna that he should have seen coming.

Kennedy wanted to vent, but how did he play the outcome of the meeting to a media entourage that had become such an extension of himself? Did he spin it as an amiable exchange, as he had instructed his Soviet expert Bohlen to do in his planned press briefings?

No. Kennedy decided to leave behind in Vienna his press secretary, Pierre Salinger, to brief the journalism industry's top reporters about the summit's "somber" outcome. Before leaving, the president would meet privately in a room at the ambassador's residence with *New York Times* writer James "Scotty" Reston. He told O'Donnell he wanted to get across to Americans "the seriousness of the situation, and the *New York Times* would be the place to do it. I'll give Scotty a grim picture."

Still, he was not yet convinced Khrushchev would deliver on his Berlin threat. Perhaps de Gaulle was right when he said Khrushchev would bluff and bluster and continue to delay on Berlin as he had thus far. "Anybody who talks the way he did today and really means it would be crazy, and I'm sure he's not crazy," Kennedy told O'Donnell, not feeling very certain about that at all.

At age fifty-two, the Scottish-born Reston had already won two Pulitzer Prizes and was perhaps the most influential and most broadly read journalist in Washington. He was dressed in his usual tweed and bow tie and was chewing his briar pipe while Kennedy debriefed him under ground rules that he would neither quote the president nor mention their private meeting.

Kennedy wore a hat pulled low on his forehead as he sunk into the sofa. It would be one of the most candid sessions ever between a reporter and a commander in chief.

Having an exclusive from Kennedy on the Vienna Summit with 1,500 other reporters out jockeying for access was a coup of some significance for Reston in the new TV age that he so despised. It would be made all the more meaningful by what Kennedy would tell him in a darkened room behind closed blinds so as to conceal their meeting from other reporters.

"How was it?" asked Reston.

"Worst thing in my life," said Kennedy. "He savaged me."

Reston jotted in his notebook: "Not the usual bullshit. There is a look a man has when he has to tell the truth."

Kennedy, deep in the sofa next to Reston, said Khrushchev had violently attacked him on American imperialism—and that he'd turned particularly aggressive on Berlin. "I've got two problems," he told Reston. "First, to figure out why he did it, and in such a hostile way. And second, to figure out what we can do about it."

Reston rightly concluded in his *New York Times* report, which carefully protected the confidentiality of his Kennedy meeting, that the president "was astonished by the rigidity and toughness of the Soviet leader." He called the meeting acrimonious, and rightly said that Kennedy left Vienna pessimistic on issues across the board. In particular, the president "definitely got the impression that the German question was going to be a very near thing."

Kennedy told Reston that, because of the Bay of Pigs, Khrushchev "thought that anyone who was so young and inexperienced as to get into that mess could be taken. And anyone who got into it and didn't see it through had no guts. So he just beat the hell out of me. . . . I've got a terrible problem."

Kennedy had conjured up a quick analysis of the dangers this posed and how he had to deal with them. "If he thinks I'm inexperienced and have no guts, until we remove those ideas we won't get anywhere with him. So we have to act." He told Reston that among other things he would increase the military budget and send another division to Germany.

On the flight to London, Kennedy called O'Donnell to his cabin, wanting to vent some more but out of hearing range of Rusk, Bohlen, and the others on Air Force One. Despair had already darkened the mood so much throughout the plane that Kennedy's Air Force liaison Godfrey McHugh compared it to "riding with the losing baseball team after the World Series. Nobody said very much."

Kennedy had started his presidency determined to put Berlin on a back burner. Yet now it threatened to blow up in his face. He was overwhelmed by fear that the matter of preserving certain West German and Allied rights in West Berlin could start a nuclear war.

"All wars start from stupidity," Kennedy said to O'Donnell. "God knows I'm not an isolationist, but it seems particularly stupid to risk killing a million Americans over an argument about access rights on an Autobahn in the Soviet zone of Germany, or because the Germans want Germany reunified. If I'm going to treat Russia with a nuclear war, it will have to be for much bigger and more important reasons than that. Before I back Khrushchev against the wall and put him to a final test, the freedom of all Western Europe will have to be at stake."

Those who had worked so hard to brief Kennedy ahead of the summit were most disappointed of all, particularly members of Ambassador Thompson's staff, who saw that most of their advice had been ignored. One of them, Kempton Jenkins, would reflect later that it had been "the golden opportunity for [Kennedy] to be charming, to have Jackie charm Khrushchev, and then have Kennedy come in and say, 'Now look, I want to say this perfectly straight. Get your bloody hands off Berlin or we'll destroy you.'"

They were terms Khrushchev would have understood. The U.S. had such nuclear superiority that Kennedy did not need to take the Vienna beating. Jenkins, who closely examined the transcripts later, regretted Kennedy "never did" deliver a tough message to Khrushchev: "He was constantly talking about: We've got to find a way out. What can we do to reassure you? We don't want you to distrust our motives. We're not aggressive." The president had further confirmed Khrushchev's growing impression he could be easily outmaneuvered, and from that point forward Khrushchev would act more aggressively in the conviction that there would be little price to pay.

Kennedy's predecessors had defended West Berlin so resolutely partly in hopes of eventually breaking communist control of East Germany, and to support the West German government's claim to the city as the future capital of a unified country. Kennedy believed in none of that and wanted to avoid failure in Berlin because he thought that withdrawal there could turn West Germany against the U.S. and Britain, and would likely lead to a breakup of NATO.

Speaking with O'Donnell en route to London, Kennedy expressed a surprising sympathy for Khrushchev's predicament in Berlin. He knew that the Soviet problem was an economic one, and that West Berlin's thriving capitalism was draining East Germany of its talent.

"You can't blame Khrushchev for being sore about that," he told O'Donnell.

Though he had just been beaten up by Khrushchev, Kennedy directed his venom against Adenauer and his Germans, who continually complained he wasn't tough enough with the Soviets. He was not about to go to war over Berlin—though that was precisely what postwar agreements obligated him to do. "We didn't cause the disunity in Germany," he told O'Donnell. "We aren't really responsible for the four-power occupation of Berlin, a mistake neither we nor the Russians should have agreed to in the first place. But now the West Germans would like us to drive the Russians out of East Germany."

Kennedy complained, "It's not enough for us to be spending a tremendous amount of money on the military defense of Western Europe, and particularly on the defense of West Germany, while West Germany becomes the fastest-growing industrial power in the world. Well, if they think we are rushing into a war over Berlin, except as a last desperate move to save the NATO alliance, they've got another thing coming!"

As their plane descended to London, the president told O'Donnell that he doubted Khrushchev, "for all his shouting," would actually do what he threatened. But Kennedy was also going to be careful not to provoke the Soviet into a rash countermove in response to a sudden U.S. military action. "If we're going to have to start a nuclear war," he said, "we'll have to fix things so it will be started by the President of the United States, and nobody else. Not by a trigger-happy sergeant on a truck convoy at a checkpoint in East Germany."

LONDON
MONDAY MORNING, JUNE 5, 1961

British Prime Minister Macmillan immediately sensed Kennedy's anguish— both the physical pain in his back and the psychological torment from his meeting with Khrushchev.

While they talked, U.S. officials in crisis mode fanned out across Europe to brief key allies on what amounted to a new Soviet ultimatum. Rusk in Paris visited with de Gaulle and NATO. State Department officials Foy Kohler and Martin Hillenbrand flew to Bonn to brief Adenauer.

The British prime minister called off the formal morning meeting planned with the president—"Foreign Office and all that"—and instead invited him up to his private quarters at Admiralty House, as 10 Downing Street was closed for repairs. They sat for nearly three hours on their own, from 10:30 a.m. to 1:25 p.m., an hour longer than had been scheduled, during which Macmillan mostly listened while feeding Kennedy sandwiches and whiskey. They then reconvened with Foreign Secretary Lord Home until 3:00 p.m. Their talks that day would help shape Kennedy's closest, most trusting relationship with a foreign leader. He liked the elder Brit's dry wit, deep intelligence, and nonchalance about the most serious matters.

"For the first time in his life," Macmillan would recall later, regarding the Vienna Summit, "Kennedy met a man who was impervious to his charm." The president appeared to him "rather stunned—'baffled' would perhaps be fairer . . . impressed and shocked." Macmillan saw that Kennedy had been overwhelmed by Khrushchev's ruthlessness and barbarity—rather like meeting Napoleon "at the height of his power for the first time," or like Neville Chamberlain "trying to hold a conversation with Herr Hitler."

Macmillan told Kennedy that the simple position for the West to take "would be to say that the Russians could do what they liked about a treaty with the DDR [East Germany], but the West stood on their rights and would meet any attack on these with all the force at their command."

Kennedy said it was precisely that threat which had stopped Soviet action to that point. Unfortunately, he said, Khrushchev perceived the West as weaker after recent events in Laos and "elsewhere"—a euphemism for Cuba. After all, even in 1949 when the West had a nuclear monopoly, it had not been prepared to force its way into West Berlin, and the Russians knew that they were now relatively stronger than they were twelve years earlier, said Kennedy.

Lord Home feared Khrushchev was being forced into action over Berlin due to his difficulties with the East German refugees and related problems with other satellites. Khrushchev "might feel that he had to find a way of stopping this," he said. Once Khrushchev's new aide-mémoire on Berlin was made public, Lord Home said it would put the West in an uncomfortable position, "as on the face of it, it appears fairly reasonable."

Kennedy wanted help from the British in composing a speech that he would deliver the next day in Washington. It would need to state Khrushchev's views, strongly reaffirm Western commitment to West Berlin, and restate Berliners' right of free choice about their future. The truth, said Macmillan, was that "whatever might be happening in other parts of the world, in Berlin the West was winning. It was a very poor advertisement for the Soviet system that so many people should seek to leave the Communist paradise."

Kennedy and Macmillan agreed to step up military and other contingency planning on Berlin with an emphasis on what the West should do (1) if the Russians signed a treaty with East Germany, (2) if after the signing of a treaty, civilian supplies were interrupted, and/or (3) Western military supplies were interfered with. Home wanted Kennedy to present counterproposals to the Soviets on their aide-mémoire. Kennedy disagreed, fearing a proposal for Berlin negotiations might appear yet another "sign of weakness."

While flying back to the U.S., Kennedy sat in his shorts with his top aides sitting around him. His eyes were red and watery, betraying how dead tired he felt. His back was throbbing in pain—though even Kennedy would never know how much his illnesses and the concoctions he took against them had impaired his Vienna performance. He shook his head, stared down at his feet, and at one point hugged his bare legs, muttering about Khrushchev's unbending manner and what dangers might follow.

Kennedy told his secretary Evelyn Lincoln that he wanted to get some rest to prepare himself for a busy day in Washington. He asked her to file away safely the classified documents that he had been scouring. As she worked, she came upon a slip of paper on which Kennedy had scrawled two lines:

I know there is a God—and I see a storm coming;
If He has a place for me, I believe I am ready.

Lincoln did not know what to make of the paper, but it worried her. She could not know that Kennedy had written down from memory a partial quote from Abraham Lincoln, speaking to an Illinois educator in the spring of 1860 regarding his determination to halt slavery. The note was likely not about inviting death—Evelyn Lincoln's interpretation—but rather about recognizing a calling.

Bobby sat with his brother upon his return. Tears were running down the president's cheeks, produced by a mixture of the stress he was feeling and the decisions ahead. Bobby would recall later that he had "never seen my brother cry before about something like this. I was up in my bedroom with him and he looked at me and said, 'Bobby, if nuclear exchange comes, it doesn't matter about us. We've had a good life, we're adults. We bring these things on ourselves. The thought, though, of women and children perishing in a nuclear exchange. I can't adjust to that.'"

Journalist Stewart Alsop, a longtime friend of the president, had seen Kennedy on his London visit at Westminster Cathedral during the christening of the newborn child of Stanisław Radziwill, whose third wife was Jacqueline Kennedy's younger sister, Lee Bouvier. It was a grand affair, attended by the prime minister and all the Kennedy family. The president coaxed Alsop into a corner and talked to him for fifteen minutes about all he had just been through. "I had the sense that the thing had come to him as a very great shock, which he was beginning to adjust to."

Alsop had considered the Bay of Pigs to be the moment that had "cured any illusions that Kennedy had about the certainty of success" after a life in which he had experienced very few failures. Alsop considered Vienna a more serious moment because of the difference between Cuba's lesson that one can fail at a very big thing and the prospect of another failure that could lead to nuclear war.

Kennedy had been in office four months and sixteen days, but Alsop believed it was in Vienna that he truly became the American commander in chief. He had confronted there the brutal nature of his enemy and the reality that Berlin would be their battleground.

"After that was when he really began to be president in the full sense of the word," Alsop believed.

EAST BERLIN
WEDNESDAY, JUNE 7, 1961

East German leader Walter Ulbricht could hardly believe his good fortune as he was briefed on the Vienna talks by Mikhail Pervukhin, the Soviet ambassador to East Germany. He grew all the more satisfied as he received further details from leading officers of the Soviet High Commission in Karlshorst, with whom he spoke at the end of almost every day.

The previous three days and nights of military exercises—bringing together his National People's Army with their Soviet counterparts—had demonstrated that Ulbricht was ready militarily for whatever the West might throw at him when Khrushchev finally acted on Berlin. Ulbricht's soldiers had impressed Soviet Defense Minister Rodion Malinovsky and Andrei Grechko, commander of all Warsaw Pact forces, who considered the exercise sufficiently important to oversee it themselves. East German soldiers had proved themselves to be far more disciplined in the field than Soviet officers had anticipated.

As Ulbricht ended one of his routine twelve-hour days, he was satisfied as his chauffeur drove him to his new home at Wandlitz, some twenty miles northeast of Berlin on the edge of a thick forest. Ulbricht had not felt so optimistic in months, perhaps years, as his chauffeur drove him past the neat gardens and stuccoed villas of the Pankow district.

Pervukhin had delivered to him a copy of the Soviet aide-mémoire that Khrushchev had passed to Kennedy in Vienna. Many of Ulbricht's ideas regarding Berlin's future, stubbornly repeated in numerous letters over many months, had made it into Khrushchev's official language. Pervukhin told Ulbricht that Moscow would go public with the document in two days.

Ulbricht was confident this time that Khrushchev would not be able to walk away from his Berlin ultimatum. Khrushchev was also getting tougher on Germany in other respects. Foreign Minister Gromyko had lodged an angry protest with the British, French, and U.S. embassies in Moscow about Chancellor Adenauer's decision for the first time to schedule a plenary meeting in West Berlin of the Bundesrat, the upper house of the West Berlin parliament, on June 16. He called the move a "major new provocation" against all socialist states.

After badgering Khrushchev for so long, Ulbricht wrote a letter that day to the Soviet leader that dripped with ingratiating sentiment. "We warmly thank the [Communist Party] Presidium and you, dear friend," he said, "for the great efforts which you are undertaking for the achievement of a peace treaty and the resolution of the West Berlin issue."

Ulbricht wrote that he not only fully agreed with the wording of the ultimatum, but that he also embraced Khrushchev's summit performance and his representation of the Communist Party, the Soviet government, and the socialist camp.

"This was a great political accomplishment," he wrote.

Yet Ulbricht also realized much of what had been accomplished had come due to his pressure, and he was not about to let up now. He spent much of the letter complaining about growing West German "revanchism" that threatened them both. The West German Economics Ministry had threatened to repeal its trade treaty with East Germany should a peace treaty be concluded. The cost to the East German economy would be great, as it would then be treated "as a foreign state, which would have to pay for its daily purchases in West Germany in foreign currency" it did not have.

Ulbricht told Khrushchev that Adenauer and other West German officials were lobbying neutral countries to reduce the rights of East German consulates and trade offices. Adenauer was also trying to prevent East German participation in the next Olympic Games.

Ulbricht was most concerned with preventing any further procrastination now that Khrushchev seemed fully focused on Berlin. "Comrade Pervukhin informed us here that you would find it useful if a consultation of the first secretaries [of Communist Parties of the Soviet bloc] would take place as soon as possible." Ulbricht said he thus had taken the liberty of appealing to leaders of Poland, Hungary, Romania, and Bulgaria to gather on July 20 and 21 to "discuss preparations for a peace treaty."

Ulbricht wanted the entire socialist bloc to circle around him. "The goal of this meeting," he said by way of instruction to Khrushchev, "should be an agreement on the political, diplomatic, economic and organizational preparation, and also measures for the coordination of radio and press agitation."

MOSCOW
WEDNESDAY, JUNE 7, 1961

Upon Khrushchev's return to Moscow from Vienna, he ordered multiple copies of the summit minutes to be produced and distributed among friends and allies. He wanted his proficient handling of Kennedy to be known far and wide—particularly among his critics at home and abroad. He had the papers marked "Top Secret," but he circulated them to a broader audience than was usual for such documents. One copy went to Castro in Cuba, though he was not yet considered a member of the socialist camp. Among the eighteen nations for distribution were also the noncommunist countries of Egypt, Iraq, India, Brazil, Cambodia, and Mexico. A senior Soviet would brief Yugoslavia's Josip Broz Tito.

Khrushchev was acting like the victor, wanting everyone to relive the championship match with him. He followed his tough line in Vienna with a harder and more dictatorial line at home, blaming rising Soviet civil discontent, vagrancy, crime, and unemployment on too much liberalization, sounding increasingly like his own neo-Stalinist critics. He also reversed reforms of the judicial system associated with his de-Stalinization.

"What liberals you've become!" he shot at Roman Rudenko, chief public prosecutor, as he criticized laws that were too soft on thieves, whom he thought should be shot.

"No matter how you scold me," said Rudenko, "if the law does not provide for the death penalty, we can't apply it."

"The peasants have a saying: 'Get rid of the bad seeds,'" Khrushchev responded. "Stalin had the correct position on these issues. He went too far, but we never had any mercy on criminals. Our fight with enemies should be merciless and well directed."

Khrushchev pushed through changes that increased the use of the death penalty, grew the size of police units in the KGB, and reversed many of the liberalizing trends he himself had introduced.

While Kennedy headed home, worrying about what to tell America, Khrushchev was at the Indonesian embassy celebrating the sixtieth birthday of the country's visiting leader, Sukarno.

The band struck up dance tunes out on the embassy's lawn as various party leaders, including President Leonid Brezhnev and First Deputy Premier Anastas Mikoyan, at Khrushchev's urging, got up to join a folk dance. Diplomats and prominent Russians kept time with rhythmic handclapping. Among the dancers was Prince Souvanna Phouma of Laos.

Sukarno himself took Khrushchev's wife, Nina, onto the dance floor. Khrushchev's post-Vienna high was infecting everyone. The Soviet leader took a baton at one point to lead the orchestra and told jokes throughout the evening. When Sukarno said he would want new Soviet loans in exchange for letting Khrushchev direct the band, the Soviet leader opened his coat, pulled out his pockets, and showed they were empty.

"Look, he robs me of everything," he said to the crowd's laughter.

Watching Mikoyan sway expertly, Khrushchev joked that his number two only kept his job because the party Central Committee had ruled that he was such a fine dancer. No one had seen Khrushchev so carefree since before the 1956 Hungarian uprising and the 1957 coup attempt against him.

When Sukarno said he wanted to kiss a pretty girl, Khrushchev's wife searched the crowd before settling on a reluctant partner, whose husband was at first unwilling to make her available.

"Oh, please come," said Nina. "You only have to kiss him once, not twice."

So the girl gave the Indonesian leader his kiss.

Yet the enduring memory of the evening was when Sukarno drew Khrushchev to the dance floor for an awkward pas de deux. They danced a bit hand in hand before the euphoric Khrushchev performed solo. Khrushchev described his dance style as that of "a cow on ice," heavy, uncertain, and with unsteady feet.

But on this occasion Khrushchev bent down and kicked his legs out, Cossack style. The heavyset Soviet leader looked unusually light on his feet.

12

ANGRY SUMMER

The construction workers of our capital are for the most part busy
building apartment houses, and their working capacities are fully
employed to that end. Nobody intends to put up a wall.

Walter Ulbricht, at a press conference, June 15, 1961

Somehow he does succeed in being a President, but only in the
appearance of one.

Dean Acheson, writing to President Truman about his work
on Berlin for President Kennedy, June 24, 1961

The issue over Berlin, which Khrushchev is now moving toward a
crisis . . . is far more than an issue over that city. It is broader and deeper
than even the German question as a whole. It has become an issue of
resolution between the U.S.A. and the U.S.S.R., the outcome of which will
go far to determine the confidence of Europe—indeed, of the world—in
the United States.

Dean Acheson, in a report on Berlin for President Kennedy,
June 29, 1961

HOUSE OF MINISTRIES, EAST BERLIN
THURSDAY, JUNE 15, 1961

Walter Ulbricht's decision to summon West Berlin–based correspondents to a press conference on his communist side of the border was so unprecedented that his propagandists did not even know how to go about inviting the reporters.

The problem was that Ulbricht had cut off all telephone trunk lines between the city's two parts in 1952. So Ulbricht's people had to dispatch a special operations team across the border, armed with rolls of West German ten-pfennig coins and a West Berlin press association membership list. Working from public telephone booths, they called Western correspondents one by one with a terse message: "Press conference. Chairman of the State Council of the German Democratic Republic Ulbricht. House of Ministries. Thursday. Eleven o'clock. You are invited."

Three days later, some three hundred correspondents—roughly half of them representing each side of the city—crowded into a huge banquet hall where Hermann Göring had once entertained officers of the Third Reich's Air Ministry. A huge hammer and compass, the East German national symbol, rose triumphantly behind the stage where the Nazi eagle and swastika had once stood.

By the time Ulbricht marched in, the room was already uncomfortably warm and stuffy from the combination of reporters' body warmth, the hot day outside, and the lack of air-conditioning. Beside him was Gerhard Eisler, the legendary communist who ran East Germany's broadcasting operations. Known to correspondents as East Germany's Goebbels, he looked out at the crowd through small eyes magnified by thick bifocals. Though convicted as a Soviet spy in the U.S., he had jumped bail in 1950 and dramatically escaped New York aboard a Polish steamer before making his way to the newly created East Germany. Western reporters whispered to each other what they knew about Eisler.

Mutual Broadcasting Network correspondent Norman Gelb soaked in the atmosphere. He had never seen Ulbricht so close up, and he wondered how this short, unassuming, tight-lipped gray man with the shrill voice and rimless glasses had survived so many Soviet and East German power struggles. Though his neatly trimmed goatee gave him an intended resemblance to Lenin, Gelb thought Ulbricht looked more like an aging office manager than a dictator.

Timed to coincide with Khrushchev's first public report on the Vienna Summit in Moscow, Ulbricht's long opening statement disappointed correspondents who had come expecting something of historic consequence. Ulbricht's purpose in organizing the extraordinary meeting only grew clearer after he began taking questions, two or three at a time, which he answered with long lectures that made follow-ups impossible.

Correspondents scribbled furiously as Ulbricht declared that West Berlin's character would change dramatically after East Germany signed its peace treaty with the Soviets, with or without Western agreement. As a "free city," he said, it was "self-evident that so-called refugee camps in West Berlin will be closed and persons who occupy themselves with traffic in mankind will leave Berlin." He said that would also mean the shuttering of U.S., British, French, and West German "espionage centers" operating in West Berlin. Ulbricht said East German travel thereafter would be more strictly regulated and that only those who obtained permission from the Interior Ministry would be able to leave the country.

Annamarie Doherr, a correspondent for the left-leaning *Frankfurter Rundschau*, pressed Ulbricht for more details. She wondered how Ulbricht would achieve control over travel, given the open East Berlin border. "Mr. Chairman," she said, "does the creation of a 'free city,' as you term it, mean the state boundaries of the German Democratic Republic will be erected at the Brandenburg Gate?" She wanted to know whether he was committed to carrying through his plan "with all of its consequences," which included a potential war.

Ulbricht's face was passive, and his cold eyes remained unchanged. He answered without emotion: "I understand your question as implying that there are people in West Germany who would like to see us mobilize the construction workers of the capital of the GDR for the purpose of building a wall." He paused, looked down on the short, plump Frau Doherr from the rostrum, and then continued. "I am not aware of any such intention. The construction workers of our capital are for the most part busy building apartment houses, and their working capacities are fully employed to that end. Nobody intends to put up a wall."

It was Ulbricht's first public mention ever of a "wall," though the reporter had not mentioned such a barrier herself. He had shown his hand, yet none of the media would pick up on it in their reports that would follow. It sounded to them like more of Ulbricht's usual obfuscation.

At six o'clock that evening, East Germans could watch Khrushchev's own report about the Vienna Summit's outcome on state television. The Soviet leader bluntly declared: "A peace treaty with Germany cannot be postponed any longer." By design, the edited replay of Ulbricht's press conference followed the Soviet leader's statement at eight p.m.

The chilling effect was immediate. Despite increased monitoring of borders by security officers, the following day would bring the biggest one-day outflow of refugees of the year: a record 4,770, which would have amounted to 1.74 million people on an annualized basis from a population of just 17 million. The term increasingly used to describe the flight, *Torschlusspanik*—the fear of the door's closing before you can pass through it—described the panicked mood that was spreading like a rash across East Germany after Ulbricht's speech.

Some commentators at the time believed the rapid increase in refugees showed that Ulbricht had miscalculated the potential impact of the press conference. More likely, it was all part of the East German's endgame. For all of Khrushchev's increased public expressions of determination regarding Berlin, Ulbricht knew the Soviet leader had not entirely thought through his next step after Vienna.

Yet each of Ulbricht's moves was carefully calibrated. By making matters worse for himself over the short term, he would make Khrushchev digest ever more deeply the unacceptable cost of further inaction.

Ulbricht was determined not to lose the post-Vienna momentum.

THE WHITE HOUSE, WASHINGTON, D.C.
FRIDAY, JUNE 16, 1961

Given his well-known criticism of Kennedy's Bay of Pigs performance, Dean Acheson was flattered and a little surprised that Kennedy was turning to him again for advice. The president's questions to him were as simple as they were difficult to answer: How did he counter Khrushchev after his Vienna ultimatum? How seriously should the president take the Soviet leader's Berlin threat—and what should he do about it?

The Acheson relationship to Kennedy had become an increasingly complex one. The two men had grown acquainted with each other in the late 1950s, when then Senator Kennedy had occasionally driven his Georgetown neighbor home from meetings on Capitol Hill. What the young Kennedy didn't know was how much Acheson detested Kennedy's father, not only for his support for an American foreign policy of isolationism, but also for the dishonest way in which Acheson believed he had come about his riches. Acheson believed it was those ill-gotten gains that had then bought the White House for his son.

For President Kennedy, however, Acheson provided perhaps his best option for clear answers to urgent questions. Acheson regarded his job that day as cutting through the mush of administration decision-making represented by the "Interdepartmental Coordinating Group on Berlin Contingency Planning," better known as the Berlin Task Force. Acheson assured the men in the room that his purpose "was not to interfere with any present operation but rather to stimulate further thought and activity."

He said the task force had to take Khrushchev's threats in Vienna at face value, and thus their Berlin contingency planning was no longer a theoretical exercise. Decisions had to be made, he said. The cost of inaction was enormous, as was the danger of failing to reverse Khrushchev's growing perception of American weakness. The issue of Berlin involved "deeply the prestige of the United States and perhaps its very survival."

Because he didn't believe a political solution was available, he said the question was now whether they had the political will to make difficult decisions, "regardless of the opinions of our allies." Khrushchev was "now willing to do what he [has] not been willing to do before," said Acheson, "undoubtedly due to the feeling that the U.S. [will] not oppose him with nuclear weapons."

If the U.S. was unwilling to do that, Acheson continued, it could not oppose Russian advances. Acheson was little interested in hearing the views of others in the room. He was there to convert them to his own thinking. He believed that the Kennedy administration was entering the worst of all worlds. The more Khrushchev doubted the U.S. willingness to use nuclear weapons, the more he might test Kennedy to the point that the president would have no other choice but to use them. "Nuclear weapons should not be looked upon as the last and largest weapon to be used," he said, "but as the first step in a new policy in protecting the United States from the failure of a policy of deterrence."

Acheson's hard line had won him many enemies in the Democratic Party and among the senior officials gathered in the room. He told them that inaction now regarding Berlin would have a ripple effect far beyond the city that would endanger U.S. interests around the world. "Berlin is vital to the power position of the U.S.," he said. "Withdrawal would destroy our power position." Thus, they had "to act so as neither to invite a series of defeats nor precipitate ourselves into the ultimate catastrophe."

With apologies to the Joint Chiefs and the secretary of defense, who he conceded would in the end decide the military issues, Acheson then outlined what he would propose to President Kennedy. Acheson wanted a more intensive training of U.S. reserves than their usual summer routine so that they would be in battle-ready condition. He wanted the U.S. to fly "STRAC units"—Strategic Army Corps operations—to Europe, and, after their exercises, leave part of them behind to increase Allied strength near the front. He envisioned crash programs for Polaris and other missile systems and submarines to improve nuclear capability. He wanted the U.S. to resume nuclear testing and, in violation of Kennedy's promise to Khrushchev, also restart the sort of reconnaissance flights that had triggered the capture of the U-2 and RB-47 airmen and the breakdown of U.S.–Soviet relations. He wanted aircraft carriers deployed in positions that better helped defend Berlin.

The men in the room were stunned. Acheson was proposing nothing less than a full military mobilization that would place the United States on a war footing. If Acheson reflected Kennedy's thinking in any way, they were witnessing a historic turning point in the confrontation with Moscow over Berlin.

Acheson continued in a similar vein. He wanted a substantial increase in the military budget and a proclamation of a national emergency so that Americans got the point, supported by congressional resolutions. All this would, of course, require preparing the American people and Congress psychologically. For that, Acheson suggested a large program of air raid shelter construction as a means of galvanizing the population.

He wanted a general alert of the Strategic Air Command and a movement of troops to Europe. If none of this had any impact on the Soviets, he wanted a garrison airlift for Berlin and a continued testing of checkpoints through increased ground traffic to ensure access remained open. That might be followed "by a military movement indicating the eventual use of tactical nuclear weapons and then strategic nuclear weapons."

Acheson anticipated Allied protests, particularly from the British. "It would be important to bring our allies along," he said, "but we should be prepared to go without them unless the Germans buckled." Acheson was convinced his friend Adenauer would support his plan, and that was most crucial, as it would be German troops and interests that would be most at stake. "We should be prepared to go to the bitter end if the Germans go along with us," he said.

Though the men in the room did not know to what extent Acheson spoke for Kennedy, he no doubt reflected the president's growing sense of urgency. The president had been frustrated throughout the year with the lethargic decision-making process of the State Department, which he called "a bowl of jelly," and of the Pentagon, which often took days or weeks to answer his questions. He wanted his apparatus to deal more quickly with a world where he would have only minutes to decide matters that could cost millions of lives.

Acheson gave the group just two weeks to explore his ideas. He said a decision should then be made on his proposals, and action should then begin on implementation. Gauging the surprised faces around the room, Acheson said he knew he was outlining a very risky course, but it was not foolhardy if the U.S. government was really prepared to use nuclear weapons for the protection of Berlin, on which it had staked its entire prestige. "If we [are] not prepared to go all the way, we should not start. Once having started, backing down would be devastating. If we [are] not prepared to take all the risks, then we had better begin by attempting to mitigate the eventual disastrous results of our failure to fulfill our commitments."

After Acheson ended his presentation, the room fell silent. Acheson knew that those who drove policy in Washington were those who were most determined to do so, and none among Kennedy's top foreign policy team offered a dissenting view. The State Department's Foy Kohler, an Acheson ally and the meeting's chair, broke the ice by expressing his general agreement. He added, however, that the British opposed Acheson's idea of demonstrably sending troops up the Autobahn to protest any communist restriction of access to Berlin. Macmillan had argued they would be "chewed up" by the Soviets.

The Pentagon's Paul Nitze added that Sir Evelyn Shuckburgh, who headed the British policy planning staff for Berlin and Germany, had said "it was essential not to scare people to death with our buildup."

If the NATO allies opposed actions to defend Berlin, Acheson argued, the U.S. needed to know now. "We should proceed not by asking them if they would be afraid if we said 'Boo!' We should instead say 'Boo!' and see how far they jump."

Ambassador Thompson, a known Acheson opponent who had flown in from Moscow for the meeting, warned, "We must not corner [Khrushchev] completely." As it was important for the Russians not to think the U.S. was isolated from its allies, "it would perhaps be best not to say 'Boo!' first before getting the British leaders with us."

Acheson fired back that it would be quite a problem to convince Khrushchev they were serious while, at the same time, letting the British know they were not.

Unlike Acheson, Thompson was convinced the Soviet leader did not want a military confrontation and would do much to avoid it. He believed lower-profile actions would be more effective and less likely to provoke Khrushchev into his irrational worst behavior and perhaps provoke just the war that the U.S. hoped to avoid.

Nitze, however, doubted that lower-profile actions could be effective, since it would be difficult to engage in contingency planning without introducing initiatives that would require high-profile presidential declarations and justifications to Congress.

Acheson interjected that they might be able to avoid some of that sort of noise, since Congress might be convinced to go along with many measures on the basis of existing emergency legislation, which could be followed later with a supporting resolution.

Acheson seemed to have thought through everything.

Asked about the president's timeline, Acheson said the basis for decision should come before the secretaries of state and defense by the end of the following week. It had to be done within ten days at the very outside. Acheson was issuing deadlines, and everyone was saluting smartly.

The Pentagon's Nitze said a working group should start within three days, and that its job would be to list the steps necessary regarding Berlin. It would set a target date for getting a full set of military recommendations by June 26.

That was fast for government work.

THE KREMLIN, MOSCOW
WEDNESDAY, JUNE 21, 1961

To add a theatrical touch, Khrushchev wore his wartime lieutenant general's uniform, replete with a hero's decorations, at the military celebration for the twentieth anniversary of Hitler's Soviet invasion. Khrushchev had not worn the uniform since he had served as political adviser on the Stalingrad front during World War II. Given his midsection growth since then, the Soviet army had to tailor him a new one.

As backdrop for the meeting, a documentary film about Khrushchev's life as a military and political hero, called *Our Nikita Sergeyevich*, had just opened in Moscow theaters. The review in the newspaper *Izvestia* said at its opening: "Always and in all things side-by-side with the people, in the thick of events—that is how the Soviet people know Nikita Sergeyevich Khrushchev."

Before television cameras, the cosmonaut Yuri Gagarin praised Khrushchev as "the pioneer explorer of the cosmic age." The Soviet leader received another Order of Lenin and a third golden hammer-and-sickle medal for "guiding the creation and development of the rocket industry . . . which opened a new era in the conquest of space." Khrushchev decorated seven thousand others who had contributed to the flight. To consolidate personal alliances and neutralize rivals, he gave Orders of Lenin to his Politburo ally Leonid Brezhnev and to a potential rival at the October Party Congress, Frol Kozlov. Before acting on Berlin, Khrushchev was protecting his flanks like a master politician.

Khrushchev framed the Western refusal to compromise on Berlin as a threat not only to Moscow but to the entire communist world. Like the Nazis twenty years earlier, he said, the West would suffer complete failure because of the growth in military strength of the Soviet Union and the socialist camp.

One after another, the Soviet Union's military heroes and top commanders praised Khrushchev for his leadership and sounded the alarm about Berlin. Marshal Vasily Chuikov, commander in chief of the Soviet Union's ground forces, told the crowd, "The historic truth is that during the assault on Berlin there was not a single American, British, or French armed soldier around it, except for the prisoners of war whom we freed." Thus, he said, the Allies' claims to special rights in Berlin so long after surrender "are entirely unfounded."

The crowd cheered.

General A. N. Suburov, former commander of Ukrainian partisans, bore personal witness that Khrushchev was a gifted military strategist who could evaluate a major enemy at a historic moment and prescribe the proper course of action behind an achievable plan. Defense Minister Rodion Malinovsky said the Americans and their allies were creating "a gigantic military apparatus and a system of aggressive blocks" around Soviet borders that must be resisted. He said they were stockpiling nuclear arms and rockets and creating areas of tension in Algeria, the Congo, Laos, and Cuba. They were carrying out the same policy that had led to World War II, he declared, "blinded by class hatred for socialism."

Khrushchev was developing the background story for whatever action he would order on Berlin. The Americans were Moscow's most dangerous enemy. Berlin was the battleground to be cleared. Khrushchev was the hero of the past and the present who would lead the socialists of the world at this historic moment. It was at the same time a Berlin battle cry and a campaign event in advance of the October Party Congress. The future of Berlin and Khrushchev were inextricably linked.

Khrushchev then paid his military a substantial reward for their support. Since the mid-1950s, he'd cut defense budgets and manpower while redirecting conventional arms resources to nuclear missile forces. Now he reversed the Soviet troop drawdown, provided access to new weaponry, and increased spending to give balanced support to "all the types of troops of our armed forces," because the military "must have everything necessary in order immediately to smash any opponent . . . for the liberty of our Motherland."

The delirious crowd cheered their leader.

WASHINGTON, D.C.
SATURDAY, JUNE 24, 1961

Even as Dean Acheson was putting the final touches on his new Berlin assessment, he jotted a personal note to his former boss, President Harry

Truman, containing concerns about his new boss. He was "worried and puzzled" by Kennedy, he told Truman. "Somehow he does succeed in being a President, but only in the appearance of one."

Four days later, on June 28, Acheson submitted a preliminary version of his Berlin report to Kennedy in preparation for a press conference the president would hold that day, and a crucial gathering of his National Security Council and key congressional figures the day after.

The thirteenth press conference of Kennedy's six-month-old administration was a result of rising public and media pressure. His reluctance to discuss Berlin through most of June had given rise to reporting that he was behind the curve both with the public and the Pentagon in their willingness to stand up to Khrushchev. *Time* magazine, the largest-circulation American weekly, said in its July 7 edition, "There is a wide and spreading feeling that the Administration has not yet provided ample leadership in guiding the U.S. along the dangerous paths of the cold war." It called upon Kennedy to seize the Berlin challenge "unhesitatingly and with boldness."

Kennedy complained to Salinger about such reports. "This shit has got to stop," he said. What particularly irked him was Richard Nixon's attack on Kennedy, that "never in American history has a man talked so big and acted so little."

As so often in his presidency, Kennedy's rhetoric at the press conference was tougher toward the Soviets than the reality of his policy. "No one can fail to appreciate the gravity of this threat," Kennedy said. "It involves the peace and security of the Western world." He denied that he had seen a proposal for military mobilization for Berlin, though he said he would be considering "a whole variety of measures." The statement was true only in the narrowest sense, in that Acheson was due to discuss military contingencies with the president the following day.

CABINET ROOM, THE WHITE HOUSE, WASHINGTON, D.C.
THURSDAY, JUNE 29, 1961

The first three paragraphs of Acheson's report on Berlin contained an un-
equivocal call to action.

> The issue over Berlin, which Khrushchev is now moving toward a crisis
> to take place, so he says, toward the end of 1961, is far more than an issue
> over that city. It is broader and deeper than even the German question as
> a whole. It has become an issue of resolution between the U.S.A. and the
> U.S.S.R., the outcome of which will go far to determine the confidence of
> Europe—indeed, of the world—in the United States. It is not too much
> to say that the whole position of the United States is in the balance.
>
> Until this conflict of wills is resolved, an attempt to solve the Berlin
> issue by negotiation is worse than a waste of time and energy. It is
> dangerous. This is so because what can be accomplished by negotiation
> depends on the state of mind of Khrushchev and his colleagues.
>
> At present, Khrushchev has demonstrated that he believes he will
> prevail because the United States and its allies will not do what is necessary
> to stop him. He cannot be persuaded by eloquence or logic, or cajoled by
> friendliness. As [former British Ambassador to Moscow] Sir William
> Hayter has written, "The only way of changing [Russian] purpose is to
> demonstrate . . . what they want to do is not possible."

With that as preamble, Acheson tersely laid out his proposal. Berlin was
a problem only because the Soviets had decided to make it one. Their reasons were several: They wanted to neutralize Berlin en route to taking it
over; they wanted to weaken or break up the Western alliance; and they
wished to discredit the United States. He said that the "real themes should
be that Khrushchev is a false trustee and a war monger, and these themes
should be hammered home."

Acheson's goal was to shift Khrushchev's thinking, to convince him that

Kennedy's response to any test in Berlin would be so firm that Khrushchev wouldn't risk it. He wanted the president to declare a national emergency and order a rapid buildup in American nuclear as well as conventional forces. He said American forces in Germany outside Berlin should be reinforced immediately by two or three divisions, to a total of six. The underlying message: If anyone was to back down over Berlin, it would have to be the Soviets.

The Acheson report listed three "essentials" that, if violated, would trigger a military response. The Soviets could not threaten Western garrisons in Berlin, they could not disrupt air and surface access to the city, and they could not interfere with West Berlin's viability and place in the free world. Acheson said a 1948-style airlift should be the response to any interruption of access. If the Soviets blocked the airlift more effectively this time, given their enhanced military capability and Berlin's larger supply needs, then Kennedy should send two American armored divisions up the Autobahn to force open West Berlin.

Acheson had thrown down the gauntlet, but Kennedy wasn't yet prepared to pick it up. The president said little during the meeting. He doubted the American people were ready for a course as ambitious as Acheson was proposing. The Allies would be even less willing. De Gaulle had his hands full with Algeria, and Kennedy knew Macmillan had no stomach for troops storming up the Autobahn.

Thompson led the arguments against the plan. He disagreed with Acheson that Khrushchev's motive was to humiliate the U.S., and said it was instead to stabilize his Eastern European flank. Thus, he favored a quieter Western military buildup and thought it ought to be accompanied by a diplomatic initiative for Berlin negotiations after the West German elections in September. Thompson argued that if Kennedy declared a national emergency, it would make the U.S. look "hysterical" and could force Khrushchev to make a rash countermove he would otherwise avoid.

Admiral Arleigh Burke, the U.S. Navy chief, also opposed Acheson's plan. The veteran opposed the scale of the military "probe" recommended by Acheson, or an airlift unconnected with a probe. Burke had seen Kennedy's reluctance to provide the military support required to succeed in Cuba, and he wasn't about to put his neck on the line for Acheson's Berlin scheme.

Kennedy saw his administration separating into two camps. The first was becoming known as the Hard-Liners on Berlin and the other had been disparagingly labeled by the hawks in the room as the SLOBs, or the Soft-Liners on Berlin. The hard-liners included Acheson and Assistant Secretary of State Foy Kohler, the whole of the Germany desk at the State Department, Assistant Secretary of Defense Paul Nitze, and more often than not, the Joint Chiefs at the Pentagon and Vice President Lyndon Johnson.

The soft-liners disliked the acronym that described them, which they saw as an attempt to discredit their greater willingness to find a negotiated Berlin solution, although they still supported a tough approach to the Soviets and some military buildup. They were a formidable group and were closer personally to Kennedy: Thompson, Kennedy Soviet affairs adviser Charles Bohlen, White House aide Arthur Schlesinger, White House consultant and Harvard professor Henry Kissinger, and special counsel Ted Sorensen. They also included Robert McNamara and McGeorge Bundy.

Acheson, however, had a weapon they could not match: a fully developed proposal that was specific and comprehensive down to the last soldier to be deployed. The SLOBs had provided no alternative.

After the meeting, Schlesinger organized an Acheson counterinsurgency. The forty-three-year-old historian had already served three times on Adlai Stevenson's presidential campaign staff before aligning himself with Kennedy. He believed men of ideas had to collaborate with men of power to achieve noble purposes. He could recite cases from history, when Western intellectuals of their time—Turgot, Voltaire, Struensee, Benjamin Franklin, John Adams, and Thomas Jefferson—had "assumed collaboration with power as the natural order of things." Schlesinger turned to the State Department's legal adviser Abram Chayes to begin work on a plan that was intended to provide a thinking man's alternative to Acheson.

Acheson warned his longtime friend Chayes that he'd already looked at softer options and they wouldn't fly. "Abe, you'll see. You try, but you will find it just won't write."

PITSUNDA

EARLY JULY 1961

From his Black Sea retreat, a frustrated Khrushchev demanded to see a better map of Berlin.

His ambassador to East Germany, Mikhail Pervukhin, had sent him a map that lacked sufficient detail to determine whether Ulbricht was right that it was possible to effectively divide the city. Khrushchev could see that in some parts of Berlin, sectors were divided by a line running down the center of a street. In other places, it seemed the border ran through buildings and canals. Khrushchev worried as he studied more closely that "one sidewalk was in one sector, the other in a different one. Cross the street and you have already crossed the border."

In a July 4 letter, Pervukhin had reported to Foreign Minister Gromyko that shutting down the city's border would be a logistical nightmare, as some 250,000 Berliners crossed the line each day by train, by car, and on foot. "This would necessitate building structures for the whole expanse of the border within the city and adding a large number of police posts," he stated. That said, he conceded that closing the border "in one way or the other" might be required given "the exacerbation of the political situation." Pervukhin worried about the negative reaction of the West to any such move, including a possible economic embargo.

Ulbricht had long since overcome any such doubts, and by the end of June had developed with his top security man in the Politburo, Erich Honecker, detailed plans about how the border could be closed. He brought the Soviet ambassador and Yuli Kvitsinsky, a young and rising diplomat, who acted as translator, to his home outside East Berlin on the Döllnsee to drive home his most compelling point. The situation in the GDR was growing visibly worse, he told Pervukhin, adding, "Soon it would lead to an explosion." He told Pervukhin to tell Khrushchev that his country's collapse was "inevitable" if the Soviets didn't act.

Since Vienna, Khrushchev's son Sergei had been struck by how his father's "thoughts constantly reverted to Germany." At the same time, the Soviet leader had lost interest in the notion of a war-ending peace treaty with East Germany. After lobbying for such a document since 1958, he had determined it did nothing to solve his most urgent problem: the refugees.

The fact that Kennedy cared so little about whether Khrushchev unilaterally signed such a treaty with the East Germans, a document the U.S. and its allies would have ignored, had also prompted Khrushchev to question its worth. Though Ulbricht still demanded the treaty, Khrushchev had concluded that producing such a document was not as urgent as the need to "plug up all the holes" between East and West Berlin.

Once the door to the West was closed, he told Sergei, "perhaps people would stop rushing around and begin working, the economy would take off, and it wouldn't be long before West Germans began knocking on the GDR's door" for better relations. Then he could negotiate a war-ending treaty with the West from a position of strength.

For now, however, Khrushchev's problem was the map. When the four powers drew the lines among their four sectors after World War II, no one had given any thought to the possibility that those lines might someday become an impermeable border. "History had created this inconvenience," Khrushchev would write years later, "and we had to live with it."

Khrushchev complained that those who had marked the map were either unqualified or unthinking. "It's hard to make sense of the map you sent me," he told Pervukhin. He told him to summon Ivan Yakubovsky, chief military commander in Berlin and head of the Group of Soviet Forces in Germany, and "pass on my request that his staff make a map of Berlin with the borders marked and with comments on whether it's possible to establish control over them."

After that, he wanted Pervukhin to take the map to Comrade Ulbricht and then gather his comments as to the feasibility of shutting the border all along the jagged, erratic, and undefended lines that divided the world's competing systems.

Ulbricht, as usual in 1961, was already way ahead of him.

And a world away in Miami Beach, perhaps the highest-profile East German refugee yet was providing the world with a dazzling reminder of the East German refugee problem—and Ulbricht with yet another reason to close the gate as quickly as possible.

Marlene Schmidt,
the Universe's Most Beautiful Refugee

She was Walter Ulbricht's ultimate humiliation.

As the communist leader maneuvered behind the scenes to close his Berlin border, one of his refugees was strutting down the catwalk of a Miami Beach stage in her shimmering Miss Universe crown. Amid the flashing of cameras, Ulbricht's most intractable problem had assumed the unmistakable shape of someone judges had declared "the world's most beautiful girl."

At age twenty-four, Marlene Schmidt was intelligent, radiant, blonde, a little shy, and a lot statuesque. West Germany's Der Spiegel *magazine described her as someone with an electrical engineer's brain atop a Botticelli figure. But her real draw—the one that was getting her headlines around the world—was the story of her fairy-tale flight to freedom.*

It had been only a year since Marlene had fled Jena, an East German industrial town that had been flattened by Allied bombing during World War II. Since then, Soviet expropriation had further gutted the city and communist central planners were rebuilding it in the colorless monotony of their bland block buildings. Though her new West German home of Stuttgart was just 220 miles away from Jena, it was a world apart.

U.S. and British air attacks had also destroyed most of Stuttgart, where German industry had grown around Gottlieb Daimler's automobiles and combustion engines. However, West Germany's postwar economic miracle had already transformed the city into a hilly, green boomtown of cranes, new cars, and rising aspirations—driven by West Germany's ascent to become the world's third-largest exporter.

Just a few weeks after landing in the West, Marlene had entered the Miss Germany contest, drawn by a local newspaper advertisement that announced that first prize would be a French Renault convertible. After winning in the luxurious spa town of Baden-Baden, West Germany, Marlene in Florida surpassed forty-eight competitors from around the world to become Germany's first and only Miss Universe.

Time magazine couldn't resist a dig at the communists for having let her escape. "Even allowing for the crush [of refugees]," it said, "it is hard to understand how the East German border guards failed to spot lissome, 5-ft. 8-in. Marlene. . . . The West had no such difficulty."

Marlene's triumph was projected to the world in Technicolor from a pageant organized and produced by Paramount Pictures, with then game-show host Johnny Carson as master of ceremonies and actress Jayne Meadows as color commentator. Tens of thousands of East Germans watched as well, the product of thousands of jerry-rigged antennae on rooftops that allowed most of the country to pull down the West German television signal. They hung on every detail.

Marlene, who was earning $53 a week as an electrical engineer in a Stuttgart research laboratory, spoke of her excitement over Miss Universe winnings that included $5,000 in cash, a $5,000 mink coat, a $10,000 personal appearance contract, and a full wardrobe. Newspapers reported that her victory celebration stretched until five in the morning, followed by an "American-style breakfast" of orange juice, bacon and eggs, toast, and coffee. "I'm a little tired, but so happy," conceded Marlene through her interpreter, a doting Navy lieutenant and German linguist who escorted her through news conferences, interviews, and photo sessions.

World attention forced Ulbricht's propaganda apparatus to react. The East German leader's three-pronged effort to slow the refugee flood included more assertive propaganda about the virtues of socialism and the failures of capitalism; greater repressive measures, including punishment of refugees' family members for complicity; and increased incentives for refugees who returned, ranging from jobs to housing.

Yet nothing could reverse the escalating numbers in a population awash with rumors that the opportunity to escape might vanish soon.

In the case of Marlene, the official communist youth publication, Junge Welt (Young World), accused the Americans of rigging the beauty contest to call attention to East Germany's refugee problem. It sneered at how the West German media had falsely created "a Soviet zone Cinderella" who had been saved from half-starved communism by the Golden West. The writer countered that while East Germans valued her for her engineering and socialist education, "now all that matters are her bust, butt and hips. She is no longer to be taken seriously. She is just a display piece."

When American journalists related such reports to her for comment, Marlene shrugged in resignation. "I had expected to hear this from them. I think it is uncomfortable for the East German government to have the world reminded of the situation in East Germany."

Absent the Miss Universe crown, Marlene's story had been similar to that of so many others at the time. A few weeks after helping her mother and sister escape, Marlene had chosen to follow them when she heard that authorities were investigating her for complicity in their crime of Republikflucht, or flight from the Republic. Under the 1957 Gesetz zur Änderung des Passgesetzes (Law to Change Passport Regulations), she would serve up to three years in prison if prosecuted.

Junge Welt called her Miami triumph one of those short-lived pleasures of capitalism that would quickly fade away, to be followed by a hard life in an unfriendly land. "You will only reign one year, after which the world will forget you," it said.

In this case, East German propaganda proved partially right. In 1962, she would become the third among the eight wives of Hollywood actor Ty Hardin, star of the Western television series Bronco. She divorced him four years later, and only after that ran up eleven movie credits as an actor, writer, and producer, but they included little of note aside from female nudity. "I learned that life in Hollywood wasn't for me," she said, reflecting on her choice to move back home and work on electrical engines in Saarbrücken.

When she left East Germany, however, Marlene's choice had been between freedom and prison. After release, she would have been banned from work-

ing as an engineer and would have been caught in a dreary world of limited potential. Hollywood had had its disappointments for her, but the flight to the West had been her salvation.

Marlene Schmidt would wear her Miss Universe crown for less than a month before Ulbricht moved to close the escape hatch through which she and so many others had passed.

PART III

THE SHOWDOWN

13

"THE GREAT TESTING PLACE"

The immediate threat to free men is in West Berlin. But that isolated outpost is not an isolated problem. The threat is worldwide . . . above all it has now become—as never before—the great testing place of Western courage and will, a focal point where our solemn commitments, stretching back over the years since 1945, and Soviet ambitions now meet in basic confrontation.

President Kennedy in a special television address, July 25, 1961

Khrushchev is losing East Germany. He cannot let that happen. If East Germany goes, so will Poland and all of Eastern Europe. He will have to do something to stop the flow of refugees. Perhaps a wall. And we won't be able to prevent it. I can hold the Alliance together to defend West Berlin, but I cannot act to keep East Berlin open.

President Kennedy to Deputy National Security Advisor Walt Rostow,
several days later

THE VOLKSKAMMER (PEOPLE'S CHAMBER), EAST BERLIN
THURSDAY, JULY 6, 1961

Mikhail Pervukhin, the Soviet ambassador to East Germany, ordered his aide Yuli Kvitsinsky to track down Ulbricht immediately. "We have a yes from Moscow," Pervukhin said.

At age twenty-nine, Kvitsinsky was a rising star in the Soviet foreign ministry who had made himself invaluable to Pervukhin with his sound judgment and flawless German. He sensed the historic moment. After Khrushchev had scrutinized a much-improved map of Berlin from General Yakubovsky, the commander of the Group of Soviet Forces in Germany, the Soviet leader had concluded that Ulbricht was right: it would be possible to barricade Berlin.

Years later, Khrushchev would take full credit for the decision to build the Berlin Wall. "I had been the one," he would write in his memoirs, "who thought up the solution to the problem which faced us as a consequence of our unsatisfactory negotiations with Kennedy in Vienna." Yet the truth was that Khrushchev was merely giving Ulbricht the green light to proceed with a solution that the East German leader had sought as early as 1952 from Stalin. The Soviets would help shape, refine, and provide the crucial military guarantees for the operation's success, but it was Ulbricht who had driven the outcome with his constant badgering, and it would be Ulbricht's team that would work out all the details.

Khrushchev would tell the West German ambassador to Moscow, Hans Kroll, "I don't want to conceal from you that it was I who in the end gave the order. Ulbricht had pressured me for a long time and in the last months with increasing vehemence, but I don't want to hide myself behind Ulbricht's back." Khrushchev then joked with Kroll that Ulbricht was far too thin anyway for that purpose. "The wall will disappear again someday, but only when the reasons for its construction disappear," Khrushchev told Kroll.

Khrushchev had agonized over the decision; he knew the cost would be great to socialism's global reputation. "What should I have done?" he had asked himself. "You can easily calculate when the East German economy would have collapsed if we hadn't done something soon against the mass flight. There were, though, only two kinds of countermeasures: cutting off air traffic or the Wall. The former would have brought us to a serious conflict with the United States which possibly could have led to war. I could not and did not want to risk that. So the Wall was the only remaining option."

After Khrushchev relayed his decision to East Berlin, Kvitsinsky tracked down Ulbricht at the People's Chamber, where he had been attending a session of East Germany's rubber-stamp unicameral parliament, whose decisions, like most everything else in the country, followed his dictate.

Pervukhin told a satisfied Ulbricht that he had Khrushchev's green light to begin practical preparations for closing the Berlin border, but that he must operate under the greatest of secrecy. "For the West, the action must be carried out quickly and unexpectedly," Pervukhin said.

In stunned silence, the two Soviets listened to Ulbricht as he recited without emotion each minute detail of what was already a meticulously constructed plan.

The only way to close such a border rapidly enough, Ulbricht said, and with sufficient surprise, was to use barbed wire and fencing—and a massive amount of it. He knew precisely where he would get it and how he would bring it to Berlin without alerting Western intelligence agencies. Just before he shut the border, he would bring the metro and the elevated trains to a complete stop, he said. He would put up an unbreakable glass wall at the main Friedrichstrasse train station, through which the greatest amount of cross-Berlin traffic passed, so that East Berliners could not board West Berlin–bound trains to escape the shutdown.

The Soviets should not underestimate the difficulty of the border closing, Ulbricht told Pervukhin. He would act in the early hours of a Sunday morning, when traffic across the border would be far less and many Berliners would be outside the city. The 50,000 East Berliners who worked in West Berlin during the week as so-called *Grenzgänger*, or "border crossers," would be home for the weekend and thus caught in Ulbricht's trap.

Ulbricht said he would share the details with only a handful of his most trusted lieutenants: Politburo security chief Erich Honecker, who would direct the operation; State Security chief and thus secret police chief Erich Mielke; Interior Minister Karl Maron; Defense Minister Heinz Hoffmann, and Transportation Minister Erwin Kramer. Ulbricht said he would entrust only one individual, his chief bodyguard, to hand-deliver regular updates on preparations to Pervukhin and Kvitsinsky.

THE WHITE HOUSE, WASHINGTON, D.C.
FRIDAY, JULY 7, 1961

Just one day after Ulbricht received Khrushchev's go-ahead for his bold
plan, Kennedy's special assistant Arthur Schlesinger was scheming to slow
adviser Dean Acheson's own rush to action.

Having won the Pulitzer Prize at age twenty-seven for his book *The Age
of Jackson*, Schlesinger was the Kennedy court historian who also engaged
in random troubleshooting. His sudden focus on Berlin came as a response
to what he considered his own poor performance during the run-up to the
Bay of Pigs operation. Schlesinger had been alone among the president's
closest advisers in opposing the invasion, but he reproached himself for
failing "to do more than raise a few timid questions" while military commanders and the CIA lobbied Kennedy to approve action. Schlesinger had
limited his dissent to a private memo that had warned Kennedy: "At one
stroke you would dissipate all the extraordinary goodwill which has been
rising toward the new Administration through the world."

Schlesinger was determined not to make the same mistake twice. He
considered the Acheson plan for Berlin to be every bit as foolhardy as the
Bay of Pigs blueprint. So Schlesinger asked two people who had significant
influence with Kennedy to draft an alternative. One was State Department
legal adviser Abram Chayes, a thirty-nine-year-old law scholar who had led
the team that drafted Kennedy's 1960 Democratic Convention platform. The
other was thirty-eight-year-old White House consultant Henry Kissinger, a
rising star who had shaped Kennedy's thinking on nuclear issues with his
book *The Necessity of Choice: Prospects of American Foreign Policy*. Kissinger
had supported New York Governor Nelson Rockefeller's effort to win the
Republican nomination for president in 1960, but he was working through
Harvard colleagues to gain influence in the Kennedy White House.

When Kennedy first drafted Acheson into service the previous February,
Schlesinger had concluded that the president was merely trying to get a
broader mixture of views. Now Schlesinger feared that Kennedy would adopt

Acheson's hard-line approach to Berlin as policy if no one provided him with an alternative. UN Ambassador Adlai Stevenson was equally troubled by Acheson's growing influence. "Maybe Dean is right," Stevenson told Schlesinger. "But his position should be the conclusion of a process of investigation, not the beginning."

Schlesinger wanted to combat Acheson's effort to convince the president that "West Berlin was not a problem but a pretext" for Khrushchev to test the general will of the U.S. and its new president to resist Soviet encroachment.

Schlesinger worried that "the thrust of Acheson's rhetoric, and especially of his brilliant and imperious oral presentations," would fix the debate around the idea that the Soviets had "unlimited objectives" in reigniting the Berlin Crisis. Yet those who knew Moscow best, Thompson and Averell Harriman, a former ambassador to Moscow, felt Khrushchev's game might be limited to Berlin alone and thus should be played quite differently. Although the State Department was divided over Acheson's tough approach, Schlesinger was distraught that no one was framing the other side of the debate because Rusk "was circumspect, and no one quite knew where he stood."

The British government had leaked its softer line to the *Economist* magazine, which had reported, "Unless Mr. Kennedy takes a decisive grip on the wheel, the West is in danger of bypassing one possible line of compromise after another until it reaches a dead end, where neither it nor Russia has any choice except between ignominious retreat and nuclear devastation."

Schlesinger felt he had to move fast or lose all influence, as "talk of war mobilization under the proclamation of national emergency contained the risk of pushing the crisis beyond the point of no return." He worried about repeating the prelude to the Bay of Pigs crisis, where a bad plan had gained unstoppable momentum because no one had opposed it or presented an alternative choice.

He was determined to prompt a showdown on Berlin before it was too late.

On July 7, just after a lunch meeting with Kennedy on another issue, Schlesinger handed the president his Berlin memo and asked that he look it over en route to Hyannis Port that afternoon. The timing was good, as the president would meet with senior officials there the next day on Berlin. Kennedy said he preferred to read Schlesinger's thoughts right away, because Berlin was his most urgent problem.

Schlesinger had calculated correctly that nothing would get Kennedy's attention faster than a credible warning that the president was in danger of repeating his mistakes in Cuba. Kennedy had joked after the debacle that Schlesinger's cautionary memo on Cuba would "look pretty good" when the historian got around to writing his book on the administration. He then added a word of warning: "Only he'd better not publish that memorandum while I'm still alive." In his anti-Acheson memo, Schlesinger reminded Kennedy that the Cuban fiasco was a result of "excessive concentration on military and operational problems" in the preparatory stage while underestimating the political issues.

Though Schlesinger's paper praised Acheson for "analyzing the issues of last resort," he worried that the former secretary of state was defining the issue "to put it crudely as: are you chicken or not? When someone proposes something which seems tough, hard, put-up-or-shut-up, it is difficult to oppose it without seeming soft, idealistic, mushy. . . ." He reminded the president that his Soviet expert Chip Bohlen believed that nothing could help discussion of the Soviets more than eliminating the adjectives "hard" and "soft" from the language of the debate.

"People who had doubts about Cuba," said Schlesinger, in a clear reference to himself, "suppressed those doubts lest they seem 'soft.' It is obviously important such fears not constrain free discussion of Berlin."

The president read the memo carefully. He then looked at his friend with concern. He agreed that Acheson's paper was too narrow and that "Berlin planning had to be brought back into balance." He tasked Schlesinger to expand on his memorandum immediately for use the following day in Hyannis Port.

Schlesinger worked against the clock, since Kennedy's helicopter would lift off from the White House lawn at five p.m. With only two hours remaining before the president's departure, Chayes and Kissinger, the lawyer and the political scientist, dictated as Schlesinger edited while typing furiously. By the time Schlesinger ripped the final version from his typewriter, he had something that raised a series of questions about the Acheson paper and suggested new approaches. It said:

> The Acheson premise is substantially as follows: Khrushchev's principal purpose in forcing the Berlin question is to humiliate the U.S. on a basic issue by making us back down on a sacred commitment and thus shatter our world power and influence. The Berlin crisis, in this view, has nothing to do with Berlin, Germany, or Europe. From this premise flows the conclusion that we are in a fateful test of wills . . . and that Khrushchev will be deterred only by a demonstrated U.S. readiness to go to nuclear war rather than to abandon the status quo. On this theory, negotiation is harmful until the crisis is well developed; then it is useful only for propaganda purposes; and in the end its essential purpose is to provide a formula to cover Khrushchev's defeat. The test of will becomes an end in itself rather than a means to a political end.

The three men then listed the issues that they believed Acheson had overlooked.

- *"What political moves do we make until the crisis develops?"* The memo argued, "If we sit silent or confine ourselves to rebutting Soviet contentions," Khrushchev would keep the initiative and put Kennedy on the defensive, making him look rigid and unreasonable.
- *"The [Acheson] paper indicates no relationship between the proposed military action and larger political objectives."* The memo argued, in language intended to shock, that Acheson "does not state any political objective other than [preserving] present access procedures for which we are prepared to incinerate the world." It thus argued, "It is essential to elaborate the cause for which we are prepared to go to nuclear war."
- *"The paper covers only one eventuality . . . the Communist interruption of military access to West Berlin."* Yet, the memo argues, "actually, there

is a whole spectrum of harassments, of which a full-scale blockade may well be one of the least likely."

- *"The paper hinges on our willingness to face nuclear war. But this option is undefined."* The three men counsel Kennedy, whom they already knew was troubled by his war options: "Before you are asked to make the decision to go to nuclear war, you are entitled to know what concretely nuclear war is likely to mean. The Pentagon should be required to make an analysis of the possible levels and implications of nuclear warfare and the possible gradations of our own nuclear response."

- *The memo attacked Acheson for addressing himself "almost exclusively to the problem of military access" to Berlin.* However, military traffic was only 5 percent of the whole, while 95 percent consisted of supplies for the civilian population. It noted that East Germany was already in full control of this civilian traffic, which it "has gone to surprising lengths to facilitate." It noted that civilian traffic was most essential to the U.S. objective of preserving West Berlin's freedom.

- *The memo argued that Acheson ignored sensitivities inside NATO.* "What happens if our allies decline to go along?" It was unlikely the Allies would support Acheson's idea of sending troops up the Autobahn to break a blockade through a ground probe, which de Gaulle had already opposed. "What about the United Nations? Whatever happens, this issue will go into the UN. For better or for worse, we have to have a convincing UN position."

Seldom had such an important document been composed so rapidly. Schlesinger typed quickly to keep up with the unfolding thoughts of his brilliant co-conspirators. With an eye on the clock, he created a section called "Random thoughts about unexplored alternatives." It listed in rat-a-tat fashion what questions the president should be exploring beyond those Acheson had provided.

Most of all, the men wanted to ensure that all questions and alternatives were "systematically brought to the surface and canvassed" before rushing forward with the Acheson plan. The unsigned Schlesinger paper suggested that the president consider withdrawing the Acheson paper from circulation altogether. The danger of Acheson's thoughts leaking, the memo argued, was greater than the danger to full discussion from a more limited distribution.

Oblivious to the fact that Khrushchev had already decided his course on Berlin, U.S. officials in Washington were engaged in a behind-the-scenes bureaucratic war against Dean Acheson. Although written quickly, the Schlesinger-inspired memo was thorough, even including ideas about which new individuals should be brought into the process to dilute the power of Acheson. It suggested, among others, Averell Harriman and Adlai Stevenson.

It was the revenge of the so-called SLOBs—the Soft-Liners on Berlin.

The Schlesinger memo concluded by suggesting that one of its authors drive the process. "In particular, Henry Kissinger should be brought into the center of Berlin planning," it said. It would be one of the opening acts for a man who would over time become one of the most effective foreign policy infighters in U.S. history.

At the same time, Kennedy was also hearing doubts about existing nuclear war planning regarding Berlin from Defense Secretary McNamara and National Security Advisor Bundy. In his own memo ahead of the Hyannis Port meeting, Bundy complained about the "dangerous rigidity" of the strategic war plan. It had left the president little choice between an all-out attack on the Soviet Union or no response at all. Bundy suggested that McNamara review and revise it.

THE WHITE HOUSE, WASHINGTON, D.C.
FRIDAY, JULY 7, 1961

Henry Kissinger spent only a day or two each week in Washington working as a White House consultant, commuting from his post at Harvard University, but that had proved sufficient to put him at the center of the struggle to shape Kennedy's thinking on Berlin. The ambitious young professor would happily have worked full-time for the president; that, however, had been blocked by his former dean and now D.C. boss, National Security Advisor McGeorge Bundy.

Though Kissinger had mastered the art of flattering his superiors, Bundy was more immune to it than most. Along with the president, Bundy regarded Kissinger as brilliant but also tiresome. Bundy imitated Kissinger's long, German-accented discourses and the rolling of the president's eyes that accompanied them. For his part, Kissinger would complain that Bundy had put his considerable intellectual talents to "the service of ideas that were more fashionable than substantial." Kissinger biographer Walter Isaacson concluded that their differences were a matter of class and style: the tactful, upper-class Bostonian condescending to the brash German Jew.

Still, being so near the center of American power was a new and heady experience for Kissinger, and an early introduction to the White House infighting that would be such a part of his extraordinary life. Born Heinz Alfred Kissinger in Fürth, Bavaria, in 1923, he had fled Nazi persecution with his family, arriving in New York when he was fifteen. Now he was advising America's commander in chief. While Bundy had labored to keep him at arm's length from Kennedy, Kissinger was now reaching him through another Harvard professor, Arthur Schlesinger, who was deploying him against Acheson.

Kissinger had none of Acheson's historic place or access to the Oval Office—and at age thirty-eight was thirty years Acheson's junior—but his thirty-two-page "Memorandum for the President" on Berlin was an audacious attempt to one-up the former secretary of state. It landed on Kennedy's desk just before he departed for Hyannis Port to work on developing his approach to Berlin. Though Kissinger was much more hard-line on Moscow than Schlesinger, he felt it would be foolhardy for Kennedy to embrace Acheson's complete dismissal of diplomacy as one available avenue.

Kissinger worried that Kennedy's aides, and perhaps the president himself, might be naive enough to be tempted by Khrushchev's "free city" idea, under which West Berlin would fall under United Nations control. Kissinger was also concerned about Kennedy's distaste for the great Adenauer, and the president's belief that the West's long-standing commitment to eventual German unification, through free elections, was fanciful, and should be negotiable. Kennedy, Kissinger feared, didn't sufficiently realize that inattention to Berlin could breed a crisis for the Atlantic Alliance that would hurt U.S. security interests far more than any deal with Moscow could justify.

So Kissinger put his warning to Kennedy in unmistakable terms:

> The first task is to clarify what is at stake. The fate of Berlin is the touchstone for the future of the North Atlantic Community. A defeat over Berlin, that is a deterioration of Berlin's possibility to live in freedom, would inevitably demoralize the Federal Republic. Its scrupulously followed Western-oriented policy would be seen as a fiasco. All other NATO nations would be bound to draw the indicated conclusions from such a demonstration of the West's impotence. For other parts of the world, the irresistible nature of the Communist movement would be underlined. Coming on top of the Communist gains of the past five years, it would teach a clear lesson even to neutralists. Western guarantees, already degraded in significance, would mean little in the future. The realization of the Communist proposal that Berlin become a "free city" could well be the decisive turn in the struggle of freedom against tyranny. Any consideration of policy must start from the premise that the West simply cannot afford a defeat in Berlin.

Regarding unification, Kissinger warned Kennedy that abandoning traditional U.S. support would demoralize West Germans, making them doubt their place in the West. It would at the same time encourage the Soviets to increase their pressure on Berlin, as they would conclude that Kennedy already was "cutting [his] losses." Instead, Kissinger suggested that Kennedy's response to Khrushchev's increasing of Berlin tensions "with respect to German unification should be offensive and not defensive. We should use every opportunity to insist on the principle of free elections and take our stand before the United Nations on this ground." He warned Kennedy that he should not take West Berlin morale for granted, as U.S. leaders had done since the beginning of the Berlin Crisis in November 1959. "We should give them some tangible demonstration of our confidence to maintain their hope and courage," he wrote.

It concerned Kissinger all the more that Kennedy didn't have a credible military contingency plan for a Berlin crisis. In any conventional conflict, Kissinger argued, the U.S. would be overrun by Soviet superiority, and he doubted that Kennedy would ever engage in a nuclear war over Berlin's freedom. His paper captured all of those ideas in clearer, more strategic form than any other document that had reached the White House until that time.

A cover note for the Kissinger memo, written by Bundy, said: "He and [White House officials Henry] Owen and [Carl] Kaysen and I all agree the current strategic war plan is dangerously rigid and, if continued without amendment, may leave you very little choice as to how you face the moment of thermonuclear truth. In essence, the current plan calls for shooting off everything we have in one shot, and it is so constructed as to make any more flexible course very difficult."

Kissinger advised Kennedy that his only course in the tense days ahead, should the Soviets maintain their aggressive post-Vienna position on Berlin, would be to make any unilateral Soviet action appear too hazardous to the risk-averse Khrushchev. "In other words, we must be prepared to face a showdown," he said. Kissinger dismissed the arguments of some in the administration that Kennedy should make Berlin concessions to help Khrushchev in his domestic struggles against more dangerous hard-liners ahead of his October Party Congress. "Khrushchev's domestic position is his problem, not ours," he said, adding that only a strong Khrushchev could be conciliatory, and that was not what Kennedy was facing.

What concerned Kissinger most was the apparent Kennedy course of doing nothing about Berlin and waiting for a Soviet move, which, he argued, was the riskiest approach. "What may seem watchful waiting to us may appear as insecurity [to Khrushchev]," Kissinger said. Prophetically, he indicated that such an approach would tempt Moscow to prompt a crisis at the moment of "maximum difficulty" for the U.S., causing a situation in which the world would come to doubt Kennedy's determination.

In a separate note to Schlesinger, Kissinger later said, "I am in the position of a man sitting next to a driver heading for a precipice who is being asked to make sure the gas tank is full and the oil pressure adequate." Frustrated with being at the fringes of decision making, he worried that Kennedy's White House wanted him only for brainstorming purposes, not as someone whose advice would be taken. He eventually resigned in October, having concluded that his ideas would not be taken seriously.

HYANNIS PORT, MASSACHUSETTS
SATURDAY, JULY 8, 1961

President Kennedy was displeased.

It was fine to drop the ball on Laos or even Cuba. Neither was decisive for the United States or his place in history. But this was Berlin—the central stage for the world's defining struggle! He repeated this fact several times to advisers as he expressed his dismay that while Moscow was charging ahead on Berlin, they had yet to respond even to Khrushchev's aide-mémoire delivered in Vienna—even though it had been more than a month since the summit. The news from the Soviet Union that morning was bad. Khrushchev had announced he would rescind plans to reduce the Soviet Army by 1.2 million men and would enlarge his defense budget by a third, to 12.399 billion rubles—an increase of roughly $3.4 billion. Speaking before graduates of Soviet military academies, Khrushchev said that he believed a new world war over Berlin was not inevitable, but he nevertheless told his country's soldiers to prepare for the worst.

Soviet troops roared their approval.

Khrushchev told them his measures were in response to news reports that President Kennedy would ask for an additional $3.5 billion for his defense budget. With that, the Soviet leader was abandoning his insistence on putting general economic investments ahead of the military budget and increasing missile forces at the expense of troop numbers. "These are forced measures, comrades," he said. "We take them because we cannot neglect the Soviet people's security."

Kennedy was livid that *Newsweek* had published details of the Pentagon's top-secret Berlin contingency planning, which apparently had been the basis for Khrushchev's response. Kennedy was so upset by the leak that he ordered the FBI to investigate its source.

Khrushchev had responded to the *Newsweek* article as if it were a declaration of Kennedy's policy. Realizing that London was the weakest Allied link on Berlin, Khrushchev had summoned British Ambassador Frank Roberts to his box at the Bolshoi Ballet for a dressing-down during a break in a performance by the famous British prima ballerina Dame Margot Fonteyn. Khrushchev scorned British resistance to Soviet goals in Berlin as futile. He told Roberts that six hydrogen bombs would be "quite enough" to destroy the British Isles, that nine would annihilate France, and that the Kremlin could respond a hundredfold to any new division that the West could scrape up. Knowing he was singing from Prime Minister Macmillan's song sheet, he said, "Why should two hundred million people die for two million Berliners?"

In Hyannis Port, Kennedy scolded Secretary Rusk, who sat in his usual business suit on the fantail of the Kennedys' fifty-two-foot speedboat, the *Marlin*, for having failed to come up with an answer to Khrushchev's Berlin ultimatum. While the president fumed, the First Lady dropped into the ocean to water-ski, and Robert McNamara and General Maxwell Taylor joined Kennedy's friends Charles Spalding and his wife for hot dogs and chowder.

When Rusk explained that the text had been delayed by the need to clear it with the Allies, Kennedy exploded that it wasn't the Allies but the U.S. president who carried the burden on Berlin. Inspired by the Schlesinger memo, he ordered Rusk to give him a plan for negotiations on Berlin within ten days. The president then turned on the State Department's Soviet expert, Chip Bohlen, a former ambassador to Moscow: "Chip, what's wrong with the goddamned department of yours? I can never get a quick answer, no matter what question I put to them."

Martin Hillenbrand, head of the State Department's German desk, would later insist that a draft of the reply to the Soviet aide-mémoire had actually been produced promptly. But after ten days, State had discovered that the White House had misplaced it. So special assistant Ralph Dungan had the State Department send over a new draft. However, a White House official locked it up in a safe before going on a two-week leave, and he had not left behind the combination. At the same time, NATO allies were also stuck in the slow grinding of their own response.

While fingers assessing blame were pointing in various directions, an agitated Kennedy demanded that the Pentagon give him a plan for non-nuclear resistance in the case of a Berlin confrontation. It should be significant enough, he said, to prevent a Soviet advance and give the president time to talk to Khrushchev and avoid the rush to nuclear exchange. "I want the damn thing in ten days," Kennedy said.

Kennedy told his advisers to provide him with new options beyond the current choice between "holocaust or humiliation."

LINCOLN BEDROOM, THE WHITE HOUSE, WASHINGTON, D.C.
TUESDAY, JULY 25, 1961

In the late afternoon, President Kennedy retreated to his bedroom to read through the speech he would give at ten o'clock that evening to a national television audience. It was the first time Kennedy would use the Oval Office for such a purpose, and workmen had been there all day, laying cables and wires.

Kennedy knew how high the stakes had become. At home, he had to reverse a growing impression of foreign policy weakness, which made him politically vulnerable. After mishandling Cuba and Vienna, he also had to convince Khrushchev that he was willing to defend West Berlin at any cost. His problem: Khrushchev had stopped believing Kennedy would fight for Berlin, as Soviet Ambassador Menshikov was telling anyone in Washington who would listen. At the same time, however, Kennedy wanted Khrushchev to know he remained open to reasonable compromise.

Kennedy soaked in a hot bath to ease his inescapable back pain. He then ate his supper alone from a tray, as he often did. Midway through the meal, he phoned his secretary Evelyn Lincoln and said, "Will you take this down. I want to add it to the speech I am giving tonight." He then began dictating:

Finally, I would like to close with a personal word. When I ran for the President of the United States I knew that we faced serious challenges in the Sixties, but I could not realize nor could any man who does not bear this responsibility know how heavy and constant would be its burdens.

The United States relied for its security in the late Forties on the fact that it alone had the atomic bomb and the means of delivery. Even in the early Fifties when the Soviet Union began to develop its own thermo-nuclear capacity we still had a clear lead in the means of delivery, but in the very recent years the Soviet Union has developed its own nuclear stockpile and has also developed the capacity in planes and missiles to deliver bombs against our country itself.

Lincoln scribbled furiously in shorthand as Kennedy continued to dictate, the words falling into perfect sentences and paragraphs.

This means that if the United States and the Soviet Union become engaged in a struggle in which these missiles are used, then it could mean the destruction of both of our people and our country.

What makes this so somber is the fact that the Soviet Union is attempting in a most forceful way to assert its power, and this brings them into collision with us in those areas, such as Berlin, where we have long-standing commitments. Three times in my lifetime, our country and Europe have been involved in wars, and on both sides in each case serious misjudgments were made which brought about great devastation. Now, however, through any misjudgments on either side about the intentions of the other, more devastation could be rained in several hours than we have seen in all the wars in our history.

Knowing the gravity of the president's words, Lincoln concentrated on getting each one of them right. She felt the moment of history, and heard the pain in the voice of the man carrying its *burden*—a word he used several times in the speech and increasingly each day.

> As President and Commander-in-Chief, therefore, and as Americans, you and I together move through serious days. I shall bear the responsibility of the Presidency under our Constitution for the next three-and-one-half years. I am sure you know that I shall do the very best I can for our country and our cause.
>
> Like you, I have a family which I wish to see grow up in a country at peace and in a world where freedom endures.
>
> I know that sometimes you get impatient and wish we could make some immediate action that would end our perils, but there is no easy and quick solution. We are opposed by a system which has organized a billion people and which knows that if the United States falters, their victory is imminent. Therefore, we must look to long days ahead, which if we are courageous and persevering can bring us what we all desire. I ask therefore in these days your suggestions and advice. I ask your criticisms when you think we are wrong, but above all, my fellow citizens, I want you to realize that I love this country and shall do my best to protect it. I need your good will and support and above all your prayers.

Evelyn Lincoln couldn't remember when the president had ever added so much to the end of a speech just a couple of hours before its delivery.

Kennedy said to his secretary, "Will you type this up and give it to me when I come over?"

The president arrived at the Oval Office at 9:30 p.m. to test the height of the chair behind his desk and the lighting. He asked Evelyn Lincoln if he could inspect his dictation and then took it into the Cabinet Room, where he sat and scribbled revisions and made cuts, tightening it but not removing any of its anguish. When it was time to go before the cameras, he came into Lincoln's office and asked for a hairbrush and went into her washroom to make certain every strand was in place.

Despite these preparations, the speech would be given by a perspiring and tense president in an overheated office. To improve the sound quality, technicians had shut down the air-conditioning, although temperatures that day had hit a high of 94 degrees. The office would be made all the more uncomfortable by the lights of seven news cameras and the body heat of some sixty people who jammed in to witness the historic moment.

Kennedy stepped briefly outside to mop his face and lip before returning to his desk just seconds before he spoke to a national and global audience. Under lights that made reading his recently altered text difficult, he would trip over a few lines and deliver others less eloquently than usual. But few listeners noticed. His stirring, tough rhetoric masked the series of compromises he had agreed to in the previous days that had considerably weakened the Acheson plan.

Kennedy had pulled back from Acheson's call for a declaration of national emergency, he had decided against immediate mobilization of troops, and he had reduced the increase in defense spending. In the seventeen days between his Hyannis Port meetings and the July 25 speech, the SLOBs had methodically chipped away at the Acheson approach as the workings of the U.S. foreign policy structure turned almost entirely to Berlin, including two crucial National Security Council meetings on July 13 and 19.

On July 13 in the Cabinet Room, Secretary Rusk used Acheson's own words to soften the approach, quoting a part of his friend's paper that spoke of keeping early steps as low-key as possible. "We should try to avoid actions which are not needed for sound military purposes and which would be considered provocative," he said.

With Vice President Johnson's backing, Acheson had pushed back. He believed that if, as his friend Rusk argued, one left the call-up of reserves to the end, "we would not affect Khrushchev's judgment of the shape of the crisis any more than we could do so by dropping bombs after he had forced the issue to the limit."

Bundy had left those in the room four alternatives: (1) Proceed with all possible speed with a substantial reinforcement of U.S. forces; (2) Proceed with all measures not requiring the declaration of a national emergency; (3) Proceed with a declaration of national emergency and all preparation, except a call-up of reserves or guard units; or (4) Avoid any significant military buildup for the present on the grounds that this was a crisis more of political unity and will than of military imperative.

The president listened as his senior officials debated the options. But the first time he showed his own hand was before the TV audience. In a meeting of the National Security Council's smaller Steering Group, he had said there were only two things that mattered to him: "Our presence in Berlin, and our access to Berlin."

Acheson had grown so frustrated with what he considered the drift in policy during July that he told a small working group on Berlin, "Gentlemen, you might as well face it. This nation is without leadership."

At the second key NSC meeting, at four p.m. on July 19, the Acheson plan died a quiet death after an exchange between its author and Defense Secretary McNamara. Acheson wanted a definite decision of the group to declare a national emergency and begin the call-up of reserves no later than September. McNamara preferred not to commit yet, but wanted it understood that Kennedy could declare an emergency later and call up larger ground reserves "when the situation required."

Acheson had held his ground, arguing McNamara's course wasn't sufficiently energetic or concrete.

Kennedy had kept the discussion going until it gradually became clear to Acheson that the commander in chief didn't have the stomach for a full mobilization. Acheson eventually approved the McNamara approach, which would give the secretary of defense the more flexible timetable he wanted so as not "to have a large reserve force on hand with no mission." However, deployment would be rapid in the event of a deepening crisis.

Ambassador Thompson wasn't in the room, but he had helped win the day with cables from Moscow that argued Kennedy would impress the Soviets more by keeping the Allies together around substantial military moves than by dividing them over excessive ones. Thompson's logic was that a longer-term buildup in readiness would have more impact than dramatic, immediate, publicity-getting gestures. Kennedy's intelligence advisers also argued that too strong a public posture would only prompt Khrushchev to become even more rigid and more likely to take military countermeasures of his own.

The outcome was that on July 25 the president did not declare a national emergency but said he would seek congressional standby authority to triple the draft, call up reserves, and impose economic sanctions against Warsaw Pact countries in the case of a Berlin blockade. Kennedy told the NSC meeting that a national emergency was "an alarm bell which could only be rung once," and that taking the Acheson course would only convince the Soviets not of U.S. determination but of "our panic."

Acheson had argued in favor of a national emergency because it would have impressed both the Soviets and his U.S. opponents of the gravity of the situation while enabling the president to call up one million reserves and extend terms of service.

Kennedy, however, was determined not to overreact, partly because he wished to rebuild Allied confidence in his leadership after he had so badly botched the Bay of Pigs. He also reckoned that he was in for a long series of confrontations with the Soviets and thus worried about a premature escalation to address what he thought might be "a false climax" in the confrontation. The president wanted to keep some powder dry.

So Kennedy called for $3.454 billion in new spending for the armed forces, almost exactly equal to Khrushchev's announcement, though lower than the $4.3 billion Acheson had originally sought. The increase would nevertheless bring the combined defense spending increase under Kennedy to $6 billion. He wanted an increase in the Army's authorized strength from 875,000 to 1 million. The U.S. would prepare a new Berlin airlift capability and a further capacity to move six additional divisions to Europe by Khrushchev's December deadline for a peace treaty.

Most striking, but entirely unnoticed by the media, was the speech's mention seventeen times of *West* Berlin, continuing the president's regular addition of the qualifier "West." Kennedy was repeating his message to Khrushchev in Vienna that the Soviets were free to do what they wanted with the city's eastern portion as long as they didn't touch the western part.

Just the previous day at lunch, one of the top officials of the U.S. Information Agency, James O'Donnell, had complained to speechwriter Ted Sorensen about the emphasis on "West" Berlin in a final draft of the speech. O'Donnell's opinion mattered, since he was a Kennedy family friend and veteran Berlin hand who as a conquering soldier had been the first non-Soviet to examine the interior of Hitler's bunker. He had written a book about Hitler's final days and had then lived through the Berlin blockade as a *Newsweek* correspondent. His standing was such that he had written a memo for candidate Kennedy on the four-power agreements regarding Berlin.

Sorensen had proudly shown the draft of the July 25 speech to O'Donnell, arguing that "even hard-liners" like him would like it. Yet the more closely O'Donnell scrutinized it, the more he was taken aback by the unilateral concessions it contained. The speech spoke of Kennedy's willingness to remove "actual irritants" in West Berlin while declaring that "the freedom of that city is not negotiable." According to Ulbricht, those "irritants" included West Berlin's lively and free media, the American radio station RIAS, the freedom with which Western militaries and intelligence agencies were operating, and—most important—the ability of East Germans to cross the open border and seek refuge.

Another paragraph recognized "the Soviet Union's historical concern about their security in Central and Eastern Europe, after a series of ravaging invasions, and we believe arrangements can be worked out which will help to meet those concerns, and make it possible for both security and freedom to exist in this troubled area."

What could Kennedy have meant by that? O'Donnell wondered, not knowing that this built on similar language Kennedy had privately used in Vienna. Was he buying into Moscow's complaints about resurgent German militarism? Was he ceding forever to the Soviets the captive countries of Poland, Czechoslovakia, and Hungary?

But nothing troubled O'Donnell more than repetitive references exclusively to "West" Berlin's security. That could only have been an intentional message that, in O'Donnell's view, gave the Soviets a free hand in East Berlin, though the city technically remained under four-power rule.

Kennedy's speech told Americans, "The immediate threat to free men is in West Berlin." He used the visual teaching aid of a map for the American people to show West Berlin as an island of white in a sea of communist black. Said Kennedy:

> For West Berlin, lying exposed 110 miles inside East Germany, surrounded by Soviet troops and close to Soviet supply lines, has many roles. It is more than a showcase of liberty, a symbol, an island of freedom in a communist sea. It is even more than a link with the Free World, a beacon of hope behind the Iron Curtain, an escape hatch for refugees.
>
> West Berlin is all of that. But above all it has now become—as never before—the great testing place of Western courage and will, a focal point where our solemn commitments stretching back over the years since 1945, and Soviet ambitions now meet in basic confrontation. The United States is there; the United Kingdom and France are there; the pledge of NATO is there—and the people of Berlin are there. It is as secure, in that sense, as the rest of us—for we cannot separate its safety from our own . . . we have given our word that an attack upon that city will be regarded as an attack upon us all.

Kennedy returned to West Berlin at the end of the thirty-one-minute speech.

> The solemn vow each of us gave to West Berlin in time of peace will not be broken in time of danger. If we do not meet our commitments in Berlin, where will we later stand? If we are not true to our word there, all that we have achieved in collective security, which relies on these words, will mean nothing. And if there is one path above all others to war, it is the path of weakness and disunity.

Sorensen was upset that O'Donnell was underestimating the importance of the speech's emotive commitment to defend Berlin. As for its disregard for captive East Berlin and Eastern Europeans generally, Sorensen argued to O'Donnell that the speech was merely recognizing reality. The Russians did what they wanted anyway in their sector. Americans would be reluctant enough to accept a military buildup to safeguard two million West Berliners, but it would be expecting far too much of Americans to risk their lives for the lot of a million East Berliners caught on the wrong side of history.

O'Donnell suggested an easy fix. The president could simply omit the word "West" in most of the places where it appeared before the word "Berlin." After an hour of argument, Sorensen protested: "I can't monkey around anymore with the text of this speech . . . this speech has been churned through the mills of six branches of government. We have had copies back and forth for ten days. This is the final version. This is the policy line.

"This is it."

The lunch ended on that note.

Sorensen had also pushed back similar protests from elsewhere inside the government. The so-called Berlin Mafia, the group of senior officials who had been following every comma and semicolon of the fragile Berlin standoff for years, felt that the president was committing heresy, essentially telling the Soviets they could ignore four-power agreements and do anything they wanted with their part of the city.

"There was an 'Oh, my God!' feeling as one saw the language," said the Austrian-born Karl Mautner, who served in the intelligence and research bureau of the State Department after having been posted to the American Mission in Berlin. Having fought during World War II with the 82nd Airborne at Normandy and the Battle of the Bulge, he was outraged at Kennedy's backsliding. "We knew immediately what it meant. . . . We were undercutting our own position."

The emphasis on *West* Berlin appeared all the more intentional to the Soviets five days after the speech when, on July 30, Senator William Fulbright said on the ABC Sunday-morning television talk show *Issues and Answers* that the Soviets could reduce tensions in the Berlin Crisis best by closing the West Berlin escape hatch for refugees. "The truth of the matter is, I think, the Russians have the power to close it in any case," said Fulbright. "Next week, if they chose to close their borders, they could, without violating any treaty. I don't understand why the East Germans don't close their border because I think they have a right to close it."

Fulbright's interpretation of the treaty was wrong, and he corrected himself in a statement to the Senate on August 4, saying that freedom of movement across Berlin was guaranteed by postwar agreements and that his TV interview had given "an unfortunate and erroneous impression." That said, Kennedy never repudiated him, and McGeorge Bundy reported favorably to the president on Fulbright's TV appearance by writing about "a variety of comment from Bonn and Berlin, including reference to the helpful impact of Senator Fulbright's remarks."

The truth was that West Germans despaired at the comments, while East Germans were delighted at Fulbright's suggestion. West Berlin's *Der Tagesspiegel* newspaper complained that the senator's comment was potentially as encouraging for enemy action as Acheson's words had been before the Korean War, when he had declared that South Korea was outside America's defense perimeter. The Communist Party paper *Neues Deutschland* called Fulbright's ideas "realistic."

Early in August, Kennedy mused about what was likely to happen next in Berlin during a stroll along the colonnade by the Rose Garden with Walt Rostow, an economist who was advising Kennedy. "Khrushchev is losing East Germany," he said. "He cannot let that happen. If East Germany goes, so will Poland and all of Eastern Europe. He will have to do something to stop the flow of refugees. Perhaps a wall. And we won't be able to prevent it. I can hold the Alliance together to defend West Berlin, but I cannot act to keep East Berlin open."

MOSCOW
THURSDAY, AUGUST 3, 1961

On a sweltering Moscow morning, Ulbricht drove to his meeting with Khrushchev in a limousine whose windows were closed and curtained.

Ulbricht had not announced his departure from Berlin for the emergency Warsaw Pact summit that day, and if he could avoid it, he did not want to be seen in public.

Moscow seemed serene compared with what Ulbricht faced back home. Tourist groups walked behind guides around Red Square. The day's first sightseeing boats rode up the Moskva River beside men in kayaks out for morning exercise. Giant swimming pools were opening up in public parks. With school out, the city was filled with parents and their children.

Khrushchev and Ulbricht met to work out the final details for the border closure before approaching members of the Warsaw Pact for their approval. Ulbricht also wanted his allies to consider emergency economic support should the West respond with sanctions.

The two men had been closely tracking the preparatory work of their security services and military forces for most of the previous month, so there was no need to review each detail. Khrushchev said they together would "encircle Berlin with an iron ring. . . . Our forces must create such a ring, but your troops must control it." The Soviets were sending an additional 4,000 soldiers to Berlin even as the two men talked. Khrushchev told Ulbricht he was also putting tanks on the border with West Germany, behind East German soldiers' positions.

The purpose of their meeting that morning was to finalize the timing. Khrushchev said he wanted to put off the signing of any peace treaty with Ulbricht until after the border closure. He was also unwilling to let Ulbricht take any action against access routes or air routes to West Berlin. Ulbricht agreed that although he still wished to sign a war-ending peace treaty with Moscow, that had become secondary to stopping the refugees and saving his country. Ulbricht told the Soviet leader he needed only two weeks to be ready to stop movement between East and West Berlin.

"When would it be best for you to do this?" asked Khrushchev. "Do it when you want. We can do it at any time."

Because of both the urgency of his refugee problems and the danger that plans could leak, Ulbricht wanted to move quickly. He suggested the night between Saturday, August 12, and Sunday, August 13.

Noting that the thirteenth is considered an unlucky day in the West, Khrushchev joked that "for us and for the whole socialist camp it would be a very lucky day indeed."

Khrushchev, the builder of the Moscow Metro, wanted to hear more of the logistical details. How would Ulbricht deal with streets, which he had seen on his detailed map, where one side was East Berlin and the other West?

"In those homes which have an exit to West Berlin, we will brick up the exit," Ulbricht said. "In other places, we will erect barriers of barbed wire. The wire has already been assembled. All of this can be done very quickly."

Khrushchev refused Ulbricht's request that he call for an emergency economic conference to prepare necessary support for the East German economy. The Soviet leader feared that merely scheduling such a meeting might tip off the West to their plans—and accelerate the refugee flow even further. Ulbricht would simply have to do his best to prepare.

He also wanted Ulbricht to be certain that all operations remained strictly within his own territory, "and not a millimeter more" into West Berlin. Every signal Kennedy had sent Khrushchev, from the Vienna Summit to his July 25 speech to Fulbright's television statement, had been that he was on safe ground as long as all Soviet and East German actions were limited to Soviet bloc territory and in no way interrupted Allied rights of access to Berlin. In fact, his most recent conversation with U.S. Ambassador Thompson had convinced him that Kennedy and Adenauer might even welcome the outcome. In a meeting two days earlier, he had told Ulbricht:

> When the border is closed, the Americans and West Germans will be happy. Thompson told me that this flight is causing the West Germans a lot of trouble. So when we institute these controls, everyone will be satisfied. And beyond that, they will feel your power.

Without referring to the notion of a Berlin wall by name, Khrushchev asked the Warsaw Pact group to approve a border closure as impermeable as the one that had existed between East and West German territories since 1952. "We propose that the Warsaw Pact states agree, in the interests of the cessation of the subversive activity, to implement control along the GDR borders, including the borders in Berlin, comparable to that existing along the state borders of the Western Powers."

The three-day Warsaw Pact meeting that followed gave Ulbricht some but not all of what he wanted. His socialist neighbors accepted the border closure without dissent, and they agreed to reposition their troops to back up the Soviet military. What Ulbricht's allies would not provide, much to Khrushchev's consternation, was economic insurance. One Communist Party leader after the other—Władysław Gomułka of Poland, Antonín Novotný of Czechoslovakia, and János Kádár of Hungary—worried about how the West might retaliate economically against the whole bloc and spoke of their limited resources. Gomułka even wanted Ulbricht to consider helping *him* should there be a Western boycott of the entire bloc by redirecting goods that might normally be sold to the West. He worried about how exposed Poland would be to any Berlin blowback because of its large debt and trade with the West.

Novotný warned Ulbricht that he should not count on him for foodstuffs, because of his country's problems with agricultural production. As Czechoslovakia had a greater share of its trade with the West than any other Warsaw Pact country, he feared his country would suffer most in the aftermath of any Berlin action. Kádár complained that the potential economic impact of an East German border closure had not been discussed among Soviet allies earlier, particularly as his country relied on trade with the West for nearly a third of its economy—and a quarter of that amount was with West Germany.

Khrushchev fumed:

> I think we must help the GDR. Let us, comrades, perceive this better, deeper and more keenly. . . . Now, comrades, we will all help the GDR. I will not say who of you will help most. All must help and must help more. Let us look at it this way: if we do not now turn our attention to the needs of the GDR and we do not make sacrifices, they cannot endure; they do not have enough internal strength.

"What would it mean if the GDR was liquidated?" Khrushchev demanded to know from the leaders sitting before him. Did they want the West German army on their borders? By strengthening East Germany's position, "we strengthen our position," he said, frustrated at seeing how little solidarity existed within his bloc. In an alliance where most members felt little threatened by the West but were increasingly dependent upon it economically, Khrushchev's arguments did not convince them.

When fellow communist leaders asked Khrushchev why he didn't worry more about American military response, Khrushchev told them the West had reacted far less resolutely than he had feared thus far to his escalating pressures and rhetoric. The U.S., he said, had "proved to be less tough than we assumed" regarding Berlin. Khrushchev said it was true the adversary still "could show himself, but we can already say now that we expected more pressure, but so far the strongest intimidation has been Kennedy's speech."

Khrushchev told his allies it was his view that the U.S. was "barely governed," and that the U.S. Senate reminded him of the medieval Russian principality of Novgorod, where the boyars "shouted, yelled and pulled at each other's beards; that's how they decided who was right."

He even spoke nostalgically of the time when the American secretary of state was John Foster Dulles, who although anticommunist provided "more stability" for the U.S.–Soviet relationship. As for Kennedy, Khrushchev said he "felt for him . . . he is too much of a lightweight for both Republicans and Democrats." Khrushchev was confident his weak and indecisive adversary would not respond in any meaningful way.

Ulbricht returned home as the countdown began for the most important day of his life—and that of his country. But first he would have to weather a final skirmish with the East German proletariat.

Ulbricht and Kurt Wismach Lock Horns

With less than forty-eight hours to go before launching his operation, Walter Ulbricht nevertheless kept a routine appointment with laborers of the Oberspree Cable Works in the southern part of East Berlin. Some 1,500 laborers gathered in a giant hall, wearing work overalls and wooden shoes that protected them against electrocution and molten metal. Some climbed up the struts of cranes for a better view; others sat atop twelve-foot-high cable rollers.

Reporting that he had just returned from Moscow, Ulbricht told his crowd, "It is imperative that a peace treaty be signed without delay [between East Germany] and our glorious comrade and ally, the Union of Soviet Socialist Republics." In a combative voice, he said, "Nobody can stop socialism. . . . Not even those who have fallen into the clutches of the slave-traders." He said the cost to the East German economy of the refugee flight, which he called "flesh trade and kidnappings," was two and a half billion marks a year. "Every citizen of our State will agree with me that we must put a stop to such conditions."

Kurt Wismach, who at first appeared to Ulbricht to be just another one of the workers, boiled inside as he listened to what he considered the usual communist double-talk. Imbued with a false sense of strength as he sat far above Ulbricht on a roll of cables, he began to applaud derisively and at length after each of Ulbricht's statements. It seemed that nothing could stop Wismach's hands from clapping nor his voice from shouting into the silence of the hall around him.

"Even if I am the only one to say it: Free elections!" he screamed.

Ulbricht looked up at the worker and snapped back. "Now just a moment!" he shouted. "We're going to clear this up right away!"

Wismach shouted back at the leader whom millions so feared: "Yes, and we'll see which is the right way!"

Ulbricht shouted up at him and then turned to take in all those seated and standing in the hall around him. "Free elections! What is it you want to elect freely? . . . The question is put to you by the people!"

By then Wismach spoke with the courage of a man who had gone too far to reverse himself. "Have you the slightest idea what the people really think?" he yelled, seeing that most of his coworkers' hands were frozen at their sides. No one was coming to his support.

Ulbricht waved his hands and barked back that it had been Germany's free elections in the 1920s and 1930s that had brought the country Hitler and World War II. "Now I ask you: Do you want to travel along this same road?"

"Nein, nein," shouted a vocal minority of party loyalists in the crowd. With each additional rebuttal from Ulbricht and his request for the crowd to support him, this group shouted more encouragement to the communist leader.

Other workers who might have sided with Wismach—likely the majority—remained silent. They realized that to do otherwise would expose them to whatever retribution their vocal fellow laborer would assuredly face.

"The one lonely heckler thinks he shows special courage!" Ulbricht bellowed. "Have the courage to fight against German militarism!"

The party faithful cheered their leader again.

"Whoever supports free elections supports Hitler's generals!" a red-faced Ulbricht shouted.

The crowd applauded one last time as Ulbricht stormed out.

The next day, party disciplinarians interrogated Wismach on, among other matters, his possible membership in Western flesh-trading and spy agencies. He was required to write a statement retracting his outburst, and he had to accept a pay cut and a demotion that could only be reversed through hard work and "political awareness."

Wismach left East Berlin as a refugee a few days later with his wife and child. He would be among the last to pass so easily.

14

THE WALL:
SETTING THE TRAP

The GDR had to cope with an enemy who was economically very powerful and therefore very appealing to the GDR's own citizens. . . . The resulting drain of workers was creating a simply disastrous situation in the GDR, which was already suffering from a shortage of manual labor, not to mention specialized labor. If things had continued like this much longer, I don't know what would have happened.

Premier Khrushchev, explaining in his memoirs his decision
to approve the Berlin border closure

In this period we are entering, it will be shown whether we know everything and whether we are firmly anchored everywhere. Now we must prove whether we understand the politics of the party and are capable of carrying out its orders.

Erich Mielke, chief of East German secret police, providing final
instructions on August 12, 1961

COMMUNIST PARTY HEADQUARTERS, EAST BERLIN
WEDNESDAY, AUGUST 9, 1961

Like a veteran stage producer preparing for the performance of a lifetime, Walter Ulbricht rehearsed every scene with his lieutenants in the last crucial hours before his August 13 curtain call. His drama, code-named "Operation Rose," would play for one night only. He would have no second chance to get it right.

No detail was too small for Ulbricht's attention nor that of the man he had deputized to direct the show, Erich Honecker, the Central Committee's chief for security matters. At age forty-eight, Honecker had two qualities that had recommended him: unquestioned loyalty and unmatched organizational capability.

With his combed-back, graying hair and *Mona Lisa* smile, Honecker had come a long way from his days as the young, handsome communist rabble-rouser who had spent a decade in Hitler's jails during the 1930s. He knew his operation could catapult him past rivals to become the front-runner for Ulbricht's eventual succession. It also could save German socialism. Failure would cost him his career and perhaps his country.

Honecker's final checklist was as long as it was precise.

He needed to know whether his people had purchased sufficient quantities of barbed wire to wrap around West Berlin's entire ninety-six-mile circumference. To avoid suspicion, Honecker's team had distributed the barbed-wire orders among a number of innocuous East German purchasers and they, in turn, had negotiated with several different manufacturers in both Great Britain and West Germany.

Thus far, none of their Western business partners had sounded an alarm. Honecker saw no evidence that Western intelligence agencies had any clue about what was about to transpire. A sales order was a sales order. Lenin's prediction came to mind: "The capitalists will sell us the rope with which we will hang them." In this case, the capitalists were peddling at bulk discounts barbed wire with which the communists would enclose their own people. To avoid any diplomatic backlash, Honecker's people had removed hundreds of British and West German manufacturer labels from the barbed wire and burned them.

East German teams and their Soviet advisers had mapped every meter of the twenty-seven-mile-long internal border that ran through the city center between West and East Berlin and the remaining sixty-nine miles that separated West Berlin and the East German countryside. They noted precisely what peculiarities faced them on each stretch of the border.

On July 24, Honecker's deputy, Bruno Wansierski, a fifty-six-year-old party technocrat and trained carpenter, had updated his boss on the massive construction project it was his job to oversee. To conceal its purpose, Wansierski's report was innocuously labeled: "Overview of the Scope of the Engineering Operations on the Western Outer Ring of Berlin." Those who would read the documents later would compare their precision to Nazi blueprints for building and operating concentration camps. Though Ulbricht's project was less murderous, its execution would be no less cynically exacting.

With only three weeks until the target date, Wansierski—director of the Department for Security Questions of the Socialist Unity Party's Central Committee—complained that he still lacked sufficient supplies for nearly two-thirds of the task. After taking inventory of "all available materials," he reported that he was short some 2,100 concrete pillars, 1,100 kilograms of metal cramps, 95 fathoms of timber, 1,700 kilograms of connecting wire, and 31.9 tons of mesh wire. Most problematic, he lacked 303 tons of barbed wire, the project's most essential raw material.

Furious activity had filled all the supply gaps in the two weeks since Wansierski's report. By August 9, Ulbricht was satisfied that everything was in place. Dozens of trucks had already transported hundreds of concrete uprights secretly from Eisenhüttenstadt, an industrial town on the Oder River near the Polish border, to a stockpile at a police barracks in the Berlin district of Pankow and several other locations.

Several hundred police from across East Germany had assembled at the vast State Security Directorate compound at Hohenschönhausen on East

Berlin's outskirts. Many were constructing wooden sawhorses, known in German as "Spanish riders," that would form the first physical street barriers. They hammered in nails and hooks from which others would string the barbed wire while wearing thousands of pairs of specially ordered protective gloves.

Ulbricht was equally painstaking in determining which army and police units would be deployed. Beginning at 1:30 a.m., their first task would be to form a human chain around West Berlin to stop any spontaneous escape attempts or other acts of resistance until construction brigades could raise the first physical barriers. For this, Ulbricht would deploy only his most trusted forces: border police, reserve police, police school cadets, and crack troops known as factory fighting militia, organized around workplaces.

Plans for each small section of the border detailed how they would operate. For example, Border Police Commander Erich Peter planned to deploy precisely ninety-seven officers at the city's most important crossing point on East Berlin's Friedrichstrasse. That would produce the required density for that point of one man per square meter. His plan dictated that a further thirty-nine officers there would construct the initial barrier of barbed wire, concrete posts, and sawhorses.

Regular army soldiers would form the second line of defense and would, in an emergency, move up to fill in any breaches in the forward line. The mighty fail-safe power of the Soviet military would stand back in a third ring, which would advance only if Allied forces disrupted the operation or East German units collapsed.

Ulbricht's lieutenants were just as meticulous in how they planned ammunition allocations, distributing it in sufficient quantities for the task but in a manner that was designed to avoid any reckless shooting. At the most sensitive border points, police units would be issued two five-bullet clips of blanks that would be loaded into their carbines in advance. They would have instructions to shoot the blanks as a warning should East Berliners or West Berliners rush them in a rage. Should the blanks fail in their purpose, police would have a further three clips of live ammunition in reserve. These they would load and fire only with the approval of commanding officers.

On the second line of defense, soldiers of the National People's Army would be armed with submachine guns and limited quantities of live ammunition. To avoid accidents, the soldiers would not preload their guns but instead keep the ammo inside satchels attached to their belts. Ulbricht's insurance policy was that the most trusted units would be fully armed from the outset: the First Motorized Rifle Division, some factory militia, and two elite *Wachregimenten*—guard units that specialized in internal security—one from the army and the other attached to the Stasi (Staatssicherheit), the State Security Ministry.

From the moment that police and military units received their first orders at 1:00 a.m., all East Berlin streetlights would be doused and they would have thirty minutes under the moonlight to close the border with their human chain. They would have a further 180 minutes to put up barriers around the city, including the complete closure of sixty-eight of the existing eighty-one crossing points to West Berlin. That would leave only a manageable thirteen checkpoints for East German police to monitor the following morning.

At precisely 1:30 a.m., East German authorities would shut down all public transportation. They would prevent all trains arriving from West Berlin from unloading passengers at Friedrichstrasse, the main East–West station. At key crossings that would never reopen, teams equipped with special tools would split train tracks. Still other units would unroll and place the barbed wire while an additional eight hundred transport police beyond the usual staffing would man stations to dissuade unrest.

If all went well, the whole job would be done by six a.m.

Ulbricht cleared the final language for the official statement that he would circulate in the early hours of August 13 to all corners of East Germany and throughout the world. He would blame his action on the West German government's "systematic plans for a civil war" that were being executed by "revenge-seeking and militaristic forces." The statement said the "sole purpose" of the border closure was to provide East German citizens security from these nefarious forces.

From that point forward, East Germans would be allowed to enter West

Berlin only with special passes issued by the Interior Ministry. After ten days' time, West Berliners again would be allowed to visit East Berlin.

Ulbricht had not overlooked a single detail. Those who knew him best had seldom seen him so calm and content.

SOVIET EMBASSY, EAST BERLIN
WEDNESDAY AFTERNOON, AUGUST 9, 1961

Without emotion, Ulbricht walked Soviet Ambassador Pervukhin through his final preparations. "Comrade Cell" Ulbricht, so nicknamed in his younger years for his organizational skill, was in his element. He spoke without notes, as he had committed every aspect to his legendary memory. Despite the operation's many moving parts, he still saw no sign that Western intelligence services either suspected what was about to happen or were planning countermeasures. Pervukhin would report to Khrushchev that the operation could proceed on the agreed-upon timetable.

Khrushchev received the news with resignation and determination. The refugee exodus had reached the monstrous proportions of 10,000 refugees weekly and more than 2,000 on many individual days. The Soviet leader would recall later how he had agonized about the decision to go ahead. "The GDR had to cope with an enemy who was economically very powerful and therefore very appealing to the GDR's own citizens. West Germany was all the more enticing to East Germans because they all spoke the same language. . . . The resulting drain of workers was creating a simply disastrous situation in the GDR, which was already suffering from a shortage of manual labor, not to mention specialized labor. If things had continued like this much longer, I don't know what would have happened."

Khrushchev had been forced to choose between an action that said nothing good about communism and a failure to act that might have prompted the crumbling of his western front. "I spent a great deal of time trying to think of a way out. How could we introduce incentives in the GDR to counteract the force behind the exodus of East German youths to West

Germany? How could we create conditions in the GDR which would enable the state to regulate the steady attrition of its working force?"

He knew that critics, "especially in bourgeois societies," would say the Soviets had locked down East German citizens against their will. People would claim that "the gates of the Socialist paradise are guarded by armed troops." But Khrushchev had concluded the border closing was "a necessary and only temporary defect." Still, the Soviet leader remained certain none of this trouble would have been necessary if Ulbricht had more effectively tapped "the moral and material potential that would someday be harnessed by the dictatorship of the working classes."

But that was Utopia, and Khrushchev had to deal with the real world.

He knew that East Germany, along with the Soviet Union's other Eastern European satellites, had "yet to reach a level of moral and material development where competition with the West is possible." He had to be honest with himself: There was no way to improve the East German economy rapidly enough to stem the flow of refugees and stop the collapse of East Germany in the face of such overwhelming West German material superiority.

The only option was containment.

EAST BERLIN
FRIDAY, AUGUST 11, 1961

Less than thirty-six hours before the operation was to begin, Soviet war hero Marshal Ivan Konev sat down for his first meeting with Ulbricht. To ensure discipline and success, Khrushchev had dispatched him to lead all Soviet forces in Germany, replacing General Ivan Yakubovsky, who he would slot in as his deputy. Khrushchev's move was rich in symbolism. One of the great men of Soviet history was heading to Berlin for a return engagement.

At age sixty-three, Konev was a tall, brutal, energetic man with a cleanly shaven bald head and wicked blue eyes with a knowing twinkle. During

World War II, after having liberated Eastern Europe, his troops had swooped into the German capital from the south and conquered the Nazis, together with the soldiers of Marshal Zhukov, in the bloody Battle of Berlin of May 1945. For his heroics, he had won six Orders of Lenin, was twice recognized as "Hero of the Soviet Union," and had then served as the Warsaw Pact's first commander.

Most appropriate for the task at hand, he had led the Soviet military crackdown in Budapest in 1956 that resulted in deaths of 2,500 Hungarians and 700 Soviet troops. Some 200,000 Hungarians had fled the country as refugees. Given Konev's past behavior toward Germans, Khrushchev also knew he would not shrink from the bloodiest decisions.

Near World War II's end, Konev had pursued a German division in retreat to the small Soviet town of Shanderovka. After surrounding the town to prevent the escape of German soldiers who had taken shelter there in a blizzard, he'd firebombed his enemies. His T-34 tanks then crushed under their tracks the evacuating German troops that his soldiers had failed to machine-gun down. The story went that his Cossack cavalry had then butchered the last survivors with their sabers, even cutting off arms that had been raised in surrender. His men killed some 20,000 Germans.

Khrushchev had taken a risk in sending such a high-profile military commander to East Germany just a few days before an ostensibly secret operation. On the previous afternoon, General Yakubovsky had contributed to the provocative move by inviting the military liaison officers representing the three Western Allies in Berlin to meet his previously unannounced successor.

"Gentlemen, my name is Konev," the general had said to them in a gravelly voice. "You may perhaps have heard of me."

Konev savored the surprised look on the Western Allies' faces as his statement was translated into their three languages by their three interpreters. "You are of course accredited to the commander in chief of the Group of Soviet Forces in Germany," he said. "Well, I am now the commander in chief, and it is to me that you will be accredited from here on out." He asked the liaison officers to inform their commanders of the change and the fact that his friend General Yakubovsky would serve as his deputy.

He asked if any of the three had questions. Initially speechless, the U.S. and British officers awkwardly conveyed the greetings of their commanders. The French officer, however, said he could not do the same because his commander was unaware either of Konev's presence or his assumption of command.

"As one soldier to another," Konev said, smiling to the French officer, "let me tell you this, so that you can repeat it to your general. I have always reminded my officers that a commander should never be taken by surprise."

Given what would follow, the theater was rich.

Konev lacked specific orders on how to respond should Western powers respond more aggressively than expected to the border closure. Khrushchev trusted his ruthless commander to make the right decision. Acting as Ulbricht's direct superior, Konev reminded the East German leader that success required two nonnegotiable aspects. While closing the border, he said, East German units at no point could be allowed to disrupt the ability of West Berliners or the Western Allies to move by air, road, or rail to and from West Germany.

Second, said Konev, the operation had to be as fast as the wind.

Khrushchev had constructed the plan so that "our establishing of the border control in the GDR didn't give the West either the right or the pretext to resolve our dispute by war." To achieve that, Konev considered speed essential to create a fait accompli, to ensure the loyalty of East German forces, and to dissuade any trigger-happy American commander from improvising. A rapidly executed operation could also demonstrate to the West the impossibility of reversing the facts that communist troops would establish on the ground.

THE VOLKSKAMMER, EAST BERLIN
10:00 A.M., FRIDAY, AUGUST 11, 1961

At age twenty-six, Adam Kellett-Long of Reuters was the only Western news correspondent based in communist East Berlin, and that suited him just fine. A gaggle of reporters fought over each shred of news in West Berlin, but he had the communist side to himself under an arrangement through which the East German government paid its bills to the news agency through supplying his office and accreditation. Ulbricht called Kellett-Long "my little shadow," acknowledging his frequent presence.

Still, the East German press office's telephone call that morning was unusual, urging the young reporter to cover an emergency session of the Volkskammer, the country's parliament, on Luisenstrasse at 10:00 a.m. on Friday, August 11. The British reporter usually skipped the Volkskammer's mundane meetings, as his editors were unlikely ever to print a report on them. But if his East German minders were so eager for him to attend, there must be a reason.

The council that day passed what Kellett-Long regarded as an "enigmatic resolution," saying that its members approved whatever measures the East German government wished to undertake to address the "revanchist" situation in Berlin. It was an all-purpose rubber stamp for Ulbricht.

Outside the meeting hall, Kellett-Long buttonholed his most reliable source, Horst Sindermann, who ran the Communist Party's propaganda operations. "What is all this about?" asked Kellett-Long.

Sindermann was less talkative than usual. He studied the young Brit through thick glasses, strands of dark hair combed across his balding head, then spoke in a measured, businesslike manner. "If I were you, and were planning to leave Berlin this weekend, I would not do so," he said.

The East German then disappeared into the crowd.

Kellett-Long would later recall, "You could not have a stronger tip in a communist country that whatever was going to happen was going to happen that weekend."

The British reporter checked out news reports, but found no further clues. Sender Freies Berlin, the U.S.-funded West Berlin radio station, had that morning reported yet another record number of East Germans arriving at the Marienfelde emergency refugee camp. Kellett-Long had joked to his wife that, by his calculations, East Germany would be entirely empty by 1980 or so.

The official East Berlin radio station Deutschlandsender didn't report on refugees at all that day—or anything else that would help Kellett-Long. It was running a feature on the second human to orbit the Earth, Soviet cosmonaut Gherman Titov, who had circled the globe seventeen times in twenty-five hours and eighteen minutes before safely returning to Earth. The accomplishment was "unprecedented in human history," the radio station said, noting that it further proved the socialist superiority that the refugee flood so stubbornly contradicted.

In a further effort to follow up Sindermann's tip, the British reporter drove to the Ostbahnhof, East Berlin's main station for those arriving from elsewhere in East Germany, where he often tried to monitor the refugee flow. The number of travelers seemed greater than usual, but what struck Kellett-Long even more was the larger presence of uniformed and plain-clothes police.

The police were aggressively working the crowd, fishing out dozens of travelers seemingly at random, arresting some and turning back others. The Brit scribbled in his notebook: "an escalated police operation." However, it seemed to Kellett-Long that East German authorities were losing the battle, trying to hold back the sea with outstretched palms. He could see the tension in their eyes.

Kellett-Long returned to his office and wrote a story that rang bells in editorial rooms around the world. "Berlin is holding its breath this sunny weekend," he wrote, "waiting for drastic measures to stem the refugee flow to West Berlin." Based on the Sindermann steer, he said authorities would be responding "imminently."

It was strong and pessimistic language, just the sort of brash report that had made Kellett-Long so unpopular with his superiors. But he was confident of it. Kellett-Long reckoned there were now several possibilities as to what could happen next. He listed them for his readers: East German authorities could tighten their controls on travelers. They could impose stiffer penalties on those apprehended while trying to flee. A far bigger story, of course, would be if the East Germans shut off transit routes altogether.

Kellett-Long couldn't imagine that alternative. Then he would be writing about a potential war.

STASI HEADQUARTERS, NORMANNENSTRASSE, EAST BERLIN
LATE FRIDAY AFTERNOON, AUGUST 11, 1961

In the first briefing for his lieutenants ahead of their weekend work, Stasi chief Erich Mielke gave the historic moment its code name. "The name of this operation will herewith be known as 'Rose,'" he said. He did not explain the reasoning behind the name, though the suggestion was that behind the tens of thousands of barbed-wire thorns was a plan of organizational beauty.

Mielke exuded self-confidence. Though he was only five feet, five inches tall—about the same height as Ulbricht and Honecker—he was more powerfully built, more athletic, and more handsome than either of them. He wore a permanent five-o'clock shadow on his jowls and had bags under his dark eyes.

Back in 1931, at only twenty-four years of age, Mielke had begun his thuggish communist career with the murder of two Berlin police officers who had been lured to a political rally for the planned hit in front of the Babylon Cinema. After the killings, Mielke crowed among comrades at a local pub, "Today we celebrate an act that I have staged!" ("*Heute wird ein Ding gefeiert, das ich gedreht habe!*") Party comrades smuggled Mielke out of Germany, where he was convicted in absentia. He then began his education and training in Moscow as a Soviet political intelligence officer.

Mielke had run East German state security since 1957, but the coming hours would be the most crucial test yet for his elaborate apparatus of 85,000 full-time domestic spies and 170,000 informants. Most of his senior officers, gathered in the canteen at secret police headquarters, had known nothing about the operation until that moment.

"Today we begin a new chapter of our Chekist work," he told them, with one of his frequent references to the Cheka, the original state security arm of the Bolshevik revolution. "This new chapter demands the mobilization of each individual member of the State Security Forces. In this period we are entering, it will be shown whether we know *everything* and whether we are firmly anchored *everywhere*. Now we must prove whether we understand the politics of the party and are capable of carrying out its orders."

Mielke kept fit, drank little, and didn't smoke, but he had three indulgences: a passion for Prussian marching music, hunting on private grounds he kept for top communist officials, and the success of the security forces' soccer team, Sportsvereinigung Dynamo, which would regularly win championships with the help of his manipulation of matches and players. Yet none of that compared with the game he was fixing now.

He told his officers that the work they were about to perform would "demonstrate the strength of our republic. . . . What is the main thing to remember: always be watchful, demonstrate *extreme* efficiency and eliminate *all* negative occurrences. *No* enemy must be allowed to become active; *no* conglomeration of enemies must be permitted."

He then issued instructions for the weekend ahead. They ranged from how to control individual factories to assessing precisely the "enemy forces" on a district-by-district level. He wanted secret police present within the armed forces to ensure combat readiness and political loyalty through the closest possible contact to officers. "Whoever may confront us with antagonistic actions will be arrested," he said. "Enemies must be seized outright. Our goal is to prevent all negative phenomena. Enemy forces must be immediately and discreetly arrested . . . if they become active."

Mielke had taken leadership after the June 1953 failure of his mentor

Wilhelm Zaisser to stop worker protests from spreading. Back then, soldiers and police had in many cases joined ranks with the protesters. Strikes had spread like waves across the country, and it had taken Soviet tanks and troops to restore order.

Mielke was determined to preclude all such problems by anticipating them and dousing dissent before it gained momentum.

EAST AND WEST BERLIN
SATURDAY, AUGUST 12, 1961

It was like any other summer weekend for most Berliners.

The weather was a pleasant 75 degrees (24 degrees Celsius), with just enough cloud cover to provide relief from the sun. After the downpours of the previous week, Berliners gathered at sidewalk cafés, in parks, and at lakeside beaches.

One neighborhood near Berlin's East–West border had been closed to traffic, but it was for the annual Kreuzberg *Kinderfest*, or children's fair, on the Zimmerstrasse. Flags and streamers decorated the narrow street, where children from all sectors of Berlin were laughing, playing, and begging their parents for ice cream and cake. Doting adults tossed children wrapped candies from their apartment windows above the streets.

Most Allied military officers had taken the day off to be with their families. Some steered sailboats on the Wannsee and up it through the undulating Havel. Major General Albert Watson II, the U.S. commandant in Berlin, played golf at the Blue-White Club, where membership was part of occupation rights.

The Severin + Kühn company tour buses were having a bumper day showing off the Cold War's epicenter to tourists, including stops in the Soviet sector. They instructed passengers not to photograph certain public buildings but urged them to snap as many shots as they liked of the Soviet memorial in Treptower Park, with its statue of a giant Red Army soldier cradling a German baby in one arm while crushing a swastika with his boot.

The biggest story of the day in West Berlin papers was that of the record inflow of refugees. A flat nasal voice at the Marienfelde refugee center provided the count over loudspeakers for all who were waiting in line—"seven-hundred sixty-five, seven hundred sixty-six, seven hundred sixty-seven"—to reach more than two thousand by day's end.

Church workers, members of civic clubs, and other volunteers, including the spouses of Allied forces, had gathered to help feed hungry refugees and console weeping babies. The camp's facilities overflowed, so refugees had been distributed around the city to sleep in church naves and in classrooms on military camp beds and hospital cots. Heinrich Albertz, Mayor Brandt's chief of staff, telephoned George Muller, the deputy political adviser at the American Mission, to ask for field rations, as Marienfelde had run out of food. "The matter just can't continue like this," he said.

Muller extracted several thousand C rations from the U.S. garrison to help. They would last only a few days, but Albertz would take what he could get.

Not since 1953 had West Berlin seen such a stampede. Marienfelde's twenty-five three-story apartment blocks were filled to bursting, as were twenty-nine other temporary camps set up to absorb the flood. Twenty-one daily charter flights were ferrying thousands of the new refugees from West Berlin to other parts of West Germany where jobs were plentiful.

Yet none of that was sufficient to manage the human tide. Processors had all but given up trying to sift out real from bogus refugees, among them certainly dozens of East German spies that Ulbricht's foreign intelligence chief Markus Wolf was planting in the West.

As dark settled over Berlin, a fireworks display for the children's festival illuminated the sky. Dancing couples on the rooftop terrace of the new Berlin Hilton stopped to take in the pyrotechnics. West Berlin movie houses were sold out that weekend, and more than half of the customers were East Berliners. It was no wonder, considering the hits they could see for a mark and twenty-five pfennigs in Eastern or Western currency: *The Misfits*, with Clark Gable and Marilyn Monroe, at Atelier am Zoo; *Ben-Hur*, with Charlton Heston; or *The Old Man and the Sea*, with Spencer Tracy, at the Delphi Filmpalast. Or they could watch *For Whom the Bell Tolls*, with Gary Cooper and Ingrid Bergman, at the Studio on Kurfürstendamm, or *The Third Man*, with Orson Welles, at the Ufa Pavillion.

On a live stage, Leonard Bernstein's new musical, *West Side Story*, was taking West Berlin by storm. East Berlin also had its stage attractions. Hundreds of West Berliners crossed each evening to see the latest Bertolt Brecht performance at the famous Berliner Ensemble, or political cabaret in the Distel. Some made the trip for cheap drinks at places like the Rialto Bar in the northeast Pankow district, which had no closing hour.

Soviet troops were restricted to barracks that night, due to nonfraternization policies. However, British, French, and American soldiers were doing the town, enjoying their considerable attraction to Berlin girls whose own German men had far less pocket money to entertain them. The First Welsh Regiment had gathered at a British sector dance hall. The French had a dance floor at the Maison du Soldat. American GIs gathered in their own service clubs and favorite pubs—and as so often on Saturdays, they would make it a long and liquid night.

NUREMBERG, WEST GERMANY
SATURDAY EVENING, AUGUST 12, 1961

Berlin's mayor Willy Brandt launched the final phase of his national campaign for chancellor in Nuremberg in Bavaria, some one hundred miles north of Munich. Before 60,000 voters on the city's cobbled market square, he attacked his opponent Adenauer for refusing to engage him in a public debate of the Nixon–Kennedy variety.

In a raspy, emotional voice, the forty-seven-year-old mayor rhetorically asked the crowd why so many refugees came to West Berlin every day. "The answer," he said, "is because the Soviet Union is preparing a strike against our people, the seriousness of which only a very few understand." He said East Germans fear "the Iron Curtain will be cemented shut" and they will be left "locked into a giant prison. They are agonizingly worried that they might be forgotten or sacrificed on the altar of indifference and lost opportunities."

As prophetic as he was poetic, Brandt fired another shot across the bow of his opponent Adenauer. "Today we stand in the most serious crisis of our postwar history, and the chancellor belittles that matter. . . ."

He called for all Germans on both sides of the divide to join in a plebiscite about their future, confident they would choose a democratic, Western course. If East Germans could not be included in such a referendum, West Germans and West Berliners should vote on their own, he said. "We also have a claim to self-determination," he said, in reference to Germany's wartime defeat, "not because we are better than others, but rather because we are no worse than other people."

The crowd cheered wildly, wanting even more of Brandt when he retreated in exhaustion to the two railway carriages that had been carrying him from one campaign stop to another. The train would drive overnight to Kiel on the North Sea coast.

While Brandt was in Nuremberg, Adenauer was campaigning closer to his Bonn home in Lübeck. His less focused, more meandering speech asked East Germans to stop their westward stampede and stay home, helping to prepare East Germany for unification.

"It is our duty," he said, employing the emotive German concept of *Pflicht*, "to say to our German brothers and our German sisters on the other side of the zone border: Don't panic." Germans together would someday overcome their difficult separation, he said, and become as one again.

GROSSER DÖLLNSEE, EAST GERMANY
5:00 P.M., SATURDAY, AUGUST 12, 1961

Walter Ulbricht appeared uncharacteristically relaxed to guests attending his garden party at Grosser Döllnsee, some twenty-five miles outside Berlin. The government guest quarters, known as "House Among the Birches," had once served as the hunting lodge for Luftwaffe commander Hermann Göring, something Ulbricht's guests knew but did not mention.

Ulbricht's party had a dual purpose. First, he was quarantining government officials who would later sign off on his operation in an environment that he could hermetically seal. Second, he was executing a diversionary maneuver. Any Western intelligence agency monitoring his movements would report that East Germany's leader was throwing a summer party at his countryside retreat.

His guests speculated among themselves about why they had been summoned. Some noticed a larger-than-usual number of soldiers and military vehicles in the woods surrounding the guesthouse. But none of them had risen in Ulbricht's hierarchy by asking too many questions.

The August sun beat down as they gathered in the shade of birch trees in the meadow beside a serene lake. For those who remained inside, Ulbricht was showing a film, the popular Soviet comedy with the German title of *Rette sich wer kann!* (or *Each Man for Himself*), about the chaos aboard a Russian freighter carrying lions and tigers.

Only a handful of Ulbricht's guests knew that at four p.m. their boss had signed the final order that gave Honecker the green light to put Operation Rose into motion. Standing by his side had been the crucial players in that evening's chain of command: Politburo members Willi Stoph and Paul Verner, who ran the government; Defense Minister Heinz Hoffmann; Minister of State Security Erich Mielke; Minister of Interior Karl Maron; Minister for Transport Erwin Kramer; People's Police President Fritz Eikemeier and his chief of staff Horst Ende.

While standing before them, Honecker had briefed his senior officers on their assignments for the evening, and none had raised any questions or objections. He had then provided each of them their written instructions, having signed them as he would all the other orders for that evening: "With socialist greetings, E. Honecker."

HYANNIS PORT, MASSACHUSETTS
MIDDAY, SATURDAY, AUGUST 12, 1961 (6:00 P.M. IN BERLIN)

Apparently unaware of what was occurring in Berlin, President Kennedy was trying to beat the 90-degree heat on Cape Cod with a midday boat outing. He had spent Saturday morning reading reports that followed up on Friday discussions about how to prepare for a possible Berlin crisis with Secretary of State Rusk and Secretary of Defense McNamara.

The day's diplomatic traffic contained some reason for concern.

Khrushchev had given a speech at a Soviet–Romanian Friendship Rally a day earlier, and the U.S. embassy in Moscow worried about his blatant threats "of complete destruction" of NATO members Greece, Italy, and West Germany should war break out. At the same time, Khrushchev had talked more emphatically than before of Soviet willingness to provide guarantees of access to West Berlin and ensure noninterference in the city's internal affairs.

Both could be viewed as messages to Kennedy—a stick and a carrot.

Secretary of State Rusk had sent a sharply worded cable to U.S. Ambassador to Germany Dowling that began, "The situation in East Germany is causing us increasing concern." He warned that an "explosion along 1953 lines at this time would be highly unfortunate."

He feared that such an uprising, in response to the danger of "the escape hatch being closed," would come "before the military and political measures now under way for dealing with the Berlin problem have become effective." He said, "It would be particularly unfortunate if an explosion in East Germany were based on the expectation of immediate Western military assistance."

He wanted Dowling to report on what the West German government thought about the "likelihood of early explosion" and "what action it contemplates to prevent one, and what action by the U.S. and other Allies it would consider useful." He reminded Dowling to tell the West Germans "that as a matter of policy, the Allies should do nothing to exacerbate the situation."

Despite such clear worries about coming trouble, Kennedy set his papers aside at midday and, with the sun burning through the overcast sky, set off on his motorboat into Nantucket Sound with his wife, three-year-old Caroline, and Lem Billings, his longtime friend and New York advertising man. The president dropped anchor in Cotuit Harbor after the Coast Guard and police boats cleared a swimming area for the First Family. Jackie set aside her pink parasol and jumped into the water dressed in a blue-and-white bathing suit.

The latest report on Khrushchev's activities included little of interest. The Soviet leader had left for a weekend retreat in the Crimea, where he was preparing for his October Party Congress, and the word was that he planned to be away until the first week of September. More excitement was swirling around the New York Yankees' extraordinary baseball year. Mickey Mantle had just hit his forty-fourth homer and Roger Maris his forty-second.

After a four-and-a-half-hour cruise, the Kennedys returned to their private dock, where they swam, joined by Caroline in an orange life jacket. The *Los Angeles Times* reported that although "the president did not swim vigorously . . . he showed no trace of his recent back ailment when he agilely climbed a ladder at the stern of the *Marlin*."

While soldiers in East Germany were secretly loading trucks with tank traps, barbed wire, pillars, and sawhorses, Kennedy drove his white golf cart into Nantucket village, where he bought Caroline and four of her cousins some ice cream at a local candy store. Jackie looked like something out of a fashion magazine in her blue blouse and red shorts.

EAST BERLIN
7:00 P.M., SATURDAY, AUGUST 12, 1961

Reuters correspondent Kellett-Long had created such a stir with his Friday story, in which he had predicted an imminent Berlin event, that his news editor David Campbell had flown in that afternoon to track the story personally.

By early evening on Saturday, the two men were still searching for factual confirmation of Kellett-Long's apparent scoop. "You put us out on a real limb here," Campbell told his young reporter. "Something better happen."

In rereading his story, Kellett-Long wondered whether he should have used somewhat less hyperbolic language. He and Campbell drove around East Berlin in his car, looking in vain for the crisis he had predicted. Yet all Kellett-Long saw was a beautiful day with crowded swimming pools and overflowing cafés.

Perhaps it would happen later in the evening, the reporter told his boss.

PEOPLE'S ARMY HEADQUARTERS, STRAUSBERG, EAST GERMANY
8:00 P.M., SATURDAY, AUGUST 12, 1961

General Heinz Hoffmann, who was both East German defense minister and army commander, stood proudly before his officers. At age fifty, he looked like something out of a World War II film, standing ramrod-straight in his perfectly pressed uniform with eight rows of medals, wavy blond hair with gray streaks, combed back. With his square and high cheekbones, he was almost too handsome.

Like so much of the East German leadership, he had been a rambunctious young communist in prewar Germany. Convicted of assault during anti-Nazi demonstrations, he had done hard jail time. In 1937 and 1938, Hoffmann had been seriously wounded while fighting in the Spanish Civil War, where he had served in an international brigade under the cover name Heinz Roth. After two years in an internment camp, he'd moved to the Soviet Union, where he had been educated for his future work. In 1949, he had taken charge of creating the East German armed forces that he would now deploy against their own people.

Beside him stood his most impressive workhorse officer, Ottomar Pech, a man of a quite different background who had fought in the Third Reich's Wehrmacht before his capture by the Russians on the Eastern Front. His job was to train the most elite military units and oversee coordination between the secret police and the military, which would be so crucial that evening.

Arrayed before them were the army's top commanders and senior border police officers at the People's Army headquarters in Strausberg, some thirty kilometers east of Berlin. They had eaten generously from a cold buffet table groaning with the sort and quality of food that was not easily accessible to all East Germans: sausage, ham, veal, caviar, and smoked salmon. Though alcohol had been available, most of the men drank coffee, for rumors had indicated they would be involved in a secret operation that evening.

Hoffmann briefed officers on what was to come after they watched a morale-building film extolling the might of socialist combat forces. At precisely 8:00 p.m., Hoffmann handed his senior officers the first sealed orders. Successively lower-ranking officers were briefed thereafter, many by telephone. They were ready to mobilize soldiers and police, thousands of whom had been held by their superiors in their barracks and at training grounds throughout the weekend.

By 10:00 p.m., Honecker was confident his apparatus had responded exactly as planned and was ready for full mobilization. He would receive reports throughout the night from commanding officers, district party committees, and government departments. His tentacles stretched everywhere. Honecker would later reflect that the operation that he had begun "in the dawning day, Sunday" would make the world "prick up its ears."

The little information that had leaked out to the West on the operation wasn't resulting in any response. The head of West Germany's Free Democratic Party, Erich Mende, had contacted Ernst Lemmer, Adenauer's minister responsible for *gesamtdeutsche Fragen*, or German-German relations, after hearing reports from West German intelligence that they were picking up "indications" that showed Ulbricht was planning at some point soon to introduce *Sperrmassnahmen*, or measures to blockade the middle of Berlin. The intelligence had been convincing enough that Mende had come to Lemmer's office to discuss the danger while they inspected an outspread city map together. The two men agreed that sealing the border would be impossible.

"It just wouldn't work," Mende concluded.

Yet at midnight on the dot, Honecker rang army headquarters and issued the order to begin the unimaginable.

"You know the assignment!" he said. "March!"

Hoffmann immediately set his units in motion: some 3,150 soldiers of the 8th Motorized Artillery Division began to roll on East Berlin from Schwerin, with 100 battle tanks and 120 armored personnel carriers. They would park in the stockyards of the Friedrichsfelde district of East Berlin. Hoffmann would dispatch a further 4,200 troops of the 1st Motorized Division from their barracks in Potsdam with 140 tanks and 200 personnel carriers. They would form the second ring of defense behind the border's front lines, which would be made up of 10,000 men from units of the East Berlin Volkspolizei, the 1st Brigade of the Readiness Police, and the Berlin Security Command.

In all, some 8,200 People's Police and 3,700 members of the mobile police forces—reinforced with 12,000 factory militia men and 4,500 State Security men—would move into action in the hours ahead. They would be supported by a further 40,000 East German soldiers around the country, just in case the border closure triggered anything similar to the national uprising of June 1953. Soldiers from Saxony, who were considered particularly reliable, would reinforce the 10,000 soldiers of the People's Army stationed in Berlin.

It was a cool and clear night—perfect for the purpose.

Perhaps Mother Nature was a communist.

GROSSER DÖLLNSEE, EAST GERMANY
10:00 P.M., SATURDAY, AUGUST 12, 1961

Ulbricht looked at his watch. "We're going to have a little meeting," he said to his guests.

It was precisely 10:00 p.m. and thus time to assemble his garden party's guests in a single room for the announcement. They were tired, overfed, and ready to go home, having already been with him for more than six hours. More than a few were drunk or at least tipsy. All gathered obediently.

Ulbricht then informed them that the sector border between East and West Berlin would be closed in three hours' time. In a printed edict, which the ministers there would approve, he would authorize action by East German security forces to place "under proper control the still open border between socialist and capitalist Europe."

"Alle einverstanden?"—All agreed?—Ulbricht asked, noting the nodding of his mostly silent guests.

He informed his guests that they, like his domestic staff, would not be able to leave Döllnsee until the operation was well under way to ensure complete security. But, he offered, there was still plenty of food and alcohol for them to enjoy.

No one protested. As Ulbricht had told Soviet Ambassador Pervukhin three days earlier: "We will eat together. I'll share with them the decision to close the border, and I am entirely convinced that they will approve this measure. But above all else, I will not let them leave until we have completed the operation.

"Sicher ist sicher," he had said: Better safe than sorry.

REUTERS NEWS AGENCY OFFICE, EAST BERLIN
10:00 P.M., SATURDAY, AUGUST 12, 1961

Kellett-Long was worried more about his career than about Berlin's fate.

It was past ten o'clock, and he had no additional facts to back up his Friday story that Berlin was facing a decisive weekend. He returned to the Ostbahnhof to look for any unusual activity and seek out the vendor who regularly provided him with an early edition of *Neues Deutschland*, the Communist Party paper that contained any news of importance.

He hungrily scanned its pages, feeling "shattered" to read only routine stories with "nothing to suggest anything was about to happen."

Kellett-Long's London editors, under pressure from subscribers, were pressing him to either file a story to support his earlier report or knock it down. "I can't just bury my head in the sand," he thought to himself as he began to compose leads.

"Contrary to expectations . . ." he typed out.

"Contrary to expectations, *what?*" he asked himself.

"What an amateur I am," he mumbled to himself.

He crumpled up the paper and tossed it away. In a state of nerves, he smoked one cigarette after another.

RÖNTGENTAL, EAST GERMANY
MIDNIGHT, SUNDAY, AUGUST 13, 1961

Three long, penetrating wails of a siren wrenched Sergeant Rudi Thurow from his slumber. Thurow turned on his light and looked at his watch. It was a minute past midnight. Probably just another drill, he cursed to himself. There had been so many lately. Yet the slender, blond, twenty-three-year-old leader of the 4th Platoon, 1st Brigade, of the East German border police knew his job was to take each one of them seriously.*

Thurow had also seen enough military activity the previous afternoon to suspect something more than an exercise was in the works. Soviet T-34 and T-54 tanks had rumbled by all afternoon past his post in Röntgental, forty kilometers north of Berlin, and he had seen several trainloads of East German soldiers rolling into East Berlin.

It had been six years since Thurow had volunteered to join the border guards, attracted by the good pay and privileged access to scarce consumer goods. He had earned decorations of all sorts since then, and had distinguished himself as his brigade's top sharpshooter.

He dressed quickly, then ran to the adjoining room, where he awakened his men, who cursed in complaint while he abruptly pulled off their blankets. Once assembled in the parade yard, First Lieutenant Witz, the

---

*Thurow himself escaped to the West on February 21, 1962. As a deserter he thereafter was hounded by State Security; he evaded one confirmed order to murder him and at least one effort to kidnap him.

company commander, told his men and dozens of others that on this night, they would undertake measures that had been forced upon them by the enemy.

For too long, said Witz, the government had tolerated the loss of its workforce to the West. He said the flesh merchants in West Berlin, who preyed on the citizens of the GDR, would be put in their place. He spoke of eighty-three espionage and terror centers in West Berlin that would be dealt a crippling blow by his men's action that night.

Witz, who said he had been briefed only an hour earlier, carefully tore open a large brown envelope marked "Top Secret," then took out its contents. Thurow and the others impatiently listened while Witz read for five minutes from the document before it came to the point.

> In order to prevent the enemy activities of the vengeful and militaristic powers of West Germany and West Berlin, controls will be introduced on the borders of the German Democratic Republic, including the border of the Western sector of Greater Berlin. . . .

Berlin was to be split in two, and Thurow's men would help draw the dividing line. Thurow heard a fellow sergeant, a loyal communist, whisper a question: "Would the Allies simply stand by and let this happen?"

Or were they at war?

REUTERS NEWS AGENCY OFFICE, EAST BERLIN
1:00 A.M., SUNDAY, AUGUST 13, 1961

Shortly before 1:00 a.m., Adam Kellett-Long watched his East German news agency printer cough out its daily good-night message. He decided "to pack it up" and think about finding new employment in the morning.

Just then, his phone rang and a voice he did not recognize advised him in German not to go to bed that night. At 1:11 a.m., his teleprinter came to life. Kellett-Long read as it spat out a 10,000-word Warsaw Pact decree. The

British correspondent was frustrated that the printer would not pump out the copy as quickly as he could read it. It spoke of how "deceived people," namely the refugees, were being recruited as spies and saboteurs. In response, Warsaw Pact member states were ensuring that "reliable safeguards and effective control be established around the whole territory of West Berlin." The declaration reassured NATO allies that the Warsaw Pact would not touch access routes to West Berlin.

Kellett-Long raced to his car and drove toward the border to see what was happening. Aside from the occasional couple embracing in a doorway, he saw only a deserted city as he steered down the Schönhauser Allee near his home and then turned on Unter den Linden toward the Brandenburg Gate.

There a policeman waved a red flare to stop his car.

"I'm afraid you can't go any further," the policeman said calmly. *"Die Grenze ist geschlossen."* (The border is closed.)

Kellett-Long then drove up Unter den Linden on his way back to the office to file his report, but he was blocked at Marx-Engels Square, a main parade ground for East German soldiers. Another policeman with another flare stood before its empty expanse, blocking traffic so that a huge convoy of personnel vehicles could pass, carrying uniformed police and soldiers. It seemed to go on forever.

Kellett-Long rushed back to his office to file a "snap" report that would ring news agency machines around the world. It was easy to write: "The East–West border was closed early today. . . ."

He followed that with a first-person account:

> Earlier today, I became the first person to drive an East Berlin car through the police cordons since the border controls began shortly after midnight. . . . The Brandenburg Gate, main crossing point between the two halves of the city, was surrounded by East German police, some armed with submachine guns, and members of the paramilitary "factory fighting guards."

Kellett-Long then turned on East German radio and heard announcers read one decree after another about new restrictions on travel and how they would be enforced. He filed new reports as quickly as he could type. The British reporter found it curious that East German radio was playing modern, soothing jazz between the endless decrees.

"So that's all they are doing," he thought to himself. "They are just reading decrees and playing nice music."

FRENCH SECTOR, WEST BERLIN
1:50 A.M., SUNDAY, AUGUST 13, 1961

Twenty minutes after the operation began, West Berlin police sergeant Hans Peters saw the blazing headlights of a half dozen East German army trucks as they rolled down the road he was patrolling. Strelitzer Strasse was a street like 193 others that crossed the previously unmarked boundary between two Berlins.

The trucks belched out soldiers, who scattered up both sides of the street. Each carried long, dark objects that he took to be machine guns. Peters, a Third Reich army veteran who had served on the Eastern Front, pulled his Smith & Wesson revolver from his holster. Yet even as he slipped bullets into the chamber, he knew it was an inadequate defense against such numbers. He sought cover in a doorway, from which he watched a scene that would be repeated throughout the night at dozens of other locations.

Two squads of six soldiers each sprawled and squatted on the sidewalks facing west, pointing their machine guns on tripods in his direction. They had no intention of invading the West and were merely setting up a line to deter a no-show opponent. Behind them, two other squads carried barbed wire. They uncoiled the rolls and hung the strands from wooden sawhorses they had placed across the street. Their cordon was safely within the Soviet zone and well behind the demarcation line.

Though Peters was technically in the French sector, all French soldiers remained in bed. That left only him, a lone West Berlin policeman, to observe a flawless operation. He watched the enemy seal the street so quietly and smoothly that none of the residents of Strelitzer Strasse even rose to turn on a light.

Once the border line was secure, the East German soldiers turned their guns to the East, prepared to contain their own people. Peters alerted his superiors to what he had witnessed.

U.S. MISSION, WEST BERLIN
2:00 A.M., SUNDAY, AUGUST 13, 1961

After receiving the first reports of the border closure at around 2:00 a.m., the top U.S. official in Berlin, E. Allan Lightner Jr., was reluctant to awaken his superiors. Washington tended to overreact, and Lightner wanted to get his story straight before reporting in. It was also a summer weekend, and his bosses would be more unhappy than usual about an unnecessary wake-up call.

Senior officials of the U.S, British, and French Allied missions in West Berlin were already burning up phone lines among themselves, piecing together what seemed to be occurring. "There seems to be something going on in East Berlin," Lightner said with some understatement to diplomatic officer William Richard Smyser, who served in the Eastern affairs section. He wanted them to check it out.

At just past three in the morning in the early light of a northern European dawn, Smyser drove his Mercedes 190SL with his colleague Frank Trinka up to Potsdamer Platz, where East German Vopos (Volkspolizei) and factory militia were unrolling the first strands of barbed wire. When they told the Americans they could not pass, Smyser protested, "We are officials of the American forces. You have no right to stop us."

It would be the first test of whether the Soviets and their East German clients would prevent Allied right of free passage in Berlin, a potential trigger for a U.S. military response. After an exchange by radio with superiors, the East German police rolled back the barbed wire to let the diplomats pass. They would stop any ordinary East Germans from crossing that night, but the police had clear orders not to impede the movement of Allied officials. Khrushchev's decision to operate within Kennedy's guidelines was now operational.

During an hour's drive around East Berlin, Smyser and Trinka witnessed a city of frenetic police activity and private despair. All along the border, Vopos were unloading concrete posts and barbed wire and blocking all streets leading from East to West. At Bahnhof Friedrichstrasse, East Berlin's main station from the West, armed police were blocking the dimly lit platforms as anguished would-be travelers sat in the cavernous halls on their suitcases and bundles, many of them weeping. As he looked into their faces, Smyser could imagine them thinking, "Oh my God, if we'd only gone twenty-four hours earlier."

Children were separated from parents, lover from lover, and friend from friend. One of border police sergeant Rudi Thurow's men had been so ashamed of stopping people from continuing their lives as before that he had vaulted the barbed wire to freedom that morning.

Smyser and Trinka drove back to West Berlin through the Brandenburg Gate, cleared through again after a short delay by an East German policeman who had gained approval from a senior East German Communist Party official who was supervising the crossing.

The diplomats had gathered such a partial picture that the American Mission chose not to file a full report to Washington as the crisis was unfolding. Lightner's team concluded that they had neither the resources nor the manpower to match news agency reports on what had become a breaking story. Due to State Department bureaucracy, it would take four to six hours anyway to send an official telegram through channels at the U.S. embassy in Bonn from Berlin and then to Washington. The border closure had also disrupted U.S. intelligence efforts to get hold of their usual contacts, thus impeding independent confirmation of what was occurring in East Berlin.

When Lightner debriefed his scouts, he was particularly keen to hear that they had not seen Soviet forces taking any direct part in the operation. On the one hand, that meant the closure was less of a military threat to the

U.S., since Soviet troops weren't massing in Berlin. On the other hand, the East German regime was violating existing four-power agreements that prohibited the presence of its troops in East Berlin at all, let alone their use to occupy the city and seal its border.

At 11:00 a.m. Berlin time, Lightner cabled Rusk his first full report, before that having only sent partial information bursts through a so-called critical channel that didn't require the same clearances. He reported simply: "Early morning Aug 13 East German regime introduced drastic control measures which have effect of preventing entry into West Berlin of Sovzone and East Berlin residents." He said the move was "evidently as a result of increased refugee flow with attendant economic loss to GDR and prestige loss to socialist camp."

Lightner didn't cable again until 10:00 p.m. that night, when he wrapped up the mission's best knowledge of what had happened in the previous twenty-four hours. He put his emphasis on the massive military deployment, including significant backup by the Soviets, which was "designed to intimidate people from the outset and thus nip in the bud any possible resistance [by showing] civilian disobedience would be ruthlessly suppressed."

He concluded that the sizable Soviet military mobilization throughout East Germany revealed Moscow's doubts about the reliability of Walter Ulbricht's military. He also noted, however, that the East German authorities were allowing Western military and civilian personnel to pass freely to and from East Berlin. Lightner reported that eight hundred new refugees had registered in West Berlin between 10:00 a.m. and 4:00 p.m. on the first day of the city's physical division, having either crossed on August 12 or "through canals and fields today."

NEAR POTSDAMER PLATZ, WEST BERLIN
9:00 A.M., SUNDAY, AUGUST 13, 1961

West Berliners' mood of disorientation and confusion shifted to rage as the morning wore on. West Berlin policeman Klaus-Detlef Brunzel, new at his job and only twenty years old, arrived for duty at Potsdamer Platz only to discover how drastically the world had changed in just a few hours.

On the previous evening, he had worked a routine shift, confiscating contraband and chitchatting with the prostitutes who loitered on the vacant, war-flattened square, which until that day had been an excellent spot for them to attract clientele from both sides of the city. Now he saw only East German border police in their place, using jackhammers to dig holes for concrete pillars, from which they were stringing barbed wire. Brunzel had only been four years old when World War II ended, but he feared a new war had begun as he watched East German tanks track him with their gun barrels as he walked back and forth in front of them.

By late morning, a crowd of angry West Berliners had gathered at the border, throwing stones at the East German police and calling them pigs and Nazis. Brunzel took cover "to avoid being hit by masonry thrown by our own people!"

Before long, the West Berlin fury turned on absent American soldiers, protectors who they felt should have saved them from this fate. All the rhetoric about American commitment to Berlin's freedom had not produced a single U.S. rifle company.

U.S. MILITARY HEADQUARTERS, CLAYALLEE, WEST BERLIN
SUNDAY MORNING, AUGUST 13, 1961

General Watson, the American commandant in Berlin, had felt hamstrung by his reporting lines and instructions. He had also doubted his own judgment, having been in Berlin just three months.

He had considered Berlin a sufficiently calm place to have relocated his mother-in-law to the city. He compared the divided city's role in the U.S.–Soviet standoff to the "quiet in the eye of the cyclone." His time in Berlin had been spent less on military response and more on learning German, reducing his golf handicap, and playing what he called "elderly doubles" tennis with his wife.

In profiling the fifty-two-year-old commander, the Berlin press wrote of his fondness for horseback riding, bridge, light opera, and reading paperback mysteries. Watson was resigned to leading a command where he was so outnumbered by the enemy that he knew West Berlin would have been impossible to defend against a concerted Soviet conventional attack. Yet even if he had had the troops, he still lacked the independent authority to use them.

The bureaucracy of getting things done in Berlin was the worst Watson had experienced in the military, and that said a lot. He had one reporting line directly to U.S. Ambassador Walter Dowling, who sat three hundred miles away in Bonn. His second reporting line was to General Bruce Clarke, the U.S. Army Commander in Europe, headquartered in Heidelberg. Then there was a third line to NATO Commander General Lauris Norstad in Paris. Watson's orders came from all three, and they were rarely consistent.

There were also times, like the night of August 12–13 and the following morning, when all those channels fell mostly silent. Watson's instinct in such times of doubt was to stand whatever ground he occupied and hope for the best. For weeks, his instructions from the Pentagon had more often than not included warnings that he should not allow himself to be provoked by the East Germans or Soviets into a military action that could escalate into violent conflict, as if his superiors had known what was coming. So Watson played it safe in the early hours of August 13 and did nothing but observe the operation.

The East Germans hadn't crossed any of his lines. They had not set a foot in any of the non-Soviet Allied zones. And for all the Soviet military activity around the city, his scouts had not reported any major movement inside Berlin. So Watson saw no reason to wake up General Clarke or General Norstad. The State Department folks would alert Ambassador Dowling in Bonn, so Watson didn't contact him, either.

Early that morning, Watson had sent a helicopter over East Berlin airspace to monitor the situation. Yet he opted not to dispatch U.S. troops to the newly reinforced border. A show of U.S. force might have satisfied Berliners looking for a timely demonstration of American commitment, but Watson's superiors would have considered it a reckless provocation.

Watson felt justified in showing such restraint at 7:30 a.m., when Colonel Ernest von Pawel reported in to his emergency operations center in the basement of U.S. headquarters on Clayallee. Von Pawel told Watson that four Soviet divisions had moved out of their usual garrison areas in East Germany and had surrounded Berlin.

At age forty-six, "Von" was the crucially important chief of the U.S. Military Liaison Mission to the Commander in Chief, Group of Soviet Forces, Germany. Though his name had the ring of German nobility, Von's roots and manner were pure Laramie, Wyoming. He had won a reputation with Watson for getting things right.

Just four days earlier, Von had predicted during the regular meeting of the Berlin Watch Committee that Ulbricht was going to put up a "wall." The committee was a secret interagency intelligence group in the city whose job it was to raise alarm bells at the first indication of hostile military action. Though no one had paid attention then, that gave Von credibility with his commander now.

Lieutenant Colonel Thomas McCord, head of the U.S. Army's 513th Military Intelligence Group, Berlin, had been studying a number of pictures and reports of large quantities of construction material—concrete blocks, barbed wire, and other supplies—stockpiled near the city's dividing line. But the material was in so many places and had been ordered by so many sources that his men had difficulty interpreting what they were seeing.

"Do you think they plan to build a wall, Tom?" Colonel David Goodwin, the chief of intelligence on General Watson's staff, had asked at the meeting. McCord responded that he had three sources and they were contradictory. One "reliable" but untested source said there would be a wall and it was "imminent." But two sources, who were judged as more reliable, had said there would be nothing of the sort.

All eyes had then turned to von Pawel. He reminded the group that during World War II the Germans had built a wall in Warsaw sealing off the Jewish ghetto, a comparison that seemed outlandish at the time. "If you think a wall is the least likely option," he had said, "then that is where I place my bet, because we've never outguessed the Soviets before." The problem was that von Pawel had lacked any hard evidence at the time to support his conviction.

The deputy chief of the CIA base, John Dimmer, dismissed von Pawel's notion. It would be "political suicide" for Ulbricht to build a wall, he had said, and with that he had swayed the group to conclude a wall was the "least likely" of the many alternatives they were discussing.

Von Pawel's report on the morning of August 13 left no room for doubt about what was occurring. Hiding under a bridge in East Germany from 4:00 to 6:00 a.m., one of his men had seen a whole Soviet division rumble down the Autobahn. Von himself had counted a hundred tanks while making his way to Potsdam. He reported to Watson:

> The Soviet 19th Motorized Rifle Division, combined with the 10th Guards
> Tank Division and possibly the 6th Motorized Rifle Division, moved out
> early this morning and moved into position around Berlin. Elements
> of the 1st East German Army Motorized Rifle Division moved out from
> Potsdam and are presently unlocated. Soviet units deployed and moved
> off the autobahn, deploying units into small outposts and roadblocks
> composed of three or four tanks, an armed personnel carrier and several
> troops. These outposts were established 3 or 4 kilometers apart, and ap-
> pear completely to ring Berlin.

It was an elaborately and perfectly organized operation, about which U.S. military intelligence had reported nothing in advance. What von Pawel's report meant to Watson was that Soviet troops were primed to pounce in such numbers that they would overwhelm his paltry force if it dared respond.

It was 10:00 a.m. before the three Western commandants—the French, the British, and the American—and their staffs met on the Correnplatz, at Allied headquarters in the suburban Dahlem district of the American sector. All had been taken by surprise—and none had any good ideas about how to respond. Watson chaired the meeting by the coincidence of their monthly rotation. Yet for all Watson's lack of Berlin experience, he knew how to count. His twenty-seven tanks, less than one for every mile of the West Berlin–East Berlin internal border, and six 105-millimeter howitzers were not sufficient to take on the Soviet army and their East German clients.

REUTERS NEWS AGENCY OFFICE, EAST BERLIN
MID-MORNING, SUNDAY, AUGUST 13, 1961

Mary Kellett-Long looked out their East Berlin office window and saw an angry and growing crowd that had been building in size with every hour of the morning. It had never struck Mary before how close their apartment at Schönhauser Allee was to the Berlin border, just four hundred yards away, as the line had never been so clearly defined.

Most of the crowd was made up of furious East Berlin youth who saw their connection to the West cut off. Her husband, Adam, who by then had made his way into the crowd, thought they looked like angry soccer fans after a heartbreaking defeat, looking for someone to take it out on. Police and the paramilitary factory forces pushed back the line of protesters, which by then was twenty deep.

When the explosions began, Mary feared that East German units had fired on civilians and perhaps her husband. But the blasts were the sound of police firing tear-gas canisters into the protesters, who responded by running in all directions.

Adam recalled a more innocent time. Not long before August 13, a Vopo had stopped his car for a routine check as he returned from a West Berlin shopping trip. As he searched the trunk, Adam pulled a can of baked beans out of a bag and threw it in the air saying, *"Das ist eine Bombe!"* The police officer fell to the ground and his colleagues pulled their guns. The Vopo then dusted himself off and laughed, letting the reporter pass. Clearly, the time for practical jokes was over.

Like the few sporadic protests that had occurred across East Germany

June 21. Khrushchev dons his old uniform and prepares his military for the possibility of war, during a speech in the Grand Kremlin Palace. (*ITAR-TASS/Sovfoto*)

July 8. Kennedy, aboard the *Marlin*, summons his top advisers to Hyannis Port to discuss the growing crisis. Left to right: JFK, military adviser Maxwell Taylor, Secretary of State Dean Rusk, and Secretary of Defense Robert McNamara. (*AP Photo*)

Meanwhile, every week the flood of East German refugees to West Berlin rises even higher, making the crisis greater. An overhead shot of the Marienfelde refugee center on the outskirts of Berlin. (*USIS/National Archives*)

A mother watches over her children while they wait for processing at Marienfelde. (*USIS/National Archives*)

One refugee is Marlene Schmidt, who wins the Miss Universe pageant in Miami on July 15, less than a month before the border closes. (*UPI/Library of Congress*)

July 25. A pensive JFK before his first live TV speech to the nation from the Oval Office. (*Cecil Stoughton/JFK Library*)

Giving his secretary, Evelyn Lincoln, last-minute edits for the speech. (*Robert Knudsen/ JFK Library*)

August 13. The border closes. East German infantrymen seal off the crossing point at the Brandenburg Gate. (*USIS /National Archives*)

An East German policeman breaks up a West Berlin demonstration with a high-pressure water hose. (*USIS/National Archives*)

Children in East Berlin look across the low barbed wire into West Berlin. (*UPI/Library of Congress*)

August 16. Mayor Willy Brandt rallies his city. A quarter million West Berliners hear him warn that the existence of the entire noncommunist world is at stake. (*AP Photo, above, and USIS/National Archives, below*)

August 18. After resisting the president's request that he visit West Berlin, Vice President Johnson basks delightedly in the adoring crowd. (*USIS/National Archives*)

August 21. West Germany's largest newspaper, *Bild*, heralds the arrival of symbolic troop reinforcements from the 18th Infantry, 1st Battle Group. (*National Archives*)

August 22. Adenauer finally appears in Berlin nine days after the border closes, to much criticism because of the delay. (*AP Photo/Library of Congress*)

Walter Ulbricht speaks to factory militia men to thank them for protecting his country against imperialist subterfuge. (*AP Photo/Library of Congress*)

The wall grows. East Berlin workmen pile up the blocks. (*AP Photo/Library of Congress*)

A West German stands on a car to wave over the wall. (*UPI/Library of Congress*)

West Berliners stand on ladders and wave to loved ones on the other side. (*USIS/National Archives*)

Great escapes: East German border guard Conrad Schumann discards his rifle while leaping over barbed wire to freedom. (*USIS/National Archives*)

An elderly East Berlin woman is lowered from a window of her building, which rested in the communist zone, to freedom in West Berlin, with the help of neighbors and West Berlin firemen. (*UPI/National Archives*)

General Lucius Clay, hero of the 1948 Berlin Airlift. (*AP Photo/ Library of Congress*)

September 19. An honor guard of U.S. soldiers and West Berlin police greets Clay, Kennedy's special representative to Berlin, upon his arrival at Tempelhof Airport. (*AP Photo/Werner Kreusch*)

September 24. Kennedy warns the UN of the dangers of nuclear war facing the world, just as he is approving revised first-strike nuclear plans. (*Cecil Stoughton/JFK Library*)

October 18. Khrushchev shocks the world by announcing at the 22nd October Party Congress that he will explode the largest nuclear test bomb in history. (*ITAR-TASS/Sovfoto*)

October 25. The showdown begins. Three jeeps with armed U.S. military police escort an American automobile into East Berlin at the Friedrichstrasse checkpoint. (*UPI/National Archives*)

One of several American tanks is brought up to Checkpoint Charlie. (*USIS/National Archives*)

Soviet tanks from an American tank gunner's viewpoint. (*dpa/National Archives*)

Spectators lining the Friedrichstrasse. (*U.S. Army Signal Corps/National Archives*)

U.S. Army tanks, in the foreground, face off against Soviet tanks at Checkpoint Charlie.
(*AP Photo*)

August 1962. A year after the border closing, eighteen-year-old Peter Fechter is shot in the back by communist border police and lies bleeding to death for more than an hour before his corpse is retrieved. The incident causes widespread protests in West Berlin. (*UPI/National Archives*)

June 26, 1963. Kennedy, Brandt, and Adenauer stand in an open car as they drive past half a million cheering Berliners, en route to the president's historic speech. (*U.S. Army Signal Corps/ National Archives*)

"Ich bin ein Berliner." (*Robert Knudsen/JFK Library*)

that day, the demonstration lacked the scale, determination, or reach to challenge Ulbricht's victory. In contrast to 1953, Ulbricht was firmly in charge, well prepared, and enjoyed the full military and political support of the Soviets. He had prevented any organized opposition both through the element of surprise and the deployment of thousands of police and soldiers at every strategic point throughout the city.

Ulbricht's lieutenants used water cannons at several key locations to keep riotous West Berliners at bay. As long as the Allied troops stayed put in West Berlin, as they seemed determined to do, Ulbricht knew he could handle anything East Berliners or West Berliners might throw at him. Khrushchev's insurance policy—the Soviet tanks waiting in Berlin's hinterland—would not be necessary.

Marshal Konev had won his second battle of Berlin, this time with no bloodshed.

Under four-power agreements, Kennedy would have had every right to order his military to knock down the barriers put up that morning by East German units that had no right to operate in Berlin. On July 7, 1945, the U.S., Soviet, British, and French military governors of Germany had agreed that they would ensure unrestricted movement throughout Berlin. That had been reconfirmed again by the four-power agreement that had ended the Berlin blockade.

However, Kennedy had made clear through several channels before August 13 that he would not respond if Khrushchev and the East Germans restricted their actions to their own territory. Beyond that, Konev had sent a clear message about the cost of intervention through his massive military mobilization. Not only had Soviet troops ringed Berlin in a manner the Allies could not miss, but Khrushchev had gone a step further, putting his missile forces on full alert throughout Eastern Europe.

Nonetheless, it had still been a tense night for Konev. If fighting had been necessary, he had doubted whether the East German military and police forces would have remained loyal, despite their training, indoctrination, and careful supervision. Hundreds among their ranks already had fled as refugees, and many had relatives in the West.

Konev had been confident that East German soldiers, militia, and police would put up their border barriers properly, but he had doubted how they would have responded if Allied troops had moved forward to tear down the barricades and restore free movement.

To his relief, it had never come to that. Kennedy had never tested them.

WEST BERLIN
SUNDAY MORNING, AUGUST 13, 1961

When he first heard the news of the border closing, RIAS radio director Robert H. Lochner had been up late, preparing for a series of meetings the next morning for his boss, the legendary U.S. television journalist Edward R. Murrow. Murrow was visiting from Washington on an inspection trip as chief of the United States Information Service.

Lochner laid his work aside and ordered RIAS to alter its program from the usual weekend rock and roll to more serious music and news bulletins every quarter hour. He knew RIAS, with the largest transmitter in Europe, would be expected to provide East Berliners a lifeline at a time of crisis, just as it had done on June 17, 1953.

Then he set off for East Berlin in his car with State Department plates, making three trips across the Soviet zone throughout the evening, recording whatever he saw on a hidden tape recorder. He told stories of families divided and of forlorn lovers, using their recorded, troubled voices to dramatize the moment. Lochner had never seen as large a group of miserable human beings as those gathered at shuttered East Berlin train stations that morning, having failed to hear or believe overnight radio reports that the Berlin border had been closed.

At 10:00 a.m. he walked through the vast waiting hall of the Friedrichstrasse station, which overflowed with thousands of people "with desperate faces, cardboard boxes, some with suitcases." They sat on packed bags with nowhere to go.

On a staircase leading up to the elevated S-Bahn tracks stood black-suited Transportpolizei, or Trapos, blocking public access. They reminded Lochner of Hitler's SS in their threatening uniforms and with their stony, young, obedient faces.

An old woman timidly walked up to one of the Trapos, standing about three steps above her, and asked when the next train was due for West Berlin. Lochner would never forget the sneering tone of the officer's answer.

"That is all over," he said. "You are all sitting in a mousetrap now."

Lochner the next day showed the new East Berlin to Murrow, who doubted whether his friend Kennedy understood the seriousness of the situation that had been spawned by his inaction. He wrote a cable that evening telling the president that he was confronting a political and diplomatic disaster. If the president didn't show resolve quickly, Murrow predicted a crisis of confidence that could undermine the U.S. far beyond Berlin's borders. "What is in danger of being destroyed here is that perishable quality called hope," he wrote.

POLICE HEADQUARTERS, EAST BERLIN
6:00 A.M., SUNDAY, AUGUST 13, 1961

Erich Honecker was in an agitated state of excitement throughout the night, driving along the border and relishing the near-perfect execution of his plan.

He supervised every detail: he saw police checking out entry shafts to sewer systems for would-be escapees. Boats patrolled waterways that couldn't be closed as easily as streets. The extra troops he had ordered for the Friedrichstrasse station had been sufficient to manage the Sunday numbers.

Honecker had praised every commander he met throughout the night, occasionally suggesting changes in some finer details. At 4:00 a.m., satisfied that the most critical phase had been executed without a hitch, he returned to his office. By 6:00 a.m., all commanders had reported in that their missions had been carried out as instructed.

There was much work yet to be done to complete the job in the days ahead, but Honecker could not have been more satisfied. A few hundred East Berliners had rushed through the border in areas that had not yet been reinforced, and some had swum across lakes or canals. Other East Berliners would simply remain in the West, where by luck they had been spending the weekend. A few West Berliners would smuggle out their partners or friends in car trunks or under car seats in the first hours. A couple of more inventive East Berliners had replaced their own license plates with friends' West Berlin plates and had driven through.

From noon on Saturday to 4:00 p.m. on Monday, Marienfelde welcomed a record 6,904 refugees, the most of any weekend in East German history. But West Berlin authorities estimated that all but 1,500 had crossed the border before communist security forces had closed it down. The numbers were acceptably small, considering the fact that the refugee exodus had been brought to an end.

Honecker phoned Ulbricht with his final report. He then told his staff, "Now we can all go home."

Khrushchev would reflect later: "The establishment of border control restored order and discipline in the East Germans' lives, and Germans have always appreciated discipline."

15

THE WALL:
DESPERATE DAYS

Why would Khrushchev put up a wall if he really intended to seize West Berlin? . . . This is his way out of his predicament. It's not a very nice solution, but a wall is a hell of a lot better than a war.

President John F. Kennedy, August 13, 1961

The Russians . . . feel strongly that if they can break our will in Berlin that we will never be able to be good for anything else and they will have won the battle in 1961.

U.S. Attorney General Robert Kennedy, August 30, 1961

HUMBOLDT HARBOR, EAST BERLIN
THURSDAY, AUGUST 24, 1961

Günter Litfin, a twenty-four-year-old tailor whose boldest acts until that point had been performed with a needle and thread, summoned the courage to flee East Berlin eleven days after the communists had sealed the border.

Until August 13, Litfin had lived divided Berlin's ideal life, taking maximum advantage of each side's benefits as one of the city's 50,000 *Grenzgänger*, or "border jumpers." By day, he worked in West Berlin earning hard *Westmark*, which he exchanged on the black market at a five-to-one rate for

East German money, or *Ostmark*. He worked out of an atelier near West Berlin's Zoo Station, where he had already become a tailor to show-business greats: Heinz Rühmann, Ilse Werner, and Grete Weiser. Actresses in particular were drawn to his boyish manner, dark eyes, and curly black hair. At night he retreated to a comfortable East Berlin apartment in the Weissensee district, which he rented cheaply for those plentiful *Ostmark*.

Overnight, Litfin's dream life became a nightmare. The border closure prevented him from traveling to West Berlin, so he lost his job and his social position. Worse yet, an East German–mandated job placement process was about to land Litfin in a mind-numbing textile factory job with longer hours and a fraction of his previous pay.

Litfin damned himself for not moving to West Berlin when he had had the chance. A few days before the border closed, he had even rented a studio apartment in West Berlin's Charlottenburg district on the leafy Suarez-strasse. He and his brother had been slowly transporting his household goods in small loads, using two different cars, to avoid police suspicion. They had already smuggled out his most precious belonging, his modern sewing machine, by dismantling it and moving it in pieces.

Even more maddening was that Günter Litfin had been at a house-warming party in West Berlin with his brother, Jürgen, on the night the city was divided. When they'd returned home on the elevated S-Bahn at just past midnight, they had noticed nothing amiss.

It wasn't until the next morning at 10:00 a.m., after Jürgen had heard the bad news on the radio, that he woke up his brother: "All access routes are closed and everything is shut down," he told Günter. The two brothers then reflected on the last time Ulbricht had shut down Berlin's border: on June 17, 1953, after Soviet tanks had put down the worker uprising. Life had returned to normal several days later, so they expected the same was likely this time. Even during the 1948 Berlin Airlift, the city's border had remained open. The Litfins at first dismissed the notion that the Americans would allow the border closure to stand, given all that was at stake. Though the brothers distrusted the British and French commitment to Berlin's freedom, they had little doubt that the Americans would come through.

The Litfins set off on their bicycles to size up the new landscape. They rolled to a stop at Günter's usual border crossing at the Bornholmer Bridge, where a two-lane highway passed over multiple train tracks. Police had blocked the pavement with barbed wire and tank traps. Günter sighed to his brother, "I can't believe this will stay."

But with each successive day the brothers grew more convinced the Americans would not rescue them. The communists had begun replacing the temporary barriers of sawhorses and barbed wire with a ten-foot-high wall built of prefabricated concrete sections and connecting mortar. Ulbricht was rapidly closing all escape hatches. So Günter decided to risk escape before it was too late.

He closely followed the reports on RIAS radio about the many escapes that had succeeded after August 13. Since then, some 150 East Germans had swum to their liberty across the Teltow Canal, many towing children. In a single action, a dozen teenagers had made it across the waterway in a group sprint. One daring young man had driven his Volkswagen right through one border section's barbed wire safely into the French sector. Another bold East Berliner had disarmed a border guard, taking his sub-machine gun right out of his hands so that he could not shoot, and then had run across the border with it.

Encouraged by these success stories and despite a heart condition, Litfin decided to act. At just after four in the afternoon on Thursday, August 24, in the spotlight of a 77-degree midday sun, Günter crossed a railway yard that lay between Friedrichstrasse in the east and the Lehrter train station in the West. Wearing a light brown jacket and black pants, he jumped into the warm waters of the Spree Canal at the Humboldt harbor. Günter wasn't a particularly strong swimmer, but he reckoned that he was strong enough to make it across the thirty meters or so of water to freedom.

Standing above him on a nearby bridge, a transit policeman, or Trapo, shouted five times at Günter to stop. But the tailor only swam with more determination. The officer fired two warning shots that struck the water just beyond Günter's head. When Litfin continued to swim, the Trapo sprayed machine-gun fire all around him. The first bullets struck the tailor when he was still ten meters short of the shore.

Wounded, Günter flailed and dived deep to avoid subsequent shots from what by then were three police. When he came up for air and raised his hands in surrender, the Trapos screamed derisively at him. A shot pierced his neck, and Günter sank like a stone.

Günter Litfin would be the first person shot dead while trying to escape East Berlin, a victim of bad timing. What he couldn't have known was that police that morning had received their first shoot-to-kill orders to stop all those attempting the crime of "flight from the Republic." Had Litfin fled a day earlier, he would have succeeded. Instead, two East German fireboats carrying police units searched the Spree Canal for more than two hours before three army frogmen pulled Günter's body from the water at about seven p.m.

The day after Günter was killed, eight secret police tore apart his mother's apartment while she wept uncontrollably. They ripped off her oven door and disassembled the oven. They slashed open mattresses and dumped out dresser drawers. An officer explained to Günter's wailing mother, "Your son has been shot dead. He was a criminal."

To further punish the family, authorities prohibited Günter's mother and brother from viewing the body before its burial, not even for identification. The family lowered Günter into his grave in a closed casket at Weissensee Cemetery on a bright summer day, Wednesday, August 30. Jürgen was satisfied with the polished black granite headstone he had chosen, and he ran his fingers across its gold script: OUR UNFORGOTTEN GÜNTER.

Hundreds of Berliners gathered at the graveside: school friends, family members, and dozens of others who didn't know Günter at all but had come to make a statement by their presence.

Even with so many watching, Jürgen could not let his brother disappear without confirming it was really him. So he jumped down into the grave site and broke open the coffin with a crowbar that he had concealed until that moment. Though Günter's skin had blackened and a bandage covered a broad area beneath his mouth and over his neck, concealing the large exit wound from the shot that had killed him, Jürgen had no doubt about the identity.

He looked up and nodded to his mother that it was her son.

Berlin was in shock in the days following August 13. The city passed through stages of grief: denial, disbelief, rage, frustration, depression, and ultimately resignation. How Berliners responded depended on where they sat, in the East or the West.

For West Berliners, initial anger at the communists was now accompanied by a growing fury over American betrayal. The talk around town was all about how the Americans had not sent a single platoon on August 13 to demonstrate solidarity, nor had they imposed a single sanction on the East Germans or Soviets to punish them for their action.

By comparison, the East Berliner response was one of self-loathing for having missed the opportunity to escape mixed with disgust for the cynical communist leaders who had imprisoned them. Mielke's omnipresent Stasi agents had succeeded in their mission. Those who might have considered rebellion were deterred by the constant watch kept by Stasi agents at every factory, school, and apartment building.

AT THE BORDER, BERNAUER STRASSE, EAST BERLIN
TUESDAY AFTERNOON, AUGUST 15, 1961

A little more than two days after the border closure, East German workmen operating giant cranes began to lower prefabricated concrete segments onto Bernauer Strasse. Each block was precisely 1.25 meters square and 20 centimeters thick. Hundreds more sat nearby on a flatbed truck. Satisfied that the U.S. and its allies were unlikely to do anything to upset his project, Ulbricht was taking the next step. He had issued orders for construction crews to begin replacing the temporary border barriers in several sensitive locations with something more lasting.

CBS correspondent Daniel Schorr rushed to Bernauer Strasse to tell the story. "We noticed slabs of concrete being moved into place as though to build a *wall*," he said tentatively, among the first to employ the term "wall" to describe what eventually would divide Berliners. With his distinctive baritone laced with disbelieving emotion, he compared it to what Germans had built in Warsaw to contain Jews.

Schorr tried to explain to his American listeners why the U.S. military was watching passively while the communists made the figurative Iron Curtain a physical reality of concrete and mortar. "We might have been willing to go to war to defend our right to stay in Berlin," he said, "but can we go to war to defend the right of East Germans to get out of their own country?"

Construction crews had also begun operating at Potsdamer Platz, laboring under huge floodlights that allowed round-the-clock work. However, it was Bernauer Strasse that would become both the focus and the symbol of Ulbricht's intention to make Berlin's divide both permanent and impermeable.

A fluke of prewar planning had put Bernauer Strasse directly on the dividing line between the East Berlin district of Mitte, in the Soviet zone, and the West Berlin borough of Wedding, in the French sector. Until 1938, the demarcation line had been down the middle of the cobblestoned, kilometer-long Bernauer Strasse, but in that year Wedding's street cleaners protested. To simplify their job, Berlin's Third Reich authorities expanded Wedding's territory to the edge of the four-story apartment buildings on the street's eastern side so that their cleaners could rule over the entire thoroughfare.

As a result, Berlin's Cold War division left Bernauer Strasse's pavement and the apartment buildings on its northern side in West Berlin, and all the homes on the southern side in East Berlin. So in the first two days after August 13, these East Berlin residents could escape to the West—depending on their apartments' locations in their buildings—either by walking out the front door or climbing down a rope or sheet through an open window.

Like many of the soldiers dispatched to East Berlin for Operation Rose, nineteen-year-old Hans Conrad Schumann was born in rural Saxony, where his father had raised sheep in the village of Leutewitz. These were roots that authorities knew from experience would make young Schumann less politically susceptible. Yet as Schumann patrolled the East German side of the border along Bernauer Strasse on August 15, he failed to see the threat to his socialist homeland that he had been instructed to resist. Instead, all he saw were justifiably angry, unarmed protesters shaking their fists and shouting that he was a pig, a traitor, or—more hurtful, given the German past—a concentration camp guard.

It had been a confusing experience, as Schumann had felt greater sympathy for the crowd than for the soldiers who then dispersed them with smoke bombs and water cannons. It was then that Schumann began to consider his own escape. At the fast pace the construction crews were working, Schumann thought to himself, within days a concrete wall would replace all the barbed-wire fencing that still marked most of the border on Bernauer Strasse. Within weeks, all of East Berlin would be enclosed, and his chance would be gone.

As he visualized his flight, Schumann pressed down on the top of the coiled wire where he was standing watch and tested how much it would give against what amount of pressure.

"What are you doing there?" asked a colleague.

Though Schumann's heart beat wildly, he responded calmly.

"The wire is rusting already," he responded. It had the benefit of truth.

A young photographer began to watch Schumann from a few paces away in West Berlin. Peter Leibing, working on behalf of the photo agency Conti-Press in Hamburg, had rushed the 160 miles to Berlin to capture history as it unfolded. The images were powerful: East German soldiers cradling submachine guns, crying women, angry and sad faces, all framed through strands of barbed wire. When Leibing arrived at the epicenter of this drama, Bernauer Strasse, he joined a large crowd of West Berliners who had already gathered to watch the wall's construction. Standing on a corner of Ruppinerstrasse in the West, Leibing looked through his lens at Conrad

Schumann as he stood against a building in the East, smoking a cigarette. Some in the crowd told Leibing they had watched Schumann return to the barbed-wire coil on several occasions, always pushing the wire down a little farther to test its resistance to pressure.

The larger his audience, Schumann thought to himself, the greater the chance of a safe escape, since his colleagues would be less likely to shoot him as he fled. Schumann shouted at a young West Berliner who was approaching the border that he should get back. But then he confided to the same individual under his breath, *"Ich werde springen"* (I'm going to jump).

The young man raced off, and before long a police van pulled up as closely as possible without attracting the suspicion of the other East German soldiers. Leibing trained his lens on the spot in the barbed wire that Schumann had been testing. It struck him as ironic that he was using an East German camera, an Exakta. The longer he waited, the more it seemed to Leibing that Schumann had lost his courage or never intended to jump.

At about 4:00 p.m., Schumann saw his two colleagues disappear around a corner and out of sight. He tossed away his cigarette, raced forward, and jumped onto the top of the coil with his right boot, pressing down just hard enough to propel himself forward but not to sink into the concertina wire. As he soared, he released his Kalashnikov submachine gun with his right hand while extending his left arm for balance. It looked to the cheering crowd as if he were extending his wings for flight. His flat steel helmet remained steady on his head as he pulled his neck into his shoulder. Like a champion hurdler, he landed on his left boot and then ran without shortening his stride up to and then through the Opel Blitz police van's open door.

Drawing upon his previous experience photographing horse jumps in Hamburg, Leibing snapped a photo that perfectly captured the soldier in flight over the obstacle beneath him. His manual shutter would give him only one shot, but that was enough to produce an iconic photo.

"Welcome to the West, young man," said a West Berlin police officer to a shaking, silent Schumann, and he collapsed in the van.* The door slammed shut and the vehicle sped away. It was but a brief triumph.

Within a week, Ulbricht had grown so confident that Kennedy would not intervene that on August 22, he began to expand his wall construction to multiple sites. Though history would record August 13 as the Berlin Wall's birthdate, the truth was that it rose only gradually in the days that followed, once the communists could be certain they would face no resistance.

RATHAUS SCHÖNEBERG, CITY HALL OF WEST BERLIN
4:00 P.M., WEDNESDAY, AUGUST 16, 1961

Willy Brandt had never been so worried before a speech.

As he stood before the Rathaus Schöneberg, he looked down on 250,000 angry Berliners and knew it would be difficult to strike the right tone. He had to channel the crowd's rage, but not so ferociously that it incited them to storm across the border, only to be shot down.

He also knew this crucial moment was a campaign opportunity. Elections were only one month off, and Brandt wanted to show Germans that he could more effectively defend their interests than the aging Chancellor Adenauer, who with his American friends had done nothing to stop the border closure nor reverse it. Adenauer had turned down Brandt's invitation to join him at the rally, and he had not set foot in Berlin since August 13.

Thus far, Adenauer had resisted pressure from his party and the public to visit the city because, he said, his appearance might incite political unrest and encourage false expectations. What he didn't say was that it would also

---

*Schumann later settled in Bavaria in West Germany, where he met his wife. After the fall of the Berlin Wall, he said, "Only since 9 November 1989 [the date of the fall] have I felt truly free." Still, he continued to suffer tensions with former colleagues and family in Saxony. On June 20, 1998, suffering from depression, he committed suicide, hanging himself in an orchard.

underscore his impotence. Adenauer was also eager to avoid giving the Soviets any excuse to expand on their success and threaten West Berlin or West
German freedoms—a line Moscow had been careful not to cross.

So while Brandt prepared for his speech, Adenauer met in Bonn with
the Soviet ambassador to West Germany, Andrei Smirnov. He agreed to sign
a communiqué the Soviet had brought to the meeting: "The Federal Republic would not undertake any step that could damage its relationship with
the Soviet Union or endanger the international situation."

It reeked of appeasement.

Within forty-eight hours of the border closure, Adenauer had announced that he would not cut trade ties with East Germany, reversing his
initial threats. Even his hawkish defense minister Franz Josef Strauss had
appealed for calm. "If shooting starts," he told a West German crowd, "no
one knows with what kind of weapons it will end."

British Prime Minister Macmillan, the ally so reluctant to provoke the
Russian bear, had praised Adenauer for having responded with a "heated
heart and cool head." It seemed as though, after all his concern about Kennedy's leadership, Adenauer was now adopting the U.S. president's position
on the wall.

However, Adenauer's response was one more of resignation than conviction. He had seen his worst fears realized regarding Kennedy's indecisive
leadership. Heinrich Krone, the chairman of Adenauer's party faction in the
Bundestag, wrote in his diary, "This was the hour of our greatest disillusion-
ment." The building of the wall ended whatever residual confidence Adenauer had that membership in "the strongest alliance in the world" could
guarantee absolute security.

He was also taking the long view. His West Germany remained intact
and anchored in NATO. There was no advantage in denying the reality that
East Berlin had landed ever more securely in communist hands. Therefore,
his most important purpose was to win the September 17 elections and
keep his country out of socialist control.

Smirnov wooed and threatened Adenauer along the usual Soviet lines.
He spoke of how constructively Moscow had worked with Adenauer while

reminding him of his country's certain destruction should he forget Germany's role in the last two world wars and pursue what he called warlike activities and escalation now.

During his meeting with Smirnov, Adenauer chose not to condemn the Soviets or Khrushchev. Instead, he extended thanks to the Soviet leader for his greetings, warmly recalled his last meeting with Khrushchev, and spoke of his focus on winning the September 17 elections.

Only at that point did he mention Berlin. "We're dealing in my view here with an aggravating and unpleasant matter, which has been played up way beyond the necessary," he told Smirnov. "I would be grateful if the Soviet government could calm the situation." Adenauer said he worried and "quite openly feared" that developments in Berlin and the Soviet zone "under some conditions could lead to bloodshed." He said plaintively, "I would be grateful if the Soviet government could prevent such an occurrence."

If his approach to the Soviets was one of restraint, it was quite the opposite when it came to his political opponent, Willy Brandt. Adenauer knew the border closure would hurt him with voters. He also knew an increasing number of them were questioning whether the old man was still fit enough to lead, and that Brandt had moved his Social Democrats to the more acceptable political center. He hoped voters would weigh all that against West Germany's thriving economy and the stability he had achieved for his country within the Western alliance.

Less than forty-eight hours after the communists had closed the border, Adenauer had campaigned in the Bavarian city of Regensburg rather than rushing to Berlin. He told the crowd he did not wish to inflame the situation by grandstanding in Berlin. Instead of attacking the communists, he took a nasty swipe at Brandt's character, for the first time referring publicly to his illegitimate birth. "If ever anyone has been treated with the greatest consideration by his political opponents," said Adenauer, "it is Herr Brandt, alias Frahm," a reference to his unwed mother's maiden name, which Brandt had discarded while in wartime exile.

At an August 29 campaign speech that followed in Hagen, Westphalia, Adenauer told a partisan crowd that Khrushchev had shut down the Berlin border so as to help the socialist Brandt in the upcoming elections. The German press attacked Adenauer for turning so viciously on Brandt, but among voters Adenauer was effectively sowing doubts about his opponent.

Brandt, who until then had responded with restraint, lashed back. "The old gentleman really cannot grasp what's going on anymore." He advised Adenauer to seek *"ein friedliches Lebensabend"*—a peaceful retirement. Brandt calculated that his best strategy was to announce that he was abandoning electioneering altogether. "For me all that matters is the struggle for Berlin," he said, announcing that he would reduce his election work to one day each week and otherwise focus on "Germany's destiny."

Brandt realized that perhaps the most important factor with voters was how he handled the Americans. On the day of his rally, West Germany's most-read newspaper, *Bild-Zeitung*, with its circulation of 3.7 million, covered the entire top half of its front page with a headline that captured the public mood: THE EAST ACTS—AND THE WEST? THE WEST DOES NOTHING.

The editors had placed large photographs of the three Allied leaders under the story with derisive cutlines: "President Kennedy remains silent / Macmillan goes hunting / And Adenauer insults Brandt."

In an accompanying front-page editorial, *Bild* said:

> We entered the Western alliance because we believed this would be the best solution for Germany as well as for the West. The majority of Germans, the overwhelming majority, is still convinced of this. But this conviction is not strengthened if some of our partners, at a moment when the German cause is in great danger, coolly declare: "Allied rights have not been touched."
>
> The German cause is in the greatest danger. Three days already and so far nothing has happened apart from a paper protest by the Allied commandants.
>
> We are disillusioned!

The more sober Berlin broadsheet *Der Tagesspiegel* captured the spirit of the day in a giant four-panel cartoon that was so popular it was being passed from person to person around Berlin.

The primary character in each panel, labeled THE WEST, is portrayed as an aging, bald American man in a dark suit and a bow tie and with a raised, lecturing finger.

In the first frame, the West winces from Stalin's blows to his head with a club labeled GERMANY'S VISION. He says only, "[Hit me] Once more and I'll take out my big stick." The second panel shows the West with two bumps, the new one marked HUNGARY. The third frame has a diminutive Ulbricht bashing the West with a club stamped CLOSING OF THE INTERCITY BORDER. The final panel shows a bruised and beaten West, standing by himself pathetically above the caption UND SO WEITER—"And so on."

After wiping the sweat from his brow, Brandt told the 250,000 Berliners standing before him that through the border closure the Soviets had "given their pet dog Ulbricht a little extra leash" with his "regime of injustice." Brandt captured the frustration of the crowd, saying, "We cannot help our fellow citizens in the sector and our countrymen in the Zone bear this burden, and that is for us the bitterest pill to swallow! We can only help them bear it in showing them that we will rise to stand with them in this desperate hour!"

The crowd exploded with relief that Brandt had finally expressed their dismay.

Brandt drew parallels between the Ulbricht dictatorship and the Third Reich. He called the border closure "a new version of the occupation of the Rhineland by Hitler. Only today the man is named Ulbricht." He had to shout above the crowd's deafening cheers in a raspy voice made hoarse from the campaign trail and his chain-smoking.

Brandt paused before the most sensitive part of the speech, during which he directly addressed the U.S. and Kennedy. He began by defending the Americans, to the displeasure of many of his listeners. "Without them," he said, "the tanks would have rolled on."

The crowd only began to applaud when he voiced their own disappointment with Kennedy.

"[But] Berlin expects more than words," he said. "It expects political action." The crowd erupted in cheers when he told them that he had written to President Kennedy with that opinion. "I told him our views in all frank-ness," he said to roars of approval. Brandt saw in their eyes the political appeal of an attack on the Americans even as they knew how powerless they were to take on the Soviets alone.

OVAL OFFICE, THE WHITE HOUSE, WASHINGTON, D.C.
WEDNESDAY MORNING, AUGUST 16, 1961

President Kennedy was enraged.

He considered the letter from Mayor Brandt, which rested atop his morning correspondence, to be insulting and impertinent. Even given Ber-lin's situation, it overstepped the sort of language any city mayor should use with the American president. With each line that he read, Kennedy grew more certain that the letter's primary purpose was to serve Brandt's electoral campaign.

Brandt called the border closure an encroachment that was "the most serious in the postwar history of this city since the blockade." In a surpris-ingly direct rebuke of the Kennedy administration, he wrote, "While in the past Allied Commandants have even protested against parades by the so-called National People's Army in East Berlin, this time, after military oc-cupation of the East Sector by the People's Army, they have limited themselves to delayed and not very vigorous steps." He charged that the Allies had thus endorsed the "illegal sovereignty of the East Berlin government."

Brandt protested, "We now have a state of accomplished extortion."

He told Kennedy that although this had not weakened West Berliners' will to resist, "it has tended to arouse doubts as to the determination of the three powers and their ability to react." He conceded Kennedy's argument that existing four-power guarantees applied only to West Berlin and its people, the presence of troops there, and their access routes. "However," he stressed, "this is a matter of a deep wound in the life of the German people."

Brandt warned Kennedy that Berlin could become "like a ghetto" and lose "its function as a refuge of freedom and a symbol of hope for unification. Worse," he said, "instead of flight to Berlin, we might then experience the beginning of flight *from* Berlin" as its citizens lost confidence in the city's future.

Brandt's letter then set out a series of proposals, again ignoring the fact that he was only a city mayor or that this was a level of bilateral exchange that belonged more properly to the chancellor. He called upon Kennedy to introduce a new, three-power status for West Berlin that would exclude the Soviets but include the French and British. He wanted Kennedy to bring the Berlin question before the United Nations, as the Soviet Union "has violated the Declaration of Human Rights in most flagrant manner." Finally, he said, "It would be welcomed if the American garrison were to be demonstratively strengthened."

Brandt closed with the line "I consider the situation serious enough, Mr. President, to write to you in all frankness as is possible only between friends who trust each other completely." Then he signed it "Your Willy Brandt."

Kennedy fumed. The letter was political dynamite. Already stung by charges that he had demonstrated weakness in Cuba, Laos, and Vienna, Kennedy considered it salt on an open wound. The final line, in which Brandt referred to his relationship of trust with the president, irked Kennedy most.

"*Trust?*" Kennedy spat as he angrily waved the letter at his press secretary, Pierre Salinger. "I don't trust this man at all. He's in the middle of a campaign against old Adenauer and wants to drag me in. Where does he get off calling me a friend?"

The State Department and the White House were furious that Brandt had revealed the existence of the letter at a rally before Kennedy had even received it—driving home its electoral purpose. Administration officials briefed the press in that fashion, setting off a storm of negative U.S. media comment. The *Daily News* called Brandt's letter "rude and presumptuous." The *Washington Evening Star*'s commentator William S. White condemned Brandt as a "mere mayor" trying to "take over the foreign policy, not only of his own country, but of all the West by addressing personal notes to the

President of the United States. . . . It is easy for demagogues to whip up excited crowds, as Mr. Brandt is doing, to pour scorn on the West for inaction."

Brandt would later take credit for his letter shifting Kennedy to a more active defense of Berlin, yet perhaps more decisive was the journalist Marguerite Higgins, to whom Kennedy had shown the letter with disgust while sitting in his rocking chair in the Oval Office. The well-known U.S. war reporter, who had covered both World War II and the Korean conflict, was at age forty-one a personal friend of the president. "Mr. President, I must tell you quite openly," she said, "that in Berlin the suspicion is growing that you want to sell out the West Berliners."

Kennedy came to accept that he had to take some action quickly to reassure Berliners, Americans, and Soviets alike that he remained ready to stand up to the Kremlin. Two days after receiving the Brandt letter, Kennedy wrote back to the mayor that he planned to dispatch to Berlin both Vice President Johnson and General Lucius Clay, the hero of the Berlin Airlift in 1948 and a friend of Marguerite Higgins.

He *would* take Brandt's advice that he send more troops to Berlin, but his letter would make clear it wasn't a lowly mayor who had prompted the decision. "On careful consideration," he wrote to Brandt, "*I myself* have decided that the best immediate response is a significant reinforcement of the Western garrisons."

He said that what was important wasn't the number of troops, which would be small, but that the reinforcements would be seen as the U.S. response to Moscow's demand that Allied soldiers leave Berlin altogether. "We believe that even a modest reinforcement will underline our rejection of this concept," he said.

However, Kennedy rejected Brandt's other suggestions. He said the mayor's notion of three-power status for West Berlin would weaken the four-power basis for an Allied protest of the border closing. He would also not pursue Brandt's idea of an appeal to the United Nations, as it was "unlikely to be fruitful." "Grave as the matter is," he wrote, "there are, as you say, no steps available to us which can force a significant material change in this present situation. Since it represents a resounding confession of failure and of political weakness, this brutal border closing evidently represents a basic Soviet decision which only war could reverse. Neither you nor we, nor any of our Allies, have ever supposed that we should go to war on this point."

Kennedy's logic was that the Soviet action was "too serious for inadequate responses." By that measure, any action short of war seemed inadequate to him, and thus he objected to all the remedies he had heard thus far, including "most of the suggestions in your own letter."

Tossing the mayor a bone that would cost Kennedy nothing, he supported Brandt's notion of "an appropriate plebiscite demonstrating the continuing conviction of West Berlin that its destiny is freedom in connection with the West."

Kennedy didn't like rewarding Brandt for pulling him into his messy, petty German politics. On the other hand, he had his own domestic political reasons for a demonstration of strength. If anyone understood how deeply intertwined America's domestic and foreign policies were, it was Kennedy.

Brandt read Kennedy's response with disappointment, believing the U.S. president had "thrown us in the frying pan." American reporters were writing with the confidence of the well-briefed that the border closure had shocked and depressed Kennedy. But the truth was quite different.

Among those who were closest to him, Kennedy did not hide his relief. He considered the border closure a potentially positive turning point that could help lead to the end of the Berlin Crisis that had been hanging over him like a Damoclean nuclear sword. He thought the fact that West Berlin had remained untouched illustrated the limits of Khrushchev's ambitions— and the relative caution with which he would execute them.

"Why would Khrushchev put up a wall if he really intended to seize West Berlin?" Kennedy said to his friend and aide Kenny O'Donnell. "There wouldn't be any need of a wall if he planned to occupy the whole city. This is his way out of his predicament. It's not a very nice solution, but a wall is a hell of a lot better than a war."

The communist move also allowed Kennedy to score public opinion points for the U.S. across the world. The communist enemy had been forced to build a barrier around its people to lock them in. Nothing could have been more damning. One couldn't buy a better argument in favor of the free world, even if the cost was the freedom of East Berliners, and, more broadly, Eastern Europeans.

Kennedy thought of himself as a pragmatic man, and the Eastern Europeans were beyond any reasonable hope of liberation anyway.

Kennedy had little sympathy for the East Germans, and told journalist James "Scotty" Reston that the U.S. had given them ample time to break out of their jail, as the Berlin border had been open from the establishment of the Soviet zone after World War II to August 13, 1961.

In the first days after the Wall went up, a similar Kennedy remark reached an alarmed West German ambassador, Wilhelm Grewe, and Chancellor Konrad Adenauer: "After all, the East Germans have had more than fifteen years to reflect on whether they wanted to stay in East Germany or go to the West." Grewe watched and worried as this callous statement further poisoned the already toxic atmosphere with Adenauer.

"Also," Grewe would later recall of Kennedy, "I got the feeling that sometimes he was not absolutely sure himself whether it was appropriate to preserve a completely passive attitude at that time, or whether he should have tried a more active policy to prevent the erection of the wall." Kennedy expressed his self-doubt with the sort of question he posed to Grewe: "Well, do you feel we should have handled this business otherwise?" The matter would occupy the president more with each day's distance from August 13 and the greater realization that the border closure was not making relations with Khrushchev any easier.

THE KREMLIN, MOSCOW
MID-AUGUST, 1961

Khrushchev congratulated himself on having outmaneuvered the U.S., the British, and the French without military conflict, political backlash, or even the most modest of economic sanctions.

His son Sergei saw him initially sigh with relief after August 13, and then grow more delighted over time as he reflected upon his achievement. Had Khrushchev not acted at all, the Soviet bloc might have begun to unravel with the implosion of its westernmost outpost. With refugees bleeding out of Berlin, his enemies would have sought his head on a platter at the Party Congress, egged on by Mao.

Khrushchev also reflected later on how "war could have broken out" if he had miscalculated. He had read Kennedy's signals perfectly, which had provided a road map for his action. The only interest Kennedy had professed was in preserving West Berlin's status and access to the city, which Khrushchev had been careful not to touch. He had been confident that Kennedy would do nothing to help liberate East Germans or contest whatever the Soviets chose to do within their own zone.

Khrushchev believed he had achieved even more than he could have expected from a peace treaty. In a treaty, Kennedy would have forced him to accept language recognizing the need for German unification over time through free elections. Now he had every reason to hope that the Western commitment to the city would continue to erode, along with the morale of West Berliners, who might decide to abandon their city in droves, doubting that the Allies would continue to defend their freedoms and connection to West Germany.

Khrushchev concluded beyond any doubt that the Vienna talks had "represented a defeat" for Kennedy. The Kremlin had decided to act and "there was nothing he could do—short of military action—to stop us. Kennedy was intelligent enough to know that a military clash would be senseless. Therefore the United States and its Western Allies had no choice but to swallow a bitter pill as we began to take certain unilateral steps."

In a nod to his country's national sport, Khrushchev spoke of himself as a skilled chess player. When the U.S. ratcheted up military pressure in Berlin, he moved in Marshal Konev. "To use the language of chess," he said, "the Americans had advanced a pawn, so we protected our position by moving a knight." Khrushchev enjoyed this turn of phrase, because he was also employing a play on words, as the Russian word for a knight in chess is *kon*, or horse, which was the root of Konev's surname. The pawn referred to Kennedy's later decision to bring Clay to Berlin.

What he was telling Kennedy, he said, was that "if you insist on holding up the shield of war against us and thwarting us in our intentions, then we're ready to meet you on your own terms."

In Vienna, Khrushchev recalled, the president had argued that under the Potsdam Agreement there was only one Germany, which a peace treaty would have to recognize. Yet now he had brought about a de facto Western recognition of two Germanys in as dramatic a manner as he could have imagined.

But Khrushchev was not done yet. Throughout August, encouraged by Kennedy's inaction, the Soviet leader reinforced East German troop positions and took other actions to hammer home his victory and solidify his position ahead of his Party Congress. He launched Soviet military maneuvers on August 16 that for the first time included nuclear-tipped battlefield missiles in tactical exercises that simulated a potential war over Berlin access. So that the Kennedy administration would not miss his point, for the first time since 1936 the Soviets invited Western military attachés to observe their ground exercises.

The tactical maneuver involved a mobilized battalion of the sort operating around the Berlin Autobahn. The Soviet guide for the attachés told them the rockets were equipped with nuclear warheads. The Soviets even simulated a nuclear cloud over a hypothetical enemy position in the village of Kubinka, west of Moscow.

More dramatic yet, at the end of August, Khrushchev announced that he would break his three-year self-imposed moratorium on nuclear testing. Then, two days later, the Soviet Union began new atmospheric blasts that were heard around the world from Semipalatinsk in Central Asia.

"Fucked again," President Kennedy groaned when he received the news after an afternoon nap.

On August 30, the president met with his military advisers to discuss a potential response. In a gloomy mood, his brother Bobby worried that the Russians "feel strongly that if they can break our will in Berlin that we will never be good for anything else and they will have won the battle in 1961.... Their plan is obviously not to be most popular but to be the most fearsome and terrorize the world into submission."

Bobby recalled what Chip Bohlen had said at the outset of 1961: "This was the year that the Russians were going to come the closest to nuclear war. I don't think there is any question but that that is true." After the meeting, when President Kennedy asked for his brother's further thoughts, Bobby said, "I want to get off."

The president didn't understand him at first.

"Get off what?"

"Get off the planet," Bobby said.

Bobby joked he was going to discard adviser Paul Corbin's suggestion that he run against his brother in the 1964 elections. He didn't want the job.

WEST BERLIN
WEEKEND OF AUGUST 18–20, 1961

It was not the first time Vice President Johnson had been displeased about an assignment from the president. The mission Kennedy wanted him to accept was to lead a morale-building trip to West Berlin with General Lucius Clay. Coming just five days after the border closure, Johnson immediately saw that what the mission lacked in substance it made up for in danger.

Just a few months earlier, Kennedy had made Johnson Chancellor Adenauer's hand-holder at the LBJ ranch during the botched Bay of Pigs invasion. So when Kennedy phoned during his dinner on August 17 to make the Berlin request, Johnson had responded, "Is that necessary?"

"Yes, it's necessary," Kennedy had insisted. It would send the wrong message for the president himself to rush so quickly to Berlin. He had to send a message to the world that the U.S. would not abandon West Berlin, but at the same time he didn't want to provoke a Soviet response. Kennedy could not publicly express his genuine relief that the communists had closed the border, but at the same time he didn't want to express false outrage too loudly.

Johnson grew all the more reluctant to make the trip when he learned that part of his mission would be to receive a battle group of 1,500 soldiers in West Berlin, troops who would storm up the Autobahn from Helmstedt, West Germany, to reinforce the 12,000 Allied troops who were already there. Though their paltry numbers might do little to defend Berliners, LBJ knew their arrival would be fraught with risk.

"Why me?" he asked Kennedy's aide Kenny O'Donnell. "There'll be a lot of shooting and I'll be in the middle of it."

After some coaxing, the vice president took on the mission with a more willing Clay.

During their overnight flight on August 18 on an Air Force Boeing 707, Clay regaled Johnson with stories of his own Berlin heroics back in 1948. He told Johnson he had converted President Truman to that operation, which Clay had begun single-handedly. What he had learned, Clay told Johnson, was that the only way to deal with the Soviets was to stand up to them.

He would tear down the Wall if he were president, he told Johnson. He believed the Korean War might have been avoided if the U.S. had shown the Soviets it was willing to be more aggressive even earlier in Berlin, when Truman had at first refused to allow Clay to bring an armored column down the Autobahn to demonstrate American commitment.

Nothing could have demonstrated just how eager West Berliners were for U.S. reassurance than Johnson and Clay's joyous reception at Tempelhof Airport, once the stage for the Berlin Airlift. Here they were, a largely powerless vice president and a retired general who commanded no troops, but a police band played "The Star-Spangled Banner," seven U.S. tanks fired a salute, and 100,000 Berliners shouted their approval.

To keep Johnson on message, the White House had scripted every word he would speak publicly with the usual Kennedy poetry. "Divided, you have never been dismayed," Johnson told Berliners. "Threatened, you have never faltered. Challenged, you have never weakened. Today, in a new crisis, your courage brings hope to all who cherish freedom and is a massive and majestic barrier to the ambitions of tyrants."

Speaking to the West Berlin city Senate later in the day, Johnson said, "To the survival and creative future of this city we Americans have pledged, in effect, what our ancestors pledged in forming the United States: 'Our lives, our fortunes, and our sacred honor.' These are the final words of our Declaration of Independence."

His words electrified a city that had been drained of its energy since August 13. The crowd of 300,000 gathered on the square before City Hall were the same Berliners who had stood depressed and angry just three days earlier before Brandt. Now many of them wept for joy. Even Clay could not hold back tears.

As Johnson made his way from appointment to appointment, he turned from reluctant traveler to eager campaigner, often climbing out of his car to bathe in the glow of an adoring crowd. The intermittent rain could not dissuade him or tens of thousands of West Berliners, whose mood reminded *New York Times* correspondent Sydney Gruson of what he had witnessed during the triumphant liberation of Paris at the end of World War II.

"The city was like a boxer who had thrown off a heavy punch and was gathering stamina for another round. . . ." he wrote. "The Vice President said nothing essentially new. That did not seem to matter. The West Berliners wanted the words said at this time in their city and, above all, they wanted his presence as a tangible expression of the link that sustains them."

Johnson elicited a huge roar from the crowd when he said the men of the 18th Infantry, 1st Battle Group, were already rolling up the Autobahn to reinforce West Berlin's garrison.

For Kennedy, the troop deployment was the first moment during the Berlin Crisis when he feared a violent exchange. Though the U.S. contingent was small, he had told White House special counsel Ted Sorensen that he saw the troops as "our hostage to that intent" of U.S. commitment to defend West Berlin.

Kennedy had postponed his usual weekend retreat to Hyannis Port in order to receive reports every twenty minutes during the night as the troops rolled toward Berlin. The Pentagon demanded to have every detail of the planned mission in advance, including each and every rest stop the soldiers would use to relieve themselves on the Autobahn as they drove through East German territory to West Berlin.

Kennedy's military advisers, Joint Chiefs chairman Lyman Lemnitzer and White House military aide Maxwell Taylor, had opposed sending the reinforcements. British Prime Minister Macmillan considered the gesture politically provocative and military "nonsense." General Bruce C. Clarke, the sixty-year-old commander of U.S. forces in Europe, who had helped swing World War II's Battle of the Bulge in America's favor, also didn't like the looks of it.

The operation's commander, Colonel Glover S. Johns Jr., was a proud Texan himself, a former commandant of the Virginia Military Institute and decorated World War II combat commander. Tall, blond, German-speaking, and with a flair for the theatrical, Johns knew his mission had no military value and posed considerable risk. Kennedy had handpicked him because he had heard this was a man who would not lose his cool commanding a small battle group of 1,500 through hostile terrain surrounded by at least a quarter of a million Soviet soldiers.

For all the details his superiors had demanded, none of them had said how Johns should respond if he was fired upon. Without any specific instructions about what weaponry to carry, he had decided himself what to put in the ammunition boxes of each vehicle. As was his habit, Johns also carried his own antique Colt pistol. If hostilities did start, Johns knew, "we were in for certain destruction." If the Soviets didn't want them heading up the Autobahn, they would be like lambs heading for slaughter.

While Johns was working out his defense plan, Johnson was working on his footwear. Johnson looked down at Brandt's fashionable loafers and issued a challenge to the mayor while the two men toured Berlin in an open Mercedes convertible, standing and waving at crowds. "You've been asking us for action instead of words," he said. "I'd like to see whether you can act, too."

He pointed to the shoes. "Where do you get a pair like that?" he asked.

"I can get a pair like that for you right here in Berlin," said Brandt, reckoning Berlin's defense was worth a pair of shoes for America's vice president.

Shortly after noon on Saturday, August 19, the U.S. embassy in Bonn reached General Bruce Clarke in Heidelberg and informed him that Vice President Johnson would be leaving for home from Berlin at 2:00 p.m. on Sunday, whether or not U.S. troop reinforcements had arrived in the city. Clarke protested angrily through his Berlin commander to Washington that Johns and his men could not risk so much if Johnson would not even stay in place to greet them.

National Security Advisor McGeorge Bundy phoned Clarke on Saturday night at 7:00 p.m. "General, I understand you're chewing out everybody in sight because you're not happy with the vice president leaving before the troops get in."

"That puts it mildly, Mr. Bundy," replied Clarke. "The men will go all-out to get there to be received by the vice president." He couldn't imagine anything Johnson had to do in Washington that was more important "than to be receiving the troops with all the world watching." Clarke knew nothing of Johnson's concerns about the possible dangers.

"What time are you going to have all the men in Berlin?" asked Bundy.

Clarke shot back, "If I could guarantee that, we wouldn't be having a crisis, would we? Who can say where we may get stopped?"

Bundy replied, "General, I'll see what we can do."

At 12:30 p.m. on Sunday, August 20—6:30 a.m. in the White House—and just a week after the border was closed, the first sixty trucks carrying the American soldiers crossed into Berlin without incident. Khrushchev had stood by his commitment not to impede Allied access, aside from a three-hour delay at a checkpoint while Soviet troops head-counted the number of troops who were entering Berlin.

West Berliners greeted Johns's men like conquering gladiators; thousands waited along bridges and roads. A few hundred Berliners stood with Vice President Johnson, who had opted to delay his departure, at the U.S.

checkpoint at Dreilinden, where the Autobahn entered West Berlin. Flowers rained upon them from all directions, surprising and delighting the weary soldiers in their soiled vehicles and battle dress.

Colonel Johns had never seen anything like it, "with the possible exception of the liberation of France." Johns's men had been on the road for four days without relief, having been pulled from field maneuvers in West Germany since they were the only fully equipped battle group that was capable of getting to Berlin with such speed. Even as they cruised through a city of cheers, many slept off their exhaustion.

The Soviet response was muted. The Kremlin dismissed the reinforcement as being of "no military significance," and said it merely put more men "in West Berlin's mousetrap." An article in *Pravda* signed "Observer"— which denoted a commentary reflecting Soviet government opinion—said it was "a provocation that cannot be ignored."

Among the troops stationed in Berlin who watched the show, Military Police Lieutenant Vern Pike was displeased, but for another reason. Like most U.S. soldiers in Berlin, he thought Kennedy and Johnson could have simply pushed the Wall down before it was built without the Soviets' doing much more than whimpering in retreat.

"Johnson was a joke, a total joke," he said. "All he wanted was to see the crowd."

As for the arriving battle group, Pike considered it "a rotten lousy outfit" that was little fit for battle but acted arrogantly toward the troops who had been in place for so long. When the new arrivals came to stay in Roosevelt Barracks, they rubbed the long-resident soldiers the wrong way, claiming they had been sent to rescue them after their failure to stop the border closure.

"We took offense to that," said Pike, "as they were only going to be here for ninety days, then they would be rotated out. We didn't need saving, and we knew they were only in Berlin for symbolic reasons." Worse, Johns's unit was "drunk and disorderly, caught fighting, resisting arrest."

However, Berliners knew only that America had finally shown its colors. Seldom had so many so loudly celebrated so little rescue. Pike thought it was a measure of Berliners' despair that they would so loudly cheer so modest a gesture.

Johnson stayed clear of East Berlin during his stay, wanting to avoid either provoking Moscow or inciting a crowd. But after General Clay quietly toured the amputated Soviet part of the city, Clay declared East Berlin to be "an armed camp" with a population that looked "totally oppressed."

For all the historic moment, Johnson didn't lose sight of his mission's other purpose: shopping.

At 5:30 on Sunday morning, his State Department escort Lucian Heichler woke Johnson's valet to get the vice president's shoe size so that Brandt could produce the shoes that he had wanted. Because Johnson had feet of two different sizes, which required him to wear handmade shoes, Brandt's people had a Leiser shoe-shop owner send twenty different pairs over to Johnson. From them, he picked two pairs that fit the bill.

On Sunday afternoon, a famous Berlin porcelain maker, the Königliche Porzellan-Manufaktur, opened its showroom at Johnson's request because he had admired the china at Willy Brandt's official City Hall dinner the night before. He had told the mayor he wanted a set for his new vice presidential residence, a mansion called "the Elms" that he had purchased in Washington, D.C.

They showed the vice president one set after another, but he protested that they were all too expensive for him. He wondered whether they had any "seconds." With his American escort, Heichler, looking for a hole to crawl into, Deputy Mayor Franz Amrehn saved the day by announcing, "The Senate and people of Berlin want to give you this as a present."

Replied Johnson, "Oh, well, in that case . . ."

The vice president then picked the fanciest china he could find, thirty-six place settings in all, and then arranged for his office to send the vice presidential insignia to be painted on every plate, saucer, cup, and bowl.

Shopping aside, Johnson had been infected by Berlin's spirit. In a report marked SECRET, he wrote to Kennedy:

I returned from Germany with new pride in America's leadership but with an unprecedented awareness of the responsibility which rests upon this country. The world expects so much from us, and we must measure up to the need, even while we seek more help from our allies. For if we fail or falter or default, all is lost, and freedom may never have a second chance.

With that, an order for thirty-six place settings of china, and two pairs of shoes, and having safely seen 1,500 more troops land in Berlin, Johnson returned home.

EAST BERLIN
TUESDAY, AUGUST 22, 1961

Ulbricht was too busy consolidating his victory to engage in self-congratulation.

His determination to change Berlin's status, which at the beginning of 1961 had neither Soviet approval nor means of execution, had been accomplished more successfully than he could have hoped. He had played a bad hand with enormous skill, and now he hoped to press his advantage.

On August 22, Ulbricht announced publicly that he would establish a no-man's-land that would stretch for a hundred meters on both sides of the Berlin Wall. East German authorities, without Soviet approval, declared they would shoot West Berliners if they strayed into the buffer zone that very soon would be known to them as "the death strip."

Swelling with confidence, the following day Ulbricht shrugged off objections from Soviet Ambassador Pervukhin and also reduced crossing points that Westerners could use from seven to only one, Checkpoint Charlie at Friedrichstrasse.

Two days later, Pervukhin and Konev summoned Ulbricht to reprimand him for these unilateral measures. The Soviets, Pervukhin said, could not accept the concept of a no-man's-land running into West Berlin territory, which "could lead to a clash between the GDR police and the forces of the Western powers."

So Ulbricht reversed those orders, protesting to his Soviet counterparts that he had "no intention of interfering" in West Berlin affairs. It was an easy compromise to make, as he had won more rights over Berlin than he had dared imagine at the beginning of the year. However, he refused to back off his decision to reduce the Western crossing points to just one.

As would happen so often in 1961, the Soviets ceded the point to Ulbricht.

TEMPELHOF AIRPORT, WEST BERLIN
WEDNESDAY, AUGUST 23, 1961

Chancellor Adenauer finally surfaced in Berlin, but only ten days after the communists had shut down the Berlin border, and after Vice President Johnson and General Clay had safely left town. Only a few hundred people cheered Adenauer when he landed at Tempelhof Airport, and perhaps only another 2,000 awaited him when he arrived for a visit to the Marienfelde refugee camp.

Many West Berliners demonstratively turned away from him as he drove through the city. Others held signs that criticized how he had handled the crisis. One typical placard read SIE KOMMEN ZU SPÄT—"You've come too late." Another said sarcastically, HURRAH, THE SAVIOR HAS COME. At Marienfelde and elsewhere, the signs suggested voters would punish him for his weak response to the border closure.

When he viewed the wall at spots along the border, the Ulbricht regime taunted him from the eastern side from a loudspeaker truck, comparing him to Adolf Hitler while pointing a high-pressure water hose in his direction. At another spot along the way, however, older East Germans wept and cheered as they waved white handkerchiefs by way of greeting.

Adenauer visited the king of West German media, Axel Springer, who had built his headquarters beside the Berlin border, and whose *Bild-*

Zeitung, West Germany's largest-circulation newspaper, had been most critical of Adenauer and American impotence during the border closing. "Herr Springer, I don't understand you," said the chancellor. "Nothing has changed here in Berlin" except that the media was stirring the pot more.

He warned Springer that his newspaper's antics might revive National Socialism.

Springer stormed from the room in anger.

BERNAUER STRASSE, EAST BERLIN
WEDNESDAY, OCTOBER 4, 1961

Berliners grew accustomed to their post-Wall reality with surprising speed. The refugee outflow came to an almost complete halt as escape attempts became riskier and border controls tightened. In increasing numbers, West Berliners were relocating to West Germany rather than taking a chance that the Soviets might not be done quite yet.

At Bernauer Strasse, tour buses visited and dozens of Berliners continually loitered on the Western side of the border, observing their street's post–August 13 phases: the initial border closure, the removal of Bernauer Strasse's East Berlin residents, the bricking up of windows and doors, and the construction of the Berlin Wall.

West Berlin police officer Hans-Joachim Lazai and his colleagues had strung a rope between trees near Bernauer Strasse beyond which they would not allow spectators to pass. But on some days the crowd grew so angry that it was difficult to restrain them. Guilt overcame Lazai on the occasions when the hard stream of the police water cannons was required to keep back West Berlin crowds. Far worse were the times when Lazai had to stand by and watch East German border police arrest and cart away those who tried to escape. Following his orders to remain in place and provoke no one, he felt "a sense of helplessness as I stood across from complete injustice."

Worst of all were the tragic deaths of those desperate days. The first one that Lazai witnessed was that of Ida Siekmann, who on August 21, just one day before her fifty-ninth birthday, became the first fatality at Bernauer Strasse. Lazai had been turning left onto the street on his way to work when he saw a dark ball descend from one of the buildings. Siekmann had thrown her mattress from the third-floor window ahead of herself in a vain hope that it would absorb her fall.

She had died instantly.

After that, West Berlin police used reinforced, sheetlike fireman nets in which they could catch jumpers. Nevertheless, would-be refugees had to jump with great accuracy, as the sixteen men who typically gripped the nets' edges could not move quickly enough in any direction to compensate for an errant leap.

It was nearly eight on the evening of October 4 when Lazai first shouted through the dark at Bernd Lünser, a twenty-two-year-old East Berlin engineering student, to jump into just such a net from the roof of a four-story apartment building at Bernauer Strasse 44.

For some time, Lünser and two friends had been trying to summon the nerve to rappel down to West Berlin from the rooftop, using a clothesline they had brought with them. By shouting their encouragement, a growing crowd of West Berliners below alerted nearby East German police to their flight attempt.

Gerhard Peters, a nineteen-year-old member of the East German border police contingent, led the pursuit after gaining access to the roof through a trapdoor. Lünser pulled off roof tiles and threw them at Peters, who, after a short time, was joined by three other officers. After a dramatic chase, Lünser's two friends were taken into custody by police after falling and sliding down the roof into a protective rail.

When one of the East German police shot at the would-be refugees, West German officers below pulled their pistols and exchanged twenty-eight shots with the East Germans. Under orders only to use their guns defensively, the West German police later argued that they had only acted once they had been fired upon.

Given a last chance to escape after a West Berlin policeman's bullet struck the pursuing East German officer in the leg, Lünser broke free and ran. Some in the crowd shouted for him to throw the policeman off the roof. Others, including Lazai, shouted for him to jump into the outstretched net. When the student finally leapt, he caught a foot on a rain gutter and fell headfirst to the ground some twelve feet from where the men held out their net.

He landed with a deathly splat.

Lazai would later condemn his own role in the incident: "Man, you drew him out into his own death."

On the following day, East German authorities sent roses to the border policeman Peters. East German Interior Minister Karl Maron decorated him for his sacrifice in fulfilling his duty. A headline in the West Berlin newspaper *BZ* sneered, DECORATION FOR MURDER.

Regine Hildebrandt, who lived nearby at Bernauer Strasse 44, had seen many failed and successful escape attempts by the time Lünser died that day.

As she wrote in her diary, she smoked a cigarette from a pack that had been pulled up by rope to her window in a basket given to her from West Berlin friends, a basket that also contained oranges, bananas, and other goods: "some small condolence for a ruined life."

"Two huge West German tourist buses just drove by," she wrote. "Yes, we've become Berlin's number-one tourist attraction. Oh how gladly we'd just be ignored! How gladly we'd turn back the wheels of time and leave things the way they were! Oh, not again! Another bus. This is a ghastly time in which we live. Our lives have lost their spirit. Nobody enjoys work or life anymore. A petulant feeling of resignation hangs over all of us. There is no point. They will do with us as they like, and we can do nothing to stop them.

"Bow your heads, friends, we are all become sheep. Two more buses. Countless faces looking our way, while we sit with balled fists in our pockets."

Berlin had some unlikely heroes in the days that followed, but their efforts failed as often as they succeeded.

Eberhard Bolle Lands in Prison

Eberhard Bolle was so focused on the potential danger he faced that he glanced only briefly at the news kiosk front pages at West Berlin's Zoo train station. They reported on the arrival of Vice President Johnson, General Clay, and the U.S. troop reinforcements. But Bolle had other concerns: the philosophy student was about to take the biggest risk of his life.

Before buttoning closed his light blue jacket, Bolle felt to confirm that the two identity cards were in its inside pocket. Though it was not a particularly warm day, he was sweating uncontrollably. His mother adored his disarming smile, but at the moment Bolle wore only a troubled frown.

The first of the two identity cards in his pocket was his own, and he would show it if asked when he crossed into East Berlin. Under the rules after the border closing six days earlier, West Berliners could still cross freely into the Soviet zone with ID. What Bolle planned to do with the second West Berlin identity card was to help the escape to the West of his friend and fellow Free University student Winfried Kastner,* with whom he shared a love of American jazz music. Like most other Berlin students that summer, they had also spent a great deal of their vacation time listening to Ricky Nelson's latest hit, "Hello Mary Lou," which had taken West Berlin by storm.

Though the Free University was in West Berlin, about a third of all its 15,000 students before August 13 had been East Berlin residents. Overnight, the border closure had ended their studies. For Kastner it was a particular disappointment, as he was in his last year of history studies and would not be accepted into an East German school because his family was considered politically unreliable. So Bolle was bringing him the ID of a West Berlin friend

---

*At the request of the former student, this book does not use his real last name.

who closely resembled Kastner, and their simple plan was that he would use it to show border police as he crossed into West Berlin.

Bolle was an apolitical, conservative student who lacked any natural taste for danger, and on the day after the border closure he had refused to help another classmate escape. What had changed his mind since then was Willy Brandt's speech before City Hall on August 16, which had so impressed him that he had written its call to action in his diary. "We now have to stand tall," Brandt had said, "so that the enemy does not celebrate while our countrymen sink into despair. We have to show ourselves worthy of the ideals that are symbolized in the Freedom Bell that hangs above our heads."

Two days later, Kastner's mother had been in tears as she appealed to Bolle to help her son during a visit he had made to their apartment in the East Berlin district of Köpenick. Rumors were flying that the border controls would grow gradually tougher, she said, and so anyone who wanted to leave East Berlin had to do so immediately. Though she and her husband did not want to be separated from their son, she said they had to think first about how to best satisfy his dream of becoming a history professor, which he would never fulfill in the East.

Bolle had suggested that his friend swim across one of the canals, but Kastner protested that he was too poor a swimmer for that. Kastner insisted the safest way of escape was by getting access to a West Berlin ID, so he provided Bolle a photo of himself and the name and contact details of a Catholic priest who was said to be producing such documents.

After the priest refused Bolle, the philosophy student turned to a friend who looked like Kastner. He was happy to part with his ID, which he would replace after reporting it lost. However, he refused to make the delivery to East Berlin himself, since it would be too risky to try to return west without it. Speaking with false confidence, Bolle declared he would transport the ID himself. "They don't hang people they can't catch," he boasted.

On the evening before his risky mission, Bolle had asked his mother if she would help someone escape if she were in his position. Only if it were a family member or a close friend, she had replied. His father admired his son's good *intentions, but he worried that his boy Eberhard had too panicky a nature to succeed.*

"Now eat something," said his father. "Who knows when your next meal will be?" Bolle forced down a few bites while his father tested him on how he would respond if East German police discovered the second ID. His responses were unconvincing, so they both hoped it would not come to that.

Bolle got out of the commuter train at Bahnhof Friedrichstrasse, where all travelers heading for East Berlin disembarked. Perspiring and trembling, he sighed with relief as border guards waved him through. He was on the last couple of stairs out of the station when a border guard appeared from his right and took him firmly by the arm.

Several years later, after interrogation, trial, conviction, and imprisonment, Bolle would still wonder why the guard had been able to pick him from the crowd for arrest. Sadly, he knew the answer.

Fear had given him away.

It would take the return of a retired U.S. general to help restore West Berliners' courage.

16

A HERO'S HOMECOMING

We have lost Czechoslovakia. Norway is threatened.... When Berlin falls, western Germany will be next. If we mean ... to hold Europe against Communism, we must not budge.... If America does not understand this now, does not know that the issue is cast, then it never will and Communism will run rampant. I believe the future of democracy requires us to stay.

*General Lucius Clay, making his case to superiors on why the U.S.
must stay in Berlin, April 10, 1948*

Why would anyone write a book about an administration that has nothing to show for itself but a string of disasters?

*President Kennedy to journalist Elie Abel, in response to a request
to write a book on his presidency, September 22, 1961*

TEMPELHOF AIRPORT, WEST BERLIN
TUESDAY, SEPTEMBER 19, 1961

General Lucius D. Clay's triumphal return to Berlin came on an unseasonably warm and sunny September afternoon.

Berlin's myriad outdoor cafés, often closed by late September, over-flowed their sidewalks. The Berlin Zoo reported record business. A gentle breeze blew a flotilla of sailboats across the Wannsee, Berlin's broad city lake, and the several waterways to which it was connected. The war years, the city's division, and now the Wall had only heightened Berliners' penchant for savoring pleasurable moments.

That said, it was more General Clay's arrival than the weather that buoyed West Berlin spirits that day. Locals regarded President Kennedy's decision to appoint Clay as his "personal representative" to their city as the most convincing proof yet that America remained determined to defend West Berlin's freedoms. Certainly, Berliners concluded, a man of Clay's pedigree would never have accepted the job unless he was convinced that Kennedy was finally ready to stand up to the Soviets.

In 1948, as Military Governor for the U.S. Zone in Germany, Clay became a German folk hero for ordering and executing, with the British, the airlift that ultimately rescued West Berlin's two million residents from the choice between starvation and communist domination. His 324-day operation was all the more remarkable because it came only three years after the U.S. and its allies had defeated Nazi Germany. At the time, it was still uncertain if Americans would risk their lives and treasure for European security, let alone for the western half of Hitler's former capital, floating as it did as an indefensible island inside communist territory.

Berliners still spoke with astonishment about Clay's "bonbon bombers"—the American pilots who had parachuted sweets to the city's children while breaking the Soviet blockade. Seldom had history seen such a risky and successful humanitarian action on behalf of a vanquished foe. City fathers named one of their broadest and longest boulevards, the Clay-allee of the Dahlem district, for the man who had made it happen.

Clay's determination to keep West Berlin free grew out of a conviction that had only grown over time, relayed to superiors as early as April 1948, that no location on the planet was more important to America's standing in the world. "We have lost Czechoslovakia. Norway is threatened," he said. "If we mean . . . to hold Europe against Communism, we must not budge." His view was that if America did not grasp the importance of West Berlin, then communism would run rampant. "I believe the future of democracy requires us to stay. . . ."

There was only one flaw in Clay's inspiring sense of mission: His motivations for accepting the new job were nobler than Kennedy's reasons for offering it to him.

For Clay, it was a chance to return to the Cold War's central battleground at another historic moment when his actions could again be decisive. For Kennedy, dispatching Clay had more to do with domestic politics and public relations.

Clay's appointment would help neutralize Kennedy's conservative critics, for the retired general was not just a Berlin hero but also an American and Republican one. He had been instrumental in persuading Eisenhower to run for president and then had helped manage his campaign. Getting Clay under the Kennedy administration tent would also minimize the damage he could do sniping at the president from the outside.

That said, Kennedy's indecision about just how much power he should give Clay in Berlin underscored his ambivalence about how best to counter Khrushchev. Although Kennedy had made Clay the only American in Berlin with a direct reporting line to the president, he had at the same time failed to give the general formal command over anyone or anything.

Kennedy had even rewritten his original letter of instruction for Clay to water down the broad authority he had initially offered him, to be "fully and completely responsible for all decisions on Berlin." The president apologized to Clay for the change: "I'm sorry this letter is not the way I wanted it, the way I originally wrote it, but this is the way the State Department feels it will have to be without cutting across all kinds of channels."

Clay had little choice but to accept the downgraded terms, as he had already left his well-paying job as chief executive of the Continental Can Company. Ever the loyal soldier, he had told the president, "As the situation exists in Berlin it is going to be very difficult no matter how it is done. . . . If it is easier for you for the letter to be written this way, it is all right with me." The two men agreed Clay would phone the president on any matter of significance.

The manner of Clay's appointment spoke again to Kennedy's greater comfort at appearing tough than at actually being so. Kennedy increasingly feared Khrushchev might push him to the precipice of unleashing atomic weapons to defend Berlin, but he had not yet determined under what circumstances and in what manner he might be willing to do so. He had no idea what role, if any, Clay would play in the decision-making process.

Whatever his dilemmas, Kennedy's popularity remained impregnable. A Gallup poll showed most Americans considered the string of Kennedy setbacks in 1961 to have been bad breaks rather than poor leadership. Kennedy's approval rating would rise to 77 percent in October after hovering above 70 percent all year, having hit a high of 83 percent as the public circled its wagons around him following the Bay of Pigs. In the quarter century since Gallup had begun polling, only Franklin Roosevelt after Pearl Harbor and Harry Truman after Roosevelt's death had enjoyed comparable popularity—and they had not sustained it nearly as long.

Kennedy was a keen reader of public opinion polls, which showed that a remarkable 64 percent of Americans would approve U.S. military intervention should the Soviets or the East Germans block access to West Berlin, while only 19 percent would be opposed. And more than 60 percent of Americans accepted that there would be war if the Soviets were determined to control Berlin.

With such a hawkish American electorate, Kennedy's choice of Clay was a popular one. It was even more so for Berliners, who celebrated Clay's arrival like that of a homecoming gladiator. From the tarmac of Tempelhof Airport, the site of his 1948 heroics, American tanks greeted him with a nineteen-gun salute. The West Berlin elite gathered to receive him in a hangar beneath a giant American flag flanked by two Berlin city banners. Unlike Kennedy, Clay spoke to all Berliners and not just to those of the West. He spoke of "our determination that *Berlin* and its people will always be free. . . . I came here with complete faith in our cause and with confidence in the courage and steadfastness of the people of *Berlin*."

Licking the wounds from his election defeat two days earlier, West Berlin Mayor Willy Brandt met Clay in Frankfurt and escorted him to Berlin on a Pan American Airlines flight. His defeat by Chancellor Adenauer was a bitter disappointment after an ugly campaign, during which his opponent had so sullied his character. However, Brandt had inflicted considerable damage on Adenauer as well, whom voters had punished due to worries about his age and his tepid response to the Berlin border closure. Adenauer's Christian Democrats had remained the country's largest political party, but the chancellor had lost his absolute majority and was left to bargain for his political survival with new coalition partners, the Free Democrats.

The Christian Democrats and their Bavarian partners, the Christian Social Union, had lost 5 percent of the vote from the previous election, for a total of just 45.3 percent. Brandt's Social Democrats had gained 4.5 percent to achieve 36.2 percent of the vote. The liberal Free Democrats had become the third force in German politics, expanding their share of the vote by 4 percent to some 12.8 percent. The Berlin border closure had realigned German politics, and Adenauer would never fully recover.*

Brandt had appealed publicly to Berliners to provide Clay with a warm homecoming, but they had required little encouragement. Hundreds of thousands of Berliners stood two to three deep along Clay's ten-mile motor route. Children waved small U.S. flags while sitting atop the shoulders of parents who had lived through the airlift. So many well-wishers showered bouquets on Clay that he was soon bathing in flowers in the back of his black Mercedes sedan.

Clay's limited job description was to "report, recommend and advise." Yet his intention from the beginning was to define his mandate more broadly and take full charge of American policy in the city in the manner of a military governor. That would put him on a collision course with men who had strongly opposed his appointment and whose authority was threatened by his arrival: General Lauris Norstad, NATO Supreme Commander, in Paris; General Bruce Clarke, commander of U.S. forces in Europe, in Heidelberg; and the U.S. ambassador to Germany, Walter Dowling, in Bonn.

Clay trumpeted that his new role would be to "demonstrate United States strength and determination" and to force the Soviets to acknowledge

---

*Adenauer would resign in 1963, and Brandt would become the first Social Democratic chancellor of the postwar period in 1969.

responsibility for their sector. He was determined to make clear that the four powers still ran Berlin and not East Germany, which he would expose as the puppet state that it was. Clay was distraught that the U.S. and its allies had allowed so many of their rights in Berlin to erode since his earlier days there, and he was determined to reverse that trend by the force of his will.

The State Department's Martin Hillenbrand worried that Clay didn't realize how much less freedom to maneuver he would have in Berlin now that the U.S. had lost its nuclear monopoly. Yet it was just that sort of defeatist thinking that Clay had rejected his entire career. Clay had launched the 1948 airlift on his own authority after President Truman had turned down his initial plan to send a full brigade storming up the Autobahn to reopen Berlin access. At the airlift's peak operations, one cargo plane was landing every three minutes—shiny new C-54s and war-battered C-47s—filled with food and supplies.

Clay's unexpected initial success had convinced President Truman to support the operation's continuation, against resistance from Pentagon and State Department officials who complained that Clay was risking a new war just three years after the last one had ended. The so-called military experts of that time had told Clay that two million Berliners could not be sustained by air, which would require 4,000 tons of supplies per day. That was more than ten times the size of the Nazi airlift to the German Sixth Army in Stalingrad, an operation which had failed in the end.

Clay had defied the naysayers and won. It had been his life's defining moment, and it would inform every decision he would make from the minute he landed in Berlin in September 1961.

WEST BERLIN
MID-SEPTEMBER, 1961

A month after the August 13 border closure, construction crews along the entire border zone were replacing temporary barriers with a more formidable and permanent *Todesstreifen*, or death strips. East German authorities each day were dispatching brigades of so-called volunteers to help dig the trenches and clear the trees and shrubbery from a broad no-man's-land that would contain the quickly expanding Wall.

The East German newspaper *Sonntag* bragged that construction teams included scientists, philologists, historians, doctors, filmmakers, street builders, journalists, and retail sales staff. "An entire people are working at the wall," it declared proudly. The inmates were laying the foundation for their own prison. Each week, a handful of these "volunteers" used their proximity to the wall to jump over or slip through one of its vanishing weak spots. The more dramatic stories became legend.

At age twenty-one, agricultural engineering student Albrecht Peter Roos began to plot his escape while working on just such a construction crew near the Brandenburg Gate. His two sisters already lived in West Germany, and he wanted to join them rather than build a better barrier to make that impossible. When the workers took a break for lunch, Roos sought his police minder's permission to relieve himself.

The guard shrugged. "Just be quick," he replied.

So Roos retreated to the adjacent woods, only to stumble over two other students hiding in the underbrush who had the same hope of escape. Leading their westward sprint, Roos scrambled through a ditch and under a fence and then rushed to a barbed-wire coil just beyond the fence that ensnared him. With the help of the two others, he negotiated his way out and then helped them through. Bleeding from dozens of cuts through their shredded clothes, the three then ran in a furious zigzag course to the West, fearing guards that had come up from behind would fire upon them.

A West Berlin policeman embraced them on free ground with the reward of a bottle of wine and the first banana Roos had ever seen or eaten.

Each day, West Berlin newspapers splashed across their pages similarly harrowing stories of escape. There was the tale of the twenty-four-year-old ambulance driver who drove his vehicle through the barbed wire at Prinzenstrasse in a hail of machine-gun fire. Photos showed him smiling and unscratched beside his bullet-pierced vehicle. There were the three East Berliners who crashed through the barrier at Bouchestrasse in their 6.5-ton truck, only to be stranded atop the curb that marked the borderline. They scampered the rest of the way to freedom, eluding police shots. A West Berlin policeman triumphantly threw their keys back over the barrier to the Vopos.

What the border closure altered most for Berliners was Sunday afternoon, the traditional German gathering time for family and friends. With phone connections cut off, East and West Berliners communicated with each other from opposite sides of the barrier from platforms and ladders, some holding up newborn babies for viewing by grandparents, some bearing placards with loving messages in big, bold letters that could be read from afar.

Quickly, the bizarre had become routine. West Berlin brides and grooms in wedding costume made their way to the Wall so that family members could wave congratulations from the East. At designated times, children came to the Wall to climb ladders and visit from afar with parents and grandparents. East German police who had wearied of West Berlin hecklers dispersed them across the divide with water cannons and tear gas at border points in the districts of Neukölln, Kreuzberg, and Zehlendorf.

Tour buses showed off the city's newest attractions: a bricked-up church on the border, blocked cemetery gates, sad people behind barbed wire— strange animals in a surreal zoo. One tour guide told a busload from the Netherlands that another handful of refugees would escape that night— another aspect of Berliners' new way of life.

STEINSTÜCKEN ENCLAVE, WEST BERLIN
THURSDAY, SEPTEMBER 21, 1961

General Clay acted immediately to ensure that the East Germans and Soviets didn't miss his arrival.

Within forty-eight hours of landing in Berlin, he directed his irresistible focus on the curious drama of some 190 stranded residents of Stein-

stücken, some 42 families in all. Through an accident of geography, the tiny
exclave of West Berlin's Zehlendorf district—located in the southwest corner of the U.S. sector of Berlin—was separated from West Berlin by a sliver
of Soviet zone. The only access was a short winding road, which since 1945
had been controlled by East German police.

As a result of August 13, the secluded hamlet became the most vulnerable part of West Berlin and thus the West. East German police had surrounded Steinstücken with barbed wire and barriers, later reinforcing them
with watch towers and a hundred-meter-wide no-man's-land. They denied
access to all nonresidents, and with each day those inside the landlocked
community lived in growing despair about their future.

East German authorities threatened to storm the village to recover an
East German who had taken refuge there, only to discover that he had no
way out. Widespread rumor had it that Ulbricht would claim the community as his own by year's end if the West continued to show no intention of
protecting it. East Germany had done the same with other, similarly pre-
carious pieces of West Berlin territory, but those areas were less sensitive,
since they were uninhabited garden plots or forestland.

Without divulging his plans to U.S. superiors or communist authorities, on September 21, at a few minutes before eleven a.m., Clay flew to
Steinstücken aboard a military helicopter, with two other helicopters protecting his flanks. He delivered the community two things it lacked: a TV
set and hope. A large crowd quickly surrounded his chopper as it landed in
a grassy field. At Clay's request, the mayor met with him at Restaurant
Steinstücken, the village's only dining establishment, bar, and grocery store.
They broke open a bottle of wine and drank generously from it while discussing the village's fears and what could be done about them.

General Clay spent only fifty minutes in Steinstücken, but it was enough
to prompt East Berlin's *Neues Deutschland* newspaper to brand his action as
a "war-like move in an otherwise calm situation." The British embassy protested in Washington that Clay was taking too much risk for too little gain.

To show he would not be bullied, the following day Clay helicoptered
in a three-man detachment from the 278th Military Police Company to

establish Steinstücken's first U.S. outpost, and it would remain for the next decade. Military Police Lieutenant Vern Pike flew in to help set up command in the mayor's basement, running the communications antennas up his chimney. Clay then ordered General Watson, the local commander, to organize a ground offensive scheduled for three days later, on September 24, to "liberate" Steinstücken by using two companies to punch a corridor through Berlin's new barrier to the community.

By coincidence, European Commander General Bruce C. Clarke arrived by train that morning from Heidelberg to inspect his Berlin operation. Over breakfast, Watson and Brigadier General Frederick O. Hartel happily told their direct superior he had arrived on "an interesting morning" because three hours later they would begin the Steinstücken operation.

"Who told you to do *that?*" Clarke protested to Watson.

"General Clay," Watson responded.

"Al," Clarke complained, "don't you know who you work for? Don't you know who writes your efficiency report?"

Clarke instructed his underlings to take no further orders from Clay and to withdraw their troops from the woods and send them back to their barracks. He then found Clay in his office and, pointing to a red phone on his desk, angrily challenged him to call Kennedy, or to "take your cotton-picking fingers off my troops."

Responded Clay, "Well, Bruce, I can see that we are not going to get along."

Clay was convinced he knew how far to push the Soviets and that he was on safe ground because Moscow "could not allow a minor issue [like Steinstücken] to become an international incident through mishandling by their East German puppets."

A few days later, U.S. troops evacuated seven East Germans who had driven their truck through the mayor's backyard fence while seeking refuge. Military police cut their hair short so they looked like GIs, put them in MP uniforms and helmets, and then evacuated them in a U.S. military helicopter. Although East German authorities threatened to shoot down the helicopter, Clay had gambled right that Moscow would not let them risk it.

The flights to and from Steinstücken became routine practice, usually ferrying MPs back and forth from their base but sometimes ushering out refugees. Clay not only felt he had proved a point to Berliners and his own superiors, but that he had also reinforced his own conviction, born in 1948, that the Soviets would back down when confronted by a determined West.

Emboldened, Clay pressed on. He announced that the U.S. military would resume patrols that Washington had stopped six years earlier along the Autobahn. It was his answer to new East German police harassment of American vehicles, which were sometimes held up for hours for inspections. The patrols would intervene in any incident involving an American car. Within a short time, the problems ended.

West Berliners were elated. The *Berliner Morgenpost* splashed a photo on its front page of General Clay kissing his wife, Marjorie, as she arrived in Tempelhof Airport. The caption read: "Every Berlin child knows the accomplishments of this American for our city's freedom. His latest actions warm the hearts of Berliners: the stationing of a U.S. commando in Steinstücken and the resumption of military patrols of the Autobahn."

What they couldn't know was that Clay's most dangerous enemies were already planning a counterattack—in Washington. The last time Clay had exceeded orders in Berlin, President Truman had covered his back. Clay had no way of knowing whether Kennedy would do the same now, but he was about to find out.

HYANNIS PORT, MASSACHUSETTS
SATURDAY, SEPTEMBER 23, 1961

The usual ilk of weekend guests were gathering at the Kennedys' Hyannis Port compound, where President Kennedy was working on a speech that he would deliver to the United Nations General Assembly the next day.

They included the president's brother Teddy; their brother-in-law, the actor Peter Lawford; Frank Sinatra; and the Dominican playboy Porfirio Rubirosa and his latest wife. Sinatra had arrived with what father Joseph

Kennedy's chauffeur Frank Saunders called "a crowd of jet-setters and beautiful people," among them women who looked liked prostitutes to him. The maids were abuzz about it all.

Saunders would later claim that he heard party noises during the night and wandered to the main house from his cabin to return Joe Kennedy's riding boots to him. He said he had stumbled upon the old man in the back hallway fondling a giggling, buxom female.

"My riding boots!" Saunders heard him exclaim. "Just in time!"

It was all part of the raucous background noise of the Kennedy administration and the barely controlled chaos of Kennedy's personal life and that of those around him. The public image of the workaholic, speed-reading, family-man president was in stark contrast to the reality that would emerge only years later through the eyewitness reports from, among others, his Secret Service agents. They were men who lacked the single-minded motivation of his closest aides and family to burnish the Kennedy image—and they worried about the security dangers of Kennedy's womanizing.

Larry Newman, who had joined the Secret Service in 1960, was less worried about the morality issues involved than he was that the president's chief procurer of women, Dave Powers, would not allow security checks or searches of any of the women who were escorted past bodyguards. This was at a time when all the agents around the president had been warned that Fidel Castro might be planning a revenge hit over the Bay of Pigs. "We didn't know if the President the next morning would be dead or alive," Newman recalled later to investigative journalist Seymour Hersh. Newman said agents only half jokingly debated among themselves who would draw the black bean to testify before the appropriate House subcommittee should the president be harmed.

Tony Sherman, a member of the Kennedy security detail from Salt Lake City, would later recall days when Kennedy "would not work at all." Sherman had not liked the fact that his job responsibilities included alerting Kennedy's aides when his wife's sudden arrival might uncover his philandering. Agent William T. McIntyre of Phoenix worried that as a sworn law enforcer, he was being asked to look the other way at illegal procurement of prostitutes. Agent Joseph Paolella of Los Angeles adored Kennedy and the fact that he always remembered his security men's names, but he worried that the U.S. president could be blackmailed by an enemy over his infidelities. He and other agents referred to one of Kennedy's guests that weekend, Peter Lawford, as "Rancid Ass," for his overdrinking and aggressiveness with women.

With all that revelry in the background, Kennedy was putting the final touches on one of the most important speeches of his presidency, and his first important signal to the world of how he intended to handle Moscow and nuclear arms control after the Berlin border closure. It would also come just four days after an airplane crash in Africa had killed United Nations Secretary-General Dag Hammarskjöld. The Soviets were campaigning to have Hammarskjöld replaced by a three-person directorate that would represent the West, the communist world, and "neutrals."

Kennedy's public approval ratings defied gravity, but the president knew that beneath them lay a string of foreign policy setbacks and festering domestic problems that over time could undermine his leadership. Before he left Washington that Friday for Hyannis Port, he had met briefly with *Detroit News* Washington bureau chief Elie Abel, who had been asked by a New York publisher to write a book on the president's first term and was seeking Kennedy's cooperation. Sitting together in the White House living quarters, with *Marine One*'s engines roaring in the background, Abel drank a Bloody Mary while Kennedy tried to dissuade him from the project. "Why would anyone write a book about an administration that has nothing to show for itself but a string of disasters?" he asked.

Abel found himself in the curious position of trying to convince Kennedy that, despite his rough start, in the end he would do great things, and he and his friends would all be proud of his administration.

On Sunday, Kennedy landed with Lawford at the Marine Air Terminal of New York's La Guardia Airport at 6:35 p.m., where they were greeted by Mayor Robert Wagner, Secretary of State Rusk, and U.S. Ambassador to the United Nations Adlai Stevenson. Pierre Salinger, the president's portly, bon vivant press secretary, had arrived ahead of them in response to an urgent call from Soviet spy Georgi Bolshakov, who had continued to play his role as unofficial conduit to Khrushchev. Bolshakov had said it was urgent that Salinger meet with Mikhail Kharlamov, the Soviet Foreign Ministry press director, who had an urgent message for the president.

Bolshakov had grown increasingly comfortable in his role, having operated without a leak and to the satisfaction of his superiors for several months. Though he remained a mid-ranking military intelligence agent, he was now custodian of a well-established and frequently employed direct line to Khrushchev. Salinger considered Bolshakov to be "a one-man troika in himself . . . interpreter, editor and spy."

Following Salinger's instructions, at 7:15 p.m. on Sunday Bolshakov brought Kharlamov through a little-watched side entrance into the Carlyle, the hotel that served as the president's residence in New York. Reporters constantly loitered in the lobby, hoping for presidential sightings, so a Secret Service agent took the two Soviets up a back elevator.

Salinger was taken aback by Kharlamov's opening words: "The storm in Berlin is over."

By his reckoning, Salinger had told Kharlamov, the Berlin situation couldn't be much worse.

"Just wait, my friend," he said.

Kharlamov asked whether the president had received a message that Khrushchev had sent to him through *New York Times* Paris correspondent Cyrus L. Sulzberger, who had conducted an interview with the Soviet leader in early September.

Salinger said he hadn't. The fact was, however, that on September 10 Sulzberger had relayed to Kennedy a personal note that Khrushchev had given him during an interview just five days earlier, although Kennedy had not yet responded.

Khrushchev had told Sulzberger, "If you are personally able to meet with President Kennedy, I wish you would tell him I would not be loath to establishing some sort of informal contact with him to find a means of settling the [Berlin] crisis without damaging the prestige of the United States— on the basis of a German peace treaty and [the establishment of the] Free

City of West Berlin." He had suggested Kennedy use informal contacts to relay his view on Khrushchev's ideas, and "to figure out various forms and stages and how to prepare public opinion and not endanger the prestige of the United States."

Kharlamov repeated for Salinger the essence of the Khrushchev message, speaking faster and more excitedly than Bolshakov could translate. So Salinger asked him to slow down, explaining that they had time. The president was out for dinner and a Broadway play, he said, and he wouldn't be back at the hotel until past midnight.

Taking a deep breath, Kharlamov said the situation was urgent. Khrushchev considered Kennedy's plans for a U.S. military buildup in Europe to be an imminent danger. That was why the Soviet leader had told Sulzberger about his eagerness to establish a private channel to Kennedy to reach a German settlement.

Khrushchev wanted another summit with Kennedy to consider American proposals on Berlin, Kharlamov said. He would leave the timing to Kennedy because of the president's "obvious political difficulties." But he was in a hurry. Kharlamov talked of the continuing "intense pressure" within the communist bloc on Khrushchev to conclude a peace treaty with East Germany. Beyond that, he said, the danger of a major military incident in Berlin remained far too great to delay a settlement.

Khrushchev also wanted to influence or at least know the content of Kennedy's Monday speech because he wished to avoid anything, at a time of rising tensions, that might give new hope to his opponents ahead of the Party Congress at the end of October. Kharlamov told Salinger that the Soviet leader "hopes your president's speech to the UN won't be another warlike ultimatum like the one on July 25. . . . He didn't like that at all."

Salinger left a message for Kennedy to call as soon as he returned to his room. He then poured scotch and soda for his Russian guests. When they left nearly two hours later, Salinger promised he'd give them the president's response the next morning at 11:30, ahead of Kennedy's UN speech.

Kennedy called Salinger at 1:00 a.m. and invited him to his thirty-fourth-floor duplex at the Carlyle. It was his New York "home," rented by his father and furnished with fine French antiques. With the draperies open as they were that night, the apartment offered a glittering view of New York's skyline. Salinger found Kennedy in bed in white pajamas, chewing on an unlit cigar and reading. At the president's request, Salinger repeated the key points of his conversation with Kharlamov several times.

The president told Salinger that Sulzberger had communicated nothing to him from his Khrushchev meeting, so the message had likely not reached Kennedy. Kennedy rose from his bed and looked out over Manhattan. He told Salinger that it was good news "if Khrushchev is ready to listen to our views on Germany," and it probably meant that he would not unilaterally sign a peace treaty with the Ulbricht regime that year and prompt yet another crisis. Yet Kennedy believed Moscow's continued insistence on a peace treaty recognizing East Germany still raised the specter of war if Khrushchev endangered West Berlin access.

The president called Secretary Rusk at 1:30 a.m., and together they settled on a message that Salinger would deliver to the Soviets the next morning. Salinger scribbled on hotel stationery as the president dictated. He would tell the Soviets that Kennedy was "cautiously receptive" to the proposal for an early summit on Berlin, but he wanted the Soviets to demonstrate good faith in achieving Laotian neutrality. Only then would a summit on the more difficult question of Germany be likely to produce "significant agreement."

The tone was to be cordial but cautious. Though Kennedy and Khrushchev had agreed on a unified, neutral Laos in Vienna, the Soviets had stood by as North Vietnam added to the military capability of the communist Pathet Lao, and Moscow was contributing two-thirds of the cost to maintaining its expanding secret army. Salinger would repeat the president's exact words to Kharlamov: "We would be watching and waiting," was the message Kennedy wanted Salinger to pass to the Soviets.

Kennedy reviewed his UN speech with Salinger until 3:00 a.m. The final text was more moderate than the Soviets might have anticipated. The language was particularly cautious regarding Berlin.

The president had been agonizing over the speech for weeks. Though the next election was not for another three years, Kennedy's domestic opponents had begun to sense his weakness. Barry Goldwater, the Arizona senator and leading Republican, had abandoned his previous restraint on attacking Kennedy over Berlin and said West German fears of abandonment were "perfectly justified." Said Goldwater, "Anytime diplomats begin talking of negotiations in a Soviet-created situation where there is nothing to negotiate, it is time for the defenders of freedom to become wary." He told a conference of Republicans on September 28 that if elections were held the next day, they would win with the largest Republican landslide ever.

Kennedy needed to retake the initiative. Khrushchev "had spit in our eye three times," Kennedy complained to his ambassador to the UN, Adlai Stevenson. "He has had a succession of apparent victories—space, Cuba, the thirteenth of August. . . . He wants to give out the feeling that he has us on the run."

Vice President Lyndon Johnson argued to the president that he couldn't demand disarmament in New York and then return to Washington and call out more divisions and restart underground nuclear testing, which is exactly what Kennedy planned to do. The president had learned from ten months of dealing with Khrushchev that one could combat the man only in contradictions.

Kennedy's performance at the UN was formidable, fed by his increasing fixation on the prospect of nuclear conflict. That, in turn, had been shaped by secret meetings spent determining with his top advisers the rich detail of exactly how he would execute a nuclear war plan, right down to specific Soviet body counts. Every word of his speech reflected his increasing preoccupation with that burden.

"A nuclear disaster," Kennedy told the General Assembly, "spread by wind and water and fear, could well engulf the great and the small, the rich and the poor, the committed and the uncommitted alike. Mankind must put an end to war—or war will put an end to mankind."

He outlined his proposal for "general and complete disarmament" under effective international control. "Today, every inhabitant of this planet must contemplate the day when this planet may no longer be habitable," he said. "Every man, woman and child lives under a nuclear sword of Damocles, hanging by the slenderest of threads, capable of being cut at any moment by accident or miscalculation or by madness. The weapons of war must be abolished before they abolish us."

Buried within the speech was a conciliatory message for Moscow on Berlin. Noticed by only the initiated, it suggested Soviet concerns over East Germany had been justified and repeated Kennedy's view, one that had so distressed veteran diplomats, that U.S. interests in Europe did not stretch beyond West Berlin. Though Salinger would later insist Kennedy had not altered his speech that night, the language would satisfy Khrushchev.

"We are committed to no rigid formulas," he said. "We see no perfect solution. We recognize that troops and tanks can, for a time, keep a nation divided against its will, however unwise that policy might seem to us. But we believe a peaceful agreement is possible which protects the freedom of West Berlin and Allied presence and access, while recognizing the historic and legitimate interests of others in assuring European security."

Kennedy closed with his growing sense of historic moment: "The events and the decisions of the next ten months may well decide the fate of man for the next ten thousand years.... And we in this hall shall be remembered either as part of the generation that turned this planet into a flaming funeral pyre or the generation that met its vow to 'save succeeding generations from the scourge of war.'"

Though put in poetic terms, he closed again with an offer of talks, without using a word of his speech to reproach Moscow over the August border closure. "We shall never negotiate out of fear, and we shall never fear to negotiate.... For together we shall save our planet, or together we shall perish in its flames."

The speech's soaring rhetoric would help establish Kennedy's reputation as a world leader. U.S. Senator Mike Mansfield called it "one of the great speeches of our generation." Yet those hearing the speech in West Berlin could not miss Kennedy's willingness to compromise further at their expense or his lack of resolve to remove the barrier that divided them.

Perhaps most telling was East German praise for the speech. The Ulbricht regime hailed it as a milestone toward peaceful coexistence. The party newspaper *Neues Deutschland* called it "remarkable; remarkable because it showed American willingness to negotiate."

West German editorialists focused not on the speech's flourishes but on its wishy-washy language. *Bild-Zeitung* wondered bitterly whether Kennedy's reference to "the historic and legitimate interests of others" was suggesting that Moscow had the right "to split Germany or renounce reunification."

West German Foreign Minister Heinrich von Brentano told a party caucus of his Christian Democratic Union that the country must "brace itself with all its strength against tendencies to get a Berlin settlement at West Germany's expense."

West German Chancellor Konrad Adenauer complained to friends that the president didn't mention German unification once at the United Nations. Kennedy also left out the ritual call for all-German free elections. He seemed to be retreating on all questions of principle regarding Berlin. Kennedy had not even done the bare minimum: demand that free circulation of people return to Berlin. Adenauer set in motion a trip to Washington in hopes of getting Kennedy back on message, if it wasn't already too late.

Adenauer's fears that Kennedy might abandon West Germany had grown so great that on August 29 he had reached out to Khrushchev with a secret message through West German Ambassador Kroll. Despite his public stance against any talks with Moscow, privately he was urging the Soviet to join new negotiations. "The two greatest dangers," he said, "are when tanks stand opposite tanks, at a distance of just some meters, as is the case now in Berlin, and the even greater danger of an incorrect assessment of the situation."

In the *Berliner Morgenpost*, a readers' debate raged over whether or not one could still trust the Americans to defend Berlin's freedom. One contributor from the city district of Steglitz asked whether the West was writing the Soviet Union a blank check to do what it wanted in West Berlin by the end of that year. Another writer said Marxists had it right that U.S. capital-

ism's abundance had created an indecisive and indifferent society—
"although it is five minutes before midnight."

Beside these letters was one from Raymond Aron, the famous French
philosopher, echoing French leader Charles de Gaulle's warning in a television appearance that week. "What is at stake," wrote Aron, "isn't just the
fate of two million Berliners. It is the capability of the United States to
convince Khrushchev that it has the tenacity not to give in to horse trading."

West Berliners were confused by their guarantor's mixed messages.
One day General Clay had landed in Steinstücken and flexed U.S. muscle
through his patrols on their Autobahn. The next day Kennedy gave a speech
that continued the American retreat. Kennedy had not even mentioned the
Wall's existence or the fact that East Germans were further fortifying it
every day.

New York Times columnist James "Scotty" Reston wrote that Kennedy
"has talked like Churchill but acted like Chamberlain." In the same column,
Reston reported on a leaked Kennedy memo regarding Clay's confrontational Berlin measures in which the president asked senior officials why his
policy of seeking negotiations on Berlin was being misunderstood.

Reading the tea leaves and intelligence reports, Khrushchev was beginning to sense that Clay's hard line in Berlin was nothing more than a retired
general's bold improvisation that lacked presidential blessing. There was
sufficient sign of disagreement in U.S. policy circles that it was time to
probe the differences.

So Marshal Konev dispatched a sharp note to General Watson demanding that Clay's "illegal" Autobahn patrols end. His letter, he stressed, wasn't
a "protest but a warning." The Kennedy administration ordered Clay's
Autobahn patrols to stop after a week of successful operations. General
Konev's allies had been Clay's American enemies.

On September 27, General Clarke flew to Berlin to reprimand his
commander again. After a ceremonial lunch with Clay for press purposes,
General Clarke again advised General Watson, his Berlin commander, that
U.S. forces could no longer be used to counteract Soviet or East German

actions without his approval. The East German press got wind of Clay's differences with the Kennedy administration and made much of it.

Clarke then got wind of another secret Clay operation.

Clay had ordered army engineers to construct barriers in a secluded forest on the outskirts of Berlin that would replicate the Wall as closely as possible. U.S. troops then mounted bulldozer attachments on their tanks, and Clay supervised as they crashed through the barriers, using different speeds and height placements for the shovels to achieve maximum efficiency. Clay's purpose was to determine the best way to punch a hole through the barrier should the opportunity or necessity present itself.

"As soon as I learned of it," General Clarke would later write in a private correspondence, "I stopped it and got rid of what had been done."

Clarke didn't report the Clay operation or his action against it to Washington, hoping the whole matter would simply disappear.

Kennedy would never know about it—but Khrushchev would. A Soviet agent hiding in the forest had snapped photos. Khrushchev had no way of knowing that General Clarke had shut down the exercise. He now had what he considered concrete evidence that the Americans might well be planning an operation in Berlin that would challenge or humiliate him during his Party Congress.

17

NUCLEAR POKER

In a certain sense there is an analogy here—I like this comparison—with Noah's Ark, where both the "clean" and the "unclean" found sanctuary. But regardless of who lists himself with the "clean" and who is considered to be "unclean," they are all equally interested in one thing, and that is that the Ark should successfully continue its cruise.

Premier Khrushchev to President Kennedy, in the first letter
of their secret correspondence, September 29, 1961

Our confidence in our ability to deter Communist action, or resist Communist blackmail, is based upon a sober appreciation of the relative military power of the two sides. The fact is that this nation has a nuclear retaliatory force of such lethal power than any enemy move which brought it into play would be an act of self-destruction on his part.

Deputy Secretary of Defense Roswell Gilpatric,
Hot Springs, Virginia, October 21, 1961

CARLYLE HOTEL, NEW YORK
SATURDAY, SEPTEMBER 30, 1961

Carrying two folded newspapers under his arm, Georgi Bolshakov appeared as arranged at Pierre Salinger's door at the Carlyle at 3:30 p.m., having been escorted up the back elevator by a Secret Service agent.

Concealed inside one of the papers was a thick manila envelope, from which Bolshakov removed a bundle of pages. With conspiratorial flamboyance, the Soviet spy announced that he held before him a personal twenty-six-page letter from Khrushchev to Kennedy, a manuscript he said he had spent the entire night translating. The bags under Bolshakov's eyes were such a permanent fixture that Salinger could not know if that was true.

"You may read this," Bolshakov told Salinger. "Then it is for the eyes of the president only." It had been only a week since Bolshakov and Salinger had last met in the same room ahead of Kennedy's United Nations speech. Khrushchev was impatient to test Kennedy's conciliatory words and his expressed willingness to open new talks on Berlin, despite French and West German opposition. Bolshakov handed Salinger both the English and Russian versions of the letter so that U.S. government translators could compare them for accuracy.

Thus began what National Security Advisor McGeorge Bundy would dub the "pen pal letters," uniquely direct and private correspondence between the two leading adversaries of their time. Over the next two years, Khrushchev would continue to use the cloak-and-dagger means of having Bolshakov and others slip his letters to Salinger, to Robert Kennedy, or to Ted Sorensen on street corners, in a bar, or elsewhere, often in unmarked envelopes slipped out from folded newspapers.

Khrushchev considered the matter of such urgency that Bolshakov had phoned Salinger a day earlier with an offer to charter a plane to deliver the letter to Newport, Rhode Island, where Kennedy had been on a week's autumn vacation at the home of Jacqueline's mother, Janet Lee Bouvier, and stepfather, Hugh Auchincloss. However, Kennedy and Rusk wanted to avoid a potential "media sensation" in the event that one of two dozen reporters with the president spotted the Russian agent. So they dispatched Salinger to New York the next day.

"If you knew the importance of what I have, you wouldn't keep me waiting that long," Bolshakov had replied.

Salinger would later paraphrase the message in Khrushchev's 6,000-word letter: *You and I, Mr. President, are leaders of two nations that are on a collision course. . . . We have no choice but to put our heads together and find ways to live in peace.*

The man who had so battered Kennedy in Vienna opened on a warm and personal note, explaining that he was resting with his family at his Black Sea retreat in Pitsunda. In the secretive Soviet Union, not even his own citizens knew where he was. "As a former Naval officer," Khrushchev wrote to Kennedy, "you would surely appreciate the merits of these surroundings, the beauty of the sea and the grandeur of the Caucasian mountains." Khrushchev said it was difficult in such a setting to think that problems lacking solutions "cast a sinister shadow on peaceful life, on the future of millions of people."

But because that was the case, Khrushchev was suggesting a confidential exchange between the two men whose actions would determine the future of the planet. If Kennedy was uninterested, the Soviet leader said the president could ignore the letter and Khrushchev would never mention it again.

Salinger was struck by the peasant simplicity of Khrushchev's language, "in contrast to the sterile gobbledygook that passes for this level of diplomatic correspondence." The letter had none of Khrushchev's usual threats and instead solicited Kennedy's alternative proposals should he differ with Khrushchev's suggestions.

Khrushchev's initiative had several possible motivations. Most important, his Party Congress would begin in a little more than two weeks, and engaging Kennedy in such an exchange would give him greater assurance that the U.S. would do nothing to disrupt his painstaking choreography. Second, he hoped to calm the rising tensions that had produced a much larger expansion of U.S. defense spending than he had anticipated.

Khrushchev knew the Soviet Union lacked the economic depth to match a sustained arms race with the far wealthier United States. For the first time, he had to worry that the West might challenge his conventional military dominance around Berlin. Kennedy's defense buildup was also inflaming Soviet hard-liners' arguments that Khrushchev was doing too little to combat the West and should have gone further to neutralize West Berlin. In his letter, Khrushchev warned Kennedy that the tit-for-tat military spending, spurred by Berlin, was further reason why Moscow was "attaching such exclusive significance to the German question."

The Soviet leader said he was willing to reexamine positions frozen through fifteen years of cold war. Writing to the Catholic Kennedy, the atheist Soviet compared the postwar world to Noah's Ark, aboard which all parties wanted to continue their voyage, whether they were clean or unclean. "And we have no other alternative: either we should live in peace and cooperation so that the Ark maintains its buoyancy, or else it sinks."

Khrushchev also said he was willing to expand on the quiet contacts between Secretary of State Rusk and Foreign Minister Gromyko, whose first meeting had been in New York on September 21. In addition, he was willing to take up Kennedy's suggestion of preparatory talks between the U.S. and Soviet ambassadors to Yugoslavia, America's legendary diplomat George Kennan and General Alexei Yepishev, a Khrushchev confidant.

Just a day after the border closure on August 14, the State Department had authorized Kennan to open that channel, but at the time Moscow had shown no interest. Now Khrushchev was eager, though he worried that without clear instructions the ambassadors would "indulge in tea-drinking" and "mooing at each other when they should talk on the substance." Khrushchev suggested instead the use of U.S. Ambassador Thompson, since he was a trusted and proven interlocutor, though he immediately apologized, saying he understood that this would be Kennedy's choice.

Khrushchev protested at length about Western suspicions that Moscow still intended to seize West Berlin. "It is ridiculous to even think of that," he said, arguing that the city was of no geopolitical importance. To show his good intentions, he suggested moving the United Nations headquarters to West Berlin, an idea he had floated earlier that month in separate meetings with Belgian Foreign Minister Paul-Henri Spaak and former French Prime Minister Paul Reynaud.

Apart from opening his new channel to Kennedy, Khrushchev was taking other measures to avoid further escalation of tensions with the U.S. Khrushchev's party Presidium had put on ice a far-advanced plan to provide Cuba with more advanced weaponry, including missiles that could reach the U.S. Khrushchev had also warned Ulbricht against a series of measures he was implementing to expand his hold on East Berlin, lecturing his troublesome client that he should be satisfied with his 1961 gains.

In his most important gesture, Khrushchev responded to Kennedy's appeal of the previous week for progress on Laos. He confirmed their agreement of Vienna that Laos would become a neutral, independent state like Burma and Cambodia. However, he disagreed with Kennedy's concern about specifically who should take which leadership positions in Laos, saying that should not be a matter for Moscow and Washington to decide.

With that, Khrushchev closed with best wishes to Kennedy's wife and for his and his family's health.

HYANNIS PORT, MASSACHUSETTS
SATURDAY, OCTOBER 14, 1961

It would take two weeks before Kennedy was ready to respond.

Working over the weekend on Cape Cod, Kennedy wrote and rewrote a draft that would balance his heightened distrust for Khrushchev with his desire to use all means to avoid war through miscalculation. A negative reply could hasten another Kremlin move on Berlin, but too positive a reply would look naive to his domestic and Allied critics. Both Charles de Gaulle and Konrad Adenauer worried that any Kennedy–Khrushchev talks were simply a recipe for new concessions on West Berlin.

Adenauer's concerns would have been even greater if he had known the instructions Kennedy had given Rusk to dramatically reconstruct U.S. positions for a new round of Berlin talks, with a peace conference as their goal. Kennedy had ruled out as a negotiator U.S. Ambassador to West Germany Walter Dowling, because "he reflects Bonn's opinion too much." He also wanted Rusk to leave on the table only issues acceptable to Moscow and remove Adenauer's insistence on talks aimed at German and Berlin reunification through free elections. "These are not negotiable proposals," he said. "Their emptiness in this sense is generally recognized; and we should have to fall back from them promptly." What he was willing to consider were many of Moscow's previously unacceptable ideas, including making West Berlin an internationalized "free city" as long as it was NATO that guaranteed its future and not a foreign troop contingent including the Soviets.

Considering how much he was willing to compromise, Kennedy was disappointed by the Soviet response. Soviet aircraft increasingly buzzed U.S. planes traveling to Berlin, Khrushchev had resumed nuclear testing, and the Soviet leader again was threatening to sign an East German peace treaty. On the other hand, Khrushchev had abandoned earlier threats of war and was promising to preserve West Berlin's independence.

One matter was certain: after having tried to put the Berlin issue on the back burner at the beginning of his presidency, Kennedy was now overwhelmed by it. Unable to get the president to focus any attention on his land conservation agenda, Secretary of the Interior Stewart Udall complained, "He's imprisoned by Berlin. That's all he thinks about. He has a restless mind, and he likes to roam over all subjects, but ever since August, Berlin has occupied him totally."

Kennedy considered reaching out to his allies to get their advice and buy-in on how to respond to Khrushchev, but experience had taught him that that would only produce muddle and press leaks. He would then lose Khrushchev's trust. But what was that trust worth, anyway? Chip Bohlen, the former U.S. ambassador to Moscow, told Kennedy that his response to Khrushchev "may be the most important letter the President will ever write."

In a letter dated October 16, more than two weeks after Khrushchev's correspondence, Kennedy seized upon Khrushchev's personal tone and wrote about the value of getting away from Washington and spending time on the shore with his children and their cousins. He embraced Khrushchev's offer of confidential correspondence, and said he would not hint at it in public or disclose it to the press. However, Kennedy added to Khrushchev that he would share the letter with Rusk and a few other of his closest associates.

Kennedy embraced Khrushchev's Noah's Ark analogy. Due to the dangers of the nuclear age, he said, U.S.–Soviet collaboration to keep the peace now was even more important than their partnership during World War II. Kennedy could not have been clearer in his de facto acceptance of Berlin's border closure. He called his attitude toward Berlin and Germany "one of reason, not belligerence. There is peace in that area now—and this government shall not initiate and shall oppose any action which upsets that peace."

Although he had been willing to allow the construction of the Berlin Wall, he was now drawing the line he would not cross regarding Berlin. He rejected Khrushchev's efforts to open negotiations to change Berlin's status to a so-called "free city" where Soviet troops would join the other three Allies in ensuring the city's freedom and the East Germans would control access. "We would be 'buying the same horse' twice," he said, "conceding objectives which you seek, merely to retain what we already possess." But Kennedy expressed willingness to begin exploratory talks through the American whom Khrushchev had suggested for the purpose, Ambassador Thompson.

Kennedy also wanted Khrushchev to give the U.S. more on Laos as a test case for Berlin. Said the president, "I do not see how we can expect to reach a settlement on so bitter and complex an issue as Berlin, where both of us have vital interests at stake, if we cannot come to a final agreement on Laos, which we have previously agreed should be neutral and independent after the fashion of Burma and Cambodia." Now that it was clear that the neutralist Prince Souvanna Phouma would become prime minister, Kennedy said that he and Khrushchev should ensure that the prince "is assisted by the kind of men we believe necessary to meet the standard of neutrality." He said the acceleration of communist attacks on South Vietnam, many from Laotian territory, were "a very grave threat to peace."

However, more important to Khrushchev than the content of Kennedy's letter was the fact that the president had taken his bait and replied at all. Now the Soviet leader could be relatively certain that Kennedy was ready to engage in new talks regarding Berlin, and thus would refrain from confrontational speeches or actions that might disrupt Khrushchev's careful planning for his crucial, fast-approaching Party Congress. Only two months after closing the Berlin border, the Soviet was drawing Kennedy into new negotiations on the city's status, without having suffered even the modest hand-slap of economic sanctions.

What Kennedy would get out of the exchange was less satisfying. Khrushchev's next communication would come in the form of a fifty-megaton hydrogen bomb.

PALACE OF CONGRESSES, MOSCOW
TUESDAY, OCTOBER 17, 1961

Sunlight glimmered through the morning mist off the golden domes of the Kremlin's fifteenth- and sixteenth-century churches. The red flags of the fifteen Soviet republics fluttered in front of the modern, glass-walled red and gold Palace of Congresses, just finished for the 22nd Soviet Party Congress.

The massive auditorium was filled to capacity. Not one of its red seats was vacant. Never had so many communists met in one place at the same time. Some 4,394 voting delegates and 405 nonvoting delegates—nearly 5,000 in all—had gathered from eighty communist and noncommunist countries. That was three and a half times more delegates than in the preceding three congresses.

The numbers were a reflection of the party's growth, now reaching the 10 million mark in membership, after having added nearly 1.5 million members since the 21st Party Congress in 1959. Khrushchev wanted a record crowd for his 1961 show, so he had entitled each party organization to send additional delegates.

The Palace of Congresses was unique, if only because everything worked so much better than in most Soviet government buildings. It had escalators with nearly silent motors, the latest stereophonic sound, West German–made central air-conditioning, British-manufactured refrigerators, and hot and cold running water in marble lavatories. Western correspondents gathered for drinks and food on the seventh floor, which they called the "Top of the Marx."

Time magazine assessed the crowd: "comrades from small Russian villages, café-sophisticated Parisians, bamboo-tough agitators from Asia." The stars included the Viet Minh's Ho Chi Minh; Red China's Chou En-lai; America's seventy-one-year-old labor activist Elizabeth Gurley Flynn; the Spanish Civil War's famed "Pasionaria," Dolores Ibárruri; and János Kádár, the leader who had helped put down the 1956 rebellion in Hungary. They filed in beneath a giant silver bas-relief of Lenin on a purple background.

Western reporters habitually called Khrushchev the "absolute leader" of the Soviet Union, but the truth was more complicated. After only a year in power, Khrushchev had narrowly survived a coup in 1957. After the G-2 incident and the Paris Summit failure in May 1960, Stalinist remnants began to rally against Khrushchev. In particular, they seized upon what they considered his irresponsible reduction of Soviet armed forces, his alienation of communist China, and his embracing of the imperialist Americans. Through early votes on prefabricated resolutions, Khrushchev monitored potential rivalries that could be his undoing.

Kennedy's three leading American political opponents—Republican Arizona Senator Barry Goldwater, New York Governor Nelson Rockefeller, and former Vice President Richard Nixon—were meek compared with Khrushchev's less visible and more dangerous opponents, men bred in Stalin's bloodiest times.

Though he owed his position to Khrushchev, Presidium member Frol Kozlov personified the sort of thug that had begun to plot against Khrushchev after the Paris Summit failure. He was ill-educated, short, boorish, Stalinist, and hostile to the West. American diplomat Richard Davies described him as a nasty drunk who ate like a pig and drank like a fish. Yet Khrushchev also faced a smoother and more ruthless kind of potential enemy in Mikhail Suslov, the party's leading ideologist and intellectual.

Khrushchev had strengthened his hold on power during 1961 through favors, factional purges, and visits throughout the country with local party leaders. The Gagarin space shot, the Bay of Pigs, the Vienna Summit, and the Berlin border closure had also neutralized would-be opponents. It seemed to party colleague Pyotr Demichev that Khrushchev was enjoying a rare "time in the sun." *Time* magazine put it this way: "In 44 years and 15 Party Congresses since the October 1917 Revolution, Communism's inner hierarchy has never seemed more stable or more successful."

Nevertheless, Khrushchev knew better than anyone how vulnerable his position could be. For all his work to advance communism in Africa and Asia, only Cuba had joined the Soviet camp under Khrushchev's leadership, and by luck more than design. Some party leaders would never forgive Khrushchev for having denounced Stalin, which they saw not only as an attack on an individual but also on communist history and legitimacy. China remained poised against Khrushchev, and the head of Beijing's delegation, Chou En-lai, would leave the Congress in a huff after laying a wreath at Stalin's tomb.

Still, Khrushchev looked leaner and fitter than he had been for months, as if he had been training for the event. "I propose we begin to work," he told the gathering, interpreted into twenty-nine languages. "The Twenty-second Congress is now in session."

Even Stalin would have envied Khrushchev's choreography. The Soviet leader monopolized the first two days with his two speeches, each some six hours in length. He navigated from one topic to another with inexhaustible energy, describing richly how the Soviet economy would surpass that of the United States by 1980—increasing its gross national product five times, expanding its industrial production six times, and providing every family a rent-free apartment. By 1965, he said, the Soviet Union would produce three pairs of shoes per person per year!

He renewed his attacks on the dead Stalin, and by the end of the Congress would remove the dictator from the Red Square mausoleum, where he rested beside Lenin, and rebury him in less prominent ground beside a lower rank of communist heroes near the Kremlin wall.

What most caught the attention of delegates and the world, however, were two bombshells related to Berlin. One was figurative and the other very real.

Disappointing East Germany's Ulbricht, Khrushchev said he would drop his insistence on signing a peace treaty by year's end. His explanation was that Gromyko's recent talks with Kennedy showed that the Western powers "were disposed to seek a settlement" on Berlin.

Having offered Kennedy that carrot, Khrushchev then swung the nuclear stick. He departed from his prepared text to talk about Soviet military prowess, particularly when it came to missile development. He laughed that the Soviets had come so far that American spy ships were tracking and confirming the remarkable accuracy of their rockets.

Still in a jocular tone and speaking impromptu, Khrushchev then jolted his listeners with a revelation: "Since I have already wandered from my written text, I want to say that our tests of new nuclear weapons are also coming along very well. We shall shortly complete these tests—presumably at the end of October. We shall probably wind them up by detonating a hydrogen bomb with a yield of fifty million tons of TNT."

The delegates stood and broke into stormy applause. No one to that date had ever tested such a powerful weapon. Reporters scribbled furiously.

"We have said that we have a hundred-megaton bomb," he added, encouraged by the crowd reaction. "This is true. But we are not going to explode it, because even if we did so at the most remote site, we might knock out all of the windows."

Delegates roared and applauded wildly.

The atheist leader then turned his words to the Almighty. "But may God grant, as they used to say, that we are never called upon to explode these bombs over anybody's territory. This is the greatest wish of our lives."

It was classic Khrushchev. He had taken some pressure off Kennedy by lifting the deadline on negotiating a Berlin treaty even as he smacked him over the head with news of a coming nuclear test. On the final day of the Congress, the Soviet Union would detonate the most powerful nuclear weapon ever to be constructed. The "Tsar Bomba," as it would later be nicknamed in the West, had the equivalent of a thousand times the explosives used in the World War II bombings of Hiroshima and Nagasaki.

Again caught flat-footed, Kennedy knew that he had to respond.

THE WHITE HOUSE, WASHINGTON, D.C.
WEDNESDAY, OCTOBER 18, 1961

During an otherwise genial White House luncheon for Texas news executives the next day, the conservative publisher of the *Dallas Morning News*, E. M. "Ted" Dealey, challenged the president. "We can annihilate Russia," he said, "and should make that clear to the Soviet government."

Reading from a five-hundred-word statement that he had extracted from his pocket, Dealey declared, "The general opinion of the grassroots thinking of this country is that you and your administration are weak sisters." He said that what was needed was "a man on horseback," but that "many people in Texas and the Southwest think you are riding Caroline's tricycle."

On edge from Khrushchev's announcement and weeks of unrelenting pressure over Berlin, Kennedy responded with irritation. "The difference between you and me, Mr. Dealey, is that I was elected president of this country and you were not. I have the responsibility for the lives of a hundred eighty million Americans, which you have not. . . . Wars are easier to talk about than they are to fight. I'm just as tough as you are—and I didn't get elected President by arriving at soft judgments."

Kennedy was facing the hardest judgment call of his life over how he would conduct a nuclear war with the Soviet Union, and Khrushchev was making the exercise more than academic. The plan he was reviewing after weeks of intensive, highly classified meetings had as its goal the preemptive destruction of the Soviet nuclear arsenal so as not to leave a single weapon for reprisal. In rich detail, it spelled out U.S. bombers' flight paths, altitudes they must maintain to avoid detection, and which targets they would hit with what kind of nuclear weapons.

By the time the plan had percolated through the bureaucracy, dozens of drafts had been debated and the Berlin Wall had already been up for three weeks. Blandly titled "Strategic Air Planning and Berlin," the thirty-three-page memo reached General Maxwell Taylor, the president's military representative, on September 5. Author Carl Kaysen, one of the administration's young geniuses, concluded, "We have a fair probability of achieving a substantial measure of success" at a cost of "only" half a million to a million Soviet casualties. It included charts, however, showing that if surviving Soviet missiles hit the U.S., the fatalities could range between five and ten million, because of the population concentration in places like New York and Chicago. "In thermonuclear warfare," Kaysen dryly observed, "people are easy to kill."

For the previous month, Kaysen had been working as deputy special assistant to National Security Advisor Bundy after gaining influence inside the administration on a number of widely differing projects, ranging from international trade to the cost factors of airborne alert systems. The forty-one-year-old Harvard economics professor had served in London during World War II, picking out European bomb targets for the Office of Strategic Services, the then-new U.S. spy service.

Kaysen began his paper by noting the flaws in the so-called Single Integrated Operational Plan, or SIOP-62, the existing blueprint determining how Kennedy would use strategic striking power in the case of war. SIOP-62 called for sending 2,258 missiles and bombers, carrying a total of 3,423 nuclear weapons, against 1,077 "military and urban-industrial targets" through the "Sino-Soviet bloc." It estimated that the attack would kill 54 percent of the Soviet population (including 71 percent of the urban population) and destroy 82 percent of its buildings "as measured by floor space." Kaysen thought SIOP-62 actually underestimated casualties, as it was making estimates only for the first seventy-two hours of war.

Kaysen maintained that two circumstances required that SIOP-62 be replaced or significantly altered. First, he worried about a false alarm, which could arise from a "deliberate feint" from Khrushchev or a "misinterpretation of events" by either side. He argued that "if the present state of tension over Berlin persists over a period of months, it is likely that, at some point, a Soviet action will appear to threaten an attack on the United States with sufficient likelihood and imminence" to trigger nuclear response.

Kaysen asserted that the problem would come if Kennedy, following a nuclear decision, decided he wanted to recall the force because he had either been mistaken or misled. Kaysen said the current plan left him little capability to do that. A recall would also require a stand-down of about eight hours for the part of the force that was launched, providing Moscow a "period of degradation" that it could exploit.

Kaysen believed the larger problem—reinforced by Kennedy's August inaction over Berlin—was that the president would never accept the level of massive nuclear retaliation that would be demanded of him to repulse any Soviet conventional attack on West Germany or West Berlin. He asked bluntly: "Will the president be ready to take it? Soviet retaliation is inevitable; and most probably, it will be directed against our cities and those of our European allies."

The clear message was that Kennedy, some ten months into his administration, was facing a Berlin crisis that threatened to worsen and a strategic plan to address it that he was unlikely to use. Kaysen was asserting that the ongoing Berlin crisis made it necessary not only to theorize but to get specific about a first-strike plan if matters turned against the U.S. on the ground.

"What is required in these circumstances is something quite different," he said. "We should be prepared to initiate general war by our own first strike, but one planned for this occasion, rather than planned to implement a strategy of massive retaliation. We should seek the smallest possible list of targets, focusing on the long-range striking capacity of the Soviets, and avoiding, as much as possible, casualties and damage in Soviet civil society."

The idea as well was to "maintain in reserve a considerable fraction of our own strategic striking power." The author's logic was that such a force would deter Khrushchev from unleashing his surviving forces against American population centers. Kaysen was wagering as well that U.S. efforts to minimize Soviet civilian casualties might also reduce the enemy's lust for revenge that could broaden the war. Kaysen then provided in vivid detail a "more effective and less frightful" plan than SIOP-62 if the current crisis over Berlin resulted in a "major reverse on the ground in Western Europe."

It gave the president what he had been asking for throughout most of the year: a more *rational* nuclear war. It would allow him to destroy the Soviet Union's long-range nuclear capability while limiting damage to the United States and its allies.

Kaysen then laid out the details of a plan that Kennedy would read and reread before responding. U.S. strategic air forces—in small numbers, using wide dispersal and low-altitude penetration to avoid interception—would strike an estimated forty-six home bases for Soviet nuclear bombers, the bombers' twenty-six staging bases, and up to eight intercontinental ballistic missile sites with two aiming points for each site. The total targets for the first strike would be eighty-eight.

Kaysen reckoned that the first strike could be executed by fifty-five bombers, particularly B-47s and B-52s, assuming a 25 percent attrition rate that would leave the required forty-one planes. One could succeed with so few aircraft, he said, as they would "fan out and penetrate undetected at low altitude at a number of different points on the Soviet early-warning perimeter, then bomb and withdraw at low altitude."

Kaysen conceded the need for more studies and exercises to test his assumptions. "Two questions immediately arise about this concept," he said. "How valid are the assumptions, and do we possess the capability and skill to execute such a raid?" He answered that the assumptions were reasonable, that the U.S. had the military means, and that "while a wide range of outcomes is possible, we have a fair probability of achieving a substantial measure of success."

If one could avoid bombing mistakes, Kaysen figured, Soviet deaths from the initial raid could be limited to no more than a million and perhaps as few as 500,000—still horrendous, but a considerable margin less than SIOP-62's assumption that 54 percent, or more than a hundred million, of the Soviet population would perish.

In a White House that was unaccustomed to such cavalier discussion of carnage, Kaysen's report came as a shock. Chief Counsel Ted Sorensen shouted at Kaysen, "You're crazy! We shouldn't let guys like you around here." Marcus Raskin, a friend of Kaysen's on the NSC, never spoke to him again after he got wind of the report. "How does this make us any better than those who measured the gas ovens or the engineers who built the tracks for the death trains in Nazi Germany?" he frothed at Kaysen.

Kennedy didn't have the same misgivings, as he had been seeking precisely the analysis that he had been given. "Berlin developments may confront us with a situation where we may desire to take the initiative in the escalation of conflict from the local to the general war level," the president wrote in the list of questions he wanted to discuss at a meeting on September 19 with General Taylor, General Lyman Lemnitzer, chairman of the Joint Chiefs of Staff, and General Thomas S. "Tommy" Power, the commander in chief of the Strategic Air Command. The level of detail in his questions underscored the president's increasing scrutiny and understanding of nuclear strike issues. Kennedy was preparing himself to wage war.

Question #1: "Is it possible to get some alternatives into the plan soon, such as having alternative options for use in different situations?" Kennedy asked. He in particular wanted to know whether he could move away from the "optimum mix" of civilian and military targets and in certain contingencies exclude urban areas, or extract China or European satellites from the target list. "If so, at what risk?"

Question #2: If Berlin developments confronted Kennedy with a situation where he wanted to escalate from a local conflict to a general war level, the president wanted to know whether a successful surprise first strike was feasible against the Soviet long-range capability.

Question #3: Kennedy worried that a surprise attack on Soviet long-range striking power would leave "a sizable number" of medium-range missiles still poised to attack Europe. In short, he wanted to know the costs of protecting Europe as well as the U.S. He asked whether including these medium-range strike targets in the initial attack would "so enlarge the target list as to preclude tactical surprise."

Question #4: "I am concerned," Kennedy said, "over my ability to control our military effort once a war begins. I assume I can stop the strategic attack at any time, should I receive word the enemy has capitulated. Is that correct?"

He posed four more questions along similar lines, wondering whether he could avoid "redundant destruction" and recall subsequent weapons if the first nuke aimed at a target achieved its "desired results." If his decision to attack turned out to have been prompted by a false alarm, he wanted to know his options for recall.

The following day's National Security Council meeting failed to provide clear answers to many of the president's questions. It also showed how divided Kennedy's advisers remained over the notion of a limited nuclear war. The Strategic Air Command's General Tommy Power said, "The time of our greatest danger of a Soviet surprise attack is now and during the coming year. If a general atomic war is inevitable, the U.S. should strike first" after identifying the essential Soviet nuclear targets.

Power had directed the firebombing raids on Tokyo in March 1945 and was deputy chief of operations for U.S. Strategic Air Forces in the Pacific during the atomic bomb strikes on Hiroshima and Nagasaki. He had assisted General Curtis E. LeMay in building up the Strategic Air Command after he joined it in 1948, and under them it had become its own fiefdom. Brutal and easily angered, Power passionately believed the only way to keep nuclear-armed communists in check was if they believed they would be annihilated if they misbehaved.

When briefed on the long-term genetic harm done by nuclear fallout, Power once responded with perverse humor, "You know, it's not yet been proved to me that two heads aren't better than one." National Security Advisor Bundy was thinking of Power when he warned Kennedy that a subordinate commander had authority "to start the thermonuclear holocaust on his own initiative" if he couldn't reach the president after a Soviet attack.

Power argued to Kennedy that the Soviets were concealing "many times more" missiles than CIA spy photos revealed. He complained that he lacked intelligence on Soviet ICBM sites, and added that he believed the U.S. had only 10 percent photographic coverage of the Soviet Union. He told the president that twenty ICBM pads had been located, but that many times more might be in unmonitored areas. Lacking crucial data on the extent of the Soviet missile force, Power strongly recommended to Kennedy that he resume the U-2 flights he had promised Khrushchev he would prohibit.

Kennedy brushed aside Power's advice. Instead, he was fixated on getting the answer to his question of whether he really could launch a surprise strike on the Soviet Union without devastating retaliation. He also tasked the generals "to come up with an answer to this question: How much information does the Soviet Union need, and how long do they need to launch their missiles?"

Martin Hillenbrand, director of the Office of German Affairs at the State Department, noticed that with each additional day Kennedy lived through the Berlin Crisis, "he became more and more impressed with its complexity and its difficulties." For previous presidents, war was a cruel but desirable alternative to matters like Nazi viciousness or Japanese aggression. But for Kennedy, in Hillenbrand's view, war had become "almost identical with the problem of human survival."

With that sense of moment, on October 10 Kennedy called together top administration officials and military commanders in the Cabinet Room to finalize nuclear contingency plans for Berlin. Assistant Secretary of Defense Paul Nitze brought with him a document entitled *Preferred Sequence of Military Actions in a Berlin Conflict.*

Cool and rational, at age fifty-four Nitze had already become perhaps the most crucial U.S. player behind the scenes influencing policies that guided the development of nuclear weapons and governed their control. Reflecting on the failure of well-meaning actors to avoid conflict, he never forgot his experience as a young boy when he witnessed the beginning of World War I while traveling through his ancestral home of Germany, where he saw Munich crowds cheer the coming disaster.

Assigned by presidents Roosevelt and Truman to survey the impact of World War II strategic bombing, Nitze saw German big cities in ruins and scrutinized the impact of atomic weapons on Hiroshima and Nagasaki. However, nothing shaped his views about the importance of U.S. nuclear capability more than a preoccupation with strategic vulnerability that had grown out of his study of Pearl Harbor.

As Truman's chief of policy planning after the war, replacing the fired George Kennan, Nitze was the principal author in 1950 of the pivotal paper *United States Objectives and Programs for National Security*, or NSC 68. In a world where the U.S. had lost its nuclear monopoly, NSC 68 provided the rationale for significantly increased defense spending and formed the core of U.S. security policy for the next four decades, with its warning of the "Kremlin's design for world domination." Nitze believed that if Truman had not approved the development of the hydrogen bomb in that year, against considerable opposition, "the Soviets would have achieved unchallengeable nuclear superiority by the late 1950s."

As two Democratic hawks, Acheson and Nitze were chairman and vice chairman of the party's Foreign Affairs and Defense Committee, which laid the foundation for Kennedy's defense stance and notions of "flexible response" after his nomination.

Like Acheson, Nitze considered Berlin a proving ground for broader communist objectives to psychologically defeat the West by showing its impotence in the face of increased Soviet capabilities. Thus, he agreed with Acheson that the notion new talks could defuse the crisis was nonsense.

On August 13, Nitze had been at first furious that the U.S. had failed to respond in any way to the Berlin border closure. However, as the Pentagon further considered its response, he saw intelligence indicating that three Soviet divisions and two East German divisions had encircled Berlin. This suggested that Moscow was setting a trap in which the U.S. might knock down the barrier only to see the Soviets occupy all of Berlin. The Pentagon opted not to recommend a move against the Wall for fear it would bring a general war for which the U.S. was unready.

Now it was Nitze's task to sketch out how the U.S. should get ready in preparation for another Berlin confrontation. After August 13, he was asked to bring together military representatives from Britain, France, and West Germany to agree on how to respond to the next Soviet provocation in Berlin.

To safeguard Berlin access, the document they produced laid out four
detailed scenarios that would gradually escalate from small-scale conventional action to nuclear war. In drafting it, Nitze had seen "permutations
expanded like possible successive moves in a game of chess," until someone
suggested "it would take a piece of paper the size of a horse blanket to write
them all down." It was then that the group came up with an abbreviated
military response plan for Berlin that they called the "Pony Blanket." Nitze
was satisfied that he had transformed a program of mounting pressures
into an organized and coherent framework that gave America and its allies
greater confidence.

Kennedy arrived late at the NSC meeting to discuss the paper. Rusk had
reported to the group that Moscow would withdraw its deadline on the East
German peace treaty if talks with the U.S. proved promising. However, Rusk
still believed a military buildup was necessary in Europe. Secretary Mc-
Namara then sketched out his recommendations.

Kennedy quickly approved them all. They included the deployment to
Europe, starting on November 1, of eleven Air National Guard squadrons;
the return to Europe from the U.S. of seven Air Force squadrons from the
Tactical Air Command; and the pre-positioning of sufficient equipment in
Europe for one armored division and one infantry division. Through rotation, Kennedy would ensure he had at least two combat-ready battle groups
plus their support elements. At the same time he would deploy to Europe
the 3rd Armored Cavalry Regiment and its intelligence detachment from
Fort Meade, Maryland.

The president remained most concerned with how he would manage a
limited nuclear conflict. His nightmare was losing control and witnessing
the "funeral pyre" he'd spoken of at the United Nations less than a month
earlier. Questioning Nitze's document, what concerned him most was
whether it would really be possible to use nuclear weapons selectively without escalation to all-out war.

On that point, Nitze disagreed with his boss McNamara and believed
that an initial limited use of nuclear weapons "would greatly increase the
temptation" of the Soviets for a strategic strike. Thus, he argued, "it would

be best for us, in moving toward the use of nuclear weapons, to consider most seriously the option of an initial strategic strike of our own." He thought it was the only way to be victorious in a nuclear exchange, because the U.S. could lose if it allowed the Soviets the first blow.

Characteristically, Kennedy quietly absorbed the details and the gravity of their conversation, interposing occasional questions, while the men around him continued to discuss the most chilling of scenarios.

Rusk was concerned that the military strategists had forgotten the moral context: "The first side to use nuclear weapons will carry a very grave responsibility and endure heavy consequences before the rest of the world," he said.

Kennedy did not resolve the division of opinion in the room, but the group agreed to draft new instructions from the president to General Norstad, his Supreme Allied Commander Europe, to provide "clear guidance" on U.S. intentions for military contingencies.

WASHINGTON, D.C.
FRIDAY, OCTOBER 20, 1961

In the ten days that followed, the president was occupied by little else apart from Berlin and its related nuclear questions, his hopes for negotiations with Moscow, and his growing difficulties with his own allies.

The *Washington Post* reported on efforts to end racial discrimination in Maryland restaurants. A story on the front page of the *New York Times* reported that Supreme Court justices were hearing arguments related to antidiscrimination sit-ins in the South. Police were enforcing carefully laid school desegregation plans while white-robed-and-hooded Ku Klux Klansmen protested.

However, the president was preoccupied by thoughts of war and how he would conduct it. His concerns were infecting the American public. *Time* magazine ran on its cover a color portrait of Virgil Couch, head of the Office for Civil Defense. A banner headline announced: [NUCLEAR]

SHELTERS: HOW SOON—HOW BIG—HOW SAFE? Couch advised Americans that planning for nuclear attack should be as normal as getting smallpox vaccinations.

With Khrushchev's fifty-megaton announcement from three days earlier still reverberating, the president called together his top national security team to put the final touches on military instructions for NATO. It would not be an easy meeting.

His Joint Chiefs were engaged in verbal combat over Kennedy's planned conventional military buildup in Europe and its potential impact on the credibility of the U.S. nuclear deterrent.

Already, France's de Gaulle and Germany's Adenauer were arguing that Kennedy was too eager to negotiate West Berlin's future with Khrushchev while doing too little to convince Khrushchev that the president would be willing to use nuclear weapons to defend the city.

It seemed that only Macmillan agreed with Kennedy's heightened desire for talks with Moscow. Having been so at odds with Kennedy's hawkish approach toward the Soviets the previous spring, the prime minister saw with satisfaction that Kennedy was now embracing the more conciliatory British position toward Moscow. He was encouraged as he watched Kennedy grow increasingly "fed up" with both de Gaulle and Adenauer.

With the Allies deeply at odds over how to handle Berlin strategy, Kennedy made his move to settle differences. At the table for the 10:00 a.m. meeting in the Cabinet Room were the president's brother Bobby, Rusk, McNamara, Bundy, and Lemnitzer. Beside him was Deputy Secretary of Defense Roswell Gilpatric, who had taken the Pentagon lead on Russian nuclear threat issues. The other major players on Berlin policy were also there: Nitze; Berlin Task Force chief Foy Kohler; the State Department's leading German hand, Martin Hillenbrand; and—so often during crucial moments of the Berlin Crisis—the outside agitator, Dean Acheson.

Lemnitzer opened the meeting by reporting to the president on the "significant disagreement" within the Joint Chiefs about the necessity for a rapid military buildup. Air Force chief General Curtis LeMay and the Navy's

Admiral George Whelan Anderson Jr. shared General Norstad's view that no large-scale conventional buildup was required in "the immediate future." But Lemnitzer and General George Decker, chief of staff of the U.S. Army, agreed with McNamara that such a buildup was required right away.

Rusk laid out Norstad's logic that a Berlin dispute would escalate so rapidly to nuclear war that a conventional buildup would be irrelevant. Beyond that, said Rusk, Norstad feared that the conventional buildup could "degrade both the credibility and capability of nuclear forces." In representing this view, Norstad had joined ranks with both the French and Germans against the president.

As so often happened at complex times related to Berlin, Kennedy sought Acheson's opinion. The memo summing up the meeting, drafted by Bundy, said with a tone of derision: "From that point on the meeting was dominated by Mr. Acheson's arguments." Bundy put it more graciously later: "As usual, Mr. Acheson was the belle of the ball."

Acheson had no patience for Allied sensitivities. He said U.S. officials at a moment of great national urgency were spending too much time getting agreement from the French, British, West Germans, and others, when it was the U.S. that would have to shoulder the burden. Acheson argued that the U.S. needed to move new divisions to Europe by November, irrespective of what the Allies might think or say.

Acheson believed the president's demonstration of intent by sending conventional forces to Europe would help "diplomatically and politically." He disagreed that nuclear logic diminished the need for American conventional action. Serious military movement by the U.S. is "an ominous thing," he said, that conveyed "the serious purpose of the American government."

Kennedy said he worried about "the gold drain," meaning the cost of such a move. McNamara and Gilpatric assured him that further negotiations with Allies could help spread or defray the costs.

A few hours after the meeting, Bundy would send a top-secret presidential letter to Norstad to which he attached the so-called Pony Blanket. Titled "U.S. Policy on Military Actions in a Berlin Conflict," it would be

approved by the president three days later as National Security Action
Memorandum No. 109. Organized under four Roman-numeral stages, it
laid out the graduated steps to be taken if the Soviets cut off access to Berlin.

- *Stage I:* If the Soviets and East Germans interfered with West Berlin
  access but didn't block it entirely, the plan prescribed U.S., French, and
  British probes up the Autobahn of a platoon or less on the ground and
  a fighter escort in the air. The document noted that such a response
  was sufficiently limited to avoid any risk of war.

- *Stage II:* If the Soviets persisted in blocking access despite Allied
  actions, the West would escalate and NATO would begin supportive
  noncombatant activities such as economic embargoes, maritime
  harassment, and UN protests. The Allies would reinforce their troops
  and mobilize to prepare for further escalation. The document warned
  that without further buildup, Allied options would be limited and
  could create delays that could weaken nuclear credibility, threaten West
  Berlin's viability, and erode Alliance resolve.

- *Stage III:* The West would escalate further against a continued
  communist blockade of West Berlin. That would include expanding
  ground operations on East German territory by such measures as
  sending three armored divisions up the Autobahn to West Berlin and
  establishing local air superiority through strikes on non-Soviet air-
  fields. "Military overpowering of determined Soviet resistance is not
  feasible," the report conceded, then added, "The risks rise, as do the
  military pressures on the Soviets." Most controversially, Kennedy was
  calling at this point for global actions against Soviet interests. That
  would include exploiting U.S. naval superiority as part of a maritime
  blockade, which would further delay the moment of nuclear truth
  while diplomats bargained.

- That brought the report to the most ominous *Stage IV:* Only if the
  Soviets still did not respond to substantial use of Allied conventional
  weapons would Kennedy escalate to nuclear war. He would then have
  the choice of one or all of the following: selective strikes to demonstrate

the will to use nuclear weapons; limited use of nuclear weapons to achieve tactical advantage; and, finally, general war.

With considerable understatement, the paper warned, "The Allies only partially control the timing and scale of nuclear weapons use. Such use might be initiated by the Soviets, at any time after the opening of small-scale hostilities. Allied initiation of limited nuclear action may elicit a reply in kind; it may also prompt unrestrained preemptive attack."

It was a sobering document. Ten months into his presidency, Kennedy had laid out the military sequence that could result in nuclear war over Berlin.

In his accompanying letter to General Norstad, Kennedy wrote, "This requires vigor in preparation, readiness for action, and caution against going off half-cocked." He said all contingencies required rapid additions to his forces and deployment to the central front. He told Norstad that if the Soviets deployed sufficient forces to defeat the West, then the response, for which he would receive specific directions, would be nuclear.

Kennedy argued to a skeptical Norstad—and by association, the French and Germans—that building up Allied conventional forces would not contradict the message he wished to send the Soviets that he was ready to go to nuclear war if necessary. "It seems evident to me," Kennedy wrote Norstad, "that our nuclear deterrent will not be credible to the Soviets unless they are convinced of NATO's readiness to become engaged on a lesser level of violence and are thereby made to realize the great risks of escalation to nuclear war."

A flurry of diplomatic activity—memos, phone calls, meetings— accompanied Kennedy's preparations for war. As so often at times of high stress, the president asked a wide group of experts to weigh in. Kennedy had asked them to be frank, and his trusted ambassador to the United Kingdom, David Bruce—a former ambassador to Germany—did not hold back.

Bruce said that through Kennedy's acceptance of the Wall without any military response, the president had made the U.S. presence in Berlin more vulnerable and had eroded West Berlin and West German morale. The Soviets had always accepted the U.S. role in the city only because of the military impossibility of removing it.

Bruce warned the president that the Soviet objective wasn't West Berlin itself but rather possession over time of "West Germany with its immense resources." He worried as well about Kennedy's wavering on the American commitment to the long-term goal of German unification. Bruce told Kennedy that it was those promises that had convinced Adenauer in 1953 to refuse "the tricky but tempting Soviet offer of reunification in favor of alliance with the NATO countries." In other words, Bruce was saying, Kennedy's willingness to depart from this commitment invited a German response that Washington might not like.

Using a captivating turn of phrase, Bruce argued that the reality of Germany's division was not sufficient reason to give it official recognition as a permanent matter: "For no government in Western Germany could survive the open acceptance by its allies that what *has at least until now been hope deferred is to be dismissed as forever hopeless*" (italics added). Bruce was blunt: Kennedy had to face the historic burden of the problems he had helped to create. "We are close, I suppose, to the moment of decision," he wrote. "I would consider it essential that we take, and make credible, the decision to engage if necessary in nuclear war rather than lose West Berlin, and consequently, West Germany."

HOT SPRINGS, VIRGINIA
SATURDAY, OCTOBER 21, 1961

Kennedy sensed that time was short.

Worried that Khrushchev might take military action soon, the president opted to launch a preemptive nuclear strike of a different sort that would reach Khrushchev as a humiliating blow at his October Party Congress.

Kennedy decided to make public previously secret details about the size, power, and superiority of the U.S. nuclear arsenal. Kennedy's satellite intelligence was making increasingly clear the extent of American nuclear dominance, but he reckoned Khrushchev lacked similar intelligence on U.S. capabilities.

President Eisenhower had never revealed what he knew about Soviet military inferiority because he did not want to accelerate Soviet efforts to arm up. It was lack of that intelligence that led Kennedy to falsely charge that Eisenhower had allowed a "missile gap" to form in Moscow's favor. Ironically, Kennedy now argued that showing America's hand was necessary to keep America safe. Not coincidentally, it was also smart politics.

Kennedy feared that he was looking weak to Moscow, the Allies, and Americans, when in truth he was strong enough to defeat Moscow or any other country in any military conflict. The president thought it would be too belligerent for him to send that message personally, so he picked for the job the number-two official at the Defense Department, Roswell Gilpatric, who was already scheduled to speak on October 21 to the Business Council in Hot Springs, Virginia.

It was an unlikely audience for such a significant moment, but the spokesman Kennedy had chosen was ideal. Gilpatric had become a personal friend of Jacqueline Kennedy, who called him "the second most attractive man" at the Pentagon, after McNamara. Kennedy liked and trusted the smooth, Yale-educated Wall Street lawyer. A young Pentagon strategist named Daniel Ellsberg drafted the speech, but the president himself collaborated on it with Bundy, Rusk, and McNamara.

Knowing nothing of the Bolshakov back channel or the exchange of private letters with Khrushchev, Ellsberg asked Kaysen whether it wouldn't be more effective for Kennedy to send a more private message to the Soviet leader about U.S. superiority? Why all the noise? Couldn't Kennedy just send him the precise coordinates of Soviet ICBMs and perhaps enclose copies of satellite photos?

However, that overlooked Kennedy's desire for a highly public response to reassure his domestic and West European audiences. White House spokesmen invited top national reporters to Hot Springs and briefed them beforehand so that the speech's importance wouldn't be missed. "Berlin is the emergency of the moment because the Soviets have chosen to make it so," Gilpatric said.

> We have responded immediately with our Western Allies by reinforcing our garrisons in that beleaguered city. We have called up some 150,000 reservists, increased our draft calls and extended the service of many who are in uniform. . . .
>
> But our real strength in Berlin—and at any other point in the perimeter of the free world's defenses that might tempt the Communist probes—is much more broadly based. Our confidence in our ability to deter Communist action, or resist Communist blackmail, is based upon a sober appreciation of the relative military power of the two sides. The fact is that this nation has a nuclear retaliatory force of such lethal power that any enemy move which brought it into play would be an act of self-destruction on his part.

Gilpatric then provided previously undisclosed details on hundreds of intercontinental bombers, including some six hundred heavy bombers, which could devastate the Soviet Union with the help of highly developed refueling techniques. He spoke of land-based and carrier-based strike forces that "could deliver additional hundreds of megatons." Gilpatric said the U.S. had tens of thousands of tactical and strategic nuclear delivery vehicles, with more than one warhead for each of them.

"Our forces are so deployed and protected that a sneak attack could not effectively disarm us," he said. Even after enduring a surprise attack, Gilpatric said that U.S. destructive power would be far greater than any enemy could muster, and that America's retaliatory force would survive better than that of the Soviets because of its concealment, its mobility, and its hardened targets.

"The Soviets' bluster and threats of rocket attacks against the free world—aimed particularly at the European members of the NATO alliance—must be evaluated against the hard facts of United States nuclear superiority," said Gilpatric. "The United States does not seek to resolve disputes by violence. But if forceful interference with our rights and obligations should lead to violent conflict—*as it well might*—the United States does not intend to be defeated" (italics added).

Finally, Kennedy had called Khrushchev's bluff.

PALACE OF CONGRESSES, MOSCOW
SUNDAY, OCTOBER 22, 1961

Given the drumbeat in Hot Springs, Virginia, Khrushchev, back in Moscow, began to worry that a Berlin conflict was coming.

During a break in the ongoing Moscow Party Congress, General Konev presented Khrushchev with evidence that the Americans were preparing for war. Though Konev remained by title the Soviet commander in Germany, Khrushchev considered much of his job to be as liaison, and the general was in Moscow as a party delegate.

Khrushchev would later recall that Konev brought him intelligence on exactly what day and hour the West would begin hostilities in Berlin. "They were preparing bulldozers to break down our border installations. The bulldozers would be followed by tanks and wave after wave of jeeps with infantry men." Khrushchev believed that the action had been timed to coincide with the first days of his Party Congress.

Though there is no reason to doubt that Khrushchev got word of Clay's unauthorized tank maneuvers, he could blame the timing of what followed more on his bothersome ally, Walter Ulbricht. Upset by Khrushchev's decision in Moscow to abandon the East German peace treaty, Ulbricht decided again to take matters into his own hands in East Berlin. This time, however, he would face an America willing to push back.

The stage was set for the first and last direct U.S.–Soviet military confrontation.

18

SHOWDOWN AT CHECKPOINT CHARLIE

I do not believe that you sent me here to live in a vacuum and I know that
I can be of no real service if it is deemed wise to be extremely cautious in
Berlin. I may add, too, that I did not come here to add to your problems
and that I am gladly expendable.

General Lucius Clay to President Kennedy, October 18, 1961

In the nature of things, we had long since decided that entry into Berlin is
not a vital interest which would warrant determined recourse to force to
protect and sustain. Having for this reason acquiesced in the building of
the wall we must recognize frankly among ourselves that we thus went a
long way in accepting the fact that the Soviets could, in the case of East
Berlin, as they have done previously in other areas under their effective
physical control, isolate their unwilling subjects.

Secretary of State Dean Rusk to General Clay, October 26, 1961

DAHLEM DISTRICT, WEST BERLIN
SUNDAY, OCTOBER·22, 1961

The evening that would trigger the year's decisive crisis began innocently.
E. Allan Lightner Jr., America's top diplomat in West Berlin, hurried his wife, Dorothy, so that they would not be late for a performance
of an experimental Czech theater company across town in East Berlin. She
had read about the show in a local paper, and it seemed an inviting diver-

sion after two months and nine days of unrelenting pressure after the Berlin border closure.

It was crisp autumn weather in West Berlin's smart Dahlem district, where the Lightners lived in a spacious villa that had been confiscated from a ranking Nazi after the war. Their neighbors were preparing for winter. Some had used the day to rake their lawns clean of brown and yellow leaves shed from beech and oak trees. Others were removing their heavy down comforters from storage to air them out across clotheslines and on balconies.

Though Lightner had failed to anticipate the Wall, it had done his career no harm. No posting had a higher profile than one on the Cold War's fault line. Like many State Department wives of the time, Dorothy embraced her husband's career and its privileges; staff considered her pushy and overly demanding of their services. The Lightners had always savored their outings in the Soviet zone, where the socialist world's top artists performed. However, since August 13, their visits had taken on greater symbolic value. East Berliners who recognized Lightner would often thank him just for showing up.

Lightner knew there was a slim chance their journey across town would be more eventful than usual. That week, the so-called East German People's Police, the Volkspolizei, or Vopos for short, had begun spot checking documents of Allied civilians. The move was not only in violation of the four-power procedures but it also contradicted Soviet instructions, most recently from Soviet Defense Minister Marshal Rodion Malinovsky, that the East Germans should change nothing at the border without Soviet sanction.

Ulbricht had apparently approved the move from his position in Moscow, where he was fuming over the content of Khrushchev's speech to the Party Congress. Though Kennedy had considered the Soviet leader's address to be belligerent, Ulbricht had focused instead on Khrushchev's decision to extend his year-end deadline for a war-ending peace treaty. In Ulbricht's view, Khrushchev was back to his old habit of dithering over Berlin at East German expense. Ulbricht's own speech three days later had called the treaty a "task of the utmost urgency." Ulbricht needed the treaty to consolidate his August triumph by further expanding his control of East Berlin while isolating and demoralizing West Berlin.

Yet words had never been enough with Khrushchev, so Ulbricht would unilaterally expand border inspections, figuring the West would complain but not resist after having accepted the far greater indignity of the border closure. In doing so, however, the East German leader was underestimating the determination of the newest U.S. factor on the ground: General Lucius Clay.

Together, Ulbricht and Clay would initiate a superpower confrontation that their masters in Moscow and Washington had neither wanted nor anticipated—though both adversaries would suspect the showdown was by the other side's design.

Encouraged by Clay, that week Lightner had instructed his U.S. Mission to resist the new East German procedures. He had prohibited his staff from submitting to the checks, and his own secretary had turned back her car just a day earlier rather than show her papers. Lightner and Clay were livid that British Prime Minister Macmillan had accepted the new controls without a peep of protest, which they considered another dose of British appeasement. London's orders to local commanders were clear: after ceding the wall, this wasn't a battle worth fighting.

Clay disagreed. If Washington permitted the East Germans to interfere further with what had been Allied rights since 1945, Clay was convinced the U.S. would undermine already fragile West Berlin morale and erode what remained of Allied legal standing. Given his preparatory conversations in Washington, he also remained confident that Kennedy was more determined than his advisers to hold the line in Berlin. For the moment, however, his enemies had been pushing back because they sensed Clay lacked the influence with Kennedy that he had won with Truman.

So for Clay, the situation presented a triple opportunity. First, he could demonstrate renewed U.S. resolve in Berlin. Second, he could restore the self-confidence of both U.S. troops and West Berliners. Finally, he could demonstrate to his opponents in Moscow and Washington that he had President Kennedy's backing.

There was only one problem: Clay himself was uncertain where his wavering president stood.

Unlike Clay, Lightner did not consider himself a Cold Warrior, but that's what he was. The fifty-three-year-old Princetonian derided as "parlor pinks" his fellow Ivy League intellectuals who wrote and spoke naively about "the great Russian experiment" of communism. He grumbled to Dorothy that a couple of months in the Soviet Union would change their tune fast enough. Experience had shaped those views. Lightner had been posted as a young man to Stalin's Russia, until 1941, when he'd evacuated wartime Moscow with the embassy's documents. After that, he had worked with anticommunist exiles in Scandinavia, shared bomb shelters in London with intrepid Brits, and had a hand in sculpting the postwar agreements that he was sorry had ceded so much of Europe to Soviet control.

Lightner told friends that if Clay had been present on August 13, the U.S. military would have broken through the earlier barriers, and the East Germans would not have risked war to replace them. He bought into Clay's argument that the U.S could not afford to retreat further, but he worried that Clay would not be able to overcome a far more bureaucratic U.S. structure in Berlin than the one he had faced in 1948. Lightner bridled at his own confusing, double reporting line—as the number two to both General Watson in Berlin and Ambassador Dowling in Bonn.

As that night's script would have it, East German police stopped Lightner's Volkswagen sedan as it snaked through the first of the checkpoint's three low red-and-white zigzag concrete barriers—two jutting out from the curbside to the left and another reaching in from the right. Following procedure, Lightner refused to show his papers to the East Germans and insisted on seeing a Soviet representative. Most often, the East German police would then wave American diplomats through. Under the new orders, however, the East German officer refused to let Lightner pass. Given it was Sunday, he said he could not reach a Soviet representative and then repeated his demand that Lightner show his papers or turn back.

Again Lightner refused, and was now egged on by Dorothy, who lectured the East German on four-power rights from the passenger side of their car. For the next forty-five minutes, tempers flared, voices rose, and arguments raged, but still no Soviet official appeared. So Lightner concluded it was time to escalate. After sending an alert through to Clay from his special car phone, Lightner prepared to muscle through. Though he knew the Vopos had shoot-to-kill orders for countrymen trying to escape, he thought it was a safe risk that they would not shoot an American diplomat trying to enter. That would be an act of war.

"Look," Lightner said to the policeman by his window, "I'm sorry, but I'm going to assert my Allied right for us to enter any sector of Berlin."

He gunned his engine.

"Get out of the way! We're coming through!"

Lightner jerked his car forward, forcing a couple of Vopos to leap aside. However, the vehicle could negotiate the tight, concrete maze only in slow motion. So an expanded group of Vopos on foot caught up to the car and stopped him again. This time they surrounded his vehicle.

One shouted angrily: "You can wait here until morning for a Russian to show up! If he shows up even then!"

In the background, Clay had begun moving the military pieces. He had ordered forward a platoon from the 2nd Battle Group to make its way the ten miles to Checkpoint Charlie from McNair Barracks in Lichterfelde with two armored personnel carriers, closely trailed by four M48 tanks mounted with bulldozers. To direct the operation, Clay and the Berlin military commander, General Watson, had retreated to the emergency operations center, known as "the bunker," established for just such an event in the basement of the U.S. consulate on the Clayallee. Though built initially in 1936 as a subheadquarters for the Third Reich's Luftwaffe, the building had served as Clay's nerve center during the Berlin Airlift and it would do so again now.

As the drama unfolded, U.S. provost marshal Lieutenant Colonel Robert Sabolyk monitored the scene at Checkpoint Charlie through binoculars from his white wooden military police shack a hundred yards away from the confrontation. With orders to keep matters under control until reinforcements arrived, the former collegiate boxer jumped into his staff car and sped forward around the first barrier, then steered wide around the second, screeching to a halt directly in front of Lightner's Volkswagen. He nearly amputated the black-booted legs of several Vopos, who jumped back and screamed in protest.

About then, four American tanks rumbled up to the thick white-painted borderline that designated the West Berlin limits. Another MP ran from the command shack to Dorothy Lightner's door and politely suggested she leave the immobilized VW. She refused to budge from her husband's side.

So the MP retreated to the shack, only to return several minutes later. "I'm sorry, but General Clay *orders* Mrs. Lightner to get out," he said.

He added in a whisper to her husband, so as not to be overheard by the Vopos: "We have a project in which we don't want Mrs. Lightner to be involved."

Once the MP had cleared her from the scene, two infantry squads of four men each unsheathed the bayonets of their M14 rifles and took up positions on either side of Friedrichstrasse. With the gun barrels of four U.S. tanks pointing directly at them, the Vopos pulled back. Lightner shifted into first gear and drove his VW slowly forward, flanked by the two U.S. Army squads. Having passed the last barrier and thus successfully penetrated communist territory, the platoon leader asked Lightner whether they should stop there.

"No," the diplomat said.

It was the first time in postwar Berlin that a fully armed infantry unit from U.S. occupying forces had marched into the Soviet sector. To further establish the continued right of Allied free passage, Lightner drove two blocks into East Berlin to the next intersection, then turned the car around and started back—all the time escorted by his armed guard. With U.S. cannons trained on them, East German police held their positions.

Safely back on American ground, Lightner prepared to drive through a second time to make his point. By this time, word of the confrontation had spread across Berlin. Reporters and photographers had gathered to track each move. With his heart beating through his chest, Albert Hemsing jumped into Lightner's passenger seat. The German-born forty-year-old public information officer had worked for the Marshall Plan's film unit in Paris after the war, making movies to support the European reconstruction effort. But he'd never been in this sort of action adventure. Vopos would later insist his breath smelled of alcohol.

When East German police blocked Lightner's path again, he waved out his window for the armed units to rejoin him. They escorted him through once more, and the East Germans again stood aside. In the meantime, the U.S. Mission's political adviser, Howard Trivers, had telephoned Soviet headquarters to request that a Russian officer come to Checkpoint Charlie and set matters straight.

By the time Lightner's VW returned from its second round-trip, a Soviet representative had arrived. Following talks with the Vopos and the Americans, the Soviet apologized that the East Germans had failed to recognize Lightner's seniority. So Lightner drove through a third time, on this occasion trailed by a second civilian car. The Vopos stood aside again, and it seemed that the U.S. victory was complete.

The two U.S. vehicles then engaged in something of a victory lap, driving up Friedrichstrasse to Unter den Linden, East Berlin's broad central boulevard, then turning left at the Brandenburg Gate, and then turning left again back to Friedrichstrasse. At about 10:00 p.m., a more senior Soviet official arrived, the deputy political adviser Colonel Lazarev. He apologized for the East German behavior, blaming it on the lack of facsimiles of Allied license plates from which they could judge which vehicles were to be checked. However, at the same time he angrily protested the U.S. "armed incursion" into the Soviet zone.

Lightner and his wife had missed their theater date, but Clay congratulated them on their performance. The next morning Clay crowed to the press that the "fiction is now destroyed" that it was the East Germans who were responsible for preventing Allied access to East Berlin.

His victory, however, would be a brief one. The same morning, the East

German government published an official decree that it would henceforth require *all* foreigners—except Allied military men in uniform—to show ID before entering "democratic" Berlin. The East German news agency ADN condemned the Sunday-evening incident as a "border provocation" prompted, it said, by an unknown civilian (Lightner) with an unknown woman (Dorothy), later to be joined by a drunk (Hemsing).

Once East German radio had the names of the Americans involved, it beamed a broadcast in English aimed at U.S. soldiers: "It will be a long time before Minister Lightner takes his girlfriend out and tries to shack up with her in East Berlin over the weekend."

Back in Washington, Kennedy was annoyed. The president was trying to launch negotiations with the Soviets, not provoke a new confrontation. "We didn't send [Lightner] there to go to the opera in East Berlin," he said, getting the event wrong and overlooking the fact that Lightner had acted according to the guidelines of his own personal representative.

At the same time, Kennedy was dealing with another problem. Just four days earlier Clay had tabled an offer to resign if he wasn't allowed to be more effective. The president could prevent a political earthquake only by providing Clay more freedom to maneuver.

U.S. MILITARY HEADQUARTERS, WEST BERLIN
WEDNESDAY, OCTOBER 18, 1961

Mounting frustration had prompted General Clay to include an offer to resign in the first personal letter he had written to President Kennedy since his return to Berlin.

National Security Advisor Bundy had warned Kennedy when he chose Clay that he was risking "another MacArthur–Truman affair," recalling the politically damaging decision by President Truman to fire General Mac-Arthur after the general had publicly disagreed with the president's Korean War policy. MacArthur had wanted to bomb China at the time, and Bundy reckoned there was every chance Clay would want to be more aggressive in Berlin than Kennedy, at a time when his administration was considering making major Berlin concessions to Khrushchev.

Though in his letter Clay offered to step down more quietly than Mac-Arthur had done, he must have known that the reasons for his departure from Berlin would almost certainly leak and then only further inflame Kennedy's critics and more deeply dishearten Berliners.

Clay began by apologizing to the president for his letter's length, 1,791 words, and for the fact that he hadn't written earlier. He explained to Kennedy that he considered the many other incidents he had confronted since his arrival in Berlin not to have been worthy of presidential attention.

Above all, he wrote the president, "we must retain the confidence of West Berliners. Otherwise, the flight of capital and responsible citizens could destroy our position here, and the indicated loss of confidence in us would spread throughout the world." While the Berliner cared little about French or British behavior, Clay argued, "if we fail, he is dismayed."

Clay held no punches. He indirectly criticized the president's handling of the August 13 border closure, which he believed could have been contested with little risk. "I do not believe we should have gone to war to stop the creation of the Wall," he said, but he added, "At a minimum, we could have moved back and forth across selected places on the border with unarmed military trucks and this limited action might well have prevented the Wall."

However, Clay was quick to blame not Kennedy but rather his Berlin underlings. "I was amazed to find that no specific action to this end was recommended here," he said. He criticized what he considered a risk-averse culture that had evolved among his Berlin ranks. "It takes only a few disapprovals to discourage independent thinking and positive recommendations," he said. He worried that Kennedy lacked access to more independent viewpoints like his own because even "as able a Commander as [NATO Supreme Commander Lauris] Norstad" was influenced by Allied reluctance.

Clay then came to the point: the "urgent need to stop the trespassing on our rights" by East German forces "while Soviet forces have been far in the background." He did not like the fact that the European Command was "tossing aside lightly" his recommendations that the U.S. must answer minor incidents. He wanted the president to give him more personal authority to address such tests of American will as the East German border checks, because their sum total was more serious than Kennedy's foreign policy advisers realized.

The general wrote with the self-assurance of a man who knew he had shaped history through the same sort of direct communication with a previous president. "If we are to react properly and promptly," he said, "the local commander must have the authority in an emergency to act immediately with my advice and consent within the full range of the authority you have delegated to our Military Command in Europe."

Clay wanted the president to free General Watson, the local Berlin commander, of the constraints being placed upon him by General Clarke in Heidelberg and General Norstad in Paris. While he acknowledged that the U.S. could not alter the Berlin situation militarily, he said, "We can lose Berlin if we are unwilling to take some risk in using force. . . . We could easily be backed into war by failing to make it clearly evident on the ground that we have reached the danger point."

Clay defended the actions he had taken thus far, which he knew Kennedy's advisers had opposed, particularly in freeing the Steinstücken refugees and running military patrols on the Autobahn. He insisted, "These few simple actions on our part have eased tension here and restored confidence in West Berlin." He told the president it had to be a priority of the U.S. to defend its right of free passage across Checkpoint Charlie, not for its own sake but because West Berliners were watching. For that reason, Clay said, he was "pushing as many vehicles as possible through each day."

Though the president had not asked him to do so, Clay then laid out a military contingency plan for Kennedy should the Soviets push back, much as he had done for Truman after the Soviet embargo: "If we are stopped on the highway [to Berlin], we must probe quickly and, I would think, from Berlin with light military strength to find out the depth of the intent [of the enemy]. If our probe is stopped by superior force and compelled to withdraw, we should resort to an immediate airlift concurrently and publicly apply economic sanction and blockade in an attempt to force Soviet action. If these steps are taken concurrently there will be no panic in West Berlin and we will gain the time for you to make the *ultimate decision* with calm and objective judgment."

When Clay mentioned "the ultimate decision," Kennedy would know he was speaking of nuclear conflict. Clay wrote coolly, "If our probe results in the destruction and capture of the force involved, it is of course evident that the Soviet government wants war."

Clay closed by promising to write shorter correspondence in the future. He wrote of how honored he was to serve as Kennedy's point man in Berlin, but added, "I realize no one knows quite what this means." He warned Kennedy that "any failure to act positively and determinedly with me here in this capacity will be assumed to have your direct approval. . . . I do not believe that you sent me here to live in a vacuum and *I know that I can be of no real service if it is deemed wise to be extremely cautious in Berlin*" (italics added).

What followed was the general's resignation offer. In his military career, Clay had gained something of a reputation for his occasional threats to step down, and in almost all of those cases it had achieved his purpose. Clay had found that a resignation offer was sometimes the only way to get his superiors' attention.

Clay weighed each word carefully, expressing the loyalty of a soldier to his commander in chief, but questioning how he could continue to serve effectively under the existing circumstances. "I may add, too, that I did not come here to add to your problems and that I am gladly expendable. I do want you to know that I would never permit myself to be made into a controversial figure in these critical times and that if you decide, or if I find that I must report to you, that I serve no useful purpose here, I would withdraw only in a manner which would meet with your approval and would not add to the problem here."

With that, he signed off:

With high respect,
>Faithfully yours,
>Lucius D. Clay,
>General, Retired,
>U.S. Army.

At Kennedy's instruction, the U.S. ambassador to Paris, General James M. Gavin, had arranged a meeting with President Charles de Gaulle to respond to the French leader's letter that Kennedy had read with considerable irritation just two days earlier.

At a time when Kennedy badly wanted a common Allied front behind his desire to engage Moscow in new Berlin talks, de Gaulle had become his most troublesome ally and was egging on West German Chancellor Adenauer as well. De Gaulle had refused to join even the preliminary discussions among the Americans, British, and West Germans regarding the possibility of new negotiations with the Soviets—and no amount of cajoling or wooing seemed to move him.

De Gaulle had disapproved of the Rusk–Gromyko talks that had taken place so soon after the border closure because they gave the impression that the U.S. had accepted Berlin's permanently divided state and was willing to discuss with Moscow a recognition of that status. He worried further that Kennedy was even willing to discuss with the Soviets the future of West Germany's alliance membership. The French leader saw no circumstances under which talks with Khrushchev could result in anything but further concessions that would negatively alter the political balance in Europe and "create a psychological demoralization, difficult to contain, in the countries that belong to our alliance, particularly in Germany, and could encourage the Soviets to undertake a further advance."

In his letter, de Gaulle had discarded all of the fatherly warmth he had shown during Kennedy's Paris visit ahead of Vienna. His language was clear and tough: "I must say, Mr. President, that today more than ever, I believe the policy to be pursued should be as follows: to refuse to consider changing the status quo of Berlin and the present situation in Germany, and consequently [to refuse] to negotiate concerning them, so long as the Soviet Union does not refrain from acting unilaterally and so long as it does not cease to threaten."

As harsh as it was, de Gaulle's letter had merely built upon a confrontational tone he had established with Kennedy immediately following August 13. As early as two weeks after that, Kennedy had asked for de Gaulle's help in influencing Third World opinion against communism. He also had said he wanted French assistance in his efforts to reach out to Moscow for new negotiations on Berlin.

De Gaulle rejected Kennedy's plea for help in the Third World, arguing that underdeveloped countries lacked the West's burden of responsibility, and "for the most part have already made up their minds, and you know in what way." De Gaulle was all the more clear in his opposition to new talks with the Soviets due to "the threats that they are hurling at us and the actual acts that they are committing in violation of agreements."

The French president warned Kennedy that any negotiations so closely following the August border closure would be understood by the Soviets as "notice of our surrender" and thus would be a grave blow to NATO. Khrushchev, he wrote, would only use the talks to apply greater pressures to Berliners.

Despite two months of U.S. diplomatic efforts since then to win over de Gaulle, including Kennedy's personal correspondence, the French leader had only hardened his position. On October 14, Kennedy had informed de Gaulle that he had achieved a "breakthrough" with Moscow in that Khrushchev had agreed to negotiate directly with the Allies over Berlin and not require them to deal with East Germany. Kennedy had said that he hoped to organize a mid-November meeting of Allied foreign ministers to prepare for new Berlin negotiations with Moscow. Kennedy had assured de Gaulle,

"We have no intention of withdrawing from Berlin nor do we intend to give our rights away in any negotiations." He argued, however, that the Allies should make every diplomatic effort possible before Berlin moved "to the stage of great and dramatic crisis." Kennedy said what he wanted was Allied clarity of purpose and military preparation "before the ultimate confrontation."

De Gaulle scoffed at Kennedy's notion that Khrushchev had made a concession regarding East Germany. He dismissed Kennedy's fear of war, saying Khrushchev "does not give the impression that the Kremlin is really prepared to hurl the thunderbolt. A wild beast that is going to spring does so without waiting that long."

With that as prelude, Ambassador Gavin knew that he was in for a difficult meeting. Kennedy had chosen Gavin for the Paris job in part because his military record made him one of the few men available whom de Gaulle respected. He had been the youngest major general to command a division in World War II, and his men called him "Jumping Jim" for his willingness despite his rank to join combat drops with his paratroopers. Nevertheless, de Gaulle spoke to him with characteristic condescension.

De Gaulle told Gavin that although he would do nothing to prevent the U.S. from holding a November meeting of the Allies, Kennedy would have to do so without French participation.

Gavin asked whether de Gaulle didn't think it would be better to participate and make clear in a common Allied front "our intent to engage in hostilities" if the Soviets pursued their current course.

De Gaulle told Gavin he believed the Soviets had only two options, and neither of them required negotiations. Either the Soviets did not want to wage a general and nuclear war, as de Gaulle believed was the case—thus there was no hurry to talk to them—or they did want to go to war, in which circumstance the Allies should refuse talks because they then "would be negotiating under direct threat."

"One cannot make working arrangements with people who are threatening them," de Gaulle told Gavin. Driving home his point, de Gaulle said the Allies could not negotiate with the Soviets "when they have threatened us with the atomic bomb, built the wall in Berlin, threatened to sign a treaty with East Germany with no promise to guarantee access to Berlin, and indulged in saber-rattling in general." His recipe: "If they apply force, we will do the same and see what happens. Any other stand would be very costly for not only Germany but for all alike."

As had been the case with his predecessors in the White House, Kennedy was losing his patience with de Gaulle, who was all too willing to risk American lives over Berlin. Kennedy's frustrations were mounting as he wrestled with the incalculable Soviets, uncooperative allies, and a retired general in Berlin who was playing by his own rules and now even trying to interfere in diplomacy.

U.S. MILITARY HEADQUARTERS, WEST BERLIN
MONDAY, OCTOBER 23, 1961

Emboldened by the success of his military escorts, Clay decided it was time to provide Washington with advice about how it could couple a negotiating initiative with military muscle-flexing. He wrote down his thoughts in a cable to Secretary of State Rusk, one of his key opponents in Washington.

Clay said he agreed with Rusk's view that the matter of showing identification papers at East German border points was not by itself a matter of "major import," but nevertheless he insisted that the U.S. had to push back. "I do not believe," he told Rusk, repeating the message he had sent to the president, "that we can afford to have any remaining right taken away from us prior to and without negotiation as we would then enter into negotiations with only those rights left which we are committed to maintain by force if necessary."

Therefore he "urgently recommended" that Rusk summon the Russian ambassador and advise him that the U.S. rejected the new East German border regime and would refuse to join any talks with the Russians on Berlin until the East Germans reversed their decree. He argued that this would improve the American position in Berlin, test Khrushchev's goodwill for negotiations, and more closely align the U.S. approach on Berlin talks with the harder-line views of the French and the West Germans.

Clay made the case to Rusk that using the border dispute for diplomatic leverage right away was a more promising track than the continuation of his armed escorts, for he realized they would ultimately run up against vast Soviet conventional superiority. Clay thus announced that he would stop his probes at Checkpoint Charlie after only one day's execution so that Rusk could pursue the diplomatic path that Clay believed he had made possible.

"We will avoid a test at Friedrichstrasse today awaiting your consideration of this recommendation," he said, then added, "We must probe not later than tomorrow."

OVAL OFFICE, THE WHITE HOUSE, WASHINGTON, D.C.
TUESDAY, OCTOBER 24, 1961

The White House staff considered West German Ambassador Wilhelm Grewe to be the most unpleasant member of the foreign diplomatic corps. Humorless and condescending, Grewe had been so open about his disdain for Kennedy's so-called New Frontiersmen that Adenauer himself had reproached him.

Given Ambassador Gavin's failure to move de Gaulle the day before, Kennedy did not look forward to his morning meeting with Grewe in the Oval Office. He was irritated by increasing leaks to the U.S. and European media about French and German opposition to his desire for a new round of Berlin negotiations, and he wanted them to stop.

Ambassador Grewe dispensed with small talk and spoke of the chancellor's concern about Kennedy's lack of commitment to West Berlin and to German unification more generally. Grewe had the dry, prosecutorial bearing that came with being one of his country's leading international lawyers. He had negotiated the end of the Allied occupation of West Germany and had been instrumental in creating the so-called Hallstein Doctrine, the tough policy which dictated that West Germany would not establish or maintain diplomatic relations with any country that recognized East Germany.

Grewe said Adenauer was prepared to go to war to defend Berlin's freedom. To prepare for that, he said, the chancellor was increasing his military budget and building up forces even as he built his new coalition government. However, Grewe said that Adenauer worried about Kennedy's plan for a conventional buildup in Europe. He "considered that such operations would only be convincing if we were prepared to follow them with a preemptive nuclear strike if that became necessary."

The German fear, Grewe said, was that a greater Allied reliance on conventional forces could create a situation where a lack of clearly defined or believable nuclear deterrent encouraged Soviet forces to "cross the border and occupy considerable areas" of West Germany, a potential he compared to the Chinese situation in 1947 when communist troops took the mainland. "The decision to use nuclear weapons," said Grewe, "must be made clear to the Soviets as well as the fact that the Soviet Union itself would be a target."

Kennedy did not betray his growing impatience with Allied lectures about what sorts of risks he should take with American lives over Berlin. He lied to Grewe that he was eager to meet with Adenauer, a meeting that was planned for mid-November, and that he hoped they could get on the same page regarding policy toward the Soviets. The president said he "deplored" press reports suggesting the two sides were at odds over opening talks with Moscow. He wanted to probe Khrushchev's more flexible ideas about what might constitute a free West Berlin. "I personally would feel much better if we did this before we got to the nuclear stage," he told Grewe.

Kennedy complained to Grewe that de Gaulle "apparently felt that every move toward the Soviets was a manifestation of weakness."

Grewe knew Adenauer had the same concerns. Like de Gaulle, Adenauer was deeply displeased by the Rusk–Gromyko talks. Beyond that, Grewe said Adenauer worried that the U.S. was abandoning its traditional support of German unification through its de facto recognition of East Germany, by encouraging closer contacts between the two Germanys, and by abandoning its support for the ultimate goal of German unity through free elections.

Impatient with the same old complaints, Kennedy responded that the U.S. and West Germany "should be looking for new approaches" to the Soviets. Kennedy told Grewe that he saw no prospect of unification in the foreseeable future and did not believe the Allies should stand pat on the West Berlin situation. He was looking for ways to improve the city's current status, and for that he wanted Adenauer's help.

Reflecting Adenauer's own contempt for Kennedy's belief in "new approaches," Grewe echoed de Gaulle's view that there was no practical possibility of achieving any improvement with the Soviets, as Moscow's approach for the moment was to seek further concessions that the West must resist. He detailed for Kennedy the cost thus far to Germans and Adenauer of the president's acquiescence to the border closure.

Before August 13, Grewe said, Berlin had enjoyed a daily average of 500,000 border crossings of families, friends, and workers, which closely linked the two cities and their peoples. These had been reduced to about 500, he said. Because of Adenauer's "reserved and moderate" response to the Berlin Wall's construction, Grewe told Kennedy that the chancellor had lost his majority and had nearly lost the elections a little more than a month earlier.

Kennedy reminded Grewe that the alternative to talks with the Soviets on Berlin was "the real prospect of a military engagement." The U.S. would not give Berlin away, he said, but on the other hand he wanted to be sure "when we come to the end of the road" that no one wondered whether force might have been avoided through more effort at talks. Kennedy impatiently told Grewe that instead of just shooting down U.S. ideas, Germany should provide "proposals of its own which it would regard as acceptable."

Stung, Grewe said that the West Germans were also looking for ways to change the Berlin situation for the better but did not believe for the moment that such an outcome could be achieved. He dismissed as unattainable the notion he had heard from some Kennedy administration sources of

Berlin hosting the UN headquarters. At best, he said, such a far-fetched idea could be an opening gambit in negotiations.

After a perfunctory handshake, Grewe returned to the embassy to send home another grim cable to Adenauer.

U.S. STATE DEPARTMENT, WASHINGTON, D.C.
TUESDAY AFTERNOON, OCTOBER 24, 1961

Secretary Rusk was irritated that General Clay was providing him with un-solicited advice on how to conduct diplomacy with Moscow, then unilater-ally making deployment decisions at Berlin's border connected to those suggestions. On Rusk's behalf, Berlin task force chief Foy Kohler called Allan Lightner at nine in the evening German time to get him back on the State Department reservation and to pull him out from under General Clay's seductive spell.

Speaking to Lightner, Kohler shot down Clay's advice that Rusk should use the unfolding border dispute as leverage for negotiations with Moscow. Beyond that, he reminded a defensive Lightner that he reported to Rusk and not to Clay. In his memo to Rusk afterward that reported on his chat with Lightner, Kohler complained, "The conversation was almost entirely in double-talk."

Lightner assured Kohler that his role in the border-crossing incident two days earlier had been "entirely unexpected and rather embarrassing." In all his life as a diplomat, Lightner had never encountered so much media attention, ranging from sneering insinuations in the communist press that he was crossing to meet with his mistress to excessive praise in the West Berlin press that the top American in Berlin was finally demonstrating U.S. testicles.

Kohler joked that Lightner's name had become "a household word in the U.S." overnight, which in the publicity-shy State Department wasn't a compliment. What bothered Kohler more, he said, was that Clay had sus-pended the border crossings without Washington's clearance, which Kohler called "a serious tactical mistake." He believed the Soviet official's eventual appearance at the border crossing on October 22 had achieved the U.S. purpose of showing that it remained the Soviets and not the East Germans who would guarantee U.S. free passage in East Berlin.

In putting a stop to the military escorts, Lightner apologized to his superiors in Washington that he had been "overruled by a higher authority," namely Clay. At the same time, he wanted to know what Rusk thought of Clay's ingenious idea of calling in the Soviet ambassador and informing him that the U.S. would refuse to negotiate with Russia until the East Germans canceled their expanded border inspections.

Kohler said Clay's proposal was being considered but that many other factors would play into the decision of when and how to talk to the Russians. Thus, Rusk wanted Clay to resume his probes with "both armed and unarmed escorts of U.S. vehicles" if the East Germans continued to refuse American rights of free passage.

With that, General Clay had clear instructions to resume his escorts. The slap on Clay's hand, however, was just as unmistakable. Rusk wanted him to stay out of U.S.–Soviet diplomacy, which was none of his business. For whatever reason, Clay's superiors were encouraging his more assertive course but refusing to connect it with a more assertive diplomacy.

The outcome was destined to be an unhappy one.

CHECKPOINT CHARLIE, WEST BERLIN
FRIDAY AFTERNOON, OCTOBER 27, 1961

United States Army First Lieutenant Vern Pike had two concerns as he looked down the enemy tank barrels, adjusted his green army helmet with the bold white "MP" emblazoned across its front, and ensured his M14 rifle had its safety off, a bullet in its chamber, and its bayonet unsheathed.

Foremost in his mind, the twenty-four-year-old U.S. military police officer was worried for his wife, Renny, who at age twenty was increasingly pregnant with their twins. Pike had decided against sending her home for

Christmas, as the young couple didn't want to be separated for that long, but now that decision looked irresponsible.

That was due to his second fear. Pike knew from his training that the scene unfolding before him could escalate to war—perhaps even a nuclear one—and take with it him, his young bride, and their unborn twins, not to mention a good portion of the planet. All it would take was one nervous U.S. or Soviet trigger finger, he thought to himself.

It was just past nine in the evening, and ten American M48 Patton tanks were poised at the Friedrichstrasse crossing, facing an identical number of Soviet T-54 tanks about a hundred paces away. The showdown had begun to unfold several hours earlier in the afternoon when U.S. tanks had clanked up to the border as they had the two previous days to back up what were already becoming routine military escorts of American civilian cars into East Berlin.

At precisely 4:45 p.m., after another successful and uneventful operation, U.S. commanders had ordered the American tanks withdrawn to Tempelhof Air Base. Pike, whose military police platoon supervised Checkpoint Charlie, then took a cigarette break with Major Thomas Tyree, who commanded the tank group. From the warmth of a drugstore on the corner of Friedrichstrasse and Zimmerstrasse, they looked out the window toward the East and turned to each other in disbelief.

"Do you see what I see?" said Tyree to Pike.

"Sir, those are tanks!" Pike responded with alarm. "And they aren't ours." He calculated that they were no more than seventy to a hundred yards from where they stood.

Though they looked to be newly built Soviet T-54 tanks, their national markings were obscured. All the more mysterious, the military personnel driving them and manning their guns appeared to be wearing unmarked black uniforms. If they were Soviet—and it was hard to imagine they were anything else—they were preserving deniability.

"Vern," said Tyree, "I don't know whose tanks those are, but get the hell to Tempelhof and get me my tanks back, quick as you can."

"Yes, sir," said Pike, glancing at his watch. The U.S. tanks had left ten minutes earlier, so it would not take long for him to catch them. He jumped into his military police car, a white Ford, and raced through Friday rush-hour traffic, weaving in and out with his siren blaring and his "gumball machine," as he called his rooftop light, rotating. He caught up with the tanks just as they were arriving at their base.

Pike shouted out his window at the lead tank, which was driven by his Berlin neighbor, Captain Bob Lamphir. "Sir, we've got trouble at Checkpoint Charlie; follow me and let's get back there as fast as we can go."

"Whoopee!" yelped Lamphir as he ordered all the tanks to turn around and head back to the border. Pike later recalled how the thrill of impending danger surged through him: "Here we are at five o'clock in the afternoon rush hour on an October Friday in Berlin, racing down Mariendamm towards Checkpoint Charlie with my little MP car going *bebop, bebop* out in the front. And every living Berliner within eyesight gets the hell out of the way."

Just before the American tanks had returned to the scene at 5:25 p.m., the Soviet tanks had withdrawn to parking areas on a vacant lot near East Berlin's main boulevard of Unter den Linden. If not for all the potential peril, the scene had the atmosphere of a French farce, with the Soviet actors rumbling behind the curtain just as their American counterparts rushed onto the stage. In expectation that their opponents might return, the U.S. tanks remained and arranged themselves in defensive positions.

Some forty minutes later, at just past six in the evening, what appeared to be Russian tanks returned and assembled themselves with guns pointed across the line. A *Washington Post* reporter who had gathered at the crossing with dozens of other correspondents announced it was "the first time that the forces of the two wartime allies, now the world's biggest powers, had met in direct and hostile confrontation."

In reference to the lack of national markings, CBS Radio correspondent Daniel Schorr called them, "to borrow a term from Orwell . . . the un-tanks. Or we may one day hear that they were just Russian-speaking volunteers who had bought some surplus tanks and come down on their own." Schorr reported on the curious scene: In the West, the American GIs sat atop their tanks, smoking, chatting, and eating dinner from mess kits. West Berliners, held back behind rope barriers, bought pretzel sticks from street vendors, and presented flowers to GIs. The Western scene was all lit by enormous floodlights beamed from the communist side—an effort to intimidate using superior wattage. On the Eastern side, the apparently Russian tanks sat in darkness with their black-uniformed crews. "What a picture for the history books!" Schorr exclaimed.

Clay required confirmation for his masters in Washington that they were Soviet. It was not an academic point: for the U.S., the danger of a confrontation with Soviet tanks was that it could turn into a general war. East German tanks posed another sort of difficulty, because their deployment was prohibited in East Berlin under the four-power agreements.

Under orders to ascertain the tanks' origin, Pike and his driver Sam McCart climbed into an Army sedan and weaved through the barricades and down a side street well past the tanks, where they parked and then walked back. It was part of the surreal nature of the showdown that both sides continued to respect military freedom of movement at the border, so Pike could drive through without impediment.

Pike was surprised at the tanks' illogical two-three-two formation, which made it impossible for the rear tanks to fire upon the enemy. Beyond that, they also were making themselves easy targets. Pike walked up to the rear tank and saw nothing to help his investigation: "no Russians, no East Germans, no one." So he climbed onto the tank and down into the driver's compartment. There he confirmed it was Soviet by the Cyrillic script on the controls and the Red Army newspaper by the brake handle, which Pike could identify, given his smattering of Russian. "Hey, McCart, look at this," he said as he climbed out of the tank and showed him the newspaper that he had taken as evidence.

The tanks' crews, about fifty men in all, were sitting on the ground a short distance away, apparently getting briefed on their mission. Pike walked up close enough to hear they were speaking Russian. When one of the Soviet officers spotted him, Pike turned to McCart and said, "Let's get the hell out of here."

After driving back, they reported to Colonel Sabolyk, who was Pike's superior, that the tanks were Soviet. When Pike explained how he had found out and showed the newspaper, Sabolyk said in shock, "You did *what?*"

The disbelieving colonel put Pike on the phone to the emergency operations center, which connected him with Kennedy's special representative so he could hear for himself. "Whose tanks are they?" Clay asked.

"They are Soviet, sir," Pike said.

"How do you know?"

When Pike told him, Clay was silent on the other end of the line. Pike felt as though he could hear him thinking, "Oh, God, a lieutenant has started World War Three."

Pike had dared to undertake the mission partly because he felt young and invulnerable, but also because by then American soldiers thought little of Soviet discipline, morale, or military capability. Though GIs knew they were outnumbered, they also felt superior. When driving into West Berlin on the Helmstedt Autobahn from West Germany, Pike had seen Russian grunts hawking their belt buckles, caps, and even Soviet medals as souvenirs in exchange for *Playboy* magazines, chewing gum, ink pens, or especially cigarettes.

At less generous moments, GIs would flick burning cigarettes to the ground just to watch the Russians scramble to recover them for a few drags. Pike recalled later that their gear was of poor quality, their boots flimsy, their field jackets old; they looked to Pike like hand-me-downs from previous conscripts. He told friends that "their body odor would chase a buzzard off a shit wagon."

Pike had little more regard for their tanks, which maneuvered badly. The drivers were often from Asian minorities, Pike had noticed, because he reckoned they were the only ones able to fit into compartments that had been built too small. He and his men chuckled when the first tanks had rolled up that day and officers standing on the road struggled to position them using exaggerated hand movements and semaphores, apparently to overcome language and handling difficulties.

But nothing was very funny about Pike's realization that the Soviet army could "simply swat us out of the way if they ever decided to take the Western half of the city." Pike recalled his orientation briefing when he had reported for duty in West Berlin.

"You are the first line of defense," his commander had said. "The best way to get out of here if the balloon goes up is to put on a *Strassenmeister* [street cleaner] armband on your left arm, pick up a broom, and start sweeping down the Autobahn all the way to West Germany. That's the only way you're going to get out of Berlin alive."

Pike had laughed then, but not now. He calculated the possible outcomes as he stamped his feet to stay warm. Either U.S. or Soviet leaders would blink and withdraw from the battlefield, or someone would shoot and a war would begin. In any case, he couldn't imagine his wife, Renny, heavy with twins, grabbing for a broom and sweeping her way out of Berlin.

The scene before Pike varied between one of imminent threat and touching human drama.

At one point, an eighty-year-old East Berlin woman decided to take advantage of the confusion to simply walk across the border to escape as a refugee. From the West Berlin side and only thirty feet away from her, her son shouted repeatedly at her to keep walking though an East Berlin policeman blocked her path. The crowd watched in fear as her son shouted over and over again: *"Mutter, komm doch, bitte!"* ("Mother, come on, please!").

The officer, whose standing orders were to shoot to kill those trying to flee, stood to the side and called off his dog in a random act of mercy. The old woman took ten more faltering steps before falling into her son's arms as she crossed the line to freedom amid onlookers' cheers.

Down the street from the unmarked Soviet tanks in the capitalist West, bathed in light from six high-powered searchlights mounted by the East Germans on wooden towers just the day before, four U.S. M48 Patton tanks rested, the first pair on the white painted line on Friedrichstrasse separating East and West. Two more tanks were in a lot just off Friedrichstrasse, and four more were poised for action a quarter mile away. Near them were five personnel carriers and five jeeps loaded with MPs wearing bulletproof vests and with bayonets fixed to rifles.

U.S. commanders had placed their entire 6,500-man garrison in Berlin on alert. The French command had ordered its 3,000 men held in barracks. The British had brought out two antitank guns near the Brandenburg Gate, about 600 yards away, and had sent armed patrols right up to the barbed-wire barricade at the gate. A *New York Times* reporter chronicled the scene for his readers: "It was like two chess players trying to come to grips in the middle of a disorganized board, with General Clay moving the American pieces and, presumably, Marshal Ivan S. Konev, the recently appointed Soviet Commander in East Germany moving the Soviet men. . . . As personal representative of President Kennedy, General Clay does not have a place in the regular chain of command. But . . . it is clear that his special position has given him the decisive voice in local decisions."

Pike and his MPs were eager to stand up to the communists, having been frustrated that their commanders had kept them in barracks on August 13. It was three weeks after the border had been closed, and Pike and his men had been reduced to watching helplessly across the border as East German Young Pioneer construction brigades replaced the flimsy barbed-wire barrier with cinder blocks.

Pike had sought guidance from his superiors over whether he should do something to disrupt their handiwork, but he got what became a consistent message: U.S. soldiers should sit on their hands and watch the Wall rise.

On the evening of September 1, Pike would recall that one of the East Germans building the wall had glanced left and right to make sure no one was watching, and then said to him over the barbed wire, "Lieutenant, look how slowly I'm working. What are you waiting for?" He wanted the Americans to intervene.

Later, a police officer standing behind the worker said much the same: "Look, Lieutenant, my machine gun isn't loaded. What are you waiting for?" In order to avoid an unwanted firefight, East German officers had not put bullets in the chambers of such border troops, and he was sharing that information with Pike so the U.S. would know it could strike.

Pike passed all that information to his superiors but was again told to show restraint.

The orders to begin the military escorts the previous Sunday were the biggest morale-booster of the year. Pike's men were to hold the line, be vigilant, and fire upon communist border police should they engage. With rifles loaded and tanks protecting their rear, they had repeatedly guided Allied civilian cars and tourist buses through the border's zigzag barriers.

Until Soviet tanks had rolled up that afternoon, the operation had worked as planned. Now all forces were frozen in place as commanders huddled in opposing headquarters on opposite sides of Berlin, awaiting instructions from Washington and Moscow.

Pike was relieved his fatigues were still dry. The paraphernalia he carried was hardly the stuff to stop Soviet tanks or infantry: an MP brassard wrapped around his upper left arm, a first-aid pouch, a canteen, handcuffs, a billy club, a .45 caliber automatic, and his rifle. Pike braced for a long and cold night. Looking through his binoculars at the young, frightened faces of his enemies, he worried "what would happen if one of those idiots took a shot at us—and then if the showdown became a shootout."

Even as the Soviets were escalating their tank presence, Clay received new instructions from Washington to retreat. Rusk was warning Clay off the aggressive course Rusk himself had endorsed just three days earlier. Foy Kohler, the lead man at the State Department handling the Checkpoint Charlie showdown, had attached a note to Rusk's cable that was intended to convince Clay that any appeal to Kennedy would be a waste of time. It read: "Approved by [Rusk] after consideration by the President." Clay had seen plenty of political mushiness from Washington over the years, but nothing topped the message that followed.

"In the nature of things," Rusk wrote, "we had long since decided that entry into Berlin is not a vital interest which would warrant determined recourse to force to protect and sustain. Having for this reason acquiesced in the building of the wall we must recognize frankly among ourselves that we thus went a long way in accepting the fact that the Soviets could, in the case of East Berlin, as they have done previously in other areas under their effective physical control, isolate their unwilling subjects."

Rusk's message was unmistakable: Clay should view Kennedy's lack of resistance to the border closure as de facto acceptance that the Soviets could do whatever they wished on territory they currently controlled. Rusk said U.S. allies would not support stronger measures, "especially on the issue of showing credentials," where the British had already caved.

Rusk conceded to Clay that Kennedy was having difficulty convincing the Allies of the "real prospect" of armed conflict over West Berlin. Consequently, while the Kennedy administration wanted to demonstrate the illegality of the East German and Soviet actions of August 13, "we have not wished this to go so far as to constitute simply a demonstration of impotence, to focus world-wide public attention on the wrong issue and to arouse hopes and expectations on the part of West Berliners and the West Germans who in the end could only be disillusioned," Rusk explained.

Clay had never been more convinced that appeasement would only encourage the Russian bear. Because of that, earlier that same day he had sent a telegram calling for "a raid in force" to knock down portions of the Wall should the East Germans respond to ongoing U.S. actions by shutting down Friedrichstrasse altogether, which he considered possible.

He outlined how it would work: tanks with bulldozer mounts would cross legally into East Germany, which was technically allowed under four-power rights, but then they would plow demonstratively through sections of the Wall on their way back. On October 26, NATO Supreme Commander Norstad had authorized General Watson to use "the present [Clay] plan for 'nosing' down the Friedrichstrasse barrier" if the East Germans blocked the crossing entirely. He instructed Watson to prepare an alternative plan in which the tanks would "nose down" different portions of the Wall simultaneously, "if practicable from a military standpoint, at several [two or more] other places as well as the Friedrichstrasse."

He had added as an unmistakable message to Clay: "This alternate plan will not under any circumstances be placed in action without specific approval from me."

In fact, Rusk's new cable had shot down Norstad and Clay at the same time. "I am unable to see what national purpose would be accomplished by the proposed raid in force," wrote Rusk. He added that Clay's lesser goal of using a tank to open up the Friedrichstrasse crossing would be discussed that afternoon with the president.

However, said Rusk, given the importance of keeping "the three principal Allies together it seems quite possible that we cannot get agreement on even this much." Rusk expressed his appreciation for Clay's counsel but told him that at the moment it was far more important to keep the Allies together "in the face of the grave Soviet threat while at the same time building up pressures on Soviets against further unilateral action."

The great General Lucius Clay of the 1948 Berlin Airlift was being hogtied by Washington while Soviet tanks were pointing their barrels down his throat.

He had never felt so powerless.

THE KREMLIN, MOSCOW
FRIDAY, OCTOBER 27, 1961

Marshal Konev complained to Khrushchev that the U.S. tanks were gunning their engines at the border and seemed prepared for a major operation. Having already provided the Soviet leader with the photographic evidence of Clay's exercises in the woods, where tanks had practiced knocking down replicas of the Wall, he believed that Khrushchev needed to take seriously the prospect that the Americans might try to undo the Soviet success of August 13.

Khrushchev, who by this time was managing the crisis personally from Moscow despite his ongoing Party Congress, had already called for an additional twenty-three Soviet tanks to be brought into Berlin. "Take our tanks to the neighboring street," he told Konev, "but let their engines run there in the same high gear. And put the noise and the roar from the tanks through amplifiers."

Konev warned Khrushchev that if he challenged the Americans in such a way, the U.S. tanks "may rush forward." He worried that the impetuous Khrushchev might overplay the Soviet hand and start a war.

"I don't think so," Khrushchev replied, "unless, of course, the minds of the American military have been made blind with hatred."

CABINET ROOM, THE WHITE HOUSE, WASHINGTON, D.C.
6:00 P.M., FRIDAY, OCTOBER 27, 1961

An aide handed General Clay a note informing him of the Soviet increase in armor at Checkpoint Charlie just while he was in the midst of a telephone conversation with President Kennedy, who was huddled in the Cabinet Room in an emergency session with his national security team. By that time it seemed that all of Washington had turned against Clay except Kennedy, who had not yet revealed his hand.

To counteract the concerns of the president's advisers, Clay reassured Kennedy that matters in Berlin were under control. He insisted that the Soviet decision to move twenty more tanks forward was a message of moderation, as the Soviets were merely mathematically matching the U.S. force capability in Berlin.

That said, the Soviets were nervous enough about the Checkpoint Charlie showdown, and its potential for escalation, that Khrushchev had put his nuclear strike forces on special alert status for the first time ever over a U.S.–Soviet dispute. Khrushchev could not be sure that matters would not spin out of control, and he was preparing for all possibilities.

Clay's view was clear: "If the Soviets don't want war over West Berlin, we can't start it. If they do, there's nothing we can do to stop them." The general was willing to gamble they didn't want a war and believed that the U.S. should push back. However, the president was holding the dice and was unwilling to take the risk.

W hat Clay would never know was that Kennedy was so unnerved by
the Checkpoint Charlie showdown that he had dispatched his
brother to solve the crisis with his regular interlocutor of the past six months,
the Soviet spy Georgi Bolshakov. At the same time he was again working a
second, more traditional channel through Ambassador Thompson in
Moscow, just as he had done before the Vienna Summit.

The president wasn't turning to the Bolshakov back channel because
of its proven success. Bobby's meetings with Bolshakov before Vienna had
done little to prepare him for Khrushchev's ambush on Berlin. At a dangerous moment, however, Bolshakov was the fastest and most direct line to
Khrushchev.

By late October, Bobby knew how to arrange a meeting with Bolshakov
rapidly, and where the media would not find them. James Symington, Bobby's assistant at the Office of the Attorney General, thought his boss had
warmed up to "Georgi" partly due to his "predilection for harmless buf-
foons." They met every fortnight or so, and Bobby discussed with him
"most of the major matters dealing with the Soviet Union and the United
States."

The president's brother made arrangements for the meetings himself,
and would later regret that "unfortunately—stupidly—I didn't write many
of the things down. I just delivered the messages verbally to my brother and
he'd act on them and I think sometimes he'd tell the State Department and
sometimes he didn't."

The first Bobby Kennedy–Bolshakov meeting about the rising border
tensions at Checkpoint Charlie came at 5:30 p.m. on October 26, one day
before Soviet tanks rolled up to the crossing. According to the recollection of the president's brother, the second and crucial negotiations came at
11:30 p.m. Washington time on October 27, or 5:30 in the morning on
October 28 in Berlin, at a time when the two sides' tanks and soldiers were
positioned across from each other in the damp, cold autumn dawn.

Bobby Kennedy recalled that he told Bolshakov, "The situation in Berlin has become more difficult." He complained that Foreign Minister Gromyko had rebuffed Ambassador Thompson's efforts that day to defuse the crisis. "It is our opinion that such an attitude is not helpful at a time when efforts are being made to find a way to resolve this problem," said Kennedy. He appealed for a "period of relative moderation and calm over the course of the next four to six weeks."

The attorney general would later recall that he then told Bolshakov, "The President would like them to take their tanks out of there in twenty-four hours." And that's precisely what Khrushchev would do. Bobby would later say that their exchange on the tank showdown at Checkpoint Charlie demonstrated that Bolshakov "delivered effectively when it was a matter of importance."

What no one recorded were the details of the agreement. However, from that point forward, the U.S. stopped its military escorts of civilians, and Clay no longer challenged East German authority at the border points. Whatever contingencies Clay had scripted to knock through portions of the Wall were shelved, and the shovels mounted to tanks to knock portions of the Wall were removed and put in storage.

Absent any resistance, East Germany further reinforced and expanded its Wall.

WASHINGTON, D.C.
10:00 P.M., FRIDAY, OCTOBER 27, 1961

On Friday night, October 27, Secretary of State Rusk sent a telegram to the U.S. Mission in Berlin that declared victory while engaging in retreat. The cable noted that the crucial decision ending the Berlin Crisis had been taken at a meeting at the White House at 5:00 p.m. attended by the president, Rusk, McNamara, Bundy, Kohler, and Hillenbrand. It would be sent to NATO and all the U.S. embassies in the three chief Allied capitals. Almost as an afterthought, Clay was copied as well.

"Probes to date have accomplished their purpose," Rusk lied. Kennedy and Clay could argue that Soviet tanks' appearance at the border was their victory, proving their point that it was Moscow and not East Berlin that still controlled events in the city.

Yet it was clear Rusk was waving the white flag. The cable declared, "Further probes by U.S. personnel wearing civilian clothes and riding in official U.S. vehicles or privately owned vehicles bearing plates of U.S. Armed Forces and using armed guards or military escort will be deferred."

Just in case his point was missed, Rusk's next instruction made clear that the president wanted Clay to avoid any further confrontation with the East Germans or the Soviets. "U.S. civilian officials," it said, "will for the time being refrain from going into East Berlin except that one civilian official will attempt daily to enter East Berlin in a privately owned vehicle without armed escort."

Clay would stay for another several months, but his enemies had won. Rusk drove home that reality further, saying, "For the time being nothing further can be done on the spot since the matter has now moved to the highest government levels. . . . Instructions have been issued to defer any further civilian probes with armed escorts into East Berlin."

Even as stubborn a man as Clay knew he had to stand down.

PALACE OF CONGRESSES, MOSCOW
SATURDAY MORNING, OCTOBER 28, 1961

After an evening of tension at the Berlin border, Marshal Konev met with Khrushchev in Moscow as his long Party Congress entered its final two days. Konev reported to Khrushchev that the situation at the border in Berlin was unchanged. No one was moving, he told the Soviet leader, "except when the tank operators on both sides would climb out and walk around to warm up."

Khrushchev instructed Konev to withdraw Soviet tanks first. "I'm sure that within twenty minutes or however long it takes them to get their instructions, the American tanks will pull back, too," he said, speaking with the confidence of a man who had made a deal.

"They can't turn their tanks around and pull them back as long as our guns are pointing at them," Khrushchev said. "They've gotten themselves into a difficult situation, and they don't know how to get out of it. . . . So let's give them one."

Shortly after 10:30 on Saturday morning, the first Soviet tanks retreated from Checkpoint Charlie. Some of them were covered by flowers, garlands put on them that morning by members of the Freie Deutsche Jugend, the party's youth organization.

After a half hour's wait, the U.S. tanks pulled back as well.

With that, the Cold War's most perilous moment ended with a whimper. However, the aftershocks of Berlin 1961 would be dramatic and long-lasting. They would shake the world a year later in Cuba—and they would shape the world for three decades to come.

Epilogue

AFTERSHOCKS

I recognize fully that Khrushchev's main intention may be to increase his chances at Berlin, and we shall be ready to take a full role there as well as in the Caribbean. What is essential at this moment of highest test is that Khrushchev should discover that if he is counting on weakness or irresolution, he has miscalculated.

President Kennedy, in a secret cable informing
British Prime Minister Harold Macmillan of the photographic
evidence of Cuban missiles, October 21, 1962

There are many people in the world who really don't understand, or say they don't, what is the great issue between the free world and the Communist world. Let them come to Berlin. There are some who say that Communism is the wave of the future. Let them come to Berlin. And there are some who say in Europe and elsewhere we can work with the Communists. Let them come to Berlin. . . .

All free men, wherever they may live, are citizens of Berlin, and therefore, as a free man, I take pride in the words *"Ich bin ein Berliner."*

President Kennedy, in a speech to Berliners, June 26, 1963

BERLIN AND HAVANA
MID-AUGUST 1962

A year after President John F. Kennedy acquiesced to the communist construction of the Berlin Wall, two dramas occurring five thousand miles apart illustrated the high cost of one of the worst inaugural-year performances of any modern U.S. president.

The first scene unfolded on August 17 under the spotlight of a Berlin summer sun just minutes after two in the afternoon, when eighteen-year-old bricklayer Peter Fechter and his friend Helmut Kulbeik began their sprint toward freedom across the so-called death strip, the no-man's-land that lay before the Wall. The first of thirty-five police shots came after the two had squirmed through an intermediary barrier of barbed wire. Two bullets pierced Fechter's back and stomach as he watched his more agile friend leap to freedom over strands of barbed wire that adorned the barrier's crown. Fechter collapsed at the base of the wall, where he lay in a quivering fetal position with his arms folded across his chest, his left shoe half off and the white of his ankle showing. For most of an hour, his failing voice cried out for help as his life bled out through multiple wounds.

At the same time and more than an ocean away, Soviet ships had begun landing secretly at eleven different Cuban ports with the makings of a Soviet nuclear missile force of sufficient range and potency to obliterate New York City or Washington, D.C. On July 26, the Soviet freighter *Maria Ulyanova*, named for Lenin's mother, had docked in the port city of Cabañas as the first of eighty-five Soviet ships that would make 150 round-trips in the following ninety days. They were transporting combat forces and the components for some twenty-four medium-range and sixteen longer-range launchers, each of which would be equipped with a nuclear warhead and two ballistic missiles.

Back in West Berlin, police and news reporters—standing atop ladders to get a better view over the Wall—tracked and photographed Fechter's bitter end. U.S. troops in battle dress stood by, following orders that they not assist would-be refugees unless they had already escaped communist territory. A gathering crowd of West Berliners screamed their protests, condemning the East Germans as murderers and the Americans as cowards. A U.S. military police lieutenant told one of the onlookers, "It's not my problem," an expression of resignation that would spread among outraged West Berliners through the next day's newspapers.

For their part, East German border guards balked at hauling away the dying victim, needlessly fearful that they would be shot by American troops. Only after Fechter's body went limp and the East Germans exploded smoke bombs to cover their work did a border patrol carry away the corpse. Still, a photographer captured a tableau oddly reminiscent of the removal of Jesus from the cross. Appearing the following day on the front page of the *Berliner Morgenpost*, it showed three helmeted police, two of them with tommy guns, holding Fechter aloft with his arms splayed and his wrists bloodstained.

Fechter's murder snapped something inside West Berliners. The following day, tens of thousands of demonstrators took to the streets, protesting American impotence as angrily as they did communist inhumanity. Their accumulated feelings of anger and frustration produced what *New York Times* correspondent Sydney Gruson called an "almost unbelievable scene" of West Berlin police firing water cannons and tear gas to prevent their own people from storming the Wall. Wrote Gruson: "More than any single event since the wall was built, Peter Fechter's lonely and brutal death has made the West Berliners feel a sense of helplessness in the face of the creeping encroachment being worked so subtly by the Communists."

Meanwhile, over Cuba, CIA aerial photography by mid-August had captured the intensive Soviet maritime activity, given the volume of the deliveries and the sloppiness of execution. Soldiers unloaded vessels at night with streetlights doused and then forwarded shipments over dirt roads in camouflaged vehicles that were so long, troops had to knock down peasant homes to negotiate the turns. Frontline commanders—when not waging war on mosquitoes, heat, or monsoons—communicated their steady progress back to Moscow through couriers to avoid U.S. electronic intercepts.

On August 22, the CIA alerted the White House that as many as 5,000 Soviet personnel had arrived on more than twenty vessels with large quantities of transport, communication, and construction equipment. CIA analysts said the speed and magnitude of this influx of Soviet personnel and matériel to a non–Soviet bloc country was "unprecedented in Soviet military aid activities; clearly something new and different is taking place." The missiles themselves would not arrive for another two months, however, and America's spy services for the moment concluded that Moscow was likely augmenting Cuba's air defense system.

U pon first reflection, there would seem to be little to connect the public killing of a teenage bricklayer in East Berlin and the clandestine arrival of Soviet troops and missile launcher parts in Cuba. Yet, taken together, they dramatically symbolized the two most significant aftershocks of Kennedy's mishandling of the events surrounding Berlin in 1961:

- The first would be longer-lasting: the freezing in place of the Cold War division of Europe for three more decades, with all of its human costs. The Wall's construction not only stopped East Germany's unraveling at a time when the country's viability was in doubt; it also condemned another generation of tens of millions of East Europeans to authoritarian, Soviet-style rule with its limits on individual and national freedom.
- The second aftershock would be more immediate: the Cuban Missile Crisis in late 1962 with its threat of nuclear war. Though history would celebrate Kennedy for his management of the Cuban crisis, Khrushchev would not have risked putting nuclear weapons in Cuba at all if he had not concluded from Berlin in 1961 that Kennedy was weak and indecisive.

The world now knows what President Kennedy did not envision at the time: that the Berlin Wall would fall in November 1989, that Germany and Berlin would be unified a year later in October 1990, and that the Soviet

Union itself would collapse a year after that, at the end of 1991. Given the Cold War's happy ending, it has been tempting for historians to give Kennedy more credit than he deserves for that outcome. By avoiding undue risk to stop the Berlin Wall's construction, their argument goes, Kennedy prevented war and set the stage for Germany's eventual unification, for the liberation of the Soviet bloc's captive nations, and for the enlargement of a free and democratic Europe.

However, the record—informed by new evidence and a closer examination of existing accounts and documents—demands a less generous judgment. Two-time National Security Advisor Brent Scowcroft correctly notes in this book's foreword, "History, sadly, does not reveal its alternatives." But it does provide unmistakable clues. We will never know whether a more resolute Kennedy could have brought an earlier end to the Cold War. What's beyond dispute, however, is that Kennedy's actions allowed East German leaders to stop just the sort of refugee flow that would be the country's undoing twenty-eight years later. The facts also make clear that Kennedy's actions in 1961 were never motivated primarily by a desire to keep West Berlin free.

During his first year in office, Kennedy was not focused on rolling back communism in Europe, but instead was trying to stop its spread to the developing world. Regarding Berlin, he was most concerned about avoiding instability and miscalculations that would lead to nuclear war. Unlike his predecessors, Presidents Eisenhower and Truman, he was dismissive both of Chancellor Konrad Adenauer and his dreams of German unification.

Perhaps the best judge of Kennedy's poor showing in 1961 was the president himself. He was privately candid about his mishandling of the Bay of Pigs crisis and the Vienna Summit. When, on September 22—more than a month after the border closure—*Detroit News* journalist Elie Abel sought Kennedy's cooperation for a book he wished to write on Kennedy's first year in office, the president responded, "Why would anyone want to write a book about an administration that has nothing to show for itself but a string of disasters?"

It was a refreshing expression of self-awareness about a year that had been marked by Kennedy's inconsistency, indecision, and policy failure.

Though Kennedy's election campaign had focused on fresh ideas and the urgent need for change, when it came to Berlin, he was more focused on maintaining the fragile status quo. He believed that one should only address the more intractable Berlin situation after a confidence-building process of negotiations on a nuclear test ban agreement and other arms control matters.

Then, in the first days of his administration, Kennedy failed to seize the best opportunity that would be available to him for a breakthrough in relations due to an amateur's misreading of Khrushchev's signals. The Soviet leader had demonstrated a new willingness to cooperate with the U.S. through a series of unilateral gestures that included the release of captured U.S. airmen on the morning after Kennedy's inauguration. Instead, Kennedy decided that Khrushchev was escalating the Cold War to test him, a conclusion he had reached largely by overinterpreting the harsh rhetoric of a routine speech delivered to rally party propagandists.

What followed was Kennedy's alarmist State of the Union speech. With considerable hyperbole, Kennedy told the nation what he had learned in less than two weeks in office that had prompted him to alter the far more cautious tone of his inaugural speech:

> Each day, the crises multiply. Each day, their solution grows more diffi-
> cult. Each day, we draw nearer the hour of maximum danger. I feel I must
> inform the Congress that our analyses over the last ten days make it clear
> that, in each of the principal areas of the crisis, the tide of events has been
> running out—and time has not been our friend.

The iconic moment for Kennedy's first-year indecisiveness came with the Bay of Pigs debacle in April, when the president neither canceled an operation that had been spawned in the Eisenhower administration nor gave it the resources required for success. From that point forward, Kennedy rightly worried that Khrushchev had concluded he was weak, particularly given the Soviet leader's more resolute response to the Hungarian uprising of 1956. As Kennedy told columnist James Reston after the Soviet leader had mauled him at the Vienna Summit, Khrushchev "thought anyone who was so young and inexperienced as to get into that mess could be taken. And anyone who got into it and didn't see it through had no guts. He just beat the hell out of me," he told Reston. "I've got a terrible problem."

After Khrushchev's threat in Vienna to unilaterally change Berlin's status by year's end, Kennedy countered with escalated rhetoric, increased defense spending, greater troop readiness, and a review of military contingencies, including the U.S. nuclear response plan. Yet he was always a step behind the Soviets. When East German forces with Soviet backing closed the Berlin border on August 13 with such remarkable speed and efficiency, the U.S. and its allies seemed to have been caught flat-footed.

Accounts from the period suggest Kennedy was caught entirely by surprise. However, upon closer scrutiny, it is clear not only that Kennedy anticipated some Soviet action similar to what followed, but also that he helped write the script for it. Kennedy privately responded with relief rather than outrage, opting neither to disrupt the border closure when he had the chance nor punish his communist rivals with sanctions. He famously told aides, "It's not a very nice solution, but a wall is a hell of a lot better than a war."

The consistent message he had sent Khrushchev—directly in Vienna and indirectly thereafter through public speeches and back-channel messages—was that the Soviet leader could do whatever he wished on the territory he controlled as long as he didn't touch West Berlin or Allied access to the city.

As Kennedy told White House economic adviser Walter Rostow several days before the border closure, "Khrushchev is losing East Germany. He cannot let that happen. If East Germany goes, so will Poland and all of Eastern Europe. He will have to do something to slow the flow of refugees. Perhaps a wall. And we won't be able to prevent it. I can hold the Alliance together to defend West Berlin, but I cannot act to keep East Berlin open."

On August 13, 1961, Khrushchev and Ulbricht could act with relative confidence that Kennedy would not respond as long as they remained within the guardrails he himself had established. Probably for that reason they constructed the Wall in its entirety not directly on the border but safely a few paces back in East Berlin. Disdainful of German unification aspirations and willing to accept the existing European balance of power, Kennedy was driven by the mistaken hope that by making the Soviets feel more secure in Berlin, he would increase the chances for fruitful negotiations on a wider range of issues. Instead, as the Cuban crisis would later show, Kennedy's inaction in Berlin only encouraged greater Soviet misbehavior.

Scholars have long wondered whether Kennedy provided even more explicit approval in advance for the Berlin Wall's construction. If such communication occurred, it likely would have come during the regular meetings of the president's brother Robert and Soviet intermediary Georgi Bolshakov, the Soviet military intelligence agent who had established himself as the secret conduit between Kennedy and Khrushchev. Bobby would later apologize for failing to keep a record of those conversations. Bolshakov's own available account sheds no light on his talks with Bobby just before or after the border closure, and Kremlin and Soviet intelligence archives that could provide clues remain closed.

In spite of that, however, the resemblance is so striking between the course Kennedy had endorsed and what the Soviets and East Germans executed as to be more than coincidental. Kennedy provided Khrushchev greater latitude for action in Berlin than any of his predecessors had done. The declassified transcripts of their Vienna Summit detail the de facto deal Kennedy was willing to strike: He would give Khrushchev a free hand to seal Berlin's border in exchange for a guarantee that the Soviets would not disrupt West Berlin's continued freedom or Allied access to the city. Senior U.S. officials who would read the Vienna transcripts later would be shocked by Kennedy's unprecedented willingness to recognize the postwar division of Europe as permanent in the interest of achieving stability. As Kennedy told Khrushchev on the first day of their Vienna talks, "It was crucial to have the changes occurring in the world and affecting the balance of power take place in a way that would not involve the prestige of the treaty commitments of our two countries."

The next day Kennedy would extend this line of argument more explicitly to Berlin, repetitively restricting America's commitment to "*West* Berlin" and not to all of Berlin as his predecessors had. Kennedy drove home that distinction publicly on July 25 in a live, televised speech whose message of retreat to Khrushchev over Berlin was so clear that it unsettled U.S. policymakers who had so carefully crafted the language of diplomacy since World War II.

Two weeks before the Berlin border closure, on July 30, Senate Foreign Relations Committee chairman William Fulbright said of the Berlin border on national television: "The truth of the matter is, I think, the Russians have the power to close it in any case.... Next week, if they chose to close their borders, they could, without violating any treaty. I don't understand why the East Germans don't close their border, because I think they have a right to close it."

With that, the Arkansas senator had said publicly what Kennedy was thinking privately. The president did nothing to repudiate him, and National Security Advisor McGeorge Bundy privately told Kennedy that he considered Fulbright's words "helpful." Without any countervailing presidential statement, Khrushchev concluded that Fulbright had delivered a deliberate signal, and he said as much both to East German leader Walter Ulbricht and visiting Italian President Amintore Fanfani. "When the border is closed," Khrushchev told Ulbricht, "the Americans and West Germans will be happy. [U.S. Ambassador to Moscow Llewellyn] Thompson told me that this [refugee] flight is causing the West Germans a lot of trouble. So when we institute these controls, everyone will be satisfied. And beyond that, they will feel your power."

"Yes," replied Ulbricht, "and we will have achieved stability." It was the one thing that unified Ulbricht, Khrushchev, and Kennedy: the desire for East German stability.

Throughout 1961, Berlin was an unwanted, inherited problem for Kennedy, and never a cause that he wished to champion. Speaking from the steaming waters of his giant golden bathtub in Paris during a break in his talks with de Gaulle, Kennedy complained to aides Kenny O'Donnell and

Dave Powers, "It seems silly for us to be facing an atomic war over a treaty preserving Berlin as the future capital of a unified Germany when all of us know that Germany will probably never be reunified." On the plane to London after the Vienna Summit, Kennedy again complained to O'Donnell, "We didn't cause the disunity in Germany. We aren't really responsible for the four-power occupation of Berlin, a mistake neither we nor the Russians should have agreed to in the first place."

If establishing the Cold War's terms for another three decades was the powerful long-term outcome of Berlin 1961, the Cuban Missile Crisis was the most significant short-term aftershock. In the minds of Kennedy and Khrushchev, the Cuban and Berlin situations were inextricably linked.

Critics called Khrushchev's scheme to put nuclear missiles in Cuba a reckless gamble, but from the Soviet leader's perspective it was a calculated risk based on what he knew of Kennedy. At the end of 1961, he told a group of Soviet officials that he had learned Kennedy would do almost anything to avoid nuclear war. "I know for certain," he had said, "that Kennedy doesn't have a strong background, nor, generally speaking, does he have the courage to stand up to a serious challenge." Regarding Cuba, he told his son Sergei that Kennedy "would make a fuss, make more of a fuss, and then agree."

Despite all his first-year setbacks, Kennedy remained so willing to provide Khrushchev concessions to reach a Berlin deal that a proposal he made in April 1962 triggered a significant clash with West German Chancellor Konrad Adenauer. What Kennedy called a "Principles Paper" proposed an "International Access Authority" that would transfer control of access to Berlin from the four powers to a newly created body through which the Soviets and East Germans could block entry by anyone they wished. All Kennedy sought in return was Kremlin acceptance of continued Allied military presence and rights in West Berlin.

The document so directly lifted Soviet language that in a copy passed by Washington to Moscow, the drafters had underscored sections to show what they had borrowed. Beyond that, the paper dropped any mention of

German reunification as an eventual goal to be achieved through free elections, which had previously been a nonnegotiable point with Moscow. Never had U.S. proposals so closely resembled Soviet positions or strayed so far from those of Adenauer. At first, Kennedy provided Adenauer only one day for response to a draft. He extended that to forty-eight hours only after angry West German protests.

Adenauer no longer could conceal his disgust with Kennedy. He protested to Paul Nitze, the U.S. assistant secretary of defense who visited him in Bonn, that if Kennedy's principles went forward, West Berlin would not have sufficient moving vans for all those who wished to flee the city. He then shot off a brusque note to Kennedy that said, "I have considerable objections against some of these proposals. I ask you most urgently, my dear Mr. President, to call an immediate pause to these proceedings. . . ."

A leak of the paper, almost certainly blessed by Adenauer, created such an uproar that commentators on both sides of the Atlantic attacked Kennedy for engaging in retreat while his adversaries continued to gun down would-be refugees, harass Allied soldiers, and further reinforce their Wall. Kennedy was forced to withdraw his proposal. Most humiliating of all, an emboldened Khrushchev was in the process of rejecting Kennedy's principles anyway because they did not include a complete withdrawal of U.S. forces.

Khrushchev was playing for larger stakes.

Even as he put in place his Cuban operation, on July 5, 1962, he countered with his most detailed proposal yet to Kennedy to end what he labeled the "West Berlin occupation regime." Under his plan, United Nations police forces would replace Allied troops. They would be drawn from the existing three Western powers but also from neutral states and two Warsaw Pact countries. Through gradual cuts to this contingent of 25 percent per year, after four years West Berlin would have no remaining foreign forces of any kind. Kennedy rejected that proposal two weeks later, on July 17, but every step of the way Khrushchev continued to move his Berlin strategy forward even as he secretly finalized his Cuban plans.

The Soviet military's high-seas operation to Cuba was so large in scale that Khrushchev had to have assumed that Kennedy and his intelligence services would discover it, but that the president would lack the will to stop the missile deployments.

On September 4, Kennedy told select members of Congress that the CIA had determined the Soviets were helping Castro build up his defense capabilities. That evening, Kennedy issued a press statement that said much the same, and warned Khrushchev "the gravest issues would arise" if the U.S. found evidence of Soviet combat troops or offensive capability. The tone and commitment to respond was far more resolute than Khrushchev had anticipated.

Two days later, on September 6, Khrushchev flew a surprised Interior Secretary Stewart Udall, who had been in Russia visiting electrical plants, to meet with him at his Black Sea retreat at Pitsunda. He explored with Udall what shift in domestic politics might be providing Kennedy a new backbone even while he repeated his conviction that Kennedy was fundamentally weak. "As a president he has understanding," Khrushchev told Udall, "but what he does not have is courage—courage to solve the German question." With his Cuban operation far advanced, Khrushchev told Udall, "So we will help him solve the problem. We will put him in a situation where it is necessary to solve it. . . . We will not allow your troops to be in Berlin."

Khrushchev told Udall that to avoid damaging Kennedy in the November elections, he would not press the issue until afterward. Without any reference to Cuba, he told Udall that the Soviets' enhanced position of strength had already changed the balance of power: "It's been a long time since you could spank us like a little boy—now we can swat your ass." War over Berlin, Khrushchev said, would mean that with "the space of an hour" there would be "no Paris and no France."

On October 16, 1962, with most of the Cuban launchers already in place, Khrushchev told Foy Kohler, who was Thompson's successor as ambassador to the USSR, that he wanted to meet with the president at the UN General Assembly session in New York during the second half of November to talk about Berlin and other issues. By then, the Soviet leader would have significantly shifted the strategic balance, giving Moscow for the first time a capability of reliably hitting the U.S. with nuclear weapons. That, in turn, would leave him in a better position either to negotiate or impose the Berlin solution he wanted. Khrushchev told his new ambassador to the United States, Anatoly Dobrynin, that Berlin remained "the primary issue in Soviet–American relations."

As Khrushchev would recall later:

> My thinking went like this: If we installed the missiles secretly, and then the United States discovered the missiles after they were poised and ready to strike, the Americans would think twice before trying to liquidate our installations by military means. I knew that the United States could knock out some of our installations, but not all of them. If a quarter or even a tenth of our missiles survived—even if only one or two big ones were left—we could still hit New York, and there wouldn't be much of New York left. I don't mean to say everyone in New York would be killed—not everyone, of course, but an awful lot of people would be wiped out. . . . And it was high time that America learned what it feels like to have her own land and her own people threatened.

Of all Khrushchev's moves linking Cuba and Berlin during this period, perhaps none was as telling as the Soviet construction of an aboveground oil pipeline across East Germany to fuel Soviet troop deployments to the West German border. The pipelines would send an unmistakable message to Kennedy that Khrushchev would be willing to go to war in Berlin over any Cuban pushback. Said Khrushchev: "The Americans knew that if Russian blood were shed in Cuba, American blood would surely be shed in Germany."

Kennedy's words and actions during the thirteen days of the Cuban crisis, from October 16 to 29, underscored his conviction that Khrushchev's Cuba and Berlin strategies were interlinked. From the beginning, he suspected that Khrushchev's Cuban strategy was ultimately aimed at winning Berlin, the Soviet leader's greater priority. Thus, Kennedy told the Joint Chiefs:

Let me just say a little, first, about what the problem is, from my point of view. First, in general, I think we ought to think of why the Russians did this. Well, actually, it was a rather dangerous but rather useful play of theirs. We do nothing and they have a missile base there with all the pressure that brings to bear on the United States and our prestige. If we attack Cuban missiles, or Cuba in any way, that gives them a clear line to take Berlin, as they were able to do in Hungary under the Anglo war in Egypt [the Suez Crisis]. We would be regarded as the trigger-happy Americans who lost Berlin. We would have no support among our allies. We would affect the West Germans' attitude towards us. And [people would believe] that we let Berlin go because we didn't have the guts to ensure a situation in Cuba. After all, Cuba is five or six thousand miles from them. They don't give a damn about Cuba. But they do care about Berlin and about their own security.

Kennedy's decision to take a harder line with the Soviets over Cuba in 1962 than he had done regarding Berlin in 1961 had at least three motivations. First, the perils were greater to the U.S., as the danger was closer to home. Second, the domestic politics of mishandling Cuba were more dangerous to Kennedy's reelection chances than they had been regarding faraway Berlin. Finally, Kennedy had at long last learned that his demonstrations of weakness had only encouraged Khrushchev to test him further. The Soviet leader had brazenly misled him, saying that he was postponing Berlin talks in deference to U.S. elections when he was merely buying time to put his missiles in place.

Kennedy drove home the Berlin connection again when he informed British Prime Minister Harold Macmillan of the photographic proof of the missiles in a secret teletype message that was received in London on October 21 at 10:00 p.m. He wrote:

I recognize fully that Khrushchev's main intention may be to increase his chances at Berlin, and we shall be ready to take a full role there as well as in the Caribbean. What is essential at this moment of highest test is that

Khrushchev should discover that if he is counting on weakness or irresolution, he has miscalculated.

Kennedy repeated his Berlin concern to Macmillan in a second message
a day later, just a few hours before his historic television address informing
Americans of the danger, demanding the Soviets remove the missiles, and
introducing a naval quarantine of Cuba. "I need not point out to you the
possible relation of this secret and dangerous move on the part of Khrushchev to Berlin," he said.

In 1962, Kennedy also rejected the advice of the so-called SLOBs, the
Soft-Liners on Berlin. Ambassador Thompson, who had returned from
Moscow to the State Department, wanted Kennedy to stop military traffic
to Berlin during the Cuban showdown so as not to provoke the Kremlin, a
notion the president rejected. National Security Advisor Bundy wondered
whether some deal was possible under which one could trade Berlin for the
missiles. Kennedy refused that as well, not wanting to be the president who
lost Berlin.

For all his newfound resolve, however, Kennedy opposed his military's
suggestion of an attack on the Cuban bases, in no small part due to concern
about a Soviet tit-for-tat military retaliation in Berlin. At one point General Curtis E. LeMay, the Air Force chief of staff, protested Kennedy's
unwillingness to strike by saying, "This is almost as bad as the appeasement
at Munich." LeMay's argument: "If we don't do anything to Cuba, they're
going to push on Berlin and push real hard because they've got us on
the run."

Kennedy told the Executive Committee, the body he had created from
his National Security Council to handle the crisis, that he worried even a
quarantine could prompt a corresponding Soviet blockade of Berlin. The
president appointed a subcommittee of that group, chaired by Paul Nitze,
to wrestle with Berlin-related issues. He even lined up General Lucius Clay
to return to Berlin if needed to coordinate U.S. actions.

In his October 22 speech to the nation, Kennedy publicly warned

Khrushchev on Berlin: "Any hostile move anywhere in the world against the safety and freedom of peoples to whom we are committed—including in particular the brave people of West Berlin—will be met by whatever action is needed."

With that, Kennedy's Berlin Crisis had moved to Cuba.

In his meeting with U.S. Ambassador to London David Bruce on the evening of Kennedy's speech, Prime Minister Macmillan worried: "Was it not likely that Khrushchev's real purpose was to trade Cuba for Berlin? If he were stopped, with great loss of face, in Cuba, would he not be tempted to recover himself in Berlin? Indeed, might not this be the whole purpose of the exercise—to move forward one pawn in order to exchange it for another?" For his part, Kennedy worried to Macmillan that Khrushchev might preemptively take military action in Berlin that would require a proportionate U.S. response against Cuba. "That's really the choice we now have," he wrote. "If [Khrushchev] takes Berlin, then we will take Cuba."

Instead, Khrushchev backed down in Cuba once challenged by a decisive Kennedy, exactly as General Clay had predicted he would a year earlier in regard to Berlin. When Soviet Deputy Foreign Minister Vasili Kuznetsov suggested a diversionary strike on Berlin to Khrushchev, the Soviet leader warned him, "Keep that sort of talk to yourself. We don't know how to get out of one predicament, and you [want to] drag us into another?" Khrushchev also rejected Ambassador Dobrynin's idea of responding to Cuba through the "first step" of closing ground routes to Berlin. "Father considered any action in Berlin to be unduly dangerous," Khrushchev's son Sergei would recall later, insisting that "not for a moment" did he consider a nuclear strike on the U.S. After Kennedy's speech, Khrushchev began to withdraw Soviet troops from the West German border so that it would be clear he had no intention of escalating the conflict.

All that said, Kennedy was never as uncompromising in Cuba as it appeared to the U.S. public. On October 27, the president's brother Bobby and Dobrynin reached an agreement that the U.S. would withdraw its Jupiter nuclear missiles from Turkey. When Khrushchev mentioned the concession the following day in a letter to Kennedy, Bobby returned the letter to the Soviets and denied that such a trade had been made. But Khrushchev considered the Turkey retreat crucial to his agreement.

Nevertheless, Kennedy had even won over his biggest Allied critics. De Gaulle famously told Kennedy's emissary Dean Acheson, who had been sent to brief him during the crisis, that he did not need to see the proof of spy photographs from "a great nation" in order to support Kennedy. Adenauer said he would throw his lot behind Kennedy even if the U.S. found it must bomb or invade Cuba. "Absolutely, the missiles must go," he said, thereafter bracing his country for a Berlin blockade or even a nuclear exchange. Tellingly, Kennedy rejected the dovish Macmillan's offer to mediate with Moscow and call a summit on Cuba, which he felt would be disastrous for Berlin. "I don't know quite what we will discuss at the meeting," Kennedy said, "because he'll be back with the same old position on Berlin, probably offering to dismantle the missiles if we'll neutralize Berlin."

Most surprised of all by Kennedy's demonstration of strength was Khrushchev himself, who had bet so much against it. General Clay suggested to diplomat William Smyser that the Cuban Missile Crisis never would have occurred had it not been for Khrushchev's perception of Kennedy's weakness, and Clay believed as well that the threat to Berlin only receded once Kennedy made it clear he would no longer tolerate Moscow's bullying.

West Berliners celebrated the outcome of the Cuban Missile Crisis more enthusiastically than any others. They concluded that the Soviet threat to them had passed.

RATHAUS SCHÖNEBERG, CITY HALL OF WEST BERLIN
WEDNESDAY, JUNE 26, 1963

Kennedy would make his first and last presidential trip to Berlin eight months after the Cuban crisis, on June 26, 1963. After visiting Checkpoint Charlie and walking along the Wall, he came to speak before City Hall, where some 300,000 Berliners had gathered. Most would remember the moment the rest of their lives.

Perhaps another million Berliners had also lined the thirty-five-mile route from Tegel. For most of the ride, Kennedy stood up on the far right side in the backseat of his open Lincoln convertible beside Mayor Willy Brandt and Chancellor Konrad Adenauer. To catch a glimpse of their American hero, Berliners were hanging from trees and lampposts and standing on rooftops and balconies. The Red Cross, which had mobilized to handle casualties in the crowd, would report that more than a thousand people fainted.

At the airport and as they rolled through Berlin in their motorcade, some in the Kennedy delegation sneered that Hitler had drawn delirious German crowds as well. Berliners' enthusiasm for Kennedy was so extreme that it unsettled Adenauer, who whispered to Rusk, "Does this mean Germany can one day have another Hitler?" At one point Kennedy was so dismayed that he told his military aide, General Godfrey T. McHugh, "If I told them to go tear down the Berlin Wall, they would do it."

Yet the more time Kennedy and his entourage spent on the ground in West Berlin, the more they were smitten by its subjects. Kennedy was both stirred by West Berliners' courage and shocked by the sight of the Wall, whose construction he had done so little to prevent. "He looks like a man who just glimpsed Hell," observed *Time* correspondent Hugh Sidey. As Kennedy drove through the city, he redrafted the most important of the three speeches he would deliver, tossing out the wishy-washy language that had been crafted back in Washington so as not to provoke the Soviets. His speech outside West Berlin's city hall would be the most emotional and powerful he would ever deliver abroad.

There are many people in the world who really don't understand, or say they don't, what is the great issue between the free world and the Communist world. Let them come to Berlin. There are some who say that Communism is the wave of the future. Let them come to Berlin. And there are some who say in Europe and elsewhere we can work with the Communists. Let them come to Berlin. And there are even a few who say that it is true that Communism is an evil system, but it permits us to make economic progress.

At that point, Kennedy threw in a German line that had not appeared in his original text, but one that he had practiced before the event with Robert Lochner, the head of Radio in the American Sector of Berlin, or RIAS, and Adenauer's interpreter Heinz Weber. He had written out what he wished to say phonetically on index cards. "Let them come to Berlin . . . *Lasst sie nach Berlin kommen,*" he said. "All free men, wherever they may live, are citizens of Berlin and, therefore, as a free man, I take pride in the words '*Ich bin ein Berliner.*'"

Or as Kennedy had written on his cards: "*Ish bin ine Bear-LEAN-er.*"

Years later, amateur linguists would argue that Kennedy had misspoken and by using the article *ein* in front of *Berliner*, which was the name of a German pastry, he had actually told the crowd, "I am a jelly doughnut." Yet the president had debated just that point with his two tutors, who had rightly concluded that by leaving out the article he would be suggesting he was born in Berlin and perhaps confuse the crowd, and thus lose the emphasis of his symbolic point. In any case, no one in the delirious crowd had any doubt about Kennedy's meaning.

Expressing all the outrage he had not shown in August 1961, Kennedy renounced communism. He conceded that democracy was imperfect, "but we have never had to put up a wall to keep our people in." Much to the delight of Adenauer, for the first time during his presidency he also talked of the right to reunification that Germans had earned through their eighteen years of good behavior. He spoke of his faith that Berlin, the German nation, and the European continent would someday be unified.

It was a new Kennedy.

The president summoned General Clay, who had traveled with him to Berlin, to stand beside him at the podium. Together they basked in the crowd's roars—the man who had privately condemned Kennedy for lacking the will to stand up to the Soviets, and the commander in chief who now was acting so Clay-like, much to the consternation of his advisers. After the speech, Bundy told the president, "I think you went a little too far."

With one speech Kennedy had shifted U.S. policy regarding Germany and Berlin to one that conformed to the new resolve he had shown in Cuba. For the first time in his presidency, Kennedy was treating Berlin as a place to be defended, a place where he would build his legacy, and no longer as an inherited inconvenience inhabited by a people for whom he had little sympathy. From that point forward, neither Kennedy nor any other U.S. president could retreat in Berlin.

As Kennedy told Ted Sorensen on their flight to Ireland from Berlin, "We'll never have another day like this as long as we live."

Less than five months later, on November 22, 1963, an assassin shot President John F. Kennedy dead in Dallas, Texas. Less than a year after that, on October 14, 1964, fellow communists ousted Soviet leader Nikita Khrushchev. He died of heart disease in 1971 after smuggling his memoirs to the West.

In October 1963, Adenauer stepped down from office as part of the co-alition deal he had reached to remain in power following the September 1961 elections. He died of natural causes in 1967, at age ninety-one, leaving as his legacy a democratic, economically buoyant West Germany and a dream—which, though it seemed unrealistic, remained U.S. policy—that it someday would be reunified. His final words to his daughter: "There is nothing to weep about."

A little less than a decade after the Berlin border closure, in May 1971, East German leader Walter Ulbricht resigned and was replaced by Erich Honecker, the man he had assigned to lead the Berlin Wall project. Ho-necker resigned a month before the Wall that he had constructed collapsed. He died of cancer in 1994, exiled in Chile, having been indicted but not tried on charges that included ordering border guards to shoot his own country's citizens if they tried to escape.

But in Berlin in 1961, their fates were cast in a city whose name would come to embody the central ideological and geopolitical struggle of the second half of the twentieth century. Ultimately, the story would end well, but only because in Cuba Kennedy would reverse the perilous course he had set the previous year in Berlin.

What Kennedy could not undo was the Wall that had risen as he passively stood by, which for three decades and perhaps for all of history would remain the iconic image of what unfree systems can impose when free leaders fail to resist.

Acknowledgments

My association with Berlin began in the womb.

My mother, Johanna Schumann Kempe, was born on January 30, 1919, in the Pankow district of what would later become communist East Berlin. She immigrated with her family to America in 1930, three years before the beginning of the Third Reich. She often told me how she, as a teenager, returned to Berlin in 1936 to watch Adolf Hitler host the Olympic Games, where his "master race" won the most medals but was upstaged by black U.S. athlete Jesse Owens, whose four golds were so enthusiastically cheered by Berliners. My mother brought back a souvenir photograph book, which still stands in my bookcase as a reminder of Berlin's many dramas.

Like most Berliners, my mother was extraordinarily proud of her origins. Berliners consider themselves a breed apart from their fellow Germans. My mother insisted Berliners were more free-spirited and flexible than other Germans, and more witty and worldly.

Given my father's more provincial German pedigree, he suffered under my mother's notions about Berliners' exceptionality. Born on May 21, 1909, in the provincial Saxon village of Leubsdorf, he grew up in Kleinzschachwitz near Dresden before immigrating to the United States in 1928. What unified my mother, a schoolteacher, and my father, a baker, was that they were both raised in parts of Germany that would fall under Soviet occupation after

World War II. The rise of the Berlin Wall in 1961 severed our extended family; I remember my parents sending large Christmas packages every year to relatives in East Germany, filled with goods they couldn't buy themselves. One of my great regrets is that my parents would both die a year before they could see the Berlin Wall collapse of its own oppressive weight in 1989.

So, first and foremost, I am indebted to my mother and father, without whom this book would never have been written. I learned from them about Berlin's significance as the dividing line between the free and unfree worlds. It was my parents who instilled in me an indignation both toward those who imposed and those who tolerated the oppressive system that encased seventeen million of their fellow Germans (and, by association, tens of millions of other East Europeans) behind Berlin's concrete walls, barbed wire, watchtowers, and armed guards.

There is also plenty of other thanks to go around. My gratitude again goes to Neil Nyren, my four-time editor at Putnam, who was crucial at every stage of this project, from the development of the concept to the final tweaks. His deft touch and creative eye much improved this manuscript's narrative. Thanks also to one of the world's most gifted agents, Esther Newberg, who along with Neil quite properly steered me away from less promising projects and toward this one.

Thanks go as well to the enormously creative Ivan Held, president of Putnam; Marilyn Ducksworth and her publicity team; and the remarkable group under Meredith Dros, including Sara Minnich, who put together the enhanced e-book. Special thanks go to John Makinson, dear friend of so many years, and Penguin visionary. His advice was always wise.

I owe much to the many chroniclers who preceded me in capturing portions of this history. I have provided a comprehensive bibliography for the reader that lists the many texts I studied over more than six years of research and reporting. But it is nonetheless appropriate to list those who influenced my understanding most: Hope Harrison and Mario Frank, on Walter Ulbricht and his relationship with Khrushchev; Hans Peter Schwartz and Charles Williams, on Adenauer; Strobe Talbott and his remarkable work on Khrushchev's memoirs; and Michael Beschloss, Robert Dallek, Christopher

Hilton, Fred Kaplan, Timothy Naftali and Aleksandr Fursenko, Robert Slusser, Jean Edward Smith, W. M. Smyser, Frederick Taylor, Theodore Sorensen, and Peter Wyden, who all have contributed important work. Two books that focus squarely on August 1961, by Norman Gelb and Curtis Cate, are of particular merit, as they were written by witnesses with great proximity to events of the time.

Despite all that good work, it still struck me that none of these books had put together all the pieces that had contributed to the historic occurrences around Berlin 1961. My goal was to produce a readable, authoritative narrative for both the expert and the general reader that would investigate all the available historical accounts and combine those with more recently declassified materials in the United States, Germany, and Russia.

To take on that challenge, my thanks go above all to the talented and resourceful Nicholas Siegel, my research assistant during the most crucial period of this project. Thanks also to Roman Kilisek, whose careful, thorough, painstaking work in the later stages was invaluable. I am deeply grateful to Natascha Braumann and Alexia Huffman, my personal assistants, who contributed richly to the book itself while also brilliantly managing the executive office of the Atlantic Council. A tip of the hat is also due many others who provided valuable research along the way: Milena Brechenmacher, Bryan Hart, Petra Krischok, Maria Panina, and Dieter Wulf. Susan Hormuth's expert photo research helped unearth unique material for the book and its various electronic incarnations—and Natascha again played a crucial role in making sense of mountains of material. Thanks as well to Maryrose Grossman and Michelle DeMartino at the John F. Kennedy Library, and to William Burr at the National Security Archive.

I owe much to colleagues at my former employer, the *Wall Street Journal,* and at the Atlantic Council of the United States, where I now work. Thanks in particular go to my former *Wall Street Journal* boss, Paul Steiger, and to Jim Pensiero, who made it possible for me to write this book. At the Atlantic Council, our always wise Chairman Emeritus Henry Catto and then President Jan Lodal encouraged me to continue this project. I owe a particular thanks to General Brent Scowcroft, one of America's most extraordinary individuals, and to Virginia Mulberger, a woman of unique judgment and character, for their friendship, inspiration, and support. Throughout this project, I have benefited from the wise counsel of Richard Steele.

I have had the remarkable luck to serve as Atlantic Council President and CEO under two chairmen who are among this country's finest leaders and mentors: Senator Chuck Hagel and General Jim Jones. Senator Hagel, our current chairman, embodies the consistent, principled, bipartisan leadership the United States so badly needs. All Americans have profited from forty-two years of General Jones's remarkable public service, most recently as President Obama's national security advisor.

Special thanks to Walter Isaacson for his early encouragement of this project. Thanks to the many Americans and Berliners who shared their stories, and to David Acheson for providing access to his father's correspondence. I'm grateful to Vern Pike for sharing his still-unpublished manuscript about his days in Berlin.

No project of this sort happens without friends and family. Pete and Maria Bagley provided kindness and support that can never be repaid. My dear friends Pete and Alex Motyl offered crucial organizational and editing suggestions that improved the manuscript significantly.

In adulthood as in childhood, I rely for ballast on my sisters Jeanie, Patty, and Teresa, and I thank them for their encouragement and understanding when this project took time that might have been spent with them. We are bound by a common heritage as first-generation Americans.

This book is quite properly dedicated to my wife, Pam, who has been my extraordinary friend, partner, editor, and counselor through every early-morning hour, every weekend day, and every vacation week spent on this project. Throughout it all, our remarkable daughter, Johanna Natalie (aka "Jo-Jo"), named for the Berliner who brought me into this world, sustains our happiness with her infectious joy and boundless curiosity. I can't wait to show her Berlin.

Notes

SOURCES

The sources for the facts, quotes, and reenactment of crucial meetings and episodes in this text are many and varied—in English, German, and Russian. They include declassified documents, manuscript collections, oral histories, interviews, memoirs, diaries, recordings, and media reports of that time. I have carefully cited all relevant sources in the endnotes and bibliography. Some of this material was not available to or used by earlier chroniclers, and thus it has allowed me to provide a more accurate and more complete account. Many important potential documents are still classified or unavailable, so the telling of this history will be even more complete over time. I and other authors will then be able to expand upon what is in these pages, and I will also provide any new insights at the websites berlin1961.com and fredkempe.com.

To improve readability, I have added articles and other connecting words, such as "the," "a," and "and," to my quotations from State Department and other government cable traffic; these had been left out at that time for reasons of brevity. I have also taken the liberty of using as direct quotes citations from these cables when it was apparent the note-taker was quoting a specific person's words. In some cases—and the accounts of the Robert Kennedy–Georgi Bolshakov meetings are a good example—I have had to rely on accounts that were only partial and left a great many questions open. In these cases, I have used my best judgment while citing what sources were available in the endnotes.

LIST OF ABBREVIATIONS

(See the bibliography for full citations and locations.)

AVP-RF: Arkhiv Vneshnei Politiki Russkoi Federatsii (Russian Ministry of Foreign Affairs Archives)

BstU: Behörde der Bundesbeauftragten für die Unterlagen des Staatssicherheitsdienstes der Ehemaligen Deutschen Demokratischen Republik

CWIHP: Cold War International History Project

DDEL: Dwight D. Eisenhower Presidential Library

DNSA: Digital National Security Archive

FRUS: Foreign Relations of the United States (U.S. Department of State, Office of the Historian)

GRU: Archive of the Main Intelligence Administration of the General Staff of the Armed Forces of the Russian Federation

HSTL: Harry S. Truman Presidential Library

JFKL: John F. Kennedy Presidential Library
MfS: Ministeriums für Staatssicherheit
OH: Oral History
RGANI: Rossiiskii Gosudarstvennyi Arkhiv Noveishei Istorii (Russian State Archive of
    Contemporary History)
SAPMO-BArch: Stiftung Archive der Parteien und Massenorganisationen im Bundesarchiv
SED Archives, IfGA, ZPA: Sozialistische Einheitspartei Deutschland Archives, Institut für
    Geschichte der Arbeiterbewegung, Zentrales Parteiarchiv
TsK KPSS: Declassified Materials from CPSU Central Committee Plenums
TsKhSD: Tsentr Khraneniia Sovremmenoi Dokumentatsii (Soviet Central Committee Archive)
TsAmo: Tsentral'nyi derzhavnyi arkhiv hromads' kykh ob'ednan' Ukrainy (Central Archive of
    Ministry of Defense, Podalsk, Russian Federation)
ZAIG: Zentrale Auswertungs- und Informationsgruppe Hauptverwaltung Aufklärung des
    Ministeriums für Staatssicherheit der DDR

FOREWORD

Page ix "Berlin was the worst moment of the Cold War": Interview with Professor William
    Kaufmann, 08/30/1996, National Security Archive, George Washington University.

INTRODUCTION

Page xiii "Who possesses Berlin": Antony Beevor, *Berlin: The Downfall 1945.* New York: Viking,
    2002, 139; quoting Archive of the Ministry of Defense (TsAMO) 233/2356/5804, 320–321.
Page xiii "Berlin is the most dangerous place": William Taubman, *Khrushchev: The Man and His Era.*
    New York: W. W. Norton, 2004, 407.
Page xiii Undaunted by the damp: Russian State Archive for Contemporary History (RGANI),
    5/30/367, Bl. 179–182, Bericht des Verteidigungsministeriums an das ZK der KPdSU über die
    Situation in Berlin und in der DDR, 28.10. 1961; Matthias Uhl, *Krieg um Berlin? Die
    sowjetische Militär- und Sicherheitspolitik in der zweiten Berlin-Krise 1958 bis 1962.* Munich:
    Oldenbourg Wissenschaftsverlag, 2008, 146–147.
Page xiv Reporting from the scene: Daniel Schorr, Schorr Script Collection, Manuscript Division,
    Library of Congress, Berlin, October 27, 1961.
Page xiv The situation was sufficiently tense: Interview with Adam Kellett-Long, October 15–16, 2008.
Page xiv "The scene is weird, almost incredible": Daniel Schorr, Schorr Script Collection, Berlin,
    October 27, 1961.
Page xiv Rumors swirled through the crowd: Norman Gelb, *The Berlin Wall—Kennedy, Khrushchev,
    and a Showdown in the Heart of Europe.* New York: Dorset Press, 1986, 256; Interview with
    Vern Pike, November 17, 2008; RIAS (Radio in the American Sector) radio reports, October
    25–28, 1961; retrieved from Chronik-der-Mauer.de.
Page xv Clay, who had commanded the 1948: Andrei Cherny, *The Candy Bombers: The Untold Story
    of the Berlin Airlift and America's Finest Hour.* New York: G. P. Putnam's Sons, 2008, 253; U.S.
    Department of State, Office of the Historian, Foreign Relations of the United States (FRUS),
    1961–1963, vol. XIV, Berlin Crisis, 1961–1962, Doc. 186, Telegram from the Mission at
    Berlin to the Department of State, Berlin, October 23, 1961, 2:00 p.m.; Curtis Cate, *The Ides
    of August: The Berlin Wall Crisis—1961.* New York: M. Evans, 1978, 477.
Page xv Convinced from personal experience: William R. Smyser, "Tanks at Checkpoint Charlie," *The
    Atlantic Times,* October 2005: http://www.atlantic-times.com/archive_detail
    .php?recordID=319; NYT, 10/24/1961; Cate, *The Ides of August,* 479.
Page xvi Since then, the communists had fortified: Gelb, *The Berlin Wall,* 3. Winston Churchill,
    "'Iron Curtain' Speech," Westminster College, Fulton, Missouri, March 5, 1946; as quoted in
    Katherine A. S. Sibley, *The Cold War.* Westport, CT: Greenwood Press, 1998, 136–137.

Page xvi the tank showdown at Checkpoint Charlie: RIAS radio reports, October 25–28, 1961; Raymond L. Garthoff, "Berlin 1961: The Record Corrected," *Foreign Policy*, no. 84 (Fall 1991), 142–156.

Page xvi Reuters correspondent Adam Kellett-Long: Interview with Adam Kellett-Long, October 15–16, 2008.

Page xvii From there they phoned: John F. Kennedy Presidential Library (JFKL), *Lucius D. Clay OH.*

Page xviii "Mr. President," responded Clay: FRUS, 1961–1963, vol. XIV, Berlin Crisis, 1961–1962, Doc. 195, 196; Cate, *The Ides of August,* 485–486.

Page xix Between the establishment of the East German state: Berlin Wall Statistics (Der Polizeipräsident von Berlin), chronik-der-mauer.de.

1. KHRUSHCHEV: COMMUNIST IN A HURRY

Page 3 "We have thirty nuclear": Michael R. Beschloss, *The Crisis Years: Kennedy and Khrushchev 1960–1963.* New York: HarperCollins, 1991, 52; Taubman, *Khrushchev: The Man and His Era,* 449.

Page 3 "No matter how good": Pravda, no. 2 (15492), February 2, 1961.

Page 4 At home, Khrushchev was suffering: Aleksandr Fursenko and Timothy Naftali, *Khrushchev's Cold War: The Inside Story of an American Adversary.* New York: W. W. Norton, 2006, 343–344.

Page 4 Khrushchev was fond: Dean Rusk, *As I Saw It: A Secretary of State's Memoirs.* London: I. B. Tauris, 1991, 227.

Page 5 Given Khrushchev's increased capability: Bryant Wedge, "Khrushchev at a Distance: A Study of Public Personality," *Society (Social Science and Modern Society),* 5, no. 10 (October 1968), 24–28.

Page 6 Another top-secret personality: CIA, Office of Current Intelligence (OCI), No. 2391-61, Copy No. 22.

Page 6 During the campaign: Arkady N. Shevchenko, *Breaking with Moscow.* New York: Alfred A. Knopf, 1985, 108–109.

Page 7 As the countdown: Taubman, *Khrushchev: The Man and His Era,* 106–107.

Page 7 Though still vigorously youthful: Fursenko and Naftali, *Khrushchev's Cold War,* 16; Beschloss, *The Crisis Years,* 47; Taubman, *Khrushchev: The Man and His Era,* 39, 191; Marshall MacDuffie, *The Red Carpet: 10,000 Miles Through Russia on a Visa from Khrushchev.* New York: W. W. Norton, 1955, 202; Michael R. Beschloss, *Mayday: The U-2 Affair: The Untold Story of the Greatest US–USSR Spy Scandal.* New York: Harper & Row, 1986, 163–164, 199.

Page 7 He recognized many faces: MacDuffie, *Red Carpet,* 198.

Page 7 Given his purpose: Beschloss, *Crisis Years,* 50–52.

Page 8 "We consider the socialist": Pravda, no. 2 (15492), February 2, 1961.

Page 9 World War II's battles: Sidney Pollard, *The International Economy Since 1945.* New York: Routledge, 1997, 2; Leon Clarck, *The Beginnings of the Cold War—Civilizations Past and Present the Bipolar "North," 1945–1991,* accessed at http://history-world.org/beginnings_of_the_cold_war.htm: *"The Elusive Peace—Soviet And American Spheres,"* Introduction.

Page 10 That didn't count the millions: William H. Chamberlin, "Khrushchev's War with Stalin's Ghosts," *Russian Review,* 21, no. 1 (January 1962), 3–10.

Page 10 Khrushchev blamed Stalin: Taubman, *Khrushchev: The Man and His Era,* 332; Nikita S. Khrushchev, "Memuary Nikity Sergeevicha Khrushcheva," *Voprosy Istorii,* no. 2 (1995), 76.

Page 11 Kroll had been born: Hans Kroll, *Lebenserinnerungen eines Botschafters.* Cologne: Kiepenheuer & Witsch, 1967, 15–17; Fursenko and Naftali, *Khrushchev's Cold War,* 205–206.

Page 12 "Ulbricht lobby": Eberhard Schulz, Hans-Adolf Jacobsen, Gert Leptin, and Ulrich Scheuner, *GDR Foreign Policy.* Armonk, NY: M. E. Sharpe, 1982, 197.

Page 14 Marta Hillers's only consolation: Anonymous, *A Woman in Berlin: Eight Weeks in the*

Conquered City: A Diary. Translation of *Eine Frau in Berlin* by Philip Boehm. New York: Picador, 2006; Jens Bisky, "Kleine Fussnote zum Untergang des Abendlandes." *Süddeutsche Zeitung,* 06/10/2003, 10.

Page 14 *Published for the first time:* Ilko-Sascha Kowalczuk and Stefan Wolle, *Roter Stern über Deutschland: Sowjetische Truppen in der DDR.* Berlin: Christoph Links, 2010, 38.

Page 15 *One such review:* Maria Sack, "Schlechter Dienst an der Berlinerin / Bestseller im Ausland—Ein Verfälschender Sonderfall," *Tagesspiegel,* 12/06/1959, 35.

Page 15 *The East German relationship:* Kowalczuk and Wolle, *Roter Stern über Deutschland,* 105.

Page 16 *The East German pity:* Silke Satjukow, *Besatzer: "Die Russen" in Deutschland 1945–1994.* Göttingen: Vandenhoeck & Ruprecht, 2008, 41, 43.

Page 16 *The latest escape:* "Vopo feuert auf Sowjet-Soldaten—Sie wollten in den Westen," *Bild-Zeitung,* 01/04/1958; "Sowjets jagen Deserteure," *Abendzeitung* (Munich), 01/03/1958.

Page 16 *That dread had grown:* Jan Foitzik, *Berichte des Hohen Kommissars der UdSSR in Deutschland aus den Jahren 1953/1954,* in *Machtstrukturen und Entscheidungsmechanismen im SED Staat und die Frage der Verantwortung* (Materialien der Enquete-Kommission "Aufarbeitung von Geschichte und Folgen der SED-Diktatur in Deutschland," Band II, 2), Baden-Baden, 1995, 1361; http://www.ddr-wissen.de/wiki/ddr.pl?17._Juni_1953.

2. KHRUSHCHEV: THE BERLIN CRISIS UNFOLDS

Page 19 *"West Berlin has turned":* The Current Digest of the Soviet Press, 10, nos. 40–52 (1958), 17.

Page 19 *"The next President in his first year":* Freedom of Communications: Final Report of the Committee on Commerce, United States Senate, Part III: *The Joint Appearances of Senator John F. Kennedy and Vice President Richard M. Nixon and Other 1960 Campaign Presentations.* 87th Congress, 1st Session, Senate Report No. 994, Part 3. Washington, D.C.: U.S. Government Printing Office, 1961.

Page 19 *Standing at the center:* Taubman, *Khrushchev: The Man and His Era,* 396; Nikita S. Khrushchev, *For Victory in Peaceful Competition with Capitalism.* New York: E. P. Dutton, 1960, 38.

Page 20 *"The time has obviously arrived":* U.S. Department of State, Documents on Germany 1944–1985, Office of the Historian, *Khrushchev Address, November 10, 1958.* Washington D.C.: Government Printing Office, 1985, 542–546.

Page 20 *The Poles weren't the only surprised:* Fursenko and Naftali, *Khrushchev's Cold War,* 195–211; Taubman, *Khrushchev: The Man and His Era,* 396–403.

Page 21 *Khrushchev explained to Gomułka:* "New Evidence on the Berlin Crisis 1958–1962," "Minutes from the Discussion between the Delegation of the People's Republic of Poland and the Government of the USSR" (October 25–November 10, 1958), *Cold War International History Project Bulletin* (CWIHP-B), Woodrow Wilson International Center for Scholars, No. 11 (1998); retrieved from Douglas Selvage, *Khrushchev's November 1958 Berlin Ultimatum: New Evidence from the Polish Archives,* 200–203, www.wilsoncenter.org; Fursenko and Naftali, *Khrushchev's Cold War,* 207–209.

Page 21 *"Now the balance of forces":* CWIHP-B, No. 11 (1998), in Selvage, *Khrushchev's November 1958 Berlin Ultimatum,* 202; Matthias Uhl and Vladimir I. Ivkin, "'Operation Atom': The Soviet Union's Stationing of Nuclear Missiles in the German Democratic Republic, 1959," CWIHP-B, No. 12/13 (2001), 299–307.

Page 21 *What he told his Polish:* CWIHP-B, No. 11 (1998), in Selvage, *Khrushchev's November 1958 Berlin Ultimatum,* 200–201; Nikita S. Khrushchev, *For Victory in Peaceful Competition with Capitalism,* 738.

Page 21 *He had also:* Matthew Evangelista, "'Why Keep Such an Army?' Khrushchev's Troop Reductions," CWIHP Working Paper No. 19, Washington, D.C.: December 1997, 4–5; Taubman, *Khrushchev: The Man and His Era,* 379.

Page 22 *The second source of Khrushchev's:* Robert Service, *Comrades! A History of World*

Communism. Cambridge, MA: Harvard University Press, 2007, 314; Fursenko and Naftali, *Khrushchev's Cold War*, 148.

Page 22 The third source of Khrushchev's: Service, *Comrades!*, 310; Nikita S. Khrushchev, "Khrushchev Remembers, Part III: The Death of Stalin, the Menace of Beria," *Life*, December 11, 1970, 54–72.

Page 22 At the time, Khrushchev: Hope M. Harrison, *Driving the Soviets up the Wall—Soviet–East German Relations. 1953–1961.* Princeton, NJ: Princeton University Press, 2003, 27; Mark Kramer, "The Early Post-Stalin Succession Struggle and Upheavals in East-Central Europe: Internal-External Linkages in Soviet Policy Making (Part1)," *Journal of Cold War Studies*, 1, nos. 1–3 (1999), 12–28.

Page 23 The March 1953 figure of 56,605: Bundesministerium für Gesamtdeutsche Fragen (BMG), ed., *Die Flucht aus der Sowjetzone und die Sperrmassnahmen des Kommunistischen Regimes vom 13. August 1961 in Berlin,* 1961; Helge Heidemeyer, *Flucht und Zuwanderung aus der SBZ/DDR 1945/1949–1961, Die Flüchtlingspolitik der Bundesrepublik Deutschland bis zum Bau der Berliner Mauer.* Düsseldorf: Droste, 1994, 338.

Page 23 "All we need is a peaceful": Feliks Chuev, *Sto sorok besed s Molotovym.* Moscow: Terra, 1991, 332–334; *Izvestia*, 12/23/2003.

Page 23 Beria wanted to negotiate: Vladislav M. Zubok and Constantine Pleshakov, *Inside the Kremlin's Cold War: From Stalin to Khrushchev.* Cambridge, MA: Harvard University Press, 1996, 159–160; Andrei Gromyko, *Memories.* London: Hutchinson, 1989, 316.

Page 23 The post-Stalin collective leadership: Harrison, *Driving the Soviets up the Wall*, 24; "Memorandum, V. Chuikov, P. Iudin, L. Il'ichev to G. M. Malenkov, 18 May 1953, Secret," retrieved from Christian F. Ostermann, "'This Is Not a Politburo, but a Madhouse'—The Post-Stalin Succession Struggle, Soviet *Deutschlandpolitik* and the SED: New Evidence from Russian, German, and Hungarian Archives," CWIHP-B, No. 10 (1998), 74–78.

Page 23 At the party plenary: "Postanovlenie plenuma TsK KPSS o prestupnykh antipartiinykh i antigosudarstvennykh deistviiakh Beriia," in "Delo Beriia," Plenum TsK KPSS Iiuli 1953 goda, Stenograficheskii Otchet, 203, 304.

Page 24 In the first days following Khrushchev's: FRUS, 1958–1960, vol. VIII, Berlin Crisis, 1958–1959, Thompson cables to Washington on November 11 and 14, 1958, 47–48, 62; and Eisenhower—Herter phone conversation of November 28, 1958, p. 114.

Page 24 "West Berlin has turned": Oleg Grinevskii, "Berlinskkii krizis 1958–1959." *Zvezda*, no. 2 (1996), 127.

Page 25 Khrushchev's son Sergei: Sergei N. Khrushchev, *Nikita S. Khrushchev: Krizisy i Rakety. Vzgliad Iznutri.* Moscow: Novosti, vol. 1, 1994, 416.

Page 25 In answer to similar doubts: Oleg Troyanovsky, *Cherez godi i rasstoiania: Istoriia Odnoi Semyi.* Moscow: Vagrius, 1997, 211–213.

Page 26 Giving him only a half hour's: Hubert Horatio Humphrey Papers. Trip Files, Russian, in Senatorial Files, 1949–1964, Box 703, Minnesota Historical Society, Minneapolis, MN; FRUS, 1958–1960, vol. VIII, Berlin Crisis, 1958–1959, 149–153; JFKL, Memorandum of conversation (Memcon) between Sen. Humphrey and Acting Secretary of State Christian Herter, December 8, 1958, Box 126; Hubert H. Humphrey, "Eight Hours with Khrushchev," *Life*, January 12, 1959, 80–91.

Page 26 To show off his knowledge: FRUS, 1958–1960, vol. VIII, Berlin Crisis, 1958–1959, 149–153.

Page 26 "somebody who has risen": Humphrey, "Eight Hours with Khrushchev," 82.

Page 26 In recounting his meeting: Quoted in Department of State, Central Files, 762.00/12-358.

Page 28 Eisenhower responded to Khrushchev's: Christian Bremen, *Die Eisenhower-Administration und die zweite Berlin-Krise 1958–1961.* Veröffentlichungen der Historischen Kommision zu Berlin, Bd. 95, Berlin and New York: de Gruyter, 1998, 383–386.

Page 28 Khrushchev congratulated himself: Taubman, *Khrushchev: The Man and His Era*, 416, quoting Sergei N. Khrushchev, *Krizisy i Rakety*, 442–443; Troyanovsky, *Cherez godi*, 218.

Page 28 For that reason, Khrushchev's considerations: Taubman, *Khrushchev: The Man and His Era*,

421; Nikita S. Khrushchev, "Memuary Nikity Sergeevicha Khrushcheva," *Voprosy Istorii*, no. 4 (1993), 36.

Page 29 "the capitalists never missed": Nikita S. Khrushchev, *Khrushchev Remembers: The Last Testament.* Boston: Little, Brown, 1974, 372.

Page 29 Disregarding the advice of his pilot: Nikita S. Khrushchev, *Khrushchev Remembers: The Last Testament,* 372. Sergei N. Khrushchev, *Nikita Khrushchev and the Creation of a Superpower.* University Park: Pennsylvania State University Press, 2000, 328–330; Fred Kaplan, *1959: The Year Everything Changed.* Hoboken, NJ: John Wiley & Sons, 2009, 107.

Page 30 "From a ravaged, backward, illiterate Russia": Nikita S. Khrushchev, "Memuary Nikity Sergeevicha Khrushcheva," *Voprosy Istorii*, no. 4 (1993), 38–39.

Page 30 To Khrushchev's relief and delight: Morton Schwartz, *The Foreign Policy of the USSR: Domestic Factors.* Encino, CA: Dickenson, 1975, 89; Nikita S. Khrushchev, *Khrushchev Remembers: The Last Testament,* 377.

Page 30 "We do not contemplate": JFKL, Memcon, USSR–Vienna Meeting, Background Documents, 1953–1961, September 15, 1959, Box 126.

Page 30 For his part, Eisenhower called: Jean Edward Smith, *The Defense of Berlin.* Baltimore: Johns Hopkins Press, 1963, 212; Gelb, *The Berlin Wall*, 43.

Page 31 His trip had nearly ended: Los Angeles Times, September 20, 1959, p. 1.

Page 31 The climactic Camp David meeting: FRUS, 1958–1960, vol. IX, Berlin Crisis, 1959–1960, 35–53; vol. X, Part I, Eastern Europe, Soviet Union, Cyprus, Doc. 129–136 (132), 459–485; Beschloss, *Mayday*, 206–215.

Page 31 The following morning, Khrushchev agreed: Fursenko, *Khrushchev's Cold War*, 238; JFKL, Eisenhower and Khrushchev meetings, September 26–27, 1959. USSR–Vienna Meeting, Background Documents 1953–1961, Box 4, National Archives and Records Administration (NARA).

Page 32 Initially, Khrushchev celebrated the incident: Sergei N. Khrushchev, *Creation of a Superpower*, 365–367.

Page 33 Years later, Khrushchev would concede: Dr. A. McGhee Harvey, "A Conversation with Khrushchev: The Beginning of His Fall from Power," *Life*, December 18, 1970, 48B.

Page 34 Eisenhower removed Khrushchev's: FRUS, 1958–1960, vol. X, Part I, Eastern Europe Region, Soviet Union, Cyprus, Doc. 82, Memo of Conference with President Eisenhower, July 8, 1959.

Page 34 In what would be the one and only session: Taubman, *Khrushchev: The Man and His Era*, 465, 495, quotes *Pravda*, May 19, 1960; Beschloss, *Mayday*, 299; A. Merriman Smith, *A President's Odyssey.* New York: Harper, 1961, 199; Thomas P. Whitney, ed., *Khrushchev Speaks—Selected Speeches, Articles, and Press Conferences, 1949–1961.* Ann Arbor: University of Michigan Press, 1963, 389–390.

Page 35 It concerned the sad story: Stanislaw Gaevsk, "Kak Nikita Sergeyevich vstrech v verkhak sorval." *Kievski Novosi*, no. 1 (1993).

Page 35 For all his theatrics, however, Khrushchev: Beschloss, *Mayday*, 305; Fursenko and Naftali, *Khrushchev's Cold War*, 282; Beschloss, *Crisis Years*, 31–32.

Page 35 To the surprise of U.S. diplomats: Pravda, May 21, 1960, 1–2; "Text of the Address by Khrushchev in East Berlin," *New York Times*, 05/20/1960; "Mr. K. Quiet in East Berlin," *Christian Science Monitor*, May 20, 1960; "Back Home in Berlin, Mr. K. Smiles Again," *New York Times*, 05/20/1960.

Page 36 Instead of flying to America: Taubman, *Khrushchev: The Man and His Era*, 472; Sergei N. Khrushchev, *Creation of a Superpower*, 408–409; Nikita S. Khrushchev, *Khrushchev Remembers: The Last Testament*, 463.

Page 36 When one of the Soviet sailors: Taubman, *Khrushchev: The Man and His Era*, 474; Nikita S. Khrushchev, *Khrushchev Remembers: The Last Testament*, 467.

Page 37 "So, another dirty trick": Shevchenko, *Breaking with Moscow*, 105–106.

Page 37 The only saving grace: Shevchenko, *Breaking with Moscow*, 96–101; Martin Ebon, *The Andropov File: The Life and Ideas of Yuri V. Andropov, General Secretary of the Communist*

Party of the Soviet Union. New York: McGraw-Hill, 1983, 26; Taubman, *Khrushchev: The Man and His Era,* 474.

Page 37 None of that dampened: Aleksei I. Adzhubei, *Krushenie illiuzii.* Moscow: Interbuk, 1991, 235; Nikolai Zakharov, "Kak Khrushceve Ameriku Pokarial," in *Argumenty I Fakty,* no. 52 (2004), 12; Khrushchev, *Khrushchev Remembers: The Last Testament,* 471.

Page 37 By September 26, only a week into: New York Times, 09/26/1960.

Page 37 Khrushchev was determined to use: Robert Divine, *Blowing on the Wind: The Nuclear Test Ban Debate, 1954–1960.* New York: Oxford University Press, 1978, 100; Stephen E. Ambrose, *Eisenhower: The President,* vol. 2. New York: Simon & Schuster, 1984, 349–350; Dwight D. Eisenhower Presidential Library (DDEL). Eisenhower–Bulganin, 10/21/1956.

Page 37 In public, Khrushchev hedged: Shevchenko, *Breaking with Moscow,* 108.

Page 37 But behind the scenes: John Bartlow Martin, *Adlai Stevenson and the World: The Life of Adlai E. Stevenson.* Garden City, NY: Doubleday, 1977, 471–475.

Page 37 Stevenson responded that: Adlai E. Stevenson Papers. Memorandum (Memo) 01/16/1960: Tucker conversation; Martin, *Adlai Stevenson,* 471–475.

Page 38 Republican Henry Cabot Lodge Jr.: Nikita S. Khrushchev, *Khrushchev Remembers: The Last Testament,* 489–490.

Page 38 By autumn, the Eisenhower administration: Beschloss, *Crisis Years,* 35; DDEL, Lodge–Christian Herter, 02/09/1960; Nikita S. Khrushchev, *Khrushchev Remembers: The Last Testament,* 489–491; Richard Nixon Papers, Nixon tel. note 02/27/1960.

Page 38 "We thought we would have more hope": Nikita S. Khrushchev, *Khrushchev Remembers: The Last Testament,* 489.

Page 38 Though Kennedy's campaign rhetoric: Fursenko and Naftali, *Khrushchev's Cold War,* 340; Soviet Central Committee Archive (TsKhSD), Gromyko to N.S. Khrushchev, August 3, 1960, Folio 5, List 30, File 335, 92–108; reproduced in CWIHP-B, No. 4 (1994), 65–67.

Page 39 The candidates continued to shower attention: New York Times, 09/27/1960.

Page 39 Kennedy predicted that the next president: New York Times, 10/07/1960.

Page 40 Yet before a national television audience: Washington Post, 10/08/1960.

Page 40 During their third debate: JFKL, *"Face-to-Face, Nixon-Kennedy" Vice President Richard M. Nixon and Senator John F. Kennedy Third Joint Television-Radio Broadcast,* October 13, 1960: http://www.jfklibrary.org/Historical+Resources/Archives/Reference+Desk/Speeches/JFK/ JFK+Pre-Pres/1960/Third+Presidential+Debate+101360.htm; The American Presidency Project: http://www.presidency.ucsb.edu; Smith, *The Defense of Berlin,* 229.

Page 41 Behind the scenes: Donald S. Zagoria, *The Sino-Soviet Conflict 1956–1961.* Princeton, NJ: Princeton University Press 1962, 245–251; Nikita S. Khrushchev, *Khrushchev Remembers: The Last Testament,* 254–255.

Page 41 The Soviet embassy in Beijing: Vladislav M. Zubok, "Khrushchev and the Berlin Crisis (1958–1962)," CWIHP Working Paper No. 6, May 1993, 17.

Page 41 Mao opposed Khrushchev's foreign policy: Nikita S. Khrushchev, *Khrushchev Remembers.* Boston: Little, Brown, 1970, 461–479; Nikita S. Khrushchev, *Khrushchev Remembers: The Last Testament,* 245–248.

Page 42 "Think of it": Beschloss, *Crisis Years,* 42.

Page 42 Mao had shocked Khrushchev: Nikita S. Khrushchev, *Khrushchev Remembers: The Last Testament,* 254–255; Nikita S. Khrushchev, *Memoirs of Nikita Khrushchev,* ed. Sergei Khrushchev. University Park: Pennsylvania State University, 2004–2007, vol. 3, 458.

Page 42 "They understood the implications": Nikita S. Khrushchev, *Khrushchev Remembers,* 471.

Page 43 On the same trip: Zhisui Li and Anne F. Thurston, eds., *The Private Life of Chairman Mao: The Memoirs of Mao's Personal Physician.* New York, 1994, 261; Taubman, *Khrushchev: The Man and His Era,* 391–392.

Page 43 "The interpreter is translating": Taubman, *Khrushchev: The Man and His Era,* 391–392; Sergei N. Khrushchev, *Memoirs of Nikita Khrushchev,* vol. 3, 458; Mikhail Romm, *Ustnye rasskazy.* Moscow: Kinotsentr, 1991, 154.

Page 43 Just two days before the gathering: Edward Crankshaw, *The New Cold War: Moscow v. Pekin.*
Harmondsworth, England, and Baltimore: Penguin Books, 1963/1970, 97–105; Taubman,
Khrushchev: The Man and His Era, 470.

Page 44 He attacked the absent Mao: Taubman, *Khrushchev: The Man and His Era,* 471; Crankshaw,
New Cold War, 107.

Page 44 "Within the short span": Chinese Communist Party Central Committee letter of February
29, 1964 to Soviet Central Committee, excerpted in John Gittings, ed., *Survey of the Sino-
Soviet Dispute: A Commentary and Extracts from Recent Polemics, 1963–1967.* London and
New York: Royal Institute of International Affairs, 1968, 130–131, 139; Jung Chang and Jon
Halliday, *Mao: The Unknown Story.* New York: Alfred A. Knopf/Doubleday, 2005, 456.

Page 45 Khrushchev called Mao: Beschloss, *Crisis Years,* 42–43; Beschloss, *Mayday,* 323–325; Chang,
Mao, 456; David Floyd, *Mao Against Khrushchev—A Short History of the Sino-Soviet Conflict.*
New York: Praeger, 1964, 280; *New York Times,* 12/02/1960; *New York Times,* 02/12/1961.

Page 45 Deng attacked the Soviet leader's: Crankshaw, *New Cold War,* 131–133; Nikita S.
Khrushchev, *Khrushchev Remembers,* 475– 477.

Page 45 Mao's interpreter Yan Mingfu: Taubman, *Khrushchev: The Man and His Era,* 472.

Page 46 Ulbricht sat forward and erect: Russian Ministry of Foreign Affairs Archives (AVP-RF),
Record of Meeting of Comrade N.S. Khrushchev with Comrade W. Ulbricht, 30 November
1960, Fond 0742, Opis 6, Por 4, Papka 43, Secret, in Hope Harrison, "Ulbricht and the Concrete
'Rose': New Archival Evidence on the Dynamics of Soviet–East German Relations and the
Berlin Crisis, 1958–61," CWIHP Working Paper No. 5, May 1993, 68–78, Papers, Appendices.

Page 46 The Soviet ambassador in East Berlin: Harrison, *Driving the Soviets up the Wall,* 147:
TsKhSD, Pervukhin, "Otchet o rabote Posol'stva SSR. V GDR za 1960 god," 15.12.60, R, 8948,
Fond 5, Opis 49, D. 287, 85; AVP-RF, Pervukin Report to Gromyko, October 19, 1960, "K
voprosu o razyryve zapadnoi Germaniei soglasheniia o vnutrigermanskoi gorgovle s GDR,"
Fond 5, Papka 40, D. 40, 3.

Page 46 A second secretary: Harrison, *Driving the Soviets up the Wall,* 149: TsKhSD, "Zapis' besedy s
sekretarem Berlinskogo okruzhkoma SEPG G. Naemliisom," October 17, 1960, from the
diary of A. P. Kazennov, Second Secretary of the USSR embassy in the GDR, October 24,
1960, R. 8948, Fond 5, Opis 49, D. 288, 5; Harrison, *Driving the Soviets up the Wall,* 147.

Page 46 Ulbricht had created a new National Defense Council: Armin Wagner, *Walter Ulbricht und
die geheime Sicherheitspolitik der SED: Der Nationale Verteidigungsrat der DDR und seine
Vorgeschichte (1953–1971).* Berlin: Christoph Links, 2002, 189; Matthias Uhl and Armin
Wagner, "Another Brick in the Wall: Reexamining Soviet and East German Policy During the
1961 Berlin Crisis: New Evidence, New Documents," CWIHP Working Paper, published
under "Storming On to Paris: The 1961 'Buria' Exercise and the Planned Solution of the
Berlin Crisis," in Vojtech Mastny, Sven G. Holtsmark, and Andreas Wenger, eds., *War Plans
and Alliances in the Cold War: Threat Perceptions in the East and West.* New York: Routledge,
2006, 46–71; Harrison, *Driving the Soviets up the Wall,* 149.

Page 47 In his most recent letter: Stiftung Archive der Parteien und Massenorganisationen im
Bundesarchiv (SAPMO-BArch), Letter from Ulbricht and the SED delegation in Moscow to
the First Secretary of the CC of the CPSU, Comrade Khrushchev, Moscow, November 22,
1960, ZPA, DY, 30/J IV 2/202/336, Bd. 2, 1;11.

Page 47 Khrushchev assured a skeptical Ulbricht: Fursenko and Naftali, *Khrushchev's Cold War,*
340–341.

Page 47 Though Ulbricht remained distrustful: Fursenko and Naftali, *Khrushchev's Cold War,* 341;
Letter from Ulbricht to Khrushchev, September 15 1961. SED Archives, IfGA, ZPA, Central
Committee files, Walter Ulbricht's office, Internal Party Archive, J IV 2/202/130, in Harrison,
"Ulbricht and the Concrete 'Rose,'" CWIHP Working Paper No. 5, 126–130, Appendices;
Letter from Ulbricht and the SED CC delegation to the CPSU 22nd Congress in Moscow to
Khrushchev, October 30, 1961, SED Archives, IfGA, ZPA, NL 182/1206, in Harrison,
"Ulbricht and the Concrete 'Rose,'" 132–139.

Page 47 "The situation in Berlin": Harrison, *Driving the Soviets up the Wall,* 151.

Page 48 "We still have not taken": AVP-RF, Record of Meeting of Comrade N. S. Khrushchev with Comrade W. Ulbricht, November 30, 1960, Fond 0742, Opis 6, Por 4, Papka 43, Secret, in Harrison, "Ulbricht and the Concrete 'Rose,'" CWIHP Working Paper No. 5, 69, Appendices.

Page 48 "Luckily, our adversaries": AVP-RF, Record of Meeting of Comrade N. S. Khrushchev with Comrade W. Ulbricht, 30 November 1960, Fond 0742, Opis 6, Por 4, Papka 43, Secret, in Harrison, "Ulbricht and the Concrete 'Rose,'" CWIHP Working Paper No. 5, 73.

3. KENNEDY: A PRESIDENT'S EDUCATION

Page 49 "We can live with the status quo": Fursenko and Naftali, *Khrushchev's Cold War,* 342; quotation retrieved from David G. Coleman, "'The Greatest Issue of All': Berlin, American National Security, and the Cold War, 1948–1963," unpublished dissertation (University of Queensland, 2000), 236–237.

Page 49 "So let us begin anew": The National Archives, *Our Documents: 100 Milestone Documents from the National Archives.* New York: Oxford University Press, 2003, 222.

Page 50 Eisenhower worried about Kennedy's: Robert Dallek, *An Unfinished Life: John F. Kennedy, 1917–1963.* Boston: Little, Brown, 2003, 302; DDEL, *Earl Mazo OH* (Columbia Oral History Project); Herbert S. Parmet, *JFK—The Presidency of John F. Kennedy.* New York: The Dial Press, 1983, 72; Geoffrey Perret, *Eisenhower.* New York: Random House, 1 999, 597.

Page 50 Eisenhower doubted young Kennedy: Michael O'Brien, *John F. Kennedy: A Biography.* New York: St. Martin's Press, 2005, 175–176, 189–190; John Hersey, "Reporter at Large: Survival," *New Yorker,* June 17, 1944.

Page 51 On the cold, overcast morning: Washington Post, 01/19/1961; *New York Times,* 01/19/1961.

Page 51 Ahead of the meeting: JFKL, President's Office Files (POF), Memo of Subjects for Discussion at Meeting of President Eisenhower and Senator Kennedy on Thursday, January 19, 1961, Box 29a.

Page 51 Eisenhower told Democratic political operative: Dallek, *An Unfinished Life,* 303; *New York Times,* 12/07/1960; JFKL, *Robert F. Kennedy OH;* JFKL, *Clark Clifford OH;* O'Brien, *JFK,* 501.

Page 51 Kennedy had been less taken with: JFKL, *Robert F. Kennedy OH;* JFKL, *Charles Spalding OH;* Dallek, *An Unfinished Life,* 302.

Page 52 In contrasting Eisenhower with Kennedy: JFKL, *Hervé Alphand OH.*

Page 52 Kennedy was perplexed: JFKL, *Robert F. Kennedy OH;* Arthur M. Schlesinger, *A Thousand Days: John F. Kennedy in the White House.* Boston: Houghton Mifflin, 1965, 118–119; Gary A. Donaldson. *The First Modern Campaign: Kennedy, Nixon, and the Election of 1960.* Lanham, MD: Rowman & Littlefield, 2007, 150; O'Brien, *JFK,* 499; Geoffrey Perret, *Jack: A Life Like No Other.* New York: Random House, 2002, 271–272; JFKL, *John Sharon OH.*

Page 52 And his coattails: New York Times, 11/10/1960; Schlesinger, *A Thousand Days,* 125; Perret, *Jack: A life like no other,* 272; Benjamin C. Bradlee, *Conversations with Kennedy.* New York: W. W. Norton, 1975, 33–34; JFKL, *Clark Clifford OH.*

Page 53 During his transition briefings: Lawrence Freedman, *Kennedy's Wars—Berlin, Cuba, Laos and Vietnam.* New York: Oxford University Press, 2000, 61; O'Brien, *JFK,* 550, 624, 644, 664.

Page 53 Instead, the two teams: O'Brien, *JFK,* 509–513, 644.

Page 53 "Current Soviet tactics": DDEL, *Dwight D. Eisenhower Papers as President of the United States, Presidential Transition Series,* Box 1, Topics suggested by Mr. Kennedy.

Page 54 Martin Hillenbrand, the director: JFKL, *Martin Hillenbrand OH.*

Page 54 "We can live with the status quo": Fursenko and Naftali, *Khrushchev's Cold War,* 342; quote retrieved from David G. Coleman, "'The Greatest Issue of All': Berlin, American National Security, and the Cold War, 1948–1963," unpublished dissertation (University of Queensland, 2000), 236–237.

Page 55 In February 1959, Kennedy: New York Times, 02/23/1959.

Page 55 "Our position in Europe": Washington Post, 08/02/1959.

Page 55 In an article published by: New York Times, 06/15/1960.

Page 55 The president had only 5,000 troops: Kowalczuk and Wolle, *Roter Stern über Deutschland,* 97; Alan John Day, ed. *Border and Territorial Disputes.* Detroit: Gale Research, 1982, 42.

Page 56 The CIA document warned Kennedy: CIA, *National Intelligence Estimate (NIE) 11-4-60 Main Trends in Soviet Capabilities and Policies,* 1960–1965; reproduced in Loch K. Johnson, *Strategic Intelligence,* vol. 1. Westport, CT: Praeger, 2007, Appendix E, 257–263 (263).

Page 56 So, with Berlin on hold: O'Brien, *JFK,* 355, 512, 613–614, 624.

Page 56 Eisenhower portrayed Laos as: O'Brien, *JFK,* 512–513; Mark K. Updegrove, *Second Acts: Presidential Lives and Legacies after the White House.* Guilford, CT: The Lyons Press, 2006, 29.

Page 57 Kennedy was struck by Eisenhower's: JFKL, POF, JFK Memo, Special Correspondence, Greenstein and Immerman, January 19, 1961, Box 29a, 573, 577; POF, Clark Clifford to JFK, Special correspondence, January 24, 1961, Box 29a; Robert S. McNamara, *In Retrospect: The Tragedy and Lessons of Vietnam.* New York: Vintage Books, 1996, 35–36; *Time,* 01/27/1961, 10; Perret, *Eisenhower,* 599–600; DDEL, Memcon, January 19, 1961; Harry S. Truman Library. Memo, Clark Clifford to LBJ, November 29, 1967; DDEL, *Major General Wilton B. Persons OH* (Columbia Oral History Project); Dallek, *An Unfinished Life,* 302–305; Hugh Sidey, *John F. Kennedy, President.* New York: Atheneum, 1964, 37; Parmet, *JFK,* 80.

Page 57 Eisenhower made no reference to: Freedman, *Kennedy's Wars,* 47–48; Fursenko and Naftali, *Khrushchev's Cold War,* 258.

Page 57 "You have an invaluable asset": Perret, *Jack: A Life Like No Other,* 278.

Page 58 Eisenhower picked up a special phone: Perret, *Jack: A Life Like No Other,* 278. "Kennedy Given Example of Fast Helicopter Service," *Washington Post,* 01/20/1961; *Times Herald,* "The Unusual and the Routine Fill Eisenhower's Final Day at the White House," *New York Times,* 01/20/1961.

Page 58 Two-thirds of the sold-out crowd: Christian Science Monitor, 01/21/1961.

Page 58 The skies opened: Beschloss, *Crisis Years,* 48; Charles C. Kenney, *John F. Kennedy: The Presidential Portfolio: History as told through the collection of the John F. Kennedy Library and Museum.* New York: Public Affairs, 2000; Richard M. Nixon, *RN: The Memoirs of Richard Nixon.* New York: Warner Books, 1979, 23; Theodore C. Sorensen, *Kennedy.* New York: HarperCollins, 1965, 240–242.

Page 59 Dean Acheson, who had been President Truman's: Beschloss, *Crisis Years,* 19.

Page 60 On December 1, 1960, Kennedy: Aleksandr Fursenko and Timothy Naftali, *One Hell of a Gamble: Khrushchev, Castro, and Kennedy, 1958–1964.* New York: W. W. Norton, 1997, 81–82; JFKL, RFK Pre-Administration Political Files, *1960 telephone log,* Box 54; Harrison, *Driving the Soviets up the Wall,* 166–167; Fursenko and Naftali, *Khrushchev's Cold War,* 349–351.

Page 60 Less encouraging to Khrushchev: Fursenko and Naftali, *One Hell of a Gamble,* 81–82, quoting Archive of the Foreign Intelligence Service. Shelepin to N. S. Khrushchev, December 3, 1960.

Page 60 A few days later, on December 12: Sidey, *JFK,* 39; Beschloss, *Crisis Years,* 32.

Page 61 The ambassador, whom U.S. officials: Beschloss, *Crisis Years,* 32; Adlai E. Stevenson Papers, Stevenson memo: Tucker conversation, January 16, 1960.

Page 61 Menshikov argued to Bobby: JFKL, Memo, Robert F. Kennedy to Rusk, Robert F. Kennedy Papers, December 12, 1960.

Page 61 Two days after meeting with: Beschloss, *Crisis Years,* 42; JFKL, Harriman Memcon, Harriman Papers, November 21 and December 14, 1960.

Page 61 "I think it's important to find out": Martin, *Adlai Stevenson,* 571.

Page 62 Beyond that, West German Chancellor: Baltimore Sun, 10/20/1960.

Page 62 After much eating and drinking: David K. E. Bruce diary entry, January 5, 1961, Department of State, Bruce Diaries, Lot 64, D 327, Secret; FRUS, 1961–1963, vol. V, Soviet Union, Doc. 10.

Page 63 Just nine days before his inauguration: George F. Kennan and T. Christopher Jespersen, eds., *Interviews with George F. Kennan.* Jackson: University Press of Mississippi, 2002, 56–57.

Page 63 Yet Kennan now opposed: JFKL, *George Kennan OH.*

Page 63 During the campaign, Kennan told Kennedy: David Mayers, *George Kennan and the Dilemmas of US Foreign Policy.* New York: Oxford University Press, 1988, 208.

Page 64 Asked by Kennedy why Khrushchev was so eager: Kennan and Jespersen, *Interviews with Kennan,* 59.

Page 65 A first version read: Sorensen, *Kennedy,* 242.

Page 66 Just as important as his words: Dallek, *An Unfinished Life,* 176, 317, 322, 342; Lincoln Papers, *Evelyn Lincoln Diary,* January 2, 4, 11, 16, 20, 1961; JFKL, *Janet Travell OH.*

Page 66 It quoted his physicians: New York Times, 01/17/1961.

Page 67 The article listed adult health issues: New York Times, 01/21/1961.

Page 68 David Murphy: David E. Murphy, Sergei A. Kondrashev, and George Bailey, *Battleground Berlin: CIA vs. KGB in the Cold War.* New Haven, CT: Yale University Press, 1997, 343–349, 359; Cable, Berlin, January 4, 1961, in Dispatch, Berlin, February 15, 1961, CIA-HRP (Historical Review Program); "Goleniewski's Work with the Soviets," Memo, January 4, 1964, CIA-HRP.

Page 68 Murphy had warned the CIA: David C. Martin, *Wilderness of Mirrors: Intrigue, Deception, and the Secrets That Destroyed Two of the Cold War's Most Important Agents.* Guilford, CT: Lyons Press, 2003, 97–98.

Page 69 The CIA also needed: Martin, *Wilderness of Mirrors,* 91.

4. KENNEDY: A FIRST MISTAKE

Page 72 "The United States Government": FRUS, 1961–1963, vol. V, Soviet Union, Doc. 12.

Page 72 "Each day, the crises": Brian R. Dirck, *The Executive Branch of Federal Government: People, Process, and Politics.* Santa Barbara, CA: ABC-CLIO, 2007, 457–459 (457).

Page 72 Nikita Khrushchev summoned the U.S. ambassador: Beschloss, *Crisis Years,* 54–55; JFKL, Thompson to Rusk, January 21 and January 24, 1961.

Page 73 Khrushchev then nodded: FRUS, 1961–1963, vol. V, Soviet Union, Doc. 9–10, Telegram from the Embassy in the Soviet Union to the Department of State, Moscow, January 21, 1961, 4 p.m. and 7 p.m.

Page 73 Khrushchev had carefully calculated: Beschloss, *Crisis Years,* 149; Fursenko and Naftali, *Khrushchev's Cold War,* 290, 338; David Knight, *The Spy Who Never Was and Other True Spy Stories.* New York: Doubleday, 1978.

Page 74 Back in November: JFKL, National Security Files NSF, Harriman to JFK, November 12 and November 15, 1960, Box 176; also see FRUS, 1961–1963, vol. V, Soviet Union, Doc. 10–11.

Page 74 The aide-mémoire said: JFKL, POF, Telegram, Thompson to JFK, January 21, 1961, Box 125a.

Page 75 When Khrushchev's offer to release: JFKL, Rusk to Thompson, January 23, 1961; Beschloss, *Crisis Years,* 55, 56; Philip A. Goduti Jr., *Kennedy's Kitchen Cabinet and the Pursuit of Peace: The Shaping of American Foreign Policy, 1961–1963.* Jefferson, NC: McFarland, 2009, 20–21.

Page 75 Secretary of State Dean Rusk: FRUS, 1961–1963, vol. V, Soviet Union, Doc. 11, Telegram from the Department of State to the Embassy in the Soviet Union, January 23, 1961, 5:57 p.m.

Page 75 In the meantime, Khrushchev: Zubok and Pleshakov, *Inside the Kremlin's Cold War.*

Page 76 Eager to be useful to Kennedy: JFKL, POF, Telegram, Thompson to JFK, January 19, 1961, Box 125a.

Page 76 The president had initially responded: Taubman, *Khrushchev: The Man and His Era,* 487; JFKL, Memo, Bundy to JFK, February 27, 1961.

Page 77 Kennedy radiated calm self-satisfaction: FRUS, 1961–1963, vol. V, Soviet Union, Doc. 12.

Page 78 But among friends and advisers: JFKL, JFK to Bundy, February 6, 1961; JFKL, McNamara to Bundy, February 23, 1961, Box 328 NSF/NSWTB; Schlesinger, *A Thousand Days,* 303–306,

344, 346–347. Richard Reeves, *President Kennedy: Profile of Power.* New York: Simon & Schuster, 1993, 40–41.

Page 78 "You've got to understand": JFKL, *Robert F. Kennedy OH;* Beschloss, *Crisis Years,* 61; Ralph G. Martin, *A Hero of Our Time: An Intimate Story of the Kennedy Years.* New York: Macmillan, 1983, 351; *Saturday Evening Post,* 03/31/1962.

Page 78 The text: For text of Khrushchev's January 6 speech, see *Pravda,* January 24, 1961; extracts printed also in *American Foreign Policy, Current Documents,* 1961, 555–558; CIA, *Current Intelligence Weekly Review,* January 26, 1961, Job 79-S01060A; FRUS, 1961–1963, vol. V, Soviet Union, Doc. 15.

Page 78 The text spoke of Kremlin support: JFKL, NSF, Box 176; "Khrushchev Report on Moscow Conference of Representatives of Communist and Working Parties," Papers of President Kennedy: NSF, Countries, Box 189.

Page 78 With its timing just ahead of: JFKL and DDEL, Thompson–Herter, January 19, 1961; Beschloss, *Crisis Years,* 61.

Page 79 Then Secretary of State Christian A. Herter had told: Digital National Security Archive (DNSA). Memo for the President, Christian A. Herter, December 9, 1960, Subject: Analysis of the Moscow Statement of Communist Parties.

Page 80 He began by listing: JFKL, John F. Kennedy, January 30, 1961.

Page 81 Four days after that, McNamara: Beschloss, *Crisis Years,* 65–66. Andrew Bacevich, "Field Marshal McNamara," *The National Interest* online, May 1, 2007.

Page 81 On February 11, Khrushchev returned: Beschloss, *Crisis Years,* 78–79; Alexander Rabinowitch, ed., *Revolution and Politics in Russia: Essays in Memory of B. I. Nicolaevsky.* Bloomington: Indiana University Press, 1972, 281–292.

Page 82 Twelve days after his State of the Union: JFKL, NSF, N. S. Khrushchev speech, Thompson telegrams, Buildup to 02/11/1961 meeting, and Preparation for Thompson trip to Moscow, Box 176.

Page 82 The long-awaited meeting: Sidey, *JFK,* 164; Sorensen, *Kennedy,* 164, 542; JFKL, NSF, *Notes on Discussion,* February 11, 1961, Countries Series, USSR, Top Secret, "*The Thinking of the Soviet Leadership,*" Cabinet Room; Bundy drafted.

Page 83 At age fifty-six, Thompson: David Mayers, "After Stalin: The Ambassadors and America's Soviet Policy, 1953–1962," *Diplomacy and Statecraft,* 5, no. 2 (July 1994), 213–247; David Mayers, *The Ambassadors and America's Soviet Policy.* New York: Oxford University Press, 1995, 201.

Page 83 He agreed with Khrushchev's view: Taubman, *Khrushchev: The Man and His Era,* 399.

Page 83 "We have refused these overtures": DNSA, Relationship of Berlin Problem to Future of Germany and Overall Relations with Soviet Union, Secret, Cable, 1773, March 9, 1959.

Page 84 "He is the most pragmatic": JFKL, Memcon, February 11, 1961; JFKL, Kennan, Bohlen, Thompson OHs; JFKL, Thompson–DFR, February 13, 1961, BOX 176, Documents for Thompson Telegrams; Beschloss, *Crisis Years,* 69.

Page 84 Pointing to Khrushchev's Kremlin opposition: FRUS, 1961–1963, vol. V, Soviet Union, Doc. 20.

Page 84 He said the Soviets were "deeply concerned": JFKL, Thompson–Rusk, February 4, 1961, also in Declassified Documents, 1977/74B; Marc Trachtenberg, *History and Strategy.* Princeton, NJ: Princeton University Press, 1991, 172.

Page 84 Thompson said Khrushchev would be influenced: JFKL, Thompson–Rusk, February 4, 1961, also in Declassified Documents, 1977/74B; Beschloss, *Crisis Years,* 175.

Page 84 Walter Dowling, the U.S. ambassador: Department of State, Telegram 1218 from Bonn, Central Files, 762.00/2-861, also in Declassified Documents, 1977/74C.

Page 85 "I am sure we would err": FRUS, 1961–1963, vol. V, Soviet Union, Doc. 20.

Page 85 The February 11 meeting: JFKL, *Charles Bohlen OH,* May 21, 1964; FRUS, 1961–1963, vol. V, Soviet Union, Doc. 26, Notes on Discussion, drafted by Bundy, "The Thinking of the Soviet Leadership," Cabinet Room, February 11, 1961; Dallek, *An Unfinished Life,* 342, 546.

Page 86 The men arrayed before him: Beschloss, *Crisis Years,* 68–70; JFKL, Memcon, February 11,

1961; JFKL, *Kennan, Bohlen, Thompson OHs*; JFKL, Thompson–DFR, February 13, 1961; *New York Times*, 02/10/1961, 02/12/1961, 02/19/1961; Schlesinger, *A Thousand Days*, 303–306; Sorensen, *Kennedy*, 510, 541–542.

Page 86 Thompson argued that the U.S. "hope for the future": JFKL, NSF, Notes on Discussion, February 11, 1961, Countries Series, USSR, Top Secret, "The Thinking of the Soviet Leadership," Cabinet Room; Bundy drafted; FRUS, 1961–1963, vol. V, Soviet Union, Doc. 26.

Page 87 Bohlen opposed Khrushchev's suggestion: FRUS, 1961–1963, vol. V, Soviet Union, Doc. 26.

Page 87 As he had told his aide: Kenneth P. O'Donnell and David F. Powers, with Joe McCarthy, *"Johnny, We Hardly Knew Ye": Memories of John Fitzgerald Kennedy.* Boston: Little, Brown, 1972, 286.

Page 87 Beyond that, other countries: Sidey, *JFK*, 164.

Page 87 "It is my duty to make decisions": Sorensen, *Kennedy*, 542–543.

Page 88 On February 27, Bundy instructed: DNSA, *Crisis over Berlin*, February 27, 1961, vol. 7.

Page 88 But by the time Thompson phoned: Beschloss, *Crisis Years*, 80.

Page 88 Khrushchev delivered a speech: *New York Times*, 03/07/1961.

5. ULBRICHT AND ADENAUER: UNRULY ALLIANCES

Page 90 "Whatever elections show": John F. Kennedy, "A Democrat Looks at Foreign Policy," *Foreign Affairs*, 36, no. 1 (October 1957), 49.

Page 90 "West Berlin is experiencing a growth": SAPMO-BArch, ZPA, J IV 2/2/743. "Stichwort Protokoll der Beratung des Politbüros am 4. Januar 1961 über 'Die Gegenwärtige Lage und die Hauptaufgaben 1961,' " Politbüro, "Reinschriftenprotokoll Nr. 1 vom 4.1.1961."

Page 91 At age sixty-seven: Mario Frank, *Walter Ulbricht: Eine Deutsche Biographie.* Berlin: Siedler, 2001, 282.

Page 92 "Our task was to dispel": Konrad Adenauer, *Memoirs, 1945–1953.* Chicago: Henry Regnery, 1966, 41, 79.

Page 92 Speaking to his subjects: *Berliner Zeitung*, 01/01/1961.

Page 93 Ulbricht had never been: SAPMO-BArch, ZPA, J IV 2/2/743. "Stichwort Protokoll der Beratung des Politbüros am 4. Januar 1961 über 'Die Gegenwärtige Lage und die Hauptaufgaben 1961,' " Politbüro, "Reinschriftenprotokoll Nr. 1 vom 4.1.1961."

Page 93 Ulbricht's party lieutenants: Frank, *Walter Ulbricht*, 344–345.

Page 94 Like his mentor Stalin, Ulbricht: Frank, *Walter Ulbricht*, 287; Thomas Grimm, *Das Politbüro Privat—Ulbricht, Honecker, Mielke & Co. aus der Sicht ihrer Angestellten.* Berlin: Aufbau-Verlag, 2004, 203; Wolfgang Weber, *DDR—40 Jahre Stalinismus: Ein Beitrag zur Geschichte der DDR.* Essen: Arbeiterpresse, 1993, 63; Catherine Epstein, *The Last Revolutionaries: German Communists and Their Century.* Cambridge, MA: Harvard University Press, 2003, 20–22.

Page 95 Ulbricht was also a man: Grimm, *Das Politbüro Privat*, 203.

Page 95 At six in the morning: Weber, *DDR—40 Jahre Stalinismus*, 159.

Page 95 Wolfgang Leonhard, the youngest member: Wolfgang Leonhard, *Child of the Revolution.* Chicago: Henry Regnery, 1958, 300, 303.

Page 96 Ulbricht snapped: Leonhard, *Child of the Revolution*, 312.

Page 96 One example came in 1946: Weber, *DDR—40 Jahre Stalinismus*, 16–17.

Page 96 As late as April 1952: "Record of Conversation of Leaders of the Socialist Unity Party of Germany W. Pieck, W. Ulbricht, and O. Grotewohl with J. V. Stalin," April 7, 1952, reprinted in Christian F. Ostermann, *Uprising in East Germany 1953: The Cold War, the German Question, and the First Major Upheaval Behind the Iron Curtain.* Budapest and New York: Central European University Press, 2001, 38.

Page 98 Though the chancellor: Henning Köhler, *Adenauer: Eine politische Biographie.* Frankfurt am Main: Propyläen, 1994, 730.

Page 98 Yet Kennedy's undisciplined: Terence Prittie, *Konrad Adenauer, 1876–1967.* London: Tom Stacey, 1972, 283.

Page 98 Nevertheless, the chancellor smiled: Der Spiegel, 01/11/1961.

Page 99 Adenauer's young country: Eric Owen Smith, *The West German Economy.* New York: St. Martin's Press, 1983, 18.

Page 99 For all that accomplishment: Charles Williams, *Adenauer: The Father of the New Germany.* New York: John Wiley & Sons, 2000, 177; Hans-Peter Schwarz, *Konrad Adenauer: A German Politician and Statesman in a Period of War, Revolution and Reconstruction.* Vol. 1: *From the German Empire to the Federal Republic, 1876–1952.* Trans. Louise Willmot. Providence, RI: Berghahn Books, 1995, 154, 160, 357, 402, 602, 604.

Page 99 Dean Acheson, President Truman's: Dean Acheson, *Sketches from Life of Men I Have Known.* New York: Harper & Brothers, 1961, 169–170.

Page 99 An automobile accident: Schwarz, *Konrad Adenauer,* vol. 1, 108–109.

Page 99 Some likened his profile: Valentin Falin, *Politische Erinnerungen.* Munich: Droemer Knaur, 1993, 328.

Page 100 Just eight years after: "Man of the Year: We Belong to the West," *Time,* 01/04/1954.

Page 100 "The aim of the Russians": Adenauer, *Memoirs,* 78–79.

Page 100 In Adenauer's view: Adenauer, *Memoirs, 1945–1953,* 79.

Page 101 Over the two days: Anneliese Poppinga, *"Das Wichtigste ist der Mut": Konrad Adenauer—Die letzten fünf Kanzlerjahre.* Bergisch Gladbach, Germany: Gustav Lübbe, 1994, 282.

Page 101 During his election campaign: Prittie, *Konrad Adenauer,* 283.

Page 101 Kennedy had been born: Frank A. Mayer, *Adenauer and Kennedy: A Study in German-American Relations, 1969–1963.* New York: St. Martin's Press, 1996.

Page 102 Eisenhower's National Security Council: DDEL, White House Office, Office of the Special Assistant for National Security Affairs (OSANSA), Records, 1952–1961, NSC, Policy Papers Subseries, Box 23, Folder NSC 5803, "U.S. Policy Toward Germany (1)," Operations Coordinating Board, Report on Germany (The Federal Republic, Berlin, East Germany: NSC 5803), November 2, 1960, printed in FRUS, 1958–1960, vol. IX, Berlin Crisis, 1959–1960, p. 697; Adrian W. Schertz, *Die Deutschlandpolitik Kennedys und Johnsons: Unterschiedliche Ansätze innerhalb der amerikanischen Regierung.* Cologne: Böhlau, 1992, 47.

Page 102 U.S. ambassador to Bonn: DNSA, *The German Scene at the Turn of the Year.* Confidential, Dispatch, 1122, February 8, 1961, Berlin Crisis, Item Number: BC01991.

Page 103 With France's de Gaulle: Eckart Conze, *Die gaullistische Herausforderung: Die Deutsch-Französischen Beziehungen in der Amerikanischen Europapolitik 1958–1963.* Munich: R. Oldenbourg, 1995, 91–94.

Page 103 Kennedy's election had fed: Köhler, *Adenauer,* 1094.

Page 104 Adenauer was painfully aware: Walter Stützle, *Kennedy und Adenauer in der Berlin-Krise 1969–1962.* Bonn and Bad Godesberg: Neue Gesellschaft, 1973, 19–20; Mayer, *Adenauer and Kennedy,* 7; John Fitzgerald Kennedy, *A Compilation of Statements and Speeches Made During His Service in the United States Senate and House of Representatives.* Washington, D.C.: U.S. Government Printing Office, 1964, 979–980.

Page 104 Schumacher, who had lost: Schwarz, *Konrad Adenauer,* vol. 1, 596–603.

Page 104 Acheson had considered Schumacher: Acheson, *Sketches,* 171.

Page 104 Even after his death: Die Zeit, 12/15/1955.

Page 104 "Went to bed early": JFKL, JFK Personal Papers, *Diary of European Trip,* ms., Box 1; Herbert S. Parmet, *Jack: The Struggles of John F. Kennedy.* New York: The Dial Press, 1983, 51.

Page 104 "We should be ready": John F. Kennedy and Allan Nevins, *The Strategy of Peace.* New York: Harper & Row, 1960, 7, 11, 12, 30; Mayer, *Adenauer and Kennedy,* 8, citing his interview with McGeorge Bundy, August 25, 1988, on "chancellor's veto."

Page 105 Nothing in Adenauer's life: Rolf-Dietrich Keil, *Mit Adenauer in Moskau—Erinnerungen eines Dolmetschers.* Bonn: Bouvier, 1997, 79, 95, 97.

Page 105 Adenauer had been shaken: Anneliese Poppinga, *Meine Erinnerungen an Konrad Adenauer.* Stuttgart: Deutsche Verlags-Anstalt, 1970, 166.

Page 105 Khrushchev got the better: Henry Ashby Turner, *The Two Germanies Since 1945*. New Haven, CT: Yale University Press, 1987, 87.

Page 105 "The freedom of 10,000": Guido Knopp, *Die Gefangenen*. Munich: Goldmann, 2005, 370.

Page 105 Having never forgotten: Mayer, *Adenauer and Kennedy*, 8, quoting Georg M. Schild, "John F. Kennedy and Berlin," Paper Presented at the Nineteenth Annual Meeting of the Society for Historians of American Foreign Relations, University of Virginia, Charlottesville, June 17–20, 1993; Kennedy and Nevins, *The Strategy of Peace*, 212–213.

Page 105 Adenauer even sent Nixon: Köhler, *Adenauer*, 1093; Stiftung Bundeskanzler-Adenauer-Haus, III, 6.

Page 105 The morning began: *Frankfurter Allgemeine Zeitung*, 01/05/1961.

Page 105 The official explanation: Williams, *Adenauer*, 340.

Page 106 Born Herbert Frahm: Williams, *Adenauer*, 488.

Page 107 The SPD's shift: Schwarz, *Konrad Adenauer*, vol. 1, 524; Bonner Rundschau, 01/06/1961; SPD Press Service, January 4, 1960, P/XV/2.

Page 107 Still, Adenauer did not trust: Williams, *Adenauer*, 488; Schwarz, *Konrad Adenauer*, vol. 1, 487.

Page 107 "Whoever wants to be": Köhler, *Adenauer*, 1090; Archiv für Christlich-Demokratische Politik, VIII-001-1503/3; Willy Brandt, *Begegnungen und Einsichten*. Hamburg: Hoffmann & Campe, 1976, 49.

Page 108 He was convinced Khrushchev: Schwarz, *Konrad Adenauer*, vol. 1, 645.

Page 108 Waving his hand, Adenauer: Poppinga, *Meine Erinnerungen an Adenauer*, 41–42, 51.

Page 109 Friedrich Brandt was hiding: Erika Von Hornstein, *Flüchtlingsgeschichten: 43 Berichte aus den frühen Jahren der DDR*. Nördlingen, Germany: F. Greno, 1985.

6. ULBRICHT AND ADENAUER: THE TAIL WAGS THE BEAR

Page 113 "We are a state": SAPMO-BArch, ZPA, J IV 2/202/129, 1–2. Letter from Ulbricht to Khrushchev, January 18, 1961; SED Archives, IfGA, ZPA, J IV, 2/202/129.

Page 113 "The probe which": SED Archives, IfGA, ZPA, J IV, 2/202/129, Letter from Khrushchev to Ulbricht, January 30, 1961, in Harrison, "Ulbricht and the Concrete 'Rose,'" CWIHP Working Paper No. 5, Appendix C.

Page 114 "Since Comrade Khrushchev's statement": SAPMO-BArch, ZPA, J IV 2/202/129, 9-2. Letter from Ulbricht to Khrushchev, January 18, 1961; SED Archives, IfGA, ZPA, J IV, 2/202/129.

Page 116 "The booming economy": Hope M. Harrison, *Driving the Soviets up the Wall: Soviet–East German Relations. 1953–1961*. Princeton, NJ: Princeton University Press, 2003, 163–164; SAPMO-BArch, ZPA, J IV 2/202/129, January 18, 1961, "Möglichkeiten des taktischen Vorgehens in der Frage Friedensvertrag und Westberlin" and "Massnahmeplan zu organisatorischen Fragen im Zusammenarbeit mit der Vorbereitung des Abschlusses eines Friedensvertrages mit der DDR und der Einberufung einer Friedenskonferenz," English translation in Harrison, "Ulbricht and the Concrete 'Rose,'" CWIHP Working Paper No. 5, Appendix B.

Page 116 An East German worker: "West Berlin Shows Progress, Enjoys Best Year Since War," *New York Times*, 01/10/1961; "German Reds Say Production Is Up—but Reported Increase Falls Short of Plan; Lags Seen in Vital Industries," *New York Times*, 01/10/1961.

Page 117 Because of all that: Harrison, *Driving the Soviets up the Wall*, 150.

Page 117 Ulbricht did not seek Khrushchev's: Donald S. Zagoria, *The Sino-Soviet Conflict, 1956–1961*. Princeton, NJ: Princeton University Press, 1962, 396.

Page 117 Yuri Andropov: Harrison, *Driving the Soviets up the Wall*, 164–165; Zagoria, *The Sino-Soviet Conflict*; Chen Jian, *Mao's China and the Cold War*. Chapel Hill: University of North Carolina Press, 2001; Vladislav M. Zubok, "'Look What Chaos in the Beautiful Socialist Camp!': Deng Xiaoping and the Sino-Soviet Split, 1956–1963," CWIHP-B, No. 10 (1998), http://www.wilsoncenter.org/topics/pubs/ACF185.pdf, 152–162; Chen Jian, "Deng Xiaoping,

Mao's 'Continuous Revolution,' and the Path Toward the Sino-Soviet Split: A Rejoinder,"
CWIHP-B, No. 10 (1998), 162–164, 165–183; Joachim Krüger, "Die Volksrepublik China in
der Aussenpolitischen Strategie der DDR (1949–1989)," in Kuo Heng-yue and Mechthild
Leutner, eds., *Deutschland und China. Beiträge des Zweiten Internationalen Symposiums zur
Geschichte der deutsch-chinesischen Beziehungen Berlin 1991* (Berliner China-Studien 21),
Munich: Minerva, 1994, 49.

Page 118 But everything about: Harrison, *Driving the Soviets up the Wall*, 165. Harrison draws on a
one-page report that was sent by Yuri Andropov to the Central Committee on January 18,
1961, written by I. Kabin, chairman of the German section in the CPSU CC Department on
Relations with Communist and Workers' Parties of Socialist Countries, TsKhSD, R. 8978,
F. 5, Op. 49, D. Workers' Parties of Socialist Countries; TsKhSD, R. 8978, F. 5, Op. 49, D. 377;
SAPMO-BArch, ZPA, J IV 2/2/745.

Page 118 The Chinese view: "Vermerk über den Antrittsbesuch Botschafter Hegens bei
Ministerpräsident der VR China, Genossen Tschou En-lai am 9.6.1961," written by Hegen,
June 12, 1961, Staatsekretär Winzer, MfAA A17879, 2–3, 6.

Page 118 "We aren't China": AVP-RF, "'Zapis' besedy tovarischcha N.S. Khrushcheva s
tovarishchem V. Ul'brikhtom, 30 noiabria 1960 goda," F. 0742, Op. 6, Por. 4, Pap. 43, 14.

Page 119 During the Fourth Congress: James S. O'Donnell, *A Coming of Age: Albania Under Enver
Hoxha*. Boulder, CO: East European Monographs (distributed by Columbia University
Press), 1999, 52–53.

Page 119 Khrushchev's response landed: SED Archives, IfGA, ZPA, J IV, 2/202/129, Letter from
Khrushchev to Ulbricht, January 30, 1961, in Harrison, "Ulbricht and the Concrete 'Rose,'"
CWIHP Working Paper No. 5, Appendix C.

Page 120 The clouds were already gathering: Köhler, *Adenauer*, 1081.

Page 121 The West German foreign office: Auswärtiges Amt—Politisches Archiv (AA-PA), 3, Betreff:
Political Relations of BRD with United States, 1961.

Page 121 In exasperation: Boston Herald, 03/13/1961.

Page 121 "The Germans are acutely aware": DNSA, Discussion with Foreign Minister von
Brentano, Position Paper, Washington, February 16, 1961; retrieved from Honoré Marc
Catudal, *Kennedy and the Berlin Wall Crisis: A Case Study in U.S. Decision Making*. Berlin:
Berlin Verlag, 1980, 302: Appendix III: Secret Position Paper for visit by Heinrich von
Brentano to Washington, February 16, 1961, with anticipated German position and
recommended U.S. position.

Page 121 Detractors said that Brentano: "Gentleman in Politics: Heinrich von Brentano," *New York
Times*, 02/18/1961.

Page 122 Rusk had supported: JFKL, POF, Memo, Visits of Chancellor Adenauer and Mayor Brandt,
Confidential, February 21, 1961, Box 117, Countries. Germany-Security. January–June 1961.

Page 122 Kennedy reassured Brentano: Rolf Steininger, *Der Mauerbau: Die Westmächte und
Adenauer in der Berlinkriese 1958–1963*. Munich: Olzog, 2001, 168; FRUS, 1969–1963, vol.
XIV, Berlin Crisis, 1969–1962, Doc. 5.

Page 123 Brentano described to Kennedy: FRUS, 1969–1963, vol. XIV, Doc. 5; JFKL, POF, Memo,
Discussion with German Foreign Minister, February 15, 1961, Secret, Box 117, Countries.
Germany-Security. January–June 1961.

Page 124 More often than not: Prittie, *Konrad Adenauer*, 255–256; "West Germany: In the Master's
Footsteps," *Time*, 10/31/1960.

Page 124 "An entirely abnormal situation'": FRUS, 1969–1963, vol. XIV, Berlin Crisis, 1969–1962,
Docs. 9–31, January–May 1961; *Documents on Germany, 1944–1985*, 723–727; *Documents on
International Affairs, 1961*, 272–277; Bundesministerium für Innerdeutsche Beziehungen,
ed., *Dokumente zur Deutschlandpolitik*, IV. Reihe, Band 6, Erster Halbband, 1. Januar–30. Mai
1961, Frankfurt am Main, 1975, 345–350. See also *Aide-mémoire der Regierung der UdSSR an
die Regierung der Bundesrepublik Deutschland, 17. Februar 1961*: http://www.chronik-der-
mauer.de/index.php/de/Start/Detail/id/758537/page/0).

7. SPRINGTIME FOR KHRUSHCHEV

Page 129 "West Berlin is a bone": FRUS, 1969–1963, vol. XIV, Berlin Crisis, 1969–1962, Doc. 8.

Page 129 "It seems more likely": National Security Archive, Memo, Acheson to the President, April 3, 1961, "April 1961 Folder," Nuclear History Box 12.

Page 129 The Soviet leader's face: FRUS, 1969–1963, vol. V, Soviet Union, Doc. 42; Michael R. Beschloss, *The Crisis Years: Kennedy and Khrushchev, 1960–1963.* New York: HarperCollins, 1991, 80–81; William Taubman, *Khrushchev: The Man and His Era.* New York: W. W. Norton, 2004, 489.

Page 130 It had taken Thompson: FRUS, 1969–1963, vol. XIV, Berlin Crisis, 1969–1962, Doc. 8; Hugh Sidey, *John F. Kennedy, President.* New York: Atheneum, 1964, 163–165; *New York Times,* 03/04/1961, 03/08/1961, 03/10/1961.

Page 130 Just that week: Beschloss, *The Crisis Years,* 81.

Page 130 Moscow's ally in the Congo: Beschloss, *The Crisis Years,* 81.

Page 130 Facing such an array: New York Times, 03/04/1961.

Page 131 Khrushchev's adviser Oleg Troyanovsky: "Who's Who with Khrushchev," *Time,* 09/21/1959; Troyanovsky, *Cherez godi,* 233–236; *New York Times,* 04/03/1955.

Page 131 A new Soviet statistical: V. M. Kudrov, "Comparing the Soviet and US Economies: History and Practices," in Nicholas Eberstadt and Jonathan Tombes, eds., *Comparing the US and Soviet Economies: The 1990 Airlie House Conference.* Vol. 1, *Total Output and Consumption.* Washington, DC: The American Enterprise Institute, 2000, 58–59; Alexander Chubarov, *Russia's Bitter Path to Modernity: A History of the Soviet and Post-Soviet Eras.* New York: Continuum, 2001, 139; Hannes Adomeit, *Imperial Overstretch: Germany in Soviet Policy from Stalin to Gorbachev; An Analysis Based on New Archival Evidence, Memoirs, and Interviews.* Baden-Baden, Germany: Nomos Verlagsgesellschaft, 1998, 103.

Page 132 In confessing his inadequacy: Stenographic account, February 16, 1961, Declassified Materials from CPSU Central Committee Plenums (TsK KPSS), Meeting of the CC CPSU Presidium, Protocol No. 328 (February 16, 1961), Information from comrade Khrushchev of the meeting on agriculture in the regions of Ukraine, North Caucasus, Transcaucasus and Central Black Earth area, in Aleksandr Fursenko et al., eds., *Archivii Kremlya: Prezidium TsK KPSS, 1954–1964 Chernoviie protokolnie zapisi zasedanii. Stenogrammi. Postanovlenia,* vol. 1 [Archives of the Kremlin: Presidium of the Central Committee of the Communist Party of the Soviet Union, 1954–1964, Notes of State Meetings, Stenographic Accounts], Moscow: Rosspen, 2004.

Page 132 At one local Communist Party: Stenographic account, March 25, 1961, TsK KPSS, Meeting of the CC CPSU Presidium, Protocol No. 321 (March 25, 1961), TsK KPSS; Fursenko and Naftali, *Khrushchev's Cold War,* 344–345.

Page 132 The Soviet public's awareness: Harrison E. Salisbury, *A New Russia.* New York: Harper & Row, 1962, 120–121.

Page 133 Speaking calmly and wearily: FRUS, 1969–1963, vol. XIV, Berlin Crisis, 1969–1962, Doc. 8.

Page 134 The American ambassador warned: FRUS, 1969–1963, vol. XIV, Berlin Crisis, 1969–1962, Doc. 8.

Page 135 Because Berlin lacked political: FRUS, 1969–1963, vol. XIV, Berlin Crisis, 1969–1962, Doc. 8.

Page 135 To further illustrate West Berlin's: FRUS, 1961–1963, vol. V, Soviet Union, Doc. 44.

Page 135 He said the U.S.: FRUS, 1961–1963, vol. V, Soviet Union, Doc. 43.

Page 135 Instead of embracing: FRUS, 1969–1963, vol. XIV, Berlin Crisis, 1969–1962, Doc. 8; FRUS, vol. V, Soviet Union, Doc. 43.

Page 136 Khrushchev complained: FRUS, 1969–1963, vol. XIV, Berlin Crisis, 1969–1962, Doc. 8.

Page 137 Thompson returned by plane: New York Times, 03/10/1961.

Page 137 "All my diplomatic colleagues": FRUS, 1961–1963, vol. V, Soviet Union, Doc. 46; vol. XIV, Berlin Crisis, 1961–1962, Doc. 11.

Page 137 A week later, Thompson: FRUS, 1969–1963, vol. XIV, Berlin Crisis, 1969–1962, Doc. 11.

Page 138 With uncanny clairvoyance, Thompson: Telegram from U.S. Embassy (Moscow) to State Department, March 16, 1961, cited in Catudal, *Kennedy and the Berlin Wall Crisis*, 62, FN 15, 240–241.

Page 139 The best minds: DNSA, Berlin Situation [Summary of Report by U.S. Intelligence Board Berlin Sub-Committee Report], Memorandum, March 7, 1961.

Page 140 Acheson's paper: Department of State, Memo for the President, April 3, 1961, 4 pp; JFKL, *Dean G. Acheson OH*, no. 1, April 27, 1964.

Page 140 With a gaggle: James Chace, *Acheson: The Secretary of State Who Created the American World.* New York: Simon & Schuster, 1998, 382.

Page 140 Acheson then helped dissuade: Douglas Brinkley, *Dean Acheson: The Cold War Years, 1953–1971.* New Haven, CT: Yale University Press, 1994, 113.

Page 141 Even at almost age sixty-eight: Robert L. Beisner, *Dean Acheson: A Life in the Cold War.* New York: Oxford University Press, 2006, 7, 89–95.

Page 141 Shortly after Kennedy's election: Acheson letters, 11/22/1960, from Democratic Party 1960 Campaign, Truman Correspondence (courtesy David Acheson). Also in David S. McLellan and David C. Acheson, eds., *Among Friends: Personal Letters of Dean Acheson.* New York: Dodd, Mead, 1980, 199.

Page 142 Acheson listed for Kennedy: JFKL, *Dean G. Acheson OH.*

Page 144 Acheson conceded that reducing: Brinkley, *Dean Acheson*, 141.

Page 144 The French and Germans: Fred M. Kaplan, *The Wizards of Armageddon.* New York: Simon & Schuster, 1983 / Stanford, CA: Stanford University Press, 1991, 283, 338; Andreas Wenger, *Living with Peril: Eisenhower, Kennedy, and Nuclear Weapons.* Lanham, MD: Rowman & Littlefield, 1997, 201; Brinkley, *Dean Acheson*, 130–131.

Page 144 He advised Kennedy: JFKL, POF, Memo, Bundy to the President, March 27, 1961, "Bundy, McGeorge 2/69-4/61 Folder," Box 62, Staff Memoranda; DDRS (Declassified Document Reference System), "Bundy to Kennedy, April 4, 1961," 1986/2903; Nigel Fisher, *Harold Macmillan: A Biography.* New York: St. Martin's Press, 1982, 257; Arthur M. Schlesinger, *A Thousand Days: John F. Kennedy in the White House.* Boston: Houghton Mifflin, 1965, 380–382; Victor Lasky, *JFK: The Man and the Myth.* New York: Macmillan, 1963, 6–7; Alistair Horne, *Harold Macmillan.* vol. 2, *1957–1986.* New York: Viking, 1989, 289–290.

Page 145 British Prime Minister Macmillan was taken aback: FRUS, 1969–1963, vol. XIV, Berlin Crisis, 1969–1962, Doc. 14, Memcon, The President's Meetings with Prime Minister Macmillan, Washington, April 1961, "East–West Issues: Berlin," April 5, 1961, 3:10 p.m.; Fisher, *Harold Macmillan*, 261.

Page 145 But the two men: Chace, *Acheson*, 174.

Page 146 A keen student of history: Anthony Sampson, *Macmillan: A Study in Ambiguity.* Harmondsworth, England: Penguin Press, 1967, 65–66.

Page 147 Macmillan had worried to columnist: JFKL, *Henry Brandon OH*; Henry Brandon, *Special Relationships: A Foreign Correspondent's Memoirs from Roosevelt to Reagan.* New York: Atheneum, 1988, 155.

Page 147 Eisenhower's ambassador to London: Horne, *Harold Macmillan*, 282; Harold Macmillan Archives, *Harold Macmillan, Diaries*, 17 November 1960 (scheduled publication date: 04/03/2011).

Page 147 "I wonder how it is": Horne, *Harold Macmillan*, 290.

Page 147 Perhaps the most disliked: Lord Longford, *Kennedy.* London: Weidenfeld & Nicolson, 1976, 79–81; Corey Ford, *Donovan of OSS: The Untold Story of William J. Donovan.* Boston: Little, Brown, 1970, 89.

Page 147 To further influence Kennedy's: Horne, *Harold Macmillan*, 282; Harold Macmillan Archives, Letter of November 9, 1960; Harold Macmillan, *Pointing the Way, 1959–1961.* London: Macmillan, 1972, 308.

Page 148 De Gaulle in Paris: Constantine A. Pagedas, *Anglo-American Strategic Relations and the French Problem, 1960–1963: A Troubled Partnership.* London: Frank Class, 2000, 124.

Page 148 When they met in London: Harold Macmillan Archives. Harold Macmillan, Diaries, February 23, 1961.

Page 148 Ahead of Macmillan's White House: Horne, *Harold Macmillan*, 286, from interview with the economist John Kenneth Galbraith.

Page 149 To the prime minister's relief: Horne, *Harold Macmillan*, 287–290, 295.

Page 149 Macmillan had been taken by: Macmillan, *Pointing the Way*, 352–353: diary entry for April 12, 1961.

Page 149 Yet that positive beginning: FRUS, 1969–1963, vol. XIV, Berlin Crisis, 1969–1962, Doc. 14, 15; Fisher, *Harold Macmillan*, 261.

Page 149 Acheson crisply listed: Schlesinger, *A Thousand Days*, 380.

Page 152 With the return of Acheson's: FRUS, 1969–1963, vol. XIV, Berlin Crisis, 1969–1962, Doc. 15.

Page 153 A final internal: Rolf Steininger, *Der Mauerbau: Die Westmächte und Adenauer in der Berlinkrise 1958–1963.* Munich: Olzog, 2001, 184.

Page 153 In the brisk spring: New York Times, 04/09/1961; Washington Post, 04/09/1961.

Page 153 British officials surprised: Steininger, *Der Mauerbau*, 182–185, 183; *New York Times*, 04/09/1961; *Washington Post*, 04/10/1961; JFKL, POF, CO: United Kingdom Security, 3/27/69-4/61, Box 127a, Item 7a.

8. AMATEUR HOUR

Page 154 "The European view": Dean G. Acheson, *Remarks at Foreign Service lunch*, Washington, D.C. (transcribed June 29, 1961), S 3, B 51, F62, DGA-Yale. The speech was delivered sometime between June 13 and 25, 1961; retrieved from Brinkley, *Dean Acheson*, 127.

Page 154 "I don't understand Kennedy": Sergei N. Khrushchev, *Nikita S. Khrushchev: Krizisy i Rakety*, vol. 1, 102–106.

Page 154 It was Washington's first: JFKL, *Dean G. Acheson OH*, no. 1; Douglas Brinkley, *Dean Acheson: The Cold War Years, 1953–1971.* New Haven, CT: Yale University Press, 1994, 127.

Page 154 Truman's former secretary: Chace, *Acheson*, 386–388; Brinkley, *Dean Acheson*, 127.

Page 155 Acheson said he would not: Richard J. Walton, *Cold War and Counterrevolution: The Foreign Policy of John F. Kennedy.* New York: Viking, 1972, 44.

Page 156 The two men talked: JFKL, *Dean G. Acheson OH*; Walton, *Cold War and Counterrevolution*, 44.

Page 156 The eighty-five-year-old: Catudal, *Kennedy and the Berlin Wall Crisis*, 57.

Page 157 Acheson spent much of the day: JFKL, *Dean G. Acheson OH*; *New York Times*, 04/10/1961; Catudal, *Kennedy and the Berlin Wall Crisis*, 58–60.

Page 157 Beyond that, Adenauer: Brinkley, *Dean Acheson*, 130–131.

Page 158 So Acheson instead focused: Brinkley, *Dean Acheson*, 129.

Page 158 For the moment, Kennedy: Catudal, *Kennedy and the Berlin Wall Crisis*, 97; Brinkley, *Dean Acheson*, 129; James Chace, *Acheson: The Secretary of State Who Created the American World.* New York: Simon & Schuster, 199, 383–384.

Page 158 Instead, Kennedy would put: http://www.jfklibrary.org/Historical+Resources/Archives/Reference+Desk/New+York+Times+Chronology/1961/May 10; David E. Murphy, Sergei A. Kondrashev, and George Bailey, *Battleground Berlin: CIA vs. KGB in the Cold War.* London and New Haven, CT: Yale University Press, 1997, 359.

Page 158 In short, Kennedy's evolving: Murphy, Kondrashev, and Bailey, *Battleground Berlin*, 360.

Page 158 When Acheson was near victory: Brinkley, *Dean Acheson*, 130; Chace, *Acheson*, 388.

Page 159 On the day of Adenauer's flight: Norman Cousins, *The Improbable Triumvirate: John F. Kennedy, Pope John, Nikita Khrushchev.* New York: W. W. Norton, 1972, 83–87.

Page 159 Khrushchev would later explain: Beschloss, *The Crisis Years*, 111; Taubman, *Khrushchev: The Man and His Era*, 5.

Page 159 It was a measure: Taubman, *Khrushchev: The Man and His Era*, 490; Beschloss, *The Crisis Years*, 110–111.

Page 160 With the schedule for the space launch: Ronald Steel, *Walter Lippmann and the American Century.* Boston and Toronto: Little, Brown, 526–527.

Page 160 Khrushchev had accelerated: Gerhard Kowalski, *Die Gargarin-Story: Die Wahrheit über den Flug des ersten Kosmonauten der Welt.* Berlin: Schwarzkopf & Schwarzkopf, 1999, 55; Beschloss, *Crisis Years,* 113.

Page 160 Lippmann savored his access: Steel, *Walter Lippmann and the American Century,* 419, 445; Barry D. Riccio, *Walter Lippmann: Odyssey of a Liberal.* New Brunswick, NJ: Transaction, 1994, 46–47.

Page 161 During a lunch break: Washington Post, 04/19/1961.

Page 161 A German solution: Steel, *Walter Lippmann and the American Century,* 527–528.

Page 162 Khrushchev laid out his Berlin: Walter Lippmann Papers. Soviet transcript of conversation between Khrushchev and Lippmann, 10 April 1961, New Haven, CT: Yale University, Sterling Memorial Library, Series VII, Box 239; Steel, *Walter Lippmann and the American Century,* 3, 203; Vladislav M. Zubok, "Khrushchev and the Berlin Crisis (1958–1962)," CWIHP Working Paper No. 6, May 1993, 21–23; Taubman, *Khrushchev: The Man and His Era,* 490–491.

Page 162 Khrushchev told Lippmann: Zubok, "Khrushchev and the Berlin Crisis (1958–1962)," CWIHP Working Paper No. 6, 22; Beschloss, *Crisis Years,* 111.

Page 163 Khrushchev said he was ready: Walter Lippmann Papers. Soviet transcript of conversation between Khrushchev and Lippmann, April 10, 1961, Yale University; Taubman, *Khrushchev,* 490–491; Deborah Welch Larson *Anatomy of Mistrust: U.S.–Soviet Relations During the Cold War.* Ithaca, NY: Cornell University Press, 2000, 287.

Page 164 Khrushchev had only one question: Pravda, April 13, 1961, 2; Sergei N. Khrushchev, *Nikita Khrushchev and the Creation of a Superpower.* University Park: Pennsylvania State University Press, 2000, 432; Taubman, *Khrushchev,* 490–491; Sergei N. Khrushchev, *Krizisy i Rakety,* vol. 2, 100–101.

Page 164 Yes, Korolyov declared: http://www.youtube.com/watch?v=Qfz5B2uERcE.

Page 164 Khrushchev exulted to: Taubman, *Khrushchev,* 491; Sergei N. Khrushchev, *Krizisy i Rakety,* vol. 2, 100–101; Sergei N. Khrushchev, *Creation of a Superpower,* 432–433.

Page 165 The Soviet leader ordered: Aleksandr Fursenko and Timothy Naftali, *Khrushchev's Cold War: The Inside Story of an American Adversary.* New York: W. W. Norton, 2006, 346. (At a Presidium meeting in June 1961, Khrushchev discussed the problem of collapsing balconies. See stenographic account, June 16, 1961, TsK KPSS); Sergei N. Khrushchev, *Creation of a Superpower,* 433–434.

Page 165 From atop the Lenin: Taubman, *Khrushchev,* 492.

Page 166 Kennedy had told Brandt: FRUS, 1969–1963, vol. XIV, Berlin Crisis, 1969–1962, Doc. 10; JFKL, Memcon, Meeting Kennedy–Brandt at White House, Washington, March 13, 1961, 3–3:40 p.m., Subject: Germany and Berlin, National Security Files (NSF), Germany, Confidential, drafted by Foy Kohler and approved by the White House on March 23, 1961.

Page 166 Brandt joined the list: Ibid.; Briefing Paper for meeting, transmitted by Rusk to the President on March 10, 1961, in Department of State, Central Files, 762.00/3–1061; Memcon, Brandt–Rusk covering similar topics, March 14, 1961, in Department of State, Central Files, 762.0221/3-1461. For Brandt's account of his conversation with the president and visit to Washington, see Willy Brandt, *Begegnungen und Einsichten, Die Jahre 1960–1975.* Hamburg: Hoffmann u. Campe, 1976, 17–18, 80–83.

Page 166 Brandt had used his forty minutes: Willy Brandt, *Begegnungen mit Kennedy.* Munich: Kindler, 1964, 49–45.

Page 166 Brandt was relieved: Wall Street Journal, Washington Post, New York Times, Christian Science Monitor, 03/14/1961.

Page 166 A month later, Kennedy's conversations: FRUS, 1969–1963, vol. XIV, Berlin Crisis, 1969–1962, Doc. 17.

Page 167 Adenauer delivered an elderly man's: New York Times, 2/17/1961.

Page 168 Kennedy said he was concerned: FRUS, at http://www.state.gov/r/pa/ho/frus/kennedyjf/

xiv/15854.htm 9. Memorandum of Conversation/1/Washington, March 10, 1961; Source: JFKL, NSF, Germany, Confidential, drafted by Kohler and approved by the White House on March 20; ibid., Doc. 10: Memcon, Washington, March 13, 1961, 3–3:40 p.m.; Bundesarchiv, Kabinettsprotokolle Online "1. Deutsche Maßnahmen zur Entlastung der US-Zahlungsbilanz" retrieved from http://www.bundesarchiv.de.

Page 168 *The communiqué:* Williams, *Adenauer: The Father of the New Germany*, 490; FRUS, 1969–1963, vol. XIV, Berlin Crisis, 1969–1962, Doc. 9, 10; Konrad Adenauer, *Erinnerungen 1959–1963*. Stuttgart: Deutsche Verlags-Anstalt, 1968, 91–97.

Page 168 *The correspondent of the German magazine: Der Spiegel*, 04/12/1961, 04/19/1961.

Page 169 *At the end of the visit: Christian Science Monitor*, 04/14/1961.

Page 169 *Little noticed was Adenauer's: Washington Post*, 04/14/1961.

Page 170 *Johnson's central Texas: Christian Science Monitor*, 04/17/1961.

Page 170 *When Adenauer visited:* Poppinga, "Das Wichtigste ist der Mut": *Konrad Adenauer*, 297.

Page 170 *With star German reporters:* Schwarz, *Konrad Adenauer*, vol. 1, 519.

Page 171 *On their drive to the airport:* Poppinga, *"Das Wichtigste ist der Mut": Konrad Adenauer*, 297; Schwarz, *Konrad Adenauer*, vol. 1, 519–520.

Page 171 *With Adenauer safely back:* "The Presidency: Interlude," *Time*, 04/28/1961; Sidey, *JFK*, 131; Peter Wyden, *Bay of Pigs: The Untold Story*. New York: Simon & Schuster, 1979, 269–270.

Page 171 *Two days earlier, eight B-26 bombers:* Wyden, *Bay of Pigs*, 184–185; Howard Jones, *The Bay of Pigs*. New York: Oxford University Press, 2008, 76–77, 100–102; also see for chronology of events: National Security Archive, "The Bay of Pigs—40 Years After," April 15–18, 1961: http://www.gwu.edu/~nsarchiv/bayofpigs/chron.html.

Page 171 *Castro's fighters sank:* FRUS, 1961–1963, vol. X, Cuba, 1961–1962, Doc. 109, 119; The National Security Archive, "The Bay of Pigs—40 Years After," April 15–18, 1961.

Page 172 *Most of the military brass:* Jones, *The Bay of Pigs*, 76–77, 96;

Page 172 *Most important at the meeting:* JFKL, *Richard M. Bissell OH*; JFKL, POF, Bundy to JFK, February 25, 1961, Staff Memoranda, Box 62; Evan Thomas, *The Very Best Men: Four Who Dared: The Early Years of the CIA*. New York: Simon & Schuster, 1995, 237, 240; "Nation: When It's in the News, It's in Trouble" and "Cuba: The Massacre," *Time*, 04/28/1961; Lawrence Freedman, *Kennedy's Wars: Berlin, Cuba, Laos, and Vietnam*. New York: Oxford University Press, 2000, 124–126; Harris Wofford, *Of Kennedys and Kings: Making Sense of the Sixties*. New York: Farrar, Straus & Giroux, 1980, 362.

Page 173 *Now working for Kennedy:* Wyden, *Bay of Pigs*, 139; Richard M. Bissell, Jonathan E. Lewis, and Frances T. Pudlo. *Reflections of a Cold Warrior: From Yalta to the Bay of Pigs*. New Haven, CT: Yale University Press, 1996, 190.

Page 173 *Kennedy had never questioned:* Gus Russo, *Live by the Sword: The Secret War Against Castro and the Death of JFK*. Baltimore: Bancroft Press, 1998, 13–15; Jones, *The Bay of Pigs*, 38, 76–78, 96, 100–102.

Page 173 *Also, leaks had been:* Russo, *Live by the Sword*, 16.

Page 173 *The April 17 invasion:* FRUS, 1961–1963, vol. VI, Kennedy–Khrushchev Exchanges, Doc. 9.

Page 174 *Khrushchev wasn't buying Kennedy's:* FRUS, 1961–1963, vol. VI, Kennedy–Khrushchev Exchanges, Doc. 9.

Page 174 *Kennedy had responded:* FRUS, 1961–1963, vol. VI, Kennedy–Khrushchev Exchanges, Doc. 10.

Page 174 *With that exchange:* Bissell, *Reflections of a Cold Warrior*, 189; Laurence Leamer, *The Kennedy Men: 1901–1963*. New York: HarperCollins, 2001, 501, 508.

Page 174 *Just six days earlier:* Thomas, *The Very Best Men*, 253; Beschloss, *The Crisis Years*, 114; Leamer, *The Kennedy Men: 1909–1963*, 501, 508; "Nation: Bitter Week," *Time*, 04/28/1961; Wofford, *Of Kennedys and Kings*. New York: Farrar, Straus & Giroux, 1980, 347–348.

Page 175 *If the president:* E. B. Potter, *Admiral Arleigh A. Burke*. Annapolis, MD: U.S. Naval

Institute Press, 2005; Gordon M. Goldstein, *Lessons in Disaster: McGeorge Bundy and the Path to War in Vietnam*. New York: Times Books/Henry Holt, 2008, 39; Sidey, *JFK*, 110; Wyden, *Bay of Pigs*, 270–271.

Page 175 Kennedy ended the three-hour: Wyden, *Bay of Pigs*, 271; https://www.cia.gov/library/center-for-the-study-of-intelligence/csi-publications/books-and-monographs/agency-and-the-hill/12-The%20Agency%20and%20the%20Hill_Part2-Chapter9.pdf: chapter 9, *Oversight of Covert Action*, 268.

Page 175 Acheson immediately grasped: JFKL, *Dean G. Acheson OH*; Chace, *Acheson*, 387.

Page 176 Speaking before diplomats: Brinkley, *Dean Acheson*, 127.

Page 176 With a tone of dismay: Acheson Letter to Truman, May 3, 1961 (courtesy David Acheson), in David S. McLellan and David C. Acheson, eds., *Among Friends: Personal Letters of Dean Acheson*. New York: Dodd, Mead, 1980, 206–207.

Page 177 He had known in advance: Vladislav M. Zubok and Constantine Pleshakov, *Inside the Kremlin's Cold War: From Stalin to Khrushchev*. Cambridge, MA: Harvard University Press, 1996, 243.

Page 177 Though Kennedy had avoided: Taubman, *Khrushchev*, 492; Beschloss, *The Crisis Years*, 121.

Page 177 "I don't understand Kennedy": Sergei N. Khrushchev, *Krizisy i Rakety*, 102–106.

Page 177 That said, Khrushchev was concerned: Fursenko and Naftali, *Khrushchev's Cold War*, 348–349.

Page 179 Paris's Left Bank: Jörn Donner, *Report from Berlin*. Bloomington: Indiana University Press, 1961.

Page 179 Donner considered the difference: Donner, *Report from Berlin*, XI.

Page 180 Like West Berlin: Interview with Vern Pike, Washington, D.C., November 17, 2008.

9. PERILOUS DIPLOMACY

Page 184 "The American government": Archive of the Main Intelligence Administration of the General Staff of the Armed Forces of the Russian Federation (GRU), "Kratkoye Soderzhanye: Besed G. Bolshakova s R. Kennedi (9 Maya 1961 goda-14 Dekabria 1962 roga)" [Summary: Meeting of G. Bolshakov with R. Kennedy, May 9, 1961–December 14, 1962].

Page 184 "Berlin is a festering sore": FRUS, 1961–1963, vol. XIV, Berlin Crisis, 1961–1962, Doc. 24, Telegram from the Embassy in the Soviet Union to the Department of State, Moscow, May 24, 1961.

Page 184 Wearing a white shirt: GRU, "Kratkoye Soderzhanye: Besed G. Bolshakova s. R. Kennedi."

Page 186 Bolshakov was just one of two: FRUS, 1961–1963, vol. V, Soviet Union, Doc. 65.

Page 187 Thompson put down the phone: FRUS, 1961–1963, vol. V, Soviet Union, Docs. 65, 66.

Page 188 After a day of reflection: FRUS, 1961–1963, vol. V, Soviet Union, Doc. 67.

Page 189 Special envoy Averell Harriman: FRUS, 1961–1963, vol. XXIV, 199–200, 209–210.

Page 189 Beyond that, Rusk told: FRUS, 1961–1963, vol. V, Soviet Union, Doc. 67.

Page 189 It suited Bolshakov: Aleksandr Fursenko and Timothy J. Naftali, *One Hell of a Gamble: Khrushchev, Castro, and Kennedy, 1958–1964*. New York: W. W. Norton, 1997, 119–123; interview with Frank Holeman, August 6, 1995, Washington, D.C.; Georgi Bolshakov, "Goryachaya Linaya" (Hot Line), *Novoye Vremya*, no. 4 (1989), 38–40; *Pravda, Bolshakov Meetings*; GRU, "Kratkoye Soderzhanye: Besed G. Bolshakova s. R. Kennedi."

Page 190 What gave Bolshakov: Fursenko and Naftali, *One Hell of a Gamble*, 119–113, citing GRU, *Biography of Georgi Bolshakov*; Dino Brugioni and Robert F. McCort, eds., *Eyeball to Eyeball: The Inside Story of the Cuban Missile Crisis*. New York: Random House, 1991, 176–178; *Zvezda*, no. 7 (1997); Benjamin C. Bradlee, *Conversations with Kennedy*. New York: W. W. Norton, 1975, 194; James W. Symington., *The Stately Game*. New York: Macmillan, 1971, 144–145.

Page 190 However, Bolshakov's most important: *Washington Times*, September 27, 1996.

Page 191 Bolshakov had worked Holeman: Fursenko and Naftali, *One Hell of a Gamble*, 111, citing interview with Frank Holeman, August 6, 1995.

Page 191 When Bolshakov returned: Fursenko and Naftali, *One Hell of a Gamble,* 111; Beschloss, *The Crisis Years,* 153–154; interview with Frank Holeman; Richard Nixon Papers, National Archives, *Rose Mary Woods–Nixon,* 12/18/1958.

Page 191 When Bolshakov replaced Gvozdev: Fursenko and Naftali, *One Hell of a Gamble,* 109–112; Brugioni and McCort, *Eyeball to Eyeball,* 176–177; Foreign Broadcast Information Service, USSR, International Service, "Kennedy Sees Soviet Journalists," Daily Report No. 12327, June 1961; Bolshakov, "Goryachaya Linaya," 38–40.

Page 191 With Guthman's blessing: Bolshakov, "Goryachaya Linaya," 38–40.

Page 192 At the Justice Department: Bolshakov, "Goryachaya Linaya," 38–40.

Page 192 "The American government": GRU, "Kratkoye Soderzhanye: Besed G. Bolshakova s. R. Kennedi."

Page 193 The two countries: FRUS, 1961–1963, vol. VII, *Arms Control and Disarmament,* Doc. 4.

Page 193 Behind Bobby's proposal: FRUS, 1961–1963, vol. VII, *Arms Control and Disarmament,* Doc. 19, 31.

Page 193 And Moscow wanted any verification: Fursenko and Naftali, *Khrushchev's Cold War,* 351.

Page 195 In Geneva, Soviet officials: Freedman, *Kennedy's Wars,* 302–304; Roger Kershaw, *Monarchy in South-East Asia: The Faces of Tradition in Transition.* New York: Routledge, 2001, 39–40; Timothy N. Castle, *At War in the Shadow of Vietnam: U.S. Military Aid to the Royal Lao Government 1955–1975.* New York: Columbia University Press, 1993, 40–42, 46–48.

Page 195 On the same day, Khrushchev delivered: New York Times, 05/13/1961; Memo, Lucius Battle–Bundy, May 25, 1961.

Page 195 The letter made no mention: FRUS, 1961–1963, vol. VI, Kennedy–Khrushchev Exchanges, Doc. 15.

Page 196 Kennedy sent cables: JFKL, Kennedy–Adenauer, May 16, 1961.

Page 196 On May 17, State Department: JFKL, *Henry Owen, National Security Council,* May 17, 1961, NSF Box 81, Germany, Berlin, General, 5/61.

Page 196 He suggested putting more money: DNSA, Memorandum, May 17, 1961, Secret, *Berlin Crisis,* BC02046.

Page 197 Western European and U.S. commentators: "Kennedys welker Lorbeer," *Die Zeit,* 5/26/1961; *Wall Street Journal,* 06/01/1961.

Page 197 In its review of European: Wall Street Journal, 06/01/1961.

Page 197 Although Vienna was technically: Wall Street Journal, 06/01/1961.

Page 198 "Our friends," said the ambassador: AVP-RF, Letter from Ambassador Pervukhin to Foreign Minister Gromyko, 19 May 1961, Top secret file, Fond: referentyra po GDR, Opis 6, Por 34, Inv. 193/3, vol. 1, Papka 46, retrieved from Harrison, "Ulbricht and the Concrete 'Rose,'" CWIHP Working Paper No. 5, 90–95, Appendix D; Murphy, Kondrashev, and Bailey, *Battleground Berlin,* 362.

Page 198 Two weeks ahead of the summit: Mikhail Boltunov, *Nevidimoe Oruzhie GRU* [Invisible GRU Weapon]. Moscow: Olma-Press, 2002, 281–283; Fursenko and Naftali, *One Hell of a Gamble,* 122–123.

Page 198 Bobby made clear: Boltunov, *Nevidimoe Oruzhie GRU,* 281–283; Beschloss, *Crisis Years,* 156; Fursenko and Naftali, *Khrushchev's Cold War,* 349–350, 354.

Page 199 One of Bolshakov's Moscow bosses: Fursenko and Naftali, *One Hell of a Gamble,* 112.

Page 200 Thompson did not take notes . . . Thompson probed, asking: FRUS, 1961–1963, vol. XIV, Berlin Crisis, 1961–1962, Doc. 24, Telegram from the Embassy in the Soviet Union to the Department of State, Moscow, May 24, 1961.

Page 202 Khrushchev responded calmly: DNSA, Thompson's Conversation with Khrushchev on Berlin, Prior to the Vienna Summit, Secret, Cable, 2887, May 24, 1961.

Page 202 Thompson's later cable to Washington: FRUS, 1961–1963, vol. XIV, Berlin Crisis, 1961– 1962, Doc. 28, Telegram from the Embassy in the Soviet Union to the Department of State, Moscow, May 27, 1961, 1 p.m.

Page 203 On the same day, Kennedy: FRUS, 1961–1963, vol. XIV, Berlin Crisis, 1961–1962, Doc. 27,

Telegram from the Mission at Berlin to the Department of State, Berlin, May 25, 1961, 7 p.m.

Page 204 Kennedy called for a defense: New York Times, 05/26/1961.

Page 205 Directly responding to what: Fursenko and Naftali, *Khrushchev's Cold War*, 355–357; AVP-RF, *Kuznetsov*, May 26, 1961, 3.66.311, 58–61; Stenographic account, May 26, 1961, and Protocol No. 331, May 26, 1961, TsK KPSS.

Page 207 Khrushchev ended his war council: Anatoly Fedorovich Dobrynin, *In Confidence: Moscow's Ambassador to America's Six Cold War Presidents (1962–1986).* New York: Times Books/Random House, 1995, 44–45; AVP-RF, *Kuznetsov*, May 26, 1961, 3.66.311, 58–61; Stenographic account, May 26, 1961, and Protocol No. 331, May 26, 1961, TsK KPSS; AVP-RF, List Commemorative Gifts and Souvenirs for Possible Delivery at the Time of N. S. Khrushchev's Stay in Austria, May 27, 1961.

Page 208 Kennedy lifted off: Beschloss, *Crisis Years*, 178; Edward M. Kennedy, *The Fruitful Bough: A Tribute to Joseph P. Kennedy.* Privately printed, 1965, 264; Sidey, *JFK*, 173.

Page 208 He was using crutches: "1961 Man of the Year—John F. Kennedy," *Time*, 01/05/1962; Goduti, *Kennedy's Kitchen Cabinet: Shaping of American Foreign Policy, 1961–1963*, 102.

10. VIENNA: LITTLE BOY BLUE MEETS AL CAPONE

Page 209 "So we're stuck": Kenneth P. O'Donnell and David F. Powers, with Joe McCarthy, *"Johnny, We Hardly Knew Ye": Memories of John Fitzgerald Kennedy.* Boston: Little, Brown, 1972, 292.

Page 209 "The U.S. is unwilling": FRUS, 1961–1963, vol. V, Soviet Union, Doc. 87, Memcon, p. 219.

Page 210 "God, we ought": Edward Klein, *All Too Human: The Love Story of Jack and Jackie Kennedy.* New York: Pocket Books, 1997, 267.

Page 210 So began what the three men: O'Donnell and Powers, with McCarthy, *"Johnny, We Hardly Knew Ye,"* 292; Seymour M. Hersh, *The Dark Side of Camelot.* Boston: Little, Brown, 1997, 10, 228.

Page 210 Between 500,000 and 1 million people: Klein, *All Too Human*, 266–268.

Page 211 At Orly Airport: New York Times, 06/01/1961.

Page 211 The cheers grew: Washington Post, 06/01/1961.

Page 211 Abroad, Kennedy's failure: Richard Reeves, *President Kennedy: Profile of Power.* New York: Simon & Schuster, 1993, 60.

Page 212 It seemed just another of his presidency's: Robert Dallek, *An Unfinished Life: John F. Kennedy, 1917–1963.* Boston: Little, Brown, 2003, 397–399; Janet G. Travell, *Office Hours: Day and Night—The Autobiography of Janet Travell, M.D.* New York: World, 1968, 3, 6, 385.

Page 212 Kennedy's personal physician: JFKL, Janet G. Travell OH, Dr. Janet Travell medical records; Parmet, *JFK*, 118–123; Beschloss, *Crisis Years*, 188–191; Janet G. Travell, *Office Hours: Day and Night.*

Page 213 Known as "Dr. Feelgood": Dallek, *An Unfinished Life*, 398–399; Hersh, *Dark Side of Camelot*, 5, 235–236; Klein, *All Too Human*, 239.

Page 213 Kennedy was so pleased: Reeves, *Kennedy: Profile of Power*, 147; Beschloss, *Crisis Years*, 187–191.

Page 213 On the night of their grand: Klein, *All Too Human;* 271.

Page 213 "You feel like Superman": Klein, *All Too Human*, 240.

Page 213 "acute and chronic intravenous amphetamine poisoning": Robert H. Ferrell, *Ill Advised: Presidential Health and Public Trust.* Columbia: University of Missouri Press, 1992, 156.

Page 214 At Bobby's urging: Reeves, *Kennedy: Profile of Power*, 147, 243, 699n; John Whitcomb and Claire Whitcomb, *Real Life at the White House: Two Hundred Years of Daily Life at America's Most Famous Residence.* New York: Routledge, 2000, 359.

Page 214 Eisenhower had warned Kennedy: Dallek, *An Unfinished Life*, 662; Otis L. Graham Jr. and Meghan Robinson Wander, eds., *Franklin D. Roosevelt: His Life and Times: An Encyclopedic View.* Boston: Da Capo Press, 1985, 94–96; DDEL, Herter Papers, Meetings with the

President, 1961; in FRUS, 1961–1963, vol. XXIV, Laos Crisis, Doc. 1, Memo of Conference with President Eisenhower, January 2, 1961.

Page 214 *In contrast to his predecessors:* Klein, *All Too Human*, 268; *New York Times*, 06/01/1961; O'Donnell and Powers, with McCarthy, *"Johnny, We Hardly Knew Ye,"* 289; Beschloss, *The Crisis Years*, 184; Schlesinger, *A Thousand Days*, 350–351; JFKL, *Charles E. Bohlen OH*.

Page 215 *Safely back:* O'Donnell and Powers, with McCarthy, *"Johnny, We Hardly Knew Ye,"* 289.

Page 215 *While Kennedy endured:* Sergei N. Khrushchev, *Creation of a Superpower*, 440.

Page 215 *Communist Party cells: Washington Post*, 06/28/1961.

Page 215 *"I believe Khrushchev":* Department of State, Telegram from the Embassy in the Soviet Union to the Department of State, May 27, 1961, Central Files, 611.61/5-2761, Secret, Priority, Limit Distribution, in FRUS, 1961–1963, vol. V, Soviet Union, Doc. 79.

Page 215 *Without confidence, Thompson: New York Times*, 06/28/1961.

Page 216 *Khrushchev swelled with pride:* TASS Dispatches. N. Novikov, in *Pravda*, May 31 and June 2, 1961.

Page 217 *De Gaulle recalled how he had told the Soviet leader:* FRUS, 1961–1963, vol. XIV, Berlin Crisis, 1961–1962, Doc. 30, Memcon, Paris, May 31, 1961.

Page 217 *Kennedy doubted dealing:* FRUS, 1961–1963, vol. XIV, Berlin Crisis, 1961–1962, Doc. 30, Memcon, Paris, May 31, 1961.

Page 219 *In his comments, Kennedy:* John F. Kennedy. *Public Papers of the Presidents of the United States: John F. Kennedy—Containing the Public Messages, Speeches, and Statements of the President, 1961–1963.* Washington, D.C.: U.S. Government Printing Office, 1962–1964, vol. 1, 423.

Page 219 *The view through long: Washington Post*, 06/02/1961.

Page 220 *Yet the star that evening: New York Times*, 06/02/1961.

Page 220 *During their "tub talk":* O'Donnell and Powers, with McCarthy, *"Johnny, We Hardly Knew Ye,"* 292.

Page 220 *Kennedy's advance team:* Monika Sommer and Michaela Lindinger, eds., *Die Augen der Welt auf Wien gerichtet: Gipfel 1961 Chruschtschow–Kennedy.* Innsbruck and Vienna: Katalog Wien Museum, 2005, 68; *Die Illustrierte Krone*, 06/03/1961, 06/04/1961; *Österreichische Neue Tageszeitung*, 06/03/1961, 06/04/1961.

Page 221 *The bald top:* O'Donnell and Powers, with McCarthy, *"Johnny, We Hardly Knew Ye,"* 292–293; Dallek, *An Unfinished Life*, 404.

Page 222 *In chronicling the first: New York Times*, 06/04/1961.

Page 222 *The German intellectual paper:* "Die Gefangenen von Wien: Das Treffen der Zwei," *Die Zeit*, 06/02/1961.

Page 223 *Viennese teenager:* Sommer/Lindinger. *Augen der Welt auf Wien: Gipfel 1961.*

Page 223 *Anticipating two long days:* FRUS, 1961–1963, vol. V, Soviet Union, Doc. 83, Memcon, Vienna, June 3, 1961; 12:45p.m.

Page 225 *In pre-summit conversations:* FRUS, 1961–1963, vol. V, Soviet Union, Doc. 76.

Page 225 *Continuing to disregard his experts':* JFKL, *Robert F. Kennedy OH*.

Page 227 *"'Miscalculation'! 'Miscalculation'! 'Miscalculation'!":* Khrushchev's reaction according to Kennedy's own account, as quoted in Donald Kagan. *On the Origins of War and the Preservation of Peace.* New York: Anchor Books, 1996, 468–469; O'Donnell and Powers, with McCarthy, *"Johnny, We Hardly Knew Ye,"* 295.

Page 228 *Khrushchev remained in full voice:* Beschloss, *The Crisis Years*, 197.

Page 228 *Khrushchev boasted about:* FRUS, 1961–1963, vol. V, Soviet Union, Doc. 84, Memcon, Vienna, June 3, 1961, Luncheon.

Page 228 *At the end of the lunch:* "Contest of Wills," *Time*, 06/16/1961.

Page 229 *The two men's after-meal:* FRUS, 1961–1963, vol. V, Soviet Union, Doc. 84, Memcon, Vienna, June 3, 1961, Luncheon.

Page 229 *"Don't spread that story":* Paul F. Boller, *Presidential Anecdotes*. New York: Oxford

University Press, 1996, 302–303; O'Donnell and Powers, with McCarthy, *"Johnny, We Hardly Knew Ye,"* 294.

Page 229 Khrushchev raised his glass: FRUS, 1961–1963, vol. V, Soviet Union, Doc. 84; Taubman, *Khrushchev,* 494; Beschloss, *The Crisis Years,* 189–191; Reeves, *Kennedy: Profile of Power,* 42–43, 669n; Hersh, *Dark Side of Camelot,* 234–237.

Page 230 After lunch, Kennedy invited: Dallek, *An Unfinished Life,* 406; FRUS, 1961–1963, vol. V, Soviet Union, Doc. 85, Memcon, Vienna, June 3, 1961, 3 p.m.

Page 230 Kennedy's friends O'Donnell: Beschloss, *The Crisis Years,* 198–199; O'Donnell and Powers, with McCarthy, *"Johnny, We Hardly Knew Ye,"* 296.

Page 230 When the two men: FRUS, 1961–1963, vol. V, Soviet Union, Doc. 85.

Page 234 After a Soviet limo: JFKL, *Llewellyn E. Thompson OH;* Beschloss, *The Crisis Years,* 205; Dallek, *An Unfinished Life,* 408.

Page 235 Kennedy had reinforced: Oleg Troyanovsky, *Cherez godi i rasstoiania: Istoriia odnoi semyi.* Moscow: Vagrius, 1997, 234.

Page 235 In the years that followed: Herbert Hoover Presidential Library (HHL). H. Hoover Papers, Oral History Transcripts, *Washington Tapes, 1965–1971: William L. Stearman OH.*

Page 236 Mercifully, the U.S. embassy: O'Donnell and Powers, with McCarthy, *"Johnny, We Hardly Knew Ye,"* 293–294.

Page 236 Dave Powers told the president: O'Donnell and Powers, with McCarthy, *"Johnny, We Hardly Knew Ye,"* 296.

Page 236 "What did you expect": Dallek, *An Unfinished Life,* 406.

Page 236 Kennedy told his friends: Beschloss, *Crisis Years,* 199, 205; Taubman, *Khrushchev: The Man and His Era,* 497; O'Donnell and Powers, with McCarthy, *"Johnny, We Hardly Knew Ye,"* 296.

Page 237 On the one hand, Khrushchev: Fursenko and Naftali, *Khrushchev's Cold War,* 34.

Page 237 It was Austria's coming-out: Die Presse, 06/01/1961; Das Kleine Volksblatt, 06/04/1961.

Page 237 Aside from the fact: Sommer and Lindinger, *Augen der Welt auf Wien: Gipfel 1961,* 73; "First Lady Wins Khrushchev Too," *New York Times,* 06/04/1961.

Page 238 "Mr. Khrushchev": Reeves, *Kennedy: Profile of Power,* 166.

Page 238 Kennedy's performance: Washington Post, 06/04/1961; Reeves, *Kennedy: Profile of Power,* 166.

11. VIENNA: THE THREAT OF WAR

Page 239 "The U.S. is unwilling": FRUS, 1961–1963, vol. V, Soviet Union, Doc. 87, Memcon, p. 219.

Page 239 "I never met a man": Hersh, *Dark Side of Camelot,* 253.

Page 240 "I greet you": Sidey, *JFK,* 196.

Page 240 After some nine minutes: Beschloss, *Crisis Years,* 209–211.

Page 240 In the conference room: FRUS, 1961–1963, vol. V, Soviet Union, Doc. 87, Memcon, Vienna, June 4, 1961, 10:15 a.m.

Page 241 However, the Soviets would doctor: O'Donnell and Powers, with McCarthy, *"Johnny, We Hardly Knew Ye,"* 294.

Page 246 Khrushchev said that even: Norman Davies, *No Simple Victory: World War II in Europe, 1939–1945.* New York: Viking, 2007, 24.

Page 248 With an actor's sense: U.S. Department of State, *Documents on Germany, 1944–1985.* Washington, D.C.: Office of the Historian, Bureau of Public Affairs, 729–732; also in Department of State Bulletin, August 7, 1961, 231–233.

Page 249 Reuters correspondent Adam Kellett-Long: Interview with Adam Kellett-Long, London, October 15–16, 2008.

Page 249 From the upstairs window: New York Times, 06/05/1961.

Page 249 The two men conversed: FRUS, 1961–1963, vol. V, Soviet Union, Doc. 88, Memcon, Vienna, June 4, 1961; Beschloss, *Crisis Years,* 220.

Page 251 The gift Kennedy: Sidey, *JFK,* 200.

Page 251 With their two days of talks: O'Donnell and Powers, with McCarthy, *"Johnny, We Hardly Knew Ye,"* 297; Dallek, *An Unfinished Life,* 412.

Page 251 When the president's staff: Beschloss, *The Crisis Years,* 220; O'Donnell and Powers, with McCarthy, *"Johnny, We Hardly Knew Ye,"* 297; Sidey, *JFK,* 200.

Page 252 Kennedy opened their last: FRUS, 1961–1963, vol. V, Soviet Union, Doc. 88, Memcon, Vienna, June 4, 1961, 3:15 p.m.

Page 253 The Berlin newspapers: Tagesspiegel, 06/04/1961.

Page 254 Fewer refugees registered: New York Times, 06/04/1961; *Kurier; Österreichische Neue Tageszeitung; Neues Deutschland.*

Page 254 Khrushchev knew he had won . . . The Soviet leader: Nikita S. Khrushchev, *Khrushchev Remembers: The Last Testament,* 499.

Page 255 After seeing off Kennedy: Nikita S. Khrushchev, *Khrushchev Remembers: The Last Testament,* 500–501.

Page 255 As he drove away: Beschloss, *Crisis Years,* 224.

Page 256 Kennedy carried with him: DNSA, Soviet Translation of the Aide-Mémoire on Germany and Berlin, For Official Use Only, Cable, June 5, 1961, Berlin Crisis: BC02081.

Page 256 No. Kennedy decided to leave: O'Donnell and Powers, with McCarthy, *"Johnny, We Hardly Knew Ye,"* 297; Pierre Salinger, *With Kennedy.* Garden City, NY: Doubleday, 1966, 182.

Page 257 "How was it?": John F. Stacks, *Scotty: James B. Reston and the Rise and Fall of American Journalism.* Boston: Little, Brown, 2003, 4, 198, 200.

Page 257 Reston rightly concluded: New York Times, 06/04/1961, 06/05/1961, 06/06/1961; Stacks, *Scotty,* 199.

Page 257 Kennedy told Reston: James Reston, JFK interview, *New York Times,* 06/05/1961; "Vienna Talks End," *New York Times,* 06/05/1961; Salinger, *With Kennedy,* 181–182; David Halberstam, *The Best and Brightest.* New York: Modern Library, 2001, 85–86; O'Donnell and Powers, with McCarthy, *"Johnny, We Hardly Knew Ye,"* 298; Taubman, *Khrushchev: The Man and His Era,* 495.

Page 258 On the flight to London: Heymann, C. David. *A Woman Named Jackie: An Intimate Biography of Jacqueline Bouvier Kennedy Onassis.* New York: Carol, 1994, 306.

Page 258 "All wars start": O'Donnell and Powers, with McCarthy, *"Johnny, We Hardly Knew Ye,"* 299.

Page 258 Those who had worked: Association for Diplomatic Studies and Training, *Interview with Kempton B. Jenkins, Foreign Affairs OH.* Interview conducted February 23, 1995 (copyright 1998 ADST), Box: 1 Fold: 34 Jenkins, Kempton B. (1951–1980): http://www.library .georgetown.edu/dept/speccoll/cl999.htm.

Page 259 Speaking with O'Donnell: O'Donnell and Powers, with McCarthy, *"Johnny, We Hardly Knew Ye,"* 299–300.

Page 260 British Prime Minister Macmillan: Macmillan, Harold. *Pointing the Way, 1959–1961,* 355–359, 400; O'Brien, *JFK,* 550.

Page 260 While they talked, U.S. officials: FRUS, 1961–1963, vol. XIV, Berlin Crisis, 1961–1962, Doc. 34, Record of Conversation, London, June 5, 1961.

Page 260 The British prime minister called off: Beschloss, *The Crisis Years,* 226; O'Brien, *JFK,* 551, 888; Schlesinger, *A Thousand Days,* 374–377; Alistair Horne. *Harold Macmillan: 1957–1986.* vol. 2, 303–305.

Page 261 "For the first time in his life": Macmillan. *Pointing the Way, 1959–1961,* 357.

Page 261 Macmillan told Kennedy: FRUS, 1961–1963, vol. XIV, Berlin Crisis, 1961–1962, Doc. 34.

Page 262 Kennedy and Macmillan agreed to step up: DNSA, Note of Points Made during the Private Conversation between Kennedy and Prime Minister Macmillan, June 8, 1961.

Page 262 While flying back to the U.S.: "1961 Man of the Year—John F. Kennedy," *Time,* 01/05/1962.

Page 262 Kennedy told his secretary: Evelyn Lincoln, *My Twelve Years with John F. Kennedy.* New York: D. McKay, 1965, 274.

Page 263 Bobby sat with his brother: Hersh, *The Dark Side of Camelot,* 383.

Page 263 Journalist Stewart Alsop: New York Herald Tribune, 04/06/1961.

Page 263 "I had the sense": JFKL, Joseph W. Alsop OH, no. 1, June 18, 1964.

Page 264 East German leader: Cate. The Ides of August, 24.

Page 265 After badgering Khrushchev: SED Archives, IfGA, ZPA, J IV, 2/202/129, Letter from Ulbricht to Khrushchev, June 1961, in Harrison, "Ulbricht and the Concrete 'Rose,'" CWIHP Working Paper No. 5, 96–97, Appendix E.

Page 266 Upon Khrushchev's return: Fursenko and Naftali, Khrushchev's Cold War, 365–366.

Page 266 "What liberals you've become": Fursenko and Naftali, Khrushchev's Cold War, 365–366.

Page 267 While Kennedy headed home: Washington Post, 06/07/1961.

Page 268 But on this occasion, Khrushchev: Washington Post, 06/07/1961.

12. ANGRY SUMMER

Page 269 "The construction workers": Neues Deutschland, June 16, 1961.

Page 269 "Somehow he does succeed": Acheson Letter to Truman, June 24, 1961 (courtesy David Acheson); Harry S. Truman Presidential Library (HSTL), Dean G. Acheson Papers, Acheson–Truman Correspondence File (1947–1971), 1961, Box 161.

Page 269 "The issue over Berlin": FRUS, 1961–1963, vol. XIV, Berlin Crisis, 1961–1962, Doc. 49, Report by Dean Acheson, Washington, June 28, 1961.

Page 270 The problem was that Ulbricht: Gelb, The Berlin Wall, 97.

Page 270 By the time Ulbricht marched in: Gelb, The Berlin Wall, 98.

Page 271 Timed to coincide with Khrushchev's: http://www.youtube.com/watch?v=jLhYIqiJlEA; Neues Deutschland, June 16, 1961; DNSA, Summary of Walter Ulbricht's Press Conference in East Berlin of June 15, Limited Official Use, Airgram, June 16, 1961, Berlin Crisis, BC02090.

Page 272 It was Ulbricht's first public mention: Harrison, Driving the Soviets up the Wall, 180.

Page 272 At six o'clock that evening: Curtis Cate, The Ides of August: The Berlin Wall Crisis, 1961. New York: M. Evans, 1978, 64–65.

Page 272 The term increasingly used: "Newsfronts: In Berlin 'Torschlusspanik,'" Life, July 28, 1961, 25.

Page 273 The Acheson relationship to Kennedy: Brinkley, Dean Acheson, 108–109.

Page 273 Acheson regarded his job: FRUS, 1969–1963, vol. XIV, Berlin Crisis, 1969–1962, Doc. 42, Record of Meeting of the Interdepartmental Coordinating Group on Berlin Contingency Planning, Washington, June 16, 1961; Robert Slusser, The Berlin Crisis of 1961: Soviet–American Relations and the Struggle for Power in the Kremlin, June–November 1961. Baltimore: Johns Hopkins University Press, 1973, 29; Catudal, Kennedy and the Berlin Wall Crisis, 138, 141.

Page 274 Acheson's hard line: FRUS, 1961–1963, vol. XIV, Berlin Crisis, 1961–1962, Doc. 42.

Page 275 Though the men in the room: "Newsfronts: JFK's Triple Play Against Khrushchev," Life, July 28, 1961, 32–33; John C. Ausland and Colonel Hugh F. Richardson, "Crisis Management: Berlin, Cyprus, Laos," Foreign Affairs, 44, no. 2 (January 1966), 291–303.

Page 276 Acheson gave the group: Catudal, Kennedy and the Berlin Wall Crisis, 141.

Page 278 Before television cameras: Pravda, June 18, 1961, in The Current Digest of the Soviet Press, 13, no. 23 (1961), 15.

Page 278 Khrushchev framed the Western refusal: Slusser, Berlin Crisis of 1961, 11–13, 18.

Page 278 One after another, the Soviet Union's: The Current Digest of the Soviet Press, 13, no. 25 (1961), 4–6 (6); Slusser, Berlin Crisis of 1961, 14–17.

Page 279 Even as Dean Acheson: Acheson Letter to Truman, June 24, 1961 (courtesy David Acheson); see also HSTL, Dean G. Acheson Papers, 1961, Box 161; Brinkley, Dean Acheson, 137–138; JFKL, Dean G. Acheson OH.

Page 280 Time magazine: "The People: The Summer of Discontent," Time, 07/07/1961; Newsweek, 07/03/1961.

Page 280 Kennedy complained to Salinger: JFKL, News Conference No. 13, Washington, D.C., June 28, 1961, 10:00 a.m., EDST; quoted in Reeves, Kennedy: Profile of Power, 188–189.

Page 281 The first three paragraphs of Acheson's: FRUS, 1961–1963, vol. XIV, Berlin Crisis, 1961–1962, Doc. 49, Report by Dean Acheson, Washington, June 28, 1961.

Page 281 He said that the "real themes": FRUS, 1961–1963, vol. XIV, 1961–1962, Doc. 52, Memo for the Record, Washington, undated, Discussion at NSC Meeting June 29, 1961.

Page 282 The veteran opposed: FRUS, 1961–1963, vol. XIV, 1961–1962, Doc. 52.

Page 283 After the meeting, Schlesinger: John Patrick Diggins, *The Liberal Persuasion: Arthur Schlesinger, Jr., and the Challenge of the American Past.* Princeton, NJ: Princeton University Press, 1997, 29–31; Arthur M. Schlesinger, *The Crisis of Confidence: Ideas, Power, and Violence in America.* Boston: Houghton Mifflin, 1969, 54, 60; Schlesinger, *A Thousand Days,* 384; JFKL, *Abram Chayes OH,* no. 4, July 9, 1964, 244–245, 248.

Page 284 His ambassador to East Germany: Sergei N. Khrushchev, *Creation of a Superpower,* 453.

Page 284 In a July 4 letter, Pervukhin: Harrison, *Driving the Soviets up the Wall,* 185; AVP-RF, Letter from Ambassador Pervukhin to Foreign Minister Gromyko sent to the Central Committee on 4 July 1961. Top secret file, Russian Foreign Ministry Archive, Fond: referentyra po GDR, Op. 6, Por 34, Pap. 46, Inv. 193/3, vol. 1, in Harrison,"Ulbricht and the Concrete 'Rose,'" CWIHP Working Paper No. 5, 55, 98–105, Appendix F.

Page 284 Ulbricht had long since overcome: Yuli A. Kvitsinsky (Julij A. Kwizinskij), *Vor dem Sturm: Erinnerungen eines Diplomaten,* Berlin: Siedler, 1993, 175, 179.

Page 285 Since Vienna, Khrushchev's son: Sergei N. Khrushchev, *Nikita Khrushchev and the Creation of a Superpower,* 453; Harrison, *Driving the Soviets up the Wall,* 186, 216.

Page 285 Though Ulbricht still demanded: Nikita S. Khrushchev, *Khrushchev Remembers: The Last Testament,* 505–508 (506).

Page 285 Khrushchev complained that: Sergei N. Khrushchev, *Nikita Khrushchev and the Creation of a Superpower,* 454.

Page 287 She was Walter Ulbricht's: Karl-Eduard von Schnitzler, "Die schönste Frau der Welt—eine Deutsche!" *Junge Welt,* 07/20/1961; "Marlene Schmidt, Die Anti-Miss von 1961," *Der Spiegel,* 4/30/2001.

Page 287 At age twenty-four: "Marlene Schmidt, Die Anti-Miss von 1961," *Der Spiegel,* 4/30/2001.

Page 288 Time magazine couldn't resist: "Universal Appeal," *Time,* 7/28/1961.

Page 288 Marlene's triumph was: http://www.youtube.com/watch?v=6i9sllFNZqs.

Page 288 Marlene, who was earning: Lee Rutherford, "Refugee Takes Universe Title," *Washington Post,* 07/18/1961.

Page 289 In the case of Marlene: "Die schönste Frau der Welt—eine Deutsche!" *Junge Welt,* 07/20/1961.

Page 289 In 1962, she would: "Marlene Schmidt, Die Anti-Miss von 1961," *Der Spiegel,* 4/30/2001.

13. "THE GREAT TESTING PLACE"

Page 293 "The immediate threat": JFKL, Radio and Television Report to the American People on the Berlin Crisis, President Kennedy, The White House, July 25, 1961: http://www.jfklibrary.org/Historical+Resources/Archives/Reference+Desk/Speeches/JFK/003POF03BerlinCrisis07251961.htm.

Page 293 "Khrushchev is losing": JFKL, *Walt W. Rostow OH*; Walt W. Rostow, *The Diffusion of Power: An Essay in Recent History,* New York: Macmillan, 1972, 231. Schlesinger, *A Thousand Days,* 394.

Page 293 Mikhail Pervukhin, the Soviet Ambassador: Kvitsinsky, *Vor dem Sturm,* 179–180; Klaus Wiegrefe, "Die Schandmauer," *Der Spiegel,* 08/06/2001, 71.

Page 294 Years later, Khrushchev would take: Nikita S. Khrushchev, *Khrushchev Remembers: The Last Testament,* 508; Nikita S. Khrushchev, *Khrushchev Remembers: The Glasnost Tapes.* Boston: Little, Brown, 1990, 169.

Page 294 Khrushchev would tell the West German: Hans Kroll, *Lebenserinnerungen eines Botschafters.* Cologne: Kiepenheuer & Witsch, 1967, 512, 526.

Page 294 Khrushchev had agonized: Sergei N. Khrushchev, *Creation of a Superpower,* 454–455; Kroll, *Lebenserinnerungen,* 512, 527; Nikita S. Khrushchev, *Khrushchev Remembers: The Glasnost Tapes,* 169.

Page 295 Pervukhin told a satisfied Ulbricht: Harrison, *Driving the Soviets up the Wall,* 186; Wiegrefe, "Die Schandmauer," 71; Kvitsinsky, *Vor dem Sturm,* 180–181.

Page 295 The only way to close such a border: Kvitsinsky, *Vor dem Sturm,* 179–181; Central Analysis and Information Group of the Ministry for State Security (ZAIG), *Protokol über die Besprechung am 07.07.1961,* Top secret, Ministerium für Staatssicherheit (MfS) 4899, 9; Uhl and Wagner, "Another Brick in the Wall: Reexamining Soviet and East German Policy During the 1961 Berlin Crisis: New Evidence, New Documents," CWIHP Working Paper, published under "Storming On to Paris: The 1961 'Buria' Exercise and the Planned Solution of the Berlin Crisis," in Mastny, Holtsmark, and Wenger, *War Plans and Alliances in the Cold War,* 46–71; Wiegrefe, "Die Schandmauer," 71.

Page 295 The Soviets should not underestimate: SAPMO-BArch, ZPA, J IV 2/202/130, "Besondere Informationen an Genossen Walter Ulbricht," Bd. 6, July 15, 1961; Patrick Major, *Behind the Berlin Wall: East Germany and the Frontiers of Power.* New York: Oxford University Press, 2010, 110.

Page 296 Having won the Pulitzer Prize: Schlesinger, *A Thousand Days,* 255–256; A. J. Langguth, *Our Vietnam: The War 1954–1975.* New York: Simon & Schuster, 2000, 136–137.

Page 296 Schlesinger was determined: Schlesinger, *A Thousand Days,* 383–384, 386–387.

Page 296 When Kennedy first drafted: Schlesinger, *A Thousand Days,* 381; Chace, *Acheson,* 391; McGeorge Bundy, *Danger and Survival: Choices About the Bomb in the First Fifty Years.* New York: Random House, 1988, 375–376.

Page 297 On July 7, just after a lunch meeting: FRUS, 1961–1963, vol. XIV, Berlin Crisis, 1961–1962, Doc. 57, JFKL, POF, Memo from the President's Special Assistant (Schlesinger) to President Kennedy; Under Secretary of State Bowles sent Rusk a similar memo on July 7, expressing concern about trend of U.S. thinking on Berlin; see Department of State, Central Files, 762.00/7-761.

Page 298 Schlesinger had calculated: Schlesinger, *A Thousand Days,* 386.

Page 299 "The Acheson premise": FRUS, 1961–1963, vol. XIV, Berlin Crisis, 1961–1962, Doc. 57.

Page 301 At the same time, Kennedy was also hearing: Schlesinger, *A Thousand Days,* 388; Catudal, *Kennedy and the Berlin Wall Crisis,* 160.

Page 301 Henry Kissinger spent only a day: Walter Isaacson, *Kissinger: A Biography.* New York: Simon & Schuster Paperbacks, 2005, 110–113; W. R. Smyser, *Kennedy and the Berlin Wall.* Lanham, MD: Rowman & Littlefield, 2010, 35–38.

Page 302 Kissinger would complain: Henry Kissinger, *White House Years.* Boston: Little, Brown, 1979, 13–14.

Page 303 So Kissinger put his warning: JFKL, Henry Kissinger, Memorandum for the President, Subject: Berlin, July 7, 1961, 1–2.

Page 304 In a separate note to Schlesinger: W. R. Smyser, *Kennedy and the Berlin Wall,* 38; Jeremy Suri, *Henry Kissinger and the American Century.* Cambridge, MA: Harvard University Press, 2007, 175–176.

Page 305 President Kennedy was displeased: "Kennedy Confers on Berlin Issues," *New York Times,* 07/09/1961; "Kennedy to Meet 3 Aides on Berlin," *New York Times,* 07/08/1961; Reeves, *Kennedy: Profile of Power,* 192.

Page 305 It was fine to drop the ball: Schlesinger, *A Thousand Days,* 390.

Page 305 The news from the Soviet Union: Nikita S. Khrushchev, *Communism—Peace and Happiness for the Peoples,* vol. 1, *January-September 1961.* Moscow: Foreign Languages Publishing House, 1963, 288–309, Speech at a Reception Given by the Central Committee of the C.P.S.U. and the Council of Ministers of the U.S.S.R. for Graduates of Military Academies, July 8, 1961; "Khrushchev Halts Troop Reduction; Raises Arms Fund," "Excerpts From Khrushchev's Address on Arms Policy," *New York Times,* 07/09/1961.

Page 306 Kennedy was livid: Newsweek, 07/03/1961.

Page 306 Khrushchev had responded to the Newsweek: Beschloss, *Crisis Years*, 244; "West Is Drafting Reply to Soviet on German Issues," *New York Times*, 06/30/1961, 07/01/1961, 07/05/1961, 07/14/1961; "British Envoy Tells Khrushchev Soviet Policy on Berlin Is Illegal," *New York Herald Tribune*, 07/06/1961; "Matter of Fact: Khrushchev as Hitler," *Washington Post*, 07/12/1961; Martin McCauley, ed., *Khrushchev and Khrushchevism*, Bloomington: Indiana University Press, 1987, 222.

Page 306 When Rusk explained: Reeves, *Kennedy: Profile of Power*, 192; Catudal, *Kennedy and the Berlin Wall Crisis*, 153–154.

Page 306 The president then turned on: Gelb, *The Berlin Wall*, 112.

Page 306 Martin Hillenbrand, head: Beschloss, *The Crisis Years*, 246–248; *New York Times*, 07/09/1961, 07/14/1961; Schlesinger, *A Thousand Days*, 752; Catudal, *Kennedy and the Berlin Wall Crisis*, 153–154.

Page 307 "I want the damn thing": Reeves, *Kennedy: Profile of Power*, 192.

Page 307 Kennedy soaked in a hot bath: Evelyn Lincoln, *My Twelve Years with John F. Kennedy*. New York: D. McKay, 1965, 232–233, 278.

Page 308 "Finally, I would like to close": Radio and Television Report to the American People on the Berlin Crisis, July 25, 1961: http://www.jfklibrary.org/Historical+Resources/Archives/Reference+Desk/Speeches/JFK/003POF03BerlinCrisis07251961.htm.

Page 309 Kennedy said to his secretary: Lincoln, *My Twelve Years with John F. Kennedy*, 233–234.

Page 310 On July 13 in the Cabinet Room: FRUS, 1961–1963, vol. XIV, Berlin Crisis, 1961–1962, Doc. 66, Memo of Discussion in the National Security Council, Washington, July 13, 1961, prepared by Bundy on July 24, 1961; Brinkley, *Dean Acheson*, 144.

Page 310 Bundy had left: FRUS, 1961–1963, vol. XIV, Berlin Crisis, 1961–1962, Doc. 66n3, memo drafted by Bundy on military choices in Berlin planning outlining four alternatives.

Page 311 The president listened: JFKL, NSF, NSC Meetings, Top Secret, prepared by Bundy on July 24, 1961, Memo of Discussion in the National Security Council; in FRUS, 1961–1963, vol. XIV, Berlin Crisis, 1961–1962, Doc. 66.

Page 311 Acheson had grown: Catudal, *Kennedy and the Berlin Wall Crisis*, 182.

Page 311 At the second key NSC: FRUS, 1961–1963, vol. XIV, Berlin Crisis, 1961–1962, Doc. 77, Memo of Minutes of the National Security Council Meeting, Washington, July 19, 1961, prepared by Bundy on July 25, 1961.

Page 311 Ambassador Thompson wasn't in the room: Theodore C. Sorensen, *Kennedy*. New York: HarperCollins, 1965, 589.

Page 312 Kennedy told the NSC: Catudal, *Kennedy and the Berlin Wall Crisis*, 180; Beschloss, *The Crisis Years*, 257.

Page 312 Just the previous day at lunch: Cate, *The Ides of August*, 108–111; author interview with James O'Donnell.

Page 314 "For West Berlin, lying exposed": JFKL, Radio and Television Report to the American People on the Berlin Crisis, President Kennedy, The White House, July 25, 1961: http://www.jfklibrary.org/Historical+Resources/Archives/Reference+Desk/Speeches/JFK/003POF03BerlinCrisis07251961.htm.

Page 315 O'Donnell suggested an easy: Gelb, *The Berlin Wall*, 118.

Page 315 "There was an 'Oh, my God!'": Gelb, *The Berlin Wall*, 118; author's interview with Karl Mautner.

Page 315 The emphasis on West *Berlin:* Beschloss, *Crisis Years*, 264; *New York Times*, 08/03/1961; *Der Tagesspiegel*, 08/02/1961; *Neues Deutschland*, 08/02/1961; JFKL, Bundy–JFK, August 4, 1961; Catudal, *Kennedy and the Berlin Wall Crisis*, 201–203.

Page 316 Fulbright's interpretation of the treaty: Ann Tusa, *The Last Division: A History of Berlin, 1945–1989*. London: Hodder and Stoughton, 1997, 257; *Washington Post*, 07/31/1961; *New York Times*, 08/03/1961.

Page 316 Early in August, Kennedy: JFKL, *Walt W. Rostow OH*; Rostow, *Diffusion of Power*, 231;

Beschloss, *The Crisis Years*, 265; Schlesinger, *A Thousand Days*, 394; Catudal, *Kennedy and the Berlin Wall Crisis*, 201.

Page 316 On a sweltering Moscow morning: Harrison, *Driving the Soviets up the Wall*, 192–194; SAPMO-BArch, ZPA, DY, 30/3682; Uhl and Wagner, "Another Brick in the Wall," CWIHP Working Paper, published under "Storming On to Paris," in Mastny, Holtsmark, and Wenger, *War Plans and Plliances in the Cold War*, 46–71; Aleksandr Fursenko, "Kak Byla Postroena Berlinskaia Stena," in *Istoricheskie Zapiski*, no. 4 (2001), 78–79.

Page 317 The two men had been closely: Fursenko and Naftali, *Khrushchev's Cold War*, 377, 379–380.

Page 317 "When would it be best": Fursenko, "Kak Byla Postroena Berlinskaia Stena," 78.

Page 318 Noting that the thirteenth: Nikita S. Khrushchev, *Khrushchev Remembers: The Last Testament*, 506.

Page 318 "In those homes": Fursenko, "Kak Byla Postroena Berlinskaia Stena," 79.

Page 318 "When the border is closed": RGANI, Khrushchev–Ulbricht, August 1, 1961, Document No. 521557, 113–146. Document and citation graciously provided by Dr. Matthias Uhl.

Page 320 He even spoke nostalgically: Taubman, *Khrushchev: The Man and His Era*, 502; Vladislav M. Zubok, "Khrushchev's Secret Speech on the Berlin Crisis, August 1961," CWIHP-B, No. 3, Fall 1993, 58–61; Catudal, *Kennedy and the Berlin Wall Crisis*, 50. The conference of first secretaries of Central Committee of Communist and Workers Parties of socialist countries for exchange of views on the questions related to preparation and conclusion of German peace treaty, 3–5 August 1961 [Transcripts of the meeting were found in the miscellaneous documents of the International Department of the Central Committee, TsKhSD], 11, 142–144, 156–157.

Page 322 Wismach left East Berlin: Bundesministerium für Gesamtdeutsche Fragen, ed., *Die Flucht aus der Sowjetzone und die Sperrmassnahmen des kommunistischen Regimes vom 13. August 1961 in Berlin.* Bonn/Berlin, 7. September 1961, vol. 2, Doc. No. 95, 81–82; Archiv Deutschlandradio. Sendung: Die Zeit im Funk, Reporter: Hans-Rudolf Vilter, *RIAS-Interview mit dem nach West-Berlin geflüchteten Kurt Wismach, der Walter Ulbricht während seiner Rede im Kabelwerk Oberspree am 10. August 1961 mehrfach unterbrach, 17. August 1961:* http://www.chronik-der-mauer.de/index.php/de/Start/Index/id/631935/item/34/page/0.

14. THE WALL: SETTING THE TRAP

Page 323 "The GDR had to cope": Nikita S. Khrushchev, *Khrushchev Remembers.* Boston: Little, Brown, 1970, 454.

Page 323 "In this period": Bernd Eisenfeld and Roger Engelmann, *13.8.1961: Mauerbau— Fluchtbewegung und Machtsicherung.* Bremen: Temmen, 2001, 48; Behörde der Bundesbeauftragten für die Unterlagen des Staatssicherheitsdienstes der Ehemaligen Deutschen Demokratischen Republik (BStU), MfS, ZA, ZAIG No. 4900, Aus dem Protokoll über die Dienstbesprechung im MfS am 11. August 1961, Bl.3–6.

Page 325 With only three weeks: Harrison, *Driving the Soviets up the Wall*, 187–188; Uhl and Wagner, "Another Brick in the Wall," CWIHP Working Paper, published under "Storming On to Paris," in Mastny, Holtsmark, and Wenger, *War Plans and Alliances in the Cold War*, 46–71; SAPMO-BArch, ZPA, J IV 2/202–65; Klaus Froh and Rüdiger Wenzke, eds., *Die Generale und Admirale der NVA: Ein biographisches Handbuch.* Berlin: Christoph Links, 2007, 198; Peter Wyden, *Wall: The Inside Story of Divided Berlin.* New York: Simon & Schuster, 1989, 88.

Page 325 Furious activity had filled: Cate, *The Ides of August*, 222.

Page 325 Several hundred police: Wyden, *Wall—The Inside Story of Divided Berlin*, 134, 140.

Page 327 From the moment that police: Eisenfeld, *13.8.1961*, 49.

Page 327 Ulbricht cleared the final language: William I. Hitchcock, *The Struggle for Europe: The Turbulent History of a Divided Continent, 1945–2002.* New York: Doubleday, 2003, 218.

Page 328 Without emotion, Ulbricht: Fursenko and Naftali, *Khrushchev's Cold War*, 380; AVP-RF,

Pervukhin to Khrushchev, August 10, 1961, 3-64-745, p. 125; Nikita S. Khrushchev, *Khrushchev Remembers: The Last Testament*, 505.

Page 328 Khrushchev received the news: Nikita S. Khrushchev, *Khrushchev Remembers*, 454, 456–457.

Page 329 At age sixty-three, Konev: Fursenko and Naftali, *Khrushchev's Cold War*, 382; Cate, *The Ides of August*, 178–182.

Page 330 Near World War II's end: Antony Beevor, *Berlin: The Downfall, 1945*. New York: Viking, 2002, 16.

Page 331 Khrushchev had constructed the plan: Nikita S. Khrushchev, *Khrushchev Remembers*, 458.

Page 332 At age twenty-six, Adam Kellett-Long: Christopher Hilton, *The Wall: The People's Story*. Stroud, England: Sutton, 2001, 25; Cate, *The Ides of August*, 236–238.

Page 332 Kellett-Long would later recall: Interview with Adam Kellett-Long, London, October 15–16, 2008.

Page 333 Kellett-Long returned to his office: Peter Wyden, "Wir machen Berlin dicht—Die Berliner Mauer (III) Der. 13. August," *Der Spiegel*, 10/16/1989.

Page 334 Mielke exuded self-confidence: Henning Köhler, *Adenauer: Eine politische Biographie*. Frankfurt am Main: Propyläen, 1994, 39.

Page 334 Back in 1931: Heribert Schwan, *Erich Mielke: Der Mann, der die Stasi war*. Munich: Droemer Knaur, 1997, 31, 58.

Page 335 "Today we begin a new chapter": Eisenfeld, *13.8.1961*, 47–49; BStU, MfS, ZA, ZAIG Nr. 4900, Aus dem Protokoll über die Dienstbesprechung im MfS am 11. August 1961, Bl. 3–6.

Page 336 One neighborhood near Berlin's: Cate, *The Ides of August*, 207; interview with Klaus Schulz-Ladegast, Berlin, October 12, 2008.

Page 336 The Severin + Kuhn company: Cate, *The Ides of August*, 3, 68–69, 208, 211, 230.

Page 338 In a raspy, emotional voice: Rede des Regierenden Bürgermeisters von Berlin, Willy Brandt, auf dem Kongress anlässlich des Deutschlandtreffens der SPD (Brandt speech at SPD congress), August 12, 1961, in Sozialdemokratische Partei Deutschlands, ed., *Tatsachen—Argumente*, no. 21, 08/21/1961, 4–11; chronik-der-mauer.de; *Chicago Daily Tribune*, 08/13/1961.

Page 339 While Brandt was in Nuremberg: Rede von Bundeskanzler Dr. Konrad Adenauer auf einer CDU-Wahlkampfkundgebung in Lübeck (Adenauer speech at Lübeck CDU election campaign rally), August 12, 1961, Stiftung Bundeskanzler Adenauer-Haus, www.chronik-der-mauer.de.

Page 339 Walter Ulbricht appeared: Frederick Taylor, *The Berlin Wall: A World Divided, 1969–1989*. New York: HarperCollins, 2007, 159; Grimm, *Politbüro Privat*, 161; Klaus Wiegrefe, "Die Schandmauer," *Der Spiegel*, 08/06/2001, 64–65.

Page 340 His guests speculated: Wiegrefe, "Die Schandmauer."

Page 340 Only a handful of Ulbricht's: Erich Honecker, *From My Life*. New York: Pergamon, 1981, 121; Hilton, *The Wall*, 31, 34–35.

Page 341 Apparently unaware: *Los Angeles Times*, 08/13/1961.

Page 341 Khrushchev had given a speech: DNSA, Analysis of Khruschev's Speech at a Soviet–Romanian Friendship Rally on August 11, Confidential Cable, August 12, 1961.

Page 341 Secretary of State Rusk had sent: FRUS, 1961–1963, vol. XIV, Berlin Crisis, 1961–1962, Doc. 103, Telegram from the Department of State to the Embassy in Germany, August 12, 1961, 6:26 p.m.

Page 344 Hoffmann briefed officers: Cate, *The Ides of August*, 229–224; Wyden, *Wall*, 137–138; Lt. Col. Martin Herbert Löffler's description, made in Bonn on September 21, 1961, *Berliner Morgenpost*, 09/22/1962; Foreign Broadcast Information Service, DPA Dispatch (English version), September 24, 1962; *Washington Post*, 09/22/1962; *New York Times*, 09/22/1962; *Rheinische Merkur, Christ + Welt*, 09/28/1962; Wiegrefe, "Die Schandmauer."

Page 344 By 10.00 p.m., Honecker: Honecker, *From My Life*, 211.

Page 344 The little information: Norbert F. Pötzl, *Erich Honecker: Eine Deutsche Biographie*.

Stuttgart and Munich: Deutsche Verlags-Anstalt, 2nd ed., 2002, 71; *Die Welt*, 06/08/2001; Armee für Frieden und Sozialismus, *Geschichte der Nationalen Volksarmee*. Berlin: Militärverlag der DDR, 1985, 244, 246.

Page 345 In all, some 8,200 People's Police: Pötzl, *Erich Honecker*, 72.

Page 345 Ulbricht looked at his watch: Honecker, *From My Life*, 210; Pötzl, *Erich Honecker*, 72.

Page 346 No one protested: Kvitsinsky, *Vor dem Sturm*; *Berliner Zeitung*, 03/22/1993.

Page 346 Kellett-Long was worried: Wyden, *Wall—The Inside Story of Divided Berlin*, 140–141; Kellett-Long interview.

Page 347 Three long, penetrating wails: Michael Mara, Rudi Thurow, Eckhardt Schaller, and Rainer Hildebrandt, eds., *Kontrollpunkt Kohlhasenbrück—Die Geschichte einer Grenzkompanie des Ringes um West-Berlin*. Bad Godesberg, Germany: Hohwacht-Verlag, 1964; Gelb, *The Berlin Wall*, 151–153.

Page 347 Witz, who said: Gelb, *The Berlin Wall*, 153.

Page 348 Shortly before 1:00 a.m.: Interview with Adam Kellett-Long, London, October 15–16, 2008.

Page 349 In response, Warsaw Pact: Statement by Warsaw Treaty Member, August 13, 1961, in *Pravda*, August 15, 1961; for extract, see Harry Hanak, *Soviet Foreign Policy Since the Death of Stalin*. Boston: Routledge, 1972, 113.

Page 349 "Earlier today, I became": Adam Kellett-Long, "Demonstrators Defy Armed Policemen: Tense Atmosphere in East Berlin," Manchester *Guardian*, 08/14/1961; http://www.guardian .co.uk/world/1961/aug/14/berlinwall.germany.

Page 350 The trucks belched out: Cate, *The Ides of August*, 248–249.

Page 351 Senior officials of the U.S., British: Gelb, *The Berlin Wall*, 158–159, 162–163.

Page 352 During an hour's drive: William R. Smyser, *Kennedy and the Berlin Wall: "A Hell of a Lot Better Than a War,"* Lanham, MD: Rowman & Littlefield, 2009, 101–103, 174; "Wir machen Berlin dicht—Die Berliner Mauer (III) Der. 13. August," *Der Spiegel*, 10/16/1989; Mara et al., *Kontrollpunkt Kohlhasenbrück*.

Page 352 The diplomats had gathered: Gelb, *The Berlin Wall*, 161–162.

Page 353 At 11:00 a.m. Berlin time: DNSA, East German Regime to Seal East Berlin from West, Confidential, Cable 176, August 13, 1961, 1 a.m.; DNSA, Summary of Events in Berlin from Early Morning to Mid-Afternoon, Confidential, Cable 186, August 13, 1961, 10 p.m.; Department of State, Central Files, 862.181/8-1361, in FRUS, 1961–1963, vol. XIV, Berlin Crisis, 1961–1962, Doc. 104.

Page 353 West Berliners' mood: Interview with Klaus-Detlef Brunzel, Berlin, October 23, 2008.

Page 354 Before long, the West Berlin fury: Interview with Klaus-Detlef Brunzel, Berlin, October 23, 2008.

Page 354 General Watson: "Commandant in Berlin," *New York Times*, 08/14/1961.

Page 355 There were also times: Gelb, *The Berlin Wall*, 165.

Page 355 Early that morning, Watson: Gelb, *The Berlin Wall*, 165; Cate, *The Ides of August*, 301–302, 275.

Page 356 Lieutenant Colonel Thomas McCord: Catudal, *Kennedy and the Berlin Wall Crisis*, 229–230, 232.

Page 356 All eyes had then turned: Letter from Colonel Ernest von Pawel to Catudal, August 3, 1977, in Catudal, *Kennedy and the Berlin Wall Crisis*, 234.

Page 357 The deputy chief: Wyden, *Wall*, 92, from Pawel interview; Catudal, *Kennedy and the Berlin Wall Crisis*, 229–230, 232–235.

Page 357 "The Soviet 19th Motorized": Gelb, *The Berlin Wall*, 160.

Page 358 Adam recalled a more innocent: Interview with Adam Kellett-Long, London, October 15–16, 2008.

Page 359 Under four-power agreements: Smyser, *Kennedy and the Berlin Wall*, 106; Howard Trivers, *Three Crises in American Foreign Affairs and a Continuing Revolution*. Carbondale: Southern Illinois University Press, 1972, 24–25.

Page 360 When he first heard: Cate, *The Ides of August,* 162–163.

Page 360 Then he set off: Deutsches Rundfunkarchiv, *Stimmen des 20. Jahrhunderts CD—Berlin,* 13 August 1961, produced by Deutsches Historisches Museum Berlin and Deutsches Rundfunkarchiv Frankfurt am Main and Potsdam-Babelsberg: http://www.dra.de/ publikationen/cds/stimmen/cd25.html.

Page 361 Lochner the next day showed: Smyser, *Kennedy and the Berlin Wall,* 115–116; Wyden, *Wall,* 166–167; Lothar Kettenacker, *Germany 1989: In the Aftermath of the Cold War.* London: Pearson Longman, 2009, 51.

Page 362 From noon on Saturday: Washington Post, 08/14/1961, 08/15/1961; *Chicago Daily Tribune,* 08/14/1961.

Page 362 Honecker phoned Ulbricht: Washington Post, 08/14/1961.

Page 362 Khrushchev would reflect: Nikita S. Khrushchev, *Khrushchev Remembers,* 455.

15. THE WALL: DESPERATE DAYS

Page 363 "Why would Khrushchev": O'Donnell and Powers, with McCarthy, *"Johnny, We Hardly Knew Ye,"* 303.

Page 363 "The Russians . . . feel": Arthur M. Schlesinger, *Robert Kennedy and His Times.* New York: Houghton Mifflin, 1978/2002, 430.

Page 363 Until August 13, Litfin: "Erstes Maueropfer Günter Litfin—'Tod durch fremde Hand,'" *Der Spiegel* (online), 09/02/2007; Hans-Hermann Hertle, *Die Todesopfer an der Berliner Mauer 1961–1989: Ein biographisches Handbuch.* Berlin: Christoph Links, 2009, 37–39.

Page 364 The two brothers then reflected: Christian F. Ostermann, *Uprising in East Germany 1953: The Cold War, the German Question, and the First Major Upheaval Behind the Iron Curtain.* Budapest and New York: Central European University Press, 2001, 169.

Page 365 He closely followed: "Scores Flee to West Despite Red Guards," *Washington Post,* 08/15/1961.

Page 366 Günter Litfin would be the first: Tagesspiegel, 08/25/1961.

Page 367 By comparison, the East Berliner: Cate, *The Ides of August,* 399.

Page 367 A little more than two days: Wyden, *Wall,* 221.

Page 368 CBS correspondent Daniel Schorr: Wyden, *Wall,* 220; Daniel Schorr Papers, Library of Congress.

Page 368 A fluke of prewar planning: Taylor, *The Berlin Wall,* 186–187.

Page 368 As a result, Berlin's Cold War: Regine Hildebrandt, oral history interview, Gedenkstätte Berliner Mauer; also see www.dradio.de: Hörbeispiel: Erinnerungen an den Bau der Berliner Mauer vor 40 Jahren: Regine Hildebrandt (SPD), Berlinerin.

Page 369 Like many of the soldiers: Jürgen Petschull, *Die Mauer: August 1961: Zwölf Tage zwischen Krieg und Frieden.* Hamburg: Gruner + Jahr, 1981, 149–152.

Page 370 The young man raced off: Peter Leibing, oral history interview, October 8, 2001, www .jungefreiheit.de, Moritz Schwarz, "'Na, springt der?' Peter Leibing über die spektakuläre Flucht des DDR-Grenzers Conrad Schumann und das Foto seines Lebens.

Page 372 So while Brandt prepared: Horst Osterheld, *"Ich gehe nicht leichten Herzens . . ."* Adenauers letzte Kanzlerjahre: Ein dokumentarischer Bericht. Mainz: Matthias-Grünewald, 1986, 59–60; Konrad Adenauer, *Teegespräche 1959–1961* (Rhöndorfer Ausgabe), ed. Hanns Jürgen Küsters. Berlin: Siedler, 1988, 541, 546.

Page 372 Within forty-eight hours: Donald P. Steury, ed., *On the Front Lines of the Cold War: Documents on the Intelligence War in Berlin, 1946 to 1961.* Washington, D.C.: CIA, Center for the Study of Intelligence, 1999; Current Intelligence Weekly Summary, August 17, 1961, 576–582: VII-6: CIWS: Berlin, August 17, 1961 (MORI No. 28205), 582.

Page 372 British Prime Minister Macmillan, the ally: London *Times,* August 26, 1961.

Page 372 However, Adenauer's response: Heinrich Krone, *Tagebücher.* Vol. 2: *1961–1966.* Ed. Hans-Otto Kleinmann. Düsseldorf: Forschungen und Quellen zur Zeitgeschichte, 2003, 15;

Konrad Adenauer, *Erinnerungen 1959–1963 (Fragmente)*. Stuttgart: Deutsche Verlags-Anstalt, 1968, 122.

Page 373 *Only at that point:* Archiv für Christlich-Demokratische Politik, Aufzeichnung der Unterredung Adenauer's mit Smirnow, August 16, 1961, N. L. Globke Papers, I-070-(2/1.1); Hans-Peter Schwarz, *Konrad Adenauer*. Vol. 2: *The Statesman, 1952–1967*, trans. Geoffrey Penny. Providence, RI: Berghahn Books, 1997, 540–541 (English trans. of *Adenauer*. Vol. 2: *Der Staatsmann: 1952–1967*. Stuttgart: Deutsche Verlags-Anstalt, 1991).

Page 373 *Less than forty-eight hours:* Prittie, *Konrad Adenauer*, 286; *Christian Science Monitor*, *Washington Post*, *New York Times*, 08/16/1961; *New York Times*, 08/30/1961.

Page 374 *Brandt, who until then:* Peter Merseburger, *Willy Brandt 1913–1992: Visionär und Realist*. Stuttgart and Munich: Deutsche Verlags-Anstalt, 2002, 406–407; *Die Zeit*, 08/18/1961.

Page 374 *Brandt realized that perhaps:* *New York Times*, 08/17/1961; *Washington Post*, 08/17/1961; *Bild-Zeitung*, 08/16/1961.

Page 375 *After wiping the sweat:* Archiv Deutschlandradio, *Die Zeit im Funk*, RIAS, Rede von Willy Brandt auf einer Protestkundgebung vor dem Rathaus Schöneberg, Ausschnitte (excerpt of Willy Brandt speech to protesters at Schöneberg/West Berlin city hall), August, 16, 1961: www.chronik-der-mauer.de/index.php/de/Media/VideoPopup/day/16/field/audio_video/id/15023/month/August/oldAction/Detail/oldModule/Chronical/year/1961.

Page 376 *He considered the letter from Mayor:* FRUS, 1961–1963, vol. XIV, Berlin Crisis, 1961–1962, Doc. 117, Telegram from the Mission at Berlin to the Department of State, Berlin, August 16, 1961, midnight.

Page 377 *"Trust?" Kennedy spat:* Petschull, *Die Mauer*, 157; Wyden, *Wall*, 224; Jean Edward Smith, *The Defense of Berlin*, Baltimore: Johns Hopkins University Press, 1963, 283–284; Washington, D.C., *Daily News*, 08/17/1961; Washington, D.C., *Evening Star*, 08/18/1961.

Page 377 *The State Department:* Washington, D.C., *Daily News*, 08/17/1961; Washington, D.C., *Evening Star*, 08/18/1961.

Page 378 *Brandt would later take credit:* Petschull, *Die Mauer*, 159; Hermann Zolling and Uwe Bahnsen, *Kalter Winter im August. Die Berlin-Krise 1961–1963. Ihre Hintergründe und Folgen*. Oldenburg and Hamburg: Gerhard Stalling, 1967, 147.

Page 378 *Kennedy came to accept:* FRUS, 1961–1963, vol. XIV, Berlin Crisis, 1961–1962, Doc. 120, Letter from President Kennedy to Governing Mayor Brandt, Washington, August 18, 1961; JFKL, NSF, Germany, Berlin, Brandt Correspondence, Secret.

Page 379 *Brandt read Kennedy's response:* Willy Brandt, *Erinnerungen*. Frankfurt am Main: Propyläen, and Zurich: Ferenczy, 1989, 58, 63; Merseburger, *Willy Brandt*, 405.

Page 379 *"Why would Khrushchev put up":* O'Donnell and Powers, with McCarthy, *"Johnny, We Hardly Knew Ye,"* 303.

Page 380 *Kennedy had little sympathy:* James Reston, "Hyannisport—A Cool Summer Visitor from Washington," *New York Times*, 09/06/1961.

Page 380 *In the first days:* JFKL, *Dr. Wilhelm Grewe OH*, November 2, 1966, Paris; Reston, "Hyannisport—A Cool Summer Visitor from Washington."

Page 381 *Khrushchev also reflected later:* Nikita S. Khrushchev, *Khrushchev Remembers: The Glasnost Tapes*, 170.

Page 381 *Khrushchev believed:* Taubman, *Khrushchev*, 506; Sergei N. Khrushchev, *Krizisy i Rakety*, vol. 1, 132–135.

Page 381 *Khrushchev concluded beyond any doubt:* Nikita S. Khrushchev, *Khrushchev Remembers: The Last Testament*, 502–505, 509.

Page 382 *More dramatic yet:* "Russia Exhibits Atomic Infantry," *New York Times*, 08/18/1961; Fursenko and Naftali, *Khrushchev's Cold War*, 385.

Page 382 *"Fucked again":* Wyden, *Wall*, 246; Schlesinger, *A Thousand Days*, 459; Beschloss, *The Crisis Years*, 291.

Page 383 Bobby recalled what Chip: Schlesinger, *Robert Kennedy and His Times*, 429–430, citing RFK Papers, *RFK*, dictated September 1, 1961.

Page 383 It was not the first time Vice President: Theodore C. Sorensen, *Kennedy*. New York: HarperCollins, 1965, 594.

Page 384 Johnson grew all the more: Dallek, *An Unfinished Life*, 427; Petschull, *Die Mauer*, 161–162; O'Donnell and Powers, with McCarthy, *"Johnny, We Hardly Knew Ye,"* 303.

Page 384 During their overnight flight: Cate, *The Ides of August*, 405–407; JFKL, *Lucius D. Clay OH*; *Lucius D. Clay OH* (Columbia Oral History Project).

Page 385 Speaking to the West Berlin: Wyden, *Wall*, 229; "Text of VP Johnson's Address in West Berlin," *Washington Post*, 08/20/1961; *New York Times*, 08/22/1961.

Page 385 "The city was like": "300,000 Applaud," *New York Times*, 08/20/1961.

Page 385 For Kennedy, the troop: Schlesinger, *A Thousand Days*, 395; Sorensen, *Kennedy*, 594.

Page 386 British Prime Minister: Macmillan, *Pointing the Way, 1959–1961*, 393.

Page 386 The operation's commander: William D. Ellis and Thomas J. Cunningham, *Clarke of St. Vith: The Sergeants' General*. Cleveland: Dillon/Liederbach, 1974, 260–261.

Page 386 For all the details his superiors: Wyden, *Wall*, 230–232.

Page 388 Colonel Johns had never seen: *New York Times*, 08/21/1961.

Page 388 The Soviet response: "Berlin Is Called a G.I. 'Mousetrap,'" *New York Times*, 08/26/1961.

Page 388 "We took offense": Interview with Vern Pike, Washington, D.C., November 17, 2008.

Page 389 At 5:30 on Sunday: Interview with Lucian Heichler, Association for Diplomatic Studies and Training Foreign Affairs Oral History Project, initial interview date February 2, 2000, http://memory.loc.gov/cgi-bin/query/r?ammem/mfdip:@field(DOCID+mfdip2004hei01); interview with James. E. Hoofnagle, Association for Diplomatic Studies and Training Foreign Affairs Oral History Project, initial interview date March 3, 1989, http://memory.loc.gov/cgi-bin/query/r?ammem/mfdip:@field(DOCID+mfdip2004hoo01).

Page 390 "I returned from Germany": Report by Vice President Johnson, Lyndon B. Johnson Presidential Library, Vice Presidential Security Files, VP Travel, Berlin, Secret. The vice president also reported on his trip to Kennedy on August 21. The memo for the record of this meeting is in JFKL, NSF, Germany, Berlin.

Page 390 On August 22, Ulbricht: Fursenko and Naftali, *Khrushchev's Cold War*, 385, quoting MFA, *Gromyko and Malinovsky to the Central Committee*, July 7, 1962 (recounting 1961 events), 0742, 7/28/54, 10–13.

Page 390 Swelling with confidence: Fursenko and Naftali, *Khrushchev's Cold War*, 385, citing Ulbricht letter to Khrushchev, October 31, 1961, AVP-RF.

Page 391 Chancellor Adenauer finally surfaced: "Kanzler Besuch: Keen Willydrin," *Der Spiegel*, 08/30/1961.

Page 391 Many West Berliners: "Foes Taunt Adenauer in Berlin," *Washington Post*, 08/23/1961; *Die Zeit*, 03/25/1961.

Page 391 Adenauer visited the king: Schwarz, *Konrad Adenauer*. Vol. 2: *The Statesman, 1952–1967*, 542; Cable, Adenauer an Springer, 16.08.1961; Adenauer, *Teegespräche 1959–1961*, 546.

Page 392 West Berlin police officer: Doris Liebermann, "'Die Gewalt der anderen Seite hat mich sehr getroffen': Gespräch mit Hans-Joachim Lazai," in Deutschland Archiv No. 39/2006, 596–607; "Wall Victim" Ida Siekmann: http://www.chronik-der-mauer.de/index.php/de/Start/Detail/id/593816/page/1.

Page 393 It was nearly eight: "Wall Victim" Bernd Lünser: http://www.chronik-der-mauer.de/index.php/de/Start/Detail/id/593816/page/5.

Page 394 "Jörg Hildebrandt (Hg.), *Regine Hildebrandt. Erinnern tut gut. Ein Familienalbum*, Berlin 2008, S. 56.

Page 395 Eberhard Bolle was so focused: Interview with Eberhard Bolle, Berlin, October 10, 2008.

16. A HERO'S HOMECOMING

Page 398 *"We have lost Czechoslovakia"*: Teleconference, Clay and Department of the Army, April 10, 1948; communication recounted in Lucius D. Clay, *Decision in Germany*, reprint, Westport, CT: Greenwood Press, 1970, 359–362 (361).

Page 398 *"Why would anyone write"*: JFKL, *Elie Abel OH*, March 18, 1970, 3–4; Elie Abel, "Kennedy After 8 Months Is Tempered by Adversity," *Detroit News*, September 23, 1961.

Page 399 *Berliners still spoke:* Andrei Cherny, *The Candy Bombers: The Untold Story of the Berlin Airlift and America's Finest Hour*. New York: G. P. Putnam's Sons, 2008, 253.

Page 399 *Clay's determination to keep:* Teleconference, Clay and Department of the Army, April 10, 1948; communication recounted in Lucius D. Clay, *Decision in Germany*. Westport, CT: Greenwood Press, 1970, 361.

Page 400 *Clay's appointment:* Smyser, *Kennedy and the Berlin Wall*, 115.

Page 400 *Kennedy had even rewritten:* Jean Edward Smith, *Lucius D. Clay: An American Life*. New York: Henry Holt, 1990, 651–652.

Page 401 *Whatever his dilemmas:* "Public Backs Kennedy Despite 'Bad Breaks,'" *Washington Post*, 08/25/1961.

Page 401 *Unlike Kennedy, Clay spoke:* RIAS, General Clay's statement upon arrival in West Berlin, September 19, 1961: http://www.chronik-der-mauer.de/index.php/de/Media/VideoPopup/field/audio_video/id/40514/oldAction/Index/oldId/955454/oldModule/Start/page/0.

Page 402 *The Christian Democrats:* Prittie, *Konrad Adenauer*, 288–291.

Page 402 *Clay's limited job description:* Smith, *Lucius D. Clay*, 654.

Page 403 *The State Department's Martin Hillenbrand:* Gelb, *The Berlin Wall*, 246.

Page 403 *Clay had launched:* http://www.uniprotokolle.de/Lexikon/Berliner_Luftbrücke.html.

Page 404 *The East German newspaper: Washington Post*, 09/18/1961; Taylor, *The Berlin Wall: A World Divided*, 263–265.

Page 404 *At age twenty-one:* Interview with Albrecht Peter Roos, Berlin, October 13, 2008.

Page 406 *As a result of August 13:* Honoré M. Catudal, *Steinstücken: A Study in Cold War Politics*. New York: Vantage Press, 1971, 15.

Page 406 *East German authorities threatened: New York Times*, 09/22/1961; 09/23/1961; *Washington Post*, 09/22/1961; 09/23/1961; Catudal, *Kennedy and the Berlin Wall Crisis*, 139–135; Smyser, *Kennedy and the Berlin Wall*, 131.

Page 406 *Without divulging his plans:* Catudal, *Steinstücken*, 15–16, 106.

Page 406 *General Clay spent:* Smith, *Defense of Berlin*, 309–310; Interview with Vern Pike, Washington, D.C., November 17, 2008.

Page 407 *By coincidence, European Commander:* Catudal, *Kennedy and the Berlin Wall Crisis*, 133–134.

Page 407 *A few days later, U.S. troops:* Interview with Vern Pike, Washington, D.C., November 17, 2008.

Page 408 *They included the president's brother:* Frank Saunders, *Torn Lace Curtain*. New York: Holt, Rinehart, and Winston, 1982, 82–85.

Page 409 *Larry Newman:* Hersh, *Dark Side of Camelot*, 226–230, 237–246.

Page 410 *Kennedy's public approval ratings:* JFKL, *Elie Abel OH*, March 18, 1970, 3–4; *Detroit News*, September 23, 1961.

Page 410 *On Sunday, Kennedy landed:* Beschloss, *The Crisis Years*, 312–313; Schlesinger, *Robert Kennedy and His Times*, 500–501.

Page 411 *Following Salinger's instructions:* Pierre Salinger, *With Kennedy*. Garden City, NY: Doubleday, 1966, 191–192.

Page 411 *Khrushchev had told Sulzberger:* Department of State, *Presidential Correspondence*, Lot 77 D 163. Also printed in Cyrus L. Sulzberger, *The Last of the Giants*. New York: Macmillan, 1970, 801–802.

Page 412 *Taking a deep breath:* Sulzberger, *The Last of the Giants*, 788–806; C. L. Sulzberger, "Khrushchev Says in Interview He Is Ready to Meet Kennedy," *New York Times*, 09/08/1961.

Page 412 Khrushchev also wanted to influence: Salinger, *With Kennedy*, 192; Fursenko and Naftali, *Khrushchev's Cold War*, 390, 397.

Page 412 Kennedy called Salinger at 1:00 a.m.: Beschloss, *Crisis Years*, 314–315; Salinger. *With Kennedy*, 192–194.

Page 413 Though Kennedy and Khrushchev had agreed: Fursenko and Naftali, *Khrushchev's Cold War*, 395.

Page 413 Kennedy reviewed his UN speech: Christian Science Monitor, 09/26/1961.

Page 413 The president had been agonizing: Smith, *The Defense of Berlin*, 314; *New York Times*, 09/26/1961, 09/29/1961; *Christian Science Monitor*, 10/09/1961; *Washington Post*, 10/11/1961.

Page 414 Kennedy needed to retake: Ralph G. Martin, *A Hero of Our Time: An Intimate Story of the Kennedy Years*. New York: Macmillan, 1983, 661; Sidey, *JFK*, 245.

Page 414 "A nuclear disaster": "Text of Kennedy Speech to U.N. Assembly," *Wall Street Journal*, 09/26/1961; "Kennedy Meets Presidential Test, Shows Nobility of Thought, Concilliatory Mood," *Washington Post*, 09/26/1961. For text of speech: http://www.jfklibrary.org/Historical+Resources/Archives/Reference+Desk/Speeches/JFK/003POF03UnitedNations 09251961.htm.

Page 415 Perhaps most telling was East German: Smith, *The Defense of Berlin*, 314; *Neues Deutschland*, 09/26/1961.

Page 416 West German editorialists: Bild-Zeitung, 09/26/1961.

Page 416 West German Foreign Minister: Smith, *The Defense of Berlin*, 314.

Page 416 Adenauer's fears: AVP-RF, Memcon, *Kuznetsov*, Meeting with Kroll, 3-64-746, August 29, 1961; Fursenko and Naftali, *Khrushchev's Cold War*, 389.

Page 416 In the Berliner Morgenpost: *Berliner Morgenpost*, 09/26/1961.

Page 417 The New York Times *columnist:* Smith, *The Defense of Berlin*, 313.

Page 417 So Marshal Konev dispatched: Smith, *The Defense of Berlin*, 315.

Page 417 On September 27, General Clarke: Smith, *The Defense of Berlin*, 315.

Page 418 Clay had ordered army: Raymond L. Garthoff, "Berlin 1961: The Record Corrected," *Foreign Policy*, no. 84 (Fall 1991), 142–156; Freedman, *Kennedy's Wars*, 90; Donald P. Steury, "On the Front Lines of the Cold War: The Intelligence War in Berlin," presented at "Berlin: The Intelligence War, 1945–1961." Conference at the Teufelsberg and the Alliierten Museum, September 10–12, 1999; excerpts from conference speeches and panel discussions: Ambassador Raymond Garthoff on the tank confrontation of October 1961; retrieved from https://www.cia.gov/library/center-for-the-study-of-intelligence/csi-publications/csi-studies/studies/summer00/art01.html.

17. NUCLEAR POKER

Page 419 "In a certain sense": FRUS, 1961–1963, vol. VI, Kennedy–Khrushchev Exchanges, Doc. 21, Letter from Chairman Khrushchev to President Kennedy, Moscow, September 29, 1961; Department of State, Presidential Correspondence: Lot 77 D 163; also JFKL, NSF, Countries Series, USSR, *Khrushchev Correspondence*.

Page 419 "Our confidence in": Address by Roswell L. Gilpatric, Deputy Secretary of Defense, before the Business Council at the Homestead, Hot Springs, Virginia, October 21, 1961, 9:00 p.m. (EST), 10:00 p.m. (EDT): http://www.gwu.edu/~nsarchiv/NSAEBB/NSAEBB56/BerlinC6.pdf; "Our Real Strength," *Time*, 10/27/1961.

Page 419 Carrying two folded newspapers: Salinger, *With Kennedy*, 198–199.

Page 421 The man who: FRUS, 1961–1963, vol. VI, *Kennedy–Khrushchev Exchanges*, Doc. 21, Letter from Chairman Khrushchev to President Kennedy, September 29, 1961.

Page 421 Salinger was struck: Salinger, *With Kennedy*, 199.

Page 422 Khrushchev also said he was willing: FRUS, 1961–1963, vol. XIV, Berlin Crisis, 1961–1962, Doc. 137.

Page 422 Apart from opening his new channel: Fursenko and Naftali, *Khrushchev's Cold War*, 396.

Page 422 Khrushchev had also warned Ulbricht: SED Archives, IfGA, ZPA, J IV 2/202/130, Letter from Khrushchev to Ulbricht, January 28, 1961, in Harrison, "Ulbricht and the Concrete 'Rose,'" CWIHP Working Paper No. 5, 131, Appendix J.

Page 423 Adenauer's concerns: FRUS, 1961–1963, vol. XIV, Berlin Crisis, 1961–1962, Doc. 147, Memo from President Kennedy to Secretary of State Rusk, Berlin Negotiations, Washington, September 12, 1961.

Page 424 One matter was certain: Quoted in James N. Giglio, *The Presidency of John F. Kennedy.* Lawrence: University Press of Kansas, 2006, 2nd ed., 82; O'Brien, *JFK,* 552; Sidey, *JFK,* 218.

Page 424 Kennedy considered reaching out: Sorensen, *Kennedy,* 553.

Page 424 In a letter dated October 16: FRUS, 1961–1963, vol. VI, *Kennedy–Khrushchev Exchanges,* Doc. 22, Letter from President Kennedy to Chairman Khrushchev, Hyannis Port, October 16, 1961; Thomas Fensch, ed., *Top Secret: The Kennedy–Khrushchev Letters.* The Woodlands, TX: New Century Books, 2001, 69–81.

Page 426 The numbers were a reflection: New York Times, 10/16/1961, 10/17/1961, 10/18/1961; Slusser, *The Berlin Crisis of 1961,* 294.

Page 426 The Palace of Congresses was unique: Washington Post, 10/18/1961.

Page 427 Time *magazine assessed:* "Communists: The Khrushchev Code," Time, 10/20/1961.

Page 427 Though he owed his position: Beschloss, *The Crisis Years,* 44, 53, 461, 583; Fursenko and Naftali, *Khrushchev's Cold War,* 202.

Page 428 It seemed to party colleague Pyotr Demichev: Taubman, *Khrushchev,* 514.

Page 428 Still, Khrushchev looked leaner: See for Khrushchev's entire speech at the opening session of the 22nd Party Congress: *The Current Digest of the Soviet Press,* 13, no. 49 (1962); *New York Times,* 10/18/1961, 10/19/1961, 10/22/1961.

Page 430 During an otherwise genial: David Talbot, *Brothers: The Hidden History of the Kennedy Years.* New York: Free Press, 2007, 75; *New York Post,* 11/08/1961; *New York Times,* 11/05/1961.

Page 431 By the time the plan: Carl Kaysen to General Maxwell Taylor, Military Representative to the President, "Strategic Air Planning and Berlin," September 5, 1961, Top Secret. Source: National Archives, Record Group 218, Records of the Joint Chiefs of Staff, Records of Maxwell Taylor: http://www.gwu.edu/~nsarchiv/NSAEBB/NSAEBB56/BerlinC1.pdf ; also see FRUS, 1961–1963, vol. VIII, National Security Policy, Doc. 43, Memo from the President's Military Representative (Taylor) to President Kennedy, Strategic Air Planning and Berlin, Washington, September 19, 1961.

Page 431 Kaysen conceded the need: Carl Kaysen to General Maxwell Taylor, Military Representative to the President, "Strategic Air Planning and Berlin," September 5, 1961, Top Secret, excised copy, with cover memoranda to Joint Chiefs of Staff Chairman Lyman Lemnizer, Released to National Security Archive, National Archives, Record Group 218, Records of the Joint Chiefs of Staff. http://www.gwu.edu/~nsarchiv/NSAEBB/NSAEBB56/BerlinC1.pdf.

Page 433 In a White House that: Fred Kaplan, *The Wizards of Armageddon.* New York: Simon & Schuster, 1983, 299–300; Marcus G. Raskin, *Being and Doing.* New York: Random House, 1971, 62–63.

Page 434 Kennedy didn't have the same misgivings: Memo from General Maxwell Taylor to General Lemnitzer, September 19, 1961, enclosing memo on "Strategic Air Planning," Top Secret. Source: National Archives, Record Group 218, Records of the Joint Chiefs of Staff, Records of Maxwell Taylor, Box 34, Memorandums for the President, 1961. http://www.gwu.edu/~nsarchiv/NSAEBB/NSAEBB56/BerlinC3.pdf.

Page 435 The following day's National Security Council: FRUS, 1961–1963, vol. VIII, National Security Policy, Doc. 44, Memo of Conference with President Kennedy, Washington, September 20, 1961.

Page 435 Power had directed the firebombing: Kaplan, *The Wizards of Armageddon,* 246; Scott D. Sagan, *The Limits of Safety: Organization, Accidents, and Nuclear Weapons.* Princeton, NJ:

Princeton University Press, 1993, 150; U.S. Air Force, *General Horace M. Wade OH*, October 10–12, 1978, 307–308, K239.0512–1105, Air Force Historical Research Center; JFKL, NSF, Memo Bundy to Kennedy, January 30, 1961, Box 313.

Page 436 Martin Hillenbrand, director: JFKL, *Martin J. Hillenbrand OH*, Interviewed by Paul P. Sweet, American Consul General, Stuttgart, August 26, 1964, 8; Martin J. Hillenbrand, *Power and Morals.* New York: Columbia University Press, 1949, 30.

Page 436 Cool and rational, at age fifty-four Nitze: See Nitze himself in the foreword to William R. Smyser, *From Yalta to Berlin: The Cold War Struggle over Germany.* New York: St. Martin's Press, 1999, xiv–xv; Strobe Talbott, *The Master of the Game: Paul Nitze and the Nuclear Peace.* New York: Alfred A. Knopf, 1988, 37, 70, 72–73.

Page 437 As Truman's chief of policy: Paul H. Nitze, with Ann M. Smith and Steven I. Rearden, *From Hiroshima to Glasnost: At the Center of Decisions—A Memoir.* New York: Grove Weidenfeld, 1989, 91–92; Talbott, *Master of the Game,* 52, 58, 112.

Page 437 Like Acheson, Nitze considered: David Callahan, *Dangerous Capabilities: Paul Nitze and the Cold War.* New York: HarperCollins, 1990, 216–218.

Page 437 On August 13, Nitze: Callahan, *Dangerous Capabilities,* 223; Nitze, *From Hiroshima to Glasnost,* 199–200.

Page 438 To safeguard Berlin access: Nitze, *From Hiroshima to Glasnost,* 202–204; FRUS, 1961–1963, vol. XIV, Berlin Crisis, 1961–1962, Doc. 173, Minutes of Meeting, Berlin Build-up and Contingency Planning, Washington, October 10, 1961; Doc. 185, Enclosure, U.S. Policy on Military Actions in a Berlin Conflict, Washington, October 20, 1961.

Page 439 The Washington Post *reported on efforts: Washington Post, New York Times, Tagesspiegel, Der Kurier,* 10/29/1961; *Christian Science Monitor,* 09/05/1961; *New York Times,* 09/17/1961.

Page 439 Time magazine ran: Time, 10/20/1961.

Page 440 It seemed that only Macmillan: Macmillan, *Pointing the Way, 1959–1961,* 398–403; Nigel J. Ashton, *Kennedy, Macmillan and the Cold War: The Irony of Interdependence.* New York: Palgrave Macmillan, 2002, 60–61.

Page 440 With the Allies deeply at odds: FRUS, 1961–1963, vol. XIV, Berlin Crisis, 1961–1962, Doc. 184, Minutes of Meeting, Washington, October 20, 1961; also JFKL, NSF, Memo of Meeting, Washington, October 20, 1961, 10 a.m., Meetings with the President, Top Secret, drafted by Bundy.

Page 441 As so often: National Defense University, Taylor Papers, Box 34, Items for Cables to Taylor; in FRUS, 1961–1963, vol. XIV, Berlin Crisis, 1961–1962, Doc. 184.

Page 441 A few hours after the meeting: FRUS, 1961–1963, vol. XIV, Berlin Crisis, 1961–1962, Doc. 185, Letter from President Kennedy to the Supreme Commander, Allied Powers Europe (Norstad) and Enclosure, U.S. Policy on Military Actions in a Berlin Conflict, Washington, October 20, 1961.

Page 443 Bruce said that through Kennedy's: FRUS, 1961–1963, vol. XIV, Berlin Crisis, 1961–1962, Doc. 183, Telegram from the Embassy in the United Kingdom to the Department of State, London, October 20, 1961, 4 p.m.

Page 445 It was an unlikely audience: Beschloss, *The Crisis Years,* 329; Benjamin C. Bradlee, *Conversations with Kennedy.* New York: W.W. Norton, 1975, 230.

Page 445 Knowing nothing of the Bolshakov: Wyden, *Wall,* 258.

Page 446 "We have responded immediately": Address by Roswell L. Gilpatric, Deputy Secretary of Defense, before the Business Council at the Homestead, Hot Springs, Virginia, October 21, 1961: http://www.gwu.edu/~nsarchiv/NSAEBB/NSAEBB56/BerlinC6.pdf; "Gilpatric Warns U.S. Can Destroy Atom Aggressor," *New York Times,* 10/22/1961; "Our Real Strength," *Time,* 10/27/1961.

Page 447 Khrushchev would later recall that Konev: Nikita S. Khrushchev, *Khrushchev Remembers,* 459.

18. SHOWDOWN AT CHECKPOINT CHARLIE

Page 448 *"I do not believe"*: FRUS, 1961–1963, vol. XIV, Berlin Crisis, 1961–1962, Doc. 181, Letter from the President's Special Representative in Berlin (Clay) to President Kennedy, Berlin, October 18, 1961.

Page 448 *"In the nature of things"*: FRUS, 1961–1963, vol. XIV, Berlin Crisis, 1961–1962, Doc. 193, Telegram from the Department of State to the Mission at Berlin, Washington, October 26, 1961, 8:11 p.m.; Department of State, Central Files, 762.0221/10-2661.

Page 448 *E. Allan Lightner Jr.*: Slusser, *The Berlin Crisis of 1961*, 377–378; Smith, *The Defense of Berlin*, 319–320.

Page 449 *Lightner knew there was a slim chance*: Bruce W. Menning, "The Berlin Crisis of 1961 from the Perspective of the Soviet General Staff," in William W. Epley, ed., *International Cold War Military Records and History*. Proceedings of the International Conference on Cold War Military Records and History held in Washington, D.C., March 21–26, 1994, 10–13; Smyser, *Kennedy and the Berlin Wall*, 135; Gerhard Wettig, *Chruschtschows Berlin-Krise 1958 bis 1963: Drohpolitik und Mauerbau*. Munich and Berlin: R. Oldenbourg, 192.

Page 449 *Ulbricht had apparently approved*: Cate, *The Ides of August*, 476; Slusser, *The Berlin Crisis of 1961*, 353–358.

Page 450 *Encouraged by Clay*: FRUS, 1961–1963, vol. XIV, Berlin Crisis, 1961–1962, Doc. 189, Telegram from the Mission at Berlin to the Department of State, Berlin, October 24, 1961, 1 p.m., drafted by Lightner.

Page 450 *Clay disagreed*: FRUS, 1961–1963, vol. XIV, Berlin Crisis, 1961–1962, Doc. 181, Letter from the President's Special Representative in Berlin (Clay) to President Kennedy, Berlin, October 18, 1961; Smith, *Lucius D. Clay*, 642–643; 651–654; JFKL, *Lucius D. Clay OH*, July 1, 1964.

Page 451 *Unlike Clay, Lightner*: Cate, *The Ides of August*, 476; Smith, *The Defense of Berlin*, 319; Raymond L. Garthoff, *Detente and Confrontation: American-Soviet Relations From Nixon to Reagan*. Washington, D.C.: Brookings Institution Press, 1994; Smith, *Lucius D. Clay*, 659; HSTL, *E. Allan Lightner OH*, October 26, 1973.

Page 451 *Lightner told friends*: Interview with Vern Pike, Washington, D.C., November 17, 2008; Gelb, *The Berlin Wall*, 250–253; HSTL, *E. Allan Lightner OH*, October 26, 1973.

Page 451 *As that night's script*: FRUS, 1961–1963, vol. XIV, Berlin Crisis, 1961–1962, Doc. 186, Telegram from the Mission at Berlin to the Department of State, Berlin, October 23, 1961, 2 p.m.; Cate, *The Ides of August*, 476–480.

Page 452 *"Look," Lightner said to the policeman*: Cate, *The Ides of August*, 477.

Page 453 *About then, four American tanks*: "U.S. Protests to Soviet," *New York Times*, 10/24/1961.

Page 454 *By the time Lightner's VW*: *The Atlantic Times*, October 2005: William R. Smyser, "Tanks at Checkpoint Charlie. In October 1961, the World Faced a War": http://www.atlantic-times .com/archive_detail.php?recordID=319; Cate, *The Ides of August*, 479–480, 484.

Page 455 *Once East German radio*: Cate, *The Ides of August*, 479–480; Howard Trivers, *Three Crises in American Foreign Affairs and a Continuing Revolution*, 41–44.

Page 455 *Back in Washington, Kennedy*: Ashton, *Kennedy, Macmillan and the Cold War*, 62; Reeves, *Kennedy: Profile of Power*, 249; Norman Gelb, *The Berlin Wall: Kennedy, Khrushchev, and a Showdown in the Heart of Europe*. New York: Dorset Press, 1986, 253; Smyser, *Kennedy and the Berlin Wall*, 137.

Page 455 *National Security Advisor Bundy had warned*: Ann Tusa, *The Last Division: A History of Berlin, 1945–1989*. London: Hodder and Stoughton, 1997, 330; JFKL, NSF, Memo from Bundy to the President, August 28, 1961, Box 86, Berlin; Wyden, *Wall*, 264.

Page 456 *Though in his letter Clay*: FRUS, 1961–1963, vol. XIV, Berlin Crisis, 1961–1962, Doc. 181, Letter from the President's Special Representative in Berlin (Clay) to President Kennedy, Berlin, October 18, 1961; also in JFKL, NSF, Germany, Berlin, General Clay, Top Secret.

Page 458 *What followed was the general's resignation*: Smith, *Lucius D. Clay*, 662–663.

Page 459 At a time when Kennedy badly wanted: Frédéric Bozo, Two Strategies for Europe: De Gaulle, the United States, and the Atlantic Alliance. Lanham, MD: Rowman & Littlefield, 2001, 70, 71; Ashton, Kennedy, Macmillan and the Cold War, 62.

Page 459 De Gaulle had disapproved: Charles de Gaulle, Lettres, notes et carnets (1961–1963). Paris: Plon, 1986, 155–158; William R. Smyser, "Zwischen Erleichterung und Konfrontation. Die Reaktionen der USA und der UdSSR auf den Mauerbau," in Hans-Hermann Hertle, Konrad Hugo Jarausch, and Christoph Klessmann, eds., Mauerbau und Mauerfall: Ursachen—Verlauf—Auswirkungen. Berlin: Christoph Links, 2002, 147–158 (151).

Page 460 As harsh as it was, de Gaulle's letter: JFKL, POF, De Gaulle–Kennedy Letter Exchange, Box 116A.

Page 460 Despite two months of U.S. diplomatic: FRUS, 1961–1963, vol. XIV, Berlin Crisis, 1961–1962, Doc. 176, Telegram 1025 from the Department of State to the Embassy in Germany, Washington, October 13, 1961; a similar letter was sent to de Gaulle: Telegram 2136 to Paris, October 13, 1961, in Department of State, Central Files, 762.00/10-1361.

Page 461 With that as prelude: Cornelius Ryan, The Longest Day: June 6, 1944. New York: Simon & Schuster, 1994, 107.

Page 461 De Gaulle told Gavin: FRUS, 1961–1963, vol. XIV, Berlin Crisis, 1961–1962, Doc. 187, Telegram from the Embassy in France to the Department of State, Paris, October 23, 1961.

Page 462 Emboldened by the success: FRUS, 1961–1963, vol. XIV, Berlin Crisis, 1961–1962, Doc. 189, Telegram from the Mission at Berlin to the Department of State, Berlin, October 24, 1961, 1 p.m.

Page 463 The White House staff considered: Gelb, The Berlin Wall, 127–128; Cate, The Ides of August, 101.

Page 463 Given Ambassador Gavin's failure: FRUS, 1961–1963, vol. XIV, Berlin Crisis, 1961–1962, Doc. 188, Memcon, Delivery of Letter to the President from Chancellor Adenauer, Washington, October 24, 1961; New York Times, 10/25/1961, 10/26/1961.

Page 464 Grewe knew Adenauer: FRUS, 1961–1963, vol. XIV, Berlin Crisis, 1961–1962, Doc. 164; also see for Rusk–Gromyko meeting, Memcon, September 30, 1961, in Department of State, Central Files, 611.61/9-3061.

Page 466 Speaking to Lightner, Kohler: FRUS, 1961–1963, vol. XIV, Berlin Crisis, 1961–1962, Doc. 190, Memo from the Assistant Secretary of State for European Affairs (Kohler) to Secretary of State Rusk, Washington, October 24, 1961, in Department of State, Central Files, 762.00/10-2461.

Page 467 United States Army first lieutenant: Interview with Vern Pike, Washington, D.C., November 17, 2008. Also see his unpublished book Checkpoint Charlie's Angels (written with Edward W. Plaisted).

Page 472 A policeman blocking her path: Der Kurier, 10/28/1961, 10/29/1961.

Page 473 U.S. commanders had placed: "U.S. Tanks Face Soviet's at Berlin Crossing Point," New York Times, 10/28/1961.

Page 474 Even as the Soviets: Gelb, The Berlin Wall, 248; Smith, The Defense of Berlin, 324; FRUS, 1961–1963, vol. XIV, Berlin Crisis, 1961–1962, Doc. 193, Telegram from the Department of State to the Mission at Berlin, Washington, October 26, 1961, 8:11 p.m.

Page 475 Clay had never been more convinced: Department of State, Central Files, 762.0221/10-2661: Telegram 835 (Clay to Rusk), October 26, 1961, 1 p.m., mentioned in FRUS, 1961–1963, vol. XIV, Berlin Crisis, 1961–1962, Doc. 193.

Page 475 He outlined how: Department of State, Central Files, 762.0221/10-2561: Telegram 824 (Clay to Department of State), October 25, 1961, 12:34 p.m.; Secretary Ball discussing General Clay's plan: ibid., Doc. 178: Memo from Acting Secretary of State Ball to President Kennedy, Action for Dealing with the Possible Closing of the Friedrichstrasse Entry Point into East Berlin, Washington, October 14, 1961; ibid., Doc. 180, Telegram from the Department of State to the Mission at Berlin, Washington, October 18, 1961;

National Security Archive, Berlin, Norstad, dated 10/26/1961: Norstad to Clarke (CINCUSAREUR), 36.

Page 476 *"Take our tanks"*: Oleg V. Volobuev and Alexei Serov, eds., *Nikita Khrushchev: Life and Destiny*. Moscow: Novosti Press, 1989, 27; Wyden, *Wall*, 264.

Page 477 *That said, the Soviets were nervous:* Menning, "The Berlin Crisis of 1961 from the Perspective of the Soviet General Staff," 141.

Page 477 *Clay's view:* Wyden, *Wall*, 263.

Page 478 *By late October, Bobby:* James W. Symington, *The Stately Game*. New York: Macmillan, 1971, 144; Schlesinger, *Robert Kennedy and His Times*, 499–500.

Page 478 *The president's brother made arrangements:* JFKL, *Robert F. Kennedy OH*, Interview by John Bartlow Martin, March 1, 1964.

Page 478 *Bobby Kennedy recalled:* Fursenko and Naftali, *Khrushchev's Cold War*, 403–404.

Page 479 *The attorney general:* JFKL, *Robert F. Kennedy OH*, Interview by John Bartlow Martin, March 1, 1964; Schlesinger, *Robert Kennedy and His Times*, 500.

Page 479 *On Friday night, October 27:* FRUS, 1961–1963, vol. XIV, Berlin Crisis, 1961–1962, Doc. 197.

Page 480 *After an evening of tension:* Nikita S. Khrushchev, *Khrushchev Remembers: The Last Testament*, 507.

Page 481 *Shortly after 10:30 a.m. on Saturday:* Interview with Adam Kellett-Long, London, October 15–16, 2008; NPR interview: http://www.npr.org/templates/story/story .php?storyId=102618942.

EPILOGUE: AFTERSHOCKS

Page 482 *"I recognize fully"*: Harold Macmillan, *At the End of the Day*, 1961–1963. New York: Harper & Row, 1973, 182–183.

Page 482 *"There are many people"*: JFKL, Kennedy Speech to Berliners, Rudolph Wilde Platz, West Berlin, June 26, 1963: http://www.jfklibrary.org/Historical+Resources/Archives/ Reference+Desk/Speeches/JFK/003POF03BerlinWall06261963.htm.

Page 483 *The first scene unfolded:* http://www.chronik-der-mauer.de/index.php/de/Start/Detail/ id/593928/page/5; *Berliner Morgenpost*, 08/13/2006; Hilton, *The Wall*, 164–168.

Page 483 *At the same time . . . Soviet ships:* Beschloss, *Crisis Years*, 412–415; Taubman, *Khrushchev*, 549–551; Fursenko and Naftali, *Khrushchev's Cold War*, 451; Raymond L. Garthoff, *Reflections on the Cuban Missile Crisis*. Washington, D.C.: The Brookings Institution, 1987, 18–22, 208 (table showing type and numbers of missiles).

Page 484 *Fechter's murder snapped something:* "City's Mood: Anger and Frustration," *New York Times*, 08/26/1962.

Page 484 *Meanwhile, over Cuba:* Anatoli I. Gribkov and William Y. Smith, *"Operation Anadyr": U.S. and Soviet Generals Recount the Cuban Missile Crisis*. Chicago: Edition Q, 1994, 5–7, 24, 26–57; Taubman, *Khrushchev*, 550; Fursenko and Naftali, *One Hell of a Gamble*, 188–189, 191–193.

Page 485 *On August 22, the CIA:* FRUS, 1961–1963, vol. X, Cuba, January 1961–September 1962, Doc. 383, Memo from the President's Special Assistant (Schlesinger) to the President's Special Assistant for National Security Affairs (Bundy), Washington, August 22, 1962, CIA, Office of Current Intelligence (OCI), No. 3047/62, Current Intelligence Memo, August 22, 1962: "Recent Soviet Military Aid to Cuba."

Page 485 *Though history would celebrate Kennedy:* Arnold L. Horelick, "The Cuban Missile Crisis: An Analysis of Soviet Calculations and Behavior," *World Politics*, 16 (April 1964), 363–389; Graham T. Allison, *Essence of Decision: Explaining the Cuban Missile Crisis*. Boston: Little, Brown, 1971, 40–56, 102–117.

Page 490 With that, the Arkansas senator: Smyser, *Kennedy and the Berlin Wall*, 90; JFKL, Bundy–
JFK, August 4, 1961; Beschloss, *The Crisis Years*, 264; Larson, Deborah Welch. *Anatomy of
Mistrust: U.S.–Soviet Relations During the Cold War.* Ithaca, NY: Cornell University Press,
2000, 134.

Page 490 Without any countervailing presidential statement: Larson, *Anatomy of Mistrust*, 134.

Page 490 "When the border is closed": RGANI, Khrushchev–Ulbricht, August 1, 1961, Document
No. 521557, 113–146. Document and citation graciously provided by Dr. Matthias Uhl.

Page 491 Critics called Khrushchev's scheme: Arkady N. Shevchenko, *Breaking with Moscow.* New
York: Alfred A. Knopf, 1985, 117–118.

Page 491 Regarding Cuba: Sergei N. Khrushchev, *Creation of a Superpower*, 536.

Page 491 Despite all his first-year setbacks: John C. Ausland, *Kennedy, Khrushchev, and the Berlin-
Cuba Crisis, 1961–1964.* Oslo: Scandinavian University Press, 1996, 43–45; FRUS, 1961–1963,
vol. XV, Berlin Crisis, 1962–1963, Doc. 34, Memcon, Bonn, April 13, 1962; also in
Department of State, Central Files, 740.5/4-1362, Top Secret, Limit Distribution; Freedman,
Kennedy's Wars, 112–113.

Page 492 Adenauer no longer could conceal: Schwarz, *Konrad Adenauer.* Vol. 2: *The Statesman*, 608;
Archiv für Christlich-Demokratische Politik, Krone Diary, April 14, 1962.

Page 492 He then shot off a brusque note: JFKL, NSF, Germany and Europe, Box 78; Rudolf Morsey
and Hans-Peter Schwarz, eds., *Adenauer: Briefe, 1961–1963* (Rhöndorfer Ausgabe), ed. Hans
Peter Mensing, Stiftung Bundeskanzler-Adenauer-Haus, Paderborn, Germany: Ferdinand
Schoeningh, 2006, 111.

Page 492 Even as he put in place: FRUS, 1961–1963, vol. XV, Berlin Crisis, 1962–1963, Doc. 73,
Message from Chairman Khrushchev to President Kennedy, Moscow, undated, but
handwritten note: "Received at White House July 5, 1962"; also see Doc. 76: Memcon
Rusk–Dobrynin, July 12, 1962; Department of State, Presidential Correspondence:
Lot 77 D 163.

Page 493 On September 4, Kennedy: Department of State Bulletin, vol. 47 (September 24, 1962),
"U.S. Reaffirms Policy on Prevention of Aggressive Actions by Cuba: Statement by President
Kennedy," 450; also National Security Archives, Cuban Missile Crisis, President Kennedy's
Statement on Soviet Military Shipments to Cuba, September 4, 1962.

Page 493 Two days later, on September 6: FRUS, 1961–1963, vol. XV, Berlin Crisis, 1962–1963, Doc.
112, Memcon between Secretary of the Interior Udall and Chairman Khrushchev, Pitsunda,
Soviet Union, September 6, 1962.

Page 493 On October 16, 1962: FRUS, 1961–1963, vol. XV, Berlin Crisis, 1962–1963, Doc. 133,
Telegram from the Embassy in the Soviet Union to the Department of State, Moscow,
October 16, 1962.

Page 494 Khrushchev told his new ambassador: "The Cold War in the Third World and the Collapse
of Detente in the 1970s," "The Mikoyan–Castro Talks, 4–5 November 1962: The Cuban
Version," CWIHP-B, No. 8–9 (1996/1997), 320, 339–343: http://www.wilsoncenter.org/
topics/pubs/ACF199.pdf.

Page 494 "My thinking went like this": Nikita S. Khrushchev, *Khrushchev Remembers*, 493–494.

Page 494 Of all Khrushchev's moves linking: John R. Mapother, "Berlin and the Cuban Crisis,"
Foreign Intelligence Literary Scene, 12, no.1 (January 1993), 1–3; Ray S. Cline, "Commentary:
The Cuban Missile Crisis," *Foreign Affairs*, 68, no. 4 (Fall 1989), 190–196.

Page 494 Said Khrushchev, "The Americans knew": Nikita S. Khrushchev, *Khrushchev
Remembers*, 500.

Page 495 "Let me just say a little": Ernest R. May and Philip D. Zelikow, eds., *The Kennedy Tapes:
Inside the White House During the Cuban Missile.* Cambridge, MA: The Belknap Press of
Harvard University Press, 1997, 175.

Page 495 "I recognize fully": Macmillan, *At the End of the Day*, 182–183.

Page 496 Kennedy repeated his Berlin concern: FRUS, 1961–1963, vol. XI, Cuban Missile Crisis and Aftermath, Doc. 39, Telegram from the Department of State to the Embassy in the United Kingdom, Washington, October 22, 1962, 12:17 a.m.; Macmillan, *At the End of the Day,* 186.

Page 496 In 1962, Kennedy also rejected: May and Zelikow, *The Kennedy Tapes,* 309.

Page 496 National Security Advisor Bundy wondered: May and Zelikow, *The Kennedy Tapes,* 144, 183.

Page 496 At one point, General Curtis E. LeMay: May and Zelikow, *The Kennedy Tapes,* 177.

Page 496 In his October 22 speech: JFKL, Radio and Television Report to the American People on the Soviet Arms Buildup in Cuba, The White House, October 22, 1962: http://www.jfklibrary.org/jfkl/cmc/j102262.htm; May and Zelikow, *The Kennedy Tapes,* 280.

Page 497 In his meeting with U.S. ambassador to London: Macmillan, *At the End of the Day,* 187.

Page 497 "That's really the choice": Macmillan, *At the End of the Day,* 182, 199; May and Zelikow, *The Kennedy Tapes,* 385.

Page 497 When Soviet Deputy Foreign Minister: Sergei N. Khrushchev, *Creation of a Superpower,* 560.

Page 497 Khrushchev also rejected: Telegram from Soviet Ambassador to the USA Dobrynin to the USSR MFA, October 23, 1962, reproduced in "The Cuban Missile Crisis," CWIHP-B, No. 5 (Spring 1995), 70–71; Sergei N. Khrushchev, *Nikita Khrushchev and the Creation of a Superpower,* 582.

Page 497 On October 27, the president's brother: Smyser, *Kennedy and the Berlin Wall,* 192, 274, n. 18.

Page 498 De Gaulle famously told: JFKL, *Dean G. Acheson OH,* no. 1, April 27, 1964, 26.

Page 498 Adenauer said he would throw his lot: Schwarz, *Konrad Adenauer,* 629–630; Smyser, *Kennedy and the Berlin Wall,* 199.

Page 498 Tellingly, Kennedy rejected the dovish: May and Zelikow, *The Kennedy Tapes,* 256, 283–286, 388–389.

Page 498 General Clay suggested to diplomat: Smyser, *Kennedy and the Berlin Wall,* 203, citing Smyser's conversation with General Clay, Links Club, New York City, November 1962.

Page 499 Perhaps another million Berliners: Reeves, *Kennedy: Profile of Power,* 537; *New York Times,* 06/26/1963, 06/27/1963.

Page 499 some in the Kennedy: O'Donnell and Powers, with McCarthy, *"Johnny, We Hardly Knew Ye,"* 360; Dallek, *An Unfinished Life,* 624; Robert G. Torricelli and Andrew Carroll, eds., *In Our Own Words: Extraordinary Speeches of the American Century.* New York: Kodansha America, 1999, 232.

Page 499 "There are many people": JFKL, Kennedy Speech to Berliners, Rudolph Wilde Platz, West Berlin, June 26, 1963: http://www.jfklibrary.org/Historical+Resources/Archives/Reference+Desk/Speeches/JFK/003POF03BerlinWall06261963.htm.

Page 500 Years later, amateur linguists: Smyser, *Kennedy and the Berlin Wall,* 217, 221, from conversation with Heinz Weber, July 10, 2006; and Andreas W. Daum, *Kennedy in Berlin.* Washington, D.C.: German Historical Institute and New York: Cambridge University Press, 2008, 133–135.

Page 501 As Kennedy told Ted Sorensen: Sorensen, *Kennedy,* 601.

Bibliography

ARCHIVAL SOURCES

Air Force Historical Research Center, Maxwell Air Force Base, Alabama (AFHRC)

The American Presidency Project: http://www.presidency.ucsb.edu

Archiv für Christlich-Demokratische Politik (ACDP), Sankt Augustin, Germany

Arkhiv Vneshnei Politiki Russkoi Federatsii (Russian Ministry of Foreign Affairs Archives; AVP-RF), Moscow, Russian Federation

Archive of the Main Intelligence Administration of the General Staff of the Armed Forces of the Russian Federation (GRU), Moscow

Auswärtiges Amt—Politisches Archiv: *Political Relations of BRD with United States, 1961* (AA-PA), Berlin

Behörde der Bundesbeauftragten für die Unterlagen des Staatssicherheitsdienstes der Ehemaligen Deutschen Demokratischen Republik (BStU), Ministeriums für Staatssicherheit (MfS), Zentrale Auswertungs- und Informationsgruppe Hauptverwaltung Aufklärung des Ministeriums für Staatssicherheit der DDR (Central Analysis and Information Group of the Ministry for State Security; ZAIG), Berlin: www.bstu.bund.de

Bundesarchiv, Germany: http://www.bundesarchiv.de/index.html.de

Central Intelligence Agency (CIA), Office of Current Intelligence (OCI): https://www.cia.gov/library/center-for-the-study-of-intelligence/

Chronik der Mauer—Bau und Fall der Berliner Mauer: http://www.chronik-der-mauer.de/

The Current Digest of the Soviet Press: http://www.eastview.com/cdpsp/

Declassified Materials from CPSU Central Committee Plenums (TsK KPSS). "Delo Beriia," two parts, in *Izvestiia TsK KPSS*, 1 and 2 (January and February 1991), Moscow, Russian Federation

Deutsches Rundfunkarchiv (DRA), Frankfurt am Main and Potsdam–Babelsberg, Germany: http://www.dra.de/

Digital National Security Archive (DNSA). *The Berlin Crisis, 1958–1962.* Alexandria, VA: Chadwyck-Healey; Washington, D.C.: National Security Archives, 1992: http://nsarchive.chadwyck.com/marketing/index.jsp

Dwight D. Eisenhower Presidential Library. Abilene, KS (DDEL)

Foreign Broadcast Information Service (FBIS), USSR, International Service: http://www.newsbank.com/readex/index.cfm?content=370

Former Soviet Central Committee Archive (TsKhSD), Moscow

Hubert Horatio Humphrey Papers. Minnesota Historical Society, Minneapolis

Lyndon B. Johnson Presidential Library. Austin, TX (LBJL)

John F. Kennedy Presidential Library. Boston (JFKL): http://www.jfklibrary.org/
    Historical+Resources/Archives/Reference+Desk/
Walter Lippmann Papers, Yale University, Sterling Memorial Library, New Haven, CT
Harold Macmillan Archives. *Harold Macmillan Diaries*. University of Oxford, Bodleian Library,
    Oxford, England
National Security Archive (NSA), George Washington University, Washington, D.C.:
    http://www.gwu.edu/~nsarchiv/
Richard Nixon Presidential Library. College Park, MD (RNL)
SED (Sozialistische Einheitspartei Deutschland) Archives: Institut für Geschichte der
    Arbeiterbewegung, Zentrales Parteiarchiv (IfGA, ZPA), Berlin
Adlai E. Stevenson Papers, Princeton University, Mudd Manuscript Library, Princeton, NJ
Stiftung Archiv der Parteien und Massenorganisationen im Bundesarchiv (SAPMO-BArch), Berlin
Stiftung Bundeskanzler-Adenauer-Haus (Federal Chancellor Adenauer House Foundation;
    StBKAH), Bad Honnef–Rhöndorf, Germany
Harry S. Truman Presidential Library. Independence, MO (HSTL)
Tsentr Khraneniia Sovremmenoi Dokumentatsii (TsKhSD), renamed Rossiiskii Gosudarstvennyi
    Arkhiv Noveishei Istorii (Russian State Archive of Contemporary History; RGANI), Moscow,
    Russian Federation
U.S. Department of State, Central Files
U.S. Department of State, ed. Foreign Relations of the United States (FRUS), Office of the
    Historian, U.S. Government Printing Office, Washington, D.C.: http://history.state.gov/
    historicaldocuments/

GENERAL SOURCES

Acheson, Dean. *Sketches from Life of Men I Have Known*. New York: Harper & Brothers, 1960.
Adenauer, Konrad. *Erinnerungen 1959–1963. Fragmente*. Stuttgart: Deutsche Verlags-Anstalt, 1968.
———. *Memoirs, 1945–1953*. Translated by Beate Ruhm von Oppen. Chicago: Henry Regnery,
    1966.
———. *Teegespräche 1959–1961* (Rhöndorfer Ausgabe). Edited by Hanns Jürgen Küsters. Berlin:
    Siedler, 1988.
Adomeit, Hannes. *Imperial Overstretch: Germany in Soviet Policy from Stalin to Gorbachev: An
    Analysis Based on New Archival Evidence, Memoirs, and Interviews*. Baden-Baden, Germany:
    Nomos Verlagsgesellschaft, 1998.
Adzhubei, Aleksei I. *Krushenie illiuzii*. Moscow: Interbuk, 1991.
Allison, Graham T. *Essence of Decision: Explaining the Cuban Missile Crisis*. Boston: Little, Brown,
    1971.
Ambrose, Stephen E. *Eisenhower: The President*, vol. 2. New York: Simon & Schuster, 1984.
Anonymous. *A Woman in Berlin: Eight Weeks in the Conquered City: A Diary [Eine Frau in Berlin]*.
    Translated by Philip Boehm. New York: Picador, 2006.
Armee für Frieden und Sozialismus. *Geschichte der Nationalen Volksarmee*. Berlin: Militärverlag
    der DDR, 1985.
Ashton, Nigel J. *Kennedy, Macmillan and the Cold War: The Irony of Interdependence*. New York:
    Palgrave Macmillan, 2002.
Ausland, John C. *Kennedy, Khrushchev, and the Berlin–Cuba Crisis, 1961–1964*. Oslo: Scandinavian
    University Press, 1996.
Beevor, Antony. *Berlin: The Downfall, 1945*. New York: Viking, 2002.
Beisner, Robert L. *Dean Acheson: A Life in the Cold War*. New York: Oxford University Press, 2006.
Beschloss, Michael R. *The Crisis Years: Kennedy and Khrushchev, 1960–1963*. New York: Harper-
    Collins, 1991.
———. *Mayday: The U-2 Affair: The Untold Story of the Greatest US–USSR Spy Scandal*. New
    York: Harper & Row, 1986.

Bissell, Richard M., Jonathan E. Lewis, and Frances T. Pudlo. *Reflections of a Cold Warrior: From Yalta to the Bay of Pigs.* New Haven, CT: Yale University Press, 1996.

Boller, Paul F. *Presidential Anecdotes.* New York: Oxford University Press, 1996.

Boltunov, Mikhail. *Nevidimoe Oruzhie GRU [Invisible GRU Weapon].* Moscow: Olma-Press, 2002.

Bozo, Frédéric. *Two Strategies for Europe: De Gaulle, the United States, and the Atlantic Alliance.* Lanham, MD: Rowman & Littlefield, 2001.

Bradlee, Benjamin C. *Conversations with Kennedy.* New York: W. W. Norton, 1975.

Brandon, Henry. *Special Relationships: A Foreign Correspondent's Memoirs from Roosevelt to Reagan.* New York: Atheneum, 1988.

Brandt, Willy. *Begegnungen mit Kennedy.* Munich: Kindler, 1964.

———. *Begegnungen und Einsichten: Die Jahre 1960–1975.* Hamburg: Hoffmann u. Campe, 1976.

———. *Erinnerungen.* Frankfurt am Main: Propyläen, and Zürich: Ferenczy, 1989.

Bremen, Christian. *Die Eisenhower-Administration und die zweite Berlin-Krise 1958–1961.* Veröffentlichungen der Historischen Kommision zu Berlin, Bd. 95. Berlin and New York: de Gruyter, 1998.

Brinkley, Douglas. *Dean Acheson: The Cold War Years, 1953–1971.* New Haven, CT: Yale University Press, 1994.

Brugioni, Dino, and Robert F. McCort, eds. *Eyeball to Eyeball: The Inside Story of the Cuban Missile Crisis.* New York: Random House, 1991.

Bundesministerium für Gesamtdeutsche Fragen (BMG), ed. *Die Flucht aus der Sowjetzone und die Sperrmassnahmen des Kommunistischen Regimes vom 13. August 1961 in Berlin.* Bonn and Berlin, 1961.

Bundesministerium für Innerdeutsche Beziehungen, ed. *Dokumente zur Deutschlandpolitik,* IV. Reihe, Band 6, Erster Halbband, 1. Januar–30. Mai 1961, Frankfurt am Main, 1975.

Bundy, McGeorge. *Danger and Survival: Choices About the Bomb in the First Fifty Years.* New York: Random House, 1988.

Callahan, David. *Dangerous Capabilities: Paul Nitze and the Cold War.* New York: HarperCollins, 1990.

Castle, Timothy N. *At War in the Shadow of Vietnam: U.S. Military Aid to the Royal Lao Government, 1955–1975.* New York: Columbia University Press, 1993.

Cate, Curtis. *The Ides of August: The Berlin Wall Crisis, 1961.* New York: M. Evans, 1978.

Catudal, Honoré M. *Kennedy and the Berlin Wall Crisis: A Case Study in U.S. Decision Making.* Berlin: Berlin Verlag, 1980.

———. *Steinstücken: A Study in Cold War Politics.* New York: Vantage Press, 1971.

Chace, James. *Acheson: The Secretary of State Who Created the American World.* New York: Simon & Schuster, 1998.

Chang, Jung, and Jon Halliday. *Mao: The Unknown Story.* New York: Alfred A. Knopf/ Doubleday, 2005.

Cherny, Andrei. *The Candy Bombers: The Untold Story of the Berlin Airlift and America's Finest Hour.* New York: G. P. Putnam's Sons, 2008.

Chubarov, Alexander. *Russia's Bitter Path to Modernity: A History of the Soviet and Post-Soviet Eras.* New York: Continuum, 2001.

Chuev, Feliks. *Sto sorok besed s Molotovym.* Moscow: Terra, 1991.

Clay, Lucius D. *Decision in Germany.* Westport, CT: Greenwood Press, 1970.

Cold War International History Project (CWIHP). Working Paper Series and CWIHP Bulletins. Woodrow Wilson International Center for Scholars, Washington, D.C., 1994–1998: www.wilsoncenter.org.

Coleman, David G. "The Greatest Issue of All: Berlin, American National Security, and the Cold War, 1948–1963" (unpublished dissertation). University of Queensland, 2000.

Conze, Eckart. *Die gaullistische Herausforderung: Die Deutsch-Französischen Beziehungen in der Amerikanischen Europapolitik 1958–1963.* Munich: R. Oldenbourg, 1995.

Cousins, Norman. *The Improbable Triumvirate: John F. Kennedy, Pope John, Nikita Khrushchev*. New York: W. W. Norton, 1972.

Crankshaw, Edward. *The New Cold War: Moscow v. Pekin*. Harmondsworth, England, and Baltimore: Penguin Books, 1963/1970.

Dallek, Robert. *An Unfinished Life: John F. Kennedy, 1917–1963*. Boston: Little, Brown, 2003.

Daum, Andreas W. *Kennedy in Berlin*. Washington, DC: German Historical Institute, and New York: Cambridge University Press, 2008.

Davies, Norman. *No Simple Victory: World War II in Europe, 1939–1945*. New York: Viking, 2007.

Day, Alan John, and Judith Bell, eds. *Border and Territorial Disputes*. Detroit: Gale Research, 1982.

De Gaulle, Charles. *Lettres, notes et carnets (1961–1963)*. Paris: Plon, 1986.

Diggins, John Patrick. *The Liberal Persuasion: Arthur Schlesinger, Jr., and the Challenge of the American Past*. Princeton, NJ: Princeton University Press, 1997.

Dirck, Brian R. *The Executive Branch of Federal Government: People, Process, and Politics*. Santa Barbara, CA: ABC-CLIO, 2007.

Divine, Robert. *Blowing on the Wind: The Nuclear Test Ban Debate, 1954–1960*. New York: Oxford University Press, 1978.

Dobrynin, Anatoly Fedorovich. *In Confidence: Moscow's Ambassador to America's Six Cold War Presidents (1962–1986)*. New York: Times Books, 1995.

Donaldson, Gary A. *The First Modern Campaign: Kennedy, Nixon, and the Election of 1960*. Lanham, MD: Rowman & Littlefield, 2007.

Donner, Jörn. *Report from Berlin*. Translated by Albin T. Anderson. Bloomington: Indiana University Press, 1961.

Ebon, Martin. *The Andropov File: The Life and Ideas of Yuri V. Andropov, General Secretary of the Communist Party of the Soviet Union*. New York: McGraw-Hill, 1983.

Eisenfeld, Bernd, and Roger Engelmann. *13.8.1961: Mauerbau—Fluchtbewegung und Machtsicherung*. Bremen: Temmen, 2001.

Ellis, William D., and Thomas J. Cunningham. *Clarke of St. Vith: The Sergeants' General*. Cleveland: Dillon/Liederbach, 1974.

Epstein, Catherine. *The Last Revolutionaries: German Communists and Their Century*. Cambridge, MA: Harvard University Press, 2003.

Falin, Valentin. *Politische Erinnerungen*. Munich: Droemer Knaur, 1993.

Fensch, Thomas, ed., *Top Secret: The Kennedy–Khrushchev Letters*. The Woodlands, TX: New Century Books, 2001.

Fisher, Nigel. *Harold Macmillan: A Biography*. New York: St. Martin's Press, 1982.

Floyd, David. *Mao Against Khrushchev: A Short History of the Sino-Soviet Conflict*. New York: Praeger, 1964.

Foitzik, Jan, ed. Berichte des Hohen Kommissars der UdSSR in Deutschland aus den Jahren 1953/54. Dokumente aus dem Archiv für Außenpolitik der Russischen Föderation. in *Materialien der Enquete-Kommission des Deutschen Bundestages "Aufarbeitung von Geschichte und Folgen der SED-Diktatur in Deutschland,"* vol. 2. Baden-Baden: Deutscher Bundestag, 1995.

Ford, Corey. *Donovan of OSS: The Untold Story of William J. Donovan*. Boston: Little, Brown, 1970.

Frank, Mario. *Walter Ulbricht: Eine Deutsche Biographie*. Berlin: Siedler, 2001.

Freedman, Lawrence. *Kennedy's Wars: Berlin, Cuba, Laos, and Vietnam*. New York: Oxford University Press, 2000.

Freedom of Communications. Final Report of the Committee on Commerce, United States Senate . . . The Joint Appearances of Senator John F. Kennedy and Vice President Richard M. Nixon and Other 1960 Campaign Presentations. 87th Congress, 1st Session, Senate Report No. 994, Part 3, Washington, DC: U.S. Government Printing Office, 1961.

Froh, Klaus, and Rüdiger Wenzke, eds. *Die Generale und Admirale der NVA: Ein biographisches Handbuch*. Berlin: Christoph Links, 2007.

Fursenko, Aleksandr, et al., eds. *Archivii Kremlya: Prezidium TsK KPSS, 1954–1964 Chernoviie protokolnie zapisi zasedanii. Stenogrammi. Postanovlenia* [Archives of the Kremlin: Presidium of the Central Committee of the Communist Party of the Soviet Union, 1954–1964, Notes of State Meetings, Stenographic Accounts], vol. 1. Moscow: Rosspen, 2004.

Fursenko, Aleksandr, and Timothy Naftali. *Khrushchev's Cold War: The Inside Story of an American Adversary.* New York: W. W. Norton, 2006.

———. *One Hell of a Gamble: Khrushchev, Castro, and Kennedy, 1958–1964.* New York: W. W. Norton, 1997.

Garthoff, Raymond L. *Detente and Confrontation: American-Soviet Relations from Nixon to Reagan.* Washington, DC: The Brookings Institution, 1994.

———. *Reflections on the Cuban Missile Crisis.* Washington, DC: The Brookings Institution, 1987.

Gelb, Norman. *The Berlin Wall: Kennedy, Khrushchev, and a Showdown in the Heart of Europe.* New York: Dorset Press, 1986.

Giglio, James N. *The Presidency of John F. Kennedy*, 2nd ed. Lawrence: University Press of Kansas, 2006.

Gittings, John, ed. *Survey of the Sino-Soviet Dispute: A Commentary and Extracts from Recent Polemics, 1963–1967.* London and New York: Royal Institute of International Affairs, 1968.

Goduti, Philip A., Jr. *Kennedy's Kitchen Cabinet and the Pursuit of Peace: The Shaping of American Foreign Policy, 1961–1963.* Jefferson, NC: McFarland, 2009.

Goldstein, Gordon M. *Lessons in Disaster: McGeorge Bundy and the Path to War in Vietnam.* New York: Times Books/Henry Holt, 2008.

Graham, Otis L., Jr., and Meghan Robinson Wander, eds. *Franklin D. Roosevelt: His Life and Times—An Encyclopedic View.* Boston: Da Capo Press, 1985.

Gribkov, Anatoli I., and William Y. Smith. *"Operation Anadyr": U.S. and Soviet Generals Recount the Cuban Missile Crisis.* Chicago: Edition Q, 1994.

Grimm, Thomas. *Das Politbüro Privat—Ulbricht, Honecker, Mielke & Co. aus der Sicht ihrer Angestellten.* Berlin: Aufbau-Verlag, 2004.

Gromyko, Andrei A. *Memories.* Translated by Harold Shukman. London: Hutchinson, 1989.

Halberstam, David. *The Best and Brightest.* New York: Modern Library, 2001.

Hanak, Harry. *Soviet Foreign Policy Since the Death of Stalin.* Boston: Routledge, 1972.

Harrison, Hope M. *Driving the Soviets up the Wall: Soviet–East German Relations, 1953–1961.* Princeton, NJ: Princeton University Press, 2003.

Heidemeyer, Helge. *Flucht und Zuwanderung aus der SBZ/DDR 1945/1949–1961, Die Flüchtlingspolitik der Bundesrepublik Deutschland bis zum Bau der Berliner Mauer.* Düsseldorf: Droste, 1994.

Hersh, Seymour M. *The Dark Side of Camelot.* Boston: Little, Brown, 1997.

Hertle, Hans-Hermann. *Die Todesopfer an der Berliner Mauer 1961–1989: Ein Biographisches Handbuch.* Berlin: Christoph Links, 2009.

Hertle, Hans-Hermann, Konrad Hugo Jarausch, and Christoph Klessmann, eds. *Mauerbau und Mauerfall: Ursachen—Verlauf—Auswirkungen.* Berlin: Christoph Links, 2002.

Heymann, C. David. *A Woman Named Jackie: An Intimate Biography of Jacqueline Bouvier Kennedy Onassis.* New York: Carol, 1994.

Hillenbrand, Martin J. *Power and Morals.* New York: Columbia University Press, 1949.

Hilton, Christopher. *The Wall: The People's Story.* Stroud, England: Sutton, 2001.

Hitchcock, William I. *The Struggle for Europe: The Turbulent History of a Divided Continent, 1945–2002.* New York: Doubleday, 2003.

Honecker, Erich. *From My Life.* New York: Pergamon, 1981.

Horne, Alistair. *Harold Macmillan: 1957–1986*, vol. 2. New York: Viking, 1989.

Isaacson, Walter. *Kissinger: A Biography.* New York: Simon & Schuster Paperbacks, 2005.

Jian, Chen. *Mao's China and the Cold War.* Chapel Hill: University of North Carolina Press, 2001.

Johnson, Loch K. *Strategic Intelligence*, vol. 1. Westport, CT: Praeger, 2007.

Jones, Howard. *The Bay of Pigs.* New York: Oxford University Press, 2008.

Kagan, Donald. *On the Origins of War and the Preservation of Peace.* New York: Anchor Books, 1996.

Kaplan, Fred. *The Wizards of Armageddon.* New York: Simon & Schuster, 1983; Palo Alto, CA: Stanford University Press, 1991.

———. *1959: The Year Everything Changed.* Hoboken, NJ: John Wiley & Sons, 2009.

Keil, Rolf-Dietrich. *Mit Adenauer in Moskau—Erinnerungen eines Dolmetschers.* Bonn: Bouvier, 1997.

Kennan, George F., and T. Christopher Jespersen, eds. *Interviews with George F. Kennan.* Jackson: University Press of Mississippi, 2002.

Kennedy, Edward M., ed. *The Fruitful Bough: A Tribute to Joseph P. Kennedy.* Privately printed, 1965.

Kennedy, John F. *Public Papers of the Presidents of the United States: John F. Kennedy—Containing the Public Messages, Speeches, and Statements of the President, 1961–1963,* vol. 1. Washington, DC: United States Government Printing Office, 1962–1964.

Kennedy, John F., and Allan Nevins, eds. *The Strategy of Peace.* New York: Harper & Row, 1960.

Kennedy, John Fitzgerald. *A Compilation of Statements and Speeches Made During His Service in the United States Senate and House of Representatives.* Washington, DC: United States Government Printing Office, 1964.

Kenney, Charles C. *John F. Kennedy: The Presidential Portfolio: History as Told Through the Collection of the John F. Kennedy Library and Museum.* New York: Public Affairs, 2000.

Kershaw, Roger. *Monarchy in South-East Asia: The Faces of Tradition in Transition.* New York: Routledge, 2001.

Kettenacker, Lothar. *Germany 1989: In the Aftermath of the Cold War.* London: Pearson Longman, 2009.

Khrushchev, Nikita S. *Communism: Peace and Happiness for the Peoples,* vol. 1, *January–September 1961.* Moscow: Foreign Languages Publishing House, 1963.

———. *For Victory in Peaceful Competition with Capitalism.* New York: E. P. Dutton, 1960.

———. *Khrushchev Remembers.* Introduction, commentary, and notes by Edward Crankshaw. Translated and edited by Strobe Talbott. Boston: Little, Brown, 1970.

———. *Khrushchev Remembers: The Last Testament.* Foreword by Edward Crankshaw and introduction by Jerrold L. Schecter. Translated and edited by Strobe Talbott. Boston: Little, Brown, 1974.

———. *Khrushchev Remembers: The Glasnost Tapes.* Translated and edited by Jerrold L. Schecter with Vyacheslav Luchkov. Boston: Little, Brown, 1990.

———. *Memoirs of Nikita Khrushchev,* vol. 3. Edited by Sergei Khrushchev; memoirs translated by George Shriver; supplementary material translated by Stephen Shenfield. University Park: Pennsylvania State University, 2004–2007.

Khrushchev, Sergei N. *Nikita S. Khrushchev: Krizisy i Rakety,* vol 1. Moscow: Novosti Press, 1994.

———. *Nikita Khrushchev and the Creation of a Superpower.* Translated by Shirley Benson. University Park: Pennsylvania State University Press, 2000.

Klein, Edward. *All Too Human: The Love Story of Jack and Jackie Kennedy.* New York: Pocket Books, 1997.

Knight, David. *The Spy Who Never Was & Other True Spy Stories.* New York: Doubleday, 1978.

Knopp, Guido. *Die Gefangenen.* Munich: Goldmann, 2005.

Köhler, Henning. *Adenauer: Eine Politische Biographie.* Frankfurt am Main: Propyläen, 1994.

Kowalczuk, Ilko-Sascha, and Stefan Wolle. *Roter Stern über Deutschland: Sowjetische Truppen in der DDR.* Berlin: Christoph Links, 2010.

Kowalski, Gerhard. *Die Gagarin-Story: Die Wahrheit über den Flug des ersten Kosmonauten der Welt.* Berlin: Schwarzkopf & Schwarzkopf, 1999.

Kroll, Hans. *Lebenserinnerungen eines Botschafters.* Cologne: Kiepenheuer & Witsch, 1967.

Krone, Heinrich. *Tagebücher,* vol. 2: 1961–1966. Edited by Hans-Otto Kleinmann, Düsseldorf: Forschungen und Quellen zur Zeitgeschichte, 2003.

Krüger, Joachim. *Die Volksrepublik China in der Aussenpolitischen Strategie der DDR (1949–1989),* in Kuo Heng-yue and Mechthild Leutner, eds., *Deutschland und China*. Beiträge des Zweiten Internationalen Symposiums zur Geschichte der Deutsch–Chinesischen Beziehungen: Berlin, 1991. Munich: Berliner China-Studien 21, 1994.

Kudrov, V. M. "Comparing the Soviet and US Economies: History and Practices," in Nicholas Eberstadt and Jonathan Tombes, eds., *Comparing the US and Soviet Economies: The 1990 Airlie House Conference*, vol. I: Total Output and Consumption. Washington, DC: The American Enterprise Institute, 2000.

Kvitsinsky, Yuli A. (Kwizinskij, Julij A.). *Vor dem Sturm: Erinnerungen eines Diplomaten*. Berlin: Siedler, 1993.

Langguth, A. J. *Our Vietnam: The War, 1954–1975*. New York: Simon & Schuster, 2000.

Larson, Deborah Welch. *Anatomy of Mistrust: U.S.–Soviet Relations During the Cold War*. Ithaca, NY: Cornell University Press, 2000.

Lasky, Victor. *JFK: The Man and the Myth*. New York: Macmillan, 1963.

Leamer, Laurence. *The Kennedy Men: 1901–1963*. New York: HarperCollins, 2001.

Leonhard, Wolfgang. *Child of the Revolution*. Translated by C. M. Woodhouse. Chicago: Henry Regnery, 1958.

Li, Zhisui, and Anne F. Thurston, eds. *The Private Life of Chairman Mao: The Memoirs of Mao's Personal Physician*. New York: Random House, 1994.

Lincoln, Evelyn. *My Twelve Years with John F. Kennedy*. New York: D. McKay, 1965.

Longford, Lord. *Kennedy*. London: Weidenfeld and Nicolson, 1976.

MacDuffie, Marshall. *The Red Carpet: 10,000 Miles Through Russia on a Visa from Khrushchev*. New York: W. W. Norton, 1955.

Macmillan, Harold. *At the End of the Day*, 1961–1963. New York: Harper & Row, 1973.

———. *Pointing the Way, 1959–1961*. London: Macmillan, 1972.

Major, Patrick. *Behind the Berlin Wall: East Germany and the Frontiers of Power*. New York: Oxford University Press, 2010.

Mara, Michael, Rudi Thurow, Eckhardt Schaller, and Rainer Hildebrandt, eds. *Kontrollpunkt Kohlhasenbrück—Die Geschichte einer Grenzkompanie des Ringes um West-Berlin*. Bad Godesberg, Gemany: Hohwacht, 1964.

Martin, David C. *Wilderness of Mirrors: Intrigue, Deception, and the Secrets That Destroyed Two of the Cold War's Most Important Agents*. Guilford, CT: The Lyons Press, 2003.

Martin, John Bartlow. *Adlai Stevenson and the World: The Life of Adlai E. Stevenson*. Garden City, NY: Doubleday, 1977.

Martin, Ralph G. *A Hero of Our Time: An Intimate Story of the Kennedy Years*. New York: Macmillan, 1983.

Mastny, Vojtech, Sven Holtsmark, and Andreas Wenger, eds. *War Plans and Alliances in the Cold War: Threat Perceptions in the East and West (CSS Studies in Security and International Relations)*, Abingdon, England: Routledge, 2006.

May, Ernest R., and Philip D. Zelikow, eds. *The Kennedy Tapes: Inside the White House During the Cuban Missile Crisis*. Cambridge, MA: The Belknap Press of Harvard University Press, 1997.

Mayer, Frank A. *Adenauer and Kennedy: A Study in German-American Relations, 1961–1963*. New York: St. Martin's Press, 1996.

Mayers, David. *The Ambassadors and America's Soviet Policy*. New York: Oxford University Press, 1995.

———. *George Kennan and the Dilemmas of US Foreign Policy*. New York: Oxford University Press, 1988.

McCauley, Martin, ed. *Khrushchev and Khrushchevism*. Bloomington: Indiana University Press, 1987.

McLellan, David S., and David C. Acheson, eds. *Among Friends: Personal Letters of Dean Acheson*. New York: Dodd, Mead, 1980.

McNamara, Robert S. *In Retrospect: The Tragedy and Lessons of Vietnam*. New York: Vintage Books, 1996.

Menning, Bruce W. "The Berlin Crisis of 1961 from the Perspective of the Soviet General Staff," in William W. Epley, ed., *International Cold War Military Records and History*. Proceedings of the International Conference on Cold War Military Records and History Held in Washington, D.C., March 21–26, 1994. Washington, D.C.: Office of the Secretary of Defense, 1996.

Merseburger, Peter. *Willy Brandt 1913–1992. Visionär und Realist*. Stuttgart and Munich: Deutsche Verlags-Anstalt, 2002.

Morsey, Rudolf, and Hans-Peter Schwarz, eds. *Adenauer: Briefe, 1961–1963* (Rhöndorfer Ausgabe). Edited by Hans Peter Mensing. Stiftung Bundeskanzler-Adenauer-Haus. Paderborn, Germany: Ferdinand Schöningh, 2006.

Murphy, David E., Sergei A. Kondrashev, and George Bailey. *Battleground Berlin: CIA vs. KGB in the Cold War*. New Haven, CT: Yale University Press, 1997.

National Archives. *Our Documents: 100 Milestone Documents from the National Archives*. New York: Oxford University Press, 2003.

Nitze, Paul H., with Ann M. Smith and Steven I. Rearden. *From Hiroshima to Glasnost: At the Center of Decisions—A Memoir*. New York: Grove Weidenfeld, 1989.

Nixon, Richard M. *RN: The Memoirs of Richard Nixon*. New York: Warner Books, 1979.

O'Brien, Michael. *John F. Kennedy: A Biography*. New York: St. Martin's Press, 2005.

O'Donnell, James S. *A Coming of Age: Albania Under Enver Hoxha*. Boulder, CO: East European Monographs; New York: Distributed by Columbia University Press, 1999.

O'Donnell, Kenneth P., and David F. Powers, with Joe McCarthy. *"Johnny, We Hardly Knew Ye": Memories of John Fitzgerald Kennedy*. Boston: Little, Brown, 1972.

Osterheld, Horst. *"Ich Gehe Nicht Leichten Herzens . . ." Adenauers Letzte Kanzlerjahre: Ein Dokumentarischer Bericht*. Mainz: Matthias-Grünewald, 1986.

Ostermann, Christian F. *Uprising in East Germany, 1953: The Cold War, the German Question, and the First Major Upheaval Behind the Iron Curtain*. Budapest and New York: Central European University Press, 2001.

Pagedas, Constantine A. *Anglo-American Strategic Relations and the French Problem, 1960–1963: A Troubled Partnership*. London: Frank Class, 2000.

Parmet, Herbert S. *Jack: The Struggles of John F. Kennedy*. New York: The Dial Press, 1983.

———. *JFK: The Presidency of John F. Kennedy*. New York: The Dial Press, 1983.

Perlo, V. *Ekonomicheskoye sorevnovaniye SSSR I SShA* [*Economic Competition Between the USSR and the U.S.*]. Moscow, 1960.

Perret, Geoffrey. *Eisenhower*. New York: Random House, 1999.

———. *Jack: A Life Like No Other*. New York: Random House, 2002.

Petschull, Jürgen. *Die Mauer: August 1961: Zwölf Tage zwischen Krieg und Frieden*. Hamburg: Gruner & Jahr, 1981.

Pike, Vern, and Edward W. Plaisted. *Checkpoint Charlie's Angels* (unpublished).

Pollard, Sidney. *The International Economy Since 1945*. New York: Routledge, 1997.

Poppinga, Anneliese. *Meine Erinnerungen an Konrad Adenauer*. Stuttgart: Deutsche Verlags-Anstalt, 1970.

———. *"Das Wichtigste ist der Mut": Konrad Adenauer—Die letzten fünf Kanzlerjahre*. Bergisch Gladbach, Germany: Gustav Lübbe, 1994.

Potter, E. B. *Admiral Arleigh A. Burke*. Annapolis, MD: U.S. Naval Institute Press, 2005.

Pötzl, Norbert F. *Erich Honecker: Eine deutsche Biographie*, 2nd ed. Stuttgart and Munich: Deutsche Verlags-Anstalt, 2002.

Prittie, Terence. *Konrad Adenauer, 1876–1967*. London: Tom Stacey, 1972.

Rabinowitch, Alexander, ed. *Revolution and Politics in Russia: Essays in Memory of B. I. Nicolaevsky*. Bloomington: Indiana University Press, 1972.

Raskin, Marcus G. *Being and Doing*. New York: Random House, 1971.

Reeves, Richard. *President Kennedy: Profile of Power*. New York: Simon & Schuster, 1993.

Riccio, Barry D. *Walter Lippmann: Odyssey of a Liberal*. New Brunswick, NJ: Transaction, 1994.

Romm, Mikhail. *Ustnye rasskazy*. Moscow: Kinotsentr, 1991.

Rostow, Walt W. *The Diffusion of Power: An Essay in Recent History*. New York: Macmillan, 1972.

Rusk, Dean. *As I Saw It: A Secretary of State's Memoirs*. London: I. B. Tauris, 1991.

Russo, Gus. *Live by the Sword: The Secret War Against Castro and the Death of JFK*. Baltimore: Bancroft Press, 1998.

Ryan, Cornelius. *The Longest Day: June 6, 1944*. New York: Simon & Schuster, 1994.

Sagan, Scott D. *The Limits of Safety: Organization, Accidents, and Nuclear Weapons*. Princeton, NJ: Princeton University Press, 1993.

Salinger, Pierre. *With Kennedy*. Garden City, NY: Doubleday, 1966.

Salisbury, Harrison E. *A New Russia*. New York: Harper & Row, 1962.

Sampson, Anthony. *Macmillan: A Study in Ambiguity*. Harmondsworth, England: Penguin Press, 1967.

Satjukow, Silke. *Besatzer: "Die Russen" in Deutschland 1945–1994*. Göttingen: Vandenhoeck & Ruprecht, 2008.

Saunders, Frank. *Torn Lace Curtain*. New York: Holt, Rinehart, and Winston, 1982.

Schertz, Adrian W. *Die Deutschlandpolitik Kennedys und Johnsons: Unterschiedliche Ansätze innerhalb der amerikanischen Regierung*. Cologne: Böhlau, 1992.

Schlesinger, Arthur M. *The Crisis of Confidence: Ideas, Power, and Violence in America*. Boston: Houghton Mifflin, 1969.

———. *Robert Kennedy and His Times*. Boston: Houghton Mifflin, 1978.

———. *A Thousand Days: John F. Kennedy in the White House*. Boston: Houghton Mifflin, 1965.

Schultz, Eberhard, Hans-Adolf Jacobsen, Gert Leptin, and Ulrich Scheuner, eds. *GDR Foreign Policy*. Armonk, NY: M. E. Sharpe, 1982.

Schwan, Heribert. *Erich Mielke: Der Mann, der die Stasi war*. Munich: Droemer Knaur, 1997.

Schwartz, Morton. *The Foreign Policy of the USSR: Domestic Factors*. Encino, CA: Dickenson, 1975.

Schwarz, Hans-Peter. *Konrad Adenauer: A German Politician and Statesman in a Period of War, Revolution and Reconstruction*. Vol. 1: *From the German Empire to the Federal Republic, 1876–1952*. Translated by Louise Willmot. Providence, RI: Berghahn Books, 1995.

———. *The Statesman, 1952–1967*. Translated by Geoffrey Penny. Providence, RI: Berghahn Books, 1997. Translation of *Adenauer: Der Staatsmann*. Vol. 2, *1952–1967*. Stuttgart: Deutsche Verlags-Anstalt, 1991.

Service, Robert. *Comrades! A History of World Communism*. Cambridge, MA: Harvard University Press, 2007.

Shevchenko, Arkady N. *Breaking with Moscow*. New York: Alfred A. Knopf, 1985.

Sibley, Katherine A. S. *The Cold War*. Westport, CT: Greenwood Press, 1998.

Sidey, Hugh. *John F. Kennedy, President*. New York: Atheneum, 1964.

Slusser, Robert. *The Berlin Crisis of 1961: Soviet–American Relations and the Struggle for Power in the Kremlin, June–November 1961*. Baltimore: Johns Hopkins University Press, 1973.

Smith, A. Merriman. *A President's Odyssey*. New York: Harper, 1961.

Smith, Eric Owen. *The West German Economy*. New York: St. Martin's Press, 1983.

Smith, Jean Edward. *The Defense of Berlin*. Baltimore: Johns Hopkins University Press, 1963.

———. *Lucius D. Clay: An American Life*. New York: Henry Holt, 1990.

Smyser, William. R. *From Yalta to Berlin: The Cold War Struggle over Germany*. New York: St. Martin's Press, 1999.

———. *Kennedy and the Berlin Wall: "A Hell of a Lot Better than a War."* Lanham, MD: Rowman & Littlefield, 2009.

———. "Zwischen Erleichterung und Konfrontation. Die Reaktionen der USA und der UdSSR auf den Mauerbau," in Hans-Hermann Hertle, Konrad Hugo Jarausch, and Christoph Klessmann, eds., *Mauerbau und Mauerfall: Ursachen—Verlauf—Auswirkungen*. Berlin: Christoph Links, 2002.

Sommer, Monika, and Michaela Lindinger, eds. *Die Augen der Welt auf Wien gerichtet: Gipfel 1961 Chruschtschow—Kennedy*. Innsbruck and Vienna: Katalog Wien Museum; 2005.

Sorensen, Theodore C. *Kennedy*. New York: HarperCollins, 1965.

Stacks, John F. *Scotty: James B. Reston and the Rise and Fall of American Journalism*. Boston: Little, Brown, 2003.

Steel, Ronald. *Walter Lippmann and the American Century*. Boston and Toronto: Little, Brown, 1980.

Steininger, Rolf. *Der Mauerbau: Die Westmächte und Adenauer in der Berlinkriese 1958–1963*. Munich: Olzog, 2001.

Steury, Donald P., ed. *On the Front Lines of the Cold War: Documents on the Intelligence War in Berlin, 1946 to 1961*. Washington, DC: Central Intelligence Agency (CIA), Center for the Study of Intelligence, 1999.

Stützle, Walter. *Kennedy und Adenauer in der Berlin-Krise 1961–1962*. Bonn and Bad Godesberg: Neue Gesellschaft, 1973.

Sulzberger, Cyrus L. *The Last of the Giants*. New York: Macmillan, 1970.

Suri, Jeremy. *Henry Kissinger and the American Century*. Cambridge, MA: Harvard University Press, 2007.

Symington, James W. *The Stately Game*. New York: Macmillan, 1971.

Talbot, David. *Brothers: The Hidden History of the Kennedy Years*. New York: Free Press, 2007.

Talbott, Strobe. *The Master of the Game: Paul Nitze and the Nuclear Peace*. New York: Alfred A. Knopf, 1988.

Taubman, William. *Khrushchev: The Man and His Era*. New York: W. W. Norton, 2004.

Taylor, Frederick. *The Berlin Wall: A World Divided, 1961–1989*. New York: HarperCollins, 2007.

Thomas, Evan. *The Very Best Men: Four Who Dared: The Early Years of the CIA*. New York: Simon & Schuster, 1995.

Torricelli, Robert G., and Andrew Carroll, eds. *In Our Own Words: Extraordinary Speeches of the American Century*. New York: Kodansha America, 1999.

Trachtenberg, Marc. *History and Strategy*. Princeton, NJ: Princeton University Press, 1991.

Travell, Janet G. *Office Hours: Day and Night—The Autobiography of Janet Travell, M.D.* New York: World, 1968.

Trivers, Howard. *Three Crises in American Foreign Affairs and a Continuing Revolution*. Carbondale: Southern Illinois University Press, 1972.

Troyanovsky, Oleg. *Cherez godi i rasstoiania: Istoriia odnoi semyi*. Moscow: Vagrius, 1997.

Turner, Henry Ashby. *The Two Germanies Since 1945*. New Haven, CT: Yale University Press, 1987.

Tusa, Ann. *The Last Division: A History of Berlin, 1945–1989*. London: Hodder and Stoughton, 1997.

Uhl, Matthias. *Krieg um Berlin?—Die sowjetische Militär- und Sicherheitspolitik in der zweiten Berlin-Krise 1958 bis 1962*. Munich: Oldenbourg Wissenschaftsverlag, 2008.

———, and Wagner, Armin. "Another Brick in the Wall: Reexamining Soviet and East German Policy During the 1961 Berlin Crisis: New Evidence, New Documents." CWIHP Working Paper, published under "Storming On to Paris: The 1961 'Buria' Exercise and the Planned Solution of the Berlin Crisis," in Vojtech Mastny, Sven G. Holtsmark, and Andreas Wenger, eds., *War Plans and Alliances in the Cold War: Threat Perceptions in the East and West*. New York: Routledge, 2006.

Updegrove, Mark K. *Second Acts: Presidential Lives and Legacies After the White House*. Guilford, CT: The Lyons Press, 2006.

U.S. Department of State, ed. *American Foreign Policy, Current Documents, 1961*. Office of the Historian, New York: Arno Press, 1971.

———. *Documents on Germany, 1944–1985*. Office of the Historian, Washington, DC: U.S. Government Printing Office, 1986.

Volobuev, Oleg V., and Alexei Serov, ed. *Nikita Khrushchev: Life and Destiny*. Moscow: Novosti Press, 1989.

Von Hornstein, Erika. *Flüchtlingsgeschichten: 43 Berichte aus den frühen Jahren der DDR*. Nördlingen: F. Greno, 1985.

Wagner, Armin. *Walter Ulbricht und die geheime Sicherheitspolitik der SED: Der Nationale Verteidigungsrat der DDR und seine Vorgeschichte (1953–1971)*. Berlin: Christoph Links, 2002.

Walton, Richard J. *Cold War and Counterrevolution: The Foreign Policy of John F. Kennedy.* New York: Viking, 1972.

Weber, Wolfgang. *DDR—40 Jahre Stalinismus: Ein Beitrag zur Geschichte der DDR.* Essen: Arbeiterpresse, 1993.

Wenger, Andreas. *Living with Peril: Eisenhower, Kennedy, and Nuclear Weapons.* Lanham, MD: Rowman & Littlefield, 1997.

Wettig, Gerhard. *Chruschtschows Berlin-Krise 1958 bis 1963: Drohpolitik und Mauerbau.* Munich and Berlin: R. Oldenbourg, 2006.

Whitcomb, John, and Claire Whitcomb. *Real Life at the White House: Two Hundred Years of Daily Life at America's Most Famous Residence.* New York: Routledge, 2000.

Whitney, Thomas P., ed. *Khrushchev Speaks—Selected Speeches, Articles, and Press Conferences, 1949–1961.* Ann Arbor: University of Michigan Press, 1963.

Williams, Charles. *Adenauer: The Father of the New Germany.* New York: John Wiley & Sons, 2000.

Wofford, Harris. *Of Kennedys and Kings: Making Sense of the Sixties.* New York: Farrar, Straus & Giroux, 1980.

Wyden, Peter. *Bay of Pigs: The Untold Story.* New York: Simon & Schuster, 1979.

———. *Wall—The Inside Story of Divided Berlin.* New York: Simon & Schuster, 1989.

Zagoria, Donald S. *The Sino-Soviet Conflict 1956–1961.* Princeton, NJ: Princeton University Press, 1962.

Zolling, Hermann, and Uwe Bahnsen. *Kalter Winter im August: Die Berlin-Krise 1961–1963. Ihre Hintergründe und Folgen.* Oldenburg and Hamburg: Gerhard Stalling, 1967.

Zubok, Vladislav M., and Constantine Pleshakov. *Inside the Kremlin's Cold War: From Stalin to Khrushchev.* Cambridge, MA: Harvard University Press, 1996.

Index

Abel, Elie, 410
Acheson, Dean
  Berlin strategy, 140–46, 149–51, 156–59,
      310, 311–12, 440–41
  Berlin strategy, Schlesinger's alternative
      to, 283, 296–301
  contempt for Joseph Kennedy, 273
  on Cuban invasion, 155–56, 175–76
  friendship with Adenauer, 99
  influence over Kennedy, 140–41, 297
  on Kennedy's leadership ability, 176, 280,
      311
  on military buildup and response in
      Germany, 281–82
  on nuclear preparedness, 273–77
  on Soviet policy, 85
  suspicion of Khrushchev, 59
Adenauer, Konrad
  appearance in Berlin, 371–72, 391–92
  appeasement of Soviet Union, 372
  on Cuban Missile Crisis, 498
  distrust of Kennedy, 91, 98, 102, 103–4,
      156–59, 372, 416
  on East German refugees, 339
  election victory, 401–2
  with Johnson in Texas, 170–71
  on Kennedy's concessions to Khrushchev,
      423, 491–92
  Kennedy's contempt for, xx, 98, 101,
      103, 104
  on Nixon's election defeat (1960), 105
  opposition to Kennedy–Khrushchev
      negotiations, 416, 423, 440, 464–65

personality, 99
political standing, xx, 98, 107, 373–74
prisoner-of-war negotiations with
    Khrushchev, 104–5
resignation from office and death, 501
reunification goal, 92, 100, 168, 339, 416,
    444
on Sino–Soviet alliance, 42
on U.S. Berlin policy, 166–69
as West German chancellor, 92, 99–100
West German NATO membership, 91–92,
    100–101
Adzhubei, Alexei, 190
Albertz, Heinrich, 337
Allies
  access rights in Berlin, 276, 349, 351–52,
      359, 441–43
  four-power agreements, 20, 53, 115, 285,
      353, 376, 470
  impact of Bay of Pigs failure on, 175–76
  inaction on border closure, 374–75
  indecision on Berlin issue, 144, 440, 464,
      476
  troops in West Berlin, xvi, 55–56, 384,
      473
  See also de Gaulle, Charles; Macmillan,
      Harold; NATO
Alphand, Hervé, 52
Alsop, Stewart, 263
Amrehn, Franz, 389
Anderson, George Whelan, Jr., 441
Andropov, Yuri, 117
Aron, Raymond, 417